W9-ABR-998

EMERGING

CONTEMPORARY READINGS FOR WRITERS

THIRD EDITION

BARCLAY BARRIOS
Florida Atlantic University

Bedford/St. Martin's
A Macmillan Education Imprint

Boston • New York

For Bedford/St. Martin's

Vice President, Editorial, Macmillan Higher Education Humanities: Edwin Hill
Editorial Director, English and Music: Karen S. Henry
Publisher for Composition, Business and Technical Writing, Developmental Writing: Leasa Burton
Executive Editor: John Sullivan
Developmental Editor: Sarah Macomber
Associate Production Editor: Matt Glazer
Production Supervisor: Robert Cherry
Executive Marketing Manager: Joy Fisher Williams
Editorial Assistant: Evelyn Denham
Copy Editor: Jennifer S. Brett Greenstein
Photo Researcher: Sheri Blaney
Director of Rights and Permissions: Hilary Newman
Senior Art Director: Anna Palchik
Cover Design: John Callahan
Cover Photo: Cara Barer, *Road to Robinhood Bay*
Composition: Achorn International, Inc.
Printing and Binding: RR Donnelley and Sons

Manufactured in the United States of America.

0   9   8   7
f   e   d   c

For information, write: Bedford/St. Martin's, 75 Arlington Street, Boston, MA 02116
(617-399-4000)

ISBN 978-1-4576-9796-8 (Student Edition)
ISBN 978-1-319-02023-1 (Instructor's Edition)

Acknowledgments

Text acknowledgments and copyrights appear at the back of the book on pages 570–72, which constitute an extension of the copyright page. Art acknowledgments and copyrights appear on the same page as the art selections they cover. It is a violation of the law to reproduce these selections by any means whatsoever without the written permission of the copyright holder.

PREFACE FOR INSTRUCTORS

Emerging/Thinking

One of the fundamental facts of teaching writing is that when students leave our class-rooms, they go back to their increasingly busy lives: They go to other classes, go to their jobs after school, go hang out with friends, go into their disciplines, go into their careers, go into the world. The challenge for us as instructors is to help students acquire the skills of critical reading, thinking, and writing that will allow them to succeed in these diverse contexts.

Emerging seeks to address this challenge. It offers sustained readings that present complex ideas in approachable language; it encourages critical thinking and writing skills by prompting students to make connections among readings; it draws from a broad cross section of themes and disciplines in order to present students with numer-ous points of entry and identification; and it introduces emerging problems—such as cultural conflict (in social and linguistic dimensions), the impact of technology (from Facebook to brain science), race and social rights (such as conflicts between individuals and groups), and the dilemmas of ethics (concerns about genetic engineering, for in-stance, and the relations between art and philanthropy)—that have not yet been solved and settled.

The readings are organized alphabetically to open up possibilities for connections. (Alternative tables of contents highlight disciplinary concerns and thematic clusters.) Because they consist of entire book chapters or complete articles, readings can stand on their own as originally intended. However, the readings in *Emerging* were chosen because they connect to each other in interesting and illuminating ways. The issues under discussion resonate across readings, genres, and disciplines, prompting students to think about each selection in multiple dimensions. These resonant connections are shown through "tags" indicating central concepts treated in the selections. Several tags for each piece are listed in the table of contents, in each headnote, and for each assign-ment sequence—highlighting concepts such as "community," "globalism," "identity," "culture," and "trauma and violence." Thus one can see at a glance the possibilities for thematic connections among the readings. Connections with other authors are also highlighted in the table of contents, in each headnote, and through the assignment sequences (included at the back of the book; see p. 549). The assignment sequences suggest a succession of readings that are linked conceptually so that one assignment se-quence provides the structure for an entire semester. (Sequences are further explained on the next page.)

Emerging/Reading

Because students ultimately enter diverse disciplines, the readings are drawn from across fields of knowledge located both inside and outside the academy. Political science, sociology, journalism, anthropology, economics, and art are some of the disciplines one might expect to find in such a collection, but *Emerging* also includes readings from pho-tography, public health, psychology, business, philosophy, neurology, technology, and law. The author of each selection addresses his or her concerns to an audience outside the discipline — a useful model for students who eventually will need to communicate beyond the boundaries of their chosen fields. Many of the readings also represent cross-disciplinary work — an economist thinking about politics, a musician thinking about education — since the walls between departments in academia are becoming increasingly permeable.

Yet despite this disciplinary grounding, the readings, though challenging, are accessible, written as they are with a general audience in mind. The readings thus demonstrate multiple ways in which complex ideas and issues can be presented in formal yet approachable language. The accessible nature of the essays also allows for many readings longer than those typically seen in first-year composition anthologies, because the level of writing makes them comprehensible to students. Yet even the briefer readings are substantive, providing greater opportunities for nuanced arguments.

Of course, in addition to referencing emerging issues, the title of this collection refers also to the students in first-year composition courses, who themselves are emerging as readers, thinkers, and writers. By providing them with challenging texts along with the tools needed to decode, interpret, and deploy these texts, *Emerging* helps college readers develop the skills they will need as they move into working with the difficult theoretical texts presented in their choice of majors — and ultimately into their twenty-first-century careers.

Emerging/Writing

One of the philosophical tenets supporting *Emerging* is that students need to be prepared to deal with emerging issues in their jobs and lives, and to do so, they not only must acquire information about these issues (since such information will continually change) but also must possess an ability to think critically in relation to them. The editorial apparatus in *Emerging* includes the following features that will help students develop the skills needed to become fluid, reflective, and critically self-aware writers:

▶ **Part One: Emerging as a Critical Thinker and Academic Writer.** Part One presents the key skills of academic success: the ability to read critically, argue, use evidence, and revise.

▶ **Part Two: Readings.** The readings in Part Two each include a variety of questions to help students practice the skills of critical thinking, explained in detail below.

▶ **Part Three: Assignment Sequences.** In order to stress the iterative processes of thinking and writing, eight assignment sequences are included in the back of the book, each of which uses multiple selections to engage students' thinking about a central theme, issue, or problem. Each sequence frames a project extensive enough for an entire semester's work and can be easily adapted for individual classes, and two of the sequences prompt students to conduct outside research.

Additionally, the apparatus accompanying each reading provides substantial help for students while featuring innovative approaches to understanding the essays and their relation to the world outside the classroom:

▶ **Headnotes.** A headnote preceding each reading selection provides biographical information about the author and describes the context of the larger work from which the reading has been taken.

▶ **Questions for Critical Reading.** These questions at the start of each reading direct students to central concepts, issues, and ideas from the essay in order to prompt a directed rereading of the text while providing a guide for the student's own interpretive moves.

▶ **Exploring Context.** In order to leverage students' existing literacies with digital technologies, these questions ask students to use the Web and other electronic sources to contextualize each reading further, using sites and tools such as Facebook and Twitter.

▶ **Questions for Connecting.** Because thinking across essays provides particular circumstances for critical thinking, these opportunities for writing ask students to make connections between essays and to apply and synthesize authors' ideas.

▶ **Language Matters.** The Language Matters questions are a unique feature of this reader. These questions address issues of grammar and writing through the context of the essays, presenting language not as a set of rules to be memorized but as a system of meaning-making that can also be used as a tool for analysis.

▶ **Assignments for Writing.** Each reading has three Assignments for Writing questions that ask students to build on the work they've done in the other questions of the apparatus and create a piece of writing with a sustained argument supported by textual engagement.

What's New

New readings on a wider variety of topics. Twenty-one selections are new, broadening the range of topics in *Emerging*. And in response to reviewer requests, these include brief, accessible selections and new images. Authors of the readings include public intellectuals, many with familiar names. For instance, Daniel Kahneman examines our decision-making process and questions our faith in the judgments we make in "The Surety of Fools"; Chuck Klosterman considers the nature of villainy in the age of technology in "Electric Funeral"; Robin Marantz Henig considers emerging adulthood in "What Is It about 20-Somethings?"; Yo-Yo Ma suggests the need for a broad-based education including the arts in "Necessary Edges: Arts, Empathy, and Education"; and Julia Serano examines rape culture and gender stereotypes from the perspective of a transgender woman in "Why Nice Guys Finish Last." Additionally, a new visual selection by Tomas van Houtryve, "From the Eyes of a Drone," depicts everyday scenes from the perspective of a drone, calling into question the military use of drones.

More help for critical thinking, reading, and writing in Part One. A new Part One: Emerging as a Critical Thinker and Academic Writer lays the foundation for the kind of work students will do in a variety of disciplines. Expanded coverage of writing in the disciplines and argumentative writing helps students connect their work in *Emerging* to work in fields beyond composition. In addition, new disciplinary tags and an alternative table of contents that categorizes readings by discipline make it easier to find readings relevant to your students.

Fresh new assignment sequences. Eight new sequences ask challenging questions to spark students' interest: Why does race still matter? What should be the goal of an education? What do we do about bullying?

A new focus on research. Helping students connect to the world beyond the composition classroom, *Emerging* encourages students to seek out their own sources and bring unexpected ideas together. Part One includes a more in-depth look at finding, evaluating, and using sources, while two new research-focused assignment sequences challenge students to use outside sources to complicate the questions raised by the selections in *Emerging*.

Get the Most Out of Your Course with *Emerging*

Bedford/St. Martin's offers resources and format choices that help you and your students get even more out of your book and course. To learn more about or to order any of the following products, contact your Bedford/St. Martin's sales representative, e-mail sales support (**sales_support@bfwpub.com**), or visit the catalog Web site at **macmillanhighered.com/emerging/catalog**.

Select Value Packages

Add value to your text by packaging one of the following resources with *Emerging*. To learn more about package options for any of the following products, contact your Bedford/St. Martin's sales representative or visit **macmillanhighered.com/emerging /catalog**.

Writer's Help 2.0 is a powerful online writing resource that helps students find answers whether they are searching for writing advice on their own or as part of an assignment.

- **Smart search**
  Built on research with more than 1,600 student writers, the smart search in *Writer's Help 2.0* provides reliable results even when students use novice terms, such as *flow* and *unstuck*.

- **Trusted content from our best-selling handbooks**
  Choose *Writer's Help 2.0 for Hacker Handbooks* or *Writer's Help 2.0 for Lunsford Handbooks* and ensure that students have clear advice and examples for all of their writing questions.

- **Adaptive exercises that engage students**
  Writer's Help 2.0 includes LearningCurve, game-like online quizzing that adapts to what students already know and helps them focus on what they need to learn.

Student access is packaged with *Emerging* at a significant discount. Order ISBN 978-1-319-06071-8 for *Writer's Help 2.0 for Hacker Handbooks* or ISBN 978-1-319-06072-5 for *Writer's Help 2.0 for Lunsford Handbooks* to ensure your students have easy access to online writing support. Students who rent a book or buy a used book can purchase access to *Writer's Help 2.0* at **macmillanhighered.com/writershelp2**.

   Instructors may request free access by registering as an instructor at **macmillanhighered.com/writershelp2**.

   For technical support, visit **macmillanhighered.com/getsupport**.

   LaunchPad Solo for Readers and Writers allows students to work on whatever they need help with the most. At home or in class, students learn at their own pace, with instruction tailored to each student's unique needs. *LaunchPad Solo for Readers and Writers* features:

- **Pre-built units that support a learning arc**
  Each easy-to-assign unit is comprised of a pre-test check, multimedia instruction and assessment, and a post-test that assesses what students have learned about critical reading, writing process, using sources, grammar, style, mechanics, and help for multilingual writers.

- **A video introduction to many topics**
  Introductions offer an overview of the unit's topic, and many include a brief, accessible video to illustrate the concepts at hand.

- **Adaptive quizzing for targeted learning**
  Most units include LearningCurve, game-like adaptive quizzing that focuses on the areas in which each student needs the most help.

- **The ability to monitor student progress**
  Use our Gradebook to see which students are on track and which need additional help with specific topics.

LaunchPad Solo for Readers and Writers can be **packaged at a significant discount**. Visit **macmillanhighered.com/catalog/readwrite** for more information.

   ***Portfolio Keeping*, Third Edition, by Nedra Reynolds and Elizabeth Davis**, provides all the information students need to use the portfolio method successfully in a writing course. *Portfolio Teaching*, a companion guide for instructors, provides the practical information instructors and writing program administrators need to use the portfolio method successfully in a writing course. To order *Portfolio Keeping* packaged with this text, contact your sale representative for a package ISBN.

Make Learning Fun with *Re:Writing 3*
bedfordstmartins.com/rewriting

Bedford's free and open online resource includes videos and interactive elements to engage students in new ways of writing. You'll find tutorials about using common digital writing tools, an interactive peer review game, "Extreme Paragraph Makeover," and more. Visit **bedfordstmartins.com/rewriting**.

Instructor Resources

macmillanhighered.com/emerging/catalog
You have a lot to do in your course. Bedford/St. Martin's wants to make it easy for you to find the support you need—and to get it quickly.

The instructor's manual for this title, *Resources for Teaching Emerging*, is available as a PDF that can be downloaded from the Bedford/St. Martin's online catalog at the URL above. In addition to teaching tips, the instructor's manual includes detailed sample syllabi for multiple course formats, a chapter on pedagogy, lots of class activities and help with peer revision, practical advice for commenting and grading (including rubrics), sample student papers based on the readings in *Emerging*, and thorough coverage of each reading and sequence in the book.

Teaching Central offers the entire list of Bedford/St. Martin's print and online professional resources in one place. You'll find landmark reference works, sourcebooks on pedagogical issues, award-winning collections, and practical advice for the classroom—all free for instructors. Visit **macmillanhighered.com/teachingcentral**.

Bedford *Bits* collects creative ideas for teaching a range of composition topics in a frequently updated blog. A community of teachers—leading scholars, authors, and editors such as *Emerging* author Barclay Barrios, Andrea Lunsford, Elizabeth Losh, Jack Solomon, and Elizabeth Wardle—discuss assignments, activities, revision, research, grammar and style, multimodal composition, technology, peer review, and much more. Take, use, adapt, and pass the ideas around. Then, come back to the site to comment or share your own suggestion. Visit **community.macmillan.com**.

Acknowledgments

This collection itself has been a long time emerging, and I would be remiss not to thank the many people who contributed their time, energy, feedback, and support throughout the course of this project.

I would first like to acknowledge past and current colleagues who have played a role in developing this text. Richard E. Miller and Kurt Spellmeyer, both of Rutgers University, through their mentorship and guidance laid the foundations for my approach to composition as reflected in this reader. My department chairs during my time here at Florida Atlantic University, Andrew Furman and Wenying Xu, provided reassurance and support as I balanced the work of this text and the work of serving as Director of Writing Programs. The members of the Writing Committee for Florida Atlantic University's Department of English—Jeff Galin, Joanne Jasin, Jennifer Low, Julia Mason, Daniel Murtaugh, and Magdalena Ostas—generously allowed me to shape both this reader and the writing program. The dean's office of the Dorothy F. Schmidt College of Arts and Letters of Florida Atlantic University provided a Summer Teaching Development Award, which aided in the creation of the materials that form the core of the Instructor's Manual.

This third edition was made possible by the relentless work of a large group of teachers at Florida Atlantic University. I'd like to thank Gabrielle Helo for finding new readings; Adam Phillips for finding new readings and offering sample student work; Daniel Creed for also offering sample student work; Scott Rachesky for finding new readings and being a really fantastic assistant; and Mike Shier, who once again stepped up to the plate to compose headnotes despite having moved on from our program. And my very special thanks to Risa Polansky Shiman, who was exceptionally helpful, going above and beyond my expectations by finding new readings, composing headnotes, offering sample student work, and contributing to the Instructor's Manual. I could not have completed this project without all of these dedicated teachers.

I am also grateful to the reviewers who examined the manuscript of the first edition and provided valuable feedback: Sonja Andrus, Collin County Community College; Susan Bailor, Front Range Community College; Barbara Booker, Pasco-Hernando Community College; Patricia Webb Boyd, Arizona State University; John Champagne, Penn State Erie, The Behrend College; Michael Cripps, York College/CUNY; Brock Dethier, Utah State University; Kimberly Harrison, Florida International University; Karen Head, The Georgia Institute of Technology; Virginia Scott Hendrickson, Missouri State University; Lindsay Lewan, Arapahoe Community College; April Lewandowski, Front Range Community College–Westminster; Gina Maranto, University of Miami; Erica Messenger, Bowling Green State University–Main Campus; Beverly Neiderman, Kent State University; Jill Onega, Calhoun Community College; Roberta Stagnaro, San Diego State University; and Melora G. Vandersluis, Azusa Pacific University.

I am grateful as well to the reviewers who helped shape the second edition: Lena Ampadu, Towson University; John Barbour, University of Kentucky; Aaron Barrell, Everett Community College; Bridgett Blaque, Truckee Meadows Community College; Barbara B. Booker, Pasco-Hernando Community College; Patricia Boyd, Arizona State University; Sonya C. Brown, Fayetteville State University; Sakina Bryant, Sonoma State University; Michael J. Cripps, University of New England; Sarah Duerden, Arizona State University; Rebecca Gerdes, Indiana University South Bend; Rachael Groner, Temple University; Barbara E. Hamilton, Montclair State University; Susanmarie Harrington, University of Vermont; D. Alexis Hart, Virginia Military Institute; Elaine Hays, College of the Holy Cross; Wendy Hinshaw, Florida Atlantic University; Charlotte Hogg, Texas Christian University; M. Kamel Igoudjil, American University; Thomas Irwin, University of Missouri, St. Louis; Carol M. Lane, California State University, Chico; Kerry K. Lawson, Indiana University South Bend; Amy Letter, Florida Atlantic University; Lindsay Lewan, Arapahoe Community College; Gina Maranto, University of Miami; Margaret McBride, University of Oregon; Alisea Williams McLeod, Indiana University South Bend; Julia Mendenhall, Temple University; Scott Orme, Spokane Community College; Nancy Paris, Indiana University; Susan Piqueira, Central Connecticut State University; Spencer Schaffner, University of Illinois; Allison D. Smith, Middle Tennessee State University; LuAnn Sorenson, University of Illinois–Urbana-Champaign; Brian Spears, Florida Atlantic University; Christopher L. Stockdale, Sonoma State University; Christopher Walters, Normandale Community College; and Jeff Wheeler, Long Beach City College.

I also wish to thank the reviewers who helped shape the third edition: Adam Berzak, Broward College; Mary Bogue, Florida Atlantic University; Michael Cripps, University of New England; Ana Douglass, Truckee Meadows Community College; Laura Dubek, Middle Tennessee State University; Barbara Hamilton, Mercer County Community College; Megan Hesse, Florida Atlantic University; Robert Imbur, University of Toledo; Cat Mahaffey, University of North Carolina at Charlotte; Matthew Martin, Santa Rosa

Junior College; Joseph Miragliuolo, Three Rivers Community College; Scott Rachesky, Florida Atlantic University; Debra Ryals, Pensacola State College; Mary Sheffield-Gentry, Florida Atlantic University; and Linda Tucker, Southern Arkansas University.

I cannot say enough about the support I have received from Bedford/St. Martin's. The enthusiasm of Karen Henry, Leasa Burton, and John Sullivan for this project was always appreciated. And my editor Sarah Macomber patiently pushed me to make the best book possible and provided vital encouragement whenever my spirits drooped. Thanks, too, to Evelyn Denham for getting to me what I needed when I needed it. I am grateful to Margaret Gorenstein for clearing text permissions and to Sheri Blaney for obtaining art permissions. Matt Glazer expertly guided the manuscript through production, assisted by copy editor Jennifer Greenstein. I appreciate their help.

Finally, a special thanks to those who kept me centered and strong, most especially my partner, Joseph Tocio, who offered not only love and support but a compelling reason to be in Boston so that I could meet with the publisher. I offer this edition in loving memory of my mother, Elaine Montalbano Barrios.

CONTENTS

SANDRA ALLEN

A World Without Wine

A journalist explores the effects of climate change on the wine industry and its broader implications for agriculture. Allen asks, "We could live in a world without wine, of course, but would we want to?"

▶ TAGS: *economics, food and agriculture, globalism, science and technology*
▶ CONNECTIONS: *Appiah, Gilbert, Watters*

KWAME ANTHONY APPIAH

Making Conversation *and* The Primacy of Practice

A prominent philosopher argues, "In the wake of 9/11, there has been a lot of fretful discussion about the divide between 'us' and 'them.' What's often taken for granted is a picture of a world in which conflicts arise, ultimately, from conflicts between values. This is what we take to be good; that is what they take to be good. That picture of the world has deep philosophical roots; it is thoughtful, well worked out, plausible. And, I think, wrong."

observes that "Food is politics"—the decisions we make around food have complex ramifications that must be examined.

▶ TAGS: *economics, energy, ethics, food and agriculture, health and medicine*

▶ CONNECTIONS: *Appiah, Dalai Lama, Friedman, Ma, Moalem, Pollan, Wallace*

A doctor explains the mechanisms of epigenetics, in which environmental conditions and lifestyle choices change our genetic code. Epigenetics explains how a regular bee becomes a queen; it also explains how bullying can have consequences across generations. He cautions, "the choices you make can result in a big difference in this generation, the next one, and possibly everyone else down the line."

▶ TAGS: *adolescence and adulthood, food and agriculture, genetics, health and medicine, science and technology, trauma and violence*

▶ CONNECTIONS: *Dalai Lama, DeGhett, Olson, Pollan, Pozner, Restak, Rosin, Savage and Vaid, Stillman*

A journalist and fashion blogger looks at the rise of "ethnic plastic surgery," a range of niche procedures available to non-Caucasians. "The issues at stake," she writes, "are loaded: ethnic identity, standards of beauty, the politics of diversity, what constitutes race, and whether exercises of vanity can reshape it."

▶ TAGS: *beauty, community, culture, economics, health and medicine, identity, judgment and decision-making, race and ethnicity*

▶ CONNECTIONS: *Gay, Levy, Olson, Pozner, Watters, Yang, Yoshino*

A journalist writes, "When geneticists look at our DNA, they do not see a world of rigidly divided groups each going its own way. They see something much more fluid and ambiguous—something more like the social structures that have emerged in Hawaii as intermarriage has accelerated."

▶ TAGS: *community, culture, genetics, identity, judgment and decision-making, race and ethnicity, science and technology, social change, tradition*

▶ CONNECTIONS: *O'Connor, Watters, Yang, Yoshino*

last" subtly encourages men into offensive behavior. We need to dismantle that system of thinking in order to combat rape culture. She writes that "we won't get to where we want to be until the men-as-predator/sexual aggressor assumption no longer dominates our thinking. It's difficult to imagine getting there from here," she admits, "but we're going to have to try."

▶ TAGS: *culture, empathy, gender, identity, media, race and ethnicity, relationships, sexuality, social change, trauma and violence*

▶ CONNECTIONS: *Appiah, Gay, Levy, O'Connor, Padawer, Pozner, Rosin, Yang*

An ethicist examines issues of privacy in the connected digital world: "The modern Panopticon is not a physical building, and it doesn't require the threat of an inspector's presence to be effective."

▶ TAGS: *censorship, ethics, law and justice, photography and video, politics, science and technology, social change*

▶ CONNECTIONS: *Henig, Klosterman, Konnikova, Paumgarten, Restak, Wasik*

A freelance writer and blogger evaluates the relevance of art within the philosophical framework of Effective Altruism, whose goal is "doing as much good as you possibly can with your life." He asks, "if we were to consult our magic utilitarian consequences calculator, how often would it tell us to bother making art at all?"

▶ TAGS: *art, community, economics, empathy, ethics, globalism, judgment and decision-making, social change*

▶ CONNECTIONS: *Appiah, Dalai Lama, DeGhett, Klosterman, Ma, Pollan, Savage and Vaid, Wallace, Watters*

A journalist unearths the trans-generational effects of trauma on families and communities by looking at survivors of the atomic bombing of Hiroshima. She observes, "A wide range of studies have examined evidence of 'secondary trauma' in the children of Holocaust survivors, the wives of Vietnam veterans, and, more informally, in the families of U.S. veterans who've faced PTSD after deployments to Iraq and Afghanistan."

▶ TAGS: *genetics, health and medicine, psychology, trauma and violence, war and conflict*

▶ CONNECTIONS: *DeGhett, Epstein, Gilbert, Moalem, Paumgarten, Restak, Serano*

Part 3
ASSIGNMENT SEQUENCES

We tend to think of technology as a neutral tool for connection, but as the readings in this sequence make clear, technology such as social media influences our growth, development, and the ways in which we connect to others. These assignments examine the impact of technology not only on our world but also, more profoundly, on what it means to be human.

▶ TAGS: *community, conversation, culture, empathy, ethics, identity, media, photography and video, psychology, relationships, science and technology, social media*

Race remains a contentious issue even after decades of work towards civil rights and despite the reality of a diverse and deeply interconnected world.

Notwithstanding any progress made in legal and political arenas, race continues to have fractious social and cultural implications. This sequence of assignments considers the factors that cause race to persist in order to foster conversations on why racial categories continue to have such critical relevance to our world.

▶ TAGS: *beauty, civil rights, community, culture, education, empathy, genetics, globalism, identity, psychology, race and ethnicity, social change, tradition*

Gender is a fundamental category of identity that can be simultaneously enabling and disabling to our growth as human beings. Yet though gender works to determine who we are and who we can be, we also have the ability to change the meaning of gender for ourselves and our world. These assignments explore the consequences of our current system of gender and the ways in which we can work to alter the meaning, function, and relevance of gender.

▶ TAGS: *adolescence and adulthood, beauty, community, culture, gender, identity, judgment and decision-making, media, psychology, race and ethnicity, relationships, sexuality, social change, tradition, trauma and violence*

Assignments

Living in a globalized world doesn't mean we all have to get along; it does mean, however, that we must learn how to mediate cultural differences in order to solve the problems we face in common with others. War, conflict, and terrorism are the alternatives. This sequence of assignments examines an array of issues related to peace and conflict. The essays and assignments suggest tools and concepts needed to advocate for ethical solutions to conflict in a globalized world.

▶ TAGS: *censorship, community, culture, economics, empathy, ethics, globalism, judgment and decision-making, law and justice, media, photography and video, politics, psychology, science and technology, trauma and violence, war and conflict*

• •

SEQUENCE 5   561

How Can You Make a Difference in the World?

CHARLES DUHIGG, From Civil Rights to Megachurches • RHYS SOUTHAN, Is Art a Waste of Time? • KENJI YOSHINO, Preface *and* The New Civil Rights • KWAME ANTHONY APPIAH, Making Conversation *and* The Primacy of Practice • HELEN EPSTEIN, AIDS, Inc.

Assignments

Few of us are completely happy with the world around us, but each of us can work towards the world we want to see. Advocating for change is a fundamental ability we can choose to exercise. The readings in this sequence offer strategies and tools for creating small and large scale social change.

▶ TAGS: *art, civil rights, collaboration, community, conversation, culture, economics, empathy, ethics, identity, judgment and decision-making, law and justice, media, politics, psychology, race and ethnicity, relationships, social change, tradition*

Education is a political act, since the choice of what is taught, studied, and learned encodes a set of values and a particular way of looking at the world. As students, you might have a particular investment in the ends of education and, certainly, you have ideas about the goals for your own education. These assignments explore education as it exists today and as it may take shape in the future.

▶ TAGS: *adolescence and adulthood, art, community, culture, education, empathy, gender, identity, psychology, race and ethnicity, relationships, science and technology, social change, tradition*

Bullying is a deadly epidemic. It is a critical problem with no simple solution. This sequence explores the ramifications of bullying and offers the opportunity to research approaches that work towards a solution.

▶ TAGS: *adolescence and adulthood, community, conversation, culture, empathy, ethics, gender, genetics, identity, judgment and decision-making, law and justice, photography and video, psychology, relationships, sexuality, social change, social media, trauma and violence*

Food is a central problem in a world with a burgeoning population. Yet most of us don't think much about food. These assignments explore some of the practical and ethical problems around food and eating while offering a chance to conduct additional research on this issue.

▶ TAGS: *community, culture, economics, energy, ethics, food and agriculture, genetics, globalism, health and medicine, politics, science and technology, social change, tradition, trauma and violence, war and conflict*

DISCIPLINARY CONVERSATIONS

HEALTH, MEDICINE, AND NURSING

HUMANITIES

NATURAL SCIENCES

SOCIAL SCIENCES

THEMATIC CONTENTS

GETTING ALONG

GLOBAL PROBLEMS AND SOLUTIONS

GROWING UP

ME AND WE

MEDIA AND CULTURE

RIGHTS AND WRONGS

TECHNO-BIOLOGY

Part One

EMERGING AS A CRITICAL THINKER AND ACADEMIC WRITER

I N SOME CLASSES, such as biology, sociology, economics, or chemistry, what you learn and what you're tested on is *content*—a knowledge of terms and concepts. In contrast, what you need to learn in a composition class is a *process*—an approach to reading and writing that you will practice with the essays in this book, in class discussions, and by responding to essay assignments. This class is not just about the readings in this book but also about what you can do with them. What you will do with them, of course, is write. And yet it's not entirely accurate to say you're here to learn how to write, either. After all, you already did a lot of writing in high school, and if you couldn't write, you wouldn't have gotten into college. But you will learn a particular *kind* of writing in this class, one that may be new to you: *academic writing*—joining a conversation by researching, weighing, and incorporating what others say into your own work in order to make a point of your own. You'll use academic writing throughout your college career, and the skills you learn in this class will also help you throughout your life. That's because academic writing involves *critical thinking*—the ability to evaluate, assess, apply, and generate ideas—an essential skill no matter what career you choose. Thriving in a career—any career—is never about how much you know but about what you can do with the knowledge you have. College will prepare you for your career by providing you with knowledge (your job here is part memorization), but college will also help you learn how to evaluate knowledge, how to apply it, and how to create it; these are the skills of critical thinking.

> **Whenever we solve problems or make decisions, we use critical thinking because we gather, evaluate, and apply knowledge to the situation at hand.**

What's *Emerging*?

The Readings

College is also, of course, a time for change. You're not just moving into your career—you're moving into a new phase of your life. In this sense, you might think of yourself as an emerging thinker and writer, one who builds on existing skills and expands them in an academic context. In some ways, emerging is also very much the theme of the readings. Each was chosen to give you an opportunity to practice critical thinking through academic writing. But each one also concerns an emerging issue in the world today, something you might have already encountered but also something you will have to deal with as you move on in your life.

Take, for example, Thomas L. Friedman's chapter "The Dell Theory of Conflict Prevention" (p. 124), taken from his best-selling book *The World Is Flat*. Friedman is an expert in foreign relations, but he writes not to academics or economists or political theorists but to people like you and me. At the same time, his argument—that worldwide business supply chains promote political stability—requires a lot of thinking. Comprehension is not so much the issue. Friedman lays out his argument logically and supports it with many kinds of evidence (as you will learn to do as well). But the ideas he proposes about the relationship between economics and geopolitics, as well as his ideas about war, peace, and terrorism, will require you to think about the implications of his argument, and that kind of work is the start of critical thinking. Figuring out what's in the text is challenging, but even more challenging is figuring out what's *not* in the text: the examples that would challenge Friedman's argument, or new areas where his ideas have value, or modifications of his argument based on your experience or on other things you have read. That's critical thinking. What follows will help you do that thinking.

The Support

To support you, each of the readings comes with a set of tools to help you develop your skills as a critical reader, thinker, and writer:

- **Tags.** If you look in the table of contents and at the end of each headnote, you'll find that each reading comes with a number of "tags." These tags give you a quick sense of the topics—such as gender or technology—covered in the reading.

- **Headnotes.** The headnotes that appear before each reading provide context. In addition to finding out about the author, you'll learn about the larger context of writing from which the reading is taken, so that you can have a sense of the author's overall project. Headnotes help you prepare for the reading by giving you a quick sense of what you're about to encounter.

- **Questions for Critical Reading.** As you read the headnotes, you may find that you are already developing questions about the selection you're about to read, questions that can serve as the basis of your critical thinking. Your own questions can be supplemented by the Questions for Critical Reading at the start of each selection, which are specifically designed to focus your reading and thinking in ways that will develop your critical thinking skills while helping you produce the writing asked of you in this class.

- **Exploring Context.** The Exploring Context questions use technology to deepen your understanding of the essay and its context in the world. These questions also underscore the fact that the readings have a life outside of this text where their ideas are discussed, developed, refuted, and extended—a life to which you will contribute through your work in this class.

- **Questions for Connecting.** These questions prompt you to apply your critical reading and thinking skills by relating the current reading to other selections in the book. Connecting the ideas of one author to the ideas or examples of another author is a key skill in critical thinking.

- **Language Matters.** The Language Matters questions at the end of each reading will help you practice skills with language and grammar by asking you to look at how meaning is created in these readings. Thinking critically about the language used by these authors will help you think critically about the language you use in your writing as well, so that you can take these insights back to your own writing.

- **Assignments for Writing.** These questions provide opportunities to join the conversation of these essays. Your instructor may assign these to you or you may wish to use them more informally to help you develop a deeper understanding of the text.

- **Assignment Sequences.** There are also a series of assignment sequences in this text; your instructor may choose to use or adapt one for your class. They're termed *sequences* because each assignment builds on the one that came before. In this way, you'll get to see how your understanding of a reading changes as you work with it alongside other readings from the text. As you return to previous readings while developing a central theme of thinking through these assignments, you will refine your critical thinking skills by paying close attention not only to each text but also to the relationships among groups of texts.

Fortunately, just as you've entered class with many writing skills, so too do you enter with skills in critical thinking. Critical thinking, after all, involves processing information, and we live in an information-rich world. So chances are that many of the things you do every day involve some kind of critical thinking; this class will hone those skills and translate them into the academic realm.

For now, it might be helpful to focus on six skills you might already use that correspond to aspects of academic writing and that also will enable you to thrive in the world at large: the abilities to read critically, think critically, argue, support, research, and revise.

The Writer

As you develop these skills in this class, you will emerge not only as a stronger thinker and writer but also as an individual ready to enter your chosen discipline and thereafter your career. The writing you will do within your field may look very different from the writing you do in this class, but the moves you make within your writing for this class — your ability to form and support an argument — will remain the same. Moreover, you will come to find that people working within a discipline never write only for members of that discipline; they write for the general public as well. An engineer will write very specific, very complicated documents for other engineers but will also need to communicate with business associates, salespeople, managers, customers, and investors. No matter what you end up studying, you will need to communicate the concerns of your discipline to others.

The readings in *Emerging* offer good examples. Contrast, for example, the way neuroscientist Sharon Moalem writes in "Changing Our Genes: How Trauma, Bullying, and Royal Jelly Alter Our Genetic Destiny" (p. 277), intended for a general audience, with the way he writes in "Hemochromatosis and the Enigma of Misplaced Iron: Implications for Infectious Disease and Survival," which he wrote with Eugene D. Weinberg and Maire E. Percy for the journal *BioMetals*. Notice, first, that he writes with others when publishing within his field; collaboration is very common in the sciences. Notice, too, the difference in the opening of the journal article, which I have included with its MLA citation:

> Hereditary hemochromatosis is a genetic condition whereby too much iron is absorbed through the diet (Jazwinska 1998). In people with hereditary hemochromatosis, iron overload of parenchymal cells may lead to destruction of the liver, heart, and pancreas. Two mutations (C282Y and H63D) in a "nonclassical" HLA class-I gene named HFE have been found to be associated with hereditary hemochromatosis (Feder et al. 1996). (135)

Moalem uses a very different, very specialized language that probably only makes sense to others in the discipline (*parenchymal, HLA class-I gene*), and he and his co-authors cite others in their field as they begin to make their argument ("Jazwinska," "Feder et al."). The article also includes tables that summarize their research and has a full works cited page. Moalem does not use any of these features when writing for us as general readers. Yet in both pieces he works to articulate an argument and support it with evidence: What differs is how it is written and how it is supported. In this class, you will learn the basic ways of thinking and writing necessary for academic arguments. Should you become a neuroscientist like Moalem, then you will learn the specific elements of writing like a neuroscientist in your discipline.

Writing is a lifelong skill. As you practice academic writing, you will emerge as a stronger thinker, one capable of communicating your own ideas. You will take that ability with you as you move through your college career and then later as you move into your profession.

And it all begins with reading critically.

Reading Critically

We live in a world saturated with information—so much so that Richard Restak notes in "Attention Deficit: The Brain Syndrome of Our Era" (p. 373) that our brains are being rewired by the multiple and competing demands information makes on our attention. Mastering the ability to read critically is crucial to managing these demands, since doing so allows us to select just the information we're looking for. So crucial is this skill to our survival today that we don't even think about it anymore. Indeed, you probably read for information on the Web every day, and you probably find what you need, too.

Yet while it seems intuitive, reading involves a kind of critical thinking. Though reading is a way to find information, you may find it difficult to find the information you need in these readings. They are probably not the kind of texts you've read previously in your life or educational career, so they might feel very difficult. That's OK; they're supposed to be challenging, because dealing with difficulty is the best way to develop your skills with critical thinking. In other words, if you didn't have to think about what you read in this class, you wouldn't be doing any critical thinking at all.

Strategies for Reading Critically

There are a number of steps you can take to help you read these essays critically:

- **Acknowledge that the reading is hard.** The first step is to acknowledge any difficulty you're having — recognizing it forces you to activate your skills with critical thinking consciously.

- **Keep reading the essay.** The second step is to just keep reading, even if you feel you don't understand what you're reading. Often, the opening of an essay might be confusing or disorienting, but as you continue to read, you start to see the argument emerge. Similarly, the author might repeat key points throughout the essay, so by the time you complete the reading, what seemed impossible to understand begins to make sense.

- **Write down what you *did* understand.** After you've completed the reading, you might still feel confused. Write down what you *did* understand — no matter how little that might be and no matter how unsure you are of your understanding. Recognizing what you know is the best way to figure out what you need to learn.

- **Identify specific passages that confused you.** Identifying specific passages that you did not understand is an important strategy, too. By locating any points of confusion, you can focus your critical thinking skills on those passages in order to begin to decode them.

- **Make a list of specific questions.** Make a list of specific questions you have, and then bring those questions to class as a way of guiding the class's discussion to enhance your understanding of the reading.

- **Discuss the reading with peers.** The questions accompanying the reading will give you some help, but your peers are another valuable resource. Discussing the reading with them allows you and your classmates to pool your comprehension — the section you didn't understand might be the one your peers did, and vice versa.

- **Reread the essay at least once, or more.** Finally, reread the essay. Reading, like writing, is a looping process. We read and reread, just as we write and revise, and each time we get a little more out of it.

Annotating

While reading, one of the things you'll want to search for is the author's argument, the point he or she is trying to make in the selection. In addition, you'll want to search for concepts, terms, or ideas that are unique or central to the author's argument. Reading with a pen, highlighter, laptop, or sticky notes at hand will help you identify this information. In academic terms, you will be *annotating* the text, adding questions, comments, and notes while highlighting material you feel is important in some way; annotation is the start of critical reading because it identifies the most important information in the essay, and that's exactly the information you need to think about.

You might think of annotation as keeping a running guide of your thoughts while reading. That way, when you return to work with the essay, you have the start of your critical thinking. There are a number of things you might want to pay attention to during this process:

- **Look for the author's argument.** What is the overall point the author wants to make? Consider this one of the central tasks of your reading and annotation, both because you will want to engage this argument and because it will model for you how *you* can make your own point about the issue.

- **Mark key terms, concepts, and ideas.** Pay special attention to any words or phrases in italics or quotation marks. Often this indicates that the author is introducing an idea and will then go on to define it. Critical thinking often involves ideas, so it's important for you to locate and identify the ideas of the essay.

- **Mark information you will need again.** For example, there may be certain quotations that strike you as important or as puzzling. By annotating these, you will be able to find them quickly for class discussion or while you are writing your paper.

- **Mark words you don't understand.** Look them up in a dictionary. This process will enhance your comprehension of the essay.

- **Ask questions in response to the text.** Don't assume that the author's words are gospel truth. Your job as a critical thinker is to evaluate everything the author says based on your knowledge and experience. Whenever you locate a mismatch between what the author says and what you think, note it with a question about the essay.

- **Summarize key points in the margin.** Summarizing the key points will help you map the overall flow of the argument. This process will help you comprehend the essay better and, as with locating the argument, will help you see how to structure your own writing as well.

> **HOW TO ANNOTATE A READING**
>
> - Read with a pen, a highlighter, or sticky notes at hand.
> - Look for the author's argument.
> - Mark key terms, concepts, and ideas.
> - Mark information you will need again.
> - Mark words you don't understand.
> - Ask questions in reaction to the text.
> - Summarize key points in the margin.

Let's look at an example, an annotated excerpt from "Electric Funeral," Chuck Klosterman's essay about fame and infamy in the digital age:

> Necessity used to be the mother of invention, but then we ran out of things that were necessary. The postmodern mother of invention is desire; we don't really "need" anything new, so we only create what we *want*. This changes the nature of technological competition. Because the Internet is obsessed with its own version of non-monetary capitalism, it rewards the volume of response much more than the merits of whatever people are originally responding to. (p. 226)

Annotations:
- Look this up
- But we do need new things like cures for diseases, right?
- Could be important concept
- This reminds me of Wasik and flash mobs — connection?

Let's look at how these annotation strategies work in this passage. For example, in this passage you would want to mark any terms you don't understand, such as *postmodern*, as well as terms the author may be using to form ideas, such as *nonmonetary capitalism*. Another set of strategies, though, involves questions you have in reaction to the text, each of which can serve as a point for rereading the text, and relations you see between the text and other essays you have read or your own life experience. Each question you ask or comment you make during your initial reading of the text gives you a new direction for reading the text again — both for an answer to your question and for support for any alternative position you want to take.

Returning to the text and reading it again refines your reading, making it more critical. Rereading is not something we usually do if we're just reading for comprehension; generally we understand enough of what we read that we don't have to read it again. But in an academic context rereading is essential, because critical reading goes beyond comprehension to *evaluation* — determining the accuracy and applicability of the information and ideas of the text. And before we can evaluate, we have to know the key points that need evaluation. The Questions for Critical Reading located at the start of each selection will help you in this process by focusing your rereading on a significant point in the essay — a particular term, concept, or idea that will allow you to read and think critically. Rereading Klosterman's essay with these questions in mind might cause you to pay attention to those parts of the selection where he discusses villainy and examines two Internet figures, Kim Dotcom and Julian Assange. These discussions might feel like anecdotes when you read the essay for the first time, but returning to the reading through the Questions for Critical Reading might prompt you to look more closely at how Klosterman uses these two figures to discuss the nature of villainy in relation to technology.

Glossing the Text

Each of these texts is taking part in a larger conversation about a particular topic. You might find parts of a reading confusing because you are jumping into the middle of a conversation without knowing its complete history. At times, then, you will want to go beyond annotating the text by using a skill called *glossing*. A gloss is a quick explanation of a term or concept — think of it as a quick summary of the conversation that has come before what you are reading. You probably already know what a glossary is — a list of terms and their definitions. Some words have already been glossed for you. When you provide your own glosses for a text, you're building your own sort of glossary, filling in technical details you need to understand the text as a whole. There are a number of techniques you can use to gloss parts of the text while you read and annotate it:

- **Look at the context.** Often you can determine a quick sense of a term or concept by looking at the surrounding context or the way the author uses it.

- **Use a dictionary.** Using a dictionary to look up a word or term can help you confirm what you learn from the context.

- **Use Wikipedia.** Wikipedia is a controversial tool in academia because it has no single source of authority. Instead, everyone writes it, everyone edits it, and anyone can change it. In most cases, you won't want to use Wikipedia as a source for your writing. For one thing, your writing is about critical thinking, which is about ideas, and Wikipedia is more centrally concerned with factual information. At the same time, because it contains so much knowledge, it's a useful source for glossing because it can give you a quick sense of not only a technical term's meaning but also its history.

- **Use a search engine.** Wikipedia is not the only source for information on the Web. Indeed, each of its entries includes links to other sites used in compiling the information on that page. Thus you can also do a Web search to find a quick gloss.

Let's look at an example of how you might gloss a text as you read and annotate it. Here's a short passage from Francis Fukuyama's "Human Dignity":

> In the words of Nietzsche's Zarathustra, "One has one's little pleasure for the day and one's little pleasure for the night: but one has a regard for health. 'We have invented happiness,' say the last men, and they blink." Indeed both the return of hierarchy and the egalitarian demand for health, safety, and relief of suffering might all go hand in hand if the rulers of the future could provide the masses with enough of the "little poisons" they demanded. (p. 148)

Nineteenth-century German philosopher who often challenged traditional values and morality. (Web search)

Philosophical novel where Nietzsche discusses his concept of the "Superman." (Wikipedia)

"A system of organization in which people or groups are ranked one above the other according to status or authority." (Dictionary definition)

"Of, relating to, or believing in the principle that all people are equal and deserve equal rights and opportunities." (Dictionary definition)

The context of this quotation helps, too. Fukuyama is discussing how Nietzsche foresaw the implications of natural science for human dignity — specifically the possibility of a ranking or hierarchy of humans. These glosses can help you understand Fukuyama's larger argument about human dignity.

Reading Visuals

You may notice that many of the texts you read contain visual elements such as images or graphs. Indeed, some texts are entirely visual. These, too, are opportunities for critical reading. After all, *every text is an image and every image is a text.*

Consider the page you are reading now. Though not readily apparent, it has a number of visual elements — the font selected for the text, the color of the print, the amount of empty or white space around the text and in the margins. Normally, we don't pay attention to the visual elements of printed texts. That's because printed texts are designed to minimize their visual elements so that you can focus on the meaning of the words on the page. But imagine how the meaning of these words would change if they were printed in **bold** or if they used a curly, informal font.

Visual texts often invert this relationship, bringing the visual elements into the foreground and letting words sit in the background or letting them work with or against the meaning suggested by the visual elements. The words and the images together make meaning and, like in all the texts you will read, this meaning is open to interpretation and analysis. In this sense, reading a visual text isn't all that different from reading any other kind of text, and you will want to use many of the same skills with critical reading that you would use with other selections in this book:

- **Identify the elements.** To begin reading a visual text, make note of each of its elements—not only any words it might contain but also each visual item included in the overall image. Think of each element as a sentence. Together, these elements express meaning just as the sentences of a paragraph do. When you identify each element, you are using your skills with annotation.

- **Identify the connections.** Once you've located the elements, think about the relationships between them. Do the visual and textual elements reinforce each other or do they work against each other? What meaning is the author trying to convey in each case?

- **Analyze and interpret the whole.** Just as you would with other readings in the book, you will want to analyze and interpret the visual image as a whole. This again involves critical thinking because you will need to think about not only the *explicit meanings*—what the image as a whole says—but also the *implicit meanings*—what the image as a whole implies.

Reading Arguments

Finding an author's argument, as we've already noted, is a basic goal as you approach each reading. But *reading* an author's argument involves a broader set of skills. Identifying the argument—locating and summarizing it—is the first step of that process. After that, there are a number of questions you can ask yourself in order to understand not only the argument but also its context and the ways in which the author has chosen to pursue that argument. Working through these questions will help you understand the essay more fully; it will also make you more aware of these issues in your own writing.

After reading the essay, ask yourself:

- **What is the larger conversation?** Each of the essays you read here is part of a larger discussion about an issue: ethics, race, digital life. Where do you see the author acknowledging, including, and joining that conversation? How do you imagine you will join it as well?

- **What other voices are in this conversation?** Where does the author bring in other voices? How does the author use quotation? How might you use quotations from this author as you write about the essay?

- **What counts as evidence for the author?** Each discipline has a different standard for evidence, and the standards for evidence in academic and public writing differ as well. Does the author rely on anecdotes or statistics? Does the author use other credible sources? What sources should you use in your own writing?

- **How does the author acknowledge counterarguments?** Why might an author make or avoid this move? When should you acknowledge opposing positions?

- **How does the author acknowledge audience?** What sort of contextual information does the author provide? How does the style of writing reflect the needs of a particular audience?

Thinking Critically

Once you've completed a critical reading, you're ready to do some thinking. Imagine the essay is raw material. Critical thinking is the process of *doing something* with this raw material, making something out of it in order to join the conversation of the text. There are a number of methods you can use to help with your critical thinking. Responding to the essay is a good start because it allows you to record your thoughts and reactions. You can follow that by figuring out how the essay connects to other essays you've read or to your own ideas. Seeing connections is a way to begin to identify the relationships between ideas. Synthesizing these ideas then offers you a means to add to the conversation.

Responding

You can start the process of critical thinking by taking some time to respond to the reading and connecting what you read to your own life, to what you know and think and how you feel. Your instructor might ask you to keep a reading journal or a blog where you can record these initial connections.

For example, here's a short response assignment Risa Shiman, one of the instructors in the writing program in which I teach, recently gave students in one of her classes before they started discussing Peter Singer's "Visible Man: Ethics in a World without Secrets" (p. 425):

> Do the benefits of increased access to information provided by technology outweigh the costs? Why or why not?

Notice that the question isn't long or complicated. The goal is just to get you writing in response to the issues raised by the essay. Here's how one student responded:

> I believe that the benefits of increased access to information provided by technology outweigh the costs. The world as a whole is becoming a more dangerous and unstable place, and any efforts our country can make to protect us should be taken. Threats to the United States are becoming more frequent, and with terrorists successfully executing their 9/11 attacks, I believe we need to do whatever we can to prevent future occurrences from happening. Social media has definitely made it easier to monitor the world's

views, thoughts, and opinions, and I wish that information were only used to monitor potential threats. But as Singer points out, corporations use what we put out into the world through social media so they can target their ads according to our consumer habits. But if getting Target coupons in the mail for Pampers diapers and Gerber baby food after you announce your pregnancy on Facebook is one of the things we have to deal with to make our country safer, then that is a small thing I am willing to give up. I also think that having organizations such as WikiLeaks provide a sort of checks and balances on our government is a good thing. Clearly Hillary Clinton was so upset over WikiLeaks' airing the government's dirty laundry because the government got caught, and it's embarrassing. I do understand that leaking some government documents can have a negative effect on our country. But it has been known that there are many corrupt dealings happening on Capitol Hill, and if that sort of threat makes politicians and government officials think twice before making a potential shady deal, then it's about time.

This student starts by articulating his or her beliefs about the issues, relating those opinions to Singer's discussion. These opinions can then become the basis for an argument as they are refined into a definite position and then put more closely into relation with Singer's text.

Connecting as Critical Thinking

Once you've considered your own responses, then it's a good idea to look for connections. Each of the essays you will read here is already connected to the conversation taking place around that author's particular topic. When you read, you might be able to guess some of these connections, but as you think critically about these readings, you will make new connections of your own, which is essential to critical thinking.

The strongest way to evaluate the information in an essay is to test it against other information, such as the ideas expressed in another essay. Connecting the readings might mean using a concept from one piece, such as Francis Fukuyama's idea of "Factor X," to explain another essay, such as the Dalai Lama's "Ethics and the New Genetics." But it might also mean using the ideas from one essay to modify the ideas in another: elaborating Michael Pollan's idea of the "holon" through Daniel Gilbert's concept of "super-replicators," for example. (See Figure 1.)

Connecting is a kind of critical thinking used by the authors of the essays in this book, too. In "AIDS, Inc.," Helen Epstein uses this move in discussing HIV prevention programs in Africa:

Ugandans are more likely to know their neighbors and to live near members of their extended families. This in turn may have contributed to what sociologists call "social cohesion"—the tendency of people to talk openly with one another and form trusted relationships. Perhaps this may have facilitated

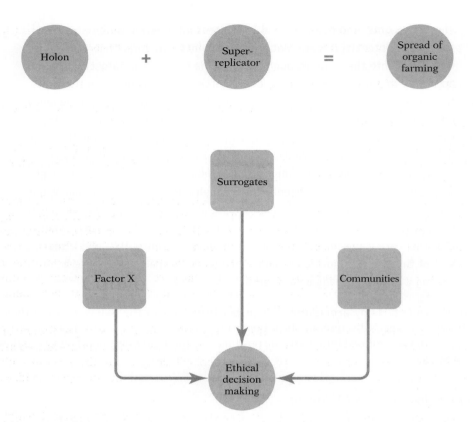

Figure 1   Clustering
Connecting and synthesizing are crucial ways of thinking critically about what you read.

> more realistic and open discussion of AIDS, more compassionate attitudes to-
> ward infected people, and pragmatic behavior change. (p. 116)

Epstein, a molecular biologist and specialist in public health, connects a concept from sociology, "social cohesion," with HIV prevention in Uganda. In making that connection, she uses the idea to support her argument and to create a new idea about what an effective prevention program should look like. It's the connections between ideas that allow authors like Epstein — and *you* — to make an argument.

   In working with these readings, you might feel like there simply are no connections between them, that the topic of each essay is unique. But keep in mind that a connection is not something you find; it's something you *make*. If the connections were already sitting there in the essays, then there wouldn't be much critical thinking involved, because there wouldn't be much thinking involved at all. The process of making connections between disparate ideas is part of critical thinking. Sociology and public health might not seem to have much in common, but when we make connections between them, we generate a new understanding of how to slow the spread of HIV.

Strategies for Making Connections

When making connections between the readings for this class, you might want to try a few different strategies:

- **Draw the connections.** Start by listing the important terms, concepts, and ideas from each essay on a sheet of paper. Once you've done that, you can literally draw lines between ideas that have some relation.

- **Use clustering.** You might also try a technique called clustering. Put the main concept of each essay in a circle on a sheet of paper. Draw other circles containing related or subsidiary ideas and connect them with lines to the circles containing the main ideas of the readings. When you find ways to connect the branches of these separate groups, you're locating relationships between the essays that you might want to pursue. Through figuring out exactly what these relationships are, you not only utilize critical thinking but also start the process of forming your own ideas, which you will express in your writing for this class.

- **Use the questions with the readings.** The Questions for Connecting at the end of each reading will also help in this process by asking you to think specifically about one essay in terms of another. These questions will direct you to think about both essays, giving you an opportunity to use each reading to test the concepts and ideas of the other.

- **Compare the tags.** The "tags" for each essay show key concepts, some of which overlap with the tags for other selections. Use the lists of the essays' tags in the table of contents to help you see some of the connections between the readings.

Synthesizing

Connecting defines relationships. Synthesizing goes one step further by combining different sources of information to generate something new. Synthesis happens a lot in the real world. For example, a doctor might combine test results, a patient's medical history, and his or her own knowledge to reach a diagnosis; and a businessperson might use a marketing report, recent sales figures, a demographic study, and data on the current economic outlook to craft a business strategy. Whenever you combine multiple sources of information to create new information or ideas, you're *synthesizing*. Synthesis always creates something new; because you'll be using it in this class to create new ideas and thus new knowledge, you'll use it to demonstrate your critical thinking.

All of the authors in this text use synthesis, because all of them are working from what's already been said and written about a subject to say and write something new. You'll do the same. After you've read a piece and connected its ideas to other contexts, you will synthesize the ideas into a new idea, your own idea. That idea will form the center of the writing you do in this class.

Strategies for Synthesizing

There are several techniques you can use to synthesize the ideas of these readings:

- **Combine ideas.** You might, for example, use ideas from two authors and combine them into a new concept that you use in your paper.

- **Apply ideas.** You might instead use a concept from one essay to show the limitations of another author's argument. In this case you would apply the first idea to the second, and in doing so, you'd produce something new, which would be the synthesis you create between the two.

- **Invent your own term.** You might even invent a term all your own, defining and deploying it through your analyses of the readings in the papers you will write. You can define the term using ideas that you pull from multiple readings, connecting and synthesizing them into a new understanding represented by your term.

- **Pay attention to similarities *and* differences.** When synthesizing, you want to ask yourself not simply how the two elements you're working with are alike but also how they're different. Paying attention to both similarities and differences allows you to discover how different ideas fit together in different ways.

Making an Argument

Introduction to Argument

All the processes we've discussed so far take place before you actually start formally writing in response to an assignment. You need to read (and reread), respond, connect, and synthesize in order to begin the process of critical thinking that forms the core of academic writing. Once you've done all that, it's time to form an argument. In academic terms, *argument* involves joining a conversation, taking a stand, or making a point. When you write in this class, you'll be doing all of these things.

You may already be familiar with this academic sense of *argument*, though you may have been introduced to it in different terms. In the grading criteria we use at my school, we make the meaning clear:

> When we use the term "argument" . . . we mean the central, problem-solving idea that drives the paper, a concept that many of us learned to think of as a "thesis." We might also think of this as a "position" or as a "project," all of which suggest that there is a central point the student is trying to make in the paper. The argument will usually show up in a thesis statement on the first page of the paper, but this is not the sole defining characteristic of an argument.
>
> The student should have a goal in a paper, something he or she is trying to accomplish, often defined by a specific, argumentative statement. But even when this statement is absent, the goal is often still apparent, whether as a summation in the conclusion or an underlying/recurring theme of the paper.
>
> An ideal argument will be spelled out in a clear thesis statement and will provide both a direction for the paper and a motivation for that direction

(a problem to solve, a goal to accomplish, a position to defend, a project to complete, etc.).

Forming an argument can be really challenging, in part because the word itself can mean so many things—an argument between lovers is quite different from an argument in a courtroom, which is also different from a scientific argument. Rather than thinking of your argument as the position you defend, like an army protecting its territory, try thinking of it as the words you send out into the world, like a participant joining a conversation.

Some Models for Argument

It might be useful to consider some models for argument to give you some sense of how you might think about your own argument. Many of these sound very similar, and that's because they are. Approaching argument from slightly different angles might be all it takes for you to get the hang of it:

- **Conversation**. We've already considered argument as a kind of conversation. With this model, you use the ideas and terms and concepts from one essay to discuss or evaluate the ideas from the other. That is, you put the authors in conversation.

- **Framing.** Think about your argument as using the ideas from one essay to "frame" the ideas from the other. That is, you examine the second essay using terms and concepts from the first, as though examining the second essay through a frame or lens provided by the first. Your goal would be to change how your readers understand the second essay by helping them view it through the frame provided by the first.

- **Theory and case.** Your argument might use a theory about something from one essay and test it using another essay as a particular case. That is, you evaluate how effective the first author's ideas are when applied to a second text. This is similar to framing, but whereas with framing you are teaching your readers something new about the second essay and its ideas, with this model you are teaching them something new about the first essay and its theories.

- **Application.** An argument might also apply the ideas of one essay to the ideas of the other. That is, you take a term or concept and apply it to the new essay, learning something new either about the term or about the new essay. Consider this a middle ground to the two models discussed above, one where your application of ideas could change the way your readers think about either essay.

Strategies for Forming an Argument

As you begin to work out what you want to argue, there are a number of matters to consider that can help you articulate your argument:

- **Think about the larger conversation.** The connections you find between essays are not just specific terms or ideas or concepts or quotations. There's also a connection in terms of the larger issues. Start by identifying the larger issue shared between the essays, and then think about how each of these essays addresses this issue. For example, if the issue is civil rights, then what does each author say about civil rights, in a larger sense? How does what each says about the topic relate to larger public debates? How might you join in?

- **Think about what you're trying to prove.** Locating the points of connection between essays does show critical thinking. But it's not enough just to prove a connection between two authors. Yes, that takes some thinking, but you also want to think about what the connections *mean*.

- **Think about what we're learning from your paper.** What have you discovered by bringing these essays together? Do the ideas of one author extend the ideas of the other author into a whole new area? Are the ideas of one author limited because of what the other author shows? Can you raise new questions based on ideas from both authors? Adding your voice to the conversation means that you are saying something new about these issues and these essays. Think about what that is.

Points to Consider

When discussing argument in the classes I teach, I share with students the kinds of questions I ask about argument when reading students' papers:

- **And so?** An argument has to have a point. It has to first assert a connection between the two essays but then also answer the question "and so?" *Essay A is like (or unlike) Essay B and so . . .*

- **What are you trying to achieve?** I often use the term *project* in class instead of *argument*. When you write, you should have a project, something you want to achieve. Other instructors might use terms like *controlling purpose* or *motive*. Regardless, anyone who reads your argument should have a good sense of what you want to achieve in the paper.

- **What knowledge are you making?** An argument is a way of making new knowledge. How do you learn something new? You think about what you know, and then you come to a conclusion. That conclusion is a new piece of knowledge that you can express. Your argument might be: If we just read Essay A we learn X, but after reading Essay B we now learn Y about Essay A. Your argument tells your readers something new, something they haven't thought about before.

Practical Help

Finding your argument is not as hard as it sounds, because you've already done a lot of the work necessary by the time you get to thinking about your argument. In forming an argument, you will probably want to draw from:

- **The assignment or prompt.** We'll talk more about these later in this section and offer some tips on how to decode the focus of an assignment, but for now, consider the assignment a foundation on which you can build your argument. It offers a central focus that you can use to organize your critical thinking and join the conversation.

- **Your annotations.** You will want to go back to your annotations of any selections connected to the assignment. Since you noted the important ideas and concepts in each essay and, most crucially, your own questions or concerns, these annotations will give you a preliminary sense of how you want to respond to each text.

- **Your connections and synthesis.** Many times strong arguments are built out of the connections you make between the texts. You may, for example, build an argument around the application of an idea from one essay to an example from another. In the process, you will offer a new insight into the essays, which represents your synthesis and your addition to the larger conversation of the texts.

Writing an Argument

All of these tips are meant to help you conceive of your argument. As you start the process of drafting it in writing, keep these points in mind:

- **Don't hide it.** Unlike some other forms of writing that build up to a central point, academic writing places the argument right at the beginning, usually in the introduction, so that the reader can follow the pursuit of that argument and the process of your thinking through the paper. Someone reading your paper should be able to point to a sentence and identify it as your argument. You may have learned to call this type of sentence a *thesis statement* for your paper.

- **Be specific.** Avoid broad statements. Instead, make your argument as specific as possible.

- **Use the essays.** One way to make sure you stay specific is to incorporate the terms from the essays in your statement of argument.

- **Make a map.** A really strong, clear argument serves as a map for the entire paper. Your reader should be able to predict the organization of the paper from reading your argument. Your argument should tell you exactly what you need to do in the paper and then should also tell your reader exactly how you will proceed in the paper.

From Argument to Draft

Once you have a good sense of your argument, you're in a good position to start drafting your paper. Let's look at a student's argument from a class I taught recently:

> A new civil rights can be achieved by replacing idle conversations with meaningful discussions that aid the presence of our true selves through Web sites that offer a safe place for human interaction.

Given this argument, it's clear the first thing the author will need to discuss is the idea of a "new civil rights," a concept from Kenji Yoshino's essay (p. 541). In the next body paragraph, the author will need to discuss how "idle conversations" prevent these new civil rights and then how "meaningful discussions" can help create them. Then the author will need to argue that such discussions support our "true selves" (another concept from Yoshino) before looking at how all of this can take place on Web sites that "offer a safe place for human interaction." The argument, in essence, contains an outline of the whole paper.

Once you have a good sense of the shape and flow of your paper as suggested by the map of your argument, it's time to think about how you will support that argument.

Using Support

Working with Quotations

As you lay out your thinking, you'll need proof to *support*, or provide evidence for, your point, which in academic writing happens through working with quotations from the texts. When you use quotation in your writing, you support your words and ideas through the words and ideas of others. Quotation supports critical thinking in two ways. First, it provides evidence for your argument, thesis, or position, showing the reader how and why you thought that way and reached the conclusions that led to your argument. Second, integrating quotation into your text itself requires some critical thinking. That's the difference between "having" quotations in your paper and "using" them. It's not enough to drop in a quotation every now and then. You need to think about the function of every quotation you use, its purpose in your paper. Is it defining a term? Supporting an assertion? Connecting ideas? To make that function clear, you will want to explain each quotation you use. That doesn't mean you should summarize or reiterate each quotation; it means you should write about what that piece of text does for your overall project. Think of it as connecting that text to your own text. You might also analyze the quotation in this process. *Analyzing* a quotation means explaining what it says and what it means.

Here's a pattern you can use to incorporate quotation into your paragraphs in ways that show your critical thinking through connection. When I share this with my students, I call it "Barclay's Super-Secret Formula" (though I suppose it's not so secret anymore):

$$C_1 \rightarrow I \rightarrow Q_1 \rightarrow E \rightarrow T \rightarrow Q_2 \rightarrow C_e$$

This pattern for a paragraph is a great way to connect and synthesize quotations from two essays in support of your argument. Let's break this formula down:

1. **C_1 is your claim.** Begin your paragraph with a sentence that contains the main idea you want to make or the connection you want to show between two essays. You might have learned to call this a topic sentence. Regardless, the key is to start with a sentence that lets the reader know exactly what the paragraph will be about. Your claim should be related to your argument and should offer the reader a clear sense of how this paragraph proves a part of the argument.

2. **I is an introduction.** After you state your claim for the paragraph, introduce the first quotation. Sometimes you will need a sentence to set up the quotation; other times you might just use an introductory phrase like "Friedman writes" or "According to Yoshino."

3. **Q₁** is your first **quotation**. After you introduce the quotation, provide it. You will want to make sure it's completely accurate and, of course, you will want to provide proper citation (we'll discuss this more below).

4. **E** is an **explanation** of the quotation. After you provide the first quotation, add a sentence that explains that quotation. This can be particularly useful if the quotation contains an idea or concept. You may want to take another sentence or two to explain that idea even more so that your reader completely understands it.

5. **T** is a **transition** sentence. Before you move on to the next quotation, offer some sort of short transition sentence. This transition should provide a sense of the kind of connection you're trying to make in the paragraph as a whole. For example, you might have a sentence like "Friedman's concept is useful for explaining the spread of HIV in Africa."

6. **Q₂** is your **second quotation**, most likely from another essay. This second quotation needs only a brief introduction or signal phrase.

7. **Cₑ** is your **explanation of the connection**. Finally, add several sentences that explain the connection you see between the quotations and the way in which this connection supports your overall argument. This part of the formula is, in many ways, the most important part of the paragraph. These sentences should also explain how the relationship between the quotations supports your argument. These sentences record your critical thinking, allowing you to use the connection you've made between these two authors to support your project for the paper.

Here's an example of what this kind of paragraph looks like:

> The political climate of our current moment is one in which people see those of opposing political parties as inhuman beings that don't need to be treated with a certain level of respect, which is dangerous because it forces people to hide their political beliefs in order to be accepted as humans. Francis Fukuyama states, "We accord beings with Factor X not just human rights but, if they are adults, political rights as well — that is, the right to live in democratic political communities where their rights to speech, religion, association, and political participation are respected" (144). Fukuyama explains that every being that we see as human is supposed to be treated with certain basic rights, evening the playing field and giving all people the opportunity to be themselves without risking the loss of human dignity. While this should be the way people are always treated, in today's politically charged climate, members of opposing parties must cover their identities or risk being treated as inhuman. Kenji Yoshino writes, "Americans have come to a consensus that people should not be penalized for being different along these dimensions. That consensus, however, does not protect individuals against demands that they mute those differences" (539). What Yoshino sees as the

demands to "mute those differences" complicates Fukuyama's argument that all beings are accorded certain rights. With the elections right around the corner, Republicans and Democrats are busy calling one another stupid, inhuman, uninformed, moronic, and immoral in attempts to strip the opposition of their Factor X and make it OK to devalue human life based on a political orientation.

This student begins with a claim about the ways in which political partisanship affects our perceptions of humanity. To prove this claim, the student begins with an idea from Francis Fukuyama: that all humans should have fundamental political rights. He or she then connects this idea to one from Kenji Yoshino about the ways in which we pressure people to hide their differences (such as differences in political points of view). Using both of these ideas, this student is able to show how political slandering devalues the humanity of those involved.

About Citation

It is absolutely essential that you acknowledge the words of others when you use them. In the real world, failure to do so can result in expensive lawsuits and ruined careers. In the academic world, failure to do so is considered plagiarism. Every time you use the words or ideas of another, you must provide a citation.

You'll no doubt notice that some of the authors you read in this collection do not use citation. Why do you have to if they don't? The answer has a lot to do with *audience.* Whenever we write, we are addressing a particular audience — that's why it's useful to think about this process as joining a conversation. The audience you select determines a lot about how you will write — your tone, for example. It also determines the need for citation. *Academic writing always requires citation because it addresses an academic audience.* Addressing an academic audience doesn't mean using complicated sentences or fancy words. A lot of academic writing has a conversational tone, but it also always uses citation.

Ultimately, there are only a few things you need to know about citation. First, know that it exists. By that I mean that you must know that there are systems in place for you to acknowledge other sources. Second, you must know *what* you are citing. For example, when you cite something from this book, you are actually citing a selection from an edited anthology. Knowing that this is an anthology (as opposed to a *monograph,* a book with a single author) is crucial to figuring out how to cite it properly. Finally, you need to know how to find the right format. A good grammar or reference handbook is an excellent source, but you can also consult reputable Web sites; there are also Web and computer programs that can help you with citation.

About Disciplines

Once you enter your major, you'll learn a specific system for providing that citation — every discipline has its own system. In this class, the system you will likely use is MLA citation, developed through the Modern Language Association, the governing body for the discipline of English. You will probably spend time in class learning the intricacies of this system, but for now remember the basics: Every time you use a quotation or paraphrase, include the author's name and the page number in parentheses at the end of the sentence, just before the period. That's true for visual images as well. Publication information for all your sources should be listed at the end of your paper. Visual images require a special format. You will want to consult a grammar handbook, a citation guide, or a reliable Web source for specific information on how to cite these sources.

If you're interested in learning more about the citation system for your discipline, you can perform a Web search to find out what system it uses. As with MLA, it will have specific rules for formatting each reference. As with all citation, it is essential that you provide these references whenever you use someone else's words or ideas.

About Research

Academic Research

Research is also an important skill of critical thinking. But *research* is a much trickier term than it used to be. It used to be that research involved looking up specific subjects on little cards or ponderous indexes of journals in the library and then hunting down books in the library stacks or finding articles on microfilm. It required a good deal of training to do well. For most of us today, though, the basic methods of research are nearly instinctive. If you were given a blank search box, you would know what to do—just type in some search terms and start looking at the results until you find what you need. And in fact we often do this kind of research every day: researching what school to attend, or information on your favorite band, or where to get the best tattoo.

But academic research is very different from this kind of research. When you research on the Web, you gather and summarize existing information. When academics do research, though, their goal is to produce *new* information. Indeed, this is what academics do for a living. Yes, teaching is an important part of our jobs, but conducting research is just as important. We are paid, in a sense, to make new knowledge. And we're not the only ones. Many careers today involve both research and its application. For example, if a medical researcher were simply to gather all the existing information on a disease, that would only be so useful. It is the move from that research to new avenues of treatment for a disease that is valuable. Making new knowledge matters.

You may be asked to produce research in this class. Even if you are not assigned a research assignment, working with the texts of this book is a kind of research since academic writing, like research, asks you to make new knowledge.

Having Sources, Finding Sources

There's an important difference between having sources, such as the ones presented for you here, and finding sources, such as doing research at the library. You might imagine it as the difference between swimming in a pool and swimming in the ocean. When you work with the texts of this book, you're practicing research in a fairly controlled environment, like swimming in a pool. You don't have to worry, for example, about the quality of the texts in this book because we've done that work for you. If you are asked to do your own research in this class, though, it's a bit like swimming in the ocean: The material you have to deal with can be just as vast, and there are extra dangers in the wild. One way to avoid those dangers is making sure you are using reliable, academic sources—a particular challenge if you are using the Web for your research. Before you use any Web site in an academic setting, you will want to make sure you evaluate it. You begin that process by asking yourself how you want to use the site. Any site on the Web can be used as an example of your ideas or the ideas of any essay. But whenever you take ideas or evidence from Web sites, you need to be careful about which sites you use. Ask yourself questions such as:

- **Who wrote the material?** Is the site authored by an individual, an organization, a governmental agency?

- **How qualified is the source?** What makes this author an expert on this material? What are this author's qualifications? If the site doesn't contain information about the qualifications of the author, then you may want to reconsider using it.

- **When was the site last updated?** Often this information will be provided on each page of the site, usually at the bottom of the page. If the site doesn't include any update information, then you will want to ask yourself how current the material is.

- **How stable is the address or URL?** Web sites come and go. Generally speaking, Web sites from established groups or organizations are more stable than Web sites with their own domain name, which in turn are more stable than Web sites hosted with a free service.

- **How do you want to use the site in your writing?** Any Web site can be used as an example, but only those Web sites that establish their authority should be used for ideas or evidence.

Ideally, academic research goes beyond what you can find on the Web. If you are asked to complete a research project for this class, your instructor will probably provide you with an orientation to the library and its resources. *How* you search will probably be familiar to you, but *what* you search will be academic books and journals.

A Formula for Academic Research

Central to academic research is the ability to work with ideas. In your prior educational experience, you may have completed research papers that were more like researching a topic on the Web. The assignments for these papers would have asked you to gather information on a topic and then present that information in a written summary. But there's not much critical thinking involved in that sort of research paper. In college, you will most likely be asked to work with ideas in your research in order to generate new knowledge.

Ideas are useful because they help us to explain, predict, or change reality; that's why we refine, revise, and use theories. For example, the theory of gravity predicts what will happen to you if you step off a cliff. With that prediction, you can wisely choose not to take that step. Similarly, various economic theories predict how changes will affect standards of living. We can use these theories to make changes to elements like the interest rate in an attempt to change reality. When you research, you will want to focus on ideas. This formula might be useful:

$$I_s(S) = K_n$$

Let's break that down:

1. I_s stands for **Ideas about Stuff**. We might also use terms like *theory, hypothesis, lens, frame,* or *secondary material*. All of these terms indicate a set of ideas about something, whether that something is models of history or of a cell's inner workings. When you do your own research, you will want to make sure you have at least one source that provides you with Ideas about Stuff.

2. **S** stands for **Stuff**. We might also use *practice* (as opposed to *theory*), *experiment* (as opposed to *hypothesis*), *case* (as opposed to *lens* or *frame*), or *primary material* (as opposed to *secondary material*). These terms all suggest materials that show what actually happened — material elements of reality. In your research, you will want a set of texts that offers you this material. Stuff is the stuff you want to study. It might be one person's story, or an account of a historical incident, or the progress of a disease. Anything can be Stuff, even ideas. That is, you might apply one theory of economic change to another in order to synthesize a new theory.

3. K_n stands for **New Knowledge**. When you apply Ideas about Stuff to Stuff, you end up with New Knowledge, whether that is a new and refined theory or a new explanation for how things happen.

In order to work with this formula, you start with a topic that interests you. Ideally, you really care about the material, because that interest will sustain you through the difficult work of performing research to create new knowledge. Once you have a topic in mind, you will want to use some of the critical thinking skills we've already discussed:

- **Start thinking.** Begin by using the methods we discussed to think critically about your topic. Try responding to the topic — writing out your feelings, thoughts, and ideas about the topic — in order to develop some avenues to start your research. You might also use clustering or other brainstorming techniques to begin to narrow your focus.

- **Be specific.** As with an argument, you will want to be very specific about your topic. If you remain broad or vague, you can become overwhelmed by the amount of information.

- **Formulate a question.** Before you start finding sources that offer you Ideas about Stuff and Stuff, you will want to develop a research question. This question is a lot like an argument for your paper. It's specific and focused. It's clear. And it offers you a map for conducting your research.

Once you've found sources, you will want to treat them as you would the essays in this book, reading them critically, annotating and glossing them, and identifying key passages you want to work with. By connecting and synthesizing your sources, you begin to create an argument, one that answers the question you started with and one that also creates new knowledge through the work you do in the research paper.

Research and Disciplines

As you enter your chosen discipline, you will learn specific methods of research that will probably involve different actions. You might, for example, design a survey for research in sociology or design an experiment for research in chemistry. Nevertheless, the essential elements of research in all disciplines are the same: using ideas in relation to reality in order to add to the conversation of the discipline.

You will also find that not only do the methods of research vary by discipline but the kinds of acceptable evidence vary as well. In the so-called "hard sciences," for example, evidence is often statistical, coming from experimental research. In the humanities, including English, evidence is often textual and supported by analysis.

Thus disciplines can approach the same topic very differently, because the knowledge that matters to the discipline (and the ways of finding it) are very different. As you read the essays in *Emerging*, you might find examples of how different disciplines treat specific topics, though it's useful to keep in mind that when these authors write for other members of their discipline, their ideas and evidence (and citation) look even more different.

Revising, Editing, and Proofreading

So far, we've discussed all the stages of critical thinking you'll need to exercise in order to produce a draft of your paper. Each stage relates to a skill you might already use, and each, too, will have value in your future career. Once you've written a draft, making an argument that contributes to the larger conversation and supporting it by working with quotation, there is still more work to be done, because every good piece of writing goes through at least one revision. This is the twelfth draft of Part One of this book, for example.

Often students think of revision as "fixing" their papers—just correcting all the errors. But that's only part of the process. Revision involves making changes and should produce something new. Again, when we produce something new in the realm of ideas, we're doing critical thinking; revision, then, is also a form of critical thinking. Instead of thinking about the readings of the class, though, revision asks you to think critically about—to evaluate, test, and assess—your own writing.

When we discussed connecting, we said that it's easier to evaluate ideas against something else. The same is true with revision. Often when we write, our initial draft looks fine to us; it seems like our best thinking. This is where connecting with others—in this case, through the process of peer revision—is again useful. As part of my job coordinating the writing classes at my university, I read the class evaluations for all the writing courses, and one thing students say over and over again is that they don't value peer review, because they believe that only the instructor has "the" answer and so only the instructor's comments count. On the contrary, I believe that *peer review is one of the most practical things you'll learn in this class*. In the rest of your life, you won't be asked to write papers, but you will be asked to work with others on committees or teams again and again. Learning to work well with others—to recognize valuable feedback and to give it in turn—is essential.

Peer review gives you practice in testing your ideas with actual readers. As noted above, every piece of writing has an audience, and your peers form part of that audience when it comes to the writing you will do for this class. Since the goal of each paper is to contribute to the conversation started in the texts, and since your classmates have also read and written about the texts, they are the interlocutors for your written conversation.

That process works in reverse, too. When you read your peers' writing, you will want to bring all your critical thinking skills to bear. You might be tempted to just write "Good job!" no matter what you think about the writing, for fear of being critical, but that shows no critical thinking. *Critical thinking is not the same as being critical.* When you offer valuable feedback, you're helping your classmates, no matter how negative that feedback might feel to you. Start by reading your peer's paper, using the same skills of critical reading that you used when you read the texts for this class. Annotate it just as you would one of the readings, marking what you think is important and asking questions in the margin when you are lost or confused. Then think critically about what your classmate is saying, using your connection skills—connect what he or she says about the text to what you know about the text, as well as to what you think and have written about the text. Finally, form your response as a way of joining the conversation.

Sample Student Paper

It might be useful for you to see how this all comes together in an actual student paper. Let's start with the assignment, taken from a recent class taught by Adam Phillips, one of the instructors in the writing program in which I teach:

In Dan Savage's essay "It Gets Better," as well as Urvashi Vaid's essay "Action Makes It Better," the authors discuss bullying with regards to the LGBTA (lesbian, gay, bisexual, transgender, and allies) community and the youth who find themselves questioning their sexuality at a young age. The advancement of social media within this generation has forced this community and many of its members to endure bullying on a much larger scale than previously encountered, which has forced many young people to fear for their safety and even take their own lives. Savage states that "[t]hings get better—things *have* gotten better, things *keep* getting better—for lesbian, gay, bisexual, and transgender people" (407). But with the rise in suicides influenced by cyberbullying, the question can be asked: Are things really getting better? **With this in mind, write an essay using ideas from Savage, Vaid, and Francis Fukuyama's "Human Dignity" in which you determine what dignity, if any, minorities such as members of the LGBTA community should receive when using social media.**

Questions to Consider:

    Whom does cyberbullying affect? Could suicides such as Billy Lucas's be avoided? How? Is it really getting better, as Savage claims? Should human dignity be afforded to all groups? Does everybody's opinion count? Should human dignity be afforded to all humans? Why or why not? Is the online community different from face-to-face communities in terms of how people treat others? Should human dignity even be considered when communicating online to others? Does "Factor X" exist in digital worlds (Facebook, *World of Warcraft*, etc.)?

    You can apply the same critical thinking skills to the text of this assignment as you would to one of the readings in this book. For starters, critically reading the assignment will help you locate key information in writing your response, and you should annotate it as you would a reading. Notice, for example, that the middle section is in bold, highlighting the main task of the assignment: "With this in mind, write an essay using ideas from Savage, Vaid, and Francis Fukuyama's 'Human Dignity' in which you determine what dignity, if any, minorities such as members of the LGBTA community should receive when using social media." In annotating the assignment, you'd probably want to highlight this sentence so that you know where to focus your own critical thinking and response.

    The questions that follow the assignment are not that different from the kinds of questions you might ask yourself when reading these three essays. Each one offers a jumping-off point for your own critical thinking, which can then lead to an argument you might use for your paper.

    Here is one student's response to the assignment:

Human rights have evolved tremendously over time. People no longer own slaves or discriminate as extremely as in previous decades. However, there is still inequality in some minority groups; one example is the LGBTA (lesbian, gay, bisexual, transgender, ally) community. Dan Savage's article "It Gets Better" shows how people's views have evolved since the 1980s and 1990s regarding homosexuality; however, the world is still not perfect for LGBTA individuals. Controversy over homosexuality still exists in politics, and same-sex relationships are still a "problem" in the eyes of some. No one aspect of any person makes them more important or worthy than another. They are all composed of the same chemical properties and share the same importance in the world. Even though some people may be leaders and others followers, they all still share the same basic attributes, as explained by Factor X in Francis Fukuyama's article "Human Dignity." Humans need to do a better job of educating the next generation and increasing awareness about minority groups, because without that awareness, people will continue to discriminate against and even bully others, even though all humans deserve to feel and be equal with one another and to live with the same rights and dignities. No group deserves to be bullied at any time, even as social media has created a new outlet for bullying of anyone who seems different. This is a difficult problem to solve but we must try. Bullying harms dignity and causes people to harm themselves, but more awareness of the problem is a partial solution.

Because all humans are equal, they all deserve the same basic rights and dignities, and bullying only works against dignity. Despite the differences among humans, Dr. Francis Fukuyama states they should all be treated equally because of the shared trait of Factor X, which is a "human essence" that "unites all human beings" (147). Fukuyama argues that "human beings [are entitled] to a higher level of respect than the rest of natural creation" (145), and that "[w]e also accept the fact that we look different, come from different races and ethnicities, are of different sexes, and have different cultures" (144). People require respect and acceptance; however, sometimes they do not provide it to those around them and they bully people instead. This bullying destroys respect. Dan Savage says "Justin Aaberg was just fifteen when he killed himself in the summer of 2010. He came out at thirteen, and endured years of bullying at the hands of classmates in a suburban Minnesota high school. Justin hanged himself in his bedroom; his mother found his body" (406). Aaberg died without a sense of equality with those around him. Without the communal idea of equality, there is a no way for people to understand why they should keep from harming or bullying others, hurting the dignity of others and sometimes leading to their deaths.

When their dignity is denied by bullying, people can act on desperate feelings. As Dan Savage explains, "A bullied teenager who ends his life is saying that he can't picture a future with enough joy in it to compensate for the pain he's in now" (407). This shows how bullying has effects that take dignity and happiness away. Savage explains that nine out of ten LGBTA students report being bullied (410). When 90 percent of these young adults are being bullied today, they are being denied their human dignity. They do not receive that "higher level of respect" that Fukuyama says all humans deserve. Savage also adds that students are eight times more likely to commit suicide or hurt themselves when they feel rejected by their families (410). These are young people who deserve the opportunity to feel equal. Nobody deserves to feel the need to end their own life, and for the most part this feeling is due to the actions of other humans and the lack of dignity that these youth feel as a result of being bullied.

In the world of social media, our interactions can quickly become impersonal and even harmful to dignity which makes it even easier to bully others. Bullying is no longer only face-to-face, which makes things even more terrifying, because it becomes anonymous or nearly invisible to everyone but the person being bullied. In this "era of social media — in a world with YouTube and Twitter and Facebook," LGBTA teens and young adults are now exposed to bullying 24/7 (408). When so much of young people's lives are lived online, that kind of constant bullying is a complete invasion of privacy and dignity, leading to even more hopeless feelings.

There is no human being on earth who deserves the pain that bullying creates, especially those in minority groups who may face other kinds of discrimination. But as Fukuyama explains, "The struggle for recognition is not economic: What we desire is not money but that other human beings respect us in the way we think we deserve" (143). Humans all desire the same respect from one another, which is a part of this Factor X that they all share. Those in the LGBTA community deserve just as much respect as the rest of humanity. Savage writes, "We weren't the same people and we didn't have or want the same things — gay or straight, not everyone wants kids or marriage; people pursue happiness in different ways" (407). The pursuit of happiness is a shared goal for humans. This is part of the dignity that we all want and deserve as humans. It is part of what makes us all the same, which shows how bullying does not make any sense. People basically strip one another of respect by bullying, but the need for respect is one thing we all share. Bullying does not make anyone respect the bully. It only hurts the dignity of the person who is bullied.

There is no easy solution for bullying, but more awareness can help protect some people. When people use social media, they know that there is the possibility that they will encounter some unpleasant souls, but that's also part of real life. Not everyone is as sensitive and respectful as they should be, especially to those in different parts of the community. According to Dan Savage, "Things get better — things *have* gotten better, things *keep* getting better — for lesbian, gay, bisexual, and transgender people" (407). The struggle is real for people in the LGBTA world. Unfortunately middle school and high school students do not get the education about the LGBTA community that they may need at that point in their lives. They do not learn how to voice their opinions with respect or how to communicate with people different than themselves without the use of negativity. The voices of LGBTA people are not always taught to younger audiences, which is unfortunate because those voices are part of the world we live in. Francis Fukuyama explains that "[h]uman beings decide to do one thing over another because one set of neurons fires rather than another, and those neuronal firings can be traced back to prior material states of the brain" (145). People react to things based on their past experiences, and those reactions sometimes come out in the wrong way. If young people are aware of what is and isn't socially acceptable when dealing with minority groups, they might change their behavior and be less prone to bullying. Young people are heavily influenced by their families and role models, and with society changing rapidly, sometimes the people we think of as wise are not as caught up to date on social norms as they should be. As a result, young people learn to act in ways that are not sensitive to the lives of those who are different from them. One easy fix to this would be advancing the amount of education young students receive on LGBTA issues. As LGBTA rights improve, more people will need to be aware and tolerant. Cyberbullying is becoming less socially acceptable. We are growing up in a technologically advanced society and with this comes a set of rules that everyone should follow, online and off, to preserve dignity for all. Raising this awareness can fight bullying and help human dignity.

Humans are capable of hurting one another with bullying in sickening ways. But there is no attribute that makes one person more worthy of respect than another. Humans are all equal in that they deserve respect and a chance for happiness. They all have the shared trait of Factor X, which makes them human, and they all prove to be human by their need for dignity and respect. Those who do bully and treat others unequally in places like social media are essentially rejecting the idea of human dignity, and their actions keep the world from being a safe and equal environment for all groups of people. By educating young people, we may be able to create a more accepting society for groups like the LGBTA. All humans are equal. They deserve to live equally, to live with the same rights and dignities, and to be protected from bullying.

Works Cited

Barrios, Barclay, ed. *Emerging: Contemporary Readings for Writers*. 3rd ed.
   Boston, MA: Bedford/St. Martins, 2016. Print.
Fukuyama, Francis. "Human Dignity." Barrios 143–65.
Savage, Dan. "It Gets Better." Barrios 406–10.

Every paper needs an argument, the main point that the author is posing. The author of this paper makes that argument clear at the end of the introduction: "Bullying harms dignity and causes people to harm themselves, but more awareness of the problem is a partial solution." The argument addresses the prompt by suggesting that all humans deserve respect and dignity when using social media since the lack of that respect causes real harms; it also suggests that raising awareness can increase dignity. It's also clear that both Savage and Fukuyama have a role to play in this argument, since Fukuyama discusses human dignity and Savage focuses on bullying.

Throughout the paper, the author supports this argument by connecting Savage and Fukuyama and synthesizing their ideas. Notice the point made in the second paragraph, for example: Fukuyama notes that humans deserve a higher level of respect, and the author connects that to Savage's statement that bullying destroys that respect. By connecting these two essays, the author is able to begin supporting the larger argument that technology is making us more human.

As the paper proceeds, each paragraph makes the same moves—connecting the authors to form a synthesis that supports the argument. There are, of course, some stumbles along the way; this author is, after all, still emerging as an academic writer. You might notice, for example, that the transitions between these paragraphs are sometimes weak. Similarly, there are grammatical and language issues that might distract us as readers. And while sometimes the author does a great job of using the texts to create a synthesis, there are certainly places where clearer analysis and connection would be useful.

This is the second, revised draft of this paper, and in many ways it is a success. By the conclusion, the author has managed to provide support and evidence for the argument. That should be your goal when you write in this class, too. Because despite its shortcomings, this paper does demonstrate critical thinking by presenting a clear argument supported with specific examples and quotations from the text. Your work in this class may look very different (in part, because the writing prompts you work with may look very different), but the skills will remain the same. And in the end, these skills are what matter—not just in this class and not just in college, but in your career and your life as well.

SANDRA ALLEN

Photo by Chris Ritter

Sandra Allen, who holds an M.F.A. from the University of Iowa's Nonfiction Writing Program, is a deputy features editor at Buzz-Feed and the co-founder of Wag's Revue, an online-only literary quarterly. Her writing has been published in the *Magazine, Paris Review Daily*, and *Hayden's Ferry Review*. She has covered topics ranging from being drugged by a stranger at a music festival to the musical *Rent* to Sandy Allen, her namesake and a 7'7" woman and folk hero.

"A World Without Wine" was originally published November 20, 2014, on BuzzFeed, the Internet-based media company. BuzzFeed features entertaining viral content such as lists and quizzes though it also includes more traditional news content, including breaking stories and serious, long-form articles. Its content is divided into twenty-eight sections including Food, Entertainment, Music, Business, and News. "How Climate Change Will End Wine As We Know It" appeared alongside stories such as "What Type Of Mac & Cheese Are You?," "What It's Like To Stop Wearing Makeup," "Hillary Clinton On Board With Obama's Immigration Actions," and "Woman With Gun Arrested Outside White House After Obama's Immigration Speech."

In this essay, Allen examines the impact that global climate change has had and will have on the wine industry. Wine grapes are particularly sensitive to climate and thus reflect changes in climate relatively rapidly. Allen uses scientific studies and interviews with vintners to consider the future of wine. As weather patterns shift, classic wine-growing regions will find themselves at risk; other regions, such as England, will benefit from new or expanded viticulture opportunities. What does this change in wine augur for agriculture in general? Allen asks us to consider the implications of climate change for more than just wine.

▶ TAGS: *economics, food and agriculture, globalism, science and technology*
▶ CONNECTIONS: *Appiah, Gilbert, Watters*

Questions for Critical Reading

1. Why should we pay attention to changes in wine growing? As you read, pay attention to those passages where Allen discusses the possible significance of the wine industry for agriculture as a whole.

2. As you read, note the kinds of evidence that Allen uncovers in relation to viticulture. Which one of these kinds of evidence is the most persuasive?

3. Allen considers many possible consequences of climate change on the production of wine. As you read the essay, make a list of these consequences. Use that list to produce a nuanced understanding of these changes: are these changes solely good and bad or more complex?

A World Without Wine

"We chose wine because it's a canary in the coal mine," says Rebecca Shaw, who co-authored the PNAS [Proceedings of the National Academy of Sciences of the United States of America] paper. Shaw is the associate vice president and senior lead scientist at the Environmental Defense Fund. She and her collaborators, most of them academics, sought to understand how agriculture at large will adapt to climate change. We're chatting in a conference room in the EDF's downtown San Francisco 28th-floor offices. The Bay Bridge looms in the window behind us, defogging itself over the course of our conversation.

On a map, the world's wine regions are particular little bands that fall in between the 30th and 50th parallels, the majority in highly biodiverse Mediterranean climates. This is because, as crops go, quality wine grape vines are super finicky. They need a cold—but not too cold—winter. They need a mostly frost-free spring during which their buds can safely emerge. They need a long, sunny growing season and eventual temperatures that are fairly warm—but not so hot that the grapes will sunburn or ripen too quickly. They need a fluctuation between daytime and nighttime temperatures, which enable the development of compounds that eventually become the complex flavors in a fine wine. Wine grapes are prima donnas; you don't give them exactly what they demand, they don't perform. Complicating things further, there are many different kinds of wine grapes, called varietals, like chardonnay, merlot, or riesling, which are even more particular about where and under which conditions they'll best grow. Go over a certain threshold of temperature? You can't grow pinot noir. Go under? You can't ripen cabernet sauvignon.

This fussiness also makes wine grapes especially useful for gathering data about weather: Each vine is like a remote sensor out in a field, and the behavior of wines across a region can paint a picture as to a given season's weather. European vintners have been keeping records for about a thousand years, which is one way climatologists have learned about Europe's historical climate, including the Little Ice Age that struck the continent between 200 and 700 years ago.

Figuring out which grapes perform best where is painstakingly slow: It takes five to seven years for a newly planted vineyard to begin producing grapes suitable for winemaking. It takes years more still before vines produce good or, with luck, great—or, with further luck, excellent—fruit. The best fine wine, and certainly the world's most expensive wines, come from regions or even individual rows of vines that have been cultivated for so long, whose behaviors are so well understood, that extremely high-quality grapes—and therefore extremely high-quality wines—are more or less guaranteed. (Certain European wine regions are steeped in so much tradition they're recognized by UNESCO as World Heritage Sites.) In Europe, the identity of a wine is so tied to a fixed place that the wines themselves are named after where they're made: Chianti is from Chianti, Champagne from Champagne. (If Americans played by the same rules, we'd call Napa Valley wines Napas.)

Worldwide, winemakers aspire to create wines that best express the personality of a given area's climate and weather, a concept called *terroir*, or the taste of the place. A given wine is thought of as an expression of a given geography's climate; much the way that you can't make New York bagels in Iowa, the idea is you can't make a Burgundy anywhere but.

Shaw says that's the other reason they chose to focus on wine — people care about where their wines originate. "No one cares about where their corn comes from, nobody cares about where their wheat comes from," she says. Wine consumers — especially in America, where wine is often believed to be snobby, unapproachable, or expensive — tend to be conservative in their selections and have internalized the idea that some wines from some places are better bets than others. Chances are, even if you prefer boxed wine over bottled, you might scoff at a wine from New Jersey.

In their study, Shaw explains, they wanted to look at the extent to which the wine industry would have to move poleward — further south in the Southern Hemisphere, further north in the Northern Hemisphere — as a result of the changing climate, and then what the impact would be upon that movement on existent ecosystems. What is the potential conservation impact of vineyards being planted in Tasmania, or British Columbia, or England? Their paper specifically mentioned the potential effects upon a giant panda habitat in China and in the Yukon-Yellowstone corridor. "Bid adieu to Bordeaux, but also, quite possibly, a hello to Chateau Yellowstone," *The Guardian* quipped in response.

Shaw expresses frustration that many in the press were distracted by the detail in their report about the pandas and missed the bigger stakes. "One of the major focuses of our work is to feed the planet without killing it," she says. "How does agriculture need to change? What are the incentives that need to be put in place that won't undermine the long-term sustainability and don't create more environmental harm?"

Wine isn't *actually* food, though. Especially if we're talking about fine wine, it's a luxury.

"Wine is food to many cultures," she responds, adding that most crops both deliver sustenance and are meaningful culturally. Corn is meaningful. Rice is meaningful. Humans have been cultivating wine for 8,000 years. "You can get into an argument about what's food and what's necessary and what's not necessary," she says. "The bottom line is wine is a very, very important part of many, many cultures."

There's a touch of emotion in her voice as she says this. We could live in a world without wine, of course, but would we want to?

This year has been one of the driest in California's history, and on the radio, there's no end to the talk about the low snowpack, the parched reservoirs, the depleted Sacramento and San Joaquin rivers. Though it's late February, the hillsides are tawny, not green. When I drive to Wine Country, many are quick to offer their opinions that the drought isn't caused by global warming. Strolling through his blocks of chardonnay, one grizzled grower in Sonoma, who declines to be interviewed when he learns my line of questioning, whistles dismissively, "I guess everybody has to do *something*."

> **We could live in a world without wine, of course, but would we want to?**

In Napa, I meet with David Graves, who co-owns a winery called Saintsbury. Graves and his business partner met while graduate students at UC Davis in the late '70s — Graves' background is in biology — and have been making climate-sensitive pinot noir and chardonnay here since 1981. The vineyard is gorgeous in the misty morning; blackbirds alight above the rows.

He is jolly and peppers his speech with quotes and anecdotes and jokes. Steel tanks loom overhead and two dogs pace around a tennis ball by our feet. We're talking about how grape growers and winemakers have to be risk-averse given that they get only a single shot each year to make do with what that year's weather produced. "If I were going to culinary school, if my sauce curdles, it doesn't cost a year's wages to do it again," he says.

He recalls once visiting a cousin who's a brewer. His cousin excused himself for a   15 moment—someone had added too much water to a batch of beer and rather than boil it down, elected to just throw it all out and start again. Graves laughs: "I said, 'This is a dream!'"

It's vital, in other words, that Graves understand what's happening in his vineyard, which he says isn't warming.

Some researchers, in particular a Southern Oregon University climatologist named Gregory Jones, argue that Napa has been experiencing overall increased temperatures. In the '80s and early '90s, long before there was scientific consensus concerning climate change, Jones was looking at the question of how it might affect wine-grape growing. (Jones had done his dissertation in Bordeaux, and his family owns a winery in Oregon.) "I didn't think we really knew enough about the basics," he explains over the phone.

To Jones, it wasn't hard to see that warming had already been affecting wine: "If you go back to Burgundy 10 years ago or Germany 10 years ago, they'd have one good vintage in eight or nine or ten. It was because they were variable and much colder," he says. "And today they have seven or eight or nine good vintages in 10." This matches what he's witnessed in Oregon: "In my region, 50 years ago it was difficult because there was too much frost and a longer growing season. Bingo—we can do it." Another way to trace climate change's effect on wine already, Jones argues, is the increased alcohol levels in wines around the world—warmer years mean more sugar in the berries, as they're sometimes called, which means more alcohol in the wine. (Others would argue that it's simply become fashionable to make more alcoholic wines.)

David Graves, convinced he hasn't seen a warming trend, partnered with a climate researcher named Dan Cayan at University of California, San Diego, and a trade group called the Napa Valley Vintners, which represents about 400 of Napa's wineries. The data they gathered was more localized than Jones'. Their study, which hasn't been published in a peer-reviewed journal, found that the warming trend in most non-urban parts of Napa Valley over the last 60 to 80 years has been "significantly less" than what Jones had claimed. (I later ask Cayan about the fact that it hasn't been published in a peer-reviewed journal. "That's partly my own fault for being a slacker," he says, adding that there is additional work they are doing, in terms of sourcing and then cleaning up the data they're gathering.)

"I really, really don't want to give aid and comfort to climate-change denialists,"   20 Graves says. All they wanted to do was shrink the proverbial pixel size: "Let's get the resolution so we're not in a grid that's a hundred kilometers by a hundred kilometers, we're in a grid that's five kilometers by five kilometers. And ultimately that really matters because that could be the difference between you growing pinot noir and syrah."

Graves says, in fact, he's seen a *cooling* trend in his vineyard in recent years; whether that's a short-term thing, he doesn't know. And it's true that the world will not warm uniformly. Some areas will encounter colder temperatures, or wetter ones, or extreme weather like heat waves or hail. Ultimately the scariest thing for grape growers and wine makers is uncertainty or large variation year to year. Graves and the polite Napa Valley Vintners representative I sit down with later that day say they don't plan to use the data they've collected to model Napa's future; climate modeling is expensive.

But it's also not hard to intuit why producers and the NVV might not want more press about how their $50 billion valley, the crown jewel of American wine, is screwed. What they seem to want is a little impossible: to acknowledge that climate change is real, but that somehow they will be unaffected. (And on some level, isn't that what we all want?)

Gregory Jones thinks people are simply afraid of speaking publicly, lest they inspire backlash like Ross Brown did after his Tasmanian purchase: "I've had conversations with the biggest winemakers in Napa," he says. "I don't have conversations with them at their front door, I have conservations at their back door."

Regardless, there is a generally split opinion between what researchers and what industry professionals are saying (or are willing to say). Many took issue with the PNAS estimate—a potential 25% to 73% loss—when it was a published and covered in the mainstream press. As pre-eminent wine writer Jancis Robinson says over email, "I think those proportions are way too high, but I have certainly witnessed considerable changes."

Noah Diffenbaugh, a Stanford professor who studies climate and food security and who has published several papers about climate change's effects on wine, says there are a few big things we can take away: "I'm confident that we'll see increasing temperatures in the areas that are currently the high-value, high-quality growing regions." He goes on, "I'm impressed with human ingenuity and the ability of humans to succeed in a variety of environments."

Worldwide, grape growers and winemakers are already adapting, as they always have, to a given year or month or day's varying demands and challenges. There are things they can do in the case of really hot weather. They're managing canopies to increase air circulation around berries. They're spraying vines with what's basically wine-grape sunscreen. They're in some cases going to turn to technology—remote sensors or drones to help monitor vineyards and use water resources more intelligently, or even cloud seeding to artificially create rain. In some cases, they are starting to replant vineyards to varietals that they anticipate will better handle the increased temperatures to come.

Many of the biggest players in American wine are starting to look into what their options will be as things worsen. One of the largest domestic producers, Constellation, has partnered with a research extension of the University of California system to identify less commonly known varietals that are more suitable to a hotter, drier climate, especially in California's San Joaquin Valley, where much of our supermarket wine originates. There are rumors of others—the largest producer, Gallo, and another giant, Bronco, which sells two-buck Chuck—experimenting with varietal cultivation and genetic modification to the same end. (Neither company responded to interview requests.) Inexpensive mass-market wines are also going to be less susceptible to climate change because they're already so loaded up with additives, like powdered tannins, a super-concentrated grape juice called Mega Purple that adds color, and what's essentially liquified oak chips. (And bottles aren't labeled with ingredients, meaning consumers are often unaware of whether their wines are natural or full of additives.) These wines are less about *terroir* and more about drinkability attained as cheaply as possible.

Throughout the world, some big producers are looking into and purchasing sites in cooler areas, as Brown Brothers did in Tasmania. J. Barrie Graham, a banker with experience in financing and advising Northern California wineries, says no one was thinking or talking about global warming seven or eight years ago when making long-term financial decisions. "I would say now it's a very common discussion."

For now, David Graves says he's not doing anything significant to react to potential changes in climate in southern Napa: "In the 25-year time frame, I'm ready to say probably we're not going to see a radical change." He adds that there are other potential changes that could threaten Californian wine—first among them the scarcity of water, changing consumer tastes, and changes in immigration that will affect California wine's primarily Hispanic labor force. He then sighs. "Beyond that, from, say, 2040 on? All bets are off."

"I'm reminded of two things," he says. "One is that Harry Truman famously said   30 he wanted a one-armed economist so the economist couldn't say 'on the other hand.' " His loud laugh echoes through the high winery roof: "The other thing is what Keynes is reputed to have said: 'In the long run we're all dead.' "

Nowhere is the story of what is going to happen to viticulture if nothing is done to curb climate change more starkly painted than in Europe. Europe is the world capital of wine, home to France, Italy, and Spain, the world's first three largest producers, respectively. (The U.S. is fourth.) Most—and some would argue all—of the world's best wines are produced there. In many European nations, laws govern which varietals can be grown where, at what density vines can be planted, whether irrigation is allowed, whether the addition of sugar is allowed—it goes on and on. Additives? Out of the question. Such laws seek to protect regional products but may end up having the opposite effect.

A much-repeated example is that in Burgundy, France, growers grow pinot noir as their red grape. If pinot noir is no longer optimal in Burgundy, growers won't be able to switch their vineyards over to different red grapes and sell them as anything but cheap table wines—forgoing the hundreds or thousands of dollars that fine Burgundies can fetch. "As one of my colleagues in Germany likes to say, 'Europeans are growing grapes and making wine in a cage,' " Gregory Jones says.

Jean-Marc Touzard, economist and research director at the French National Institute for Agricultural Research, says they've observed the effects of climate change on wine since the 1980s. For example, "The vine matures faster because of higher temperatures. In Languedoc Roussillon, the harvest used to be in September, now it's at the end of August." Hotter, more compressed growing seasons have also affected the wines themselves—acidity is lower; sugar and therefore alcohol are higher. Flavor profiles are changing.

That said, Touzard argues that the laws are starting to evolve, offering the example that in some southern growing regions, they now allow irrigation—"under certain date restrictions"—something that before would have been unheard of in French wine. It's of course debatable whether this change, which to an outsider may sound insignificant, is enough.

Two things are clear: In France and around the world, it's going to be the small producers, the ones with fewer resources to purchase new vineyard sites, or replant, or survive a few bad years, that are at greatest risk. In Europe especially, these are sometimes single-man operations. They make a handicraft. A wine blogger I speak with, Bertrand Celce, travels to France (and elsewhere) discovering and documenting the efforts of such producers. He says some grape growers he's encountering certainly are pessimistic. Wet conditions, for example, means an increased instance of disease, something such producers—who don't use herbicides—have limited means to combat.

"The problem is they have to do more work," Celce says. "They have smaller surfaces, but they tend to have little employment." If the case study of American Prohibition serves as an example, the end result of global warming will be a wine scene that is more homogenous in terms of style, and owned by fewer, richer players. Eventually, when the best wines in the world become more scarce, the bottles remaining will become even more valuable, meaning fine wine will be even more of a luxury commodity than it already is.

And yet, in more northern parts of Europe, in countries that have never been viable for commercial viticulture—and perhaps have long envied their neighbors—some see an opportunity.

The fall day I visit Denbies Wine Estate, in Surrey, England, is comically beautiful: blue skies punctuated by clouds fluffy as sheep. The parking lot is full. I am made to follow a flock of mostly gray-haired, mostly British couples as they're led into an octagonal movie theater where a loud video explains the winemaking process, then down a corridor past the winery itself. The guide is chirpy and her rather unnecessary-seeming headset malfunctions. At the end of the tour we are poured three wines and shepherded into a gift shop where the women browse tea towels and Christmas ornaments with furrowed brows and the men stand about with hands in pockets. What's most remarkable, to me, aren't the wines but the fact that this is the sort of bustling touristy affair I'd expect to find in Napa or Mendoza.

Victor Maguire is courteous and wry and leads me on a tour of the estate in a sputtering Land Rover. He's worked at Denbies, which was founded in the late '80s and is one of the largest vineyards in the country, for nearly a decade. While grapevines have been cultivated in England for a millennium, the practice has always been marginal, a cottage industry. The problem had always been it was a little too cold, a little too wet, for a consistently good crop.

But in the last few decades, England has witnessed something fairly spectacular: the first real emergence of a commercial wine culture. New wine regions often make their name on a particular wine or two, and England's is sparkling wine. We are geographically not all so far from Champagne, and the soils here are very similar. Climate change means that England will become "increasingly more ideal than Champagne" for sparkling wine, Maguire says.

As numerous people in the English wine industry point out during my visit, sparkling wine was most likely invented here, in 1662. The producers of Champagne then began replicating the process, which they dubbed the *méthode champenoise*, or Champagne method. There is some perhaps perverse excitement, then, at the notion that the

French are at risk of losing their viticulture and the English might take up that mantle. (The English have wanted this for some time: When he financed his settlement at Jamestown, King James sent along French vignerons and required each homesteader to carry with him several cuttings of French wine grapes to plant, hoping his new colony would crush the French wine industry. This project failed, and the Virginians soon instead became all about tobacco.)

The day before, I visited a shop in London that sells only English spirits and wine—a whole wall of them. There are 400 vineyards in the country—though many fewer wineries—and perhaps more importantly, English producers are being recognized internationally for their quality: Four won gold medals at the International Wine Challenge this year. And indeed, some of the sparkling wines I tasted were superb.

As Maguire grips the Land Rover's steering wheel and we wend through the rows, I ask him what he thinks of the possible effects of climate change on French wine. He pauses. "There is a school of thought that Champagne in 50 years will not have the ideal climate," Maguire says judiciously, with a small smile. He then talks more freely about the hard weather France has seen of late. This year, for the third vintage in a row, for example, Burgundy lost a significant portion of its crop to hail, and the Languedoc was hit by the worst flooding in 60 years.

"It's happening already, and we know that the continental growing and ripening seasons are becoming more compressed," he says.

Harvest is underway at Denbies. We pass a group of laborers as they relax and lunch in the sunshine. But isn't it a bad thing, I ask, if we lose French wine?   45

"I don't think we're *losing* France," he replies. "I think they'll have to learn to compensate." He adds, "I think it's great that English wine now has a place in the European arena."

The problem, though, is that England or Tasmania is probably not going to be able to ever reach the level of output as the great traditional wine regions of the world. There's the additional problem of styles. As wine writer Jancis Robinson points out to me, these newer regions "make completely different sorts of wine. Cool-climate wines are very different in style from those produced in the hot, dry regions under threat." The latter produce larger-bodied reds. Most importantly, though, whereas the French or the Italians or the Spanish have been perfecting what they do for centuries—and wine is an integral part of each of those cultures—these new wine regions are in their relative infancies. People are still figuring out what works best and where, and that trial and error can take lifetimes.

If all of New York bagels were about to disappear forever, how much of a silver lining would it be if there were new opportunities for bagels in Des Moines? Especially if in this metaphor, there were bagel shops that had been perfecting their crafts for not just decades but in some cases centuries? This is the scariest part of global warming: the fact that we won't be able to undo the damage done, that we won't be able to extricate Venice, or New Orleans, from the sea. Their disappearance will be a net loss, regardless of what mountainside civilizations will someday rise.

Maybe we aren't afraid enough. Or maybe we are too afraid. Maybe it's just wine.

We turn another corner. Robust rows, their berries full and heavy, surround us.   50
Maguire stomps his foot on the break and we lurch to a halt. His mouth falls open.

"The fruit looks spectacularly good!" he exclaims. "I've never seen it look so good!"

Exploring Context

1. Allen references the 2014 National Climate Assessment. Explore this report at nca2014. globalchange.gov/report. What other impacts might we expect from global climate change?

2. Silicon Valley Bank produces an annual report on the wine industry. Review this report at www.svb.com/wine-report. Does the most recent report reflect any of the changes that Allen suggests are coming for this industry? Why would a bank produce such a report in the first place?

3. Allen's essay was originally published online and included several links to other Web sites. Select a key quotation from Allen's text and provide links that support or elaborate the points Allen makes in the quotation.

Questions for Connecting

1. What practices must we modify in response to the coming changes in wine production? Synthesize Allen's argument with Kwame Anthony Appiah's ideas about how cultural practices change in "Making Conversation" and "The Primacy of Practice" (p. 44). What values are at stake in viticulture? Can we agree to act on climate change even if we don't all agree on the facts surrounding it?

2. In "Reporting Live from Tomorrow" (p. 179), Daniel Gilbert suggests that surrogates can help us make decisions about our future. Apply his ideas to Allen's essay. Can wine function as a surrogate for agriculture as a whole? You might want to use your work from Question 2 of Questions for Critical Reading.

3. Allen's argument seems to assume, on some level, that the loss of certain wines would be tragic. Is she just being "WEIRD"? Evaluate Allen's argument using Ethan Watters's ideas in "Being WEIRD: How Culture Shapes the Mind" (p. 493). Is wine a harbinger of larger global changes in food production or does that perception depend on a particular Western cultural outlook?

Language Matters

1. Each discipline has a specific approach to evidence. Start by finding information on how research is done in your intended major or field. How would you pursue Allen's arguments through that field? How would that discipline make this argument?

2. In small groups, select a common grammatical error, such as sentence fragments or subject-verb agreement problems. Select a key quotation from Allen's text and then change it to represent the error. Share the original and altered quotations in small groups to create a list of error examples and corrections using this essay.

3. Allen includes a number of specialized terms, including *terroir* and *viticulture*. Often, a glossary is used to define terms. Create a brief glossary for Allen's essay. How would you choose which terms to include?

Assignments for Writing

1. Rebecca Shaw of the Environmental Defense Fund asks in Allen's essay "How does agriculture need to change? What are the incentives that need to be put in place that won't undermine the long-term sustainability and don't create more environmental harm?" (p. 35). Write a paper in which you answer Shaw's question using the evidence Allen provides elsewhere in her essay. What changes might we promote in agriculture in response to climate change? Should we create new technologies or simply explore new geographical locations for food production? Use your work from Questions 1 and 3 of Questions for Critical Reading in making your response.

2. Write a paper on the significance of wine. What are its cultural functions, according to Allen? What role does it play in the economy? In food production? Consider using your work from Question 1 of Questions for Critical Reading and Question 2 of Exploring Context to support your response.

3. Do we have enough evidence to respond to climate change? Write a paper in which you determine our best response to shifts in global climate. Does Allen offer enough evidence for us to take action at personal or national levels? Or does her essay instead suggest that we need more evidence, given the costs and magnitude of change needed? You might find your work from Questions for Critical Reading useful.

KWAME ANTHONY APPIAH

© Rick Friedman/Corbis

Kwame Anthony Appiah was born in London, grew up in Ghana, and earned a Ph.D. at Cambridge University. He is a professor of philosophy and law at New York University. He has also taught at Princeton, Duke, Harvard, Yale, Cornell, Cambridge, and the University of Ghana. He has published numerous academic books and articles as well as three detective novels. In 2008, Appiah was recognized for his contributions to racial, ethnic, and religious relations when Brandeis University awarded him the first Joseph B. and Toby Gittler Prize.

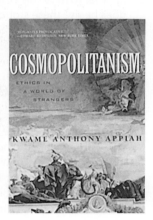

Appiah's *Cosmopolitanism: Ethics in a World of Strangers* (2006) was one of the first books published in Henry Louis Gates Jr.'s Issues of Our Time series, which aims to tackle the important concerns of the information age. In *Cosmopolitanism*, Appiah examines the imaginary boundaries that have separated people around the world and the ways we can redraw those boundaries. Appiah claims with the book's title that we are all citizens of the world. In the time of al Qaeda, we can no longer afford to draw significant lines between different groups and regions. Humanity has fundamental commonalities, Appiah suggests, and we should embrace them.

The following selections, "Making Conversation" and "The Primacy of Practice," appear in *Cosmopolitanism* as the introduction and one of the book's chapters. Appiah first defines *cosmopolitanism* and its problems but ultimately determines that practicing a citizenship of the world is not only helpful in a post-9/11 world, but necessary. There is no divide between "us" and "them," he suggests, only a basic moral obligation we have to each other. It is not necessary for people to agree to behave morally for the right reason, or the right god, or the right country or custom. It is only necessary that they agree to behave morally. Conversation, Appiah writes, is the best starting point.

It's tempting to reduce what follows to something as simple as "We should all just get along," but Appiah is also challenging us to think about how we can make that happen. How primal is practice in your own life? Is what you do more important than why you do it?

▶ TAGS: *collaboration, community, conversation, ethics, globalism, identity, judgment and decision-making, politics, social change*

▶ CONNECTIONS: *Allen, DeGhett, Duhigg, Epstein, Friedman, Southan, Stillman, van Houtryve, Yoshino*

Questions for Critical Reading

1. As you read Appiah, use his text to create a definition of what he means by *cosmopolitanism*, working with quotations from Appiah that support your interpretation. Then apply this definition to a current national or world situation. How does it show cosmopolitanism at work, or how might embracing this concept help resolve the situation?

2. According to Appiah, what are some crucial tools needed to enact his vision of cosmopolitanism? Reread his essay to locate quotations in which Appiah discusses these tools. How realistic is his vision? Based on the examples he offers, do you think these tools would be effective? Why or why not?

3. In order to make his argument, Appiah includes some stories from his own life. How does he use these stories? What sort of evidence do they provide? What other forms of evidence does he use? Support your answers by searching for specific examples from the text.

Making Conversation

Our ancestors have been human for a very long time. If a normal baby girl born forty thousand years ago were kidnapped by a time traveler and raised in a normal family in New York, she would be ready for college in eighteen years. She would learn English (along with — who knows? — Spanish or Chinese), understand trigonometry, follow baseball and pop music; she would probably want a pierced tongue and a couple of tattoos. And she would be unrecognizably different from the brothers and sisters she left behind. For most of human history, we were born into small societies of a few score people, bands of hunters and gatherers, and would see, on a typical day, only people we had known most of our lives. Everything our long-ago ancestors ate or wore, every tool they used, every shrine at which they worshipped, was made within that group. Their knowledge came from their ancestors or from their own experiences. That is the world that shaped us, the world in which our nature was formed.

Now, if I walk down New York's Fifth Avenue on an ordinary day, I will have within sight more human beings than most of those prehistoric hunter-gatherers saw in a lifetime. Between then and now some of our forebears settled down and learned agriculture; created villages, towns, and, in the end, cities; discovered the power of writing. But it was a slow process. The population of classical Athens when Socrates* died, at the end of the fifth century BC, could have lived in a few large skyscrapers. Alexander† set off from Macedon to conquer the world three-quarters of a century later with an army of between thirty and forty thousand, which is far fewer people than commute into Des Moines every Monday morning. When, in the first century, the population of Rome reached a million, it was the first city of its size. To keep it fed, the Romans had had to build an empire that brought home grain from Africa. By then, they had already

---

*Socrates: Athenian Greek (469–399 BC); one of the founders of Western philosophy known chiefly through the writings of his students, notably Plato [Ed.].

†Alexander: Alexander the Great (356–323 BC) founded an empire that eventually covered about two million square miles [Ed.].

worked out how to live cheek by jowl in societies where most of those who spoke your language and shared your laws and grew the food on your table were people you would never know. It is, I think, little short of miraculous that brains shaped by our long history could have been turned to this new way of life.

Even once we started to build these larger societies, most people knew little about the ways of other tribes, and could affect just a few local lives. Only in the past couple of centuries, as every human community has gradually been drawn into a single web of trade and a global network of information, have we come to a point where each of us can realistically imagine contacting any other of our six billion conspecifics and sending that person something worth having: a radio, an antibiotic, a good idea. Unfortunately, we could also send, through negligence as easily as malice, things that will cause harm: a virus, an airborne pollutant, a bad idea. And the possibilities of good and of ill are multiplied beyond all measure when it comes to policies carried out by governments in our name. Together, we can ruin poor farmers by dumping our subsidized grain into their markets, cripple industries by punitive tariffs, deliver weapons that will kill thousands upon thousands. Together, we can raise standards of living by adopting new policies on trade and aid, prevent or treat diseases with vaccines and pharmaceuticals, take measures against global climate change, encourage resistance to tyranny and a concern for the worth of each human life.

And, of course, the worldwide web of information—radio, television, telephones, the Internet—means not only that we can affect lives everywhere but that we can learn about life anywhere, too. Each person you know about and can affect is someone to whom you have responsibilities: To say this is just to affirm the very idea of morality. The challenge, then, is to take minds and hearts formed over the long millennia of living in local troops and equip them with ideas and institutions that will allow us to live together as the global tribe we have become.

Under what rubric to proceed? Not "globalization"—a term that once referred to a marketing strategy, and then came to designate a macroeconomic thesis, and now can seem to encompass everything, and nothing. Not "multiculturalism," another shape shifter, which so often designates the disease it purports to cure. With some ambivalence, I have settled on "cosmopolitanism." Its meaning is equally disputed, and celebrations of the "cosmopolitan" can suggest an unpleasant posture of superiority toward the putative provincial. You imagine a Comme des Garçons–clad sophisticate with a platinum frequent-flyer card regarding, with kindly condescension, a ruddy-faced farmer in workman's overalls. And you wince.

Maybe, though, the term can be rescued. It has certainly proved a survivor. Cosmopolitanism dates at least to the Cynics* of the fourth century BC, who first coined the expression cosmopolitan, "citizen of the cosmos." The formulation was meant to be paradoxical, and reflected the general Cynic skepticism toward custom and tradition. A citizen—a *politēs*—belonged to a particular *polis*, a city to which he or she owed loyalty. The cosmos referred to the world, not in the sense of the earth, but in the sense of the universe. Talk of cosmopolitanism originally signaled, then, a rejection

5

---

*Cynics: Ancient school of Greek philosophy. Cynics advocated a simple life, free from material things, rejecting desires for fame and even health [Ed.].

of the conventional view that every civilized person belonged to a community among communities.

The creed was taken up and elaborated by the Stoics,* beginning in the third century BC, and that fact proved of critical importance in its subsequent intellectual history. For the Stoicism of the Romans—Cicero, Seneca, Epictetus, and the emperor Marcus Aurelius—proved congenial to many Christian intellectuals, once Christianity became the religion of the Roman Empire. It is profoundly ironic that, though Marcus Aurelius sought to suppress the new Christian sect, his extraordinarily personal *Meditations*, a philosophical diary written in the second century AD as he battled to save the Roman Empire from barbarian invaders, has attracted Christian readers for nearly two millennia. Part of its appeal, I think, has always been the way the Stoic emperor's cosmopolitan conviction of the oneness of humanity echoes Saint Paul's insistence that "there is neither Jew nor Greek, there is neither bond nor free, there is neither male nor female: for ye are all one in Christ Jesus."[1]

Cosmopolitanism's later career wasn't without distinction. It underwrote some of the great moral achievements of the Enlightenment, including the 1789 "Declaration of the Rights of Man" and Immanuel Kant's work proposing a "league of nations." In a 1788 essay in his journal *Teutscher Merkur*, Christoph Martin Wieland—once called the German Voltaire—wrote, in a characteristic expression of the ideal, "Cosmopolitans . . . regard all the peoples of the earth as so many branches of a single family, and the universe as a state, of which they, with innumerable other rational beings, are citizens, promoting together under the general laws of nature the perfection of the whole, while each in his own fashion is busy about his own well-being."[2] And Voltaire himself—whom nobody, alas, ever called the French Wieland—spoke eloquently of the obligation to understand those with whom we share the planet, linking that need explicitly with our global economic interdependence. "Fed by the products of their soil, dressed in their fabrics, amused by games they invented, instructed even by their ancient moral fables, why would we neglect to understand the mind of these nations, among whom our European traders have traveled ever since they could find a way to get to them?"[3]

So there are two strands that intertwine in the notion of cosmopolitanism. One is the idea that we have obligations to others, obligations that stretch beyond those to whom we are related by the ties of kith and kind, or even the more formal ties of a shared citizenship. The other is that we take seriously the value not just of human life but of particular human lives, which means taking an interest in the practices and beliefs that lend them significance. People are different, the cosmopolitan knows, and there is much to learn from our differences. Because there are so many human possibilities worth exploring, we neither expect nor desire that every person or every society should converge on a single mode of life. Whatever our obligations are to others (or theirs to us) they often have the right to go their own way. As we'll see, there will be times when these two ideals—universal concern and respect for legitimate difference—clash. There's a sense in which cosmopolitanism is the name not of the solution but of the challenge.

---

*Stoics: School of philosophy influenced by the Cynics. Stoics held that destructive emotions should be controlled and that clear thinking would lead to reason [Ed.].

A citizen of the world: How far can we take that idea? Are you really supposed to   10
abjure all local allegiances and partialities in the name of this vast abstraction, humanity? Some proponents of cosmopolitan-
ism were pleased to think so; and they often
made easy targets of ridicule. "Friend of men,   **[C]osmopolitanism is the name**
and enemy of almost every man he had to do   **not of the solution but of the**
with," Thomas Carlyle* memorably said of   **challenge.**
the eighteenth-century physiocrat the Mar-
quis de Mirabeau, who wrote the treatise *L'Ami des hommes* when he wasn't too busy
jailing his own son. "A lover of his kind, but a hater of his kindred," Edmund Burke[†]
said of Jean-Jacques Rousseau,° who handed each of the five children he fathered to an
orphanage.

Yet the impartialist version of the cosmopolitan creed has continued to hold a
steely fascination. Virginia Woolf[‡] once exhorted "freedom from unreal loyalties"—
to nation, sex, school, neighborhood, and on and on. Leo Tolstoy,[§] in the same spirit,
inveighed against the "stupidity" of patriotism. "To destroy war, destroy patriotism,"
he wrote in an 1896 essay—a couple of decades before the tsar was swept away by a
revolution in the name of the international working class. Some contemporary philosophers have similarly urged that the boundaries of nations are morally irrelevant—
accidents of history with no rightful claim on our conscience.

But if there are friends of cosmopolitanism who make me nervous, I am happy to be
opposed to cosmopolitanism's noisiest foes. Both Hitler and Stalin—who agreed about
little else, save that murder was the first instrument of politics—launched regular in-
vectives against "rootless cosmopolitans"; and while, for both, anti-cosmopolitanism
was often just a euphemism for anti-Semitism, they were right to see cosmopolitanism
as their enemy. For they both required a kind of loyalty to one portion of humanity—a
nation, a class—that ruled out loyalty to all of humanity. And the one thought that
cosmopolitans share is that no local loyalty can ever justify forgetting that each human
being has responsibilities to every other. Fortunately, we need take sides neither with
the nationalist who abandons all foreigners nor with the hard-core cosmopolitan who
regards her friends and fellow citizens with icy impartiality. The position worth defending might be called (in both senses) a partial cosmopolitanism.

There's a striking passage, to this point, in George Eliot's *Daniel Deronda*, published in 1876, which was, as it happens, the year when England's first—and, so far,
last—Jewish prime minister, Benjamin Disraeli, was elevated to the peerage as Earl of
Beaconsfield. Disraeli, though baptized and brought up in the Church of England, always had a proud consciousness of his Jewish ancestry (given the family name, which
his father spelled D'Israeli, it would have been hard to ignore). But Deronda, who has
been raised in England as a Christian gentleman, discovers his Jewish ancestry only as

---

*Thomas Carlyle: Scottish essayist and historian (1795–1881) [Ed.].
[†]Edmund Burke: Anglo-Irish politician and political philosopher (1729–1797) [Ed.].
°Jean-Jacques Rousseau: French political philosopher (1712–1778) [Ed.].
[‡]Virginia Woolf: English novelist, critic, and essayist (1882–1941) [Ed.].
[§]Leo Tolstoy: Russian writer best known for his novels, such as *War and Peace* (1828–1910) [Ed.].

an adult; and his response is to commit himself to the furtherance of his "hereditary people":

> It was as if he had found an added soul in finding his ancestry—his judg-
> ment no longer wandering in the mazes of impartial sympathy, but choosing,
> with the noble partiality which is man's best strength, the closer fellowship
> that makes sympathy practical—exchanging that bird's-eye reasonableness
> which soars to avoid preference and loses all sense of quality, for the generous
> reasonableness of drawing shoulder to shoulder with men of like inheritance.

Notice that in claiming a Jewish loyalty—an "added soul"—Deronda is not rejecting a human one. As he says to his mother, "I think it would have been right that I should have been brought up with the consciousness that I was a Jew, but it must always have been a good to me to have as wide an instruction and sympathy as possible." This is the same Deronda, after all, who has earlier explained his decision to study abroad in these eminently cosmopolitan terms: "I want to be an Englishman, but I want to understand other points of view. And I want to get rid of a merely English attitude in studies."[4] Loyalties and local allegiances determine more than what we want; they determine who we are. And Eliot's talk of the "closer fellowship that makes sympathy practical" echoes Cicero's claim that "society and human fellowship will be best served if we confer the most kindness on those with whom we are most closely associated."[5] A creed that disdains the partialities of kinfolk and community may have a past, but it has no future.

In the final message my father left for me and my sisters, he wrote, "Remember you are citizens of the world." But as a leader of the independence movement in what was then the Gold Coast, he never saw a conflict between local partialities and a universal morality—between being part of the place you were and a part of a broader human community. Raised with this father and an English mother, who was both deeply connected to our family in England and fully rooted in Ghana, where she has now lived for half a century, I always had a sense of family and tribe that was multiple and overlapping: Nothing could have seemed more commonplace.

Surely nothing *is* more commonplace. In geological terms, it has been a blink of 15 an eye since human beings first left Africa, and there are few spots where we have not found habitation. The urge to migrate is no less "natural" than the urge to settle. At the same time, most of those who have learned the languages and customs of other places haven't done so out of mere curiosity. A few were looking for food for thought; most were looking for food. Thoroughgoing ignorance about the ways of others is largely a privilege of the powerful. The well-traveled polyglot is as likely to be among the worst off as among the best off—as likely to be found in a shantytown as at the Sorbonne. So cosmopolitanism shouldn't be seen as some exalted attainment: It begins with the simple idea that in the human community, as in national communities, we need to develop habits of coexistence: conversation in its older meaning, of living together, association.

And conversation in its modern sense, too. The town of Kumasi, where I grew up, is the capital of Ghana's Asante region, and, when I was a child, its main commercial thoroughfare was called Kingsway Street. In the 1950s, if you wandered down it toward the railway yards at the center of town, you'd first pass by Baboo's Bazaar, which sold imported foods and was run by the eponymous Mr. Baboo—a charming and courteous Indian—with the help of his growing family. Mr. Baboo was active in the Rotary and could always be counted on to make a contribution to the various charitable projects that are among the diversions of Kumasi's middle class, but the truth is that I remember Mr. Baboo mostly because he always had a good stock of candies and because he was always smiling. I can't reconstruct the tour down the rest of the street, for not every store had bonbons to anchor my memories. Still, I remember that we got rice from Irani Brothers; and that we often stopped in on various Lebanese and Syrian families, Muslim and Maronite, and even a philosophical Druze, named Mr. Hanni, who sold imported cloth and who was always ready, as I grew older, for a conversation about the troubles of his native Lebanon. There were other "strangers" among us, too: In the military barracks in the middle of town, you could find many northerners among the "other ranks," privates and NCOs,* their faces etched in distinctive patterns of ethnic scarification. And then there was the occasional European—the Greek architect, the Hungarian artist, the Irish doctor, the Scots engineer, some English barristers and judges, and a wildly international assortment of professors at the university, many of whom, unlike the colonial officials, remained after independence. I never thought to wonder, as a child, why these people traveled so far to live and work in my hometown; still, I was glad they did. Conversations across boundaries can be fraught, all the more so as the world grows smaller and the stakes grow larger. It's therefore worth remembering that they can also be a pleasure. What academics sometimes dub "cultural otherness" should prompt neither piety nor consternation.

Cosmopolitanism is an adventure and an ideal: But you can't have any respect for human diversity and expect everyone to become cosmopolitan. The obligations of those who wish to exercise their legitimate freedom to associate with their own kind—to keep the rest of the world away as the Amish do in the United States—are only the same as the basic obligations we all have: to do for others what morality requires. Still, a world in which communities are neatly hived off from one another seems no longer a serious option, if it ever was. And the way of segregation and seclusion has always been anomalous in our perpetually voyaging species. Cosmopolitanism isn't hard work; repudiating it is.

In the wake of 9/11, there has been a lot of fretful discussion about the divide between "us" and "them." What's often taken for granted is a picture of a world in which conflicts arise, ultimately, from conflicts between values. This is what we take to be good; that is what they take to be good. That picture of the world has deep philosophical roots; it is thoughtful, well worked out, plausible. And, I think, wrong.

I should be clear: This book [Appiah's *Cosmopolitanism*] is not a book about policy, nor is it a contribution to the debates about the true face of globalization. I'm a philosopher by trade, and philosophers rarely write really useful books. All the same, I hope to persuade you that there are interesting conceptual questions that lie beneath the facts of globalization. The cluster of questions I want to take up can seem pretty abstract. How real are values? What do we talk about when we talk about difference? Is any form of relativism right? When do morals and manners clash? Can culture be

---

*NCOs: Noncommissioned officers [Ed.].

"owned"? What do we owe strangers by virtue of our shared humanity? But the way these questions play out in our lives isn't so very abstract. By the end, I hope to have made it harder to think of the world as divided between the West and the Rest; between locals and moderns; between a bloodless ethic of profit and a bloody ethic of identity; between "us" and "them." The foreignness of foreigners, the strangeness of strangers: These things are real enough. It's just that we've been encouraged, not least by well-meaning intellectuals, to exaggerate their significance by an order of magnitude.

As I'll be arguing, it is an error—to which we dwellers in a scientific age are pe- 20 culiarly prone—to resist talk of "objective" values. In the absence of a natural science of right and wrong, someone whose model of knowledge is physics or biology will be inclined to conclude that values are not real; or, at any rate, not real like atoms and nebulae. In the face of this temptation, I want to hold on to at least one important aspect of the objectivity of values: that there are some values that are, and should be, universal, just as there are lots of values that are, and must be, local. We can't hope to reach a final consensus on how to rank and order such values. That's why the model I'll be returning to is that of conversation—and, in particular, conversation between people from different ways of life. The world is getting more crowded: In the next half a century the population of our once foraging species will approach nine billion. Depending on the circumstances, conversations across boundaries can be delightful, or just vexing: What they mainly are, though, is inevitable.

The Primacy of Practice

Local Agreements

Among the Asante,* you will be glad to hear, incest between brothers and sisters and parents and children is shunned as *akyiwadeɛ.* You can agree with an Asante that it's wrong, even if you don't accept his explanation of why. If my interest is in discouraging theft, I needn't worry that one person might refrain from theft because she believes in the Golden Rule; another because of her conception of personal integrity; a third because she thinks God frowns on it. I've said that value language helps shape common responses of thought, action, and feeling. But when the issue is what to do, differences in what we think and feel can fall away. We know from our own family lives that conversation doesn't start with agreement on principles. Who but someone in the grip of a terrible theory would want to insist on an agreement on principles before discussing which movie to go to, what to have for dinner, when to go to bed?

Indeed, our political coexistence, as subjects or citizens, depends on being able to agree about practices while disagreeing about their justification. For many long years, in medieval Spain under the Moors and later in the Ottoman Near East, Jews and Christians of various denominations lived under Muslim rule. This modus vivendi† was possible only because the various communities did not have to agree on

---

*Asante: A people living primarily in Ghana and the Ivory Coast [Ed.].
†Modus vivendi: Latin phrase meaning mode (or way) of living that accommodates divergent points of view; agreeing to disagree [Ed.].

a set of universal values. In seventeenth-century Holland, starting roughly in the time of Rembrandt, the Sephardic Jewish community began to be increasingly well integrated into Dutch society, and there was a great deal of intellectual as well as social exchange between Christian and Jewish communities. Christian toleration of Jews did not depend on express agreement on fundamental values. Indeed, these historical examples of religious toleration—you might even call them early experiments in multiculturalism—should remind us of the most obvious fact about our own society.

Americans share a willingness to be governed by the system set out in the U.S. Constitution. But that does not require anyone to agree to any particular claims or values. The Bill of Rights tells us, "Congress shall make no law respecting an establishment of religion, or prohibiting the free exercise thereof. . . ." Yet we don't need to agree on what values underlie our acceptance of the First Amendment's treatment of religion. Is it religious toleration as an end in itself? Or is it a Protestant commitment to the sovereignty of the individual conscience? Is it prudence, which recognizes that trying to force religious conformity on people only leads to civil discord? Or is it skepticism that any religion has it right? Is it to protect the government from religion? Or religion from the government? Or is it some combination of these, or other, aims?

Cass Sunstein, the American legal scholar, has written eloquently that our understanding of Constitutional law is a set of what he calls "incompletely theorized agreements."[6] People mostly agree that it would be wrong for the Congress to pass laws prohibiting the building of mosques, for example, without agreeing exactly as to why. Many of us would, no doubt, mention the First Amendment (even though we don't agree about what values it embodies). But others would ground their judgment not in any particular law but in a conception, say, of democracy or in the equal citizenship of Muslims, neither of which is explicitly mentioned in the Constitution. There is no agreed-upon answer—and the point is there doesn't need to be. We can live together without agreeing on what the values are that make it good to live together; we can agree about what to do in most cases, without agreeing about why it is right.

I don't want to overstate the claim. No doubt there are widely shared values that help Americans live together in amity. But they certainly don't live together successfully because they have a shared theory of value or a shared story as to how to bring "their" values to bear in each case. They each have a pattern of life that they are used to; and neighbors who are, by and large, used to them. So long as this settled pattern is not seriously disrupted, they do not worry over-much about whether their fellow citizens agree with them or their theories about how to live. Americans tend to have, in sum, a broadly liberal reaction when they *do* hear about their fellow citizens' doing something that they would not do themselves: They mostly think it is not their business and not the government's business either. And, as a general rule, their shared Americanness matters to them, although many of their fellow Americans are remarkably unlike themselves. It's just that what they do share can be less substantial than we're inclined to suppose.

Changing Our Minds

It's not surprising, then, that what makes conversation across boundaries worthwhile isn't that we're likely to come to a reasoned agreement about values. I don't say that we can't change minds, but the reasons we exchange in our conversations will seldom do much to persuade others who do not share our fundamental evaluative judgments already. (Remember: The same goes, mutatis mutandis,* for factual judgments.)

When we offer judgments, after all, it's rarely because we have applied well-thought-out principles to a set of facts and deduced an answer. Our efforts to justify what we have done—or what we plan to do—are typically made up after the event, rationalizations of what we have decided intuitively. And a good deal of what we intuitively take to be right, we take to be right just because it is what we are used to. If you live in a society where children are spanked, you will probably spank your children. You will believe that it is a good way to teach them right from wrong and that, despite the temporary suffering caused by a beating, they will end up better off for it. You will point to the wayward child and say, sotto voce,† that his parents do not know how to discipline him; you will mean that they do not beat him enough. You will also, no doubt, recognize that there are people who beat their children too hard or too often. So you will recognize that beating a child can sometimes be cruel.

Much the same can be said about the practice of female genital cutting. . . . If you've grown up taking it for granted as the normal thing to do, you will probably respond at first with surprise to someone who thinks it is wrong. You will offer reasons for doing it—that unmodified sexual organs are unaesthetic; that the ritual gives young people the opportunity to display courage in their transition to adulthood; that you can see their excitement as they go to their ceremony, their pride when they return. You will say that it is very strange that someone who has not been through it should presume to know whether or not sex is pleasurable for you. And, if someone should try to force you to stop from the outside, you may decide to defend the practice as an expression of your cultural identity. But this is likely to be as much a rationalization as are the arguments of your critics. They say it is mutilation, but is that any more than a reflex response to an unfamiliar practice? They exaggerate the medical risks. They say that female circumcision demeans women, but do not seem to think that male circumcision demeans men.

I am not endorsing these claims, or celebrating the argumentative impasse, or, indeed, the poverty of reason in much discussion within and across cultures. But let's recognize this simple fact: A large part of what we do we do because it *is* just what we do. You get up in the morning at eight-thirty. Why *that* time? You have coffee and cereal. Why not porridge? You send the kids to school. Why not teach them at home? You have to work. Why that job, though? Reasoning—by which I mean the public act of exchanging stated justifications—comes in not when we are going on in the usual way, but when we are thinking about change. And when it comes to change, what moves people is often not an argument from a principle, not a long discussion about values, but just a gradually acquired new way of seeing things.

> **Reasoning . . . comes in not when we are going on in the usual way, but when we are thinking about change.**

My father, for example, came from a society in which neither women nor men were traditionally circumcised. Indeed, circumcision was *akyiwadeɛ*; and since chiefs were 30

---

*Mutatis mutandis: "With the necessary modifications" (Latin) [Ed.].
†Sotto voce: Italian for "under the breath"; a dramatic lowering of volume for emphasis [Ed.].

supposed to be unblemished, circumcision was a barrier to holding royal office. Nevertheless, as he tells us in his autobiography, he decided as a teenager to have himself circumcised.

> As was the custom in those happy days, the young girls of Adum would gather together in a playing field nearby on moonlight nights to regale themselves by singing traditional songs and dancing from about 7 PM until midnight each day of the week.
>
> . . . On one such night, these girls suddenly started a new song that completely bowled us over: Not only were the words profane in the extreme, but they also constituted the most daring challenge to our manhood and courage ever flung at us. More than that, we were being invited to violate an age-old tradition of our ancestors, long respected among our people, namely the taboo on circumcision. Literally translated the words were:
>
> "An uncircumcised penis is detestable, and those who are uncircumcised should come for money from us so that they can get circumcised. We shall never marry the uncircumcised."[7]

To begin with, my father and his friends thought the girls would relent. But they were wrong. And so, after consultation with his mates, my father found himself a *wansam*—a Muslim circumcision specialist—and had the operation performed. (It was, he said, the most painful experience of his life and, if he'd had it to do again, he would have refrained. He did not, of course, have the advantage of the preparation, the companionship of boys of his own age, and the prestige of suffering bravely that would have come if the practice had been an Akan tradition.)

My father offered a reason for this decision: He and his friends conceded that "as our future sweethearts and wives, they were entitled to be heard in their plea in favor of male circumcision, even though they were not prepared to go in for female circumcision, which was also a taboo among our people." This explanation invites a question, however. Why did these young women, in the heart of Asante, decide to urge the young men of Adum to do what was not just untraditional but taboo? One possibility is that circumcision somehow became identified in their minds with being modern. If that was the point, my father would have been sympathetic. He was traditional in some ways; but like many people in Kumasi in the early twentieth century, he was also excited by a modern world that was bringing new music, new technology, new possibilities. To volunteer for circumcision in his society he surely had not just to hear the plea of the young women of Adum but to understand—and agree with—the impulse behind it. And, as I say, it may have been exactly the fact that it was untraditional that made it appealing. Circumcision—especially because it carried with it exclusion from the possibilities of traditional political office—became a way of casting his lot with modernity.

This new fashion among the young people of Adum was analogous to, if more substantial than, the change in taste that has produced a generation of Americans with piercings and tattoos. And that change was not simply the result of argument and debate, either (even though, as anyone who has argued with a teenager about a pierced belly button will attest, people on both sides can come up with a whole slew of arguments). There's some social-psychological truth in the old Flanders & Swann song "The Reluctant Cannibal," about a young "savage" who pushes away from the table and declares, "I won't eat people. Eating people is wrong." His father has all the arguments, such as they are. ("But people have always eaten people, / What else is there to eat? / If the Juju had meant us not to eat people, / He wouldn't have made us of meat!") The son, though, just repeats his newfound conviction: Eating people is wrong. He's just sure of it, he'll say so again and again, and he'll win the day by declamation.

Or take the practice of foot-binding* in China, which persisted for a thousand years—and was largely eradicated within a generation. The anti-foot-binding campaign, in the 1910s and 1920s, did circulate facts about the disadvantages of bound feet, but those couldn't have come as news to most people. Perhaps more effective was the campaign's emphasis that no other country went in for the practice; in the world at large, then, China was "losing face" because of it. Natural-foot societies were formed, with members forswearing the practice and further pledging that their sons would not marry women with bound feet. As the movement took hold, scorn was heaped on older women with bound feet, and they were forced to endure the agonies of unbinding. What had been beautiful became ugly; ornamentation became disfigurement. (The success of the anti-foot-binding campaign was undoubtedly a salutary development, but it was not without its victims. Think of some of the last women whose feet were bound, who had to struggle to find husbands.) The appeal to reason alone can explain neither the custom nor its abolition.

So, too, with other social trends. Just a couple of generations ago, in most of the industrialized world, most people thought that middle-class women would ideally be housewives and mothers. If they had time on their hands, they could engage in charitable work or entertain one another; a few of them might engage in the arts, writing novels, painting, performing in music, theater, and dance. But there was little place for them in the "learned professions"—as lawyers or doctors, priests or rabbis; and if they were to be academics, they would teach young women and probably remain unmarried. They were not likely to make their way in politics, except perhaps at the local level. And they were not made welcome in science. How much of the shift away from these assumptions is the result of arguments? Isn't a significant part of it just the consequence of our getting used to new ways of doing things? The arguments that kept the old pattern in place were not—to put it mildly—terribly good. If the *reasons* for the old sexist way of doing things had been the problem, the women's movement could have been done with in a couple of weeks. There are still people, I know, who think that the ideal life for any woman is making and managing a home. There are more who think that it is an honorable option. Still, the vast majority of Westerners would be appalled at the idea of trying to force women back into these roles. Arguments mattered for the women who made the women's movement and the men who responded to them. This I do not mean to deny. But their greatest achievement has been to change our habits. In the 1950s, if a college-educated woman wanted to go to law or business school, the natural response was "Why?" Now the natural response is "Why not?"

Or consider another example: In much of Europe and North America, in places where a generation ago homosexuals were social outcasts and homosexual acts were illegal, lesbian and gay couples are increasingly being recognized by their families, by society, and by the law. This is true despite the continued opposition of major religious

35

---

*Foot-binding: Ancient Chinese practice of wrapping female feet in order to keep them from growing more than about three inches long, resulting in terrible pain and deformity [Ed.].

groups and a significant and persisting undercurrent of social disapproval. Both sides make arguments, some good, most bad, if you apply a philosophical standard of reasoning. But if you ask the social scientists what has produced this change, they will rightly not start with a story about reasons. They will give you a historical account that concludes with a sort of perspectival shift. The increasing presence of "openly gay" people in social life and in the media has changed our habits. Over the last thirty or so years, instead of thinking about the private activity of gay *sex*, many Americans started thinking about the public category of gay *people*. Even those who continue to think of the sex with disgust now find it harder to deny these people their respect and concern (and some of them have learned, as we all did with our own parents, that it's better not to think too much about other people's sex lives anyway).

Now, I don't deny that all the time, at every stage, people were talking, giving each other reasons to do things: accept their children, stop treating homosexuality as a medical disorder, disagree with their churches, come out. Still, the short version of the story is basically this: People got used to lesbians and gay people. I am urging that we should learn about people in other places, take an interest in their civilizations, their arguments, their errors, their achievements, not because that will bring us to agreement, but because it will help us get used to one another. If that is the aim, then the fact that we have all these opportunities for disagreement about values need not put us off. Understanding one another may be hard; it can certainly be interesting. But it doesn't require that we come to agreement.

Fighting for the Good

I've said we can live in harmony without agreeing on underlying values (except, perhaps, the cosmopolitan value of living together). It works the other way, too: We can find ourselves in conflict when we do agree on values. Warring parties are seldom at odds because they have clashing conceptions of "the good." On the contrary, conflict arises most often when two peoples have identified the same thing as good. The fact that both Palestinians and Israelis — in particular, that both observant Muslims and observant Jews — have a special relation to Jerusalem, to the Temple Mount, has been a reliable source of trouble. The problem isn't that they disagree about the importance of Jerusalem: The problem is exactly that they both care for it deeply and, in part, for the same reasons. Muhammad, in the first years of Islam, urged his followers to turn toward Jerusalem in prayer because he had learned the story of Jerusalem from the Jews among whom he lived in Mecca. Nor is it an accident that the West's fiercest adversaries among other societies tend to come from among the most Westernized of the group. *Mon semblable mon frère?** Only if the *frère* you have in mind is Cain.† We all know now that the foot soldiers of al Qaeda who committed the mass murders at the Twin Towers and the Pentagon were not Bedouins from the desert; not unlettered fellahin.°

Indeed, there's a wider pattern here. Who in Ghana excoriated the British and built the movement for independence? Not the farmers and the peasants. Not the chiefs. It was the Western-educated bourgeoisie. And when in the 1950s Kwame

---

**Mon semblable mon frère?*: French for "My likeness my brother?" [Ed.].

†Cain: Biblical son of Adam and Eve who murdered his brother Abel (see Genesis 4:1–8) [Ed.].

°Fellahin: Middle Eastern peasant or farmer [Ed.].

Nkrumah—who went to college in Pennsylvania and lived in London—created a nationalist mass movement, at its core were soldiers who had returned from fighting a war in the British army, urban market women who traded Dutch prints, trade unionists who worked in industries created by colonialism, and the so-called veranda boys, who had been to colonial secondary schools, learned English, studied history and geography in textbooks written in England. Who led the resistance to the British Raj?* An Indian-born South African lawyer, trained in the British courts, whose name was Gandhi; an Indian named Nehru who wore Savile Row suits and sent his daughter to an English boarding school; and Muhammad Ali Jinnah, founder of Pakistan, who joined Lincoln's Inn in London and became a barrister at the age of nineteen.

In Shakespeare's *Tempest*, Caliban, the original inhabitant of an island commandeered by Prospero, roars at his domineering colonizer, "You taught me language and my profit on't / Is, I know how to curse." It is no surprise that Prospero's "abhorred slave" has been a figure of colonial resistance for literary nationalists all around the world. And in borrowing from Caliban, they have also borrowed from Shakespeare. Prospero has told Caliban, 40

> When thou didst not, savage,
> Know thine own meaning, but wouldst gabble like
> A thing most brutish, I endowed thy purposes
> With words that made them known.

Of course, one of the effects of colonialism was not only to give many of the natives a European language, but also to help shape their purposes. The independence movements of the post-1945 world that led to the end of Europe's African and Asian empires were driven by the rhetoric that had guided the Allies' own struggle against Germany and Japan: democracy, freedom, equality. This wasn't a conflict between values. It was a conflict of interests couched in terms of the same values.

The point applies as much within the West as elsewhere. Americans disagree about abortion, many vehemently. They couch this conflict in a language of conflicting values: They are pro-life or pro-choice. But this is a dispute that makes sense only because each side recognizes the very values the other insists upon. The disagreement is about their significance. Both sides respect something like the sanctity of human life. They disagree about such things as why human life is so precious and where it begins. Whatever you want to call those disagreements, it's just a mistake to think that either side doesn't recognize the value at stake here. And the same is true about choice: Americans are not divided about whether it's important to allow people, women and men, to make the major medical choices about their own bodies. They are divided about such questions as whether an abortion involves two people—both fetus and mother—or three people, adding in the father, or only one. Furthermore, no sane person on either side thinks that saving human lives or allowing people medical autonomy is the only thing that matters.

Some people will point to disputes about homosexuality and say that there, at least, there really is a conflict between people who do and people who don't regard homosexuality as a perversion. Isn't that a conflict of values? Well, no. Most Americans,

*British Raj: Term for British rule in India from 1858 to 1947 [Ed.].

on both sides, have the concept of perversion: of sexual acts that are wrong because their objects are inappropriate objects of sexual desire. But not everyone thinks that the fact that an act involves two women or two men makes it perverted. Not everyone who thinks these acts are perverse thinks they should be illegal. Not everyone who thinks they should be illegal thinks that gay and lesbian people should be ostracized. What is at stake, once more, is a battle about the meaning of perversion, about its status as a value, and about how to apply it. It is a reflection of the essentially contestable character of perversion as a term of value. When one turns from the issue of criminalization of gay sex — which is, at least for the moment, unconstitutional in the United States — to the question of gay marriage, all sides of the debate take seriously issues of sexual autonomy, the value of the intimate lives of couples, the meaning of family, and, by way of discussions of perversion, the proper uses of sex.

What makes these conflicts so intense is that they are battles over the meaning of the *same* values, not that they oppose one value, held exclusively by one side, with another, held exclusively by their antagonists. It is, in part, because we have shared horizons of meaning, because these are debates between people who share so many other values and so much else in the way of belief and of habit, that they are as sharp and as painful as they are.

Winners and Losers

But the disputes about abortion and gay marriage divide Americans bitterly most of all because they share a society and a government. They are neighbors and fellow citizens. And it is laws governing all of them that are in dispute. What's at stake are their bodies or those of their mothers, their aunts, their sisters, their daughters, their wives, and their friends; those dead fetuses could have been their children or their children's friends. 45

We should remember this when we think about international human rights treaties. Treaties are law, even when they are weaker than national law. When we seek to embody our concern for strangers in human rights law and when we urge our government to enforce it, we are seeking to change the world of law in every nation on the planet. We have outlawed slavery not just domestically but in international law. And in so doing we have committed ourselves, at a minimum, to the desirability of its eradication everywhere. This is no longer controversial in the capitals of the world. No one defends enslavement. But international treaties define slavery in ways that arguably include debt bondage; and debt bondage is a significant economic institution in parts of South Asia. I hold no brief for debt bondage. Still, we shouldn't be surprised if people whose income and whose style of life depend upon it are angry. Given that we have neighbors — even if only a few — who think that the fact that abortion is permitted in the United States turns the killing of the doctors who perform them into an act of heroism, we should not be surprised that there are strangers — even if only a few — whose anger turns them to violence against us.

I do not fully understand the popularity among Islamist movements in Egypt, Algeria, Iran, and Pakistan of a high-octane anti-Western rhetoric. But I do know one of its roots. It is, to use suitably old-fashioned language, "the woman question." There are Muslims, many of them young men, who feel that forces from outside their society—forces that they might think of as Western or, in a different moment, American—are pressuring them to reshape relations between men and women. Part of that pressure, they feel, comes from our media. Our films and our television programs are crammed with indescribable indecency. Our fashion magazines show women without modesty, women whose presence on many streets in the Muslim world would be a provocation, they think, presenting an almost irresistible temptation to men. Those magazines influence publications in their own countries, pulling them inevitably in the same direction. We permit women to swim almost naked with strange men, which is our business; but it is hard to keep the news of these acts of immodesty from Muslim women and children or to protect Muslim men from the temptations they inevitably create. As the Internet spreads, it will get even harder, and their children, especially their girls, will be tempted to ask for these freedoms too. Worse, they say, we are now trying to force our conception of how women and men should behave upon them. We speak of women's rights. We make treaties enshrining these rights. And then we want their governments to enforce them.[8]

Like many people in every nation, I support those treaties, of course; I believe that women, like men, should have the vote, should be entitled to work outside their homes, should be protected from the physical abuse of men, including their fathers, brothers, and husbands. But I also know that the changes that these freedoms would bring will change the balance of power between men and women in everyday life. How do I know this? Because I have lived most of my adult life in the West as it has gone through the latter phases of just such a transition, and I know that the process is not yet complete.

The recent history of America does show that a society can radically change its attitudes—and more importantly, perhaps, its habits—about these issues over a single generation. But it also suggests that some people will stay with the old attitudes, and the whole process will take time. The relations between men and women are not abstractions: They are part of the intimate texture of our everyday lives. We have strong feelings about them, and we have inherited many received ideas. Above all, we have deep *habits* about gender. A man and a woman go out on a date. Our habit is that, even if the woman offers, the man pays. A man and a woman approach an elevator door. The man steps back. A man and a woman kiss in a movie theater. No one takes a second look. Two men walk hand in hand in the high street.* People are embarrassed. They hope their children don't see. They don't know how to explain it to them.

Most Americans are against gay marriage, conflicted about abortion, and amazed (and appalled) that a Saudi woman can't get a driver's license. But my guess is that they're not as opposed to gay marriage as they were twenty years ago. Indeed, twenty years ago, most Americans would probably just have thought the whole idea ridiculous. On the other hand, those Americans who are in favor of recognizing gay marriages probably don't have a simple set of reasons why. It just seems right to them, probably, in the way that it just seems wrong to those who disagree. (And probably they're thinking not about couples in the abstract but about Jim and John or Jean and Jane.) The younger they are, the more likely it is that they think that gay marriage is fine. And if they don't, it will often be because they have had religious objections reinforced regularly through life in church, mosque, or temple. ₅₀

---

*The high street: Term used in the United Kingdom for what Americans call main street [Ed.].

I am a philosopher. I believe in reason. But I have learned in a life of university teaching and research that even the cleverest people are not easily shifted by reason alone—and that can be true even in the most cerebral of realms. One of the great savants of the postwar era, John von Neumann, liked to say, mischievously, that "in mathematics you don't understand things, you just get used to them." In the larger world, outside the academy, people don't always even care whether they *seem* reasonable. Conversation, as I've said, is hardly guaranteed to lead to agreement about what to think and feel. Yet we go wrong if we think the point of conversation is to persuade, and imagine it proceeding as a debate, in which points are scored for the Proposition and the Opposition. Often enough, as Faust said, in the beginning is the deed: Practices and not principles are what enable us to live together in peace. Conversations across boundaries of identity—whether national, religious, or something else—begin with the sort of imaginative engagement you get when you read a novel or watch a movie or attend to a work of art that speaks from some place other than your own. So I'm using the word "conversation" not only for literal talk but also as a metaphor for engagement with the experience and the ideas of others. And I stress the role of the imagination here because the encounters, properly conducted, are valuable in themselves. Conversation doesn't have to lead to consensus about anything, especially not values; it's enough that it helps people get used to one another.

NOTES

1. Galatians 3:28. In quoting the Bible, I have used the King James version, except for the Pentateuch, where I have used Robert Alter's powerful modern translation, *The Five Books of Moses* (New York: Norton, 2004).
2. Christoph Martin Wieland. "Das Geheimniß des Kosmopolitenordens," *Teutscher Merkur*, August 1788, p. 107. (Where I give a reference only to a source that is not in English, the translation is mine.)
3. *Essai sur les mœurs et l'esprit des nations*, vol. 16 of *Oeuvres complètes de Voltaire* (Paris: L'Imprimerie de la Société Litteraire-Typographique, 1784), p. 241. Voltaire is speaking specifically here of "the Orient," and especially of China and India, but he would surely not have denied its more general application.
4. George Eliot, *Daniel Deronda* (London: Penguin, 1995), pp. 745, 661–62, 183.
5. Cicero, *De officiis* 1.50.
6. Cass R. Sunstein, "Incompletely Theorized Agreements," *Harvard Law Review* 108 (1995): 1733–72.
7. Joseph Appiah, *Joe Appiah: The Autobiography of an African Patriot* (New York: Praeger, 1990), p. 22.
8. I have put this complaint in the mouth of a Muslim. But the truth is you could hear it from non-Muslims in many places as well. It is less likely to be heard in non-Muslim Africa, because there, by and large (as Amartya Sen has pointed out), women have a less unequal place in public life. See Jean Drèze and Amartya Sen, *Hunger and Public Action* (Oxford: Clarendon Press, 1989).

Exploring Context

1. Appiah uses the term *cosmopolitanism* to describe an ability to get along with others in a globalized and deeply connected world, an ability he relates to having conversation.

Locate a Web site that you think represents Appiah's understanding of *cosmopolitan*. What makes it so? What kinds of conversations happen on this site? Locate passages from Appiah's text that support your interpretation of the Web site as an example of cosmopolitanism. Does the site fit the definition you created in Question 1 of Questions for Critical Reading?

2. Appiah looks at a number of culturally specific practices, including foot-binding in China and circumcision in African nations. Select one of Appiah's examples and use information from the Web to prepare a short report on how the practice has changed in its home culture. Are the reasons for these changes consistent with Appiah's arguments?

3. Visit a social networking site such as Twitter or Facebook. If you don't currently have a profile on either site, create one. Explore the site and consider the role it might play in Appiah's vision of cosmopolitanism. Does it promote that ideal? What sorts of conversations does the site allow? Is it the kind of tool you described in Question 2 of Questions for Critical Reading?

Questions for Connecting

1. How do Appiah's insights about conversation confirm Helen Epstein's findings in "AIDS, Inc." (p. 110)? How can AIDS prevention be further promoted in Africa despite differences in values and practices? Synthesize the ideas of these authors to suggest strategies for halting the spread of HIV.

2. One of Appiah's primary concerns is the way in which conversation can create change. Synthesize Appiah's ideas with Charles Duhigg's concepts of social change in "From Civil Rights to Megachurches" (p. 86). What role does conversation have in the development of social ties? Does it create more strong ties or weak ties? How does peer pressure act to change practice?

3. Appiah uses homosexuality as one example of how practices have changed as a result of conversations. Extend his example using Dan Savage's "It Gets Better" (p. 406) and Urvashi Vaid's "Action Makes It Better" (p. 411). How do these essays contribute to social change around homosexuality and LGBTQ issues? How do they reflect Appiah's notion of cosmopolitanism? Incorporate your work with the definition of *cosmopolitanism* from Question 1 of Questions for Critical Reading.

Language Matters

1. Transition words or phrases help readers move from one idea or unit in an essay to another. In order to practice using transitions, locate a passage in Appiah that you found difficult or confusing. To clarify the thinking of your selected passage, write a short paragraph that could precede your selection, using transitions to ease the difficulty of the passage from Appiah. Think about what Appiah is trying to do in that part of his essay and then clarify that purpose with transition words or phrases. How might the paragraph you write work as a transitional paragraph for Appiah's ideas? How can you more effectively use transitions in your own writing?

2. As an exercise in being concise, summarize Appiah's argument in a haiku, a Japanese form of nonrhyming poetry that has three lines, with five syllables in the first line, seven syllables in the second line, and five in the third. For example:

> Language matters much.
> Working on a haiku can
> Clarify this text.

Use the haiku to express Appiah's argument in just a few words.

3. If you are not familiar with simple sentences — sentences with just a subject and verb — locate information on them in a grammar handbook or other reference resource. Then choose one of Appiah's key sentences and transform it into a simple sentence or into a series of simple sentences. Does breaking down Appiah's sentence into simple sentences make his ideas easier to understand? When are simple sentences useful? Why didn't Appiah write this whole essay in simple sentences? When should you use these in your own writing? What makes them useful?

Assignments for Writing

1. For Appiah, cosmopolitanism is as much a challenge as a solution to the problems of a globalized world. Using Appiah's sense of the term *cosmopolitanism*, locate the challenges presented by the examples he uses to illustrate his arguments. Then write a paper in which you propose the best strategies for overcoming the challenges presented by cosmopolitanism. In what way does Appiah offer a solution to facing these challenges in an increasingly diverse world? Is the solution Appiah finds in cosmopolitanism adequate in addressing these challenges in a way that respects the diversity of local populations? Use your work in Exploring Context to offer specific examples of successful strategies.

2. Appiah discusses his choice of cosmopolitanism as a rubric for moving forward. At the same time, he discusses the problems of realizing social change. Based on his discussion of the primacy of practice, how can we advocate for change in social practices? Write a paper in which you identify the best tools for achieving social change. In constructing and supporting your argument, you may wish to build on the cultural practice you explored in Question 2 of Exploring Context.

3. Appiah is invested in conversation as an engagement with others, but has this engagement been constructive in the ideological conflicts Appiah discusses? Using one of the examples Appiah describes in the sections "Changing Our Minds" (p. 51) and "Fighting for the Good" (p. 55), write a paper in which you determine whether conversation has helped to resolve the conflict Appiah describes, and if so, how.

THE DALAI LAMA

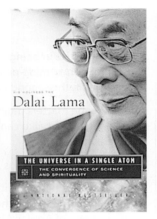

Tenzin Gyatso is the fourteenth Dalai Lama and the leader of the Central Tibetan Administration — the government-in-exile of Tibet. Gyatso was declared at two years old to be the reincarnation of an earlier Dalai Lama; at the age of fifteen he assumed the roles of religious and political leader of the Tibetan people. The only Dalai Lama to visit the West, Gyatso has become notable for gaining Western sympathy for the cause of a free Tibet and for authoring or coauthoring more than fifty books. Among his many honors are the Nobel Peace Prize (1989) and the U.S. Congressional Gold Medal (2006).

In *The Universe in a Single Atom* (2005), the Dalai Lama tries to reconcile religion with science, claiming that religion and science are parts of the same path to ultimate truth. Relying on just one, he suggests, is incomplete at best and "impoverishing" at worst. Simply following the rationale of science that everything "is reducible to matter and energy leaves out a huge range of human experience," and the opposite approach "can lock us into fundamentalist cages" that deny proven facts. According to the Dalai Lama, we must attempt to bridge this gap between our different ways of thinking.

In "Ethics and the New Genetics," a chapter from *The Universe in a Single Atom*, the Dalai Lama focuses on the field of genetic engineering. The potential benefits of this area of science are enormous, but the Dalai Lama reminds us to bear the potential costs in mind: "The higher the level of knowledge and power," he writes, "the greater must be our sense of moral responsibility" (p. 63). He argues that the speed of scientific progress in recent years has outpaced our society's ethical development, raising questions of what to do about possible breakthroughs in the future, when to trust our instinctual reactions, and what consequences science can have on culture and society.

In an age when stem cell research is controversial, the Dalai Lama urges us in this essay to craft ethical standards that can guide us in the complex decisions involved when technology intersects with life.

▶ TAGS: *ethics, genetics, health and medicine, judgment and decision-making, politics, religion, science and technology*

▶ CONNECTIONS: *Allen, Manning, Pollan, Wallace*

Questions for Critical Reading

1. What sort of ethical standards should we have for fields with profound implications like genetic engineering? As you read the Dalai Lama's essay, locate quotations that support your proposed system of ethics.

2. What are the keys to developing an ethics apart from religion? Search the Dalai Lama's essay for quotations that support your position.

3. As you read the Dalai Lama's text, look for specific quotations that suggest the conditions necessary for the use of genetic technologies. Are such technologies ever justified, in his view?

Ethics and the New Genetics

Many of us who have followed the development of the new genetics are aware of the deep public disquiet that is gathering around the topic. This concern has been raised in relation to everything from cloning to genetic manipulation. There has been a worldwide outcry over the genetic engineering of foodstuffs. It is now possible to create new breeds of plants with far higher yields and far lower susceptibility to disease in order to maximize food production in a world where the increasing population needs to be fed. The benefits are obvious and wonderful. Seedless watermelons, apples that have longer shelf lives, wheat and other grains that are immune to pests when growing in the field—these are no longer science fiction. I have read that scientists are even experimenting to develop farm products, such as tomatoes, injected with genes from different species of spiders.

But by doing these things, we are changing the genetic makeup, and do we really know what the long-term impact will be on the species of plants, on the soil, on the environment? There are obvious commercial benefits, but how do we judge what is really useful? The complex web of interdependence that characterizes the environment makes it seem beyond our capacity to predict.

Genetic changes have happened slowly over hundreds of thousands of years of natural evolution. The evolution of the human brain has occurred over millions of years. By actively manipulating the gene, we are on the cusp of forcing an unnaturally quick rate of change in animals and plants as well as our own species. This is not to say that we should turn our backs on developments in this area—it is simply to point out that we must become aware of the awesome implications of this new area of science.

The most urgent questions that arise have to do more with ethics than with science per se, with correctly applying our knowledge and power in relation to the new possibilities opened by cloning, by unlocking the genetic code and other advances. These issues relate to the possibilities for genetic manipulation not only of human beings and animals but also of plants and the environment of which we are all parts. At heart the issue is the relationship between our knowledge and power on the one hand and our responsibility on the other.

Any new scientific breakthrough that offers commercial prospects attracts tremendous interest and investment from both the public sector and private enterprise. The amount of scientific knowledge and the range of technological possibilities are so enormous that the only limitations on what we do may be the results of insufficient imagination. It is this unprecedented acquisition of knowledge and power that places us in a critical position at this time. The higher the level of knowledge and power, the greater must be our sense of moral responsibility.

If we examine the philosophical basis underlying much of human ethics, a clear recognition of the principle that correlates greater knowledge and power with a greater

5

need for moral responsibility serves as a key foundation. Until recently we could say that this principle had been highly effective. The human capacity for moral reasoning has kept pace with developments in human knowledge and its capacities. But with the new era in biogenetic science, the gap between moral reasoning and our technological capacities has reached a critical point. The rapid increase of human knowledge and the technological possibilities emerging in the new genetic science are such that it is now almost impossible for ethical thinking to keep pace with these changes. Much of what is soon going to be possible is less in the form of new breakthroughs or paradigms in science than in the development of new technological options combined with the financial calculations of business and the political and economic calculations of governments. The issue is no longer whether we should or should not acquire knowledge and explore its technological potentials. Rather, the issue is how to use this new knowledge and power in the most expedient and ethically responsible manner.

The area where the impact of the revolution in genetic science may be felt most immediately at present is medicine. Today, I gather, many in medicine believe that the sequencing of the human genome will usher in a new era, in which it may be possible to move beyond a biochemical model of therapy to a genetically based model. Already the very definitions of many diseases are changing as illnesses are found to be genetically programmed into human beings and animals from their conception. While successful gene therapy for some of these conditions may be some way off, it seems no longer beyond the bounds of possibility. Even now, the issue of gene therapy and the associated question of genetic manipulation, especially at the level of the human embryo, are posing grave challenges to our capacity for ethical thinking.

A profound aspect of the problem, it seems to me, lies in the question of what to do with our new knowledge. Before we knew that specific genes caused senile dementia, cancer, or even aging, we as individuals assumed we wouldn't be afflicted with these problems, but we responded when we were. But now, or at any rate very soon, genetics can tell individuals and families that they have genes which may kill or maim them in childhood, youth, or middle age. This knowledge could radically alter our definitions of health and sickness. For example, someone who is healthy at present but has a particular genetic predisposition may come to be marked as "soon to be sick." What should we do with such knowledge, and how do we handle it in a way that is most compassionate? Who should have access to such knowledge, given its social and personal implications in relation to insurance, employment, and relationships, as well as reproduction? Does the individual who carries such a gene have a responsibility to reveal this fact to his or her potential partner in life? These are just a few of the questions raised by such genetic research.

To complicate an already intricate set of problems, I gather that genetic forecasting of this kind cannot be guaranteed to be accurate. It is sometimes certain that a particular genetic disorder observed in the embryo will give rise to disease in the child or adult, but it is often a question of relative probabilities. Lifestyle, diet, and other environmental factors come into play. So while we may know that a particular embryo carries a gene for a disease, we cannot be certain that the disease will arise.

People's life choices and indeed their very self-identity may be significantly affected by their perception of genetic risk, but those perceptions may not be correct and the risk may not be actualized. Should we be afforded such probabilistic knowledge? In cases where one member of the family discovers a genetic disorder of this type, should all the other members who may have inherited the same gene be informed? Should this knowledge be made available to a wider community—for instance, to health insurance companies? The carriers of certain genes may be excluded from insurance and hence even from access to health care all because there is a possibility of a particular disease manifesting itself. The issues here are not just medical but ethical and can affect the psychological well-being of the people concerned. When genetic disorders are detected in the embryo (as will increasingly be the case), should parents (or society) make the decision to curtail the life of that embryo? This question is further complicated by the fact that new methods of dealing with genetic disease and new medications are being found as swiftly as the genes carrying individual disease are identified. One can imagine a scenario in which a baby whose disease may manifest in twenty years is aborted and a cure for the disease is found within a decade.

Many people around the world, especially practitioners of the newly emerging discipline of bioethics, are grappling with the specifics of these problems. Given my lack of expertise in these fields, I have nothing concrete to offer in regard to any specific question—especially as the empirical facts are changing so rapidly. What I wish to do, however, is think through some of the key issues which I feel every informed person in the world needs to reflect upon, and to suggest some general principles that can be brought to bear in dealing with these ethical challenges. I believe that at heart the challenge we face is really a question of what choices we make in the face of the growing options that science and technology provide us.

> **[A]t heart the challenge we face is really a question of what choices we make in the face of the growing options that science and technology provide us.**

Attendant on the new frontiers of genetically based medicine there is a series of further issues which again raise deep and troubling ethical questions. Here I am speaking primarily of cloning. It has now been several years since the world was introduced to a completely cloned sentient being, Dolly, the famous sheep. Since then there has been a huge amount of coverage of human cloning. We know that the first cloned human embryos have been created. The media frenzy aside, the question of cloning is highly complex. I am told there are two quite different kinds of cloning—therapeutic and reproductive. Within therapeutic cloning, there is the use of cloning technology for the reproduction of cells and the potential creation of semi-sentient beings purely for the purpose of harvesting body parts for transplantation. Reproductive cloning is basically the creation of an identical copy.

In principle, I have no objection to cloning as such—as a technological instrument for medical and therapeutic purposes. As in all these cases, what must govern one's decisions is the question of compassionate motivation. However, regarding the idea of deliberately breeding semi-human beings for spare parts, I feel an immediate, instinctive revulsion. I once saw a BBC documentary which simulated such creatures through computer animation, with some distinctively recognizable human features. I was horrified. Some people might feel this is an irrational emotional reaction that need not be taken seriously. But I believe we must trust our instinctive feelings of revulsion, as these arise out of our basic humanity. Once we allow the exploitation of such hybrid semi-humans, what is to stop us from doing the same with our fellow human beings whom the whims of society may deem deficient in some way? The willingness to step across such natural thresholds is what often leads humanity to the commission of horrific atrocities.

Although reproductive cloning is not horrifying in the same way, in some respects its implications may be more far-reaching. Once the technology becomes feasible, there could be parents who, desperate to have children and unable to do so, may seek to bear a child through cloning. What would this practice do to the future gene pool? To the diversity that has been essential to evolution?

There could also be individuals who, out of a desire to live beyond biological possibility, may choose to clone themselves in the belief that they will continue to live in the new cloned being. In this case, I find it difficult to see any justifiable motives—from the Buddhist perspective, it may be an identical body, but there will be two different consciousnesses. They will still die.

One of the social and cultural consequences of new genetic technologies is their effect on the continuation of our species, through interference with the reproductive process. Is it right to select the sex of one's child, which I believe is possible now? If it is not, is it right to make such choices for reasons of health (say, in couples where a child is at serious risk of muscular dystrophy or hemophilia)? Is it acceptable to insert genes into human sperm or eggs in the lab? How far can we go in the direction of creating "ideal" or "designer" fetuses—for instance, embryos that have been selected in the lab to provide particular molecules or compounds absent in genetically deficient siblings in order that the children born from such embryos may donate bone marrow or kidneys to cure siblings? How far can we go with the artificial selection of fetuses with desirable traits that are held to improve intelligence or physical strength or specific color of eyes for instance?

When such technologies are used for medical reasons—as in the curing of a particular genetic deficiency—one can deeply sympathize. The selection of particular traits, however, especially when done for primarily aesthetic purposes, may not be for the benefit of the child. Even when the parents think they are selecting traits that will positively affect their child, we need to consider whether this is being done out of positive intention or on the basis of a particular society's prejudices at a particular time. We have to bear in mind the long-term impact of this kind of manipulation on the species as a whole, given that its effects will be passed on to following generations. We need also to consider the effects of limiting the diversity of humanity and the tolerance that goes with it, which is one of the marvels of life.

Particularly worrying is the manipulation of genes for the creation of children with enhanced characteristics, whether cognitive or physical. Whatever inequalities there may be between individuals in their circumstances—such as wealth, class, health, and so on—we are all born with a basic equality of our human nature, with certain potentialities; certain cognitive, emotional, and physical abilities; and the fundamental disposition—indeed the right—to seek happiness and overcome suffering. Given that genetic technology is bound to remain costly, at least for the foreseeable future, once it is allowed, for a long period it will be available only to a small segment of human society, namely the rich. Thus society will find itself translating an inequality of circumstance (that is, relative wealth) into an inequality of nature through enhanced intelligence, strength, and other faculties acquired through birth.

The ramifications of this differentiation are far-reaching—on social, political, and ethical levels. At the social level, it will reinforce—even perpetuate—our disparities, and it will make their reversal much more difficult. In political matters, it will breed a ruling elite, whose claims to power will be invocations of an intrinsic natural superiority. On the ethical level, these kinds of pseudonature-based differences can severely undermine our basic moral sensibilities insofar as these sensibilities are based on a mutual recognition of shared humanity. We cannot imagine how such practices could affect our very concept of what it is to be human.

When I think about the various new ways of manipulating human genetics, I can't help but feel that there is something profoundly lacking in our appreciation of what it is to cherish humanity. In my native Tibet, the value of a person rests not on physical appearance, not on intellectual or athletic achievement, but on the basic, innate capacity for compassion in all human beings. Even modern medical science has demonstrated how crucial affection is for human beings, especially during the first few weeks of life. The simple power of touch is critical for the basic development of the brain. In regard to

> **We cannot imagine how such practices could affect our very concept of what it is to be human.**

his or her value as a human being, it is entirely irrelevant whether an individual has some kind of disability—for instance, Down syndrome—or a genetic disposition to develop a particular disease, such as sickle-cell anemia, Huntington's chorea, or Alzheimer's. All human beings have an equal value and an equal potential for goodness. To ground our appreciation of the value of a human being on genetic makeup is bound to impoverish humanity, because there is so much more to human beings than their genomes.

For me, one of the most striking and heartening effects of our knowledge of the genome is the astounding truth that the differences in the genomes of the different ethnic groups around the world are so negligible as to be insignificant. I have always argued that the differences of color, language, religion, ethnicity, and so forth among human beings have no substance in the face of our basic sameness. The sequencing of the human genome has, for me, demonstrated this in an extremely powerful way. It has also helped reinforce my sense of our basic kinship with animals, who share very large percentages of our genome. So it is conceivable if we humans utilize our newly found genetic knowledge skillfully, it could help foster a greater sense of affinity and unity not only with our fellow human beings but with life as a whole. Such a perspective could also underpin a much more healthy environmental consciousness.

In the case of food, if the argument is valid that we need some kind of genetic modification to help feed the world's growing population, then I believe that we cannot simply dismiss this branch of genetic technology. However, if, as suggested by its critics, this argument is merely a front for motives that are primarily commercial—such as producing food that will simply have a longer lasting shelf life, that can be more easily exported from one side of the world to the other, that is more attractive in appearance and more convenient in consumption, or creating grains and cereals engineered not to produce their own seeds so that farmers are forced to depend entirely upon the biotech companies for seeds—then clearly such practices must be seriously questioned.

Many people are becoming increasingly worried by the long-term consequences of producing and consuming genetically modified produce. The gulf between the scientific community and the general public may be caused in part by the lack of transparency in the companies developing these products. The onus should be on the biotech industry both to demonstrate that there are no long-term negative consequences for consumers of these new products and to adopt complete transparency on all the possible implications such plants may have for the natural environment. Clearly the argument that if there is no conclusive evidence that a particular product is harmful then there is nothing wrong with it cannot be accepted.

The point is that genetically modified food is not just another product, like a car or a portable computer. Whether we like it or not, we do not know the long-term consequences of introducing genetically modified organisms into the wider environment. In medicine, for instance, the drug thalidomide was found to be excellent for the treatment of morning sickness in pregnant women, but its long-term consequences for the health of the unborn child were not foreseen and proved catastrophic.

Given the tremendous pace of development in modern genetics, it is urgent now to 25 refine our capacity for moral reasoning so that we are equipped to address the ethical challenges of this new situation. We cannot wait for a series of responses to emerge in an organic way. We need to confront the reality of our potential future and tackle the problems directly.

I feel the time is ripe to engage with the ethical side of the genetic revolution in a manner that transcends the doctrinal standpoints of individual religions. We must rise to the ethical challenge as members of one human family, not as a Buddhist, a Jew, a Christian, a Hindu, a Muslim. Nor is it adequate to address these ethical challenges from the perspective of purely secular, liberal political ideals, such as individual freedom, choice, and fairness. We need to examine the questions from the perspective of a global ethics that is grounded in the recognition of fundamental human values that transcend religion and science.

It is not adequate to adopt the position that our responsibility as a society is simply to further scientific knowledge and enhance our technological power. Nor is it sufficient to argue that what we do with this knowledge and power should be left to the choices of individuals. If this argument means that society at large should not interfere with the course of research and the creation of new technologies based on such research, it would effectively rule out any significant role for humanitarian or ethical considerations in the regulation of scientific development. It is essential, indeed it is a responsibility, for us to be much more critically self-aware about what we are developing and why. The basic principle is that the earlier one intervenes in the causal process, the more effective is one's prevention of undesirable consequences.

In order to respond to the challenges in the present and in the future, we need a much higher level of collective effort than has been seen yet. One partial solution is to ensure that a larger segment of the general public has a working grasp of scientific thinking and an understanding of key scientific discoveries, especially those which have direct social and ethical implications. Education needs to provide not only training in the empirical facts of science but also an examination of the relationship between science and society at large, including the ethical questions raised by new technological possibilities. This educational imperative must be directed at scientists as well as laypeople, so that scientists retain a wider understanding of the social, cultural, and ethical ramifications of the work they are doing.

Given that the stakes for the world are so high, the decisions about the course of research, what to do with our knowledge, and what technological possibilities should be developed cannot be left in the hands of scientists, business interests, or government officials. Clearly, as a society we need to draw some lines. But these deliberations cannot come solely from small committees, no matter how august or expert they may be. We need a much higher level of public involvement, especially in the form of debate and discussion, whether through the media, public consultation, or the action of grassroots pressure groups.

Today's challenges are so great—and the dangers of the misuse of technology   30
so global, entailing a potential catastrophe for all humankind—that I feel we need a moral compass we can use collectively without getting bogged down in doctrinal differences. One key factor that we need is a holistic and integrated outlook at the level of human society that recognizes the fundamentally interconnected nature of all living beings and their environment. Such a moral compass must entail preserving our human sensitivity and will depend on us constantly bearing in mind our fundamental human values. We must be willing to be revolted when science—or for that matter any human activity—crosses the line of human decency, and we must fight to retain the sensitivity that is otherwise so easily eroded.

How can we find this moral compass? We must begin by putting faith in the basic goodness of human nature, and we need to anchor this faith in some fundamental and universal ethical principles. These include a recognition of the preciousness of life, an understanding of the need for balance in nature and the employment of this need as a gauge for the direction of our thought and action, and—above all—the need to ensure that we hold compassion as the key motivation for all our endeavors and that it is combined with a clear awareness of the wider perspective, including long-term consequences. Many will agree with me that these ethical values transcend the dichotomy of religious believers and nonbelievers, and are crucial for the welfare of all humankind. Because of the profoundly interconnected reality of today's world, we need to relate to the challenges we face as a single human family rather than as members of specific nationalities, ethnicities, or religions. In other words, a necessary principle is a spirit of oneness of the entire human species. Some might object that this is unrealistic. But what other option do we have?

I firmly believe it is possible. The fact that, despite our living for more than half a century in the nuclear age, we have not yet annihilated ourselves is what gives me great hope. It is no more coincidence that, if we reflect deeply, we find these ethical principles at the heart of all major spiritual traditions.

In developing an ethical strategy with respect to the new genetics, it is vitally important to frame our reflection within the widest possible context. We must first of all remember how new this field is and how new are the possibilities it offers, and to contemplate how little we understand what we know. We have now sequenced the whole of the human genome, but it may take decades for us fully to understand the functions of all the individual genes and their interrelationships, let alone the effects of their interaction with the environment. Too much of our current focus is on the feasibility of a particular technique, its immediate or short-term results and side effects, and what effect it may have on individual liberty. These are all valid concerns, but they are not sufficient. Their purview is too narrow, given that the very conception of human nature is at stake. Because of the far-reaching scope of these innovations, we need to examine all areas of human existence where genetic technology may have lasting implications. The fate of the human species, perhaps of all life on this planet, is in our hands. In the face of the great unknown, would it not be better to err on the side of caution than to transform the course of human evolution in an irreversibly damaging direction?

In a nutshell, our ethical response must involve the following key factors. First, we have to check our motivation and ensure that its foundation is compassion. Second, we must relate to any problem before us while taking into account the widest possible perspective, which includes not only situating the issue within the picture of wider human enterprise but also taking due regard of both short-term and long-term consequences. Third, when we apply our reason in addressing a problem, we have to be vigilant in ensuring that we remain honest, self-aware, and unbiased; the danger otherwise is that we may fall victim to self-delusion. Fourth, in the face of any real ethical challenge, we must respond in a spirit of humility, recognizing not only the limits of our knowledge (both collective and personal) but also our vulnerability to being misguided in the context of such a rapidly changing reality. Finally, we must all—scientists and society at large—strive to ensure that whatever new course of action we take, we keep in mind the primary goal of the well-being of humanity as a whole and the planet we inhabit.

The earth is our only home. As far as current scientific knowledge is concerned, this may be the only planet that can support life. One of the most powerful visions I have experienced was the first photograph of the earth from outer space. The image of a blue planet floating in deep space, glowing like the full moon on a clear night, brought home powerfully to me the recognition that we are indeed all members of a single family sharing one little house. I was flooded with the feeling of how ridiculous are the various disagreements and squabbles within the human family. I saw how futile it is to cling so tenaciously to the differences that divide us. From this perspective one feels the fragility, the vulnerability of our planet and its limited occupation of a small orbit sandwiched between Venus and Mars in the vast infinity of space. If we do not look after this home, what else are we charged to do on this earth?

Exploring Context

1. Visit the home page for the Human Genome Project (ornl.gov/sci/techresources /Human_Genome/home.shtml). How does the project address the kinds of ethical problems that concern the Dalai Lama? Is it consistent with your proposed system of ethics from Question 1 of Questions for Critical Reading?

2. Explore the Web site for the Presidential Commission for the Study of Bioethical Issues (bioethics.gov). Are government organizations equipped to answer the Dalai Lama's

call for a new ethics governing these technologies? Does the commission reflect your argument about a nonreligious ethics from Question 2 of Questions for Critical Reading?

3. London's Science Museum has an online exhibit about Dolly the sheep, the first cloned animal. Visit the site at sciencemuseum.org.uk/antenna/dolly/index.asp. In the aftermath of Dolly's life and death, what new ethical concerns should we consider?

Questions for Connecting

1. Francis Fukuyama's "Human Dignity" (p. 143) also addresses concerns about the potential of biotechnologies. How does Fukuyama's exploration of the matter complicate the Dalai Lama's call for a new ethics? What are their respective positions on genetic technologies? Does Fukuyama answer the Dalai Lama's call for a "moral compass"? You may wish to draw on your work on the use of genetic technologies from Question 3 of Questions for Critical Reading.

2. Sharon Moalem, in "Changing Our Genes: How Trauma, Bullying, and Royal Jelly Alter Our Genetic Destiny" (p. 277), suggests that the traumas we experience can change our genetic code. How do the genetic consequences of trauma affect the Dalai Lama's argument about biotechnology? How might we incorporate Moalem's conclusions in a "moral compass"? Consider how your answer affects your response to Question 3 of Questions for Critical Reading.

3. How does the fallibility of human judgment, as illustrated by Daniel Kahneman in "The Surety of Fools" (p. 215), enhance the Dalai Lama's call for an ethics to guide technologies like genetic engineering? Can we be sure of the consequences of this technology? How does the "illusion of validity" reinforce the need for a moral compass? Incorporate your work on ethics from Question 2 of Questions for Critical Reading.

Language Matters

1. The Dalai Lama uses a clear, simple style of writing to discuss a very complex subject. Select a key quotation from his text and break down the parts of each sentence. How does he use language to express difficult concepts clearly? How can you do the same in your writing?

2. In a small group, discuss what revision means. If you were going to revise this text, where would you start? What areas need more development?

3. If you were going to include images with this text, which ones would you choose? How would adding images change the meaning of the text? How can visual images support an argument made with words?

Assignments for Writing

1. The Dalai Lama uses the complex ethical dilemma of genetic technologies to make his argument about the necessity for a moral compass to guide us in relation to knowledge and scientific discovery. Write a paper in which you extend the Dalai Lama's argument using your own example of a technology or discovery that demands a moral compass. You may want to use your example to discuss how to utilize new knowledge and power in the most expedient and ethically responsible manner. In composing your essay, consider the gap between moral reasoning and technological capacity. Should different approaches be taken when developing ethical standards for the two different types of cloning? Why? What are the implications of probabilistic knowledge?

2. In this essay, the Dalai Lama discusses potential consequences of enabling people to forecast genetic predispositions in their children and to alter their children's genetic makeup accordingly. Write a paper in which you propose a standard for deciding when such forecasting should be used. Is such a technology ever ethical? Is it ever accurate? Why must relative probabilities be taken into consideration when thinking about genetic forecasting? To what degree must self-determination be considered a factor? You may wish to discuss the correlation of greater knowledge with a greater need for moral responsibility, and you may wish to draw on your exploration of the Web sites in Exploring Context and your understanding of the Dalai Lama's concepts from Questions for Connecting. Consider also including your work from Question 2 of Questions for Connecting.

3. The possible consequences of genetic manipulation reach far beyond the sphere of science. Consider, for example, the role of national and global politics in relation to scientific breakthroughs that have the potential to literally change the face of humanity but will almost certainly not be available to everyone. Write a paper in which you examine the consequences of technology in terms of social and economic stability. How does the Dalai Lama characterize the relationship between knowledge and responsibility? In what ways does genetic engineering have the potential to perpetuate our disparities on social, political, and ethical levels? Should new technologies be available to everyone?

TORIE ROSE DEGHETT

Photo by Stephanie
Coyne DeGhett

Freelance magazine writer **Torie Rose DeGhett** holds an M.A. from Columbia University's Graduate School of Journalism. Her work, focused largely on foreign affairs, has appeared in publications such as the *Atlantic*, the *Guardian*, and *Guernica*. DeGhett also runs *The Political Notebook*, a blog that was recognized as one of *Time*'s "30 Must-See Tumblr Blogs" and that covers diverse topics from national security to hip-hop songs. DeGhett's "The War Photo No One Would Publish" ran in August 2014 as a feature story on *TheAtlantic.com*, a National Magazine Award–winning multimedia publication that covers politics, business, technology, and culture, among other timely topics. On the day that DeGhett's essay was published, *TheAtlantic.com* also featured pieces on America's moral obligations in Iraq, the disproportionate number of women in public relations, and the spread of valley fever, a fungal infection prevalent among poor farmworkers in the American Southwest.

"The War Photo No One Would Publish" centers on the issue of censorship, detailing the account of a graphic Gulf War photo the American press refused to publish. More than twenty years later, through interviews with the photographer and media players of the time, DeGhett examines the circumstances behind taking the haunting photo and the motives behind keeping it out of the headlines. Ultimately, DeGhett argues that incomplete news coverage has the effect of shielding — and even deceiving — the public when it comes to the consequences of war.

How critical is it to expose the unpleasant, and sometimes gory, side of an issue? Should the press protect the public from what some might call unnecessarily explicit images? Or are such images necessary in painting a complete and accurate picture of an event?

▶ TAGS: *art, censorship, empathy, ethics, judgment and decision-making, media, photography and video, politics, science and technology, trauma and violence, war and conflict*

▶ CONNECTIONS: *Appiah, Dalai Lama, Friedman, Fukuyama, Pozner, Singer, Southan*

Questions for Critical Reading

1. Is censorship ever justified? Briefly write down your thoughts on the question. After you've read this essay, add to what you've written by exploring how DeGhett's essay has confirmed or challenged your thoughts about censorship.

2. As you read, take note of the reasons various decision makers used for not publishing the photo. Are these reasons sufficient justification? Support your response with quotations from the text.

3. What gives an image power? Note places in the text that discuss the ability of images to affect viewers.

The War Photo No One Would Publish

The Iraqi soldier died attempting to pull himself up over the dashboard of his truck. The flames engulfed his vehicle and incinerated his body, turning him to dusty ash and blackened bone. In a photograph taken soon afterward, the soldier's hand reaches out of the shattered windshield, which frames his face and chest. The colors and textures of his hand and shoulders look like those of the scorched and rusted metal around him. Fire has destroyed most of his features, leaving behind a skeletal face, fixed in a final rictus. He stares without eyes.

On February 28, 1991, Kenneth Jarecke stood in front of the charred man, parked amid the carbonized bodies of his fellow soldiers, and photographed him. At one point, before he died this dramatic mid-retreat death, the soldier had had a name. He'd fought in Saddam Hussein's army and had a rank and an assignment and a unit. He might have been devoted to the dictator who sent him to occupy Kuwait and fight the Americans. Or he might have been an unlucky young man with no prospects, recruited off the streets of Baghdad.

Jarecke took the picture just before a ceasefire officially ended Operation Desert Storm—the U.S.-led military action that drove Saddam Hussein and his troops out of Kuwait, which they had annexed and occupied the previous August. The image and its anonymous subject might have come to symbolize the Gulf War. Instead, it went unpublished in the United States, not because of military obstruction but because of editorial choices. It's hard to calculate the consequences of a photograph's absence. But sanitized images of warfare, the *Atlantic*'s Conor Friedersdorf argues, make it "easier . . . to accept bloodless language" such as 1991 references to "surgical strikes" or modern-day terminology like "kinetic warfare." The

> **It's hard to calculate the consequences of a photograph's absence.**

© Kenneth Jarecke /Contact Press Images

Vietnam War, in contrast, was notable for its catalog of chilling and iconic war photography. Some images, like Ron Haeberle's pictures of the My Lai massacre, were initially kept from the public, but other violent images — Nick Ut's scene of child napalm victims and Eddie Adams's photo of a Vietcong man's execution — won Pulitzer Prizes and had a tremendous impact on the outcome of the war.[1]

Not every gruesome photo reveals an important truth about conflict and combat. Last month, the *New York Times* decided — for valid ethical reasons — to remove images of dead passengers from an online story about Flight MH-17 in Ukraine and replace them with photos of mechanical wreckage.[2] Sometimes though, omitting an image means shielding the public from the messy, imprecise consequences of a war — making the coverage incomplete, and even deceptive.

In the case of the charred Iraqi soldier, the hypnotizing and awful photograph ran against the popular myth of the Gulf War as a "video-game war" — a conflict made humane through precision bombing and night-vision equipment. By deciding not to publish it, *Time* magazine and the Associated Press denied the public the opportunity to confront this unknown enemy and consider his excruciating final moments.

The image was not entirely lost. The *Observer* in the United Kingdom and *Libération* in France both published it after the American media refused. Many months later, the photo also appeared in *American Photo*, where it stoked some controversy, but came too late to have a significant impact. All of this surprised the photographer, who had

"He was fighting to save his life to the very end, till he was completely burned up," Jarecke says of the man he photographed. "He was trying to get out of that truck."

© Kenneth Jarecke /Contact Press Images

assumed the media would be only too happy to challenge the popular narrative of a clean, uncomplicated war. "When you have an image that disproves that myth," he says today, "then you think it's going to be widely published."

"Let me say up front that I don't like the press," one Air Force officer declared, starting a January 1991 press briefing on a blunt note.[3] The military's bitterness toward the media was in no small part a legacy of the Vietnam coverage decades before. By the time the Gulf War started, the Pentagon had developed access policies that drew on press restrictions used in the U.S. wars in Grenada and Panama in the 1980s. Under this so-called "pool" system, the military grouped print, TV, and radio reporters together with cameramen and photojournalists and sent these small teams on orchestrated press junkets, supervised by Public Affairs Officers (PAOs) who kept a close watch on their charges.

By the time Operation Desert Storm began in mid-January 1991, Kenneth Jarecke had decided he no longer wanted to be a combat photographer—a profession, he says, that "dominates your life." But after Saddam Hussein's invasion of Kuwait in August 1990, Jarecke developed a low opinion of the photojournalism coming out of Desert Shield, the pre-war operation to build up troops and equipment in the Gulf. "It was one picture after another of a sunset with camels and a tank," he says. War was approaching and Jarecke says he saw a clear need for a different kind of coverage. He felt he could fill that void.

After the U.N.'s January 15, 1991 deadline for Iraq's withdrawal from Kuwait came and went, Jarecke, now certain he should go, convinced *Time* magazine to send him to Saudi Arabia. He packed up his cameras and shipped out from Andrews Air Force Base on January 17—the first day of the aerial bombing campaign against Iraq.

Out in the field with the troops, Jarecke recalls, "anybody could challenge you," however absurdly and without reason. He remembers straying 30 feet away from his PAO and having a soldier bark at him, "What are you doing?" Jarecke retorted, "What do you *mean* what am I doing?"

Recounting the scene two decades later, Jarecke still sounds exasperated. "Some first lieutenant telling me, you know, where I'm gonna stand. *In the middle of the desert.*"

As the war picked up in early February, PAOs accompanied Jarecke and several other journalists as they attached to the Army XVIII Airborne Corps and spent two weeks at the Saudi-Iraqi border doing next to nothing. That didn't mean nothing was happening—just that they lacked access to the action.

During the same period, military photojournalist Lee Corkran was embedding with the U.S. Air Force's 614th Tactical Fighter Squadron in Doha, Qatar, and capturing their aerial bombing campaigns. He was there to take pictures for the Pentagon to use as it saw fit—not primarily for media use. In his images, pilots look over their shoulders to check on other planes. Bombs hang off the jets' wings, their sharp-edged darkness contrasting with the soft colors of the clouds and desert below. In the distance, the curvature of the earth is visible. On missions, Corkran's plane would often flip upside down at high speed as the pilots dodged missiles, leaving silvery streaks in the sky. Gravitational forces multiplied the weight of his cameras—so much so that if he had ever needed to eject from the plane, his equipment could have snapped his neck. This was the air war that comprised most of the combat mission in the Gulf that winter.

The scenes Corkran witnessed weren't just off-limits to Jarecke; they were also invisible to viewers in the United States, despite the rise of 24-hour reporting during the conflict. Gulf War television coverage, as Ken Burns wrote at the time, felt cinematic and often sensational, with "distracting theatrics" and "pounding new theme music," as if "the war itself might be a wholly owned subsidiary of television."

Some of the most widely seen images of the air war were shot not by photographers, but rather by unmanned cameras attached to planes and laser-guided bombs. Grainy shots and video footage of the roofs of targeted buildings, moments before impact, became a visual signature of a war that was deeply associated with phrases like "smart bombs" and "surgical strike." The images were taken at an altitude that erased the human presence on the ground. They were black-and-white shots, some with bluish or greenish casts. One from February 1991, published in the photo book *In The Eye of Desert Storm* by the now-defunct Sygma photo agency, showed a bridge that was being used as an Iraqi supply route. In another, black plumes of smoke from French bombs blanketed an Iraqi Republican Guard base like ink blots. None of them looked especially violent.

> **The images were taken at an altitude that erased the human presence on the ground.**

The burned-out truck, surrounded by corpses, on the "Highway of Death."
© Kenneth Jarecke /Contact Press Images

The hardware-focused coverage of the war removed the empathy that Jarecke says is crucial in photography, particularly photography that's meant to document death and violence. "A photographer without empathy," he remarks, "is just taking up space that could be better used."

In late February, during the war's final hours, Jarecke and the rest of his press pool drove across the desert, each of them taking turns behind the wheel. They had been awake for several days straight. "We had no idea where we were. We were in a convoy," Jarecke recalls. He dozed off.

When he woke up, they had parked and the sun was about to rise. It was almost 6 o'clock in the morning. The group received word that a ceasefire was a few hours away, and Jarecke remembers another member of his pool cajoling the press officer into abandoning the convoy and heading toward Kuwait City.

The group figured they were in southern Iraq, somewhere in the desert about 70 miles away from Kuwait City. They began driving toward Kuwait, hitting Highway 8 and stopping to take pictures and record video footage. They came upon a jarring scene: burned-out Iraqi military convoys and incinerated corpses. Jarecke sat in the truck, alone with Patrick Hermanson, a public affairs officer. He moved to get out of the vehicle with his cameras.

Hermanson found the idea of photographing the scene distasteful. When I asked   20
him about the conversation, he recalled asking Jarecke, "What do you need to take a picture of that for?" Implicit in his question was a judgment: There was something dishonorable about photographing the dead.

"I'm not interested in it either," Jarecke recalls replying. He told the officer that he didn't want his mother to see his name next to photographs of corpses. "But if I don't take pictures like these, people like my mom will think war is what they see in movies." As Hermanson remembers, Jarecke added, "It's what I came here to do. It's what I have to do."

"He let me go," Jarecke recounts. "He didn't try to stop me. He could have stopped me because it was technically not allowed under the rules of the pool. But he didn't stop me and I walked over there."

More than two decades later, Hermanson notes that Jarecke's resulting picture was "pretty special." He doesn't need to see the photograph to resurrect the scene in his mind. "It's seared into my memory," he says, "as if it happened yesterday."

The incinerated man stared back at Jarecke through the camera's viewfinder, his blackened arm reaching over the edge of the truck's windshield. Jarecke recalls that he could "see clearly how precious life was to this guy, because he was fighting for it. He was fighting to save his life to the very end, till he was completely burned up. He was trying to get out of that truck."

He wrote later that year in *American Photo* magazine that he "wasn't thinking at   25
all about what was there; if I had thought about how horrific the guy looked I wouldn't have been able to make the picture." Instead, he maintained his emotional remove by attending to the more prosaic and technical elements of photography. He kept himself steady; he concentrated on the focus. The sun shone in through the rear of the destroyed truck and backlit his subject. Another burned body lay directly in front of

the vehicle, blocking a close-up shot, so Jarecke used the full 200mm zoom lens on his Canon EOS-1.

In his other shots of the same scene, it is apparent that the soldier could never have survived, even if he had pulled himself up out of the driver's seat and through the window. The desert sand around the truck is scorched. Bodies are piled behind the vehicle, indistinguishable from one another. A lone, burned man lies face down in front of the truck, everything incinerated except the soles of his bare feet. In another photograph, a man lies spread-eagle on the sand, his body burned to the point of disintegration, but his face mostly intact and oddly serene. A dress shoe lies next to his body.

The group continued on across the desert, passing through more stretches of highway littered with the same fire-ravaged bodies and vehicles. Jarecke and his pool were possibly the first members of the Western media to come across these scenes, which appeared along what eventually became known as the Highway of Death, sometimes referred to as the Road to Hell.

The retreating Iraqi soldiers had been trapped. They were frozen in a traffic jam, blocked off by the Americans, by Mutla Ridge, by a minefield. Some fled on foot; the rest were strafed by American planes that swooped overhead, passing again and again

Iraqi prisoners of war, captured by the U.S. military on their way to Baghdad.
© Kenneth Jarecke /Contact Press Images

Impact on military

to destroy all the vehicles. Milk vans, fire trucks, limousines, and one bulldozer appeared in the wreckage alongside armored cars and trucks, and T-55 and T-72 tanks. Most vehicles held fully loaded, but rusting, Kalashnikov variants. According to descriptions from reporters like the *New York Times*' R. W. Apple and the *Observer*'s Colin Smith, amid the plastic mines, grenades, ammunition, and gas masks, a quadruple-barreled anti-aircraft gun stood crewless and still pointing skyward.[4] Personal items, like a photograph of a child's birthday party and broken crayons, littered the ground beside weapons and body parts. The body count never seems to have been determined, although the BBC puts it in the "thousands."[5]

"In one truck," wrote Colin Smith in a March 3 dispatch for the *Observer*, "the radio had been knocked out of the dashboard but was still wired up and faintly picking up some plaintive Arabic air which sounded so utterly forlorn I thought at first it must be a cry for help."

Following the February 28 ceasefire that ended Desert Storm, Jarecke's film roll with the image of the incinerated soldier reached the Joint Information Bureau in Dhahran, Saudi Arabia, where the military coordinated and corralled the press, and where pool editors received and filed stories and photographs. At that point, with the operation over, the photograph would not have needed to pass through a security screening, says Maryanne Golon, who was the on-site photo editor for *Time* in Saudi Arabia and is now director of photography for the *Washington Post*. Despite the obviously shocking content, she tells me she reacted like an editor in work mode. She selected it, without debate or controversy among the pool editors, to be scanned and transmitted. The image made its way back to the editors' offices in New York City.

Jarecke also made his way from Saudi Arabia to New York. Passing through Heathrow Airport on a layover, he bought a copy of the March 3 edition of the *Observer*. He opened it to find his photograph on page 9, printed at the top across eight columns under the heading, "The real face of war."

That weekend in March, when the *Observer*'s editors made the final decision to print the image, every magazine in North America made the opposite choice. Jarecke's photograph did not even appear on the desks of most U.S. newspaper editors (the exception being the *New York Times*, which had a photo wire service subscription but nonetheless declined to publish the image). The photograph was entirely absent from American media until far past the time when it was relevant to ground reporting from Iraq and Kuwait. Golon says she wasn't surprised by this, even though she'd chosen to transmit it to the American press. "I didn't think there was any chance they'd publish it," she says.

Apart from the *Observer*, the only major news outlet to run the Iraqi soldier's photograph at the time was the Parisian news daily *Libération*, which ran it on March 4. Both newspapers refrained from putting the image on the front page, though they ran it prominently inside. But Aidan Sullivan, the pictures editor for the British *Sunday Times*, told the *British Journal of Photography* on March 14 that he had opted instead for a wide shot of the carnage: a desert highway

> **"We would have thought our readers could work out that a lot of people had died in those vehicles. Do you have to show it to them?"**

30

littered with rubble. He challenged the *Observer*: "We would have thought our readers could work out that a lot of people had died in those vehicles. Do you have to show it to them?"

"There were 1,400 [Iraqi soldiers] in that convoy, and every picture transmitted until that one came, two days after the event, was of debris, bits of equipment," Tony McGrath, the *Observer*'s pictures editor, was quoted as saying in the same article. "No human involvement in it at all; it could have been a scrapyard. That was some dreadful censorship."

The media took it upon themselves to "do what the military censorship did not do," says   35
Robert Pledge, the head of the Contact Press Images photojournalism agency that has represented Jarecke since the 1980s. The night they received the image, Pledge tells me, editors at the Associated Press's New York City offices pulled the photo entirely from the wire service, keeping it off the desks of virtually all of America's newspaper editors. It is unknown precisely how, why, or by whom the AP's decision was handed down.

Vincent Alabiso, who at the time was the executive photo editor for the AP, later distanced himself from the wire service's decision. In 2003, he admitted to *American Journalism Review* that the photograph ought to have gone out on the wire and argued that such a photo would today.[6]

Yet the AP's reaction was repeated at *Time* and *Life*. Both magazines briefly considered the photo, unofficially referred to as "Crispy," for publication. The photo departments even drew up layout plans. *Time*, which had sent Jarecke to the Gulf in the first place, planned for the image to accompany a story about the Highway of Death.

"We fought like crazy to get our editors to let us publish that picture," former photo director Michele Stephenson tells me. As she recalls, Henry Muller, the managing editor, told her, "*Time* is a family magazine." And the image was, when it came down to it, just too disturbing for the outlet to publish. It was, to her recollection, the only instance during the Gulf War where the photo department fought but failed to get an image into print.

James Gaines, the managing editor of *Life*, took responsibility for the ultimate decision not to run Jarecke's image in his own magazine's pages, despite photo director Peter Howe's push to give it a double-page spread. "We thought that this was the stuff of nightmares," Gaines told Ian Buchanan of the *British Journal of Photography* in March 1991. "We have a fairly substantial number of children who read *Life* magazine," he added. Even so, the photograph was published later that month in one of *Life*'s special issues devoted to the Gulf War—not typical reading material for the elementary-school set.

Stella Kramer, who worked as a freelance photo editor for *Life* on four special-   40
edition issues on the Gulf War, tells me that the decision to not publish Jarecke's photo was less about protecting readers than preserving the dominant narrative of the good, clean war. Flipping through 23-year-old issues, Kramer expresses clear distaste at the editorial quality of what she helped to create. The magazines "were very sanitized," she says. "So, that's why these issues are all basically just propaganda." She points out the picture on the cover of the February 25 issue: a young blond boy dwarfed by the American flag he's holding. "As far as Americans were concerned," she remarks, "nobody ever died."

"If pictures tell stories," Lee Corkran tells me, "the story should have a point. So if the point is the utter annihilation of people who were in retreat and all the charred bodies . . . if that's your point, then that's true. And so be it. I mean, war is ugly. It's hideous." To Corkran, who was awarded the Bronze Star for his Gulf War combat photography, pictures like Jarecke's tell important stories about the effects of American and allied airpower. Even Patrick Hermanson, the public affairs officer who originally protested the idea of taking pictures of the scene, now says the media should not have censored the photo.

The U.S. military has now abandoned the pool system it used in 1990 and 1991, and the Internet has changed the way photos reach the public. Even if the AP did refuse to send out a photo, online outlets would certainly run it, and no managing editor would be able to prevent it from being shared across various social platforms, or being the subject of extensive op-ed and blog commentary. If anything, today's controversies often center on the vast abundance of disturbing photographs, and the difficulty of putting them in a meaningful context.[7]

Some have argued that showing bloodshed and trauma repeatedly and sensationally can dull emotional understanding. But never showing these images in the first place guarantees that such an understanding will never develop. "Try to imagine, if only for a moment, what your intellectual, political, and ethical world would be like if you had never seen a photograph," author Susie Linfield asks in *The Cruel Radiance*, her book on photography and political violence. Photos like Jarecke's not only show that bombs drop on real people; they also make the public feel accountable. As David Carr wrote in the *New York Times* in 2003, war photography has "an ability not just to offend the viewer, but to implicate him or her as well."[8]

As an angry 28-year-old Jarecke wrote in *American Photo* in 1991: "If we're big enough to fight a war, we should be big enough to look at it."

NOTES

1. Michael Griffin, "Media Images of War," *Media, War & Conflict* 3, no. 1 (2010): 7–41.
2. Megan Garber, "The Malaysia Air Crash: Should We Publish Pictures of Bodies?" *The Atlantic*, July 17, 2014.
3. Malcolm W. Browne, "Conflicting Censorship Upsets Many Journalists," *New York Times*, January 21, 1991.
4. R. W. Apple Jr., "Death Stalks Desert Despite Cease-Fire," *New York Times*, March 2, 1991.
5. "Flashback: 1991 Gulf War," *BBC News*, March 20, 2003. http://news.bbc.co.uk/2/hi/middle_east/2754103.stm
6. Lori Robertson, "Images of War," *American Journalism Review* (October/November 2004).
7. David Frum, "Photographs as Weapons of War in the Middle East," *The Atlantic*, August 2, 2014.
8. David Carr, "Telling War's Deadly Story at Just Enough Distance," *New York Times*, April 7, 2003.

Exploring Context

1. Explore Kenneth Jarecke's Web site at kennethjarecke.com. In what ways does his larger body of work reflect the ideas about photography that DeGhett offers? Incorporate your findings into your response from Question 3 of Questions for Critical Reading.

2. View Nick Ut's image of child napalm victims mentioned by DeGhett at goo.gl/Y1j1kw. What factors might cause this photo to be published but not Jarecke's? Use quotations from DeGhett to support your answer and then apply your analysis to the rationale for not publishing Jarecke's photograph that you traced in Question 2 of Questions for Critical Reading.

3. Use a search engine to look for images of "war photography." How has technology changed the accessibility of images of war? Support your thoughts with quotations from the essay.

Questions for Connecting

1. Does Jarecke's image meet the standards for art as explained in Rhys Southan's "Is Art a Waste of Time?" (p. 434)? Does the failure of Jarecke to get his image widely published during the war support the idea that art is not as important as Effective Altruism? Are war photographers replaceable? Consider Nick Ut's images from Question 2 of Exploring Context as an additional example in making your argument.

2. In "Visible Man: Ethics in a World without Secrets" (p. 425), Peter Singer suggests that "sousveillance" can be used to hold governments accountable. How does DeGhett's essay complicate Singer's argument? Does sousveillance require free access to publication channels?

3. How might you apply the Dalai Lama's concept of a moral compass from "Ethics and the New Genetics" (p. 63) to Jarecke's photograph? Is it more compassionate to respect the death of the soldier in the photograph by not publishing it or to call attention to the horrors of war by publishing the photo? Can censorship be moral? Incorporate your response from Question 1 of Questions for Critical Reading.

Language Matters

1. Wordle (wordle.net) is a tool for generating "word clouds" — it transforms text into a visual representation. Use Wordle to create a word cloud for this essay by typing either key quotations or key terms. How does the visual representation enhance or change your understanding of the text?

2. Select a key passage from DeGhett and replace all the verbs with blanks ("_____"). Working in small groups, fill in the blanks with verbs and then reflect on which verbs you chose and why. How does the context of each sentence determine which word to use? More important, how significant are verbs to the meaning of a sentence? Could you change DeGhett's entire argument by changing the verbs?

3. Locate the strongest transition in DeGhett's essay. What makes it strong or effective? How can you use this strategy in your own writing?

Assignments for Writing

1. One of DeGhett's central arguments is that photographs such as Jarecke's are powerful tools to examine the consequences of war. Write a paper in which you examine how images can affect conflicts such as war. Do such photographs create empathy or do they numb viewers to violence? Draw from your work on the power of images from Question 3 of Questions for Critical Reading.

2. DeGhett suggests that given the development of technologies such as social media, Jarecke's photograph would have had a very different fate had it been taken today. Write a paper in which you suggest the ways in which technology has changed the power of the media. Use your exploration of war photography from Question 3 of Exploring Context to support your position.

3. In some ways DeGhett's essay is centrally concerned with practices of censorship. Write a paper in which you propose guidelines for an ethics of censorship. In which situations might it be justified? Use your answers from Question 1 for Questions for Critical Reading and Question 3 of Questions for Connecting in making your response.

CHARLES DUHIGG

New Mexico native **Charles Duhigg** is a reporter for the *New York Times*. He won a Pulitzer Prize in 2013 for his series "The iEconomy" and has received other notable awards over the course of his career, including the Scripps Howard National Journalism Award and the Investigative Reporters and Editors Medal, among others. Duhigg studied history at Yale University and holds an M.B.A. from Harvard Business School. Duhigg is also the author of *New York Times* best-seller *The Power of Habit: Why We Do What We Do in Life and Business*, a book exploring the genesis of habits, how they can be transformed, and how they contributed to the success of figures such as Olympic swimmer Michael Phelps and civil rights leader Martin Luther King Jr., as well as companies such as Target, Alcoa, Procter & Gamble, and more. More than one million copies have been sold worldwide, and *The Power of Habit* spent more than ninety weeks on the *Times*' best-seller lists.

Andrew Toth/Getty Images

In this chapter from the book, Duhigg explores the power of relationships and social habits in creating large-scale change, citing as an example the way Rosa Parks's arrest for remaining seated on a bus sparked the civil rights movement. Parks's arrest effected change when other similar incidents didn't, Duhigg asserts, because Parks was deeply involved in many different circles within the community. The power of her diverse relationships triumphed over apathy, inspiring friends and connections to take a stand on her behalf and against racism and segregation in general. This, in turn, motivated — or, as Duhigg calls it, "peer pressured" — others outside of Parks's network to get involved due to a sense of obligation. "On a playground, peer pressure is dangerous," Duhigg writes. "In adult life, it's how business gets done and communities self-organize" (p. 92).

Strong ties, or close relationships, combined with weak ties, or distant connections, have the power to mobilize large groups toward a singular goal, he argues — especially once leaders, such as Martin Luther King Jr., instill new habits and values that allow movements to become self-directed, and therefore sustainable. Duhigg also cites the growth of Rick Warren's Saddleback Church from seven parishioners in 1979 to more than twenty thousand today as an example of the power of social habits to mobilize the masses, as Warren himself used the psychology of social habit to build his community and movement.

How important are relationships in accomplishing goals? What kinds of relationships are important when it comes to creating change? Strong ties? Weak ties? Both?

▶ TAGS: *civil rights, collaboration, community, conversation, law and justice, politics, psychology, relationships, religion, social change*

▶ CONNECTIONS: *Appiah, Epstein, Southan, Yoshino*

Questions for Critical Reading

1. Pay attention as you read to Duhigg's definition and use of the terms *strong tie* and *weak tie*. How do these ideas help him make his argument?

2. Take a moment to write down some of your experiences with peer pressure. After you've read the essay, return to these experiences and relate them to Duhigg's ideas about peer pressure. Do your experiences confirm or complicate his ideas? Refer specifically to his text in making your response.

3. What elements are useful for creating social change? As you read the essay, note places where Duhigg describes concepts or actions that help produce social change. Use these to help you compose your response.

From Civil Rights to Megachurches

I.

The 6 PM Cleveland Avenue bus pulled to the curb and the petite forty-two-year-old African American woman in rimless glasses and a conservative brown jacket climbed on board, reached into her purse, and dropped a ten-cent fare into the till.[1]

It was Thursday, December 1, 1955, in Montgomery, Alabama, and she had just finished a long day at Montgomery Fair, the department store where she worked as a seamstress. The bus was crowded and, by law, the first four rows were reserved for white passengers. The area where blacks were allowed to sit, in the back, was already full and so the woman—Rosa Parks—sat in a center row, right behind the white section, where either race could claim a seat.

As the bus continued on its route, more people boarded. Soon, all the rows were filled and some—including a white passenger—were standing in the aisle, holding on to an overhead bar. The bus driver, James F. Blake, seeing the white man on his feet, shouted at the black passengers in Parks's area to give up their seats, but no one moved. It was noisy. They might not have heard. Blake pulled over to a bus stop in front of the Empire Theater on Montgomery Street and walked back.

"Y'all better make it light on yourselves and let me have those seats," he said. Three of the black passengers got up and moved to the rear, but Parks stayed put. She wasn't *in* the white section, she told the driver, and besides, there was only one white rider standing.

"If you don't stand up," Blake said, "I'm going to call the police and have you arrested."   5

"You may do that," Parks said.[2]

The driver left and found two policemen.

"Why don't you stand up?" one of them asked Parks after they boarded.

"Why do you push us around?" she said.

"I don't know," the officer answered. "But the law is the law and you're under   10 arrest."[3]

At that moment, though no one on that bus knew it, the civil rights movement pivoted. That small refusal was the first in a series of actions that shifted the battle over race relations from a struggle fought by activists in courts and legislatures into a contest that would draw its strength from entire communities and mass protests. Over the next year, Montgomery's black population would rise up and boycott the city's buses, ending their strike only once the law segregating races on public transportation was stricken from the books. The boycott would financially cripple the bus line, draw tens of thousands of protesters to rallies, introduce the country to a charismatic young leader named Martin Luther King Jr., and spark a movement that would spread to Little Rock, Greensboro, Raleigh, Birmingham, and, eventually, to Congress. Parks would become a hero, a recipient of the Presidential Medal of Freedom, and a shining example of how a single act of defiance can change the world.

But that isn't the whole story. Rosa Parks and the Montgomery bus boycott became the epicenter of the civil rights campaign not only because of an individual act of defiance, but also because of social patterns. Parks's experiences offer a lesson in the power of social habits—the behaviors that occur, unthinkingly, across dozens or hundreds or thousands of people which are often hard to see as they emerge, but which contain a power that can change the world. Social habits are what fill streets with protesters

Social habits are why some initiatives become world-changing movements, while others fail to ignite.

who may not know one another, who might be marching for different reasons, but who are all moving in the same direction. Social habits are why some initiatives become world-changing movements, while others fail to ignite. And the reason why social habits have such influence is because at the root of many movements—be they large-scale revolutions or simple fluctuations in the churches people attend—is a three-part process that historians and sociologists say shows up again and again:

A movement starts because of the social habits of friendship and the strong ties between close acquaintances.

It grows because of the habits of a community, and the weak ties that hold neighborhoods and clans together.

And it endures because a movement's leaders give participants new habits that create a fresh sense of identity and a feeling of ownership.[4]

Usually, only when all three parts of this process are fulfilled can a movement become self-propelling and reach a critical mass. There are other recipes for successful social change and hundreds of details that differ between eras and struggles. But understanding how social habits work helps explain why Montgomery and Rosa Parks became the catalyst for a civil rights crusade.

It wasn't inevitable that Parks's act of rebellion that winter day would result in anything other than her arrest. Then habits intervened, and something amazing occurred.

Rosa Parks wasn't the first black passenger jailed for breaking Montgomery's bus segregation laws. She wasn't even the first that year. In 1946, Geneva Johnson had been arrested for talking back to a Montgomery bus driver over seating.[5] In 1949, Viola White, Katie Wingfield, and two black children were arrested for sitting in the white section and refusing to move.[6] That same year, two black teenagers visiting from New Jersey—where buses were integrated—were arrested and jailed after breaking the law by sitting next to a white man and a boy.[7] In 1952, a Montgomery policeman shot and killed a black man when he argued with a bus driver. In 1955, just months before Parks was taken to jail, Claudette Colvin and Mary Louise Smith were arrested in separate incidents for refusing to give their seats to white passengers.

None of those arrests resulted in boycotts or protests, however. "There weren't many real activists in Montgomery at the time," Taylor Branch, the Pulitzer Prize–winning civil rights historian, told me. "People didn't mount protests or marches. Activism was something that happened in courts. It wasn't something average people did."

When a young Martin Luther King Jr., arrived in Montgomery in 1954, for instance, a year before Parks's arrest, he found a majority of the city's blacks accepted segregation "without apparent protest. Not only did they seem resigned to segregation per se; they also accepted the abuses and indignities which came with it."[8]

So why, when Parks was arrested, did things change?

One explanation is that the political climate was shifting. The previous year, the U.S. Supreme Court had handed down *Brown v. Board of Education*, ruling that segregation was illegal within public schools; six months before Parks's arrest, the Court had issued what came to be known as *Brown II*—a decision ordering that school integration must proceed with "all deliberate speed." There was a powerful sense across the nation that change was in the air.

But that isn't sufficient to explain why Montgomery became ground zero for the civil rights struggle. Claudette Colvin and Mary Louise Smith had been arrested in the wake of *Brown v. Board*, and yet they didn't spark a protest. *Brown*, for many Montgomery residents, was an abstraction from a far-off courthouse, and it was unclear how—or if—its impact would be felt locally. Montgomery wasn't Atlanta or Austin or other cities where progress seemed possible. "Montgomery was a pretty nasty place," Branch said. "Racism was set in its ways there."

When Parks was arrested, however, it sparked something unusual within the city. Rosa Parks, unlike other people who had been jailed for violating the bus segregation law, was deeply respected and embedded within her community. So when she was arrested, it triggered a series of social habits—the habits of friendship—that ignited an initial protest. Parks's membership in dozens of social networks across Montgomery allowed her friends to muster a response before the community's normal apathy could take hold.

Montgomery's civil life, at the time, was dominated by hundreds of small groups that created the city's social fabric. The city's *Directory of Civil and Social Organizations* was almost as thick as its phone book. Every adult, it seemed—particularly every black adult—belonged to some kind of club, church, social group, community center, or neighborhood organization, and often more than one. And within these social networks, Rosa Parks was particularly well known and liked. "Rosa Parks was one of those rare people of whom everyone agreed that she gave more than she got," Branch wrote in his history of the civil rights movement, *Parting the Waters*. "Her character represented one of the isolated high blips on the graph of human nature, offsetting a dozen or so sociopaths."[9] Parks's many friendships and affiliations cut across the city's racial and economic lines. She was the secretary of the local NAACP chapter, attended the Methodist church, and helped oversee a youth organization at the Lutheran church near her home. She spent some weekends volunteering at a shelter, others with a botanical club, and on Wednesday nights often joined a group of women who knit blankets for a local hospital. She volunteered dressmaking services to poor families and provided last-minute gown alterations for wealthy white debutantes. She was so deeply enmeshed in the community, in fact, that her husband complained that she ate more often at potlucks than at home.

In general, sociologists say, most of us have friends who are like us. We might have a few close acquaintances who are richer, a few who are poorer, and a few of different races—but, on the whole, our deepest relationships tend to be with people who look like us, earn about the same amount of money, and come from similar backgrounds.

Parks's friends, in contrast, spanned Montgomery's social and economic hierarchies. She had what sociologists call "strong ties"—firsthand relationships—with dozens of groups throughout Montgomery that didn't usually come into contact with one another. "This was absolutely key," Branch said. "Rosa Parks transcended the social stratifications of the black community and Montgomery as a whole. She was friends with field hands and college professors."

And the power of those friendships became apparent as soon as Parks landed in jail.

Rosa Parks called her parents' home from the police station. She was panicked, and her mother—who had no idea what to do—started going through a mental Rolodex of Parks's friends, trying to think of someone who might be able to help. She called the wife of E. D. Nixon, the former head of the Montgomery NAACP, who in turn called her husband and told him that Parks needed to be bailed out of jail. He immediately agreed to help, and called a prominent white lawyer named Clifford Durr who knew Parks because she had hemmed dresses for his three daughters.

Nixon and Durr went to the jailhouse, posted bail for Parks, and took her home. They'd been looking for the perfect case to challenge Montgomery's bus segregation laws, and sensing an opportunity, they asked Parks if she would be willing to let them fight her arrest in court. Parks's husband was opposed to the idea. "The white folks will kill you, Rosa," he told her.[10]

But Parks had spent years working with Nixon at the NAACP. She had been in Durr's house and had helped his daughters prepare for cotillions. Her friends were now asking her for a favor.

"If you think it will mean something to Montgomery and do some good," she told them, "I'll be happy to go along with it."[11]

That night—just a few hours after the arrest—news of Parks's jailing began to filter through the black community. Jo Ann Robinson, the president of a powerful group of schoolteachers involved in politics and a friend of Parks's from numerous organizations, heard about it. So did many of the schoolteachers in Robinson's group, and many of the parents of their students. Close to midnight, Robinson called an impromptu meeting and suggested that everyone boycott the city's buses on Monday, four days hence, when Parks was to appear in court.

Afterward, Robinson snuck into her office's mimeograph room and made copies of a flyer.

"Another Negro woman has been arrested and thrown into jail because she re- 35
fused to get up out of her seat on the bus for a white person to sit down," it read. "This
woman's case will come up on Monday. We are, therefore, asking every Negro to stay
off the buses Monday in protest of the arrest and trial."[12]

Early the next morning, Robinson gave stacks of the flyers to schoolteachers and
asked them to distribute it to parents and coworkers. Within twenty-four hours of
Parks's arrest, word of her jailing and the boycott had spread to some of the city's most
influential communities—the local NAACP, a large political group, a number of black
schoolteachers, and the parents of their students. Many of the people who received a
flyer knew Rosa Parks personally—they had sat next to her in church or at a volunteer
meeting and considered her a friend. There's a natural instinct embedded in friendship,
a sympathy that makes us willing to fight for someone we like when they are treated
unjustly. Studies show that people have no problem ignoring strangers' injuries, but
when a friend is insulted, our sense of outrage is enough to overcome the inertia that
usually makes protests hard to organize. When Parks's friends learned about her arrest and the boycott, the social habits of friendship—the natural inclination to help
someone we respect—kicked in.

The first mass movement of the modern civil rights era could have been sparked
by any number of earlier arrests. But it began with Rosa Parks because she had a large,
diverse, and connected set of friends—who, when she was arrested, reacted as friends
naturally respond, by following the social habits of friendship and agreeing to show
their support.

Still, many expected the protest would be nothing more than a one-day event.
Small protests pop up every day around the world, and almost all of them quickly fizzle
out. No one has enough friends to change the world.

Which is why the second aspect of the social habits of movements is so important. The Montgomery bus boycott became a society-wide action because the sense
of obligation that held the black community together was activated soon after Parks's
friends started spreading the word. People who hardly knew Rosa Parks decided to participate because of a social peer pressure—an influence known as "the power of weak
ties"—that made it difficult to avoid joining in.

II.

Imagine, for a moment, that you're an established midlevel executive at a prosperous 40
company. You're successful and well liked. You've spent years building a reputation inside your firm and cultivating a network of friends that you can tap for clients, advice,
and industry gossip. You belong to a church, a gym, and a country club, as well as the
local chapter of your college alumni association. You're respected and often asked to
join various committees. When people within your community hear of a business opportunity, they often pass it your way.

Now imagine you get a phone call. It's a midlevel executive at another company
looking for a new job. Will you help him by putting in a good word with your boss,
he asks?

If the person on the telephone is a total stranger, it's an easy decision. Why risk
your standing inside your firm helping someone you don't know?

If the person on the phone is a close friend, on the other hand, it's also an easy choice. Of course you'll help. That's what friends do.

However, what if the person on the phone isn't a good friend or a stranger, but something in between? What if you have friends in common, but don't know each other very well? Do you vouch for the caller when your boss asks if he's worth an interview? How much of your own reputation and energy, in other words, are you willing to expend to help a friend of a friend get a job?

In the late 1960s, a Harvard Ph.D. student named Mark Granovetter set out to answer that question by studying how 282 men had found their current employment.[13] He tracked how they had learned about open positions, whom they had called for referrals, the methods they used to land interviews, and most important, who had provided a helping hand. As expected, he found that when job hunters approached strangers for assistance, they were rejected. When they appealed to friends, help was provided.

More surprising, however, was how often job hunters also received help from casual acquaintances—friends of friends—people who were neither strangers nor close pals. Granovetter called those connections "weak ties," because they represented the links that connect people who have acquaintances in common, who share membership in social networks, but aren't directly connected by the strong ties of friendship themselves.

In fact, in landing a job, Granovetter discovered, weak-tie acquaintances were often *more* important than strong-tie friends because weak ties give us access to social networks where we don't otherwise belong. Many of the people Granovetter studied had learned about new job opportunities through weak ties, rather than from close friends, which makes sense because we talk to our closest friends all the time, or work alongside them or read the same blogs. By the time they have heard about a new opportunity, we probably know about it, as well. On the other hand, our weak-tie acquaintances—the people we bump into every six months—are the ones who tell us about jobs we would otherwise never hear about.[14]

When sociologists have examined how opinions move through communities, how gossip spreads or political movements start, they've discovered a common pattern: Our weak-tie acquaintances are often as influential—if not more—than our close-tie friends. As Granovetter wrote, "Individuals with few weak ties will be deprived of information from distant parts of the social system and will be confined to the provincial news and views of their close friends. This deprivation will not only insulate them from the latest ideas and fashions but may put them in a disadvantaged position in the labor market, where advancement can depend . . . on knowing about appropriate job openings at just the right time.

"Furthermore, such individuals may be difficult to organize or integrate into political movements of any kind. . . . While members of one or two cliques may be efficiently recruited, the problem is that, without weak ties, any momentum generated in this way does not spread *beyond* the clique. As a result, most of the population will be untouched."[15]

The power of weak ties helps explain how a protest can expand from a group of friends into a broad social movement. Convincing thousands of people to pursue the same goal—especially when that pursuit entails real hardship, such as walking to work rather than taking the bus, or going to jail, or even skipping a morning cup of coffee because the company that sells it doesn't support organic farming—is hard. Most people don't care enough about the latest outrage to give up their bus ride or caffeine unless it's a close friend that has been insulted or jailed. So there is a tool that activists have long relied upon to compel protest, even when a group of people don't necessarily *want* to participate. It's a form of persuasion that has been remarkably effective over hundreds of years. It's the sense of obligation that neighborhoods or communities place upon themselves.

In other words, peer pressure.

Peer pressure—and the social habits that encourage people to conform to group expectations—is difficult to describe, because it often differs in form and expression from person to person. These social habits aren't so much one consistent pattern as dozens of individual habits that ultimately cause everyone to move in the same direction.

The habits of peer pressure, however, have something in common. They often spread through weak ties. And they gain their authority through communal expectations. If you ignore the social obligations of your neighborhood, if you shrug off the expected patterns of your community, you risk losing your social standing. You endanger your access to many of the social benefits that come from joining the country club, the alumni association, or the church in the first place.

In other words, if you don't give the caller looking for a job a helping hand, he might complain to his tennis partner, who might mention those grumblings to someone in the locker room who you were hoping to attract as a client, who is now less likely to return your call because you have a reputation for not being a team player. On a playground, peer pressure is dangerous. In adult life, it's how business gets done and communities self-organize.

> **On a playground, peer pressure is dangerous. In adult life, it's how business gets done and communities self-organize.**

Such peer pressure, on its own, isn't enough to sustain a movement. But when the strong ties of friendship and the weak ties of peer pressure merge, they create incredible momentum. That's when widespread social change can begin.

To see how the combination of strong and weak ties can propel a movement, fast forward to nine years *after* Rosa Parks's arrest, when hundreds of young people volunteered to expose themselves to deadly risks for the civil rights crusade.

In 1964, students from across the country—many of them whites from Harvard, Yale, and other northern universities—applied for something called the "Mississippi Summer Project." It was a ten-week program devoted to registering black voters in the South.[16] The project came to be known as Freedom Summer, and many who applied were aware it would be dangerous. In the months before the program started, newspapers and magazines were filled with articles predicting violence (which proved tragically accurate when, just a week after it began, white vigilantes killed three volunteers outside Longdale, Mississippi). The threat of harm kept many students from participating in the Mississippi Summer Project, even after they applied. More than a thousand applicants were accepted into Freedom Summer, but when it came time to head south in June, more than three hundred of those invited to participate decided to stay home.[17]

In the 1980s, a sociologist at the University of Arizona named Doug McAdam began wondering if it was possible to figure out why some people had participated in Freedom

Summer and others withdrew.[18] He started by reading 720 of the applications students had submitted decades earlier. Each was five pages long. Applicants were asked about their backgrounds, why they wanted to go to Mississippi, and their experiences with voter registration. They were told to provide a list of people organizers should contact if they were arrested. There were essays, references, and, for some, interviews. Applying was not a casual undertaking.

McAdam's initial hypothesis was that students who ended up going to Mississippi probably had different motivations from those who stayed home, which explained the divergence in participation. To test this idea, he divided applicants into two groups. The first pile were people who said they wanted to go to Mississippi for "self-interested" motives, such as to "test myself," to "be where the action is," or to "learn about the southern way of life." The second group were those with "other-oriented" motives, such as to "improve the lot of blacks," to "aid in the full realization of democracy," or to "demonstrate the power of nonviolence as a vehicle for social change."

The self-centered, McAdam hypothesized, would be more likely to stay home once they realized the risks of Freedom Summer. The other-oriented would be more likely to get on the bus.

The hypothesis was wrong.

The selfish and the selfless, according to the data, went South in equal numbers. Differences in motives did not explain "any significant distinctions between participants and withdrawals," McAdam wrote.

Next, McAdam compared applicants' opportunity costs. Maybe those who stayed home had husbands or girlfriends keeping them from going to Mississippi? Maybe they had gotten jobs, and couldn't swing a two-month unpaid break?

Wrong again.

"Being married or holding a full-time job actually enhanced the applicant's chances of going south," McAdam concluded.

He had one hypothesis left. Each applicant was asked to list their memberships in student and political organizations and at least ten people they wanted kept informed of their summer activities, so McAdam took these lists and used them to chart each applicant's social network. By comparing memberships in clubs, he was able to determine which applicants had friends who also applied for Freedom Summer.

Once he finished, he finally had an answer as to why some students went to Mississippi, and others stayed home: because of social habits—or more specifically, because of the power of strong and weak ties working in tandem. The students who participated in Freedom Summer were enmeshed in the types of communities where both their close friends *and* their casual acquaintances expected them to get on the bus. Those who withdrew were also enmeshed in communities, but of a different kind—the kind where the social pressures and habits didn't compel them to go to Mississippi.

"Imagine you're one of the students who applied," McAdam told me. "On the day you signed up for Freedom Summer, you filled out the application with five of your closest friends and you were all feeling really motivated.

"Now, it's six months later and departure day is almost here. All the magazines are predicting violence in Mississippi. You called your parents, and they told you to stay at home. It would be strange, at that point, if you weren't having second thoughts.

"Then, you're walking across campus and you see a bunch of people from your church group, and they say, 'We're coordinating rides—when should we pick you up?'

These people aren't your closest friends, but you see them at club meetings and in the dorm, and they're important within your social community. They all know you've been accepted to Freedom Summer, and that you've said you want to go. Good luck pulling out at that point. You'd lose a huge amount of social standing. Even if you're having second thoughts, there's real consequences if you withdraw. You'll lose the respect of people whose opinions matter to you."

When McAdam looked at applicants with religious orientations—students who cited a "Christian duty to help those in need" as their motivation for applying, for instance, he found mixed levels of participation. However, among those applicants who mentioned a religious orientation *and* belonged to a religious organization, McAdam found that *every single one* made the trip to Mississippi. Once their communities knew they had been accepted into Freedom Summer, it was impossible for them to withdraw.[19]

On the other hand, consider the social networks of applicants who were accepted into the program but didn't go to Mississippi. They, too, were involved in campus organizations. They, too, belonged to clubs and cared about their standing within those communities. But the organizations they belonged to—the newspaper and student government, academic groups and fraternities—had different expectations. Within those communities, someone could withdraw from Freedom Summer and suffer little or no decline in the prevailing social hierarchy.

When faced with the prospect of getting arrested (or worse) in Mississippi, most students probably had second thoughts. However, some were embedded in communities where social habits—the expectations of their friends and the peer pressure of their acquaintances—compelled participation, so regardless of their hesitations, they bought a bus ticket. Others—who also cared about civil rights—belonged to communities where the social habits pointed in a slightly different direction, so they thought to themselves, *Maybe I'll just stay home.*

On the morning after he bailed Rosa Parks out of jail, E. D. Nixon placed a call to the new minister of the Dexter Avenue Baptist Church, Martin Luther King Jr. It was a little after 5 AM, but Nixon didn't say hello or ask if he had awoken King's two-week-old daughter when the minister answered—he just launched into an account of Parks's arrest, how she had been hauled into jail for refusing to give up her seat, and their plans to fight her case in court and boycott the city's buses on Monday. At the time, King was twenty-six years old. He had been in Montgomery for only a year and was still trying to figure out his role within the community. Nixon was asking for King's endorsement as well as permission to use his church for a boycott meeting that night. King was wary of getting too deeply involved. "Brother Nixon," he said, "let me think about it and you call me back."

But Nixon didn't stop there. He reached out to one of King's closest friends—one of the strongest of King's strong ties—named Ralph D. Abernathy, and asked him to help convince the young minister to participate. A few hours later, Nixon called King again.

"I'll go along with it," King told him.

"I'm glad to hear you say so," Nixon said, "because I've talked to eighteen other people and told them to meet in your church tonight. It would have been kind of bad to be getting together there without you."[20] Soon, King was drafted into serving as president of the organization that had sprung up to coordinate the boycott.

On Sunday, three days after Parks's arrest, the city's black ministers—after speaking to King and other members of the new organization—explained to their congregations that every black church in the city had agreed to a one-day protest. The message was clear: It would be embarrassing for any parishioner to sit on the sidelines. That same day, the town's newspaper, the *Advertiser*, contained an article about "a 'top secret' meeting of Montgomery Negroes who plan a boycott of city buses Monday."[21] The reporter had gotten copies of flyers that white women had taken from their maids. The black parts of the city were "flooded with thousands of copies" of the leaflets, the article explained, and it was anticipated that every black citizen would participate. When the article was written, only Parks's friends, the ministers, and the boycott organizers had publicly committed to the protest—but once the city's black residents read the newspaper, they assumed, like white readers, that everyone else was already on board.

Many people sitting in the pews and reading the newspapers knew Rosa Parks personally and were willing to boycott because of their friendships with her. Others didn't know Parks, but they could sense the community was rallying behind her cause, and that if they were seen riding a bus on Monday, it would look bad. "If you work," read a flyer handed out in churches, "take a cab, or share a ride, or walk." Then everyone heard that the boycott's leaders had convinced—or strong-armed—all the black taxi drivers into agreeing to carry black passengers on Monday for ten cents a ride, the same as a bus fare. The community's weak ties were drawing everyone together. At that point, you were either with the boycott or against it.

On the Monday morning of the boycott, King woke before dawn and got his coffee. His wife, Coretta, sat at the front window and waited for the first bus to pass. She shouted when she saw the headlights of the South Jackson line, normally filled with maids on their way to work, roll by with no passengers. The next bus was empty as well. And the one that came after. King got into his car and started driving around, checking other routes. In an hour, he counted eight black passengers. One week earlier, he would have seen hundreds.

"I was jubilant," he later wrote. "A miracle had taken place. . . . Men were seen riding mules to work, and more than one horse-drawn buggy drove the streets of Montgomery. . . . Spectators had gathered at the bus stops to watch what was happening. At first, they stood quietly, but as the day progressed they began to cheer the empty buses and laugh and make jokes. Noisy youngsters could be heard singing out, 'No riders today.'"[22]

That afternoon, in a courtroom on Church Street, Rosa Parks was found guilty of violating the state's segregation laws. More than five hundred blacks crowded the hallways and stood in front of the building, awaiting the verdict. The boycott and impromptu rally at the courthouse were the most significant black political activism in Montgomery's history, and it had all come together in five days. It had started among Parks's close friends, but it drew its power, King and other participants later said, because of a sense of obligation among the community—the social habits of weak ties. The community was pressured to stand together for fear that anyone who didn't participate wasn't someone you wanted to be friends with in the first place.

There are plenty of people who would have participated in the boycott without such encouragement. King and the cabbies and the congregations might have made the same choices without the influence of strong and weak ties. But tens of thousands of people from across the city would not have decided to stay off the buses without the encouragement of social habits. "The once dormant and quiescent Negro community was now fully awake," King later wrote.

Those social habits, however, weren't strong enough on their own to extend a one-day boycott into a yearlong movement. Within a few weeks, King would be openly worrying that people's resolve was weakening, that "the ability of the Negro community to continue the struggle" was in doubt.[23]

Then those worries would evaporate. King, like thousands of other movement leaders, would shift the struggle's guidance from his hands onto the shoulders of his followers, in large part by handing them new habits. He would activate the third part of the movement formula, and the boycott would become a self-perpetuating force.

III.

In the summer of 1979, a young seminary student who was white, had been one year old when Rosa Parks was arrested, and was currently focused mostly on how he was going to support his growing family, posted a map on the wall of his Texas home and began drawing circles around major U.S. cities, from Seattle to Miami.[24]

Rick Warren was a Baptist pastor with a pregnant wife and less than $2,000 in the bank. He wanted to start a new congregation among people who didn't already attend church, but he had no idea where it should be located. "I figured I would go somewhere all my seminary friends didn't want to go," he told me. He spent the summer in libraries studying census records, phone books, newspaper articles, and maps. His wife was in her ninth month, and so every few hours Warren would jog to a pay phone, call home to make sure she hadn't started labor yet, and then return to the stacks.

One afternoon, Warren stumbled upon a description of a place called Saddleback Valley in Orange County, California. The book Warren was reading said it was the fastest-growing region in the fastest-growing county in one of the fastest-growing states in America. There were a number of churches in the area, but none large enough to accommodate the quickly expanding population. Intrigued, Warren contacted religious leaders in Southern California who told him that many locals self-identified as Christian but didn't attend services. "In the dusty, dimly lit basement of that university library, I heard God speak to me: 'That's where I want you to plant a church!'" Warren later wrote. "From that moment on, our destination was a settled issue.[25]

Warren's focus on building a congregation among the unchurched had begun five years earlier, when, as a missionary in Japan, he had discovered an old copy of a Christian magazine with an article headlined "Why Is This Man Dangerous?" It was about Donald McGavran, a controversial author focused on building churches in nations where most people hadn't accepted Christ. At the center of McGavran's philosophy was an admonition that missionaries should imitate the tactics of other successful movements—including the civil rights campaign—by appealing to people's social habits. "The steady goal must be the Christianization of the entire fabric which is the people, or large enough parts of it that the social life of the individual is not destroyed," McGavran had written in one of his books. Only the evangelist who helps people "to become followers of Christ *in their normal social relationship* has any chance of liberating multitudes."[26]

That article—and, later, McGavran's books—were a revelation to Rick Warren. Here, finally, was someone applying a rational logic to a topic that was usually couched in the language of miracles. Here was someone who understood that religion had to be, for lack of a better word, marketed.

McGavran laid out a strategy that instructed church builders to speak to people in their "own languages," to create places of worship where congregants saw their friends, heard the kinds of music they already listened to, and experienced the Bible's lessons in digestible metaphors. Most important, McGavran said, ministers needed to convert *groups* of people, rather than individuals, so that a community's social habits would encourage religious participation, rather than pulling people away.

In December, after graduating from seminary and having the baby, Warren loaded his family and belongings into a U-Haul, drove to Orange County, and rented a small condo. His first prayer group attracted all of seven people and took place in his living room.

Today, thirty years later, Saddleback Church is one of the largest ministries in the world, with more than twenty thousand parishioners visiting its 120-acre campus—and eight satellite campuses—each week. One of Warren's books, *The Purpose-Driven Life*, has sold thirty million copies, making it among the biggest sellers in history. There are thousands of other churches modeled on his methods. Warren was chosen to perform the invocation at President Obama's inauguration, and is considered one of the most influential religious leaders on earth.

And at the core of his church's growth and his success is a fundamental belief in the power of social habits.

"We've thought long and hard about habitualizing faith, breaking it down into pieces," Warren told me. "If you try to scare people into following Christ's example, it's not going to work for too long. The only way you get people to take responsibility for their spiritual maturity is to teach them *habits* of faith.

"Once that happens, they become self-feeders. People follow Christ not because you've led them there, but because it's who they are."

When Warren first arrived in Saddleback Valley, he spent twelve weeks going door-to-door, introducing himself and asking strangers why they *didn't* go to church. Many of the answers were practical—it was boring, people said, the music was bad, the sermons didn't seem applicable to their lives, they needed child care, they hated dressing up, the pews were uncomfortable.

Warren's church would address each of those complaints. He told people to wear shorts and Hawaiian shirts, if they felt like it. An electric guitar was brought in. Warren's sermons, from the start, focused on practical topics, with titles such as "How to Handle Discouragement," "How to Feel Good About Yourself," "How to Raise Healthy Families," and "How to Survive Under Stress."[27] His lessons were easy to understand, focused on real, daily problems, and could be applied as soon as parishioners left church.

It started to work. Warren rented school auditoriums for services and office buildings for prayer meetings. The congregation hit fifty members, then one hundred, then two hundred in less than a year. Warren was working eighteen hours a day, seven days a week, answering congregants' phone calls, leading classes, coming to their homes to offer marriage counseling, and, in his spare time, always looking for new venues to accommodate the church's growing size.

One Sunday in mid-December, Warren stood up to preach during the eleven o'clock 100 service. He felt light-headed, dizzy. He gripped the podium and started to speak, but the words on the page were blurry. He began to fall, caught himself, and motioned to the assistant pastor—his only staff—to take the lectern.

"I'm sorry, folks," Warren told the audience. "I'm going to have to sit down."[28]

For years, he had suffered from anxiety attacks and occasional bouts of melancholy that friends told him sounded like mild depressions. But it had never hit this bad before. The next day, Warren and his family began driving to Arizona, where his wife's family had a house. Slowly, he recuperated. Some days, he would sleep for twelve hours and then take a walk through the desert, praying, trying to understand why these panic attacks were threatening to undo everything he had worked so hard to build. Nearly a month passed as he stayed away from the church. His melancholy became a full-fledged depression, darker than anything he had experienced before. He wasn't certain if he would ever become healthy enough to return.

Warren, as befitting a pastor, is a man prone to epiphanies. They had occurred when he found the magazine article about McGavran, and in the library in Texas. Walking through the desert, another one struck.

"You focus on building people," the Lord told him. "And I will build the church."

Unlike some of his previous revelations, however, this one didn't suddenly make 105 the path clear. Warren would continue to struggle with depression for months—and then during periods throughout his life. On that day, however, he made two decisions: He would go back to Saddleback, and he would figure out how to make running the church less work.

When Warren returned to Saddleback, he decided to expand a small experiment he had started a few months earlier that, he hoped, would make it easier to manage the church. He was never certain he would have enough classrooms to accommodate everyone who showed up for Bible study, so he had asked a few church members to host classes inside their homes. He worried that people might complain about going to someone's house, rather than a proper church classroom. But congregants loved it, they said. The small groups gave them a chance to meet their neighbors. So, after he returned from his leave, Warren assigned every Saddleback member to a small group that met every week. It was one of the most important decisions he ever made, because it transformed church participation from a decision into a habit that drew on already-existing social urges and patterns.

"Now, when people come to Saddleback and see the giant crowds on the weekends, they think that's our success," Warren told me. "But that's just the tip of the iceberg. Ninety-five percent of this church is what happens during the week inside those small groups.

"The congregation and the small groups are like a one-two punch. You have this big crowd to remind you why you're doing this in the first place, and a small group of close friends to help you focus on how to be faithful. Together, they're like glue. We have over five thousand small groups now. It's the only thing that makes a church this size manageable. Otherwise, I'd work myself to death, and 95 percent of the congregation would never receive the attention they came here looking for."

Without realizing it, Warren, in some ways, has replicated the structure that propelled the Montgomery bus boycott—though he has done it in reverse. That boycott started among people who knew Rosa Parks, and became a mass protest when the weak ties of the community compelled participation. At Saddleback Church, it works the other way around. People are attracted by a sense of community and the weak ties that a congregation offers. Then once inside, they're pushed into a small group of neighbors—a petri dish, if you will, for growing close ties—where their faith becomes an aspect of their social experience and daily lives.

Creating small groups, however, isn't enough. When Warren asked people what 110 they discussed in one another's living rooms, he discovered they talked about the Bible and prayed together for ten minutes, and then spent the rest of the time discussing kids or gossiping. Warren's goal, however, wasn't just to help people make new friends. It was to build a community of the faithful, to encourage people to accept the lessons of Christ, and to make faith a focus of their lives. His small groups had created tight bonds, but without leadership, they weren't much more than a coffee circle. They weren't fulfilling his religious expectations.

Warren thought back to McGavran, the author. McGavran's philosophy said that if you teach people to live with Christian habits, they'll act as Christians without requiring constant guidance and monitoring. Warren couldn't lead every single small group in person; he couldn't be there to make sure every conversation focused on Christ instead of the latest TV shows. But if he gave people new habits, he figured, he wouldn't need to. When people gathered, their instincts would be to discuss the Bible, to pray together, to embody their faith.

So Warren created a series of curriculums, used in church classes and small group discussions, which were explicitly designed to teach parishioners new habits.

"If you want to have Christ-like character, then you just develop the habits that Christ had," one of Saddleback's course manuals reads. "All of us are simply a bundle of habits. . . . Our goal is to help you replace some bad habits with some good habits that will help you grow in Christ's likeness."[29] Every Saddleback member is asked to sign a "maturity covenant card" promising to adhere to three habits: daily quiet time for reflection and prayer, tithing 10 percent of their income, and membership in a small group. Giving everyone new habits has become a focus of the church.

"Once we do that, the responsibility for spiritual growth is no longer with me, it's with you. We've given you a recipe," Warren told me. "We don't have to guide you, because you're guiding yourself. These habits become a new self-identity, and, at that point, we just need to support you and get out of your way."[30]

> **These habits become a new self-identity.**

Warren's insight was that he could expand his church the same way Martin 115 Luther King grew the boycott: by relying on the combination of strong and weak ties. Transforming his church into a movement, however—scaling it across twenty thousand parishioners and thousands of other pastors—required something more, something that made it self-perpetuating. Warren needed to teach people habits that caused them to live faithfully not because of their ties, but because it's who they are.

This is the third aspect of how social habits drive movements: For an idea to grow beyond a community, it must become self-propelling. And the surest way to achieve that is to give people new habits that help them figure out where to go on their own.

As the bus boycott expanded from a few days into a week, and then a month, and then two months, the commitment of Montgomery's black community began to wane.

The police commissioner, citing an ordinance that required taxicabs to charge a minimum fare, threatened to arrest cabbies who drove blacks to work at a discount. The boycott's leaders responded by signing up two hundred volunteers to participate in a carpool. Police started issuing tickets and harassing people at carpool meeting spots. Drivers began dropping out. "It became more and more difficult to catch a ride," King later wrote. "Complaints began to rise. From early morning to late at night my telephone rang and my doorbell was seldom silent. I began to have doubts about the ability of the Negro community to continue the struggle."[31]

One night, while King was preaching at his church, an usher ran up with an urgent message. A bomb had exploded at King's house while his wife and infant daughter were inside. King rushed home and was greeted by a crowd of several hundred blacks as well as the mayor and chief of police. His family had not been injured, but the front windows of his home were shattered and there was a crater in his porch. If anyone had been in the front rooms of the house when the bomb went off, they could have been killed.

As King surveyed the damage, more and more blacks arrived. Policemen started telling the crowds to disperse. Someone shoved a cop. A bottle flew through the air. One of the policemen swung a baton. The police chief, who months earlier had publicly declared his support for the racist White Citizens' Council, pulled King aside and asked him to do something — anything — to stop a riot from breaking out.

King walked to his porch.

"Don't do anything panicky," he shouted to the crowd. "Don't get your weapons. He who lives by the sword shall perish by the sword."[32]

The crowd grew still.

"We must love our white brothers, no matter what they do to us," King said. "We must make them know that we love them. Jesus still cries out in words that echo across the centuries: 'Love your enemies; bless them that curse you; pray for them that despitefully use you.'"

It was the message of nonviolence that King had been increasingly preaching for weeks. Its theme, which drew on the writings of Gandhi and Jesus's sermons, was in many ways an argument listeners hadn't heard in this context before, a plea for nonviolent activism, overwhelming love and forgiveness of their attackers, and a promise that it would bring victory. For years, the civil rights movement had been kept alive by couching itself in the language of battles and struggles. There were contests and setbacks, triumphs and defeats that required everyone to recommit to the fight.

King gave people a new lens. This wasn't a war, he said. It was an embrace.

Equally important, King cast the boycott in a new and different light. This was not just about equality on buses, King said; it was part of God's plan, the same destiny that had ended British colonialism in India and slavery in the United States, and that had caused Christ to die on the cross so that he could take away our sins. It was the newest stage in a movement that had started centuries earlier. And as such, it required new responses, different strategies and behaviors. It needed participants to offer the other cheek. People could show their allegiance by adopting the new habits King was evangelizing about.

"We must meet hate with love," King told the crowd the night of the bombing. "If I am stopped, our work will not stop. For what we are doing is right. What we are doing is just. And God is with us."

When King was done speaking, the crowd quietly walked home.

"If it hadn't been for that nigger preacher," one white policeman later said, "we'd all be dead." 130

The next week, two dozen new drivers signed up for the carpool. The phone calls to King's home slowed. People began self-organizing, taking leadership of the boycott, propelling the movement. When more bombs exploded on the lawns of other boycott organizers, the same pattern played out. Montgomery's blacks showed up en masse, bore witness without violence or confrontation, and then went home.

It wasn't just in response to violence that this self-directed unity became visible. The churches started holding mass meetings every week—sometimes every night. "They were kind of like Dr. King's speech after the bombing—they took Christian teachings and made them political," Taylor Branch told me. "A movement is a saga. For it to work, everyone's identity has to change. People in Montgomery had to learn a new way to act."

Much like Alcoholics Anonymous—which draws power from group meetings where addicts learn new habits and start to believe by watching others demonstrate their faith—so Montgomery's citizens learned in mass meetings new behaviors that expanded the movement. "People went to see how other people were handling it," said Branch. "You start to see yourself as part of a vast social enterprise, and after a while, you really believe you are."

When the Montgomery police resorted to mass arrests to stop the boycott three months after it started, the community embraced the oppression. When ninety people were indicted by a grand jury, almost all of them rushed to the courthouse to present themselves for arrest. Some people went to the sheriff's office to see if their names were on the list and were "disappointed when they were not," King later wrote. "A once fear-ridden people had been transformed."

In future years, as the movement spread and there were waves of killings and 135 attacks, arrests and beatings, the protesters—rather than fighting back, retreating, or using tactics that in the years before Montgomery had been activist mainstays—simply stood their ground and told white vigilantes that they were ready to forgive them when their hatred had ceased.

"Instead of stopping the movement, the opposition's tactics had only served to give it greater momentum, and to draw us closer together," King wrote. "They thought they were dealing with a group who could be cajoled or forced to do whatever the white man wanted them to do. They were not aware that they were dealing with Negroes who had been freed from fear."

There are, of course, numerous and complex reasons why the Montgomery bus boycott succeeded and why it became the spark for a movement that would spread across the South. But one critical factor is this third aspect of social habits. Embedded within King's philosophy was a set of new behaviors that converted participants from followers into self-directing leaders. These are not habits as we conventionally think about them. However, when King recast Montgomery's struggle by giving protesters a new sense of self-identity, the protest became a movement fueled by people who were acting because they had taken ownership of a historic event. And that social pattern, over time, became automatic and expanded to other places and groups of students and protesters whom King never met, but who could take on leadership of the movement simply by watching how its participants habitually behaved.

On June 5, 1956, a panel of federal judges ruled that Montgomery's bus segregation law violated the Constitution.[33] The city appealed to the U.S. Supreme Court and on December 17, more than a year after Parks was arrested, the highest court rejected the final appeal. Three days later, city officials received the order. The buses had to be integrated.

The next morning, at 5:55 AM, King, E. D. Nixon, Ralph Abernathy, and others climbed on board a city bus for the first time in more than twelve months, and sat in the front.[34]

"I believe you are Reverend King, aren't you?" asked the white driver.   140

"Yes, I am."

"We are very glad to have you this morning," the driver said.[35]

Later, NAACP attorney and future Supreme Court justice Thurgood Marshall would claim that the boycott had little to do with ending bus segregation in Montgomery. It was the Supreme Court, not capitulation by either side, that changed the law.

"All that walking for nothing," Marshall said. "They could just as well have waited while the bus case went up through the courts, without all the work and worry of the boycott."[36]

Marshall, however, was wrong in one important respect. The Montgomery bus   145 boycott helped birth a new set of social habits that quickly spread to Greensboro, North Carolina; Selma, Alabama; and Little Rock, Arkansas. The civil rights movement became a wave of sit-ins and peaceful demonstrations, even as participants were violently beaten. By the early 1960s, it had moved to Florida, California, Washington, D.C., and the halls of Congress. When President Lyndon Johnson signed the Civil Rights Act of 1964 — which outlawed all forms of segregation as well as discrimination against minorities and women — he equated the civil rights activists to the nation's founders, a comparison that, a decade earlier, would have been political suicide. "One hundred and eighty-eight years ago this week, a small band of valiant men began a long struggle for freedom," he told television cameras. "Now our generation of Americans has been called on to continue the unending search for justice within our own borders."

Movements don't emerge because everyone suddenly decides to face the same direction at once. They rely on social patterns that begin as the habits of friendship, grow through the habits of communities, and are sustained by new habits that change participants' sense of self.

King saw the power of these habits as early as Montgomery. "I cannot close without giving just a word of caution," he told a packed church on the night he called off the boycott. There was still almost a decade of protest ahead of him, but the end was in sight. "As we go back to the buses let us be loving enough to turn an enemy into a friend. We must now move from protest to reconciliation. . . . With this dedication we will be able to emerge from the bleak and desolate midnight of man's inhumanity to man to the bright and glittering daybreak of freedom and justice."

NOTES

1. For my understanding of the Montgomery bus boycott, I am indebted to those historians who have made themselves available to me, including John A. Kirk and Taylor Branch. My understanding of these events also draws on John A. Kirk, *Martin Luther King, Jr.: Profiles in Power* (New York: Longman, 2004); Taylor Branch, *Parting the Waters: America in the King Years, 1954–63* (New York: Simon and Schuster, 1988); Taylor Branch, *Pillar of Fire: America in the King Years, 1963–65* (New York: Simon and Schuster, 1998); Taylor Branch, *At Canaan's Edge: America in the King Years, 1965–68* (New York: Simon and Schuster, 2006); Douglas Brinkley, *Mine Eyes Have Seen the Glory: The Life of Rosa Parks* (London: Weidenfeld and Nicolson, 2000); Martin Luther King, Jr., *Stride Toward Freedom: The Montgomery Story* (New York: Harper and Brothers, 1958); Clayborne Carson, ed. *The Papers of Martin Luther King, Jr.*, vol. 1, *Called to Serve* (Berkeley: University of California, 1992), vol. 2, *Rediscovering Precious Values* (1994), vol. 3, *Birth of a New Age* (1997), vol. 4, *Symbol of the Movement* (2000), vol. 5, *Threshold of a New Decade* (2005); Aldon D. Morris, *The Origins of the Civil Rights Movement* (New York: Free Press, 1986); James Forman, *The Making of Black Revolutionaries* (Seattle: University of Washington, 1997). Where not cited, facts draw primarily from those sources.
2. Henry Hampton and Steve Fayer, eds., *Voices of Freedom: An Oral History of the Civil Rights Movement from the 1950s Through the 1980s* (New York: Bantam Books, 1995); Rosa Parks, *Rosa Parks: My Story* (New York: Puffin, 1999).
3. John A. Kirk, *Martin Luther King, Jr.: Profiles in Power* (New York: Longman, 2004).
4. For more on the sociology of movements, see G. Davis, D. McAdam, and W. Scott, *Social Movements and Organizations* (New York: Cambridge University, 2005); Robert Crain and Rita Mahard, "The Consequences of Controversy Accompanying Institutional Change: The Case of School Desegregation," *American Sociological Review* 47, no. 6 (1982): 697–708; Azza Salama Layton, "International Pressure and the U.S. Government's Response to Little Rock," *Arkansas Historical Quarterly* 56, no. 3 (1997): 257–72; Brendan Nelligan, "The Albany Movement and the Limits of Nonviolent Protest in Albany, Georgia, 1961–1962," Providence College Honors Thesis, 2009; Charles Tilly, *Social Movements, 1768–2004* (London: Paradigm, 2004); Andrew Walder, "Political Sociology and Social Movements," *Annual Review of Sociology* 35 (2009): 393–412; Paul Almeida, *Waves of Protest: Popular Struggle in El Salvador, 1925–2005* (Minneapolis: University of Minnesota, 2008); Robert Benford, "An Insider's Critique of the Social Movement Framing Perspective," *Sociological Inquiry* 67, no. 4 (1997): 409–30; Robert Benford and David Snow, "Framing Processes and Social Movements: An Overview and Assessment," *Annual Review of Sociology* 26 (2000): 611–39; Michael Burawoy, *Manufacturing Consent: Changes in the Labor Process Under Monopoly Capitalism* (Chicago: University of Chicago, 1979); Carol Conell and Kim Voss, "Formal Organization and the Fate of Social Movements: Craft Association and Class Alliance in the Knights of Labor," *American Sociological Review* 55, no. 2 (1990): 255–69; James Davies, "Toward a Theory of Revolution," *American Sociological Review* 27, no. 1 (1962): 5–18; William Gamson, *The Strategy of Social Protest* (Homewood, Ill.: Dorsey, 1975); Jeff Goodwin, *No Other Way Out: States and Revolutionary Movements, 1945–1991* (New York: Cambridge University, 2001); Jeff Goodwin and James Jasper, eds.,

Rethinking Social Movements: Structure, Meaning, and Emotion (Lanham, Md.: Rowman and Littlefield, 2003); Roger Gould, "Multiple Networks and Mobilization in the Paris Commune, 1871," *American Sociological Review* 56, no. 6 (1991): 716–29; Joseph Gusfield, "Social Structure and Moral Reform: A Study of the Woman's Christian Temperance Union," *American Journal of Sociology* 61, no. 3 (1955): 221–31; Doug McAdam, *Political Process and the Development of Black Insurgency, 1930–1970* (Chicago: University of Chicago, 1982); Doug McAdam, "Recruitment to High-Risk Activism: The Case of Freedom Summer," *American Journal of Sociology* 92, no. 1 (1986): 64–90; Doug McAdam, "The Biographical Consequences of Activism," *American Sociological Review* 54, no. 5 (1989): 744–60; Doug McAdam, "Conceptual Origins, Current Problems, Future Directions," in *Comparative Perspectives on Social Movements: Political Opportunities, Mobilizing Structures, and Cultural Framings*, ed. Doug McAdam, John McCarthy, and Mayer Zald (New York: Cambridge University, 1996); Doug McAdam and Ronnelle Paulsen, "Specifying the Relationship Between Social Ties and Activism," *American Journal of Sociology* 99, no. 3 (1993): 640–67; D. McAdam, S. Tarrow, and C. Tilly, *Dynamics of Contention* (Cambridge: Cambridge University, 2001); Judith Stepan-Norris and Judith Zeitlin, " 'Who Gets the Bird?' or, How the Communists Won Power and Trust in America's Unions," *American Sociological Review* 54, no. 4 (1989): 503–23; Charles Tilly, *From Mobilization to Revolution* (Reading, Mass.: Addison-Wesley, 1978).

5. Phillip Hoose, *Claudette Colvin: Twice Toward Justice* (New York: Farrar, Straus and Giroux, 2009).

6. Ibid.

7. Russell Freedman, *Freedom Walkers: The Story of the Montgomery Bus Boycott* (New York: Holiday House, 2009).

8. Martin Luther King, Jr., *Stride Toward Freedom* (New York: Harper and Brothers, 1958).

9. Taylor Branch, *Parting the Waters: America in the King Years, 1954–63* (New York: Simon and Schuster, 1988).

10. Douglas Brinkley, *Mine Eyes Have Seen the Glory: The Life of Rosa Parks* (London: Weidenfeld and Nicolson, 2000).

11. John A. Kirk, *Martin Luther King, Jr.: Profiles in Power* (New York: Longman, 2004).

12. Carson, *Papers of Martin Luther King, Jr.*

13. Mark Granovetter, *Getting a Job: A Study of Contacts and Careers* (Chicago: University of Chicago; 1974).

14. Andreas Flache and Michael Macy, "The Weakness of Strong Ties: Collective Action Failure in a Highly Cohesive Group," *Journal of Mathematical Sociology* 21 (1996): 3–28. For more on this topic, see Robert Axelrod, *The Evolution of Cooperation* (New York: Basic Books, 1984); Robert Bush and Frederick Mosteller, *Stochastic Models for Learning* (New York: Wiley, 1984); I. Erev, Y. Bereby-Meyer, and A. E. Roth, "The Effect of Adding a Constant to All Payoffs: Experimental Investigation and Implications for Reinforcement Learning Models," *Journal of Economic Behavior and Organization* 39, no. 1 (1999): 111–28; A. Flache and R. Hegselmann, "Rational vs. Adaptive Egoism in Support Networks: How Different Micro Foundations Shape Different Macro Hypotheses," in *Game Theory, Experience, Rationality: Foundations of Social Sciences, Economics, and Ethics in Honor of John C. Harsanyi (Yearbook of the Institute Vienna Circle)*, ed. W. Leinfellner and E. Köhler (Boston: Kluwer, 1997), 261–75; A. Flache and R. Hegselmann, "Rationality vs. Learning in the Evolution of Solidarity Networks: A Theoretical Comparison," *Computational and Mathematical Organization Theory* 5, no. 2 (1999): 97–127; A. Flache and R. Hegselmann, "Dynamik Sozialer Dilemma-Situationen," final research report of the DFG-Project Dynamics of Social Dilemma Situations,

University of Bayreuth, Department of Philosophie, 2000; A. Flache and Michael Macy, "Stochastic Collusion and the Power Law of Learning," *Journal of Conflict Resolution* 46, no. 5 (2002): 629–53; Michael Macy, "Learning to Cooperate: Stochastic and Tacit Collusion in Social Exchange," *American Journal of Sociology* 97, no. 3 (1991): 808–43; E. P. H. Zeggelink, "Evolving Friendship Networks: An Individual-Oriented Approach Implementing Similarity," *Social Networks* 17 (1996): 83–110; Judith Blau, "When Weak Ties Are Structured," unpublished manuscript, Department of Sociology, State University of New York, Albany, 1980; Peter Blau, "Parameters of Social Structure," *American Sociological Review* 39, no. 5 (1974): 615–35; Scott Boorman, "A Combinatorial Optimization Model for Transmission of Job Information Through Contact Networks," *Bell Journal of Economics* 6, no. 1 (1975): 216–49; Ronald Breiger and Philippa Pattison, "The Joint Role Structure of Two Communities' Elites," *Sociological Methods and Research* 7, no. 2 (1978): 213–26; Daryl Chubin, "The Conceptualization of Scientific Specialties," *Sociological Quarterly* 17, no. 4 (1976): 448–76; Harry Collins, "The TEA Set: Tacit Knowledge and Scientific Networks," *Science Studies* 4, no. 2 (1974): 165–86; Rose Coser, "The Complexity of Roles as Seedbed of Individual Autonomy," in *The Idea of Social Structure: Essays in Honor of Robert Merton*, ed. L. Coser (New York: Harcourt, 1975); John Delany, "Aspects of Donative Resource Allocation and the Efficiency of Social Networks: Simulation Models of Job Vacancy Information Transfers Through Personal Contacts," Ph.D. diss., Yale University, 1980; E. Ericksen and W. Yancey, "The Locus of Strong Ties," unpublished manuscript, Department of Sociology, Temple University, 1980.

15. Mark Granovetter, "The Strength of Weak Ties: A Network Theory Revisited," *Sociological Theory* 1 (1983): 201–33.

16. McAdam, "Recruitment to High-Risk Activism."

17. Ibid.; Paulsen," Specifying the Relationship Between Social Ties and Activism."

18. In a fact-checking email, McAdam provided a few details about the study's genesis: "My initial interest was in trying to understand the links between the civil rights movement and the other early new left movements, specifically the student movement, the anti-war movement, and women's liberation movement. It was only after I found the applications and realized that some were from volunteers and others from 'no shows' that I got interested in explaining (a) why some made it to Mississippi and others didn't, and (b) the longer term impact of going/not-going on the two groups."

19. In another fact-checking email, McAdam wrote: "For me the significance of the organizational ties is not that they make it 'impossible' for the volunteer to withdraw, but that they insure that the applicant will likely receive lots of support for the link between the salient identity in question (i.e., Christian) and participation in the summer project. As I noted in [an article] 'it is a strong subjective identification with a particular identity, *reinforced by organizational ties* that is especially likely to encourage participation.'"

20. Tom Mathews and Roy Wilkins, *Standing Fast: The Autobiography of Roy Wilkins* (Cambridge, Mass.: Da Capo, 1994).

21. Branch, *Parting the Waters.*

22. King, *Stride Toward Freedom;* James M. Washington, *A Testament of Hope: The Essential Writings and Speeches of Martin Luther King, Jr.* (New York: HarperCollins, 1990).

23. King, *Stride Toward Freedom.*

24. For understanding Pastor Warren's story, I am indebted to Rick Warren, Glenn Kruen, Steve Gladen, Jeff Sheler, Anne Krumm, and the following books: Jeffrey Sheler, *Prophet of Purpose: The Life of Rick Warren* (New York: Doubleday, 2009); Rick Warren, *The Purpose-Driven Church* (Grand Rapids, Mich.: Zondervan, 1995); and the following

articles: Barbara Bradley, "Marketing That New-Time Religion," *Los Angeles Times*, December 10, 1995; John Wilson, "Not Just Another Mega Church," *Christianity Today*, December 4, 2000; "Therapy of the Masses," *The Economist*, November 6, 2003; "The Glue of Society," *The Economist*, July 14, 2005; Malcolm Gladwell, "The Cellular Church," *The New Yorker*, September 12, 2005; Alex MacLeod, "Rick Warren: A Heart for the Poor," *Presbyterian Record*, January 1, 2008; Andrew, Ann, and John Kuzma, "How Religion Has Embraced Marketing and the Implications for Business," *Journal of Management and Marketing Research* 2 (2009): 1–10.

25. Warren, *Purpose-Driven Church*.

26. Donald McGavran, *The Bridges of God* (New York: Friendship Press, 1955). Italics added.

27. Sheler, *Prophet of Purpose*.

28. In a fact-checking email a Saddleback spokesperson, provided additional details: "Rick suffers from a brain chemistry disorder that makes him allergic to adrenaline. This genetic problem resists medication and makes public speaking painful, with blurred vision, headaches, hot flashes, and panic. Symptoms usually last around fifteen minutes; by that time, enough adrenaline is expended so the body can return to normal function. (His adrenaline rushes, like any speaker might experience, whenever he gets up to preach.) Pastor Rick says this weakness keeps him dependent on God."

29. *Discovering Spiritual Maturity*, Class 201, published by Saddleback Church, http://www.saddlebackresources.com/CLASS-201-Discovering-Spiritual-Maturity-Complete-Kit-Downoad-P3532.aspx.

30. In a fact-checking email a Saddleback spokesperson said that while an important tenet of Saddleback is teaching people to guide themselves, "this implies that each person can go in any direction they choose. Biblical principles/guidelines have a clear direction. The goal of small group study is to teach people the spiritual disciplines of faith *and* everyday habits that can be applied to daily life."

31. Martin Luther King, Jr., *The Autobiography of Martin Luther King, Jr.*, ed. Clayborne Carson (New York: Grand Central, 2001).

32. Carson; King,

33. *Browder v. Gayle*, 352 U.S. 903 (1956).

34. Washington, *Testament of Hope*.

35. Kirk, *Martin Luther King, Jr.*

36. Ibid.

Exploring Context

1. Explore the Web site for Saddleback Church at saddleback.com. How does the Web site reflect the role that strong and weak ties continue to play in the church? Use your response to expand your answer to Question 1 of Questions for Critical Reading.

2. Visit the Web site for the Rosa Parks Museum at www.troy.edu/rosaparks/museum/. Does the museum record the sorts of connections that Duhigg claims were at the center of Parks's experience?

3. Review your list of friends on Facebook or another social media site. How many of these relationships would you consider strong ties? How many would you consider weak ties? How might you expect these people to act if you had an experience similar to that of Rosa Parks?

Questions for Connecting

1. Apply Maria Konnikova's work in "The Limits of Friendship" (p. 236) to Duhigg's argument. What effect might the Dunbar number have on social habits and peer pressure? Does the "rule of three" help determine the line between strong ties and weak ties? How does social media change the quantity and quality of our connections, and how might these changes in turn influence the process of social change? Use your work from Question 3 of Exploring Context in composing your response.

2. Duhigg examines the process of social change, specifically the Montgomery bus boycott and the explosive growth of Saddleback Church. How might Duhigg's insights be applied to the HIV epidemic in Africa, as explored by Helen Epstein in "AIDS, Inc." (p. 110)? Is social cohesion a form of peer pressure? Could South Africa use strong and weak ties in its HIV prevention campaigns?

3. The forces at work in the events that Duhigg examines seem quite similar to the forces Bill Wasik harnesses to create flash mobs, as explained in "My Crowd Experiment: The Mob Project" (p. 474). Does peer pressure always change social habits? Do strong and weak ties necessarily create social change? Noting the differences between group action in Duhigg and Wasik, what would you argue is the key factor in harnessing groups to create social change? Use your response to Question 3 of Questions for Critical Reading to support your argument.

Language Matters

1. Review the rules for verb tense in a grammar handbook or other reference resource. Then select two key quotations from Duhigg and change the tenses of the verbs. What difference does tense make to an argument? What are the conventions for verb tense in academic writing?

2. Apostrophes indicate possession. Go through Duhigg's text and locate some examples of the apostrophe, which is perhaps one of the most frequently misunderstood marks of punctuation. Given that an apostrophe is a kind of "tie," how might Duhigg's discussion explain the frequent misuse of this punctuation mark? What are the complexities of "possession" in today's world, in writing and in reality?

3. What counts as evidence for Duhigg? Reread his essay, noting the kinds of evidence he uses to support his argument. How would you categorize each? What is the strongest evidence? The weakest? Which kinds of evidence should you use to support your own argument?

Assignments for Writing

1. In this essay Duhigg is most concerned with examining the effects of peer pressure in the specific cases of the Montgomery bus boycott and the growth of Saddleback Church. Write a paper in which you apply Duhigg's ideas to your own example of social change. Does your example illustrate the power of strong and weak ties to create change or does it instead indicate the limits of these connections?

2. What are the risks of peer pressure? Duhigg primarily looks at the benefits of this social force. Write a paper in which you explore instead some of its negative effects. Consider using your experiences from Question 2 of Questions for Critical Reading.

3. According to Duhigg, strong and weak ties work to change social habits and thus create social change. Write a paper in which you consider instead the ways in which these same forces create personal change. How did social habit create individual change for the members of Saddleback Church? What personal changes did people make from peer pressure in the course of the civil rights movement?

HELEN EPSTEIN

Photo by Peter Peter, courtesy of Helen Epstein

After earning a Ph.D. in molecular biology from Cambridge University, **Helen Epstein** attended the London School of Hygiene and Tropical Medicine, where she earned an M.Sc. in public health in developing countries. In 1993, while working as a scientist for a biotechnology company in search of an AIDS vaccine, Epstein moved to Uganda, where she witnessed the suffering caused by the virus. Epstein still works in public health care in developing countries. She has published articles in magazines such as the *New York Review of Books* and in 2007 published her book, *The Invisible Cure: Africa, the West, and the Fight against AIDS.*

Epstein compiled the information she had gathered in her years as a scientist in Africa, along with her personal observations, to write *The Invisible Cure.* In it she explores the reasons behind the unprecedented AIDS epidemic in Africa and suggests ways to reduce infection rates on that continent. Along the way she corrects the misinformation and misconceptions that Westerners have been using as a guide for aiding Africans who suffer from or are at risk for HIV/AIDS. She points out that programs for prevention might need to be in the hands of Africans themselves in order to account for local cultures. For instance, while campaigns promoting condom usage might be successful in Western countries, this does not mean such campaigns will succeed within other cultures. Instead, listening to and understanding the traditions and customs of individual cultures might lead to more successful approaches to the AIDS epidemic.

In "AIDS, Inc.," a chapter from *The Invisible Cure*, Epstein examines HIV and AIDS prevention programs in Africa. In South Africa, Epstein witnesses a government-run campaign that focuses on creating conversations about sexual activity among the nation's youth in order to help them make informed decisions about sex. However, many of the conversations stop there, leaving out any talk of people who already have AIDS. While the campaign may open up new avenues for youth in terms of sexual responsibility and respect, the lack of conversation surrounding AIDS perpetuates the social stigmas of infected peoples as well as an "out of sight, out of mind" attitude toward the virus. Perhaps, as Epstein points out, campaigns are only as successful as the conversations surrounding them. She points to Uganda — one of the few countries in Africa where the rate of infection has dropped precipitously — as an example of effective conversation. Open conversation among Ugandans about personal experiences with the virus has succeeded in preventing its spread by breaking the cycle of social stigmas surrounding those infected.

What social stigmas concerning HIV and AIDS exist locally and globally? How do these social stigmas interfere with campaigns to successfully prevent the spread of the virus? How might class, race, gender, and religion contribute to the way prevention is approached? While Epstein points out how important conversation is among communities, is it possible to create a global conversation about HIV and AIDS?

▶ TAGS: *adolescence and adulthood, collaboration, community, conversation, culture, education, globalism, health and medicine, judgment and decision-making, media, politics, sexuality, social change*

▶ CONNECTIONS: *Appiah, Duhigg, Southan, Yoshino*

Questions for Critical Reading

1. What is a *lifestyle brand*? Make note of the definition of the term as you read Epstein's text. Then find an example of a lifestyle brand from popular culture. How might such an approach be used in health education? How effective might it be? How effective was it in South Africa?

2. Define *social cohesion* using Epstein's text. What role did it play in HIV infection rates in Uganda? How might that role be extended to other countries, including the United States?

3. What do you think would make an effective HIV prevention program for the United States? Compare your vision to Epstein's and her observations on such programs in Africa. Would the same strategies be effective in those two different cultural contexts? Support your responses with passages from the essay.

AIDS, Inc.

In response to government prevarication over HIV treatment, a vigorous AIDS activist movement emerged in South Africa and a fierce public relations battle ensued. The Treatment Action Campaign, or TAC, along with other activist groups, accused the South African health minister, Manto Tshabalala-Msimang, of "murder" for denying millions of South Africans access to medicine for AIDS. A spokesman from the ANC Youth League then called the activists "paid marketing agents for toxic AIDS drugs from America."[1] An official in the Department of Housing accused journalists who defended the AIDS activists of fanaticism, and quoted Lenin* on how the "press in bourgeois society . . . deceive[s], corrupt[s], and fool[s] the exploited and oppressed mass of the people, the poor."

Meanwhile, across the nation thousands of people were becoming infected daily, from the rural homesteads of the former Bantustans† to the peri-urban townships and squatter camps to the formerly all-white suburbs, now home to a growing black middle class. By 2005, the death rate for young adults had tripled.[2] Surveys showed that nearly everyone in South Africa knew that HIV was sexually transmitted and that it could be prevented with condoms, abstinence, and faithfulness to an uninfected partner. Children were receiving AIDS education in school and condoms were widely available,

---

*Lenin: Vladimir Lenin (1870–1924), a chief figure in the Russian revolution of 1917 (which led to the communist takeover); Lenin was the first head of the USSR [Ed.].

†Bantustans: Areas in South Africa where the black population was kept separate from whites during the policy of apartheid, or racial segregation, in the twentieth century [Ed.].

but these programs made little difference. In the din of the battle between the activists and the government, the deeper message, that HIV was everyone's problem, was lost.

In 1999, a group of public health experts sponsored by the U.S.-based Kaiser Family Foundation stepped into this fray. They were concerned about the worsening AIDS crisis in South Africa and wanted to launch a bold new HIV prevention program for young people. They also knew they had to take account of the South African government's attitudes toward AIDS and AIDS activists. Their program, called loveLife, would soon become South Africa's largest and most ambitious HIV prevention campaign. It aimed both to overcome the limitations of similar campaigns that had failed in the past and, at the same time, to avoid dealing with the issues of AIDS treatment and care that had become so controversial.

Could this work? I wondered. Was it possible to reduce the spread of HIV without involving HIV-positive people and the activists and community groups that supported them? LoveLife had been endorsed at one time or another by the archbishop of Cape Town; Nelson Mandela; the king of the Zulu tribe; Jacob Zuma, South Africa's former deputy president; and even Zanele Mbeki, the wife of the president. In 2003, loveLife's annual $20 million budget was paid for by the South African government, the Kaiser Family Foundation, UNICEF, the Bill and Melinda Gates Foundation, and the Global Fund to Fight AIDS, Tuberculosis, and Malaria. At least South Africa's leaders were beginning to take AIDS seriously, I thought, but what kind of program was this?

"What we want to do is create a substantive, normative shift in the way young people   5
behave," explained loveLife's director, David Harrison, a white South African doctor, when I met him in his Johannesburg office. The average age at which young South Africans lose their virginity — around seventeen — is not much different from the age at which teenagers in other countries do. What's different, Harrison said, was that many of the young South Africans who were sexually active were very sexually active. They were more likely to start having sex at very young ages, even below the age of fourteen — well below the national average. Those vulnerable young people were more likely to have more than one sexual partner, and they were less likely to use condoms. South African girls were more likely to face sexual coercion or rape, or to exchange sex for money or gifts, all of which placed them at greater risk of HIV infection. For Harrison, the trick was to "get inside the head-space of these young people . . . we have to understand what is driving them into sex — they know what HIV is, but they don't internalize it," he said.

LoveLife's aim was to get young people talking, to each other and to their parents, so they would really understand and act on what they knew. But to reach out to them, you had to use a special language that young people could relate to. According to Harrison, traditional HIV prevention campaigns were too depressing: They tried to scare people into changing their behavior, and this turned kids off. LoveLife's media campaign, on the other hand, was positive and cheerful, and resembled the bright, persuasive modern ad campaigns that many South African kids were very much attracted to.

In the past couple of years, nearly a thousand loveLife billboards had sprouted all along the nation's main roads. They were striking. For example, on one of them, the hands of four women of different races caressed the sculpted back and buttocks of a young black man as though they were appraising an antique newel post. The caption read, "Everyone he's slept with, is sleeping with you." On another, a gorgeous mixed-race couple—the boy looked like Brad Pitt, the girl like an Indian film star—lay in bed, under the caption "No Pressure." Some people told me they found these ads oversexualized and disturbing, but it is hard to see why. On the same roads, there are torsos advertising sexy underwear and half-naked actresses advertising romantic movies. Sex is a potent theme in marketing all sorts of products; loveLife, according to its creators, tries to turn that message around to get young people thinking and talking about sex in more responsible ways and convince them of the virtues of abstinence, fidelity, and the use of condoms.

Harrison calls loveLife "a brand of positive lifestyle." The sexy billboards and similar ads on TV and radio, as well as newspaper inserts that resemble teen gossip magazines, with articles and advice columns about clothes, relationships, and sexual health, were designed, Harrison says, to persuade young people to avoid sex in the same way a sneaker ad tries to seduce them into buying new sneakers, because the players in the ads look so cool. The idea is "to create a brand so strong that young people who want to be hip and cool and the rest of it want to associate with it," Harrison told an interviewer in 2001.[3]

The concept of a "lifestyle brand" originated with the rise of brand advertising in the 1960s, when ads for such products as Pepsi-Cola and Harley-Davidson began to promote not only soft drinks and motorcycles, but also a certain style or aesthetic. People were urged to "join the Pepsi generation" or ride a Harley-Davidson not just to get around, but to embrace a certain attitude. A Harley wasn't just a bike; it was a macho rebellion, an escape from the workaday world to the open road. In the 1970s, family-planning programs also tried to promote contraceptives in developing countries by tapping into poor people's

> **Harrison calls loveLife "a brand of positive lifestyle."**

aspirations for a glamorous Western lifestyle. Campaigns depicted small, well-dressed families surrounded by sleek new commodities, including televisions and cars. Harrison predicted that young South Africans would readily respond to this approach too.

"Kids have changed," Harrison explained. Today's young South Africans weren't like the activists who risked their lives in the anti-apartheid demonstrations at Sharpeville and Soweto. "Seventy-five percent of South African teenagers watch TV every day," Harrison informed me. "Their favorite program is *The Bold and the Beautiful*"—an American soap opera in which glamorous characters struggle with personal crises while wearing and driving some very expensive gear. "They are exposed to the global youth culture of music, fashion, pop icons, and commercial brands. They talk about brands among themselves, even if they can't afford everything they see."

The Kaiser Foundation's Michael Sinclair told me that loveLife drew much of its inspiration from the marketing campaign for the soft drink Sprite.[4] In the mid-1990s, sales of Sprite were flagging until the company began an aggressive campaign to embed Sprite in youth culture by sponsoring hip-hop concerts and planting attractive, popular kids in Internet chat rooms or college dormitories and paying them to praise or distribute Sprite in an unobtrusive way. Sprite is now one of the most profitable drinks in the world because it managed to exploit what marketing experts call "the cool effect" — meaning the influence that a small number of opinion leaders can have on the norms and behavior of large numbers of their peers. So far, corporate marketers had made the greatest use of the cool effect, but there was speculation that small numbers of trendsetters could change more complex behavior than shopping, such as criminality, suicide, and sexual behavior.[5]

For this reason, loveLife had established a small network of recreation centers for young people, known as Y-Centers, throughout the country. At Y-Centers, young people could learn to play basketball, volleyball, and other sports, as well as learn break dancing, radio broadcasting, and word processing. All Y-Center activities were led by "loveLife GroundBreakers" — older youths, usually in their early twenties, who, like the kids who made Sprite cool, were stylish and cheerful and enthusiastic about their product, in this case, loveLife and its program to encourage safer sexual behavior. If abstinence, monogamy, and condoms all happened to fail, each Y-Center was affiliated with a family-planning clinic that offered contraceptives and treatment for sexually transmitted diseases such as syphilis and gonorrhea. The centers offered no treatment for AIDS symptoms, however, and when I visited, none of them offered HIV testing either.

Any young person could become a Y-Center member, but in order to fully participate in its activities, he or she had to complete a program of seminars about HIV, family planning, and other subjects related to sexuality and growing up. The seminars emphasized the biological aspects of HIV and its prevention, but not the experience of the disease and its effects on people's lives. Members also received training to raise their self-esteem, because, as Harrison told an interviewer in 2001,

> there is a direct correlation between young people's sexual behavior and their sense of confidence in the future. Those young people who feel motivated, who feel that they have something to look forward to — they are the ones who protect themselves, who ensure that they do not get HIV/AIDS. . . . It's all about the social discount rates that young people apply to future benefits.[6]

Dr. Harrison arranged for me to visit a loveLife Y-Center in the archipelago of townships in the flat scrubland south of Johannesburg known as the Vaal Triangle. Millions of people live in these townships, many of them recent migrants from rural South Africa or from neighboring countries. The Vaal, once a patchwork of white-owned farms, is now a residential area for poor blacks. At first, only a few families moved here, because the apartheid government used the notorious pass laws to restrict the tide of impoverished blacks seeking a better life in Johannesburg. But when the apartheid laws were scrapped, people poured in. Today, the roads and other services in the area are insufficient for its huge and growing population, and many people have no electricity and lack easy access to clean water and sanitation. Unemployment exceeds 70 percent and the crime rate is one of the highest in South Africa.[7]

The loveLife Y-Center was a compound of two small lavender buildings surrounded by an iron fence and curling razor wire. Inside the compound, a group of young men in shorts and T-shirts were doing warm-up exercises on the outdoor basketball court, while girls and barefoot children looked on. Inside the main building, another group of boys in fashionably droopy jeans and dreadlocks practiced a hip-hop routine, and two girls in the computer room experimented with Microsoft Word.

15

Valentine's Day was coming up, and the Y-Center had organized a group discussion for some of its members. About thirty teenagers, most of them in school uniforms, sat around on the floor of a large seminar room and argued about who should pay for what on a Valentine's Day date. A GroundBreaker in a loveLife T-shirt and with a loveLife kerchief tied pirate-style on her head officiated. "I go with my chick and I spend money on her and always we have sex," said a husky boy in a gray school uniform. "And I want to know, what's the difference between my chick and a prostitute?" As we have seen, long-term transactional relationships—in which money or gifts are frequently exchanged—may not be the same as prostitution, but they nevertheless put many township youths at risk of HIV.[8]

"Boys, they are expecting too much from us. They say we are parasites if we don't sleep with them," said a plump girl in the uniform of a local Catholic school.

"The girls, they ask for a lot of things," another boy chimed in.

"Me, I think it is wrong. If most of the boys think Valentine's Day is about buying sex, the boys must stop," a girl said. "We girls must hold our ground."

These young people were certainly talking openly about sexual relationships all right, just as Harrison prescribed. Nevertheless, I felt something was missing. "Do you ever talk about AIDS in those discussion groups?" I asked the GroundBreaker afterward. "We do it indirectly," she replied. "We know that if we just came out and started lecturing them about AIDS, they wouldn't listen. They would just turn off. So we talk about positive things, like making informed choices, sharing responsibility, and positive sexuality." 20

Was this true? Do young people in South Africa, like their politicians, really want to avoid the subject of AIDS? I wanted to meet young people outside the Y-Center and ask them what they thought about that. A few hundred yards away from the Y-Center stood the headquarters of St. Charles Lwanga, a Catholic organization that carries out a number of activities in the township. Their AIDS program, called Inkanyezi, meaning "star" in Zulu, provides counseling to young people about AIDS and also brings food and other necessities to some four hundred orphans and people living with AIDS in the Vaal.

St. Charles Lwanga was independent of loveLife, and its budget was modest, less than a tenth of what loveLife spent on its billboards alone. The Inkanyezi program was staffed almost entirely by volunteers, whose only compensation was that they were allowed to eat some of the food—usually rice and vegetables—that they prepared for the patients. Lack of funding greatly limited the help that Inkanyezi was able to provide. Although Inkanyezi nurses were able to dispense tuberculosis medicine, antiretroviral drugs were as yet unavailable. Indeed, many of the patients they visited lacked some of the most basic necessities for life and human dignity. Sometimes destitute patients had their water and electricity cut off. But the worst thing was that many of the patients were socially isolated and lived alone in flimsy shacks. The doors were easily broken down and at night neighborhood thugs sometimes came in and stole what little they had. Sometimes the patients were raped.

Justice Showalala, who ran Inkanyezi, organized a meeting for me with a group of about twenty-five young people from Orange Farm. The HIV rate in the area was not known, but several people explained to me how their lives had been changed by the virus. They said they had witnessed extreme prejudice and discrimination against people with AIDS, and they did not know where to turn when they learned that a relative or friend was HIV positive. "People say you shouldn't touch someone with HIV," said one girl. "I have a friend at school who disclosed she has HIV, and the others won't even walk with her." Justice explained how he had offered to introduce some teachers from a local school to some of his HIV-positive clients. "They said, 'If you want me to meet people with AIDS, you better give me a rubber suit.'"

The loveLife Y-Center did little to help young people deal with such confusion, stigma, and shame. "I learned basketball at the Y-Center," one girl told me, "and at meetings we talked about resisting peer pressure, [like when] your friends advise you to break your virginity, to prove you are girl enough. But I was afraid the people there would find out my sister had HIV. We talked about it as though it was someone else's problem."

In general, although sex was openly discussed at the Y-Center, the experience of AIDS was not. The Y-Center offered individual counseling for a small number of young people with HIV, but those who were hungry, homeless, or destitute, or were suffering from the symptoms of AIDS, were told to consult other organizations, including Inkanyezi.

It turns out that talking about the pain, both physical and emotional, that the disease creates is far more difficult than getting over the embarrassment of talking about sex. "I had heard about HIV before," said an Inkanyezi girl, wearing a bright blue T-shirt and matching headband. "But then I found out my mother was HIV positive. I was so shocked, so shocked. I even talked to my teacher about it. She said it can happen to anyone; it must have been from mistakes my mother made, and that I shouldn't make those mistakes in my own life."

"Sometimes, women have no choice," said the older woman sitting next to the girl in blue. She was thin, with intense dark eyes and a deep, wry smile. She was dressed entirely in black, except for a baseball cap with a red ribbon on it—the universal symbol of solidarity with HIV-positive people. "They get infected because of their husbands, and there's nothing they can do.

"It happened like this," the older woman went on. "It was back when we were living in Soweto, before we moved here. One day my daughter and I were washing clothes together," she said, nodding at the girl in blue. "She said she'd had a dream that I was so sick, that I had cancer and I was going to die. I waited until we were done with the washing, and then I told her that I was HIV positive. She said, 'I knew it, you were always sick and always going to support groups.' She was so down, she just cried all day and all night after that. I told her, 'Only God knows why people have this disease. Don't worry, I won't die right away.'

"Once I visited the loveLife Y-Center," the woman continued, "but I just saw children playing. I sat and talked with them, and they were shocked when I said I was HIV positive. I told them about what it was like, and one of them said she would ask the managers whether I could come and talk to a bigger group. But that was about six months ago and they haven't called me. I haven't moved and my number hasn't changed. I don't know why they haven't called."

"I think there should be more counseling and support groups for people who find out their parents are HIV positive," the girl in blue said. "It puts you down, it really gets to you, it haunts you. When you are standing in class and you have to recite a poem or something, I find I can't get anything out of my mouth. I can't concentrate. [The problem] here is ignorance. I didn't care about HIV until I found out about my mother. Then I started to care about these people. I wish many people in our country would also think like that."

In 2003, the only African country that had seen a nationwide decline in HIV prevalence was Uganda. Since 1992 the HIV rate had fallen by some two-thirds, a success that saved perhaps a million lives. The programs and policies that led to this success [are discussed elsewhere], but the epidemiologists Rand Stoneburner and Daniel Low-Beer have argued that a powerful role was played by the ordinary, but frank, conversations people had with family, friends, and neighbors—not about sex, but about the frightening, calamitous effects of AIDS itself.[9] Stoneburner and Low-Beer maintain that these painful personal conversations did more than anything else to persuade Ugandans to come to terms with the reality of AIDS, care for the afflicted, and change their behavior. This in turn led to declines in HIV transmission. The researchers found that people in other sub-Saharan African countries were far less likely to have such discussions.

In South Africa, people told Stoneburner and Low-Beer that they had heard about the epidemic from posters, radio, newspapers, and clinics, as well as from occasional mass rallies, schools, and village meetings; but they seldom spoke about it with the people they knew. They were also far less likely to admit knowing someone with AIDS or to be willing to care for an AIDS patient. It may be no coincidence that the HIV rate in South Africa rose higher than it ever did in Uganda, and has taken far longer to fall.

When I was in Uganda during the early 1990s, the HIV rate was already falling, and I vividly recall how the reality of AIDS was alive in people's minds. Kampala taxi drivers talked as passionately about AIDS as taxi drivers elsewhere discuss politics or football. And they talked about it in a way that would seem foreign to many in South Africa because it was so personal: "my sister," "my father," "my neighbor," "my friend."[10]

Ugandans are not unusually compassionate people, and discrimination against people with AIDS persists in some families and institutions. But Ugandans do seem more willing to openly address painful issues in their lives. This courage owes much to the AIDS information campaigns launched by the government of Uganda early on in the epidemic. But it may have other sources as well. Maybe the difference between the ways South Africa and Uganda have dealt with AIDS has historical roots. Both South Africa and Uganda have bitter histories of conflict. But while Uganda was terrorized for decades by a series of brutal leaders, they could not destroy the traditional rhythms of rural family life. Uganda is one of the most fertile countries in Africa; there is enough land for everyone, and most people live as their ancestors did, as peasant farmers and herders. No large settler population displaced huge numbers of people or set up a system to exploit and humiliate them, as happened in South Africa and in many other African countries. This means Ugandans are more likely to know their neighbors and to live near members of their extended families. This in turn may have contributed to what sociologists call "social cohesion"—the tendency of people to talk openly with one another and form trusted relationships. Perhaps this may have facilitated more realistic and open discussion of AIDS, more compassionate attitudes toward infected people, and pragmatic behavior change.

Perhaps many attempts to prevent the spread of HIV fail because those in charge 35
of them don't recognize that the decisions people make about sex are usually a matter
of feeling, not calculation. In other words, sexual behavior is determined less by what
Dr. Harrison called "discount rates" that young people "apply to future benefits" than
by emotional attachments. I thought of the South African girls who said they had lost
a sister or a friend to AIDS. If one of them was faced with a persistent, wealthy seducer,
what would be more likely to persuade her to decline? The memory of a loveLife billboard, with its flashy, beautiful models? Or the memory of a person she had known
who had died?

On the morning before I left South Africa, I attended a loveLife motivational seminar
at a school not far from Orange Farm. "These seminars help young people see the future, identify choices, and identify the values that underpin those choices," Harrison
had told me. "We help them ask themselves, 'What can you do to chart life's journey
and control it as much as possible?'" The seminars were based on Success by Choice,
a series devised by Marlon Smith, a California-based African-American motivational
speaker. How was Mr. Smith's message of personal empowerment translated to South
Africa, I wondered, where children have to contend with poverty, the risk of being
robbed or raped, and a grim future of likely unemployment?

About twenty-five children aged ten to fourteen were in the class, and the Ground-
Breaker asked them to hold their hands out in front of them, pretend they were looking
in a mirror, and repeat the following words:

"You are intelligent!"
"You are gifted!"
"There is no one in the world like you!"   40
"I love you!"

The children spoke quietly at first, then louder, as though they were being hypno-
tized. The GroundBreaker urged them to talk more openly with their parents, to keep
themselves clean, and to make positive choices in their lives, especially when it came
to sexuality. There was little mention of helping other people, nor was there much advice about how to avoid being raped or harassed by other students as well as teachers,
relatives, or strangers, or how to plan a future in a country where unemployment for
township blacks was so high.

Then something really odd occurred. One of the GroundBreakers asked the children to stand up because it was time for an "Icebreaker." "This is a little song-and-dance
thing we do, to give the children a chance to stretch. It improves their concentration,"
another GroundBreaker told me. The words of the song were as follows:

Pizza Hut
Pizza Hut
Kentucky Fried Chicken and a Pizza Hut
McDonald's
McDonald's
Kentucky Fried Chicken and a Pizza Hut.

In the dance, the children spread their arms out as though they were rolling out a
pizza, or flapped their elbows like chickens.

What kinds of choices was Dr. Harrison really referring to? I wondered. The techniques of marketing attempt to impose scientific principles on human choices. But it seemed a mad experiment to see whether teenagers living through very difficult times could be persuaded to choose a new sexual lifestyle as they might choose a new brand of shampoo, or whether children could be trained to associate safe sex with pizza and self-esteem.

Afterward, I spoke to some of the children who had participated in the seminar. They all knew how to protect themselves from HIV, and they were eager to show off their knowledge about condoms, abstinence, and fidelity within relationships. But they all said they didn't personally know anyone with AIDS; nor did they know of any children who had lost parents to AIDS. They did mention Nkosi Johnson, the brave HIV-positive twelve-year-old boy who became world-famous in 2000 when he stood up at an International Conference on AIDS and challenged the South African president, Thabo Mbeki, to do more for people living with the virus.

In fact, their principal would tell me later, more than twenty children at the school were AIDS orphans, and many more had been forced to drop out because there was no one to pay their expenses after their parents died. The children I spoke to seemed not to know why some of their classmates wore ragged uniforms or had no shoes or stopped showing up at all.

The week before, I had met some teenage girls in Soweto and I had asked them the same question. They answered in the same way: The only person they knew with AIDS was Nkosi Johnson, the famous boy at the AIDS conference. Just as Harrison had warned me, these girls said they were tired of hearing about AIDS. The girls were orphans, although they said their parents had not died of AIDS. I later discovered that, in another part of that same orphanage, there was a nursery where thirty babies and small children, all of them HIV positive, all abandoned by their parents, lay on cots or sat quietly on the floor, struggling for life. No wonder those girls were tired of hearing about HIV. It was right in their midst, within earshot, but the world around them was telling them to look the other way.

A couple of years later, I would meet a group of primary-school students in Kigali, Rwanda. By then, the HIV infection rate in Rwanda had fallen steeply, just as it had in Uganda years earlier. The school was a typical single-story line of classrooms in one of the poorest sections of Kigali. I spoke to the principal first, and he showed me the government-issued manual used for teaching about AIDS, which contained the usual information about abstinence and condoms. The school day had just ended, and he went outside and asked a few students to stay behind and chat with me.[11]

The Rwandan students had no idea in advance what I wanted to talk to them about. But when I asked them the same question I had asked the South African children, "Do you know anyone with AIDS?" their answers floored me. Every one of them had a story about someone they knew who was HIV positive or suffering from AIDS. "I knew a man who had bad lips [sores] and tears all over his skin," said a fourteen-year-old boy. "People stigmatized him and he died because no one was caring for him." Another boy described a woman who was "so thin, she almost died." But then her relatives took her to the hospital, where she was given AIDS treatment. "She got better because people cared for her," he said.

When I asked the Rwandan children whether they had any questions for me, all   50
they wanted to know was what they could do to help people with AIDS. The responses
of the South African children were strikingly different. When I asked them if they had
questions for me, they quickly changed the subject from AIDS and asked me what
America was like and whether I knew any of the pop stars they admired on TV.

The persistent denial of AIDS in South Africa was deeply disturbing. People liked
the colorful, frank advertising and the basketball games sponsored by loveLife. But
its programs seemed to me to reinforce the
denial that posed so many obstacles to preventing HIV in the first place. In 2005, the
Global Fund to Fight AIDS, Tuberculosis,
and Malaria would come to similar conclusions and terminate its multimillion-dollar
grant to loveLife.[12]

> **The persistent denial of AIDS in South Africa was deeply disturbing.**

Epidemiologists are equivocal about whether loveLife had any effect on HIV transmission in South Africa, but during the program's first seven years, HIV infection rates
continued to rise steadily.[13]

A more realistic HIV prevention program would have paid less attention to aspirations and dreams unattainable for so many young people, and greater attention to
the real circumstances in people's lives that make it hard for them to avoid infection. It
would also have been more frank about the real human consequences of the disease.
But that would have meant dealing with some very painful matters that South Africa's
policy-makers seemed determined to evade.

It was heartening that Western donors were now spending so much money on
AIDS programs in Africa. But the problem with some large foreign-aid programs was
that distributing the funds often involved negotiating with governments with a poor
record of dealing with AIDS. In addition, the huge sums of money involved were often
very difficult to manage, so that small community-based groups that need thousands
of dollars, rather than millions — like Inkanyezi in Orange Farm — were often over-
looked in favor of overly ambitious megaprojects, whose effectiveness had not been
demonstrated and whose premises were open to question. It seemed clear to me that
more could be learned from Inkanyezi's attempt to help people deal with the reality of
AIDS than from loveLife's attempt to create a new consumerist man and woman for
South Africa.

NOTES

1. Helen Schneider, "On the fault-line: The politics of AIDS policy in contemporary South
   Africa," *Afr Stud* 61:1 (July 1, 2002), 145–67; Samantha Power, "The AIDS Rebel,"
   New Yorker, May 19, 2003, pp. 54–67.
2. Rob Dorrington et al., "The Impact of HIV/AIDS on Adult Mortality in South Africa"
   (Cape Town: Burden of Disease Research Unit, Medical Research Council of South
   Africa, September 2001); "Mortality and causes of death in South Africa, 2003 and
   2004," Statistics South Africa, May 2006.
3. Richard Delate, "The Struggle for Meaning: A Semiotic Analysis of Interpretations of
   the loveLife His&Hers Billboard Campaign," November 2001, http://www.comminit
   .com/stlovelife/sld-4389.html.

4. Personal communication, February 2003.

5. For more about this, see Malcolm Gladwell, *The Tipping Point* (Boston: Little, Brown, 2000), and Everett Rogers, *Diffusion of Innovations* (New York: Free Press, 1983).

6. Delate, "Struggle for Meaning."

7. See Prishani Naidoo, "Youth Divided: A Review of loveLife's Y-Centre in Orange Farm" (Johannesburg: CADRE Report, 2003).

8. Nancy Luke and Kathleen M. Kurtz, "Cross-Generational and Transactional Sexual Relations in Sub-Saharan Africa: Prevalence of Behavior and Implications for Negotiating Safer Sexual Practices," International Center for Research on Women, 2002, http://www.icrw.org/docs/CrossGenSex_ Report_902.pdf; J. Swart-Kruger and L. M. Richter, "AIDS-related knowledge, attitudes and behaviour among South African street youth: Reflections on power, sexuality and the autonomous self," *Soc Sci Med* 45:6 (1997), 957–66; Editorial, "Reassessing priorities: Identifying the determinants of HIV transmission," *Soc Sci Med* 36:5 (1993), iii–viii.

9. Daniel Low-Beer and Rand Stoneburner, "Uganda and the Challenge of AIDS," in *The Political Economy of AIDS in Africa*, eds. Nana Poku and Alan Whiteside (London: Ashgate, 2004).

10. See Helen Epstein, "Fat," *Granta* 49 (1995). Low-Beer and Stoneburner make this observation, too, as do Janice Hogle et al. in *What Happened in Uganda? Declining HIV Prevalence, Behavior Change and the National Response* (USAID, 2002).

11. In 2006, the *Washington Post* reported that the HIV infection rate in Rwanda, once estimated to be 15 percent, was now estimated to be 3 percent. See Craig Timberg, "How AIDS in Africa Was Overstated: Reliance on Data from Urban Prenatal Clinics Skewed Early Projections," *Washington Post*, April 6, 2006, p. A1. Timberg attributed the downward revision to a new U.S. government survey and suggested that the earlier estimate, issued by the UNAIDS program, had been inflated, perhaps to raise money or appease AIDS activists. Although the old UNAIDS statistics were in need of correction, there clearly had been a decline in the true infection rate. A population-based survey carried out in Rwanda in 1986 found that prevalence was 17.8 percent in urban areas and 1.3 percent in rural areas. (Rwandan HIV Seroprevalence Study Group, "Nationwide community-based serological survey of HIV-1 and other human retrovirus infections in a country," *Lancet* 1 (ii) (1989), 941–43.

12. A. E. Pettifor et al., "Young people's sexual health in South Africa: HIV prevalence and sexual behaviors from a nationally representative household survey," *AIDS* 19:14 (September 23, 2005), 1525–34; but see R. Jewkes, "Response to Pettifor et al.," *AIDS* 20:6 (April 4, 2006), 952–53; author reply, 956–58; and W. M. Parker and M. Colvin, "Response to Pettifor et al.," *AIDS* 20:6 (April 4, 2006), 954–55.

13. In 2005, an article in the prestigious medical journal *AIDS* reported that young people who had attended at least one loveLife program were slightly, but significantly, less likely to be HIV positive than those who had not. The author argued that this was consistent with the possibility that loveLife reduced risky sexual behavior. However, there could well be another explanation. From what I saw, loveLife attracted young people who would have been at lower risk of infection in the first place, either because they were wealthier or better educated or less vulnerable to abuse. (While the loveLife study attempted to control for education and wealth, it did not do so rigorously.) Indeed, the tendency to avoid the subject of AIDS would seem to discourage HIV-positive young people from attending loveLife's programs, and this could make it look as though loveLife protected young people when in fact it merely alienated those most at risk. Most loveLife materials were in English, and thus accessible only to young people with

higher social status. This would have sent a clear signal to those—often marginalized and vulnerable young people—who could not speak English well that loveLife was not for them. The main author of the article reporting lower HIV rates among young people exposed to loveLife admitted to me in an interview that an anthropologist hired by loveLife itself had come to these same conclusions, but her results remain unpublished. See Pettifor et al., "A community-based study to examine the effect of a youth HIV prevention intervention on young people aged 15–24 in South Africa: results of the baseline survey," *Trop Med Int Health* 10:10 (October 2005), 971–80; but see also Jewkes, "Response to Pettifor et al.," author reply, and Parker and Colvin, "Response to Pettifor." Information re the loveLife anthropologist from Pettifor, personal communication, April 2006.

Exploring Context

1. The (RED) campaign (red.org) pairs popular products with fundraising in the fight against AIDS in Africa. Explore the (RED) Web site. Given Epstein's argument, how successful might this campaign be? How does your work with lifestyle brands from Question 1 of Questions for Critical Reading inform your answer?

2. Use the Web to locate information on current HIV infection rates in Africa. Has the situation improved since Epstein wrote her essay, or is it continuing to get worse? What might account for this trend, given Epstein's argument?

3. One of Epstein's central arguments is the usefulness of conversation in combating HIV infection in Africa. How might social networking technologies like Facebook or Twitter help in such a campaign?

Questions for Connecting

1. Kwame Anthony Appiah, in "Making Conversation" and "The Primacy of Practice" (p. 44), examines the mechanisms of cultural change. Apply his ideas to the fight against HIV/AIDS in Africa. How does social cohesion leverage the power of conversation? How might we promote new practices around sex in Africa regardless of the values that people hold? Work with your definition of social cohesion from Question 2 of Questions for Critical Reading as well as your thoughts on effective HIV prevention programs from Question 3 of Questions for Critical Reading.

2. How has imagination failed in the fight against HIV/AIDS in Africa? Use Daniel Gilbert's insights from "Reporting Live from Tomorrow" (p. 179) to expand Epstein's argument. What role do super-replicators play in the spread of the disease? How could they be used to help eradicate it? Are surrogates available? Why aren't they being used, and what effect might they have?

3. Kenji Yoshino, in "Preface" and "The New Civil Rights" (p. 539), suggests that conversation has an important role to play in producing change around civil rights. How does Epstein's argument confirm or complicate Yoshino's ideas? What makes conversation useful in producing social change?

Language Matters

1. Periods are important marks of punctuation, denoting the units of meaning we call sentences. Select a key passage from Epstein's text and type it into a word processor without any capital letters or periods. In class, trade these never-ending sentences and work on replacing the missing punctuation marks. How can you tell when a period is needed in Epstein's text? How can you tell when one is needed in your own text?

2. Outlines can be helpful in creating organization before we start writing, but they can also help us see the organization of any existing piece of writing. Create an outline of Epstein's piece, using a one-sentence summary of each major move of her argument. What sections do you see in her essay? How do they relate to each other? How can you use postdraft outlines of your own papers to check your organization as you revise?

3. Because it is sexually transmitted, HIV/AIDS is a delicate issue for many people. What sort of tone and language does Epstein use to discuss the disease and its transmission? How do her choices reflect both her audience and the delicacy of the subject matter? When would you make similar choices in your own writing?

Assignments for Writing

1. Epstein explores the way children and families address the AIDS crisis in Africa. In a short paper, examine the generational response to HIV/AIDS using Epstein's essay. Here are some questions to help your critical thinking: How do adults handle the discussion of AIDS? Is this separate from the discussion of other sexually transmitted diseases? How do children and young adults handle this topic? How do *you* handle it? You might want to draw on your work on social cohesion from Question 2 of Questions for Critical Reading or your analysis of conversation's potential for combating HIV from Question 3 of Exploring Context.

2. Epstein evaluates a number of approaches to HIV prevention, both formal and informal campaigns. Write a paper in which you assess the role of government in the prevention of diseases like HIV. Consider: What should the role of the government be in addressing the HIV/AIDS crisis? Both loveLife and Inkanyezi are private organizations that address sexually transmitted diseases and HIV/AIDS; should there be a similar government outreach program? What role would that program play? Are ordinary people better at preventing disease? How can a government promote the kind of strategies that were effective in Uganda?

3. South Africa's loveLife relies heavily on an advertising campaign. Write an essay in which you evaluate the role of commercial culture in addressing national crises such as HIV/AIDS. What role should companies and advertisers take upon themselves? How does that differ from what they appear to do? Are they really just out for profit, or do companies have a conscience? Should or can they act on issues that affect national health? You might want to reference your work on (RED) from Question 1 in Exploring Context in making your argument.

THOMAS L. FRIEDMAN

AP Photo/Steven Chemin

Journalist and author **Thomas L. Friedman** holds a B.A. in Mediterranean studies from Brandeis University and an M.A. in Middle Eastern studies from Oxford University. Friedman joined the *New York Times* in 1981 and has won three Pulitzer Prizes since. His foreign affairs column appears in more than seven hundred newspapers, and his books *From Beirut to Jerusalem* (1989), *The Lexus and the Olive Tree: Understanding Globalization* (1999), *Longitudes and Attitudes: Exploring the World after September 11* (2002), *The World Is Flat: A Brief History of the Twenty-First Century* (2005), *Hot, Flat, and Crowded: Why We Need a Green Revolution — and How It Can Renew America* (2008), and, with Michael Mandelbaum, *That Used to Be Us: How America Fell Behind the World It Invented and How We Can Come Back* (2011) have been national best-sellers.

The World Is Flat examines the impact of the "flattening" of the globe, an international leveling of business competition enabled by increasing interconnectedness. Friedman argues that globalized trade, outsourcing, offshoring, supply-chaining, and six other economic, technological, and political forces have changed the world permanently. He examines the positive and negative effects flattening has had and will continue to have on global politics and business.

In "The Dell Theory of Conflict Prevention," which is the penultimate chapter in *The World Is Flat*, Friedman explores the future of war in a globalized economy. Updating a concept he first introduced in *The Lexus and the Olive Tree* — the "Golden Arches Theory of Conflict Prevention," which suggested that citizens in societies economically developed enough to support a McDonald's lose interest in fighting wars — Friedman proposes with the "Dell Theory of Conflict Prevention" that countries will hesitate to risk their place in the global supply chain by fighting a nonessential war. He warns, though, that his new theory does not apply to every kind of modern threat, for terrorists, too, have learned how to use global supply chains.

According to Friedman, the flat world will have an impact on you directly as you compete for work with others around the world. This new business environment presents tremendous opportunities for us all; but what are the geopolitical consequences of this new economic reality, and will those consequences generate peace or more conflict?

▶ TAGS: *collaboration, economics, globalism, politics, war and conflict*
▶ CONNECTIONS: *Appiah, DeGhett, Stillman, van Houtryve*

Questions for Critical Reading

1. Much of Friedman's focus in this chapter is on collaboration. What role do you imagine collaboration plays in economic systems of production? Do you think it also plays a role in terrorism? As you read Friedman's text, look for quotations that confirm or challenge your initial thoughts.

2. What is the *Dell Theory of Conflict Prevention*? As you read Friedman's text, locate a quotation that defines this concept. Can you offer any examples from current events that show the Dell Theory's success or failure in relation to conflicts around the world?

3. Friedman discusses mutant supply chains. As you read his text, take note of the reasons they can be so successful and thus so dangerous. Locate passages from Friedman that support your answer.

The Dell Theory of Conflict Prevention

> Free Trade is God's diplomacy. There is no other certain way of uniting people in the bonds of peace.
>
> —BRITISH POLITICIAN RICHARD COBDEN, 1857

Before I share with you the subject of this chapter, I have to tell you a little bit about the computer that I wrote this book on. It's related to the theme I am about to discuss. This book was largely written on a Dell Inspiron 600m notebook, service tag number 9ZRJP41. As part of the research for this book, I visited with the management team at Dell near Austin, Texas. I shared with them the ideas in this book and in return I asked for one favor: I asked them to trace for me the entire global supply chain that produced my Dell notebook. Here is their report:

My computer was conceived when I phoned Dell's 800 number on April 2, 2004, and was connected to sales representative Mujteba Naqvi, who immediately entered my order into Dell's order management system. He typed in both the type of notebook I ordered as well as the special features I wanted, along with my personal information, shipping address, billing address, and credit card information. My credit card was verified by Dell through its work flow connection with Visa, and my order was then released to Dell's production system. Dell has six factories around the world—in Limerick, Ireland; Xiamen, China; Eldorado do Sul, Brazil; Nashville, Tennessee; Austin, Texas; and Penang, Malaysia. My order went out by e-mail to the Dell notebook factory in Malaysia, where the parts for the computer were immediately ordered from the supplier logistics centers (SLCs) next to the Penang factory. Surrounding every Dell factory in the world are these supplier logistics centers, owned by the different suppliers of Dell parts. These SLCs are like staging areas. If you are a Dell supplier anywhere in the world, your job is to keep your SLC full of your specific parts so they can constantly be trucked over to the Dell factory for just-in-time manufacturing.

"In an average day, we sell 140,000 to 150,000 computers," explained Dick Hunter, one of Dell's three global production managers. "Those orders come in over Dell.com or over the telephone. As soon as these orders come in, our suppliers know about it. They get a signal based on every component in the machine you ordered, so the supplier knows just what he has to deliver. If you are supplying power cords for desktops, you can see minute by minute how many power cords you are going to have to deliver." Every two hours, the Dell factory in Penang sends an e-mail to the various SLCs nearby, telling each one what parts and what quantities of those parts it wants delivered within the next ninety minutes—and not one minute later. Within ninety minutes, trucks from the various SLCs around Penang pull up to the Dell manufacturing plant and unload the parts needed for all those notebooks ordered in the last two hours. This goes on all day, every two hours. As soon as those parts arrive at the factory, it takes thirty minutes for Dell employees to unload the parts, register their bar codes, and put them into the bins for assembly. "We know where every part in every SLC is in the Dell system at all times," said Hunter.

So where did the parts for my notebook come from? I asked Hunter. To begin with, he said, the notebook was codesigned in Austin, Texas, and in Taiwan by a team of Dell engineers and a team of Taiwanese notebook designers. "The customer's needs, required technologies, and Dell's design innovations were all determined by Dell through our direct relationship with customers," he explained. "The basic design of the motherboard and case—the basic functionality of your machine—was designed to those specifications by an ODM [original design manufacturer] in Taiwan. We put our engineers in their facilities and they come to Austin and we actually codesign these systems. This global teamwork brings an added benefit—a globally distributed virtually twenty-four-hour-per-day development cycle. Our partners do the basic electronics and we help them design customer and reliability features that we know our customers want. We know the customers better than our suppliers and our competition, because we are dealing directly with them every day." Dell notebooks are completely redesigned roughly every twelve months, but new features are constantly added during the year—through the supply chain—as the hardware and software components advance.

It happened that when my notebook order hit the Dell factory in Penang, one part was not available—the wireless card—due to a quality control issue, so the assembly of the notebook was delayed for a few days. Then the truck full of good wireless cards arrived. On April 13, at 10:15 AM, a Dell Malaysia worker pulled the order slip that automatically popped up once all my parts had arrived from the SLCs to the Penang factory. Another Dell Malaysia employee then took out a "traveler"—a special carrying tote designed to hold and protect parts—and started plucking all the parts that went into my notebook.

Where did those parts come from? Dell uses multiple suppliers for most of the thirty key components that go into its notebooks. That way if one supplier breaks down or cannot meet a surge in demand, Dell is not left in the lurch. So here are the key suppliers for my Inspiron 600m notebook: The Intel microprocessor came from an Intel factory either in the Philippines, Costa Rica, Malaysia, or China. The memory came from a Korean-owned factory in Korea (Samsung), a Taiwanese-owned factory in Taiwan (Nanya), a German-owned factory in Germany (Infineon), or a Japanese-owned factory in Japan (Elpida). My graphics card was shipped from either a Taiwanese-owned factory in China (MSI) or a Chinese-run factory in China (Foxconn). The cooling fan came from a Taiwanese-owned factory in Taiwan (CCI or Auras). The motherboard came from either a Korean-owned factory in Shanghai (Samsung), a Taiwanese-owned factory in Shanghai (Quanta), or a Taiwanese-owned factory in Taiwan (Compal or Wistron). The keyboard came from either a Japanese-owned company in Tianjin, China (Alps), a Taiwanese-owned factory in Shenzen, China (Sunrex), or a Taiwanese-owned factory in Suzhou, China (Darfon). The LCD display was made in either South Korea (Samsung or LG.Philips LCD), Japan (Toshiba or Sharp), or Taiwan (Chi Mei Optoelectronics, Hannstar Display, or AU Optronics). The wireless card came from either an American-owned factory in China (Agere) or Malaysia (Arrow), or a Taiwanese-owned factory in Taiwan (Askey or Gemtek) or China (USI). The modem was made by either a Taiwanese-owned company in China (Asustek or Liteon) or a Chinese-run company in China (Foxconn). The battery came from an American-owned factory in Malaysia (Motorola), a Japanese-owned factory in Mexico or Malaysia or China (Sanyo), or a South Korean or Taiwanese factory in either of those two countries (SDI or Simplo). The hard disk drive was made by an American-owned factory in Singapore (Seagate), a Japanese-owned company in Thailand (Hitachi or Fujitsu), or a Japanese-owned factory in the Philippines (Toshiba). The CD/DVD drive came from a South Korean–owned company with factories in Indonesia and the Philippines (Samsung); a Japanese-owned factory in China or Malaysia (NEC); a Japanese-owned factory in Indonesia, China, or Malaysia (Teac); or a Japanese-owned factory in China (Sony). The notebook carrying bag was made by either an Irish-owned company in China (Tenba) or an American-owned company in China (Targus, Samsonite, or Pacific Design). The power adapter was made by either a Thai-owned factory in Thailand (Delta) or a Taiwanese, Korean, or American-owned factory in China (Liteon, Samsung, or Mobility). The power cord was made by a British-owned company with factories in China, Malaysia, and India (Volex).

> **This supply chain symphony . . . is one of the wonders of the flat world.**

The removable memory stick was made by either an Israeli-owned company in Israel (M-System) or an American-owned company with a factory in Malaysia (Smart Modular).

This supply chain symphony—from my order over the phone to production to delivery to my house—is one of the wonders of the flat world.

"We have to do a lot of collaborating," said Hunter. "Michael [Dell] personally knows the CEOs of these companies, and we are constantly working with them on process improvements and real-time demand/supply balancing." Demand shaping goes on constantly, said Hunter. What is "demand shaping"? It works like this: At 10 AM Austin time, Dell discovers that so many customers have ordered notebooks with 40-gigabyte hard drives since the morning that its supply chain will run short in two hours. That signal is automatically relayed to Dell's marketing department and to Dell.com and to all the Dell phone operators taking orders. If you happen to call to place your Dell order at 10:30 AM, the Dell representative will say to you, "Tom, it's your lucky day! For the next hour we are offering 60-gigabyte hard drives with the notebook you want—for only $10 more than the 40-gig drive. And if you act now, Dell will throw in a carrying case along with your purchase, because we so value you as a customer." In an hour or two, using such promotions, Dell can reshape the demand for any part of any notebook or desktop to correspond with the projected supply in its global supply chain. Today memory might be on sale, tomorrow it might be CD-ROMs.

Picking up the story of my notebook, on April 13, at 11:29 AM, all the parts had been plucked from the just-in-time inventory bins in Penang, and the computer was assembled there by A. Sathini, a team member "who manually screwed together all of the parts from kitting as well as the labels needed for Tom's system," said Dell in their production report to me. "The system was then sent down the conveyor to go to burn, where Tom's specified software was downloaded." Dell has huge server banks stocked with the latest in Microsoft, Norton Utilities, and other popular software applications, which are downloaded into each new computer according to the specific tastes of the customer.

"By 2:45 PM, Tom's software had been successfully downloaded, and [was] manu- 10
ally moved to the boxing line. By 4:05 PM, Tom's system [was] placed in protective foam and a shuttle box, with a label, which contains his order number, tracking code, system type, and shipping code. By 6:04 PM, Tom's system had been loaded on a pallet with a specified manifest, which gives the Merge facility visibility to when the system will arrive, what pallet it will be on (out of 75+ pallets with 152 systems per pallet), and to what address Tom's system will ship. By 6:26 PM, Tom's system left [the Dell factory] to head to the Penang, Malaysia, airport."

Six days a week Dell charters a China Airlines 747 out of Taiwan and flies it from Penang to Nashville via Taipei. Each 747 leaves with twenty-five thousand Dell notebooks that weigh altogether 110,000 kilograms, or 242,500 pounds. It is the only 747 that ever lands in Nashville, except Air Force One, when the president visits. "By April 15, 2004, at 7:41 AM, Tom's system arrived at [Nashville] with other Dell systems from Penang and Limerick. By 11:58 AM, Tom's system [was] inserted into a larger box, which went down the boxing line to the specific external parts that Tom had ordered."

That was thirteen days after I'd ordered it. Had there not been a parts delay in Malaysia when my order first arrived, the time between when I phoned in my purchase, when the notebook was assembled in Penang, and its arrival in Nashville would have been only four days. Hunter said the total supply chain for my computer, including suppliers of suppliers, involved about four hundred companies in North America, Europe, and primarily Asia, but with thirty key players. Somehow, though, it all came together. As Dell reported: On April 15, 2004, at 12:59 PM, "Tom's system had been shipped from [Nashville] and was tenured by UPS shipping LTL (3–5-day ground, specified by Tom), with UPS tracking number 1Z13WA374253514697. By April 19, 2004, at 6:41 PM, Tom's system arrived in Bethesda, MD, and was signed for."

I am telling you the story of my notebook to tell a larger story of geopolitics in the flat world. To all the forces . . . that are still holding back the flattening of the world, or could actually reverse the process, one has to add a more traditional threat, and that is an outbreak of a good, old-fashioned, world-shaking, economy-destroying war. It could be China deciding once and for all to eliminate Taiwan as an independent state; or North Korea, out of fear or insanity, using one of its nuclear weapons against South Korea or Japan; or Israel and a soon-to-be-nuclear Iran going at each other; or India and Pakistan finally nuking it out. These and other classic geopolitical conflicts could erupt at any time and either slow the flattening of the world or seriously unflatten it.

The real subject of this chapter is how these classic geopolitical threats might be moderated or influenced by the new forms of collaboration fostered and demanded by the flat world—particularly supply-chaining. The flattening of the world is too young for us to draw any definitive conclusions. What is certain, though, is that as the world flattens, one of the most interesting dramas to watch in international relations will be the interplay between the traditional global threats and the newly emergent global supply chains. The interaction between old-time threats (like China *versus* Taiwan) and just-in-time supply chains (like China *plus* Taiwan) will be a rich source of study for the field of international relations in the early twenty-first century.

In *The Lexus and the Olive Tree* I argued that to the extent that countries tied their economies and futures to global integration and trade, it would act as a restraint on going to war with their neighbors. I first started thinking about this in the late 1990s, when, during my travels, I noticed that no two countries that both had McDonald's had ever fought a war against each other since each got its McDonald's. (Border skirmishes and civil wars don't count, because McDonald's usually served both sides.) After confirming this with McDonald's, I offered what I called the Golden Arches Theory of Conflict Prevention. The Golden Arches Theory stipulated that when a country reached the level of economic development where it had a middle class big enough to support a network of McDonald's, it became a McDonald's country. And people in McDonald's countries didn't like to fight wars anymore. They preferred to wait in line for burgers. While this was offered slightly tongue in cheek, the serious point I was trying to make was that as countries got woven into the fabric of global trade and rising living standards, which having a network of McDonald's franchises had come to symbolize, the cost of war for victor and vanquished became prohibitively high.

This McDonald's theory has held up pretty well, but now that almost every country has acquired a McDonald's, except the worst rogues like North Korea, Iran, and Iraq under Saddam Hussein, it seemed to me that this theory needed updating for the flat world. In that spirit, and again with tongue slightly in cheek, I offer the Dell Theory of Conflict Prevention, the essence of which is that the advent and spread of just-in-time global supply chains in the flat world are an even greater restraint on geopolitical adventurism than the more general rising standard of living that McDonald's symbolized.

The Dell Theory stipulates: No two countries that are both part of a major global supply chain, like Dell's, will ever fight a war against each other as long as they are both part of the same global supply chain. Because people embedded in major global supply chains don't want to fight old-time wars anymore. They want to make just-in-time deliveries of goods and services—and enjoy the rising standards of living that come with that. One of the people with the best feel for the logic behind this theory is Michael Dell, the founder and chairman of Dell.

"These countries understand the risk premium that they have," said Dell of the countries in his Asian supply chain. "They are pretty careful to protect the equity that they have built up or tell us why we should not worry [about their doing anything adventurous]. My belief after visiting China is that the change that has occurred there is in the best interest of the world and China. Once people get a taste for whatever you want to call it—economic independence, a better lifestyle, and a better life for their child or children—they grab on to that and don't want to give it up."

Any sort of war or prolonged political upheaval in East Asia or China "would have a massive chilling effect on the investment there and on all the progress that has been made there," said Dell, who added that he believes the governments in that part of the world understand this very clearly. "We certainly make clear to them that stability is important to us. [Right now] it is not a day-to-day worry for us . . . I believe that as time and progress go on there, the chance for a really disruptive event goes down exponentially. I don't think our industry gets enough credit for the good we are doing in these areas. If you are making money and being productive and raising your standard of living, you're not sitting around thinking, Who did this to us? or Why is our life so bad?"

There is a lot of truth to this. Countries whose workers and industries are woven   20 into a major global supply chain know that they cannot take an hour, a week, or a month off for war without disrupting industries and economies around the world and thereby risking the loss of their place in that supply chain for a long time, which could be extremely costly. For a country with no natural resources, being part of a global supply chain is like striking oil—oil that never runs out. And therefore, getting dropped from such a chain because you start a war is like having your oil wells go dry or having someone pour cement down them. They will not come back anytime soon.

"You are going to pay for it really dearly," said Glenn E. Neland, senior vice president for worldwide procurement at Dell, when I asked him what would happen to a major supply-chain member in Asia that decided to start fighting with its neighbor and disrupt the supply chain. "It will not only bring you to your knees [today], but you will pay for a long time—because you just won't have any credibility if you demonstrate you are going to go [off] the political deep end. And China is just now starting to develop a level of credibility in the business community that it is creating a business environment you can prosper in—with transparent and consistent rules." Neland said that suppliers regularly ask him whether he is worried about China and Taiwan, which have threatened to go to war at several points in the past half century, but his standard response is that he cannot imagine them "doing anything more than flexing muscles with each other." Neland said he can tell in his conversations and dealings with companies and governments in the Dell supply chain, particularly the Chinese, that "they recognize the opportunity and are really hungry to participate in the same things they have seen other countries in Asia do. They know there is a big economic pot at the end of the rainbow and they are really after it. We will spend about $35 billion producing parts this year, and 30 percent of that is [in] China."

If you follow the evolution of supply chains, added Neland, you see the prosperity and stability they promoted first in Japan, and then in Korea and Taiwan, and now in Malaysia, Singapore, the Philippines, Thailand, and Indonesia. Once countries get embedded in these global supply chains, "they feel part of something much bigger than their own businesses," he said. Osamu Watanabe, the CEO of the Japan External Trade Organization (JETRO), was explaining to me one afternoon in Tokyo how Japanese companies were moving vast amounts of low- and middle-range technical work and manufacturing to China, doing the basic fabrication there, and then bringing it back to Japan for final assembly. Japan was doing this despite a bitter legacy of mistrust between the two countries, which was intensified by the Japanese invasion of China in the last century. Historically, he noted, a strong Japan and a strong China have had a hard time coexisting. But not today, at least not for the moment. Why not? I asked. The reason you can have a strong Japan and a strong China at the same time, he said, "is because of the supply chain." It is a win-win for both.

Obviously, since Iraq, Syria, south Lebanon, North Korea, Pakistan, Afghanistan, and Iran are not part of any major global supply chains, all of them remain hot spots that could explode at any time and slow or reverse the flattening of the world. As my own notebook story attests, the most important test case of the Dell Theory of Conflict Prevention is the situation between China and Taiwan—since both are deeply embedded in several of the world's most important computer, consumer electronics, and, increasingly, software supply chains. The vast majority of computer components for every major company comes from coastal China, Taiwan, and East Asia. In addition, Taiwan alone has more than $100 billion in investments in mainland China today, and Taiwanese experts run many of the cutting-edge Chinese high-tech manufacturing companies.

It is no wonder that Craig Addison, the former editor of *Electronic Business Asia* magazine, wrote an essay for the *International Herald Tribune* (September 29, 2000), headlined "A 'Silicon Shield' Protects Taiwan from China." He argued that "Silicon-based products, such as computers and networking systems, form the basis of the digital economies in the United States, Japan, and other developed nations. In the past decade, Taiwan has become the third-largest information technology hardware producer after the United States and Japan. Military aggression by China against Taiwan would cut off a large portion of the world's supply of these products . . . Such a development would wipe trillions of dollars off the market value of technology companies listed in the United States, Japan, and Europe." Even if China's leaders, like former president Jiang Zemin, who was once minister of electronics, lose sight of how integrated China and Taiwan are in the world's computer supply chain, they need only ask their kids for an update. Jiang Zemin's son, Jiang Mianheng, wrote Addison, "is a partner in a wafer fabrication project in Shanghai with Winston Wang of Taiwan's Grace T.H.W. Group." And it is not just Taiwanese. Hundreds of big American tech companies now have R&D operations in China; a war that disrupted them could lead not only to the companies moving their plants elsewhere but also to a significant loss of R&D investment in China, which the Beijing government has been betting on to advance its development. Such a war could also, depending on how it started, trigger a widespread American boycott of Chinese goods—if China were to snuff out the Taiwanese democracy—which would lead to serious economic turmoil inside China.

The Dell Theory had its first real test in December 2004, when Taiwan held parliamentary elections. President Chen Shui-bian's pro-independence Democratic Progressive Party was expected to win the legislative runoff over the main opposition Nationalist Party, which favored closer ties with Beijing. Chen framed the election as a popular referendum on his proposal to write a new constitution that would formally enshrine Taiwan's independence, ending the purposely ambiguous status quo. Had Chen won and moved ahead on his agenda to make Taiwan its own motherland, as opposed to maintaining the status quo fiction that it is a province of the mainland, it could have led to a Chinese military assault on Taiwan. Everyone in the region was holding his or her breath. And what happened? *Motherboards won over motherland.* A majority of Taiwanese voted against the pro-independence governing party legislative candidates, ensuring that the DPP would not have a majority in parliament. I believe the message Taiwanese voters were sending was not that they never want Taiwan to be independent. It was that they do not want to upset the status quo right now, which has been so beneficial to so many Taiwanese. The voters seemed to understand clearly how interwoven they had become with the mainland, and they wisely opted to maintain

25

their de facto independence rather than force de jure* independence, which might have triggered a Chinese invasion and a very uncertain future.

Warning: What I said when I put forth the McDonald's theory, I would repeat even more strenuously with the Dell Theory: It does not make wars obsolete. And it does not guarantee that governments will not engage in wars of choice, even governments that are part of major supply chains. To suggest so would be naive. It guarantees only that governments whose countries are enmeshed in global supply chains will have to think three times, not just twice, about engaging in anything but a war of self-defense. And if they choose to go to war anyway, the price they will pay will be ten times higher than it was a decade ago and probably ten times higher than whatever the leaders of that country think. It is one thing to lose your McDonald's. It's quite another to fight a war that costs you your place in a twenty-first-century supply chain that may not come back around for a long time.

While the biggest test case of the Dell Theory is China versus Taiwan, the fact is that the Dell Theory has already proved itself to some degree in the case of India and Pakistan, the context in which I first started to think about it. I happened to be in India in 2002, when its just-in-time services supply chains ran into some very old-time geopolitics—and the supply chain won. In the case of India and Pakistan, the Dell Theory was working on only one party—India—but it still had a major impact. India is to the world's knowledge and service supply chain what China and Taiwan are to the manufacturing ones. By now readers of this book know all the highlights: General Electric's biggest research center outside the United States is in Bangalore, with seventeen hundred Indian engineers, designers, and scientists. The brain chips for many brand-name cell phones are designed in Bangalore. Renting a car from Avis online? It's managed in Bangalore. Tracing your lost luggage on Delta or British Airways is done from Bangalore, and the backroom accounting and computer maintenance for scores of global firms are done from Bangalore, Mumbai, Chennai, and other major Indian cities.

Here's what happened: On May 31, 2002, State Department spokesman Richard Boucher issued a travel advisory saying, "We urge American citizens currently in India to depart the country," because the prospect of a nuclear exchange with Pakistan was becoming very real. Both nations were massing troops on their borders, intelligence reports were suggesting that they both might be dusting off their nuclear warheads, and CNN was flashing images of people flooding out of India. The global American firms that had moved their back rooms and R&D operations† to Bangalore were deeply unnerved.

"I was actually surfing on the Web, and I saw a travel advisory come up on India on a Friday evening," said Vivek Paul, president of Wipro, which manages backroom operations from India of many American multinationals. "As soon as I saw that, I said, 'Oh my gosh, every customer that we have is going to have a million questions on this.' It was the Friday before a long weekend, so over the weekend we at Wipro developed

---

*de facto . . . de jure: concerning fact; concerning law. In other words, Taiwanese independence may not be officially recognized, but in practice it exists [Ed.].

†Back rooms and R&D operations: technical and logistical systems, and research and development [Ed.].

a fail-safe business continuity plan for all of our customers." While Wipro's customers were pleased to see how on top of things the company was, many of them were nevertheless rattled. This was not in the plan when they decided to outsource mission-critical research and operations to India. Said Paul, "I had a CIO from one of our big American clients send me an e-mail saying, 'I am now spending a lot of time looking for alternative sources to India. I don't think you want me doing that, and I don't want to be doing it.' I immediately forwarded his message to the Indian ambassador in Washington and told him to get it to the right person." Paul would not tell me what company it was, but I have confirmed through diplomatic sources that it was United Technologies. And plenty of others, like American Express and General Electric, with back rooms in Bangalore, had to have been equally worried.

For many global companies, "the main heart of their business is now supported here," said N. Krishnakumar, president of MindTree, another leading Indian knowledge outsourcing firm based in Bangalore. "It can cause chaos if there is a disruption." While not trying to meddle in foreign affairs, he added, "What we explained to our government, through the Confederation of Indian Industry, is that providing a stable, predictable operating environment is now the key to India's development." This was a real education for India's elderly leaders in New Delhi, who had not fully absorbed how critical India had become to the world's knowledge supply chain. When you are managing vital backroom operations for American Express or General Electric or Avis, or are responsible for tracing all the lost luggage on British Airways or Delta, you cannot take a month, a week, or even a day off for war without causing major disruptions for those companies. Once those companies have made a commitment to outsource business operations or research to India, they expect it to stay there. That is a major commitment. And if geopolitics causes a serious disruption, they will leave, and they will not come back very easily. When you lose this kind of service trade, you can lose it for good.

"What ends up happening in the flat world you described," explained Paul, "is that you have only one opportunity to make it right if something [goes] wrong. Because the disadvantage of being in a flat world is that despite all the nice engagements and stuff and the exit barriers that you have, every customer has multiple options, and so the sense of responsibility you have is not just out of a desire to do good by your customers, but also a desire for self-preservation."

The Indian government got the message. Was India's central place in the world's services supply chain the only factor in getting Prime Minister Vajpayee to tone down his rhetoric and step back from the brink? Of course not. There were other factors, to be sure—most notably the deterrent effect of Pakistan's own nuclear arsenal. But clearly, India's role in global services was an important additional source of restraint on its behavior, and it was taken into account by New Delhi. "I think it sobered a lot of people," said Jerry Rao, who heads the Indian high-tech trade association. "We engaged very seriously, and we tried to make the point that this was very bad for Indian business. It was very bad for the Indian economy . . . [Many people] didn't realize till then how suddenly we had become integrated into the rest of the world. We are now partners in a twenty-four by seven by three-sixty-five supply chain."

Vivek Kulkarni, then information technology secretary for Bangalore's regional government, told me back in 2002, "We don't get involved in politics, but we did bring to the government's attention the problems the Indian IT industry might face if there were a war." And this was an altogether new factor for New Delhi to take into consideration. "Ten years ago, [a lobby of IT ministers from different Indian states] never existed," said Kulkarni. Now it is one of the most important business lobbies in India and a coalition that no Indian government can ignore.

"With all due respect, the McDonald's [shutting] down doesn't hurt anything," said Vivek Paul, "but if Wipro had to shut down we would affect the day-to-day operations of many, many companies." No one would answer the phones in call centers. Many e-commerce sites that are supported from Bangalore would shut down. Many major companies that rely on India to maintain their key computer applications or handle their human resources departments or billings would seize up. And these companies did not want to find alternatives, said Paul. Switching is very difficult, because taking over mission-critical day-to-day backroom operations of a global company takes a great deal of training and experience. It's not like opening a fast-food restaurant. That was why, said Paul, Wipro's clients were telling him, " 'I have made an investment in you. I need you to be very responsible with the trust I have reposed in you.' And I think that created an enormous amount of back pressure on us that said we have to act in a responsible fashion . . . All of a sudden it became even clearer that there's more to gain by economic gains than by geopolitical gains. [We had more to gain from building] a vibrant, richer middle class able to create an export industry than we possibly could by having an ego-satisfying war with Pakistan." The Indian government also looked around and realized that the vast majority of India's billion people were saying, "I want a better future, not more territory." Over and over again, when I asked young Indians working at call centers how they felt about Kashmir or a war with Pakistan, they waved me off with the same answer: "We have better things to do." And they do. America needs to keep this in mind as it weighs its overall approach to outsourcing. I would never advocate shipping some American's job overseas just so it will keep Indians and Pakistanis at peace with each other. But I would say that to the extent that this process happens, driven by its own internal economic logic, it will have a net positive geopolitical effect. It will absolutely make the world safer for American kids.

Each of the Indian business leaders I interviewed noted that in the event of some outrageous act of terrorism or aggression from Pakistan, India would do whatever it takes to defend itself, and they would be the first to support that—the Dell Theory be damned. Sometimes war is unavoidable. It is imposed on you by the reckless behavior of others, and you have to just pay the price. But the more India and, one hopes, soon Pakistan get enmeshed in global service supply chains, the greater disincentive they have to fight anything but a border skirmish or a war of words.

The example of the 2002 India-Pakistan nuclear crisis at least gives us some hope. That cease-fire was brought to us not by General Powell but by General Electric.

We bring good things to life.

Infosys versus al Qaeda

Unfortunately, even GE can do only so much. Because, alas, a new source for geopolitical instability has emerged only in recent years, for which even the updated Dell Theory can provide no restraint. It is the emergence of mutant global supply chains—that is, nonstate actors, be they criminals or terrorists, who learn to use all the elements of the flat world to advance a highly destabilizing, even nihilistic agenda. I first started thinking about this when Nandan Nilekani, the Infosys CEO, was giving me [a] tour . . . of his company's global videoconferencing center at its Bangalore headquarters. As Nandan explained to me how Infosys could get its global supply chain together at once for a virtual conference in that room, a thought popped into my head: Who else uses open-sourcing and supply-chaining so imaginatively? The answer, of course, is al Qaeda.

Al Qaeda has learned to use many of the same instruments for global collaboration that Infosys uses, but instead of producing products and profits with them, it has produced mayhem and murder. This is a particularly difficult problem. In fact, it may be the most vexing geopolitical problem for flat-world countries that want to focus on the future. The flat world—unfortunately—is a friend of both Infosys and al Qaeda. The Dell Theory will not work at all against these informal Islamo-Leninist terror networks, because they are not a state with a population that will hold its leaders accountable or with a domestic business lobby that might restrain them. These mutant global supply chains are formed for the purpose of destruction, not profit. They don't need investors, only recruits, donors, and victims. Yet these mobile, self-financing mutant supply chains use all the tools of collaboration offered by the flat world—open-sourcing to raise money, to recruit followers, and to stimulate and disseminate ideas; outsourcing to train recruits; and supply-chaining to distribute the tools and the suicide bombers to undertake operations. The U.S. Central Command has a name for this whole underground network: the Virtual Caliphate. And its leaders and innovators understand the flat world almost as well as Wal-Mart, Dell, and Infosys do.

In the previous chapter [not included here], I tried to explain that you cannot understand the rise of al Qaeda emotionally and politically without reference to the flattening of the world. What I am arguing here is that you cannot understand the rise of al Qaeda technically without reference to the flattening of the world, either. Globalization in general has been al Qaeda's friend in that it has helped to solidify a revival of Muslim identity and solidarity, with Muslims in one country much better able to see and sympathize with the struggles of their brethren in another country—thanks to the Internet and satellite television. At the same time, . . . this flattening process has intensified the feelings of humiliation in some quarters of the Muslim world over the fact that civilizations to which the Muslim world once felt superior—Hindus, Jews, Christians, Chinese—are now all doing better than many Muslim countries, and everyone can see it. The flattening of the world has also led to more urbanization and large-scale immigration to the West of many of these young, unemployed, frustrated Arab-Muslim males, while simultaneously making it much easier for informal open-source networks of these young men to form, operate, and interconnect. This certainly has been a boon for underground extremist Muslim political groups. There has been a proliferation of these informal mutual supply chains throughout the Arab-Muslim world today—small networks of people who move money through *hawalas* (hand-to-hand financing networks), who recruit through alternative education systems like the madrassas, and who communicate through the Internet and other tools of the global information revolution. Think about it: A century ago, anarchists were limited in their ability to communicate and collaborate with one another, to find sympathizers, and to band together for an operation. Today, with the Internet, that is not a problem. Today even the Unabomber could find friends to join a consortium where his "strengths"

40

could be magnified and reinforced by others who had just as warped a worldview as he did.

What we have witnessed in Iraq is an even more perverse mutation of this mutant supply chain—the suicide supply chain. Since the start of the U.S. invasion in March 2002, more than two hundred suicide bombers have been recruited from within Iraq and from across the Muslim world, brought to the Iraqi front by some underground railroad, connected with the bomb makers there, and then dispatched against U.S. and Iraqi targets according to whatever suits the daily tactical needs of the insurgent Islamist forces in Iraq. I can understand, but not accept, the notion that more than thirty-seven years of Israeli occupation of the West Bank might have driven some Palestinians into a suicidal rage. But the American occupation of Iraq was only a few months old before it started to get hit by this suicide supply chain. How do you recruit so many young men "off the shelf" who are ready to commit suicide in the cause of jihad, many of them apparently not even Iraqis? And they don't even identify themselves by name or want to get credit—at least in this world. The fact is that Western intelligence agencies have no clue how this underground suicide supply chain, which seems to have an infinite pool of recruits to draw on, works, and yet it has basically stymied the U.S. armed forces in Iraq. From what we do know, though, this Virtual Caliphate works just like the supply chains I described earlier. Just as you take an item off the shelf in a discount store in Birmingham and another one is immediately made in Beijing, so the retailers of suicide deploy a human bomber in Baghdad and another one is immediately recruited and indoctrinated in Beirut. To the extent that this tactic spreads, it will require a major rethinking of U.S. military doctrine.

The flat world has also been such a huge boon for al Qaeda and its ilk because of the way it enables the small to act big, and the way it enables small acts—the killing of just a few people—to have big effects. The horrific video of the beheading of *Wall Street Journal* reporter Danny Pearl by Islamist militants in Pakistan was transmitted by the Internet all over the world. There is not a journalist anywhere who saw or even just read about that who was not terrified. But those same beheading videos are also used as tools of recruitment. The flat world makes it much easier for terrorists to transmit their terror. With the Internet they don't even have to go through Western or Arab news organizations but can broadcast right into your computer. It takes much less dynamite to transmit so much more anxiety. Just as the U.S. Army had embedded journalists, so the suicide supply chain has embedded terrorists, in their own way, to tell us their side of the story. How many times have I gotten up in the morning, fired up the Internet, and been confronted by the video image of some masked gunman threatening to behead an American—all brought to me courtesy of AOL's home page? The Internet is an enormously useful tool for the dissemination of propaganda, conspiracy theories, and plain old untruths, because it combines a huge reach with a patina of technology that makes anything on the Internet somehow more believable. How many times have you heard someone say, "But I read it on the Internet," as if that should end the argument? In fact, the Internet can make things worse. It often leads to more people being exposed to crazy conspiracy theories.

"The new system of diffusion—the Internet—is more likely to transmit irrationality than rationality," said political theorist Yaron Ezrahi, who specializes in the interaction between media and politics. "Because irrationality is more emotionally loaded, it requires less knowledge, it explains more to more people, it goes down easier." That is why conspiracy theories are so rife in the Arab-Muslim world today — and unfortunately are becoming so in many quarters of the Western world, for that matter. Conspiracy theories are like a drug that goes right into your bloodstream, enabling you to see "the Light." And the Internet is the needle. Young people used to have to take LSD to escape. Now they just go online. Now you don't shoot up, you download. You download the precise point of view that speaks to all your own biases. And the flat world makes it all so much easier.

Gabriel Weimann, a professor of communication at Haifa University, Israel, did an incisive study of terrorists' use of the Internet and of what I call the flat world, which was published in March 2004 by the United States Institute of Peace and excerpted on YaleGlobal Online on April 26, 2004. He made the following points:

> While the danger that cyber-terrorism poses to the Internet is frequently debated, surprisingly little is known about the threat posed by terrorists' use of the Internet. A recent six-year-long study shows that terrorist organizations and their supporters have been using all of the tools that the Internet offers to recruit supporters, raise funds, and launch a worldwide campaign of fear. It is also clear that to combat terrorism effectively, mere suppression of their Internet tools is not enough. Our scan of the Internet in 2003–04 revealed the existence of hundreds of websites serving terrorists in different, albeit sometimes overlapping, ways . . . There are countless examples of how [terrorists] use this uncensored medium to spread disinformation, to deliver threats intended to instill fear and helplessness, and to disseminate horrific images of recent actions. Since September 11, 2001, al Qaeda has festooned its websites with a string of announcements of an impending "large attack" on U.S. targets. These warnings have received considerable media coverage, which has helped to generate a widespread sense of dread and insecurity among audiences throughout the world and especially within the United States. . . .
>
> The Internet has significantly expanded the opportunities for terrorists to secure publicity. Until the advent of the Internet, terrorists' hopes of winning publicity for their causes and activities depended on attracting the attention of television, radio, or the print media. The fact that terrorists themselves have direct control over the content of their websites offers further opportunities to shape how they are perceived by different target audiences and to manipulate their image and the images of their enemies. Most terrorist sites do not celebrate their violent activities. Instead — regardless of their nature, motives, or location — most terrorist sites emphasize two issues: the restrictions placed on freedom of expression; and the plight of their comrades who are now political prisoners. These issues resonate powerfully with their own supporters and are also calculated to elicit sympathy from Western audiences that cherish freedom of expression and frown on measures to silence political opposition. . . .
>
> Terrorists have proven not only skillful at online marketing but also adept at mining the data offered by the billion-some pages of the World Wide Web. They can learn from the Internet about the schedules and locations of targets such as transportation facilities, nuclear power plants, public buildings, airports and ports, and even counterterrorism measures. According to Secretary

of Defense Donald Rumsfeld, an al Qaeda training manual recovered in Afghanistan tells its readers, "Using public sources openly and without resorting to illegal means, it is possible to gather at least 80 percent of all information required about the enemy." One captured al Qaeda computer contained engineering and structural architecture features of a dam, which had been downloaded from the Internet and which would enable al Qaeda engineers and planners to simulate catastrophic failures. In other captured computers, U.S. investigators found evidence that al Qaeda operators spent time on sites that offer software and programming instructions for the digital switches that run power, water, transportation, and communications grids.

Like many other political organizations, terrorist groups use the Internet to raise funds. Al Qaeda, for instance, has always depended heavily on donations, and its global fund-raising network is built upon a foundation of charities, nongovernmental organizations, and other financial institutions that use websites and Internet-based chat rooms and forums. The fighters in the Russian breakaway republic of Chechnya have likewise used the Internet to publicize the numbers of bank accounts to which sympathizers can contribute. And in December 2001, the U.S. government seized the assets of a Texas-based charity because of its ties to Hamas.

In addition to soliciting financial aid online, terrorists recruit converts by using the full panoply of website technologies (audio, digital video, etc.) to enhance the presentation of their message. And like commercial sites that track visitors to develop consumer profiles, terrorist organizations capture information about the users who browse their websites. Visitors who seem most interested in the organization's cause or well suited to carrying out its work are then contacted. Recruiters may also use more interactive Internet technology to roam online chat rooms and cyber cafes, looking for receptive members of the public, particularly young people. The SITE Institute, a Washington, D.C.–based terrorism research group that monitors al Qaeda's Internet communications, has provided chilling details of a high-tech recruitment drive launched in 2003 to recruit fighters to travel to Iraq and attack U.S. and coalition forces there. The Internet also grants terrorists a cheap and efficient means of networking. Many terrorist groups, among them Hamas and al Qaeda, have undergone a transformation from strictly hierarchical organizations with designated leaders to affiliations of semi-independent cells that have no single commanding hierarchy. Through the Internet, these loosely interconnected groups are able to maintain contact with one another—and with members of other terrorist groups. The Internet connects not only members of the same terrorist organizations but also members of different groups. For instance, dozens of sites supporting terrorism in the name of jihad permit terrorists in places as far-removed from one another as Chechnya and Malaysia to exchange ideas and practical information about how to build bombs, establish terror cells, and carry out attacks . . . Al Qaeda operatives relied heavily on the Internet in planning and coordinating the September 11 attacks.

For all of these reasons we are just at the beginning of understanding the geopolitical impact of the flattening of the world. On the one hand, failed states and failed 45 regions are places we have every incentive to avoid today. They offer no economic opportunity and there is no Soviet Union out there competing with us for influence over such countries. On the other hand, there may be nothing more dangerous today than a failed state with broadband capability. That is, even failed states tend to have telecommunications systems and satellite links, and therefore if a terrorist group infiltrates a failed state, as al Qaeda did with Afghanistan, it can amplify its power enormously. As much as big powers want to stay away from such states, they may feel compelled to get even more deeply embroiled in them. Think of America in Afghanistan and Iraq, Russia in Chechnya, Australia in East Timor.

In the flat world it is much more difficult to hide, but much easier to get connected. "Think of Mao at the beginning of the Chinese communist revolution," remarked Michael Mandelbaum, the Johns Hopkins foreign policy specialist. "The Chinese Communists had to hide in caves in northwest China, but they could move around in whatever territory they were able to control. Bin Laden, by contrast, can't show his face, but he can reach every household in the world, thanks to the Internet." Bin Laden cannot capture any territory but he can capture the imagination of millions of people. And he has, broadcasting right into American living rooms on the eve of the 2004 presidential election.

> **In the flat world it is much more difficult to hide, but much easier to get connected.**

Hell hath no fury like a terrorist with a satellite dish and an interactive website.

Too Personally Insecure

In the fall of 2004, I was invited to speak at a synagogue in Woodstock, New York, home of the famous Woodstock music festival. I asked my hosts how was it that they were able to get a synagogue in Woodstock, of all places, big enough to support a lecture series. Very simple, they said. Since 9/11, Jews, and others, have been moving from New York City to places like Woodstock, to get away from what they fear will be the next ground zero. Right now this trend is a trickle, but it would become a torrent if a nuclear device were detonated in any European or American city.

Since this threat is the mother of all unflatteners, this book would not be complete without a discussion of it. We can live with a lot. We lived through 9/11. But we cannot live with nuclear terrorism. That would unflatten the world permanently.

The only reason that Osama bin Laden did not use a nuclear device on 9/11 was not that he did not have the intention but that he did not have the capability. And since the Dell Theory offers no hope of restraining the suicide supply chains, the only strategy we have is to limit their worst capabilities. That means a much more serious global effort to stanch nuclear proliferation by limiting the supply — to buy up the fissile material that is already out there, particularly in the former Soviet Union, and prevent more states from going nuclear. Harvard University international affairs expert Graham Allison, in his book *Nuclear Terrorism: The Ultimate Preventable Catastrophe*, outlines just such a strategy for denying terrorists access to nuclear weapons and nuclear materials. It can be done, he insists. It is a challenge to our will and convictions, but *not to our capabilities.* Allison proposes a new American-led international security order to deal with this problem based on what he calls "a doctrine of the Three No's: No loose nukes, No new nascent nukes, and No new nuclear states." No loose nukes, says Allison, means locking down all nuclear weapons and all nuclear material from which bombs could be made—in a much more serious way than we have done up till now. "We don't lose gold from Fort Knox," says Allison. "Russia doesn't lose treasures from the Kremlin armory. So we both know how to prevent theft of those things that are super valuable to us if we are determined to do it." No new nascent nukes means recognizing that there is a group of actors out there who can and do produce highly enriched uranium or plutonium, which is nothing more than nuclear bombs just about to hatch. We need a much more credible, multilateral nonproliferation regime that soaks up this fissile material. Finally, no new nuclear states means "drawing a line under the current eight nuclear powers and determining that, however unfair and unreasonable it may be, that club will have no more members than those eight," says Allison, adding that these three steps might then buy us time to develop a more formal, sustainable, internationally approved regime.

It would be nice also to be able to deny the Internet to al Qaeda and its ilk, but that, alas, is impossible—without undermining ourselves. That is why limiting their capabilities is necessary but not sufficient. We also have to find a way to get at their worst intentions. If we are not going to shut down the Internet and all the other creative and collaborative tools that have flattened the world, and if we can't restrict access to them, the only thing we can do is try to influence the imagination and intentions that people bring to them and draw from them. When I raised this issue, and the broad themes of this book, with my religious teacher, Rabbi Tzvi Marx from Holland, he surprised me by saying that the flat world I was describing reminded him of the story of the Tower of Babel.

How so? I asked. "The reason God banished all the people from the Tower of Babel and made them all speak different languages was not because he did not want them to collaborate per se," answered Rabbi Marx. "It was because he was enraged at what they were collaborating on—an effort to build a tower to the heavens so they could become God." This was a distortion of the human capacity, so God broke their union and their ability to communicate with one another. Now, all these years later, humankind has again created a new platform for more people from more places to communicate and collaborate with less friction and more ease than ever: the Internet. Would God see the Internet as heresy?

"Absolutely not," said Marx. "The heresy is not that mankind works together—it is to what ends. It is essential that we use this new ability to communicate and collaborate for the right ends—for constructive human aims and not megalomaniacal ends. Building a tower was megalomaniacal. Bin Laden's insistence that he has the truth and can flatten anyone else's tower who doesn't heed him is megalomaniacal. Collaborating so mankind can achieve its full potential is God's hope."

Exploring Context

1. Friedman opens this chapter by tracing the assembly of his Dell notebook. Explore Dell's Web site (dell.com). Does it provide any sense of the global supply chains that are vital to the creation of its computers? Why would Dell highlight or obscure these global supply chains on its Web site? What global images and what national images are

created? How does the site reflect your response to Question 1 of Questions for Critical Reading about collaboration?

2. Infosys, headquartered in Bangalore, India, is one of the companies that Friedman mentions. Visit the Web site for Infosys (Infosys.com). How does the information on this site reflect Friedman's arguments? Given that Infosys's primary business is completely tied to global supply chains, how does its site compare to Dell's? Use your answer to Question 1 of Exploring Context.

3. Visit the Federal Bureau of Investigation's counterterrorism Web site at www.fbi.gov /about-us/investigate/terrorism. Does it reflect the global nature of terror networks as explained by Friedman? How does Friedman propose we fight terrorism? Are such strategies being pursued by organizations like the FBI? You may want to draw on your work on collaboration and mutant supply chains from Questions 1 and 3 of Questions for Critical Reading.

Questions for Connecting

1. Michael Pollan, in "The Animals: Practicing Complexity" (p. 344), describes a very different, very local economic system. What parallels can you find between Pollan's and Friedman's ideas about the collateral effects of economic systems? Do "holons" have a role to play in the global supply chain? Are integrated and organic farming systems a kind of supply chain? Use your work defining Friedman's concepts from Questions for Critical Reading to help make your argument.

2. Ethan Watters questions the possibility of universal human attributes in "Being WEIRD: How Culture Shapes the Mind" (p. 493). How does his argument challenge Friedman's theories? Is Friedman's "Dell Theory of Conflict Prevention" dependent on WEIRD culture? Do global supply chains rely on particularly Western notions of the self? How do mutant supply chains reflect Watters's points?

3. Does the Dell Theory of Conflict Prevention rely on strong ties, weak ties, or a combination of the two? Use Charles Duhigg's concepts from "From Civil Rights to Megachurches" (p. 86) to evaluate Friedman's arguments. Do mutant supply chains function in the same way as the Montgomery bus boycott? What role does peer pressure play in maintaining peace? Use your work on collaboration and on mutant supply chains from Questions 1 and 3 of Questions for Critical Reading.

Language Matters

1. Integrating the words of other authors into your writing is an essential skill. In small groups, select a key quotation from Friedman's text and then create three different sentences that integrate that quotation. Have different groups share their results. What general techniques or strategies did people use?

2. Systems of citation are a central aspect of academic writing. In this class, you may be asked to use MLA, APA, or some other format for in-text citations. Develop your own system and illustrate it by citing a quotation from Friedman's essay. What kind of

information would the citation have to include? What does this then say about how citation systems work — what does every system seem to need? Why are there so many citation systems?

3. Strong organization is self-evident. That is, when a paper is well organized, each paragraph clearly has a place in the whole. Imagine a different order for Friedman's essay. What sections would you place first, and why? What transitions would you need? Why do you think Friedman organized his essay the way he did?

Assignments for Writing

1. According to Friedman's theory, global supply chains promote geopolitical stability. But Friedman is careful to say that they do not guarantee peace. Write a paper in which you determine the limitations of Friedman's theory. What would cause the Dell Theory of Conflict Prevention to fail? Are there specific supply chains or commodities (oil, gas, natural resources) that fall outside this theory? You may want to build your argument using your work on the Dell Theory from Question 2 of Questions for Critical Reading.

2. Both Friedman's Dell Theory of Conflict Prevention and his earlier Golden Arches Theory seem to rely on the spread of American culture. Can we reap the benefits of globalized economics without sacrificing local culture? Write a paper in which you suggest strategies for balancing globalization and localization. You might want to draw on your work with Ethan Watters's essay from Question 2 of Questions for Connecting in making your argument. Consider, too, these questions: Are terrorist supply chains an attempt to preserve local cultures? Must global economics mean global culture? How is that possible, given Watters's argument?

3. As you learned in Question 1 of Questions for Critical Reading, collaboration is one of Friedman's central concerns in this essay. Write a paper in which you use Friedman's ideas to suggest the key factors for making collaboration a success.

FRANCIS FUKUYAMA

Eric Feferberg/Getty Images

Francis Fukuyama holds a B.A. in classics from Cornell University and a Ph.D. in political science from Harvard University. He is Olivier Nomellini Senior Fellow at the Freeman Spogli Institute for International Studies at Stanford University. As a prominent neoconservative thinker, Fukuyama signed letters to both President Bill Clinton (in 1998) and President George W. Bush (in 2001) advocating the overthrow of Saddam Hussein (at the time, the president of Iraq). However, Fukuyama ultimately disapproved of the 2003 invasion of Iraq, writing publicly that neoconservative ideas had changed and were no longer supportable. Fukuyama is the author of multiple books of political philosophy advocating liberal democracy, including his 2006 publication *America at the Crossroads*, which deals directly with his departure from the neoconservative agenda.

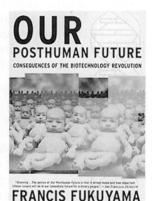

In *Our Posthuman Future: Consequences of the Biotechnology Revolution* (2002), Fukuyama updates an earlier proposal. Fukuyama had, in his book *The End of History and the Last Man* (1992), suggested that the history of humanity is an ideological struggle that is pretty much settled now, with liberal democracy as the eventual and destined end point, an argument he clarified in *America at the Crossroads*, stating that modernization is what wins the ideological struggle and that liberal democracy is merely one of the outcomes of modernization. In *Our Posthuman Future*, he reexamines this argument, taking into account the potential effects of biotechnology on liberal democracy. Now that human behavior can potentially be modified and DNA can be manipulated, Fukuyama asks, how will a political order based on natural equality survive?

In "Human Dignity," a chapter from *Our Posthuman Future*, Fukuyama examines the idea of "Factor X," an "essential human quality . . . that is worthy of a certain minimal level of respect" (p. 144) regardless of our varying individual characteristics, such as skin color, looks, or social class. Modern science, particularly the science of genetic engineering, Fukuyama claims, tends to disagree with the very idea of an essential human quality like Factor X. From this scientific perspective, human beings are the end result of genetic accidents and environmental influences. Fukuyama, however, finds merit in Pope John Paul II's assertion that science can't fully explain how human beings emerge from simple components. If that assertion is correct, Fukuyama speculates, what does this imply about science's ability to understand other complex systems? What does this mean for the future of human consciousness and political systems? In "Human Dignity," Fukuyama asks the reader to consider what happens to the idea of universal human equality when genetic engineering can be used to "improve" human genes.

Given the seemingly inevitable progress of science, which undoubtedly will influence you throughout your life, what does it mean to be human, and how can we preserve the qualities that make us so?

▶ TAGS: *civil rights, empathy, ethics, genetics, identity, science and technology, social change*
▶ CONNECTIONS: *Moalem, Rosin, Savage, Vaid*

Questions for Critical Reading

1. The idea of a *Factor X* plays a central role in Fukuyama's essay. As you read this text, locate quotations where Fukuyama defines this term and then provide a definition of the concept in your own words.

2. Do humans have an "essence"? Locate passages from Fukuyama that support your analysis. Does he think there is a human essence? What quotations make his position clear? You will need to read his text closely and critically to determine his position.

3. As the title of this selection suggests, Fukuyama is centrally concerned with the concept of human dignity in this chapter. Define *human dignity*, using quotations from Fukuyama that support your definition.

Human Dignity

Is it, then, possible to imagine a new Natural Philosophy, continually conscious that the "natural object" produced by analysis and abstraction is not reality but only a view, and always correcting the abstraction? I hardly know what I am asking for. . . . The regenerate science which I have in mind would not do even to minerals and vegetables what modern science threatens to do to man himself. When it explained it would not explain away. When it spoke of parts it would remember the whole. . . . The analogy between the *Tao* of Man and the instincts of an animal species would mean for it new light cast on the unknown thing, Instinct, by the only known reality of conscience and not a reduction of conscience to the category of Instinct. Its followers would not be free with the words *only* and *merely*. In a word, it would conquer Nature without being at the same time conquered by her and buy knowledge at a lower cost than that of life.

—C. S. LEWIS, *THE ABOLITION OF MAN*[1]

According to the Decree by the Council of Europe on Human Cloning, "The instrumentalisation of human beings through the deliberate creation of genetically identical human beings is contrary to human dignity and thus constitutes a misuse of medicine and biology."[2] Human dignity is one of those concepts that politicians, as well as virtually everyone else in political life, like to throw around, but that almost no one can either define or explain.

Much of politics centers on the question of human dignity and the desire for recognition to which it is related. That is, human beings constantly demand that others recognize their dignity, either as individuals or as members of religious, ethnic, racial, or other kinds of groups. The struggle for recognition is not economic: What we desire is not money but that other human beings respect us in the way we think we deserve. In earlier times, rulers wanted others to recognize their superior worth as king, emperor, or lord. Today, people seek recognition of their equal status as members of formerly disrespected or devalued groups—as women, gays, Ukrainians, the handicapped, Native Americans, and the like.[3]

The demand for an equality of recognition or respect is the dominant passion of modernity, as Tocqueville* noted over 170 years ago in *Democracy in America*.[4] What this means in a liberal democracy is a bit complicated. It is not necessarily that we think we are equal in all important respects, or demand that our lives be the same as everyone else's. Most people accept the fact that a Mozart or an Einstein or a Michael Jordan has talents and abilities that they don't have, and receives recognition and even monetary compensation for what he accomplishes with those talents. We accept, though we don't necessarily like, the fact that resources are distributed unequally based on what James Madison called the "different and unequal faculties of acquiring property." But we also believe that people deserve to keep what they earn and that the faculties for working and earning will not be the same for all people. We also accept the fact that we look different, come from different races and ethnicities, are of different sexes, and have different cultures.

Factor X

What the demand for equality of recognition implies is that when we strip all of a person's contingent and accidental characteristics away, there remains some essential human quality underneath that is worthy of a certain minimal level of respect—call it Factor X. Skin color, looks, social class and wealth, gender, cultural background, and even one's natural talents are all accidents of birth relegated to the class of nonessential characteristics. We make decisions on whom to befriend, whom to marry or do business with, or whom to shun at social events on the basis of these secondary characteristics. But in the political realm we are required to respect people equally on the basis of their possession of Factor X. You can cook, eat, torture, enslave, or render the carcass of any creature lacking Factor X, but if you do the same thing to a human being, you are guilty of a "crime against humanity." We accord beings with Factor X not just human rights but, if they are adults, political rights as well—that is, the right to live in democratic political communities where their rights to speech, religion, association, and political participation are respected.

The circle of beings to whom we attribute Factor X has been one of the most contested issues throughout human history. For many societies, including most democratic societies in earlier periods of history, Factor X belonged to a significant subset of the human race, excluding people of certain sexes, economic classes, races, and tribes and people with low intelligence, disabilities, birth defects, and the like. These societies were highly stratified, with different classes possessing more or less of Factor X, and some possessing none at all. Today, for believers in liberal equality, Factor X etches a bright red line around the whole of the human race and requires equality of respect for all of those on the inside, but attributes a lower level of dignity to those outside the boundary. Factor X is the human essence, the most basic meaning of what it is to be

5

---

*Tocqueville: Alexis de Tocqueville (1805–1859); French political thinker and historian best known for his two-volume book *Democracy in America* (1835 and 1840), which examined changing social conditions in American society [Ed.].

human. If all human beings are in fact equal in dignity, then X must be some characteristic universally possessed by them. So what is Factor X, and where does it come from?

For Christians, the answer is fairly easy: It comes from God. Man is created in the image of God, and therefore shares in some of God's sanctity, which entitles human beings to a higher level of respect than the rest of natural creation. In the words of Pope John Paul II, what this means is that "the human individual cannot be subordinated as a pure means or a pure instrument, either to the species or to society; he has value per se. He is a person. With his intellect and his will, he is capable of forming a relationship of communion, solidarity, and self-giving with his peers . . . It is by virtue of his spiritual soul that the whole person possesses such dignity even in his body."[5]

> **So what is Factor X, and where does it come from?**

Supposing one is not a Christian (or a religious believer of any sort), and doesn't accept the premise that man is created in the image of God. Is there a secular ground for believing that human beings are entitled to a special moral status or dignity? Perhaps the most famous effort to create a philosophical basis for human dignity was that of Kant,* who argued that Factor X was based on the human capacity for moral choice. That is, human beings could differ in intelligence, wealth, race, and gender, but all were equally able to act according to moral law or not. Human beings had dignity because they alone had free will—not just the subjective illusion of free will but the actual ability to transcend natural determinism and the normal rules of causality. It is the existence of free will that leads to Kant's well-known conclusion that human beings are always to be treated as ends and not as means.

It would be very difficult for any believer in a materialistic account of the universe—which includes the vast majority of natural scientists—to accept the Kantian account of human dignity. The reason is that it forces them to accept a form of dualism—that there is a realm of human freedom parallel to the realm of nature that is not determined by the latter. Most natural scientists would argue that what we believe to be free will is in fact an illusion and that all human decision making can ultimately be traced back to material causes. Human beings decide to do one thing over another because one set of neurons fires rather than another, and those neuronal firings can be traced back to prior material states of the brain. The human decision-making process may be more complex than that of other animals, but there is no sharp dividing line that distinguishes human moral choice from the kinds of choices that are made by other animals. Kant himself does not offer any proof that free will exists; he says that it is simply a necessary postulate of pure practical reason about the nature of morality—hardly an argument that a hard-bitten empirical scientist would accept.

Seize the Power

The problem posed by modern natural science goes even deeper. The very notion that there exists such a thing as a human "essence" has been under relentless attack by

---

*Kant: Immanuel Kant (1724–1804), German philosopher best known for *Critique of Pure Reason* (1781); he was concerned with questions of how we can know what we know [Ed.].

modern science for much of the past century and a half. One of the most fundamental assertions of Darwinism* is that species do not have essences.[6] That is, while Aristotle[†] believed in the eternity of the species (i.e., that what we have been labeling "species-typical behavior" is something unchanging), Darwin's theory maintains that this behavior changes in response to the organism's interaction with its environment. What is typical for a species represents a snapshot of the species at one particular moment of evolutionary time; what came before and what comes after will be different. Since Darwinism maintains that there is no cosmic teleology guiding the process of evolution, what seems to be the essence of a species is just an accidental by-product of a random evolutionary process.

In this perspective, what we have been calling human nature is merely the species-typical human characteristics and behavior that emerged about 100,000 years ago, during what evolutionary biologists call the "era of evolutionary adaptation" — when the precursors of modern humans were living and breeding on the African savanna. For many, this suggests that human nature has no special status as a guide to morals or values because it is historically contingent. David Hull, for example, argues,

> I do not see why the existence of human universals is all that important. Perhaps all and only people have opposable thumbs, use tools, live in true societies, or what have you. I think that such attributions are either false or vacuous, but even if they were true and significant, the distributions of these particular characters is largely a matter of evolutionary happenstance.[7]

The geneticist Lee Silver, trying to debunk the idea that there is a natural order that could be undermined by genetic engineering, asserts,

> Unfettered evolution is never predetermined [toward some goal], and not necessarily associated with progress — it is simply a response to unpredictable environmental changes. If the asteroid that hit our planet 60 million years ago had flown past instead, there would never have been any human beings at all. And whatever the natural order might be, it is not necessarily good. The smallpox virus was part of the natural order until it was forced into extinction by human intervention.[8]

This inability to define a natural essence doesn't bother either writer. Hull, for example, states that "I, for one, would be extremely uneasy to base something as important as human rights on such temporary contingencies [as human nature] . . . I fail to see why it matters. I fail to see, for example, why we must all be essentially the same to have rights."[9] Silver, for his part, pooh-poohs fears about genetic engineering on the part of those with religious convictions or those who believe in a natural order. In the future, man will no longer be a slave to his genes, but their master:

> Why not seize this power? Why not control what has been left to chance in the past? Indeed, we control all other aspects of our children's lives and identities

---

*Darwinism: Shorthand for naturalist Charles Darwin's idea of evolution by natural selection, the concept that only the species best adapted to their environment survive [Ed.].

†Aristotle: Greek philosopher and enormously important figure in Western thought. Aristotle (384–322 BC) was a student of Plato and a teacher of Alexander the Great [Ed.].

through powerful social and environmental influences and, in some cases, with the use of powerful drugs like Ritalin and Prozac. On what basis can we reject positive genetic influences on a person's essence when we accept the rights of parents to benefit their children in every other way?[10]

Why not seize this power, indeed?

Well, let us begin by considering what the consequences of the abandonment of the idea that there is a Factor X, or human essence, that unites all human beings would be for the cherished idea of universal human equality—an idea to which virtually all of the debunkers of the idea of human essences are invariably committed. Hull is right that we don't all need to be the same in order to have rights—but we need to be the same in some one critical respect in order to have *equal* rights. He for one is very concerned that basing human rights on human nature will stigmatize homosexuals, because their sexual orientation differs from the heterosexual norm. But the only basis on which anyone can make an argument in favor of equal rights for gays is to argue that whatever their sexual orientation, *they are people too* in some other respect that is more essential than their sexuality. If you cannot find this common other ground, then there is no reason not to discriminate against them, because in fact they are different creatures from everyone else.

Similarly, Lee Silver, who is so eager to take up the power of genetic engineering to "improve" people, is nonetheless horrified at the possibility that it could be used to create a class of genetically superior people. He paints a scenario in which a class called the GenRich steadily improve the cognitive abilities of their children to the point that they break off from the rest of the human race to form a separate species.

Silver is not horrified by much else that technology may bring us by way of unnatural reproduction—for example, two lesbians producing genetic offspring, or eggs taken from an unborn female fetus to produce a child whose mother had never been born. He dismisses the moral concerns of virtually every religion or traditional moral system with regard to future genetic engineering but draws the line at what he perceives as threats to human equality. He does not seem to understand that, given his premises, there are no possible grounds on which he can object to the GenRich, or the fact that they might assign themselves rights superior to those of the GenPoor. Since there is no stable essence common to all human beings, or rather because that essence is variable and subject to human manipulation, why not create a race born with metaphorical saddles on their backs, and another with boots and spurs to ride them? Why not seize *that* power as well?

The bioethicist Peter Singer, whose appointment to Princeton University caused great controversy because of his advocacy of infanticide and euthanasia under certain circumstances, is simply more consistent than most people on the consequences of abandoning the concept of human dignity. Singer is an unabashed utilitarian: He believes that the single relevant standard for ethics is to minimize suffering in the aggregate for all creatures. Human beings are part of a continuum of life and have no special status in his avowedly Darwinian worldview. This leads him to two perfectly logical conclusions: the need for animal rights, since animals can experience pain and suffering as well as humans, and the downgrading of the rights of infants and elderly people who lack certain key traits, like self-awareness, that would allow them to anticipate pain. The rights of certain animals, in his view, deserve greater respect than those of certain human beings.

But Singer is not nearly forthright enough in following these premises through to their logical conclusion, since he remains a committed egalitarian. What he does not explain is why the relief of suffering should remain the only moral good. As usual, the philosopher Friedrich Nietzsche was much more clear-eyed than anyone else in understanding the consequences of modern natural science and the abandonment of the concept of human dignity. Nietzsche had the great insight to see that, on the one hand, once the clear red line around the whole of humanity could no longer be drawn, the way would be paved for a return to a much more hierarchical ordering of society. If there is a continuum of gradations between human and nonhuman, there is a continuum within the type human as well. This would inevitably mean the liberation of the strong from the constraints that a belief in either God or Nature had placed on them. On the other hand, it would lead the rest of mankind to demand health and safety as the only possible goods, since all the higher goals that had once been set for them were now debunked. In the words of Nietzsche's Zarathustra, "One has one's little pleasure for the day and one's little pleasure for the night: But one has a regard for health. 'We have invented happiness,' say the last men, and they blink."[11] Indeed, both the return of hierarchy and the egalitarian demand for health, safety, and relief of suffering might all go hand in hand if the rulers of the future could provide the masses with enough of the "little poisons" they demanded.

It has always struck me that one hundred years after Nietzsche's death, we are much less far down the road to either the superman or the last man than he predicted. Nietzsche once castigated John Stuart Mill as a "flathead" for believing that one could have a semblance of Christian morality in the absence of belief in a Christian God. And yet, in a Europe and an America that have become secularized over the past two generations, we see a lingering belief in the concept of human dignity, which is by now completely cut off from its religious roots. And not just lingering: The idea that one could exclude any group of people on the basis of race, gender, disability, or virtually any other characteristic from the charmed circle of those deserving recognition for human dignity is the one thing that will bring total obloquy on the head of any politician who proposes it. In the words of the philosopher Charles Taylor, "We believe it would be utterly wrong and unfounded to draw the boundaries any narrower than around the whole human race," and should anyone try to do so, "we should immediately ask what distinguished those within from those left out."[12] The idea of the equality of human dignity, deracinated from its Christian or Kantian origins, is held as a matter of religious dogma by the most materialist of natural scientists. The continuing arguments over the moral status of the unborn (about which more later) constitute the only exception to this general rule.

The reasons for the persistence of the idea of the equality of human dignity are complex. Partly it is a matter of the force of habit and what Max Weber once called the "ghost of dead religious beliefs" that continue to haunt us. Partly it is the product of historical accident: The last important political movement to explicitly deny the premise of universal human dignity was Nazism, and the horrifying consequences of the Nazis' racial and eugenic policies were sufficient to inoculate those who experienced them for the next couple of generations.

But another important reason for the persistence of the idea of the universality of human dignity has to do with what we might call the nature of nature itself. Many of the grounds on which certain groups were historically denied their share of human dignity were proven to be simply a matter of prejudice, or else based on cultural and environmental conditions that could be changed. The notions that women were too irrational or emotional to participate in politics, and that immigrants from southern Europe had smaller head sizes and were less intelligent than those from northern Europe, were overturned on the basis of sound, empirical science. That moral order did not completely break down in the West in the wake of the destruction of consensus over traditional religious values should not surprise us either, because moral order comes from within human nature itself and is not something that has to be imposed on human nature by culture.[13]

All of this could change under the impact of future biotechnology. The most clear and present danger is that the large genetic variations between individuals will narrow and become clustered within certain distinct social groups. Today, the "genetic lottery" guarantees that the son or daughter of a rich and successful parent will not necessarily inherit the talents and abilities that created conditions conducive to the parent's success. Of course, there has always been a degree of genetic selection: Assortative mating means that successful people will tend to marry each other and, to the extent that their success is genetically based, will pass on to their children better life opportunities. But in the future, the full weight of modern technology can be put in the service of optimizing the kinds of genes that are passed on to one's offspring. This means that social elites may not just pass on social advantages but embed them genetically as well. This may one day include not only characteristics like intelligence and beauty, but behavioral traits like diligence, competitiveness, and the like.

The genetic lottery is judged as inherently unfair by many because it condemns certain people to lesser intelligence, or bad looks, or disabilities of one sort or another. But in another sense it is profoundly egalitarian, since everyone, regardless of social class, race, or ethnicity, has to play in it. The wealthiest man can and often does have a good-for-nothing son; hence the saying "Shirtsleeves to shirtsleeves in three generations." When the lottery is replaced by choice, we open up a new avenue along which human beings can compete, one that threatens to increase the disparity between the top and bottom of the social hierarchy.

What the emergence of a genetic overclass will do to the idea of universal human dignity is something worth pondering. Today, many bright and successful young people believe that they owe their success to accidents of birth and upbringing but for which their lives might have taken a very different course. They feel themselves, in other words, to be lucky, and they are capable of feeling sympathy for people who are less lucky than they. But to the extent that they become "children of choice" who have been genetically selected by their parents for certain characteristics, they may come to believe increasingly that their success is a matter not just of luck but of good choices and planning on the part of their parents, and hence something deserved. They will look, think, act, and perhaps even feel differently from those who were not similarly chosen, and may come in time to think of themselves as different kinds of creatures. They may, in short, feel themselves to be aristocrats, and unlike aristocrats of old, their claim to better birth will be rooted in nature and not convention.

Aristotle's discussion of slavery in Book I of the *Politics* is instructive on this score. It is often condemned as a justification of Greek slavery, but in fact the discussion is far more sophisticated and is relevant to our thinking about genetic classes. Aristotle makes a distinction between conventional and natural slavery.[14] He argues that slavery would be justified by nature if it were the case that there were people with naturally slavish natures. It is not clear from his discussion that he believes such people exist: Most actual slavery is conventional—that is, it is the result of victory in war or force, or based on the wrong opinion that barbarians as a class should be slaves of Greeks.[15] The noble-born think their nobility comes from nature rather than acquired virtue and that they can pass it on to their children. But, Aristotle notes, nature is "frequently unable to bring this about."[16] So why not, as Lee Silver suggests, "seize this power" to give children genetic advantages and correct the defect of natural equality?

The possibility that biotechnology will permit the emergence of new genetic classes has been frequently noted and condemned by those who have speculated about the future.[17] But the opposite possibility also seems to be entirely plausible—that there will be an impetus toward a much more genetically egalitarian society. For it seems highly unlikely that people in modern democratic societies will sit around complacently if they see elites embedding their advantages genetically in their children.

Indeed, this is one of the few things in a politics of the future that people are likely   25 to rouse themselves to fight over. By this I mean not just fighting metaphorically, in the sense of shouting matches among talking heads on TV and debates in Congress, but actually picking up guns and bombs and using them on other people. There are very few domestic political issues today in our rich, self-satisfied liberal democracies that can cause people to get terribly upset, but the specter of rising genetic inequality may well get people off their couches and into the streets.

If people get upset enough about genetic inequality, there will be two alternative courses of action. The first and most sensible would simply be to forbid the use of biotechnology to enhance human characteristics and decline to compete in this dimension. But the notion of enhancement may become too powerfully attractive to forgo, or it may prove difficult to enforce a rule preventing people from enhancing their children, or the courts may declare they have a right to do so. At this point a second possibility opens up, which is to use that same technology to raise up the bottom.[18]

This is the only scenario in which it is plausible that we will see a liberal democracy of the future get back into the business of state-sponsored eugenics. The bad old form of eugenics discriminated against the disabled and less intelligent by forbidding them to have children. In the future, it may be possible to breed children who are more intelligent, more healthy, more "normal." Raising the bottom is something that can only be accomplished through the intervention of the state. Genetic enhancement technology is likely to be expensive and involve some risk, but even if it were relatively cheap and safe, people who are poor and lacking in education would still fail to take advantage of it. So the bright red line of universal human dignity will have to be reinforced by allowing the state to make sure that no one falls outside it.

The politics of breeding future human beings will be very complex. Up to now, the Left has on the whole been opposed to cloning, genetic engineering, and similar biotechnologies for a number of reasons, including traditional humanism, environmental concerns, suspicion of technology and of the corporations that produce it, and fear of eugenics. The Left has historically sought to play down the importance of heredity in favor of social factors in explaining human outcomes. For people on the Left to come around and support genetic engineering for the disadvantaged, they would first have to admit that genes are important in determining intelligence and other types of social outcomes in the first place.

The Left has been more hostile to biotechnology in Europe than in North America. Much of this hostility is driven by the stronger environmental movements there, which have led the campaign, for example, against genetically modified foods. (Whether certain forms of radical environmentalism will translate into hostility to human biotechnology remains to be seen. Some environmentalists see themselves defending nature from human beings, and seem to be more concerned with threats to nonhuman than to human nature.) The Germans in particular remain very sensitive to anything that smacks of eugenics. The philosopher Peter Sloterdijk raised a storm of protest in 1999 when he suggested that it will soon be impossible for people to refuse the power of selection that biotechnology provides them, and that the questions of breeding something "beyond" man that were raised by Nietzsche and Plato could no longer be ignored.[19] He was condemned by the sociologist Jürgen Habermas, among others, who in other contexts has also come out against human cloning.[20]

On the other hand, there are some on the Left who have begun to make the case for genetic engineering.[21] John Rawls argued in *A Theory of Justice* that the unequal distribution of natural talents was inherently unfair. A Rawlsian should therefore want to make use of biotechnology to equalize life chances by breeding the bottom up, assuming that prudential considerations concerning safety, cost, and the like would be settled. Ronald Dworkin has laid out a case for the right of parents to genetically engineer their children based on a broader concern to protect autonomy,[22] and Laurence Tribe has suggested that a ban on cloning would be wrong because it might create discrimination against children who were cloned in spite of the ban.[23]

It is impossible to know which of these two radically different scenarios—one of growing genetic inequality, the other of growing genetic equality—is more likely to come to pass. But once the technological possibility for biomedical enhancement is realized, it is hard to see how growing genetic inequality would fail to become one of the chief controversies of twenty-first-century politics.

Human Dignity Redux

Denial of the concept of human dignity—that is, of the idea that there is something unique about the human race that entitles every member of the species to a higher moral status than the rest of the natural world—leads us down a very perilous path. We may be compelled ultimately to take this path, but we should do so only with our eyes open. Nietzsche is a much better guide to what lies down that road than the legions of bioethicists and casual academic Darwinians that today are prone to give us moral advice on this subject.

To avoid following that road, we need to take another look at the notion of human dignity, and ask whether there is a way to defend the concept against its detractors that is fully compatible with modern natural science but that also does justice to the full meaning of human specificity. I believe that there is.

In contrast to a number of conservative Protestant denominations that continue to hold a brief for creationism, the Catholic Church by the end of the twentieth century had come to terms with the theory of evolution. In his 1996 message to the Pontifical Academy of Sciences, Pope John Paul II corrected the encyclical *Humani generis* of Pius XII, which maintained that Darwinian evolution was a serious hypothesis but one that remained unproven. The pope stated, "Today, almost half a century after the publication of the Encyclical, new knowledge has led to the recognition of the theory of evolution as more than a hypothesis. It is indeed remarkable that this theory has been progressively accepted by researchers, following a series of discoveries in various fields of knowledge. The convergence, neither sought nor fabricated, of the results of work that was conducted independently is in itself a significant argument in favor of this theory."[24]

But the pope went on to say that while the church can accept the view that man is descended from nonhuman animals, there is an "ontological leap" that occurs somewhere in this evolutionary process.[25] The human soul is something directly created by God: Consequently, "theories of evolution which, in accordance with the philosophies inspiring them, consider the mind as emerging from the forces of living nature, or as a mere epiphenomenon of this matter, are incompatible with the truth about man." The pope continued, "Nor are they able to ground the dignity of the person."

The pope was saying, in other words, that at some point in the 5 million years between man's chimplike forebears and the emergence of modern human beings, a human soul was inserted into us in a way that remains mysterious. Modern natural science can uncover the time line of this process and explicate its material correlates, but it has not fully explained either what the soul is or how it came to be. The church has obviously learned a great deal from modern natural science in the past two centuries and has adjusted its doctrines accordingly. But while many natural scientists would scoff at the idea that they have anything to learn from the church, the pope has pointed to a real weakness in the current state of evolutionary theory, which scientists would do well to ponder. Modern natural science has explained a great deal less about what it means to be human than many scientists think it has.

Parts and Wholes

Many contemporary Darwinians believe that they have demystified the problem of how human beings came to be human through the classical reductionist methods of modern natural science. That is, any higher-order behavior or characteristic, such as language or aggression, can be traced back through the firing of neurons to the biochemical substrate of the brain, which in turn can be understood in terms of the simpler organic compounds of which it is composed. The brain arrived at its present state through a series of incremental evolutionary changes that were driven by random variation, and a process of natural selection by which the requirements of the surrounding environment selected for certain mental characteristics. Every human characteristic can thus be traced back to a prior material cause. If, for example, we today love to listen to Mozart or Beethoven, it is because we have auditory systems that were evolved, in the environment of evolutionary adaptation, to discriminate between certain kinds of sounds that were necessary perhaps to warn us against predators or to help us on a hunt.[26]

The problem with this kind of thinking is not that it is necessarily false but that it is insufficient to explain many of the most salient and unique human traits. The problem lies in the methodology of reductionism itself for understanding complex systems, and particularly biological ones.

Reductionism constitutes, of course, one of the foundations of modern natural science and is responsible for many of its greatest triumphs. You see before you two apparently different substances, the graphite in your pencil lead and the diamond in your engagement ring, and you might be tempted to believe that they were essentially different substances. But reductionist chemistry has taught us that in fact they are both composed of the same simpler substance, carbon, and that the apparent differences are not ones of essence but merely of the way the carbon atoms are bonded. Reductionist physics has been busy over the past century tracing atoms back to subatomic particles and thence back to an even more reduced set of basic forces of nature.

But what is appropriate for domains in physics, like celestial mechanics and fluid dynamics, is not necessarily appropriate for the study of objects at the opposite end of the complexity scale, like most biological systems, because the behavior of complex systems cannot be predicted by simply aggregating or scaling up the behavior of the parts that constitute them.* The distinctive and easily recognizable behavior of a flock of birds or a swarm of bees, for example, is the product of the interaction of individual birds or bees following relatively simple behavioral rules (fly next to a partner, avoid obstacles, and so on), none of which encompasses or defines the behavior of the flock or swarm as a whole. Rather, the group behavior "emerges" as a result of the interaction of the individuals that make it up. In many cases, the relationship between parts and wholes is nonlinear: That is, increasing input A increases output B up to a certain point, whereupon it creates a qualitatively different and unexpected output C. This is true even of relatively simple chemicals like water: H_2O undergoes a phase transition from liquid to solid at 32 degrees Fahrenheit, something that one would not necessarily predict on the basis of knowledge of its chemical composition.

That the behavior of complex wholes cannot be understood as the aggregated behavior of their parts has been understood in the natural sciences for some time now,[27] and has led to the development of the field of so-called nonlinear or "complex adaptive" systems, which try to model the emergence of complexity. This approach is, in a way, the opposite of reductionism: It shows that while wholes can be traced back to their simpler antecedent parts, there is no simple predictive model that allows us to move from the parts to the emergent behaviors of the wholes. Being nonlinear, they may be extremely sensitive to small differences in starting conditions and thus may appear chaotic even when their behavior is completely deterministic.

40

---

*The determinism of classical Newtonian mechanics is based in large measure on the parallelogram rule, which says that the effects of two forces acting on a body can be summed as if each were acting independently of the other. Newton shows that this rule works for celestial bodies like planets and stars, and assumes that it will also work for other natural objects, like animals.

This means that the behavior of complex systems is much more difficult to understand than the founders of reductionist science once believed. The eighteenth-century astronomer Laplace once said that he could precisely predict the future of the universe on the basis of Newtonian mechanics, if he could know the mass and motion of the universe's constituent parts.[28] No scientist could make this claim today—not just because of the inherent uncertainties introduced by quantum mechanics but also because there exists no reliable methodology for predicting the behavior of complex systems.[29] In the words of Arthur Peacocke, "The concepts and theories . . . that constitute the content of the sciences focusing on the more complex levels are often (not always) logically not reducible to those operative in the sciences that focus on their components."[30] There is a hierarchy of levels of complexity in the sciences, with human beings and human behavior occupying a place at the uppermost level.

Each level can give us some insight into the levels above it, but understanding the lower levels does not allow one to fully understand the higher levels' emergent properties. Researchers in the area of complex adaptive systems have created so-called agent-based models of complex systems, and have applied them in a wide variety of areas, from cell biology to fighting a war to distributing natural gas. It remains to be seen, however, whether this approach constitutes a single, coherent methodology applicable to all complex systems.[31] Such models may tell us only that certain systems will remain inherently chaotic and unpredictable, or that prediction rests on a precise knowledge of initial conditions that is unavailable to us. The higher level must thus be understood with a methodology appropriate to its degree of complexity.

We can illustrate the problematic relationship of parts to wholes by reference to one unique domain of human behavior, politics.[32] Aristotle states that man is a political animal by nature. If one were to try to build a case for human dignity based on human specificity, the capability of engaging in politics would certainly constitute one important component of human uniqueness. Yet the idea of our uniqueness in this regard has been challenged. . . . [C]himpanzees and other primates engage in something that looks uncannily like human politics as they struggle and connive to achieve alpha male status. They appear, moreover, to feel the political emotions of pride and shame as they interact with other members of their group. Their political behavior can also apparently be transmitted through nongenetic means, so that political culture would not seem to be the exclusive preserve of human beings.[33] Some observers gleefully cite examples like this to deflate human feelings of self-importance relative to other species.

But to confuse human politics with the social behavior of any other species is to mistake parts for wholes. Only human beings can formulate, debate, and modify abstract rules of justice. When Aristotle asserted that man is a political animal by nature, he meant this only in the sense that politics is a potentiality that emerges over time.[34] He notes that human politics did not begin until the first lawgiver established a state and promulgated laws, an event that was of great benefit to mankind but that was contingent on historical developments. This accords with what we know today about the emergence of the state, which took place in parts of the world like Egypt and Babylonia perhaps 10,000 years ago and was most likely related to the development of agriculture. For tens of thousands of years before that, human beings lived in stateless hunter-gatherer societies in which the largest group numbered no more than 50 to

100 individuals, most of them related by kinship.[35] So in a certain sense, while human sociability is obviously natural, it is not clear that humans are political animals by nature.

But Aristotle insists that politics is natural to man despite the fact that it did not exist at all in early periods of human history. He argues that it is human language that allows human beings to formulate laws and abstract principles of justice that are necessary to the creation of a state and of political order. Ethologists have noted that many other species communicate with sounds, and that chimpanzees and other animals can learn human language to a limited extent. But no other species has *human* language—that is, the ability to formulate and communicate abstract principles of action. It is only when these two natural characteristics, human sociability and human language, come together that human politics emerges. Human language obviously evolved to promote sociability, but it is very unlikely that there were evolutionary forces shaping it to become an enabler of politics. It was rather like one of Stephen Jay Gould's spandrels,* something that evolved for one reason but that found another key purpose when combined in a human whole.[36] Human politics, though natural in an emergent sense, is not reducible to either animal sociability or animal language, which were its precursors.

Consciousness

The area in which the inability of a reductionist materialist science to explain observable phenomena is most glaringly evident is the question of human consciousness. By consciousness I mean subjective mental states: not just the thoughts and images that appear to you as you are thinking or reading this page, but also the sensations, feelings, and emotions that you experience as part of everyday life.

There has been a huge amount of research and theorizing about consciousness over the past two generations, coming in equal measure from the neurosciences and from studies in computer and artificial intelligence (AI). Particularly in the latter field there are many enthusiasts who are convinced that with more powerful computers and new approaches to computing, such as neural networks, we are on the verge of a breakthrough in which mechanical computers will achieve consciousness. There have been conferences and earnest discussions devoted to the question of whether it would be moral to turn off such a machine if and when this breakthrough occurs, and whether we would need to assign rights to conscious machines.

The fact of the matter is that we are nowhere close to a breakthrough; consciousness remains as stubbornly mysterious as it ever was. The problem with the current state of thinking begins with the traditional philosophical problem of the ontological status of consciousness. Subjective mental states, while produced by material biological processes, appear to be of a very different, nonmaterial order from other phenomena. The fear of dualism—that is, the doctrine that there are two essential types of being, material and mental—is so strong among researchers in this field that it has led them to palpably ridiculous conclusions. In the words of the philosopher John Searle,

---

*A spandrel is an architectural feature that emerges, unplanned by the architect, from the intersection of a dome and the walls that support it.

Seen from the perspective of the last fifty years, the philosophy of mind, as well as cognitive science and certain branches of psychology, present a very curious spectacle. The most striking feature is how much of mainstream philosophy of mind of the past fifty years seems obviously false . . . in the philosophy of mind, obvious facts about the mental, such as that we all really do have subjective conscious mental states and that these are not eliminable in favor of anything else, are routinely denied by many, perhaps most, of the advanced thinkers in the subject.[37]

An example of a patently false understanding of consciousness comes from one of the leading experts in the field, Daniel Dennett, whose book *Consciousness Explained* finally comes to the following definition of consciousness: "Human consciousness is *itself* a huge complex of memes (or more exactly, meme-effects in brains) that can best be understood as the operation of a *'von Neumannesque'* virtual machine *implemented* in the *parallel architecture* of a brain that was not designed for any such activities."[38] A naive reader may be excused for thinking that this kind of statement doesn't do much at all to advance our understanding of consciousness. Dennett is saying in effect that human consciousness is simply the by-product of the operations of a certain type of computer, and if we think that there is more to it than that, we have a mistakenly old-fashioned view of what consciousness is. As Searle says of this approach, it works only by denying the existence of what you and I and everyone else understand consciousness to be (that is, subjective feelings).[39]

Similarly, many of the researchers in the field of artificial intelligence sidestep the question of consciousness by in effect changing the subject. They assume that the brain is simply a highly complex type of organic computer that can be identified by its external characteristics. The well-known Turing test asserts that if a machine can perform a cognitive task such as carrying on a conversation in a way that from the outside is indistinguishable from similar activities carried out by a human being, then it is indistinguishable on the inside as well. Why this should be an adequate test of human mentality is a mystery, for the machine will obviously not have any subjective awareness of what it is doing, or feelings about its activities.* This doesn't prevent such authors as Hans Moravec [40] and Ray Kurzweil[41] from predicting that machines, once they reach a requisite level of complexity, will possess human attributes like consciousness as well.[42] If they are right, this will have important consequences for our notions of human dignity, because it will have been conclusively proven that human beings are essentially nothing more than complicated machines that can be made out of silicon and transistors as easily as carbon and neurons.

The likelihood that this will happen seems very remote, however, not so much because machines will never duplicate human intelligence—I suspect they will probably be able to come very close in this regard—but rather because it is impossible to see how they will come to acquire human emotions. It is the stuff of science fiction for an android, robot, or computer to suddenly start experiencing emotions like fear, hope,

---

*Searle's critique of this approach is contained in his "Chinese room" puzzle, which raises the question of whether a computer could be said to understand Chinese any more than a non-Chinese-speaking individual locked in a room who received instructions on how to manipulate a series of symbols in Chinese. See Searle (1997), p. 11.

even sexual desire, but no one has come remotely close to positing how this might come about. The problem is not simply that, like the rest of consciousness, no one understands what emotions are ontologically; no one understands why they came to exist in human biology.

There are of course functional reasons for feelings like pain and pleasure. If we didn't find sex pleasurable we wouldn't reproduce, and if we didn't feel pain from fire we would be burning ourselves constantly. But state-of-the-art thinking in cognitive science maintains that the particular subjective form that the emotions take is not necessary to their function. It is perfectly possible, for example, to design a robot with heat sensors in its fingers connected to an actuator that would pull the robot's hand away from a fire. The robot could keep itself from being burned without having any subjective sense of pain, and it could make decisions on which objectives to fulfill and which activities to avoid on the basis of a mechanical computation of the inputs of different electrical impulses. A Turing test would say it was a human being in its behavior, but it would actually be devoid of the most important quality of a human being, feelings. The actual subjective forms that emotions take are today seen in evolutionary biology and in cognitive science as no more than epiphenomenal to their underlying function; there are no obvious reasons this form should have been selected for in the course of evolutionary history.[43]

As Robert Wright points out, this leads to the very bizarre outcome that what is most important to us as human beings has no apparent purpose in the material scheme of things by which we became human.[44] For it is the distinctive human gamut of emotions that produces human purposes, goals, objectives, wants, needs, desires, fears, aversions, and the like and hence is the source of human values. While many would list human reason and human moral choice as the most important unique human characteristics that give our species dignity, I would argue that possession of the full human emotional gamut is at least as important, if not more so.

The political theorist Robert McShea demonstrates the importance of human emotions to our commonsense understanding of what it means to be human by asking us to perform the following thought experiment.[45] Suppose you met two creatures on a desert island, both of which had the rational capacity of a human being and hence the ability to carry on a conversation. One had the physical form of a lion but the emotions of a human being, while the other had the physical form of a human being but the emotional characteristics of a lion. Which creature would you feel more comfortable with, which creature would you be more likely to befriend or enter into a moral relationship with? The answer, as countless children's books with sympathetic talking lions suggest, is the lion, because species-typical human emotions are more critical to our sense of our own humanness than either our reason or our physical appearance. The coolly analytical Mr. Spock in the TV series *Star Trek* appears at times more likable than the emotional Mr. Scott only because we suspect that somewhere beneath his rational exterior lurk deeply buried human feelings. Certainly many of the female characters he encountered in the series hoped they could rouse something more than robotic responses from him.

On the other hand, we would regard a Mr. Spock who was truly devoid of any feelings as a psychopath and a monster. If he offered us a benefit, we might accept it but would feel no gratitude because we would know it was the product of rational calculation on his part and not goodwill. If we double-crossed him, we would feel no guilt, because we know that he cannot himself entertain feelings of anger or of having been betrayed. And if circumstances forced us to kill him to save ourselves, or to sacrifice his life in a hostage situation, we would feel no more regret than if we lost any other valuable asset, like a car or a teleporter.[46] Even though we might want to cooperate with this Mr. Spock, we would not regard him as a moral agent entitled to the respect

> **[W]e would regard a Mr. Spock who was truly devoid of any feelings as a psychopath and a monster.**

that human beings command. The computer geeks in AI labs who think of themselves as nothing more than complex computer programs and want to download themselves into a computer should worry, since no one would care if they were turned off for good.

So there is a great deal that comes together under the rubric of consciousness that helps define human specificity and hence human dignity, which nonetheless cannot currently be fully explicated by modern natural science. It is not sufficient to argue that some other animals are conscious, or have culture, or have language, for their consciousness does not combine human reason, human language, human moral choice, and human emotions in ways that are capable of producing human politics, human art, or human religion. All of the nonhuman precursors of these human traits that existed in evolutionary history, and all of the material causes and preconditions for their emergence, collectively add up to much less than the human whole. Jared Diamond in his book *The Third Chimpanzee* notes the fact that the chimpanzee and human genomes overlap by more than 98 percent, implying that the differences between the two species are relatively trivial.[47] But for an emergent complex system, small differences can lead to enormous qualitative changes. It is a bit like saying there is no significant difference between ice and liquid water because they differ in temperature by only 1 degree.

Thus one does not have to agree with the pope that God directly inserted a human soul in the course of evolutionary history to acknowledge with him that there was a very important qualitative, if not ontological, leap that occurred at some point in this process. It is this leap from parts to a whole that ultimately has to constitute the basis for human dignity, a concept one can believe in even if one does not begin from the pope's religious premises.

What this whole is and how it came to be remain, in Searle's word, "mysterious." None of the branches of modern natural science that have tried to address this question have done more than scratch the surface, despite the belief of many scientists that they have demystified the entire process. It is common now for many AI researchers to say that consciousness is an "emergent property" of a certain kind of complex computer. But this is no more than an unproven hypothesis based on an analogy with other complex systems. No one has ever seen consciousness emerge under experimental conditions, or even posited a theory as to how this might come about. It would be surprising if the process of "emergence" didn't play an important part in explaining how humans came to be human, but whether that is all there is to the story is something we do not at present know.

This is not to say that the demystification by science will never happen. Searle himself believes that consciousness is a biological property of the brain much like the firing of neurons or the production of neurotransmitters and that biology will someday be able to explain how organic tissue can produce it. He argues that our present problems in understanding consciousness do not require us to adopt a dualistic ontology or abandon the scientific framework of material causation. The problem of how consciousness arose does not require recourse to the direct intervention of God.

It does not, on the other hand, rule it out, either.   60

What to Fight For

If what gives us dignity and a moral status higher than that of other living creatures is related to the fact that we are complex wholes rather than the sum of simple parts, then it is clear that there is no simple answer to the question, What is Factor X? That is, Factor X cannot be reduced to the possession of moral choice, or reason, or language, or sociability, or sentience, or emotions, or consciousness, or any other quality that has been put forth as a ground for human dignity. It is all of these qualities coming together in a human whole that make up Factor X. Every member of the human species possesses a genetic endowment that allows him or her to become a whole human being, an endowment that distinguishes a human in essence from other types of creatures.

A moment's reflection will show that none of the key qualities that contribute to human dignity can exist in the absence of the others. Human reason, for example, is not that of a computer; it is pervaded by emotions, and its functioning is in fact facilitated by the latter.[48] Moral choice cannot exist without reason, needless to say, but it is also grounded in feelings such as pride, anger, shame, and sympathy.[49] Human consciousness is not just individual preferences and instrumental reason, but is shaped intersubjectively by other consciousnesses and their moral evaluations. We are social and political animals not merely because we are capable of game-theoretic reason, but because we are endowed with certain social emotions. Human sentience is not that of a pig or a horse, because it is coupled with human memory and reason.

This protracted discussion of human dignity is intended to answer the following question: What is it that we want to protect from any future advances in biotechnology? The answer is, we want to protect the full range of our complex, evolved natures against attempts at self-modification. We do not want to disrupt either the unity or the continuity of human nature, and thereby the human rights that are based on it.

If Factor X is related to our very complexity and the complex interactions of uniquely human characteristics like moral choice, reason, and a broad emotional gamut, it is reasonable to ask how and why biotechnology would seek to make us less complex. The answer lies in the constant pressure that exists to reduce the ends of biomedicine to utilitarian ones—that is, the attempt to reduce a complex diversity of natural ends and purposes to just a few simple categories like pain and pleasure, or autonomy. There is in particular a constant predisposition to allow the relief of pain and suffering to automatically trump all other human purposes and objectives. For this will be the constant trade-off that biotechnology will pose: We can cure this disease, or prolong this person's life, or make this child more tractable, at the expense of some ineffable human quality like genius, or ambition, or sheer diversity.

That aspect of our complex natures most under threat has to do with our emotional   65
gamut. We will be constantly tempted to think that we understand what "good" and "bad" emotions are, and that we can do nature one better by suppressing the latter, by

trying to make people less aggressive, more sociable, more compliant, less depressed. The utilitarian goal of minimizing suffering is itself very problematic. No one can make a brief in favor of pain and suffering, but the fact of the matter is that what we consider to be the highest and most admirable human qualities, both in ourselves and in others, are often related to the way that we react to, confront, overcome, and frequently succumb to pain, suffering, and death. In the absence of these human evils there would be no sympathy, compassion, courage, heroism, solidarity, or strength of character.* A person who has not confronted suffering or death has no depth. Our ability to experience these emotions is what connects us potentially to all other human beings, both living and dead.

Many scientists and researchers would say that we don't need to worry about fencing off human nature, however defined, from biotechnology, because we are a very long way from being able to modify it, and may never achieve the capability. They may be right: Human germ-line engineering and the use of recombinant DNA technology on humans are probably much further off than many people assume, though human cloning is not.

But our ability to manipulate human behavior is not dependent on the development of genetic engineering. Virtually everything we can anticipate being able to do through genetic engineering we will most likely be able to do much sooner through neuropharmacology. And we will face large demographic changes in the populations that find new biomedical technologies available to them, not only in terms of age and sex distributions, but in terms of the quality of life of important population groups.

The widespread and rapidly growing use of drugs like Ritalin and Prozac demonstrates just how eager we are to make use of technology to alter ourselves. If one of the key constituents of our nature, something on which we base our notions of dignity, has to do with the gamut of normal emotions shared by human beings, then we are *already* trying to narrow the range for the utilitarian ends of health and convenience.

Psychotropic drugs do not alter the germ line or produce heritable effects in the way that genetic engineering someday might. But they already raise important issues about the meaning of human dignity and are a harbinger of things to come.

When Do We Become Human?

In the near term, the big ethical controversies raised by biotechnology will not be threats to the dignity of normal adult human beings but rather to those who possess something less than the full complement of capabilities that we have defined as characterizing human specificity. The largest group of beings in this category are the unborn, but it could also include infants, the terminally sick, elderly people with debilitating diseases, and the disabled. 70

This issue has already come up with regard to stem cell research and cloning. Embryonic stem cell research requires the deliberate destruction of embryos, while so-called therapeutic cloning requires not just their destruction but their deliberate creation for research purposes prior to destruction. (As bioethicist Leon Kass notes,

---

*The Greek root of *sympathy* and the Latin root of *compassion* both refer to the ability to feel another person's pain and suffering.

therapeutic cloning is not therapeutic for the embryo.) Both activities have been strongly condemned by those who believe that life begins at conception and that embryos have full moral status as human beings.

I do not want to rehearse the whole history of the abortion debate and the hotly contested question of when life begins. I personally do not begin with religious convictions on this issue and admit to considerable confusion in trying to think through its rights and wrongs. The question here is, What does the natural-rights approach to human dignity outlined here suggest about the moral status of the unborn, the disabled, and so on? I'm not sure it produces a definitive answer, but it can at least help us frame an answer to the question.

At first blush, a natural-rights doctrine that bases human dignity on the fact that the human species possesses certain unique characteristics would appear to allow a gradation of rights depending on the degree to which any individual member of that species shares in those characteristics. An elderly person with Alzheimer's, for example, has lost the normal adult ability to reason, and therefore that part of his dignity that would permit him to participate in politics by voting or running for office. Reason, moral choice, and possession of the species-typical emotional gamut are things that are shared by virtually all human beings and therefore serve as a basis for universal equality, but individuals possess these traits in greater or lesser amounts: Some are more reasonable, have stronger consciences or more sensitive emotions than others. At one extreme, minute distinctions could be made between individuals based on the degree to which they possess these basic human qualities, with differentiated rights assigned to them on that basis. This has happened before in history; it is called natural aristocracy. The hierarchical system it implies is one of the reasons people have become suspicious of the very concept of natural rights.

There is a strong prudential reason for not being too hierarchical in the assignment of political rights, however. There is, in the first place, no consensus on a precise definition of that list of essential human characteristics that qualify an individual for rights. More important, judgments about the degree to which a given individual possesses one or another of these qualities are very difficult to make, and usually suspect, because the person making the judgment is seldom a disinterested party. Most real-world aristocracies have been conventional rather than natural, with the aristocrats assigning themselves rights that they claimed were natural but that were actually based on force or convention. It is therefore appropriate to approach the question of who qualifies for rights with some liberality.

Nonetheless, every contemporary liberal democracy does in fact differentiate rights based on the degree to which individuals or categories of individuals share in certain species-typical characteristics. Children, for example, do not have the rights of adults because their capacities for reason and moral choice are not fully developed; they cannot vote and do not have the freedom of person that their parents do in making choices about where to live, whether to go to school, and so on. Societies strip criminals of basic rights for violating the law, and do so more severely in the case of those regarded as lacking a basic human moral sense. In the United States, they can be deprived even of the right to life for certain kinds of crimes. We do not officially strip Alzheimer's patients of their political rights, but we do restrict their ability to drive and make financial decisions, and in practice they usually cease to exercise their political rights as well.

From a natural-rights perspective, then, one could argue that it is reasonable to assign the unborn different rights from those of either infants or children. A day-old infant may not be capable of reason or moral choice, but it already possesses important elements of the normal human emotional gamut—it can get upset, bond to its mother, expect attention, and the like, in ways that a day-old embryo cannot. It is the violation of the natural and very powerful bonding that takes place between parent and infant, in fact, that makes infanticide such a heinous crime in most societies. That we typically hold funerals after the deaths of infants but not after miscarriages is testimony to the naturalness of this distinction. All of this suggests that it does not make sense to treat embryos as human beings with the same kinds of rights that infants possess.

Against this line of argument, we can pose the following considerations, again not from a religious but from a natural-rights perspective. An embryo may be lacking in some of the basic human characteristics possessed by an infant, but it is also not just another group of cells or tissue, because it has the *potential* to become a full human being. In this respect, it differs from an infant, which also lacks many of the most important characteristics of a normal adult human being, only in the degree to which it has realized its natural potential. This implies that while an embryo can be assigned a lower moral status than an infant, it has a higher moral status than other kinds of cells or tissue that scientists work with. It is therefore reasonable, on nonreligious grounds, to question whether researchers should be free to create, clone, and destroy human embryos at will.

Ontogeny recapitulates phylogeny. We have argued that in the evolutionary process that leads from prehuman ancestor to human beings, there was a qualitative leap that transformed the prehuman precursors of language, reason, and emotion into a human whole that cannot be explained as a simple sum of its parts, and that remains an essentially mysterious process. Something similar happens with the development of every embryo into an infant, child, and adult human being: What starts out as a cluster of organic molecules comes to possess consciousness, reason, the capacity for moral choice, and subjective emotions, in a manner that remains equally mysterious.

Putting these facts together—that an embryo has a moral status somewhere between that of an infant and that of other types of cells and tissue, and that the transformation of the embryo into something with a higher status is a mysterious process—suggests that if we are to do things like harvest stem cells from embryos, we should put a lot of limits and constraints around this activity to make sure that it does not become a precedent for other uses of the unborn that would push the envelope further. To what extent are we willing to create and grow embryos for utilitarian purposes? Supposing some miraculous new cure required cells not from a day-old embryo, but tissue from a month-old fetus? A five-month-old female fetus already has in her ovaries all the eggs she will ever produce as a woman; supposing someone wanted access to them? If we get too used to the idea of cloning embryos for medical purposes, will we know when to stop?

If the question of equality in a future biotech world threatens to tear up the Left, the Right will quite literally fall apart over questions related to human dignity. In the United States, the Right (as represented by the Republican Party) is divided between economic libertarians, who like entrepreneurship and technology with minimal regulation, and social conservatives, many of whom are religious, who care about a range of issues including abortion and the family. The coalition between these two groups is usually strong enough to hold up during elections, but it papers over some fundamental differences in outlook. It is not clear that this alliance will survive the emergence of new technologies that, on the one hand, offer enormous health benefits and money-making opportunities for the biotech industry, but, on the other, require violating deeply held ethical norms.

We are thus brought back to the question of politics and political strategies. For if there is a viable concept of human dignity out there, it needs to be defended, not just in philosophical tracts but in the real world of politics, and protected by viable political institutions.

NOTES

1. Clive Staples Lewis, *The Abolition of Man* (New York: Touchstone, 1944), p. 85.
2. Counsel of Europe, Draft Additional Protocol to the Convention on Human Rights and Biomedicine, On the Prohibiting of Cloning Human Beings, Doc. 7884, July 16, 1997.
3. This is the theme of the second part of Francis Fukuyama, *The End of History and the Last Man* (New York: Free Press, 1992).
4. For an interpretation of this passage in Tocqueville, see Francis Fukuyama, "The March of Equality," *Journal of Democracy* 11 (2000): 11–17.
5. John Paul II, "Message to the Pontifical Academy of Sciences," October 22, 1996.
6. Daniel C. Dennett, *Darwin's Dangerous Idea: Evolution and the Meanings of Life* (New York: Simon and Schuster, 1995), pp. 35–39; see also Ernst Mayr, *One Long Argument: Charles Darwin and the Genesis of Modern Evolutionary Thought* (Cambridge, Mass.: Harvard University Press, 1991), pp. 40–42.
7. Michael Ruse and David L. Hull, *The Philosophy of Biology* (New York: Oxford University Press, 1998), p. 385.
8. Lee M. Silver, *Remaking Eden: Cloning and Beyond in a Brave New World* (New York: Avon, 1998), pp. 256–57.
9. Ruse and Hull (1998), p. 385.
10. Silver (1998), p. 277.
11. Friedrich Nietzsche, *Thus Spoke Zarathustra*, First part, section 5, from *The Portable Nietzsche*, ed. Walter Kaufmann (New York: Viking, 1968), p. 130.
12. Charles Taylor, *Sources of the Self: The Making of the Modern Identity* (Cambridge, Mass.: Harvard University Press, 1989), pp. 6–7.
13. For a fuller defense of this proposition, see Francis Fukuyama, *The Great Disruption: Human Nature and the Reconstitution of Social Order*, part II (New York: Free Press, 1999).
14. Aristotle, *Politics* I.2.13, 1254b, 16–24.
15. Ibid., I.2.18, 1255a, 22–38.
16. Ibid., I.2.19, 1255b, 3–5.
17. See, for example, Dan W. Brock, "The Human Genome Project and Human Identity," in *Genes, Humans, and Self-Knowledge*, eds. Robert F. Weir and Susan C. Lawrence et al. (Iowa City: University of Iowa Press, 1994), pp. 18–23.
18. This possibility has already been suggested by Charles Murray. See his "Deeper into the Brain," *National Review* 52 (2000): 46–49.
19. Peter Sloterdijk, "Regeln für den Menschenpark: Ein Antwortschreiben zum Brief über den Humanismus," *Die Zeit*, no. 38, September 16, 1999.
20. Jürgen Habermas, "Nicht die Natur verbietet das Klonen. Wir müssen selbst entscheiden. Eine Replik auf Dieter E. Zimmer," *Die Zeit*, no. 9, February 19, 1998.
21. For a discussion of this issue, see Allen Buchanan and Norman Daniels et al., *From Chance to Choice: Genetics and Justice* (New York and Cambridge: Cambridge University Press, 2000), pp. 17–20. See also Robert H. Blank and Masako N. Darrough, *Biological*

Differences and Social Equality: Implications for Social Policy (Westport, Conn.: Green-wood Press, 1983).

22. Ronald M. Dworkin, *Sovereign Virtue: The Theory and Practice of Equality* (Cambridge, Mass.: Harvard University Press, 2000), p. 452.

23. Laurence H. Tribe, "Second Thoughts on Cloning," *New York Times*, December 5, 1997, p. A31.

24. John Paul II (1996).

25. On the meaning of this "ontological leap," see Ernan McMullin, "Biology and the Theology of the Human," in Phillip R. Sloan, ed., *Controlling Our Desires: Historical, Philosophical, Ethical, and Theological Perspectives on the Human Genome Project* (Notre Dame, Ind.: University of Notre Dame Press, 2000), p. 367.

26. It is in fact very difficult to come up with a Darwinian explanation for the human enjoyment of music. See Steven Pinker, *How the Mind Works* (New York: W. W. Norton, 1997), pp. 528–38.

27. See, for example, Arthur Peacocke, "Relating Genetics to Theology on the Map of Scientific Knowledge," in Sloan, ed. (2000), pp. 346–50.

28. Laplace's exact words were: "We ought then to regard the present state of the universe [not just the solar system] as the effect of its anterior state and as the cause of the one which is to follow. Given an intelligence that could comprehend at one instant all the forces by which nature is animated and the respective situation of the beings who compose it—an intelligence sufficiently vast to submit these data [initial conditions] to analysis—it would embrace in the same formula the movements of the greatest bodies in the universe and those of the lightest atom; for it, nothing would be uncertain and the future, as the past, would be present to its eyes. . . . The regularity which astronomy shows us in the movements of the comets doubtless exists also in all phenomena. The curve described by a simple molecule of air or vapor is regulated in a manner just as certain as the planetary orbits; the only difference between them is that which comes from our ignorance." Quoted in *Final Causality in Nature and Human Affairs*, ed. Richard F. Hassing (Washington, D.C.: Catholic University Press, 1997), p. 224.

29. Hassing, ed. (1997), pp. 224–26.

30. Peacocke, in Sloan, ed. (2000), p. 350.

31. McMullin, in Sloan, ed. (2000), p. 374.

32. On this question, see Roger D. Masters, "The Biological Nature of the State," *World Politics* 35 (1983): 161–93.

33. Andrew Goldberg and Christophe Boesch, "The Cultures of Chimpanzees," *Scientific American* 284 (2001): 60–67.

34. Larry Arnhart, *Darwinian Natural Right: The Biological Ethics of Human Nature* (Albany, N.Y.: State University of New York Press, 1998), pp. 61–62.

35. One exception to this appears to be the indigenous peoples of the American Pacific Northwest, a hunter-gatherer society that seems to have developed a state. See Robert Wright, *Nonzero: The Logic of Human Destiny* (New York: Pantheon Books, 2000), pp. 31–38.

36. Stephen Jay Gould and R. C. Lewontin, "The Spandrels of San Marco and the Panglossian Paradigm: A Critique of the Adaptionist Programme," *Proceedings of the Royal Society of London* 205 (1979): 81–98.

37. John R. Searle, *The Mystery of Consciousness* (New York: New York Review Books, 1997).

38. Daniel C. Dennett, *Consciousness Explained* (Boston: Little, Brown, 1991), p. 210.

39. John R. Searle, *The Rediscovery of the Mind* (Cambridge, Mass.: MIT Press, 1992), p. 3.

40. Hans P. Moravec, *Robot: Mere Machine to Transcendent Mind* (New York: Oxford University Press, 1999).

41. Ray Kurzweil, *The Age of Spiritual Machines: When Computers Exceed Human Intelligence* (London: Penguin Books, 2000).

42. For a critique, see Colin McGinn, "Hello HAL," *New York Times Book Review,* January 3, 1999.

43. On this point, see Wright (2000), pp. 306–8.

44. Ibid., pp. 321–22.

45. Robert J. McShea, *Morality and Human Nature: A New Route to Ethical Theory* (Philadelphia: Temple University Press, 1990), p. 77.

46. Daniel Dennett makes the following bizarre statement in *Consciousness Explained:* "But why should it matter, you may want to ask, that a creature's desires are thwarted if they aren't conscious desires? I reply: Why would it matter more if they were conscious — especially if consciousness were a property, as some think, that forever eludes investigation? Why should a 'zombie's' crushed hopes matter less than a conscious person's crushed hopes? There is a trick with mirrors here that should be exposed and discarded. Consciousness, you say, is what matters, but then you cling to doctrines about consciousness that systematically prevent us from getting any purchase on *why* it matters" (p. 450). Dennett's question begs a more obvious one: What person in the world would care about crushing a zombie's hopes, except to the extent that the zombie was instrumentally useful to that person?

47. Jared Diamond, *The Third Chimpanzee* (New York: HarperCollins, 1992), p. 23.

48. The dualism between reason and emotion — that is, the idea that these are distinct and separable mental qualities — can be traced to Descartes (see *The Passions of the Soul,* Article 47). This dichotomy has been widely accepted since then but is misleading in many ways. The neurophysiologist Antonio Damasio points out that human reasoning invariably involves what he labels somatic markers — emotions that the mind attaches to certain ideas or options in the course of thinking through a problem — that help speed many kinds of calculations. Antonio R. Damasio, *Descartes' Error: Emotion, Reason, and the Human Brain* (New York: Putnam, 1994).

49. That is, the Kantian notion that moral choice is an act of pure reason overriding or suppressing natural emotions is not the way that human beings actually make moral choices. Human beings more typically balance one set of feelings against another and build character by strengthening the pleasurability of good moral choices through habit.

Exploring Context

1. Fukuyama opens this chapter by quoting from a decree from the Council of Europe. Visit the council's Web site at coe.int and search for information on cloning. What else does the council have to say on the issue? How does its position reflect or complicate Fukuyama's argument?

2. Fukuyama turns to complexity theory to recuperate an understanding of the human essence. Conway's Game of Life is a classic mathematical model illustrating how simple rules governing individual parts can combine into very complex wholes. Play the Game of Life at bitstorm.org/gameoflife. Does it reflect the evolution of consciousness? How often does a stable pattern emerge in the game? How does it support or undercut Fukuyama's arguments about Factor X?

3. Fukuyama asks, "What is it that we want to protect from any future advances in bio-technology?" (p. 159). Visit the Web site of the *American Journal of Bioethics* at bioethics .net. In browsing through the site, what answers to Fukuyama's question can you find? How can we decide which biotechnologies should be pursued and which would cause us to lose our humanity?

Questions for Connecting

1. Michael Pollan's discussion of "holons" in "The Animals: Practicing Complexity" (p. 344) seems closely related to Fukuyama's use of complexity theory. In what ways are hu-mans and organic farms similar? What insight does Pollan's essay provide on Fukuyama's argument?

2. In "The End of Race: Hawaii and the Mixing of Peoples" (p. 300), Steve Olson suggests that, as a result of intermarriage, race no longer has a genetic basis. Is race part of Fac-tor X? How does Fukuyama's essay support or complicate Olson's argument about race? Is race part of being human? Is it part of human dignity? You may want to use the defi-nition of human dignity you developed in Question 3 of Questions for Critical Reading in making your argument.

3. According to Richard Restak in "Attention Deficit: The Brain Syndrome of Our Era" (p. 373), our brains are being rewired to produce attention deficit disorder. Is multi-tasking a threat to human dignity as well? If culture can change the wiring of our brains, then is that, too, a kind of biotechnology?

Language Matters

1. Select a key paragraph from the essay and then reduce each sentence of the paragraph down to a single subject and verb. What is lost by condensing the sentences in this way? What other grammatical constructions help carry the meaning of a sentence?

2. Select a particularly complex sentence from this essay. Begin by breaking this sentence down into several smaller sentences. Try substituting simpler vocabulary, too. Once you've absorbed the ideas through this process, try stating out loud a summary of what Fukuyama is trying to communicate and then write down what you say. Try these same strategies in your own writing.

3. You're probably familiar with common parts of speech like nouns and verbs. Using Fukuyama's text, create new parts of speech from common combinations of the usual parts of speech. For example, a noun and a verb together might form a "quarplat," an adverb and an adjective might be a "jerbad." Create rules for your parts of speech. When does Fukuyama use the kinds of constructions you've named? When might you?

Assignments for Writing

1. Write a paper in which you explain what it means to be human. In making your argu-ment, you should account for the fact that Fukuyama identifies many different qualities as being necessary to Factor X. Why, then, does he call them collectively "Factor X"?

How do you account for the seemingly infinite number of divergent views on what it is to be human? Use your definition of *Factor X* from Question 1 of Questions for Critical Reading.

2. Fukuyama acknowledges the difficulties that a vision of human equality presents when dealing with specific populations, including the elderly, disabled, and terminally ill. Write a paper in which you suggest standards for dealing with these boundary populations in relation to medical advances such as biotechnology. How might you change Fukuyama's working definitions of *Factor X* to be more inclusive? Consider using any specific examples you located from your work with the *American Journal of Bioethics* Web site in Question 3 of Exploring Context.

3. Fukuyama stresses the centrality of human nature in current political and ethical debate. Some environmentalists would consider his discussion anthropocentric. What about natural life beyond human beings? Write a paper in which you extend Fukuyama's discussion of human dignity to account for the natural environment, ecosystems, and other forms of life. You may want to identify those parts of Fukuyama's essay that deal directly with the distinction between the "natural" and "human" worlds as a point of departure for this discussion. What happens when we extend the concept of dignity beyond humans? Would it change the way we acquire our food or what we eat? Consider your work with Michael Pollan from Question 1 of Questions for Connecting.

ROXANE GAY

Roxane Gay earned her Ph.D. in rhetoric and technical communication from Michigan Technological University and is currently an associate professor of English at Purdue University. Gay became the talk of the literary world in 2014 with the publication of her novel *An Untamed State* and her essay collection *Bad Feminist*, both of which became *New York Times* best-sellers. Gay, editor of *The Butter* and coeditor of *PANK*, is also the author of *Ayiti* and the forthcoming *Hunger*, due out in 2016. Her work has appeared or is forthcoming in *Best American Mystery Stories 2014*, *Best American Short Stories 2012*, *McSweeney's*, *Tin House*, *Virginia Quarterly Review*, and the *New York Times Book Review*, among other publications.

Jay Grabiec/Eastern
Illinois University

In the essay collection *Bad Feminist*, Gay examines feminism and its inherent complications, often through the lens of pop culture. With honesty and wit, she tackles issues such as race, privilege, and politics with essays on topics such as the token treatment of race in Hollywood, the responsibility of writers when discussing rape culture, and the killing of Trayvon Martin. Throughout it all, she uses irreverence and wit to highlight the complex relations of gender, race, and sexuality.

In this selection, which was originally published in the *Virginia Quarterly Review*, Gay examines her own identity as a feminist in the context of cultural expectation and categorization — or, as she calls it, the "myth" of "essential feminism," which she argues "doesn't allow for the complexities of human experience or individuality" (p. 170). It also, Gay asserts, proves divisive to the movement, in that many reject the feminist label due to stereotypes and negative associations. She ultimately concludes that she is a "bad feminist," but that she "would rather be a bad feminist than no feminist at all" (p. 175).

Do you agree? What are the benefits and detriments of categorization? What are the benefits and detriments that come from rejecting labels?

▶ TAGS: *community, gender, identity, judgment and decision-making, media, race and ethnicity*
▶ CONNECTIONS: *Appiah, Duhigg, Klosterman, Levy, O'Connor, Padawer, Pozner, Rosin, Serano*

Questions for Critical Reading

1. Develop your own definition of *feminist*. As you read, pay attention to places where Gay offers her definition of the term. How do your definitions differ? Are you persuaded by Gay's definition?

2. According to Gay, what is "essential feminism"? Note places in the text where Gay discusses essential feminism. What problems are created by this concept?

3. Is Gay a "bad" feminist? Use your own understanding of *feminist* from Question 1 above in formulating your response.

Bad Feminist

My favorite definition of a feminist is one offered by Su, an Australian woman who, when interviewed for Kathy Bail's 1996 anthology *DIY Feminism*, described them simply as "women who don't want to be treated like shit." This definition is pointed and succinct, but I run into trouble when I try to expand it. I fall short as a feminist. I feel like I am not as committed as I need to be, that I am not living up to feminist ideals because of who and how I choose to be. I feel this tension constantly. As Judith Butler writes in her 1988 essay, "Performative Acts and Gender Constitution": "Performing one's gender wrong initiates a set of punishments both obvious and indirect, and performing it well provides the reassurance that there is an essentialism of gender identity after all." This tension—the idea that there is a right way to be a woman, a right way to be the most essential woman—is ongoing and pervasive.

We see this tension in socially dictated beauty standards—the right way to be a woman is to be thin, to wear make up, to wear the right kind of clothes (not too slutty, not too prude, show a little leg, ladies), and so on. Good women are charming, polite, and unobtrusive. Good women work but are content to earn 77 percent of what men earn. Depending on whom you ask, good women bear children and stay home to raise them without complaint. Good women are modest, chaste, pious, submissive. Women who don't adhere to these standards are the fallen, the undesirable. They are bad women.

Butler's thesis could also apply to feminism. There is an essential feminism, the notion that there are right and wrong ways to be a feminist, and there are consequences for doing feminism wrong.

Essential feminism suggests anger, humorlessness, militancy, unwavering principles, and a prescribed set of rules for how to be a proper feminist woman, or at least a proper white, heterosexual, feminist woman—hate pornography, unilaterally decry the objectification of women, don't cater to the male gaze, hate men, hate sex, focus on career, don't shave. I kid, mostly, with that last one. This is nowhere near an accurate description of feminism, but the movement has been warped by misperception for so long that even people who should know better have bought into this essential image of feminism.

Consider Elizabeth Wurtzel, who, in a June 2012 *Atlantic* article, says, "Real feminists earn a living, have money and means of their own." By Wurtzel's thinking, women who don't "earn a living, have money and means of their own," are fake feminists, undeserving of the label, disappointments to the sisterhood. She takes the idea of essential feminism even further in a September 2012 *Harper's Bazaar* article where she suggests that a good feminist works hard to be beautiful. She says, "Looking great is a matter of feminism. No liberated woman would misrepresent the cause by appearing

5

less than hale and happy." It's too easy to dissect the error of such thinking. She is suggesting that a woman's worth is, in part, determined by her beauty, which is one of the very things feminism works against.

The most significant problem with essential feminism is how it doesn't allow for the complexities of human experience or individuality. There seems to be little room for multiple or discordant points of view. Essential feminism has, for example, led to the rise of the phrase "sex-positive feminism," which creates a clear distinction between feminists who are positive about sex and feminists who aren't—and that in turn creates a self-fulfilling essentialist prophecy.

I sometimes cringe when someone refers to me as a feminist, as if I should be ashamed of my feminism or as if the word *feminist* is an insult. The label is rarely offered in kindness. I am generally called a feminist when I have the nerve to suggest that the misogyny deeply embedded in our culture is a real problem, requiring relentless vigilance. For example, in an essay for *Salon*, I wrote about Daniel Tosh and rape jokes. I try not to read comments because they can get vicious, but I couldn't help but note one commenter who told me I was an "angry blogger woman," which is simply another way of saying "angry feminist." All feminists are angry instead of passionate.

A more direct reprimand came from a man I was dating, during a heated discussion that wasn't quite an argument. He said, "Don't you raise your voice to me," which was strange because I had not raised my voice. I was stunned because no one had ever said such a thing to me. He expounded, at length, about how women should talk to men. When I dismantled his pseudo-theories, he said, "You're some kind of feminist, aren't you?" His tone made it clear that to be a feminist was undesirable. I was not being a good woman. I remained silent, stewing. I thought, "Isn't it obvious I am a feminist, albeit not a very good one?"

I'm not the only outspoken woman who shies away from the feminist label, who fears the consequences of accepting the label.

In an August 2012 interview with *Salon*'s Andrew O'Hehir, actress Melissa Leo, 10 known for playing groundbreaking female roles, said, "Well, I don't think of myself as a feminist at all. As soon as we start labeling and categorizing ourselves and others, that's going to shut down the world. I would never say that. Like, I just did that episode with Louis C.K."

Leo is buying into a great many essential feminist myths with her comment. We are categorized and labeled from the moment we come into this world by gender, race, size, hair color, eye color, and so forth. The older we get the more labels and categories we collect. If labeling and categorizing ourselves is going to shut the world down, it has been a long time coming. More disconcerting, though, is the assertion that a feminist wouldn't take a role on Louis C.K.'s sitcom *Louie*, or that a feminist would be unable to find C.K.'s brand of humor amusing. For Leo, there are feminists and then there are women who defy categorization and are willing to embrace career opportunities. In a July 2012 *Guardian* interview, critically acclaimed performance artist Marina Abramović, when asked how she felt about being invited to lead a woman-only lecture, said, "I really had to think about it. I am very clear that I am not a feminist. It puts you into a category and I don't like that. An artist has no gender. All that matters is whether they make good art or bad art. So I thought about it, but then I said yes."

Again, we see this fear of categorization, this fear of being forced into a box that cannot quite accommodate a woman properly. Abramović believes an artist has no gender, but there are many artists who would disagree, whose art is intimately shaped by their gender, such as artist and sculptor Louise Bourgeois, for whom feminism was a significant influence. In a 1982 *Time* article on Bourgeois and her Museum of Modern Art retrospective, Robert Hughes wrote, "The field to which Bourgeois's work constantly returns is female experience, located in the body, sensed from within. 'I try,' she told an interviewer, with regard to one work, 'to give a representation of a woman who is pregnant. She tries to be frightening but she is frightened. She's afraid someone is going to invade her privacy and that she won't be able to defend what she is responsible for.' "

Trailblazing female leaders in the corporate world tend to reject the feminist label, too. Marissa Mayer, who was appointed president and CEO of Yahoo! in July 2012, said in an interview,

> I don't think that I would consider myself a feminist. I think that I certainly believe in equal rights, I believe that women are just as capable, if not more so in a lot of different dimensions, but I don't, I think, have, sort of, the militant drive and the sort of, the chip on the shoulder that sometimes comes with that. And I think it's too bad, but I do think that feminism has become in many ways a more negative word. You know, there are amazing opportunities all over the world for women, and I think that there is more good that comes out of positive energy around that than negative energy.

For Mayer, even though she is a pioneering woman, feminism is associated with militancy. Despite the strides she has made through her career at Google and now Yahoo!, she'd prefer to eschew the label for the sake of so-called positive energy.

Audre Lorde once stated, "I am a black feminist. I mean I recognize that my power [15] as well as my primary oppressions come as a result of my blackness as well as my womaness, and therefore my struggles on both of these fronts are inseparable."

As a woman of color, I find that some feminists don't seem terribly concerned with the issues unique to women of color—the ongoing effects of racism and post-colonialism, the status of women in the Third World, working against the trenchant archetypes black women are forced into (angry black woman, mammy, Hottentot, and the like).

White feminists often suggest that by believing there are issues unique to women of color, an unnatural division occurs, impeding solidarity, sisterhood. Other times, white feminists are simply dismissive of these issues. In 2008, prominent blogger Amanda Marcotte was accused of appropriating ideas for her article, "Can a Person Be Illegal?" from the blogger "Brownfemipower," who posted a speech she gave on the same subject a few days prior to the publication of Marcotte's article. The question of where original thought ends and borrowed concepts begin was complicated significantly by the sense that a white person had yet again appropriated the creative work of a person of color.

Around the same time, feminist press Seal Press was taken to task for not devoting enough of their catalogue to women of color, which made senior editor Brooke Warner and other white feminists defensive. Warner went so far as to respond to a comment made by blogger "Blackamazon," on her eponymous blog, saying, "Seal Press here. We

WANT more WOC. Not a whole lotta proposals come our way, interestingly. Seems to me it would be more effective to inform us about what you'd like to see rather than hating." In addition to assuming a defensive posture, Warner also placed the burden of her press's diversity on women of color instead of assuming that responsibility as a senior editor. To be fair, Warner was commenting on a blog and perhaps did not think her comment through before posting, but she is neither the first nor will she be the last white feminist to suggest that the responsibility for making feminism and feminist organizations more inclusive lies with women of color.

The feminist blogosphere engaged in an intense debate over these issues, at times so acrimonious that black feminists were labeled "radical black feminists" who were "playing the race card."

Such willful ignorance and disinterest in incorporating the issues and concerns of black women into the mainstream feminist project makes me disinclined to own the feminist label until it embraces people like me. Is that my way of essentializing feminism, of suggesting there's a right kind of feminism or a more inclusive feminism? Perhaps. This is all murky for me, but a continued insensitivity toward race is a serious problem in feminist circles. 20

There's also this: lately, magazines have been telling me there's something wrong with feminism or women trying to achieve a work/life balance or just women in general. The *Atlantic* has led the way in these lamentations. In the aforementioned June 2012 article, Wurtzel, author of *Prozac Nation*, wrote a searing polemic about "1 percent wives," who are hurting feminism and the progress of women by choosing to stay at home rather than enter the workplace. Wurtzel begins the essay provocatively:

> When my mind gets stuck on everything that is wrong with feminism, it brings out the nineteenth century poet in me: Let me count the ways. Most of all, feminism is pretty much a nice girl who really, really wants so badly to be liked by everybody — ladies who lunch, men who hate women, all the morons who demand choice and don't understand responsibility — that it has become the easy lay of social movements.

There are problems with feminism, you see. Wurtzel says so, and she is vigorous in defending her position. Wurtzel goes on to state there is only one kind of equality, economic equality, and until women recognize that and enter the workforce *en masse*, feminists, and wealthy feminists in particular, will continue to fail. They will continue to be bad feminists, falling short of essential ideals of this movement.

The very next issue of the *Atlantic* included Anne-Marie Slaughter writing 12,000 words about the struggles of powerful, successful women to "have it all." She was speaking to a small, elite group of women — wealthy women with very successful careers — while ignoring the millions of women who don't have the privilege of, as Slaughter did, leaving a high-powered position at the State Department to spend more time with her sons. Many women who work do so because they have to. Working has little to do with having it all and much more to do with having food on the table.

Slaughter wrote, "I'd been the woman congratulating herself on her unswerving commitment to the feminist cause, chatting smugly with her dwindling number of college or law-school friends who had reached and maintained their place on the highest rungs of their profession. I'd been the one telling young women at my lectures that you can have it all and do it all, regardless of what field you are in."

The thing is, I am not at all sure that feminism has ever suggested women can have 25 it all. This notion of being able to have it all is always misattributed to feminism when really it's human nature to want it all.

Alas, poor feminism. So much responsibility keeps getting piled on the shoulders of a movement whose primary purpose is to achieve equality, in all realms, between men and women. I keep reading these articles and getting angry and tired because these articles tell me that there's no way for women to ever get it right. These articles make it seem like there is, in fact, a right way to be a woman and a wrong way to be a woman. And the standard appears to be ever changing and unachievable.

Which leads me to confess: I am failing as a woman. I am failing as a feminist. To freely accept the feminist label would not be fair to good feminists. If I am, indeed, a feminist, I am a rather bad one.

I want to be independent, but I want to be taken care of and have someone to come home to. I have a job I'm pretty good at. I am in charge of things. I am on committees. People respect me and take my counsel. I want to be strong and professional, but I resent how hard I have to work to be taken seriously, to receive a fraction of the consideration I might otherwise receive. Sometimes I feel an overwhelming need to cry at work so I close my office door and lose it. I want to be in charge and respected and in control, but I want to surrender, completely, in certain aspects of my life.

When I drive to work I listen to thuggish rap at a very loud volume even though the lyrics are degrading to women and offend me to my core. The classic Ying Yang Twins song "Salt Shaker"? It's amazing. "P poppin' til you percolate / First booty on duty no time to wait / Make it work, with your wet T-shirt / Bitch you gotta shake it til your calf muscle hurts."

Poetry.   30

(I am mortified by my music choices.)

I care what people think.

Pink is my favorite color. I used to say my favorite color was black to be cool, but it is pink—all shades of pink. If I have an accessory, it is probably pink. I read *Vogue*, and I'm not doing it ironically though it might seem that way. I once live-tweeted the September issue. I demonstrate little outward evidence of this, but I have a very indulgent fantasy where I have a closet full of pretty shoes and purses and matching outfits. I love dresses. For years I pretended I hated them, but I don't. Maxi-dresses are one of the finest clothing items to become popular in recent memory. I have opinions on Maxi-dresses! I shave my legs! Again, this mortifies me. If I take issue with the unrealistic standards of beauty women are held to, I shouldn't have a secret fondness for fashion and smooth calves, right?

I know nothing about cars. When I take my car to the mechanic, they are speaking a foreign language. A mechanic asks what's wrong with my car, and I lose my mind. I stutter things like, "Well, there's a sound I try to drown out with my radio." The windshield wiper fluid for the rear window of my car no longer sprays the window. It just sprays the air. I don't know how to deal with this. It feels like an expensive problem. I still call my father with questions about cars and am not terribly interested in changing any of my car-related ignorance. I don't want to be good at cars. Good feminists, I assume, are independent enough to address vehicular crises on their own; they are independent enough to care.

Despite what people think based on my writing, I very much like men. They're   35
interesting to me, and I mostly wish they would be better about how they treat women so I wouldn't have to call them out so often.

And still, I put up with nonsense from unsuitable men even though *I know better* and can do better. I love diamonds and the excess of weddings. I consider certain domestic tasks as gendered, mostly all in my favor as I don't care for chores—lawn care, bug killing, and trash removal, for example, are men's work.

> **Despite what people think based on my writing, I very much like men.**

Sometimes—a lot of the time, honestly—I totally "fake it," because it's easier. I am a fan of orgasms, but they take time, and in many instances I don't want to waste that time. All too often I don't really like the guy enough to explain the calculus of my desire. Then I feel guilty because the sisterhood would not approve. I'm not even sure what the sisterhood is, but the idea of a sisterhood menaces me, quietly reminding me of how bad a feminist I am. Good feminists don't fear the sisterhood because they know they are comporting themselves in sisterhood-approved ways.

I love babies, and I want to have one. I am willing to make certain compromises (not sacrifices) in order to do so—namely maternity leave and slowing down at work to spend more time with my child, writing less so I can be more present in my life. I worry about dying alone, unmarried and childless because I spent so much time pursuing my career and accumulating degrees. This kind of keeps me up at night, but I pretend it doesn't because I am supposed to be evolved. My success, such as it is, is supposed to be enough if I'm a good feminist. It is not enough. It is not even close.

Because I have so many deeply held opinions about gender equality, I feel a lot of pressure to live up to certain ideals. I am supposed to be a good feminist who is having it all, doing it all. Really, though, I'm a woman in her thirties, struggling to accept herself. For so long I told myself I was not this woman—utterly human and flawed. I worked overtime to be anything but this woman, and it was exhausting and unsustainable, and even harder than simply embracing who I am.

And while I may be a bad feminist, I am deeply committed to the issues important to the feminist movement. I have strong opinions about misogyny, institutional sexism that consistently places women at a disadvantage, the inequity in pay, the cult of beauty and thinness, the repeated attacks on reproductive freedom, violence against women, and on and on. I am as committed to fighting fiercely for equality as I am committed to disrupting the notion that there is an essential feminism.

I'm the kind of feminist who is appalled by the phrase "legitimate rape" and politi-   40
cians such as Missouri's Todd Akin, who reaffirmed his commitment to opposing abortion, drawing from pseudo-science and a lax cultural attitude toward rape: "If it's a legitimate rape, the female body has ways to try to shut that whole thing down. But let's assume that maybe that didn't work or something. I think there should be some punishment, but the punishment ought to be on the rapist, and not attacking the child."

Being a feminist, however, even a bad one, has also taught me that the need for feminism and advocacy also applies to seemingly less serious issues.

I'm the kind of feminist who knows it is complete hypocrisy that actress Kristen Stewart is being publicly excoriated for cheating on her boyfriend Robert Pattinson even though, if you believe the tabloid stories, Pattinson cheated on her for years. Being a bad feminist allows me to get riled up when I read that Stewart could be dropped from the *Snow White and the Huntsman* sequel while, say, Chris Brown, a known abuser with anger issues, is still performing at awards shows and selling albums, adored by a legion of ardent fans.

I'm the kind of feminist who looks at the September 2012 issue of *Vogue* with the Edith Wharton photo spread and knows there's a serious problem. Wharton is my favorite writer. I also love *Vogue* or, perhaps, hate to love *Vogue*. This photo spread would normally thrill me. But. Jeffrey Eugenides portrays Henry James, Jonathan Safran Foer portrays architect Ogden Codman Jr., and Junot Díaz portrays diplomat Walter Van Rensselaer Berry. Wharton is portrayed by model Natalia Vodianova; she is gorgeous, and *Vogue* is a fashion magazine, but a great disservice is being done.

The editors of *Vogue* are, apparently, unaware of the famous, talented, contemporary women writers who would be excellent choices for the photo essay. Zadie Smith released a book in September. There's also Karen Russell, Jennifer Egan, Aimee Bender, Nicole Krauss, Julianna Baggott, Alicia Erian, Claire Vaye Watkins, and the list could go on forever.

This disservice rises, in part, out of a culture that assumes women writers are less   45 relevant than their male counterparts, that women in general are simply not as important, that their writing is not as critical to arts and letters. This disservice rises out of a culture where Jonathan Franzen lost the Pulitzer rather than Jennifer Egan winning the award.

All too often, these seemingly smaller issues go unchecked because there are so many more serious issues facing women.

There's more to the problem. Too many women, particularly groundbreaking women and industry leaders, are afraid to be labeled feminists, afraid to stand up and say, "Yes, I am a feminist," for fear of what that label means, for fear of how to live up to it, for fear of feminism as something essential, for fear of the punishments—both obvious and indirect—that come with openly owning feminism or doing feminism wrong.

At some point, I got it into my head that a feminist was a certain kind of woman. I bought into grossly inaccurate myths about who feminists are—militant, perfect in their politics and person, man hating, humorless. I bought into these myths even though, intellectually, I *know* better. I'm not proud of this. I don't want to buy into these myths anymore. I don't want to cavalierly disavow feminism like far too many other women have done.

I also want to be myself. Bad feminism seems like the only way I can both embrace myself as a feminist and be myself.

No matter what issues I have with feminism, I am one. I cannot nor will not deny   50 the importance and absolute necessity of feminism. Like most people, I'm full of contradictions, but I also don't want to be treated like shit for being a woman.

I am, therefore, a bad feminist. I would rather be a bad feminist than no feminist at all.

Exploring Context

1. Search the Web for "women against feminism" to locate images from a controversial Tumblr campaign. How does Gay's argument respond to the reasons why these women are against feminism?

2. Explore Roxane Gay's Web site at roxanegay.com. How does her larger body of work reflect the ideas that she presents in this essay? How does your exploration confirm or change your response to Question 3 of Questions for Critical Reading?

3. Use the Meme Generator at memegenerator.net to create your own meme image about feminism. Incorporate your work from Questions 1 and 3 of Questions for Critical Reading.

Questions for Connecting

1. Ariel Levy's "Female Chauvinist Pigs" (p. 243) could be said to focus on a different kind of "bad" feminist. Using Gay's notions of feminism, examine Female Chauvinist Pigs and raunch culture. What relation do these women have to feminism, good or bad? Draw from your work in Questions 1–3 of Questions for Critical Reading and your work with women against feminism from Question 1 of Exploring Context.

2. In many ways Gay's concern is as much about stereotypes as it is about feminism. Synthesize Gay's ideas and Jennifer Pozner's arguments in "Ghetto Bitches, China Dolls, and Cha Cha Divas" (p. 359). How do stereotypes about gender and race operate, and how can they be dismantled?

3. Gay is centrally invested in changing the way women are treated. Apply Kenji Yoshino's ideas about civil rights from "Preface" and "The New Civil Rights" (p. 539) to Gay's concerns about gender. What paradigm of civil rights might produce change? Is Gay forced to "cover" her flavor of feminism? How might conversations about these issues produce change?

Language Matters

1. One common error for writers involves using commas with introductory elements. Review the rules for comma usage in these situations, using a grammar handbook or other reliable reference source. Then find examples from Gay that illustrate these rules. How can you apply these rules to your own writing?

2. Word choice and tone are important in your writing. Select a significant quotation from Gay's text, type it into a blank document in a word processor, and, using a thesaurus (the word processor's, one online, or a printed one), replace every significant word in the sentence with a synonym. Does the sentence still work? How does word choice influence tone and meaning? Why didn't Gay use "fancier" or more "academic" language in this text? Based on what you have discovered, what sort of tone do you think you should use in your writing for this class?

3. Select a key quotation from Gay's text and then translate it into another language using an online tool such as Bing Translator (bing.com/translator) or Google Translate

(translate.google.com). You might even choose to translate it several times (from English to French to German to Chinese). Then translate it back into English. The resulting sentence will probably make little sense. Describe what happened to the sentence. Did translation change parts of speech? Verb tense? Sentence structure? What elements of the sentence are key to transmitting Gay's meaning? Do they survive translation? What parts of your own sentences should you thus pay attention to the most?

Assignments for Writing

1. Use Gay's ideas about feminism to write a paper in which you create a definition of *feminism* that avoids notions of "good" or "bad." You will want to make sure the definition you create is open to people of all genders. Draw from your work in Questions for Critical Reading and Question 1 of Exploring Context to help you support your argument.

2. Gay uses several cultural references to support her argument, including popular magazines such as *Vogue*, media artists such as Louis C.K., and blogs. Write a paper in which you examine the ways in which popular culture supports stereotypes. How might we change or disable these stereotypes in culture? Incorporate your work from Question 3 of Exploring Context and Question 2 of Questions for Connecting.

3. In detailing the ways in which she is a bad feminist, Gay is also detailing the ways in which she is an individual. Thus, in some ways, Gay is using this essay to define herself. Write a paper in which you specify tools an individual can use to negotiate between individual and group identities. You might want to include what you learned about Gay from Question 2 of Exploring Context.

DANIEL GILBERT

Daniel Gilbert is a professor of psychology at Harvard University. He has won a Guggenheim fellowship, as well as the American Psychological Association's Distinguished Scientific Award for an Early Career Contribution to Psychology. In 2002, *Personality and Social Psychology Bulletin* named him one of the fifty most influential social psychologists of the decade. In addition to his book *Stumbling on Happiness* (2006) and his scholarly publications, Gilbert has published works of science fiction as well as contributed to the *New York Times,* the *Los Angeles Times, Forbes,* and *Time.* He was elected to the American Academy of Arts and Sciences in 2008.

© Rich Friedman/Corbis

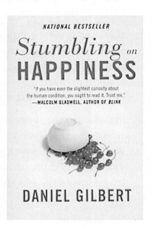

 In *Stumbling on Happiness*, a *New York Times* best-seller, Gilbert applies his expertise to the study of happiness itself. Gilbert argues that people are rarely able to predict with any accuracy how they will feel in the future, and so are often quite wrong about what will make them happy.

 In "Reporting Live from Tomorrow," a chapter from *Stumbling on Happiness*, Gilbert suggests that beliefs, just like genes, can be "super-replicators," given to spreading regardless of their usefulness. Thus even beliefs that are based on inaccurate information can provide the means for their own propagation. Gilbert explains why humans, with their unreliable memories and imaginations, are so easily susceptible to such beliefs. Though "the best way to predict our feelings tomorrow is to see how others are feeling today" (p. 190), most of us are unwilling to make use of the experiences of others because we mistakenly believe ourselves to be unique.

 The pursuit of happiness is central to our understanding of America — we all want to be happy. But this selection cautions us about predicting our future happiness and in the process provides the tools we need to correct our misapprehensions.

▶ TAGS: *adolescence and adulthood, conversation, culture, empathy, judgment and decision-making, psychology*

▶ CONNECTIONS: *Kahneman, Ma, Padawer, Wood, Yang*

Questions for Critical Reading

1. As you read Gilbert's text, look for the term *super-replicator*. What does this term mean? Develop a definition using Gilbert's text and then offer an example not included in his essay. What function does this concept serve in Gilbert's argument?

2. What does Gilbert mean by *surrogate*? You will notice as you read that Gilbert never explicitly defines the term. Instead, you should read his text critically and construct a definition out of quotations you find that discuss the idea.

3. Using Gilbert's text, define *happiness*. As with *surrogate*, you will need to analyze Gilbert's text to construct this definition. What does it mean in the context of this essay, and what does it mean for you?

Reporting Live from Tomorrow

In Alfred Hitchcock's 1956 remake of *The Man Who Knew Too Much*, Doris Day sang a waltz whose final verse went like this:

> When I was just a child in school,
> I asked my teacher, "What will I try?
> Should I paint pictures, should I sing songs?"
> This was her wise reply:
> "*Que sera, sera.* Whatever will be, will be.
> The future's not ours to see. *Que sera, sera.*"[1]

Now, I don't mean to quibble with the lyricist, and I have nothing but fond memories of Doris Day, but the fact is that this is *not* a particularly wise reply. When a child asks for advice about which of two activities to pursue, a teacher should be able to provide more than a musical cliché. Yes, of *course* the future is hard to see. But we're all heading that way anyhow, and as difficult as it may be to envision, we have to make *some* decisions about which futures to aim for and which to avoid. If we are prone to mistakes when we try to imagine the future, then how *should* we decide what to do?

Even a child knows the answer to that one: We should ask the teacher. One of the benefits of being a social and linguistic animal is that we can capitalize on the experience of others rather than trying to figure everything out for ourselves. For millions of years, human beings have conquered their ignorance by dividing the labor of discovery and then communicating their discoveries to one another, which is why the average newspaper boy in Pittsburgh knows more about the universe than did Galileo, Aristotle, Leonardo,* or any of those other guys who were so smart they only needed one name. We all make ample use of this resource. If you were to write down everything you know and then go back through the list and make a check mark next to the things you know only because somebody told you, you'd develop a repetitive-motion disorder because almost *everything* you know is secondhand. Was Yury Gagarin the first man in space? Is *croissant* a French word? Are there more Chinese than North Dakotans? Does a stitch in time save nine? Most of us know the answers to these questions despite the fact that none of us actually witnessed the launching of *Vostok I*, personally

---

*Galileo, Aristotle, Leonardo: Three geniuses. Galileo Galilei (1564–1642) was an Italian mathematician and astronomer best known for his extremely controversial belief that the earth revolves around the sun. Aristotle (384–322 BC) was a Greek philosopher and an enormously important figure in Western thought. He was a student of Plato and a teacher of Alexander the Great. Leonardo da Vinci (1452–1519) was an Italian Renaissance painter, sculptor, and scientist best known for the *Mona Lisa* and *The Last Supper* [Ed.].

supervised the evolution of language, hand-counted all the people in Beijing and Bismarck, or performed a fully randomized double-blind study of stitching. We know the answers because someone shared them with us. Communication is a kind of "vicarious observation"[2] that allows us to learn about the world without ever leaving the comfort of our Barcaloungers. The six billion interconnected people who cover the surface of our planet constitute a leviathan with twelve billion eyes, and anything that is seen by one pair of eyes can potentially be known to the entire beast in a matter of months, days, or even minutes.

The fact that we can communicate with one another about our experiences should provide a simple solution to the core problem with which this book has been concerned. Yes, our ability to imagine our future emotions is flawed—but that's okay, because we don't have to imagine what it would feel like to marry a lawyer, move to Texas, or eat a snail when there are so many people who have *done* these things and are all too happy to tell us about them. Teachers, neighbors, coworkers, parents, friends, lovers, children, uncles, cousins, coaches, cabdrivers, bartenders, hairstylists, dentists, advertisers—each of these folks has something to say about what it would be like to live in this future rather than that one, and at any point in time we can be fairly sure that one of these folks has actually *had* the experience that we are merely contemplating. Because we are the mammal that shows and tells, each of us has access to information about almost any experience we can possibly imagine—and many that we can't. Guidance counselors tell us about the best careers, critics tell us about the best restaurants, travel agents tell us about the best vacations, and friends tell us about the best travel agents. Every one of us is surrounded by a platoon of Dear Abbys who can recount their own experiences and in so doing tell us which futures are most worth wanting.

Given the overabundance of consultants, role models, gurus, mentors, yentas,* and nosy relatives, we might expect people to do quite well when it comes to making life's most important decisions, such as where to live, where to work, and whom to marry. And yet, the average American moves more than six times,[3] changes jobs more than ten times,[4] and marries more than once,[5] which suggests that most of us are making more than a few poor choices.

> **Do we listen too well when others speak, or do we not listen well enough? As we shall see, the answer to that question is *yes*.**

If humanity is a living library of information about what it feels like to do just about anything that can be done, then why do the people with the library cards make so many bad decisions? There are just two possibilities. The first is that a lot of the advice we receive from others is bad advice that we foolishly accept. The second is that a lot of the advice we receive from others is good advice that we foolishly reject. So which is it? Do we listen too well when others speak, or do we not listen well enough? As we shall see, the answer to that question is *yes*.

---

*Yenta: A Yiddish slang word meaning a person, especially a woman, who is gossipy and always ready to offer an opinion [Ed.].

Super-Replicators

The philosopher Bertrand Russell once claimed that believing is "the most mental thing we do."[6] Perhaps, but it is also the most *social* thing we do. Just as we pass along our genes in an effort to create people whose faces look like ours, so too do we pass along our beliefs in an effort to create people whose minds think like ours. Almost any time we tell anyone anything, we are attempting to change the way their brains operate — attempting to change the way they see the world so that their view of it more closely resembles our own. Just about every assertion — from the sublime ("God has a plan for you") to the mundane ("Turn left at the light, go two miles, and you'll see the Dunkin' Donuts on your right") — is meant to bring the listener's beliefs about the world into harmony with the speaker's. Sometimes these attempts succeed and sometimes they fail. So what determines whether a belief will be successfully transmitted from one mind to another?

The principles that explain why some genes are transmitted more successfully than others also explain why some beliefs are transmitted more successfully than others.[7] Evolutionary biology teaches us that any gene that promotes its own "means of transmission" will be represented in increasing proportions in the population over time. For instance, imagine that a single gene were responsible for the complex development of the neural circuitry that makes orgasms feel so good. For a person having this gene, orgasms would feel . . . well, orgasmic. For a person lacking this gene, orgasms would feel more like sneezes — brief, noisy, physical convulsions that pay rather paltry hedonic dividends. Now, if we took fifty healthy, fertile people who had the gene and fifty healthy, fertile people who didn't, and left them on a hospitable planet for a million years or so, when we returned we would probably find a population of thousands or millions of people, almost all of whom had the gene. Why? Because a gene that made orgasms feel good would tend to be transmitted from generation to generation simply because people who enjoy orgasms are inclined to do the thing that transmits their genes. The logic is so circular that it is virtually inescapable: Genes tend to be transmitted when they make us do the things that transmit genes. What's more, even *bad* genes — those that make us prone to cancer or heart disease — can become super-replicators if they compensate for these costs by promoting their own means of transmission. For instance, if the gene that made orgasms feel delicious also left us prone to arthritis and tooth decay, that gene might still be represented in increasing proportions because arthritic, toothless people who love orgasms are more likely to have children than are limber, toothy people who do not.

The same logic can explain the transmission of beliefs. If a particular belief has some property that facilitates its own transmission, then that belief tends to be held by an increasing number of minds. As it turns out, there are several such properties that increase a belief's transmissional success, the most obvious of which is accuracy. When someone tells us where to find a parking space downtown or how to bake a cake at high altitude, we adopt that belief and pass it along because it helps us and our friends do the things we want to do, such as parking and baking. As one philosopher noted, "The faculty of communication would not gain ground in evolution unless it was by and large the faculty of transmitting true beliefs."[8] Accurate beliefs give us power, which makes it easy to understand why they are so readily transmitted from one mind to another.

It is a bit more difficult to understand why *inaccurate* beliefs are so readily transmitted from one mind to another—but they are. False beliefs, like bad genes, can and do become super-replicators, and a thought experiment illustrates how this can happen. Imagine a game that is played by two teams, each of which has a thousand players, each of whom is linked to teammates by a telephone. The object of the game is to get one's team to share as many accurate beliefs as possible. When players receive a message that they believe to be accurate, they call a teammate and pass it along. When they receive a message that they believe to be inaccurate, they don't. At the end of the game, the referee blows a whistle and awards each team a point for every accurate belief that the entire team shares and subtracts one point for every inaccurate belief the entire team shares. Now, consider a contest played one sunny day between a team called the Perfects (whose members always transmit accurate beliefs) and a team called the Imperfects (whose members occasionally transmit an inaccurate belief). We should expect the Perfects to win, right?

Not necessarily. In fact, there are some special circumstances under which the Imperfects will beat their pants off. For example, imagine what would happen if one of the Imperfect players sent the false message "Talking on the phone all day and night will ultimately make you very happy," and imagine that other Imperfect players were gullible enough to believe it and pass it on. This message is inaccurate and thus will cost the Imperfects a point in the end. But it may have the compensatory effect of keeping more of the Imperfects on the telephone for more of the time, thus increasing the total number of accurate messages they transmit. Under the right circumstances, the costs of this inaccurate belief would be outweighed by its benefits, namely, that it led players to behave in ways that increased the odds that they would share other accurate beliefs. The lesson to be learned from this game is that inaccurate beliefs can prevail in the belief-transmission game if they somehow facilitate their own "means of transmission." In this case, the means of transmission is not sex but communication, and thus any belief—even a false belief—that increases communication has a good chance of being transmitted over and over again. False beliefs that happen to promote stable societies tend to propagate because people who hold these beliefs tend to live in stable societies, which provide the means by which false beliefs propagate.

Some of our cultural wisdom about happiness looks suspiciously like a super-replicating false belief. Consider money. If you've ever tried to sell anything, then you probably tried to sell it for as much as you possibly could, and other people probably tried to buy it for as little as they possibly could. All the parties involved in the transaction assumed that they would be better off if they ended up with more money rather than less, and this assumption is the bedrock of our economic behavior. Yet, it has far fewer scientific facts to substantiate it than you might expect. Economists and psychologists have spent decades studying the relation between wealth and happiness, and they have generally concluded that wealth increases human happiness when it lifts people out of abject poverty and into the middle class but that it does little to increase happiness thereafter.[9] Americans who earn $50,000 per year are much happier than those who earn $10,000 per year, but Americans who earn $5 million per year are not much happier than those who earn $100,000 per year. People who live in poor nations are much less happy than people who live in moderately wealthy nations, but people who live in moderately wealthy nations are not much less happy than people who live in extremely wealthy nations. Economists explain that wealth has "declining marginal utility," which is a fancy way of saying that it hurts to be hungry, cold, sick, tired, and scared, but once you've bought your way out of these burdens, the rest of your money is an increasingly useless pile of paper.[10]

So once we've earned as much money as we can actually enjoy, we quit working and enjoy it, right? Wrong. People in wealthy countries generally work long and hard to earn more money than they can ever derive pleasure from.[11] This fact puzzles us less than it should. After all, a rat can be motivated to run through a maze that has a cheesy reward at its end, but once the little guy is all topped up, then even the finest Stilton won't get him off his haunches. Once we've eaten our fill of pancakes, more pancakes are not rewarding, hence we stop trying to procure and consume them. But not so, it seems, with money. As Adam Smith, the father of modern economics, wrote in 1776: "The desire for food is limited in every man by the narrow capacity of the human stomach; but the desire of the conveniences and ornaments of building, dress, equipage, and household furniture, seems to have no limit or certain boundary."[12]

If food and money both stop pleasing us once we've had enough of them, then why do we continue to stuff our pockets when we would not continue to stuff our faces? Adam Smith had an answer. He began by acknowledging what most of us suspect anyway, which is that the production of wealth is not necessarily a source of personal happiness.

> In what constitutes the real happiness of human life, [the poor] are in no respect inferior to those who would seem so much above them. In ease of body and peace of mind, all the different ranks of life are nearly upon a level, and the beggar, who suns himself by the side of the highway, possesses that security which kings are fighting for.[13]

That sounds lovely, but if it's true, then we're all in big trouble. If rich kings are no happier than poor beggars, then why should poor beggars stop sunning themselves by the roadside and work to become rich kings? If no one wants to be rich, then we have a significant economic problem, because flourishing economies require that people continually procure and consume one another's goods and services. Market economies require that we all have an insatiable hunger for *stuff*, and if everyone were content with the stuff they had, then the economy would grind to a halt. But if this is a significant *economic* problem, it is not a significant *personal* problem. The chair of the Federal Reserve may wake up every morning with a desire to do what the economy wants, but most of us get up with a desire to do what *we* want, which is to say that the fundamental needs of a vibrant economy and the fundamental needs of a happy individual are not necessarily the same. So what motivates people to work hard every day to do things that will satisfy the economy's needs but not their own? Like so many thinkers, Smith believed that people want just one thing — happiness — hence economies can blossom and grow only if people are deluded into believing that the production of wealth will make them happy.[14] If and only if people hold this false belief will they do enough producing, procuring, and consuming to sustain their economies.

> The pleasures of wealth and greatness . . . strike the imagination as something grand and beautiful and noble, of which the attainment is well worth all the toil and anxiety which we are so apt to bestow upon it. . . . It is this deception which rouses and keeps in continual motion the industry of mankind. It is this

which first prompted them to cultivate the ground, to build houses, to found cities and commonwealths, and to invent and improve all the sciences and arts, which ennoble and embellish human life; which have entirely changed the whole face of the globe, have turned the rude forests of nature into agreeable and fertile plains, and made the trackless and barren ocean a new fund of subsistence, and the great high road of communication to the different nations of the earth.[15]

In short, the production of wealth does not necessarily make individuals happy, but it does serve the needs of an economy, which serves the needs of a stable society, which serves as a network for the propagation of delusional beliefs about happiness and wealth. Economies thrive when individuals strive, but because individuals will only strive for their own happiness, it is essential that they mistakenly believe that producing and consuming are routes to personal well-being. Although words such as *delusional* may seem to suggest some sort of shadowy conspiracy orchestrated by a small group of men in dark suits, the belief-transmission game teaches us that the propagation of false beliefs does not require that anyone be *trying* to perpetrate a magnificent fraud on an innocent populace. There is no cabal at the top, no star chamber,* no master manipulator whose clever program of indoctrination and propaganda has duped us all into believing that money can buy us love. Rather, this particular false belief is a super-replicator because holding it causes us to engage in the very activities that perpetuate it.[16]

The belief-transmission game explains why we believe some things about happiness that simply aren't true. The joy of money is one example. The joy of children is another that for most of us hits a bit closer to home. Every human culture tells its members that having children will make them happy. When people think about their offspring—either imagining future offspring or thinking about their current ones—they tend to conjure up images of cooing babies smiling from their bassinets, adorable toddlers running higgledy-piggledy across the lawn, handsome boys and gorgeous girls playing trumpets and tubas in the school marching band, successful college students going on to have beautiful weddings, satisfying careers, and flawless grandchildren whose affections can be purchased with candy.

> **If parenting is such difficult business, then why do we have such a rosy view of it?**

Prospective parents know that diapers will need changing, that homework will need doing, and that orthodontists will go to Aruba on their life savings, but by and large, they think quite happily about parenthood, which is why most of them eventually leap into it. When parents look back on parenthood, they remember feeling what those who are looking forward to it expect to feel. Few of us are immune to these cheery contemplations. I have a twenty-nine-year-old son, and I am absolutely convinced that he is and always has been one of the greatest sources of joy in my life, having only recently been eclipsed by my two-year-old granddaughter, who is equally adorable but who has not yet asked me to walk behind her and pretend we're unrelated. When people are asked to identify their sources of joy, they do just what I do: They point to their kids.

---

*Star chamber: Secretive and abusive English law court during the fifteenth to seventeenth centuries [Ed.].

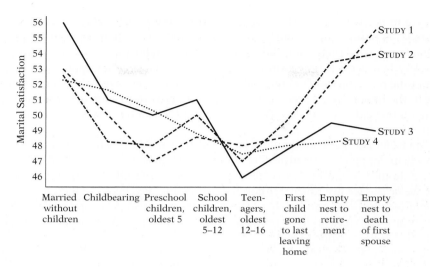

Figure 1
As the four separate studies in this graph show, marital satisfaction decreases dramatically after the birth of the first child and increases only when the last child leaves home.

Graphics are copyright © 2006 by Alfred A. Knopf, from *Stumbling on Happiness* by Daniel Gilbert. Used by permission of Alfred A. Knopf, a division of Random House, Inc.

Yet if we measure the *actual* satisfaction of people who have children, a very differ- ent story emerges. As Figure 1 shows, couples generally start out quite happy in their marriages and then become progressively less satisfied over the course of their lives together, getting close to their original levels of satisfaction only when their children leave home.[17] Despite what we read in the popular press, the only known symptom of "empty nest syndrome" is increased smiling.[18] Interestingly, this pattern of satisfaction over the life cycle describes women (who are usually the primary caretakers of chil- dren) better than men.[19] Careful studies of how women feel as they go about their daily activities show that they are less happy when taking care of their children than when eating, exercising, shopping, napping, or watching television.[20] Indeed, looking after the kids appears to be only slightly more pleasant than doing housework.

None of this should surprise us. Every parent knows that children are a lot of work—a lot of really *hard* work—and although parenting has many rewarding mo- ments, the vast majority of its moments involve dull and selfless service to people who will take decades to become even begrudgingly grateful for what we are doing. If par- enting is such difficult business, then why do we have such a rosy view of it? One reason is that we have been talking on the phone all day with society's stockholders—our moms and uncles and personal trainers—who have been transmitting to us an idea that they *believe* to be true but whose accuracy is not the cause of its successful trans- mission. "Children bring happiness" is a super-replicator. The belief-transmission net- work of which we are a part cannot operate without a continuously replenished supply of people to do the transmitting, thus the belief that children are a source of happi- ness becomes a part of our cultural wisdom simply because the opposite belief unravels the fabric of any society that holds it. Indeed, people who believed that children bring

15

misery and despair—and who thus stopped having them—would put their belief-transmission network out of business in around fifty years, hence terminating the belief that terminated them. The Shakers were a utopian farming community that arose in the 1800s and at one time numbered about six thousand. They approved of children, but they did not approve of the natural act that creates them. Over the years, their strict belief in the importance of celibacy caused their network to contract, and today there are just a few elderly Shakers left, transmitting their doomsday belief to no one but themselves.

The belief-transmission game is rigged so that we *must* believe that children and money bring happiness, regardless of whether such beliefs are true. This doesn't mean that we should all now quit our jobs and abandon our families. Rather, it means that while we *believe* we are raising children and earning paychecks to increase our share of happiness, we are actually doing these things for reasons beyond our ken. We are nodes in a social network that arises and falls by a logic of its own, which is why we continue to toil, continue to mate, and continue to be surprised when we do not experience all the joy we so gullibly anticipated.

The Myth of Fingerprints

My friends tell me that I have a tendency to point out problems without offering solutions, but they never tell me what I should do about it. In one chapter after another, I've described the ways in which imagination fails to provide us with accurate previews of our emotional futures. I've claimed that when we imagine our futures we tend to fill in, leave out, and take little account of how differently we will think about the future once we actually get there. I've claimed that neither personal experience nor cultural wisdom compensates for imagination's shortcomings. I've so thoroughly marinated you in the foibles, biases, errors, and mistakes of the human mind that you may wonder how anyone ever manages to make toast without buttering their kneecaps. If so, you will be heartened to learn that there *is* a simple method by which anyone can make strikingly accurate predictions about how they will feel in the future. But you may be disheartened to learn that, by and large, no one wants to use it.

Why do we rely on our imaginations in the first place? Imagination is the poor man's wormhole. We can't do what we'd really *like* to do—namely, travel through time, pay a visit to our future selves, and *see* how happy those selves are—and so we imagine the future instead of actually going there. But if we cannot travel in the dimensions of time, we can travel in the dimensions of space, and the chances are pretty good that somewhere in those other three dimensions there is another human being who is actually *experiencing* the future event that we are merely thinking about. Surely we aren't the first people ever to consider a move to Cincinnati, a career in motel management, another helping of rhubarb pie, or an extramarital affair, and for the most part, those who have already tried these things are more than willing to tell us about them. It is true that when people tell us about their past experiences ("That ice water wasn't really so cold" or "I love taking care of my daughter"), memory's peccadilloes may render their testimony unreliable. But it is also true that when people tell us about their *current* experiences ("How am I feeling right now? I feel like pulling my arm out of this freezing bucket and sticking my teenager's head in it instead!"), they are providing us with the kind of report about their subjective state that is considered the gold standard of happiness measures. If you believe (as I do) that people can generally say how they are feeling at the moment they are asked, then one way to make predictions about our own emotional futures is to find someone who is having the experience we are contemplating and ask them how they feel. Instead of remembering our past experience in order to simulate our future experience, perhaps we should simply ask other people to introspect on their inner states. Perhaps we should give up on remembering and imagining entirely and use other people as *surrogates* for our future selves.

    This idea sounds all too simple, and I suspect you have an objection to it that goes   20 something like this: *Yes, other people are probably right now experiencing the very things I am merely contemplating, but I can't use other people's experiences as proxies for my own because those other people are not me. Every human being is as unique as his or her fingerprints, so it won't help me much to learn about how others feel in the situations that I'm facing. Unless these other people are my clones and have had all the same experiences I've had, their reactions and my reactions are bound to differ. I am a walking, talking idiosyncrasy, and thus I am better off basing my predictions on my somewhat fickle imagination than on the reports of people whose preferences, tastes, and emotional proclivities are so radically different from my own.* If that's your objection, then it is a good one—so good that it will take two steps to dismantle it. First let me prove to you that the experience of a single randomly selected individual can sometimes provide a better basis for predicting your future experience than your own imagination can. And then let me show you why you—and I—find this so difficult to believe.

Finding the Solution

Imagination has three shortcomings, and if you didn't know that then you may be reading this book [Gilbert's *Stumbling on Happiness*] backward. If you did know that, then you also know that imagination's first shortcoming is its tendency to fill in and leave out without telling us. . . . No one can imagine every feature and consequence of a future event, hence we must consider some and fail to consider others. The problem is that the features and consequences we fail to consider are often quite important. You may recall the study [not discussed in this excerpt] in which college students were asked to imagine how they would feel a few days after their school's football team played a game against its archrival.[21] The results showed that students overestimated the duration of the game's emotional impact because when they tried to imagine their future experience, they imagined their team winning ("The clock will hit zero, we'll storm the field, everyone will cheer . . .") but failed to imagine what they would be doing afterward ("And then I'll go home and study for my final exams"). Because the students were focused on the game, they failed to imagine how events that happened *after* the game would influence their happiness. So what *should* they have done instead?

    They should have abandoned imagination altogether. Consider a study that put people in a similar predicament and then forced them to abandon their imaginations. In this study, a group of volunteers (reporters) first received a delicious prize—a gift certificate from a local ice cream parlor—and then performed a long, boring task in which they counted and recorded geometric shapes that appeared on a computer

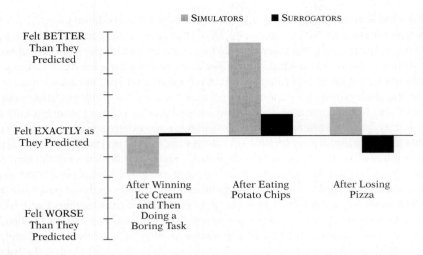

Figure 2

Volunteers made much more accurate predictions of their future feelings when they learned how someone else had felt in the same situation (surrogators) than when they tried to imagine how they themselves would feel (simulators).

Graphics are copyright © 2006 by Alfred A. Knopf, from *Stumbling on Happiness* by Daniel Gilbert. Used by permission of Alfred A. Knopf, a division of Random House, Inc.

screen.[22] The reporters then reported how they felt. Next, a new group of volunteers was told that they would also receive a prize and do the same boring task. Some of these new volunteers (simulators) were told what the prize was and were asked to use their imaginations to predict their future feelings. Other volunteers (surrogators) were not told what the prize was but were instead shown the report of a randomly selected reporter. Not knowing what the prize was, they couldn't possibly use their imaginations to predict their future feelings. Instead, they had to rely on the reporter's report. Once all the volunteers had made their predictions, they received the prize, did the long, boring task, and reported how they actually felt. As the leftmost bars in Figure 2 show, simulators were not as happy as they thought they would be. Why? Because they failed to imagine how quickly the joy of receiving a gift certificate would fade when it was followed by a long, boring task. This is precisely the same mistake that the college-football fans made. But now look at the results for the surrogators. As you can see, they made extremely accurate predictions of their future happiness. These surrogators didn't know what kind of prize they would receive, but they did know that someone who had received that prize had been less than ecstatic at the conclusion of the boring task. So they shrugged and reasoned that they too would feel less than ecstatic at the conclusion of the boring task—and they were right!

Imagination's second shortcoming is its tendency to project the present onto the future. . . . When imagination paints a picture of the future, many of the details are necessarily missing, and imagination solves this problem by filling in the gaps with details that it borrows from the present. Anyone who has ever shopped on an empty stomach, vowed to quit smoking after stubbing out a cigarette, or proposed marriage while on shore leave* knows that how we feel now can erroneously influence how we *think* we'll feel later. As it turns out, surrogation can remedy this shortcoming too. In one study, volunteers (reporters) ate a few potato chips and reported how much they enjoyed them.[23] Next, a new group of volunteers was fed pretzels, peanut-butter cheese crackers, tortilla chips, bread sticks, and melba toast, which, as you might guess, left them thoroughly stuffed and with little desire for salty snack foods. These stuffed volunteers were then asked to predict how much they would enjoy eating a particular food the next day. Some of these stuffed volunteers (simulators) were told that the food they would eat the next day was potato chips, and they were asked to use their imaginations to predict how they would feel after eating them. Other stuffed volunteers (surrogators) were not told what the next day's food would be but were instead shown the report of one randomly selected reporter. Because surrogators didn't know what the next day's food would be, they couldn't use their imaginations to predict their future enjoyment of it and thus they had to rely on the reporter's report. Once all the volunteers had made their predictions, they went away, returned the next day, ate some potato chips, and reported how much they enjoyed them. As the middle bars in Figure 2 show, simulators enjoyed eating the potato chips more than they thought they would. Why? Because when they made their predictions they had bellies full of pretzels and crackers. But surrogators—who were equally full when they made their predictions—relied on the report of someone without a full belly and hence made much more accurate predictions. It is important to note that the surrogators accurately predicted their future enjoyment of a food despite the fact that they didn't even know what the food was!

Imagination's third shortcoming is its failure to recognize that things will look different once they happen—in particular, that bad things will look a whole lot better. . . . When we imagine losing a job, for instance, we imagine the painful experience ("The boss will march into my office, shut the door behind him . . .") without also imagining how our psychological immune systems will transform its meaning ("I'll come to realize that this was an opportunity to quit retail sales and follow my true calling as a sculptor"). Can surrogation remedy this shortcoming? To find out, researchers arranged for some people to have an unpleasant experience. A group of volunteers (reporters) was told that the experimenter would flip a coin, and if it came up heads, the volunteer would receive a gift certificate to a local pizza parlor. The coin was flipped and—*oh, so sorry*—it came up tails and the reporters received nothing.[24] The reporters then reported how they felt. Next, a new group of volunteers was told about the coin-flipping game and was asked to predict how they would feel if the coin came up tails and they didn't get the pizza gift certificate. Some of these volunteers (simulators) were told the precise monetary value of the gift certificate, and others (surrogators) were instead shown the report of one randomly selected reporter. Once the volunteers had made their predictions, the coin was flipped and—*oh, so sorry*—came up tails. The volunteers then reported how they felt. As the rightmost bars in Figure 2 show, simulators felt better than they predicted they'd feel if they lost the coin flip. Why? Because simulators did not realize how quickly and easily they would rationalize the loss ("Pizza is too fattening, and besides, I don't like that restaurant anyway"). But surrogators—who had nothing to go on except the report of another randomly selected

---

*Shore leave: Time granted to a sailor to spend on land [Ed.].

individual—assumed that they wouldn't feel too bad after losing the prize and hence made more accurate predictions.

Rejecting the Solution

This trio of studies suggests that when people are deprived of the information that imagination requires and are thus *forced* to use others as surrogates, they make re-markably accurate predictions about their future feelings, which suggests that the best way to predict our feelings tomorrow is to see how others are feeling today.[25] Given the impressive power of this simple technique, we should expect people to go out of their way to use it. But they don't. When an entirely new group of volunteers was told about the three situations I just described—winning a prize, eating a mystery food, or failing to receive a gift certificate—and was then asked whether they would prefer to make predictions about their future feelings based on *(a)* information about the prize, the food, and the certificate; or *(b)* information about how a randomly selected individual felt after winning them, eating them, or los-ing them, virtually every volunteer chose the former. If you hadn't seen the results of these studies, you'd probably have done the same. If I offered to pay for your dinner at a restaurant if you could accurately predict how much you were going to enjoy it, would you want to see the restaurant's menu or some randomly selected diner's review? If you are like most people, you would prefer to see the menu, and if you are like most people, you would end up buying your own dinner. Why?

> **[I]f you are like most people, then like most people, you don't know you're like most people.**

Because if you are like most people, then like most people, you don't know you're like most people. Science has given us a lot of facts about the average person, and one of the most reliable of these facts is that the average person doesn't see herself as aver-age. Most students see themselves as more intelligent than the average student,[26] most business managers see themselves as more competent than the average business man-ager,[27] and most football players see themselves as having better "football sense" than their teammates.[28] Ninety percent of motorists consider themselves to be safer-than-average drivers,[29] and 94 percent of college professors consider themselves to be better-than-average teachers.[30] Ironically, the bias toward seeing ourselves as better than average causes us to see ourselves as less biased than average too.[31] As one research team concluded, "Most of us appear to believe that we are more athletic, intelligent, or-ganized, ethical, logical, interesting, fair-minded, and healthy—not to mention more attractive—than the average person."[32]

This tendency to think of ourselves as better than others is not necessarily a mani-festation of our unfettered narcissism but may instead be an instance of a more general tendency to think of ourselves as *different* from others—often for better but sometimes for worse. When people are asked about generosity, they claim to perform a greater number of generous acts than others do; but when they are asked about selfishness, they claim to perform a greater number of selfish acts than others do.[33] When people are asked about their ability to perform an easy task, such as driving a car or riding a bike, they rate themselves as better than others; but when they are asked about their ability to perform a difficult task, such as juggling or playing chess, they rate themselves as worse than others.[34] We don't always see ourselves as *superior*, but we almost always see ourselves as *unique*. Even when we do precisely what others do, we tend to think that we're doing it for unique reasons. For instance, we tend to attribute other people's choices to features of the chooser ("Phil picked this class because he's one of those literary types"), but we tend to attribute our own choices to features of the options ("But I picked it because it was easier than economics").[35] We recognize that our decisions are influenced by social norms ("I was too embarrassed to raise my hand in class even though I was terribly confused"), but fail to recognize that others' decisions were similarly influenced ("No one else raised a hand because no one else was as confused as I was").[36] We know that our choices sometimes reflect our aversions ("I voted for Kerry because I couldn't stand Bush"), but we assume that other people's choices reflect their appetites ("If Rebecca voted for Kerry, then she must have liked him").[37] The list of differences is long but the conclusion to be drawn from it is short: The self considers itself to be a very special person.[38]

What makes us think we're so darned special? Three things, at least. First, even if we aren't special, the way we know ourselves is. We are the only people in the world whom we can know from the inside. We *experience* our own thoughts and feelings but must *infer* that other people are experiencing theirs. We all trust that behind those eyes and inside those skulls, our friends and neighbors are having subjective experiences very much like our own, but that trust is an article of faith and not the palpable, self-evident truth that our own subjective experiences constitute. There is a difference between making love and reading about it, and it is the same difference that distinguishes our knowledge of our own mental lives from our knowledge of everyone else's. Because we know ourselves and others by such different means, we gather very different kinds and amounts of information. In every waking moment we monitor the steady stream of thoughts and feelings that runs through our heads, but we only monitor other people's words and deeds, and only when they are in our company. One reason why we seem so special, then, is that we learn about ourselves in such a special way.

The second reason is that we *enjoy* thinking of ourselves as special. Most of us want to fit in well with our peers, but we don't want to fit in too well.[39] We prize our unique identities, and research shows that when people are made to feel too similar to others, their moods quickly sour and they try to distance and distinguish themselves in a variety of ways.[40] If you've ever shown up at a party and found someone else wearing exactly the same dress or necktie that you were wearing, then you know how unsettling it is to share the room with an unwanted twin whose presence temporarily diminishes your sense of individuality. Because we *value* our uniqueness, it isn't surprising that we tend to overestimate it.

The third reason why we tend to overestimate our uniqueness is that we tend to overestimate everyone's uniqueness — that is, we tend to think of people as more different from one another than they actually are. Let's face it: All people are similar in some ways and different in others. The psychologists, biologists, economists, and sociologists who are searching for universal laws of human behavior naturally care about the similarities, but the rest of us care mainly about the differences. Social life involves selecting particular individuals to be our sexual partners, business partners, bowling partners, and more. That task requires that we focus on the things that distinguish one person from another and not on the things that all people share, which is why personal ads are much more likely to mention the advertiser's love of ballet than his love of oxygen.

A penchant for respiration explains a great deal about human behavior — for example, why people live on land, become ill at high altitudes, have lungs, resist suffocation, love trees, and so on. It surely explains more than does a person's penchant for ballet. But it does nothing to distinguish one person from another, and thus for ordinary folks who are in the ordinary business of selecting others for commerce, conversation, or copulation, the penchant for air is stunningly irrelevant. Individual similarities are vast, but we don't care much about them because they don't help us do what we are here on earth to do, namely, distinguish Jack from Jill and Jill from Jennifer. As such, these individual similarities are an inconspicuous backdrop against which a small number of relatively minor individual differences stand out in bold relief.

Because we spend so much time searching for, attending to, thinking about, and remembering these differences, we tend to overestimate their magnitude and frequency, and thus end up thinking of people as more varied than they actually are. If you spent all day sorting grapes into different shapes, colors, and kinds, you'd become one of those annoying grapeophiles who talks endlessly about the nuances of flavor and the permutations of texture. You'd come to think of grapes as infinitely varied, and you'd forget that almost all of the really *important* information about a grape can be deduced from the simple fact of its grapehood. Our belief in the variability of others and in the uniqueness of the self is especially powerful when it comes to emotion.[41] Because we can *feel* our own emotions but must *infer* the emotions of others by watching their faces and listening to their voices, we often have the impression that others don't experience the same intensity of emotion that we do, which is why we expect others to recognize our feelings even when we can't recognize theirs.[42] This sense of emotional uniqueness starts early. When kindergarteners are asked how they and others would feel in a variety of situations, they expect to experience unique emotions ("Billy would be sad but I wouldn't") and they provide unique reasons for experiencing them ("I'd tell myself that the hamster was in heaven, but Billy would just cry").[43] When adults make these same kinds of predictions, they do just the same thing.[44]

Our mythical belief in the variability and uniqueness of individuals is the main reason why we refuse to use others as surrogates. After all, surrogation is only useful when we can count on a surrogate to react to an event roughly as we would, and if we believe that people's emotional reactions are more varied than they actually are, then surrogation will seem less useful to us than it actually is. The irony, of course, is that surrogation is a cheap and effective way to predict one's future emotions, but because we don't realize just how similar we all are, we reject this reliable method and rely instead on our imaginations, as flawed and fallible as they may be.

Onward

Despite its watery connotation, the word *hogwash* refers to the feeding — and not to the bathing — of pigs. Hogwash is something that pigs eat, that pigs like, and that pigs need. Farmers provide pigs with hogwash because without it, pigs get grumpy. The word *hogwash* also refers to the falsehoods people tell one another. Like the hogwash that farmers feed their pigs, the hogwash that our friends and teachers and parents feed us is meant to make us happy; but unlike hogwash of the porcine variety, human hogwash does not always achieve its end. As we have seen, ideas can flourish if they preserve the social systems that allow them to be transmitted. Because individuals don't usually feel that it is their personal duty to preserve social systems, these ideas must disguise themselves as prescriptions for individual happiness. We might expect that after spending some time in the world, our experiences would debunk these ideas, but it doesn't always work that way. To learn from our experience we must remember it, and for a variety of reasons, memory is a faithless friend. Practice and coaching get us out of our diapers and into our britches, but they are not enough to get us out of our presents and into our futures. What's so ironic about this predicament is that the information we need to make accurate predictions of our emotional futures is right under our noses, but we don't seem to recognize its aroma. It doesn't always make sense to heed what people tell us when they communicate their beliefs about happiness, but it does make sense to observe how happy they are in different circumstances. Alas, we think of ourselves as unique entities—minds unlike any others—and thus we often reject the lessons that the emotional experience of others has to teach us.

NOTES

1. J. Livingston and R. Evans, "Whatever Will Be, Will Be (Que Sera, Sera)" (1955).
2. W. V. Quine and J. S. Ullian, *The Web of Belief*, 2nd ed. (New York: Random House, 1978), 51.
3. Half of all Americans relocated in the five-year period of 1995–2000, which suggests that the average American relocates about every ten years; B. Berkner and C. S. Faber, *Geographical Mobility, 1995 to 2000* (Washington, D.C.: U.S. Bureau of the Census, 2003).
4. The average baby boomer held roughly ten jobs between the ages of eighteen and thirty-six, which suggests that the average American holds at least this many in a lifetime. Bureau of Labor Statistics, *Number of Jobs Held, Labor Market Activity, and Earnings Growth among Younger Baby Boomers: Results from More Than Two Decades of a Longitudinal Survey*, Bureau of Labor Statistics news release (Washington, D.C.: U.S. Department of Labor, 2002).
5. The U.S. Census Bureau projects that in the coming years, 10 percent of Americans will never marry, 60 percent will marry just once, and 30 percent will marry at least twice. R. M. Kreider and J. M. Fields, *Number, Timing, and Duration of Marriages and Divorces, 1996* (Washington, D.C.: U.S. Bureau of the Census, 2002).
6. B. Russell, *The Analysis of Mind* (New York: Macmillan, 1921), 231.
7. The biologist Richard Dawkins refers to these beliefs as *memes*. See R. J. Dawkins, *The Selfish Gene* (Oxford: Oxford University Press, 1976). See also S. Blackmore, *The Meme Machine* (Oxford: Oxford University Press, 2000).
8. D. C. Dennett, *Brainstorms: Philosophical Essays on Mind and Psychology* (Cambridge, Mass.: Bradford/MIT Press, 1981), 18.
9. R. Layard, *Happiness: Lessons from a New Science* (New York: Penguin, 2005); E. Diener and M. E. P. Seligman, "Beyond Money: Toward an Economy of Well-Being," *Psychological Science in the Public Interest* 5: 1–31 (2004); B. S. Frey and A. Stutzer, *Happiness and Economics: How the Economy and Institutions Affect Human Well-Being* (Princeton, N.J.: Princeton University Press, 2002); R. A. Easterlin, "Income and Happiness: Towards a Unified Theory," *Economic Journal* 111: 465–84 (2001); and D. G. Blanchflower and A. J. Oswald, "Well-Being over Time in Britain and the USA," *Journal of Public Economics* 88: 1359–86 (2004).
10. The effect of declining marginal utility is slowed when we spend our money on the things to which we are least likely to adapt. See T. Scitovsky, *The Joyless Economy: The*

Psychology of Human Satisfaction (Oxford: Oxford University Press, 1976); L. Van Boven and T. Gilovich, "To Do or to Have? That Is the Question," *Journal of Personality and Social Psychology* 85: 1193–1202 (2003); and R. H. Frank, "How Not to Buy Happiness," *Daedalus: Journal of the American Academy of Arts and Sciences* 133: 69–79 (2004). Not all economists believe in decreasing marginal utility: R. A. Easterlin, "Diminishing Marginal Utility of Income? Caveat Emptor," *Social Indicators Research* 70: 243–326 (2005).

11. J. D. Graaf et al., *Affluenza: The All-Consuming Epidemic* (New York: Berrett-Koehler, 2002); D. Myers, *The American Paradox: Spiritual Hunger in an Age of Plenty* (New Haven: Yale University Press, 2000); R. H. Frank, *Luxury Fever* (Princeton, N.J.: Princeton University Press, 2000); J. B. Schor, *The Overspent American: Why We Want What We Don't Need* (New York: Perennial, 1999); and P. L. Wachtel, *Poverty of Affluence: A Psychological Portrait of the American Way of Life* (New York: Free Press, 1983).

12. Adam Smith, *An Inquiry into the Nature and Causes of the Wealth of Nations* (1776), book 1 (New York: Modern Library, 1994).

13. Adam Smith, *The Theory of Moral Sentiments* (1759; Cambridge: Cambridge University Press, 2002).

14. N. Ashraf, C. Camerer, and G. Loewenstein, "Adam Smith, Behavorial Economist," *Journal of Economic Perspectives* 19: 131–45 (2005).

15. Smith, *The Theory of Moral Sentiments.*

16. Some theorists have argued that societies exhibit a cyclic pattern in which people do come to realize that money doesn't buy happiness but then forget this lesson a generation later. See A. O. Hirschman, *Shifting Involvements: Private Interest and Public Action* (Princeton, N.J.: Princeton University Press, 1982).

17. C. Walker, "Some Variations in Marital Satisfaction," in *Equalities and Inequalities in Family Life*, ed. R. Chester and J. Peel (London: Academic Press, 1977), 127–39.

18. D. Myers, *The Pursuit of Happiness: Discovering the Pathway to Fulfillment, Well-Being, and Enduring Personal Joy* (New York: Avon, 1992), 71.

19. J. A. Feeney, "Attachment Styles, Communication Patterns and Satisfaction across the Life Cycle of Marriage," *Personal Relationships* 1: 333–48 (1994).

20. D. Kahneman et al., "A Survey Method for Characterizing Daily Life Experience: The Day Reconstruction Method," *Science* 306: 1776–80 (2004).

21. T. D. Wilson et al., "Focalism: A Source of Durability Bias in Affective Forecasting," *Journal of Personality and Social Psychology* 78: 821–36 (2000).

22. R. J. Norwick, D. T. Gilbert, and T. D. Wilson, "Surrogation: An Antidote for Errors in Affective Forecasting" (unpublished manuscript, Harvard University, 2005).

23. Ibid.

24. Ibid.

25. This is also the best way to predict our future behavior. For example, people overestimate the likelihood that they will perform a charitable act but correctly estimate the likelihood that others will do the same. This suggests that if we would base predictions of our own behavior on what we see others do, we'd be dead-on. See N. Epley and D. Dunning, "Feeling 'Holier Than Thou': Are Self-Serving Assessments Produced by Errors in Self- or Social-Prediction?" *Journal of Personality and Social Psychology* 79: 861–75 (2000).

26. R. C. Wylie, *The Self-Concept: Theory and Research on Selected Topics*, vol. 2 (Lincoln: University of Nebraska Press, 1979).

27. L. Larwood and W. Whittaker, "Managerial Myopia: Self-Serving Biases in Organizational Planning," *Journal of Applied Psychology* 62: 194–98 (1977).

28. R. B. Felson, "Ambiguity and Bias in the Self-Concept," *Social Psychology Quarterly* 44: 64–69.

29. D. Walton and J. Bathurst, "An Exploration of the Perceptions of the Average Driver's Speed Compared to Perceived Driver Safety and Driving Skill," *Accident Analysis and Prevention* 30: 821–30 (1998).

30. P. Cross, "Not Can But Will College Teachers Be Improved?" *New Directions for Higher Education* 17: 1–15 (1977).

31. E. Pronin, D. Y. Lin, and L. Ross, "The Bias Blind Spot: Perceptions of Bias in Self Versus Others," *Personality and Social Psychology Bulletin* 28: 369–81 (2002).

32. J. Kruger, "Lake Wobegon Be Gone! The 'Below-Average Effect' and the Egocentric Nature of Comparative Ability Judgments," *Journal of Personality and Social Psychology* 77: 221–32 (1999).

33. J. T. Johnson et al., "The 'Barnum Effect' Revisited: Cognitive and Motivational Factors in the Acceptance of Personality Descriptions," *Journal of Personality and Social Psychology* 49: 1378–91 (1985).

34. Kruger, "Lake Wobegon Be Gone!"

35. E. E. Jones and R. E. Nisbett, "The Actor and the Observer: Divergent Perceptions of the Causes of Behavior," in *Attribution: Perceiving the Causes of Behavior*, ed. E. E. Jones et al. (Morristown, N.J.: General Learning Press, 1972); and R. E. Nisbett and E. Borgida, "Attribution and the Psychology of Prediction," *Journal of Personality and Social Psychology* 32: 932–43 (1975).

36. D. T. Miller and C. McFarland, "Pluralistic Ignorance: When Similarity Is Interpreted as Dissimilarity," *Journal of Personality and Social Psychology* 53: 298–305 (1987).

37. D. T. Miller and L. D. Nelson, "Seeing Approach Motivation in the Avoidance Behavior of Others: Implications for an Understanding of Pluralistic Ignorance," *Journal of Personality and Social Psychology* 83: 1066–75 (2002).

38. C. R. Snyder and H. L. Fromkin, "Abnormality as a Positive Characteristic: The Development and Validation of a Scale Measuring Need for Uniqueness," *Journal of Abnormal Psychology* 86: 518–27 (1977).

39. M. B. Brewer, "The Social Self: On Being the Same and Different at the Same Time," *Personality and Social Psychology Bulletin* 17: 475–82 (1991).

40. H. L. Fromkin, "Effects of Experimentally Aroused Feelings of Undistinctiveness upon Valuation of Scarce and Novel Experiences," *Journal of Personality and Social Psychology* 16: 521–29 (1970); and H. L. Fromkin, "Feelings of Interpersonal Undistinctiveness: An Unpleasant Affective State," *Journal of Experimental Research in Personality* 6: 178–85 (1972).

41. R. Karniol, T. Eylon, and S. Rish, "Predicting Your Own and Others' Thoughts and Feelings: More Like a Stranger Than a Friend," *European Journal of Social Psychology* 27: 301–11 (1997); J. T. Johnson, "The Heart on the Sleeve and the Secret Self: Estimations of Hidden Emotion in Self and Acquaintances," *Journal of Personality* 55: 563–82 (1987); and R. Karniol, "Egocentrism Versus Protocentrism: The Status of Self in Social Prediction," *Psychological Review* 110: 564–80 (2003).

42. C. L. Barr and R. E. Kleck, "Self-Other Perception of the Intensity of Facial Expressions of Emotion: Do We Know What We Show?" *Journal of Personality and Social Psychology* 68: 608–18 (1995).

43. R. Karniol and L. Koren, "How Would You Feel? Children's Inferences Regarding Their Own and Others' Affective Reactions," *Cognitive Development* 2: 271–78 (1987).

44. C. McFarland and D. T. Miller, "Judgments of Self-Other Similarity: Just Like Other People, Only More So," *Personality and Social Psychology Bulletin* 16: 475–84 (1990).

Exploring Context

1. Visit Stripgenerator.com and make a comic strip that represents the argument of Gilbert's essay. Incorporate representations for your definitions of the terms in Questions for Critical Reading.

2. What is "happiness"? Enter "happy," "happiness," and related terms into Google or another search engine. What sort of results do you get? What if you search for images? What does "happiness" look like on the Web? Does it match the definition you developed in Question 3 of Questions for Critical Reading?

3. Gilbert suggests that if we want to know how happy we will be in the future, we should ask someone who's already living our goals. Use Yahoo! Answers (answers.yahoo.com) to ask questions about possible plans for your future. Can the Web function as a surrogate? Use the definition of *surrogate* that you developed in Question 2 of Questions for Critical Reading in your answer.

Questions for Connecting

1. Gilbert mostly considers surrogates and super-replicators in relation to our future happiness but can these same phenomena promote social change? Apply Gilbert's ideas to Charles Duhigg's examination of social change in "From Civil Rights to Megachurches" (p. 86). What kinds of social ties best foster super-replicators? Use your work from Questions 1 and 2 of Questions for Critical Reading.

2. What is the relationship between memes and super-replicators? Consider the impact of Bill Wasik's ideas in "My Crowd Experiment: The Mob Project" (p. 474) on what Gilbert has to say about super-replicators, drawing on the understanding of that term that you developed in response to Question 1 of Questions for Critical Reading.

3. Might Gilbert's ideas help emerging adults? Apply his ideas to Robin Marantz Henig's discussion of emerging adulthood in "What Is It about 20-Somethings?" (p. 199). What role might super-replicators play in establishing emerging adulthood as a life stage? Could surrogates help emerging adults find happiness? Use your work on super-replicators, surrogates, and happiness from Questions for Critical Reading to help you make your response.

Language Matters

1. Locate information on sentence diagrams in a grammar handbook or other reference resource. Then select a key sentence from Gilbert's text and diagram the sentence. What are the different parts of the sentence, and how are they related?

2. Locate a sentence in Gilbert's essay that uses *I* as the subject. When does Gilbert use *I*? When doesn't he? When should you?

3. Take a key sentence from Gilbert. Summarize it and then paraphrase it. What is the difference between a summary, a paraphrase, and a quotation? When would you use each in your writing, and what type of citation does each need?

Assignments for Writing

1. According to Gilbert, surrogates can offer us an accurate sense of our future happiness. Write a paper in which you assess the potential of the kind of surrogates that Gilbert describes. You will want to extend, complicate, or refute Gilbert's argument for surrogates and their reliability in predicting the future. Think about these questions: What role does individuality have in our future happiness? Is Gilbert correct in claiming that we are not as unique as we believe? Can surrogates be used to examine all future events? How can surrogates be used to control social processes? If we are not unique, why do we see ourselves as individuals? Use your definition of *surrogate* from Question 2 of Questions for Critical Reading as well as your work with Yahoo! Answers from Question 3 of Exploring Context.

2. Write a paper in which you evaluate Gilbert's argument about surrogates and their reliability in predicting the future by finding an appropriate surrogate for you and your future happiness. You may wish to use your experience finding a surrogate on the Web from Question 3 of Exploring Context in making your argument. Also consider: What role does individuality have in our future happiness? Are surrogate examples more accurate than our imagination? What event in your life did you imagine was going to make you happier than it did?

3. Gilbert defines *super-replicators* as genes or beliefs that are given to transmission regardless of their usefulness. Write a paper in which you extend Gilbert's argument through your own example of a super-replicator that persists in society. How do we communicate our ideas to others? What super-replicators are we passing along to those we come into contact with? Does the validity of a belief correlate to its speed of transmission? What is the role of super-replicators in communicating cultural ideas? Use your definition of the term from Question 1 of Questions for Critical Reading.

ROBIN MARANTZ HENIG

JB Reed. Used with permission.

Robin Marantz Henig is a journalist and author whose work focuses on science. Along with daughter Samantha Henig, she wrote the book *Twentysomething: Why Do Young Adults Seem Stuck?*, which was named a best book of the month on Amazon and a must-read on Oprah.com. Henig is also the author of *Pandora's Baby*, *The Monk in the Garden*, and *A Dancing Matrix*, among other books. Her articles have appeared in *Scientific American*, *Newsweek*, *Discover*, and other publications. Henig is the recipient of a Guggenheim fellowship, two National Association of Science Writers Science in Society Awards, and an American Society of Journalists and Authors Career Achievement Award. She holds a master's in journalism from Northwestern University and is a contributing writer for the *New York Times Magazine*.

Henig's ninth and latest book, *Twentysomething*, explores what it means to be in one's twenties today through both neuroscience and psychological research and surveys of more than 120 millennials and baby boomers. The book project came about as a result of this selection, "What Is It about 20-Somethings?," which ran as the cover story for the *New York Times Magazine* in the summer of 2010 alongside stories about elections in Pennsylvania and knockoff tennis shoes from China.

In "What Is It about 20-Somethings?," Henig analyzes the lag in today's 20-somethings' journey to what is traditionally considered adulthood, inquiring whether this period of "emerging adulthood" is a passing, circumstantial trend or a true, psychological life stage that must be accommodated the way other stages, such as adolescence, are. Henig raises this question: Does delaying conventional adult responsibilities allow for "a rich and varied period for self-discovery" or is it simply "self-indulgence" (p. 201)?

What does your experience suggest to you? What do you (or did you) expect from your twenties? What is it like to be 20-something today?

▶ TAGS: *adolescence and adulthood, economics, identity, psychology, science and technology, social change*

▶ CONNECTIONS: *Appiah, Duhigg, Gilbert, Klosterman, Konnikova, Padawer, Paumgarten, Restak, Singer, Wasik*

Questions for Critical Reading

1. What is *emerging adulthood*? As you read, pay attention to the places where Henig defines and develops this term.

2. What are the key milestones that indicate someone has reached adulthood? Use these to develop your own definition of adulthood and then, as you read, note places where Henig discusses both adulthood and emerging adulthood. Revise your response to take Henig's ideas into account.

3. While reading the essay, consider the economic impact of emerging adulthood. How has economics shaped this life stage, and what would the further economic consequences be if we truly recognized it as a life stage?

What Is It about 20-Somethings?

Why are so many people in their 20s taking so long to grow up?

This question pops up everywhere, underlying concerns about "failure to launch" and "boomerang kids." Two new sitcoms feature grown children moving back in with their parents — *$#*! My Dad Says*, starring William Shatner as a divorced curmudgeon whose 20-something son can't make it on his own as a blogger, and *Big Lake*, in which a financial whiz kid loses his Wall Street job and moves back home to rural Pennsylvania. A cover of the *New Yorker* last spring [2010] picked up on the zeitgeist: a young man hangs up his new Ph.D. in his boyhood bedroom, the cardboard box at his feet signaling his plans to move back home now that he's officially overqualified for a job. In the doorway stand his parents, their expressions a mix of resignation, worry, annoyance, and perplexity: how exactly did this happen?

It's happening all over, in all sorts of families, not just young people moving back home but also young people taking longer to reach adulthood overall. It's a development that predates the current economic doldrums, and no one knows yet what the impact will be — on the prospects of the young men and women; on the parents on whom so many of them depend; on society, built on the expectation of an orderly progression in which kids finish school, grow up, start careers, make a family, and eventually retire to live on pensions supported by the next crop of kids who finish school, grow up, start careers, make a family, and on and on. The traditional cycle seems to have gone off course, as young people remain untethered to romantic partners or to permanent homes, going back to school for lack of better options, traveling, avoiding commitments, competing ferociously for unpaid internships or temporary (and often grueling) Teach for America jobs, forestalling the beginning of adult life.

The 20s are a black box, and there is a lot of churning in there. One-third of people in their 20s move to a new residence every year. Forty percent move back home with their parents at least once. They go through an average of seven jobs in their 20s, more job changes than in any other stretch. Two-thirds spend at least some time living with a romantic partner without being married. And marriage occurs later than ever. The median age at first marriage in the early 1970s, when the baby boomers were young, was 21 for women and 23 for men; by 2009 it had climbed to 26 for women and 28 for men, five years in a little more than a generation.

We're in the thick of what one sociologist calls "the changing timetable for adulthood." Sociologists traditionally define the "transition to adulthood" as marked by   5 five milestones: completing school, leaving home, becoming financially independent, marrying, and having a child. In 1960, 77 percent of women and 65 percent of men had, by the time they reached 30, passed all five milestones. Among 30-year-olds in 2000, according to data from the United States Census Bureau, fewer than half of the women and one-third of the men had done so. A Canadian study reported that a typical 30-year-old in 2001 had completed the same number of milestones as a 25-year-old in the early '70s.

The whole idea of milestones, of course, is something of an anachronism; it implies a lockstep march toward adulthood that is rare these days. Kids don't shuffle along in unison on the road to maturity. They slouch toward adulthood at an uneven, highly individual pace. Some never achieve all five milestones, including those who are single or childless by choice, or unable to marry even if they wanted to because they're gay. Others reach the milestones completely out of order, advancing professionally before committing to a monogamous relationship, having children young and marrying later, leaving school to go to work and returning to school long after becoming financially secure.

Even if some traditional milestones are never reached, one thing is clear: Getting to what we would generally call adulthood is happening later than ever. But why? That's the subject of lively debate among policy makers and academics. To some, what we're seeing is a transient epiphenomenon, the byproduct of cultural and economic forces. To others, the longer road to adulthood signifies something deep, durable, and maybe better-suited to our neurological hard-wiring. What we're seeing, they insist, is the dawning of a new life stage — a stage that all of us need to adjust to.

Jeffrey Jensen Arnett, a psychology professor at Clark University in Worcester, Mass., is leading the movement to view the 20s as a distinct life stage, which he calls "emerging adulthood." He says what is happening now is analogous to what happened a century ago, when social and economic changes helped create adolescence — a stage we take for granted but one that had to be recognized by psychologists, accepted by society, and accommodated by institutions that served the young. Similar changes at the turn of the 21st century have laid the groundwork for another new stage, Arnett says, between the age of 18 and the late 20s. Among the cultural changes he points to that have led to "emerging adulthood" are the need for more education to survive in an information-based economy; fewer entry-level jobs even after all that schooling; young people feeling less rush to marry because of the general acceptance of premarital sex, cohabitation, and birth control; and young women feeling less rush to have babies given their wide range of career options and their access to assisted reproductive technology if they delay pregnancy beyond their most fertile years.

Just as adolescence has its particular psychological profile, Arnett says, so does emerging adulthood: identity exploration, instability, self-focus, feeling in-between, and a rather poetic characteristic he calls "a sense of possibilities." A few of these, especially identity exploration, are part of adolescence too, but they take on new depth and urgency in the 20s. The stakes are higher when people are approaching the age when options tend to close off and lifelong commitments must be made. Arnett calls it "the age 30 deadline."

The issue of whether emerging adulthood is a new stage is being debated most forcefully among scholars, in particular psychologists and sociologists. But its resolution has broader implications. Just look at what happened for teenagers. It took some effort, a century ago, for psychologists to make the case that adolescence was a new developmental stage. Once that happened, social institutions were forced to adapt: education, health care, social services, and the law all changed to address the particular needs of 12- to 18-year-olds. An understanding of the developmental profile of adolescence led, for instance, to the creation of junior high schools in the early 1900s, separating seventh and eighth graders from the younger children in what used to be called primary school. And it led to the recognition that teenagers between 14 and 18, even though they were legally minors, were mature enough to make their own choice of legal guardian in the event of their parents' deaths. If emerging adulthood is an analogous stage, analogous changes are in the wings.

But what would it look like to extend some of the special status of adolescents to young people in their 20s? Our uncertainty about this question is reflected in our scattershot approach to markers of adulthood. People can vote at 18, but in some states they don't age out of foster care until 21. They can join the military at 18, but they can't drink until 21. They can drive at 16, but they can't rent a car until 25 without some hefty surcharges. If they are full-time students, the Internal Revenue Service considers them dependents until 24; those without health insurance will soon be able to stay on their parents' plans even if they're not in school until age 26, or up to 30 in some states. Parents have no access to their child's college records if the child is over 18, but parents' income is taken into account when the child applies for financial aid up to age 24. We seem unable to agree when someone is old enough to take on adult responsibilities. But we're pretty sure it's not simply a matter of age.

If society decides to protect these young people or treat them differently from fully grown adults, how can we do this without becoming all the things that grown children resist—controlling, moralizing, paternalistic? Young people spend their lives lumped into age-related clusters—that's the basis of K–12 schooling—but as they move through their 20s, they diverge. Some 25-year-olds are married homeowners with good jobs and a couple of kids; others are still living with their parents and working at transient jobs, or not working at all. Does that mean we extend some of the protections and special status of adolescence to all people in their 20s? To some of them? Which ones? Decisions like this matter, because failing to protect and support vulnerable young people can lead them down the wrong path at a critical moment, the one that can determine all subsequent paths. But overprotecting and oversupporting them can sometimes make matters worse, turning the "changing timetable of adulthood" into a self-fulfilling prophecy.

The more profound question behind the scholarly intrigue is the one that really captivates parents: whether the prolongation of this unsettled time of life is a good thing or a bad thing. With life spans stretching into the ninth decade, is it better for young people to experiment in their 20s before making choices they'll have to live with for more than half a century? Or is adulthood now so malleable, with marriage and employment options constantly being reassessed, that young people would be better off just getting started on something, or else they'll never catch up, consigned to remain always a few steps behind the early bloomers? Is emerging adulthood a rich and varied period for self-discovery, as Arnett says it is? Or is it just another term for self-indulgence?

The discovery of adolescence is generally dated to 1904, with the publication of the massive study "Adolescence," by G. Stanley Hall, a prominent psychologist and first president of the American Psychological Association. Hall attributed the new stage to social changes at the turn of the 20th century. Child-labor laws kept children under 16 out of the work force, and universal education laws kept them in secondary school, thus prolonging the period of dependence—a dependence that allowed them to address psychological tasks they might have ignored when they took on adult roles straight out of childhood. Hall, the first president of Clark University—the same place, interestingly enough, where Arnett now teaches—described adolescence as a time of "storm and stress," filled with emotional upheaval, sorrow, and rebelliousness. He cited the "curve of despondency" that "starts at 11, rises steadily and rapidly till 15 . . . then falls steadily till 23," and described other characteristics of adolescence, including an increase in sensation seeking, greater susceptibility to media influences (which in 1904 mostly meant "flash literature" and "penny dreadfuls"), and overreliance on peer relationships. Hall's book was flawed, but it marked the beginning of the scientific study of adolescence and helped lead to its eventual acceptance as a distinct stage with its own challenges, behaviors, and biological profile.

In the 1990s, Arnett began to suspect that something similar was taking place   15
with young people in their late teens and early 20s. He was teaching human development and family studies at the University of Missouri, studying college-age students, both at the university and in the community around Columbia, Mo. He asked them questions about their lives and their expectations like, "Do you feel you have reached adulthood?"

"I was in my early- to mid-30s myself, and I remember thinking, They're not a thing like me," Arnett told me when we met last spring in Worcester. "I realized that there was something special going on." The young people he spoke to weren't experiencing the upending physical changes that accompany adolescence, but as an age cohort they did seem to have a psychological makeup different from that of people just a little bit younger or a little bit older. This was not how most psychologists were thinking about development at the time, when the eight-stage model of the psychologist Erik Erikson was in vogue. Erikson, one of the first to focus on psychological development past childhood, divided adulthood into three stages—young (roughly ages 20 to 45), middle (about ages 45 to 65), and late (all the rest)—and defined them by the challenges that individuals in a particular stage encounter and must resolve before moving on to the next stage. In young adulthood, according to his model, the primary psychological challenge is "intimacy versus isolation," by which Erikson meant deciding whether to commit to a lifelong intimate relationship and choosing the person to commit to.

But Arnett said "young adulthood" was too broad a term to apply to a 25-year span that included both him and his college students. The 20s are something different from the 30s and 40s, he remembered thinking. And while he agreed that the struggle for intimacy was one task of this period, he said there were other critical tasks as well.

Arnett and I were discussing the evolution of his thinking over lunch at BABA Sushi, a quiet restaurant near his office where he goes so often he knows the sushi chefs by name. He is 53, very tall, and wiry, with clipped steel-gray hair and ice-blue eyes, an intense, serious man. He describes himself as a late bloomer, a onetime emerging adult before anyone had given it a name. After graduating from Michigan State University in 1980, he spent two years playing guitar in bars and restaurants and experimented with girlfriends, drugs, and general recklessness before going for his doctorate in developmental psychology at the University of Virginia. By 1986 he had his first academic job at Oglethorpe University, a small college in Atlanta. There he met his wife, Lene Jensen, the school's smartest psych major, who stunned Arnett when she came to his office one day in 1989, shortly after she graduated, and asked him out on a date. Jensen earned a doctorate in psychology, too, and she also teaches at Clark. She and Arnett have 10-year-old twins, a boy and a girl.

Arnett spent time at Northwestern University and the University of Chicago before moving to the University of Missouri in 1992, beginning his study of young men and women in the college town of Columbia, gradually broadening his sample to include New Orleans, Los Angeles, and San Francisco. He deliberately included working-class young people as well as those who were well off, those who had never gone to college as well as those who were still in school, those who were supporting themselves as well as those whose bills were being paid by their parents. A little more than half of his sample was white, 18 percent African-American, 16 percent Asian-American, and 14 percent Latino.

More than 300 interviews and 250 survey responses persuaded Arnett that he was onto something new. This was the era of the Gen X slacker, but Arnett felt that his findings applied beyond one generation. He wrote them up in 2000 in *American Psychologist*, the first time he laid out his theory of "emerging adulthood." According to Google Scholar, which keeps track of such things, the article has been cited in professional books and journals roughly 1,700 times. This makes it, in the world of academia, practically viral. At the very least, the citations indicate that Arnett had come up with a useful term for describing a particular cohort; at best, that he offered a whole new way of thinking about them.

During the period he calls emerging adulthood, Arnett says that young men and women are more self-focused than at any other time of life, less certain about the future, and yet also more optimistic, no matter what their economic background. This is where the "sense of possibilities" comes in, he says; they have not yet tempered their idealistic visions of what awaits. "The dreary, dead-end jobs, the bitter divorces, the disappointing and disrespectful children . . . none of them imagine that this is what the future holds for them," he wrote. Ask them if they agree with the statement "I am very sure that someday I will get to where I want to be in life," and 96 percent of them will say yes. But despite elements that are exciting, even exhilarating, about being this

60 percent of his subjects told him they felt like both grown-ups and not-quite-grown-ups.

age, there is a downside, too: dread, frustration, uncertainty, a sense of not quite understanding the rules of the game. More than positive or negative feelings, what Arnett heard most often was ambivalence—beginning with his finding that 60 percent of his subjects told him they felt like both grown-ups and not-quite-grown-ups.

Some scientists would argue that this ambivalence reflects what is going on in the brain, which is also both grown-up and not-quite-grown-up. Neuroscientists once thought the brain stops growing shortly after puberty, but now they know it keeps maturing well into the 20s. This new understanding comes largely from a longitudinal study of brain development sponsored by the National Institute of Mental Health, which started following nearly 5,000 children at ages 3 to 16 (the average age at enrollment was about 10). The scientists found the children's brains were not fully mature until at least 25. "In retrospect I wouldn't call it shocking, but it was at the time," Jay Giedd, the director of the study, told me. "The only people who got this right were the car-rental companies."

When the NIMH study began in 1991, Giedd said he and his colleagues expected to stop when the subjects turned 16. "We figured that by 16 their bodies were pretty big physically," he said. But every time the children returned, their brains were found still to be changing. The scientists extended the end date of the study to age 18, then 20, then 22. The subjects' brains were still changing even then. Tellingly, the most significant changes took place in the prefrontal cortex and cerebellum, the regions involved in emotional control and higher-order cognitive function.

As the brain matures, one thing that happens is the pruning of the synapses. Synaptic pruning does not occur willy-nilly; it depends largely on how any one brain pathway is used. By cutting off unused pathways, the brain eventually settles into a structure that's most efficient for the owner of that brain, creating well-worn grooves for the pathways that person uses most. Synaptic pruning intensifies after rapid brain-cell proliferation during childhood and again in the period that encompasses adolescence and the 20s. It is the mechanism of "use it or lose it": the brains we have are shaped largely in response to the demands made of them.

We have come to accept the idea that environmental influences in the first three years of life have long-term consequences for cognition, emotional control, attention, and the like. Is it time to place a similar emphasis, with hopes for a similar outcome, on enriching the cognitive environment of people in their 20s?   25

NIMH scientists also found a time lag between the growth of the limbic system, where emotions originate, and of the prefrontal cortex, which manages those emotions. The limbic system explodes during puberty, but the prefrontal cortex keeps maturing for another 10 years. Giedd said it is logical to suppose—and for now, neuroscientists have to make a lot of logical suppositions—that when the limbic system is fully active but the cortex is still being built, emotions might outweigh rationality. "The prefrontal part is the part that allows you to control your impulses, come up with a long-range strategy, answer the question 'What am I going to do with my life?'" he told me. "That weighing of the future keeps changing into the 20s and 30s."

Among study subjects who enrolled as children, MRI scans have been done so far only to age 25, so scientists have to make another logical supposition about what happens to the brain in the late 20s, the 30s, and beyond. Is it possible that the brain just keeps changing and pruning, for years and years? "Guessing from the shape of the growth curves we have," Giedd's colleague Philip Shaw wrote in an e-mail message, "it does seem that much of the gray matter," where synaptic pruning takes place, "seems to have completed its most dramatic structural change" by age 25. For white matter, where insulation that helps impulses travel faster continues to form, "it does look as if the curves are still going up, suggesting continued growth" after age 25, he wrote, though at a slower rate than before.

None of this is new, of course; the brains of young people have always been works in progress, even when we didn't have sophisticated scanning machinery to chart it precisely. Why, then, is the youthful brain only now arising as an explanation for why people in their 20s are seeming a bit unfinished? Maybe there's an analogy to be found in the hierarchy of needs, a theory put forth in the 1940s by the psychologist Abraham Maslow. According to Maslow, people can pursue more elevated goals only after their basic needs of food, shelter, and sex have been met. What if the brain has its own hierarchy of needs? When people are forced to adopt adult responsibilities early, maybe they just do what they have to do, whether or not their brains are ready. Maybe it's only now, when young people are allowed to forestall adult obligations without fear of public censure, that the rate of societal maturation can finally fall into better sync with the maturation of the brain.

Cultural expectations might also reinforce the delay. The "changing timetable for adulthood" has, in many ways, become internalized by 20-somethings and their parents alike. Today young people don't expect to marry until their late 20s, don't expect to start a family until their 30s, don't expect to be on track for a rewarding career until much later than their parents were. So they make decisions about their futures that reflect this wider time horizon. Many of them would not be ready to take on the trappings of adulthood any earlier even if the opportunity arose; they haven't braced themselves for it.

Nor do parents expect their children to grow up right away — and they might not even want them to. Parents might regret having themselves jumped into marriage or a career and hope for more considered choices for their children. Or they might want to hold on to a reassuring connection with their children as the kids leave home. If they were "helicopter parents" — a term that describes heavily invested parents who hover over their children, swooping down to take charge and solve problems at a moment's notice — they might keep hovering and problem-solving long past the time when their children should be solving problems on their own. This might, in a strange way, be part of what keeps their grown children in the limbo between adolescence and adulthood. It can be hard sometimes to tease out to what extent a child doesn't quite want to grow up and to what extent a parent doesn't quite want to let go. 30

It is a big deal in developmental psychology to declare the existence of a new stage of life, and Arnett has devoted the past 10 years to making his case. Shortly after his *American Psychologist* article appeared in 2000, he and Jennifer Lynn Tanner, a developmental psychologist at Rutgers University, convened the first conference of what they later called the Society for the Study of Emerging Adulthood. It was held in 2003 at Harvard with an attendance of 75; there have been three more since then, and last year's conference, in Atlanta, had more than 270 attendees. In 2004 Arnett published a book, *Emerging Adulthood: The Winding Road from the Late Teens through the Twenties*, which is still in print and selling well. In 2006 he and Tanner published an edited volume, *Emerging Adults in America: Coming of Age in the 21st Century*, aimed at professionals and academics. Arnett's college textbook, *Adolescence and Emerging Adulthood: A Cultural Approach*, has been in print since 2000 and is now in its fourth edition. Next year he says he hopes to publish another book, this one for the parents of 20-somethings.

If all Arnett's talk about emerging adulthood sounds vaguely familiar . . . well, it should. Forty years ago, an article appeared in the *American Scholar* that declared "a new stage of life" for the period between adolescence and young adulthood. This was 1970, when the oldest members of the baby boom generation—the parents of today's 20-somethings—were 24. Young people of the day "can't seem to 'settle down,'" wrote the Yale psychologist Kenneth Keniston. He called the new stage of life "youth."

Keniston's description of "youth" presages Arnett's description of "emerging adulthood" a generation later. In the late '60s, Keniston wrote that there was "a growing minority of post-adolescents [who] have not settled the questions whose answers once defined adulthood: questions of relationship to the existing society, questions of vocation, questions of social role and lifestyle." Whereas once, such aimlessness was seen only in the "unusually creative or unusually disturbed," he wrote, it was becoming more common and more ordinary in the baby boomers of 1970. Among the salient characteristics of "youth," Keniston wrote, were "pervasive ambivalence toward self and society," "the feeling of absolute freedom, of living in a world of pure possibilities," and "the enormous value placed upon change, transformation and movement"—all characteristics that Arnett now ascribes to "emerging adults."

Arnett readily acknowledges his debt to Keniston; he mentions him in almost everything he has written about emerging adulthood. But he considers the '60s a unique moment, when young people were rebellious and alienated in a way they've never been before or since. And Keniston's views never quite took off, Arnett says, because "youth" wasn't a very good name for it. He has called the label "ambiguous and confusing," not nearly as catchy as his own "emerging adulthood."

For whatever reason Keniston's terminology faded away, it's revealing to read his old article and hear echoes of what's going on with kids today. He was describing the parents of today's young people when they themselves were young—and amazingly, they weren't all that different from their own children now. Keniston's article seems a lovely demonstration of the eternal cycle of life, the perennial conflict between the generations, the gradual resolution of those conflicts. It's reassuring, actually, to think of it as recursive, to imagine that there must always be a cohort of 20-somethings who take their time settling down, just as there must always be a cohort of 50-somethings who worry about it.

Keniston called it youth, Arnett calls it emerging adulthood; whatever it's called, the delayed transition has been observed for years. But it can be in fullest flower only when the young person has some other, nontraditional means of support—which would seem to make the delay something of a luxury item. That's the impression you get reading Arnett's case histories in his books and articles, or the essays in *20 Something Manifesto*, an anthology edited by a Los Angeles writer named Christine Hassler. "It's somewhat terrifying," writes a 25-year-old named Jennifer, "to think about all the things I'm supposed to be doing in order to 'get somewhere' successful: 'Follow your passions, live your dreams, take risks, network with the right people, find mentors, be financially responsible, volunteer, work, think about or go to grad school, fall in love and maintain personal well-being, mental health and nutrition.' When is there time to just be and enjoy?" Adds a 24-year-old from Virginia: "There is pressure to make decisions that will form the foundation for the rest of your life in your 20s. It's almost as if having a range of limited options would be easier."

While the complaints of these young people are heartfelt, they are also the complaints of the privileged. Julie, a 23-year-old New Yorker and contributor to *20 Something Manifesto*, is apparently aware of this. She was coddled her whole life, treated to French horn lessons and summer camp, told she could do anything. "It is a double-edged sword," she writes, "because on the one hand I am so blessed with my experiences and endless options, but on the other hand, I still feel like a child. I feel like my job isn't real because I am not where my parents were at my age. Walking home, in the shoes my father bought me, I still feel I have yet to grow up."

Despite these impressions, Arnett insists that emerging adulthood is not limited to young persons of privilege and that it is not simply a period of self-indulgence. He takes pains in *Emerging Adulthood* to describe some case histories of young men and women from hard-luck backgrounds who use the self-focus and identity exploration of their 20s to transform their lives.

One of these is the case history of Nicole, a 25-year-old African-American who grew up in a housing project in Oakland, Calif. At age 6, Nicole, the eldest, was forced to take control of the household after her mother's mental collapse. By 8, she was sweeping stores and baby-sitting for money to help keep her three siblings fed and housed. "I made a couple bucks and helped my mother out, helped my family out," she told Arnett. She managed to graduate from high school, but with low grades, and got a job as a receptionist at a dermatology clinic. She moved into her own apartment, took night classes at community college, and started to excel. "I needed to experience living out of my mother's home in order to study," she said.

In his book, Arnett presents Nicole as a symbol of all the young people from impoverished backgrounds for whom "emerging adulthood represents an opportunity—maybe a last opportunity—to turn one's life around." This is the stage where someone like Nicole can escape an abusive or dysfunctional family and finally pursue her own dreams. Nicole's dreams are powerful—one course away from an associate degree, she plans to go on for a bachelor's and then a Ph.D. in psychology—but she has not really left her family behind; few people do. She is still supporting her mother and siblings, which is why she works full time even though her progress through school would be quicker if she found a part-time job. Is it only a grim pessimist like me who sees how many roadblocks there will be on the way to achieving those dreams and who wonders what kind of freewheeling emerging adulthood she is supposed to be having? 40

Of course, Nicole's case is not representative of society as a whole. And many parents—including those who can't really afford it—continue to help their kids financially long past the time they expected to. Two years ago Karen Fingerman, a developmental psychologist at Purdue University, asked parents of grown children whether they provided significant assistance to their sons or daughters. Assistance included giving their children money or help with everyday tasks (practical assistance) as well as advice, companionship, and an attentive ear. Eighty-six percent said they had provided advice in the previous month; less than half had done so in 1988. Two out of three parents had given a son or daughter practical assistance in the previous month; in 1988, only one in three had.

Fingerman took solace in her findings; she said it showed that parents stay connected to their grown children, and she suspects that both parties get something out of it. The survey questions, after all, referred not only to dispensing money but also to offering advice, comfort, and friendship. And another of Fingerman's studies suggests that parents' sense of well-being depends largely on how close they are to their grown children and how their children are faring—objective support for the adage that you're only as happy as your unhappiest child. But the expectation that young men and women won't quite be able to make ends meet on their own, and that parents should be the ones to help bridge the gap, places a terrible burden on parents who might be worrying about their own job security, trying to care for their aging parents, or grieving as their retirement plans become more and more of a pipe dream.

This dependence on Mom and Dad also means that during the 20s the rift between rich and poor becomes entrenched. According to data gathered by the Network on Transitions to Adulthood, a research consortium supported by the John D. and Catherine T. MacArthur Foundation, American parents give an average of 10 percent of their income to their 18- to 21-year-old children. This percentage is basically the same no matter the family's total income, meaning that upper-class kids tend to get more than working-class ones. And wealthier kids have other, less obvious, advantages. When they go to four-year colleges or universities, they get supervised dormitory housing, health care, and alumni networks not available at community colleges. And they often get a leg up on their careers by using parents' contacts to help land an entry-level job—or by using parents as a financial backup when they want to take an interesting internship that doesn't pay.

"You get on a pathway, and pathways have momentum," Jennifer Lynn Tanner of Rutgers told me. "In emerging adulthood, if you spend this time exploring and you get yourself on a pathway that really fits you, then there's going to be this snowball effect of finding the right fit, the right partner, the right job, the right place to live. The less you have at first, the less you're going to get this positive effect compounded over time. You're not going to have the same acceleration."

Even Arnett admits that not every young person goes through a period of "emerging adulthood." It's rare in the developing world, he says, where people have to grow up fast, and it's often skipped in the industrialized world by the people who marry early, by teenage mothers forced to grow up, by young men or women who go straight from high school to whatever job is available without a chance to dabble until they find the perfect fit. Indeed, the majority of humankind would seem to not go through it at all. The fact that emerging adulthood is not universal is one of the strongest arguments against Arnett's claim that it is a new developmental stage. If emerging adulthood is so important, why is it even possible to skip it?

"The core idea of classical stage theory is that all people—underscore 'all'—pass through a series of qualitatively different periods in an invariant and universal sequence in stages that can't be skipped or reordered," Richard Lerner, Bergstrom chairman in applied developmental science at Tufts University, told me. Lerner is a close personal friend of Arnett's; he and his wife, Jacqueline, who is also a psychologist, live 20 miles from Worcester, and they have dinner with Arnett and his wife on a regular basis.

"I think the world of Jeff Arnett," Lerner said. "I think he is a smart, passionate person who is doing great work—not only a smart and productive scholar, but one of the nicest people I ever met in my life."

No matter how much he likes and admires Arnett, however, Lerner says his friend has ignored some of the basic tenets of developmental psychology. According to classical stage theory, he told me, "you must develop what you're supposed to develop when you're supposed to develop it or you'll never adequately develop it."

When I asked Arnett what happens to people who don't have an emerging adulthood, he said it wasn't necessarily a big deal. They might face its developmental tasks—identity exploration, self-focus, experimentation in love, work, and worldview—at a later time, maybe as a midlife crisis, or they might never face them at all, he said. It depends partly on why they missed emerging adulthood in the first place, whether it was by circumstance or by choice.

No, said Lerner, that's not the way it works. To qualify as a developmental stage, emerging adulthood must be both universal and essential. "If you don't develop a skill at the right stage, you'll be working the rest of your life to develop it when you should be moving on," he said. "The rest of your development will be unfavorably altered." The fact that Arnett can be so casual about the heterogeneity of emerging adulthood and its existence in some cultures but not in others—indeed, even in some people but not in their neighbors or friends—is what undermines, for many scholars, his insistence that it's a new life stage. 50

Why does it matter? Because if the delay in achieving adulthood is just a temporary aberration caused by passing social mores and economic gloom, it's something to struggle through for now, maybe feeling a little sorry for the young people who had the misfortune to come of age in a recession. But if it's a true life stage, we need to start rethinking our definition of normal development and to create systems of education, health care, and social supports that take the new stage into account.

The Network on Transitions to Adulthood has been issuing reports about young people since it was formed in 1999 and often ends up recommending more support for 20-somethings. But more of what, exactly? There aren't institutions set up to serve people in this specific age range; social services from a developmental perspective tend to disappear after adolescence. But it's possible to envision some that might address the restlessness and mobility that Arnett says are typical at this stage and that might make the experimentation of "emerging adulthood" available to more young people. How about expanding programs like City Year, in which 17- to 24-year-olds from diverse backgrounds spend a year mentoring inner-city children in exchange for a stipend, health insurance, child care, cellphone service, and a $5,350 education award? Or a federal program in which a government-sponsored savings account is created for every newborn, to be cashed in at age 21 to support a year's worth of travel, education, or volunteer work—a version of the "baby bonds" program that Hillary Clinton mentioned during her 2008 primary campaign? Maybe we can encourage a kind of socially sanctioned "rumspringa," the temporary moratorium from social responsibilities some Amish offer their young people to allow them to experiment before settling down. It requires only a bit of ingenuity—as well as some societal forbearance and financial commitment—to think of ways to expand some of the programs that now work so well for the elite, like the Fulbright fellowship or the Peace Corps, to make the chance for temporary service and self-examination available to a wider range of young people.

A century ago, it was helpful to start thinking of adolescents as engaged in the work of growing up rather than as merely lazy or rebellious. Only then could society recognize that the educational, medical, mental-health, and social-service needs of this group were unique and that investing in them would have a payoff in the future. Twenty-somethings are engaged in work, too, even if it looks as if they are aimless or failing to pull their weight, Arnett says. But it's a reflection of our collective attitude toward this period that we devote so few resources to keeping them solvent and granting them some measure of security.

The kind of services that might be created if emerging adulthood is accepted as a life stage can be seen during a visit to Yellowbrick, a residential program in Evanston, Ill., that calls itself the only psychiatric treatment facility for emerging adults. "Emerging adults really do have unique developmental tasks to focus on," said Jesse Viner, Yellowbrick's executive medical director. Viner started Yellowbrick in 2005, when he was working in a group psychiatric practice in Chicago and saw the need for a different way to treat this cohort. He is a soft-spoken man who looks like an accountant and sounds like a New Age prophet, peppering his conversation with phrases like "helping to empower their agency."

"Agency" is a tricky concept when parents are paying the full cost of Yellowbrick's comprehensive residential program, which comes to $21,000 a month and is not always covered by insurance. Staff members are aware of the paradox of encouraging a child to separate from Mommy and Daddy when it's on their dime. They address it with a concept they call connected autonomy, which they define as knowing when to stand alone and when to accept help.

Patients come to Yellowbrick with a variety of problems: substance abuse, eating disorders, depression, anxiety, or one of the more severe mental illnesses, like schizophrenia or bipolar disorder, that tend to appear in the late teens or early 20s. The demands of imminent independence can worsen mental-health problems or can create new ones for people who have managed up to that point to perform all the expected roles—son or daughter, boyfriend or girlfriend, student, teammate, friend—but get lost when schooling ends and expected roles disappear. That's what happened to one patient who had done well at a top Ivy League college until the last class of the last semester of his last year, when he finished his final paper and could not bring himself to turn it in.

The Yellowbrick philosophy is that young people must meet these challenges without coddling or rescue. Up to 16 patients at a time are housed in the Yellowbrick residence, a four-story apartment building Viner owns. They live in the apartments—which are large, sunny, and lavishly furnished—in groups of three or four, with staff members always on hand to teach the basics of shopping, cooking, cleaning, scheduling, making commitments, and showing up.

Viner let me sit in on daily clinical rounds, scheduled that day for C., a young woman who had been at Yellowbrick for three months. Rounds are like the world's most grueling job interview: the patient sits in front alongside her clinician "advocate," and a dozen or so staff members are arrayed on couches and armchairs around the room, firing questions. C. seemed nervous but pleased with herself, frequently flashing a huge white smile. She is 22, tall, and skinny, and she wore tiny denim shorts and a big T-shirt and vest. She started to fall apart during her junior year at college, plagued by binge drinking and anorexia, and in her first weeks at Yellowbrick her alcohol abuse continued. Most psychiatric facilities would have kicked her out after the first relapse, said Dale Monroe-Cook, Yellowbrick's vice president of clinical operations. "We're doing the opposite: we want the behavior to unfold, and we want to be there in that critical moment, to work with that behavior and help the emerging adult transition to greater independence."

The Yellowbrick staff let C. face her demons and decide how to deal with them. After five relapses, C. asked the staff to take away her ID so she couldn't buy alcohol. Eventually she decided to start going to meetings of Alcoholics Anonymous.

At her rounds in June, C. was able to report that she had been alcohol-free for 30 days. Jesse Viner's wife, Laura Viner, who is a psychologist on staff, started to clap for her, but no one else joined in. "We're on eggshells here," Gary Zurawski, a clinical social worker specializing in substance abuse, confessed to C. "We don't know if we should congratulate you too much." The staff was sensitive about taking away the young woman's motivation to improve her life for her own sake, not for the sake of getting praise from someone else.

C. took the discussion about the applause in stride and told the staff she had more good news: in two days she was going to graduate. On time.

The 20s are like the stem cell of human development, the pluripotent moment when any of several outcomes is possible. Decisions and actions during this time have lasting ramifications. The 20s are when most people accumulate almost all of their formal education; when most people meet their future spouses and the friends they will keep; when most people start on the careers that they will stay with for many years. This is when adventures, experiments, travels, relationships are embarked on with an abandon that probably will not happen again.

> **The 20s are like the stem cell of human development, the pluripotent moment when any of several outcomes is possible.**

Does that mean it's a good thing to let 20-somethings meander—or even to encourage them to meander—before they settle down? That's the question that plagues so many of their parents. It's easy to see the advantages to the delay. There is time enough for adulthood and its attendant obligations; maybe if kids take longer to choose their mates and their careers, they'll make fewer mistakes and live happier lives. But it's just as easy to see the drawbacks. As the settling-down sputters along for the "emerging adults," things can get precarious for the rest of us. Parents are helping pay bills they never counted on paying, and social institutions are missing out on young people contributing to productivity and growth. Of course, the recession complicates things, and even if every 20-something were ready to skip the "emerging" moratorium and act like a grown-up, there wouldn't necessarily be jobs for them all. So we're caught in a weird moment, unsure whether to allow young people to keep exploring and questioning or to cut them off and tell them just to find something, anything, to put food on the table and get on with their lives.

Arnett would like to see us choose a middle course. "To be a young American today is to experience both excitement and uncertainty, wide-open possibility and confusion, new freedoms and new fears," he writes in *Emerging Adulthood*. During the timeout they are granted from nonstop, often tedious and dispiriting responsibilities, "emerging adults develop skills for daily living, gain a better understanding of who they are and what they want from life and begin to build a foundation for their adult lives." If it really works that way, if this longer road to adulthood really leads to more insight and better choices, then Arnett's vision of an insightful, sensitive, thoughtful, content, well-honed, self-actualizing crop of grown-ups would indeed be something worth waiting for.

Exploring Context

1. Vine (vine.co) is an app that allows users to create six-second looping videos. Make a vine (or develop a script for one) that summarizes Henig's argument. What key points would you need to communicate in six seconds?

2. Clark University, where Jeffrey Jensen Arnett (who coined the term *emerging adulthood*) works, has an annual poll of emerging adults. Explore the results of these polls at www.clarku.edu/clark-poll-emerging-adults/. How does this data complicate Henig's argument?

3. This essay was originally published with a series of portraits of 20-somethings with a distinctive square ratio. Instagram, a photography app and social media service, uses that same format. Using Instagram, or looking through its Web site, select your own series of images to place alongside Henig's text. Do they confirm or complicate her argument?

Questions for Connecting

1. To what extent is emerging adulthood a uniquely Western phenomenon? Apply Henig's ideas to Helen Epstein's account of young people in African countries in "AIDS, Inc." (p. 110). Do young South Africans seem to face the same pressures and challenges as 20-something Americans? Do they have the same opportunities? What are the limitations of Henig's argument? You may want to draw from your work in Questions for Critical Reading.

2. Is Wesley Yang, author of "Paper Tigers" (p. 521), an emerging adult? Read his essay through the lens that Henig provides. How does his additional information about race and stereotypes complicate what Henig wants to say about emerging adults? How might you synthesize the kind of angst he feels with the data you located in Question 2 of Exploring Context?

3. Henig relies in part on neuroscience to support the idea of emerging adulthood. In "Attention Deficit: The Brain Syndrome of Our Era" (p. 373), Richard Restak similarly looks at the ways in which the structure of the brain has been changing. How might these changes be reflected in emerging adulthood? Are 20-somethings particularly prone to the sort of brain changes that Restak examines?

Language Matters

1. In academic writing, it's vital to state a clear, central argument so that the reader can follow that argument as it's proven with evidence in the paper. Find a quotation that you believe is a clear statement of Henig's argument. Where is it located in the essay? Why does she place it there? Where should you place your argument in your papers for this class?

2. What makes a comma unnecessary? Review information on comma usage in a grammar handbook or other reliable source. Then review Henig's essay. Are any of her commas unnecessary? How can you make sure you only use necessary commas in your own writing?

3. Locate a key sentence from Henig's text and then identify the subject, verb, and object of the sentence. How does the structure of the sentence contribute to Henig's argument? How does it make meaning, and what meaning does it make?

Assignments for Writing

1. What's the cost of growing up? Write a paper in which you use Henig's ideas to determine the price of adulthood, in terms not only of economics but also of what is lost and what is gained in the process. Use your work from Question 3 of Questions for Critical Reading and Question 1 of Questions for Connecting.

2. Henig examines the rationale for creating a new life stage called "emerging adulthood." Write a paper in which you evaluate the risks and benefits of confirming emerging adulthood as a recognized life stage. Draw from your work in Questions for Critical Reading and Question 2 of Exploring Context to support your response.

3. One of the elements of emerging adulthood, according to Henig, is a focus on exploring one's passions and life goals. Write a paper in which you balance this self-actualizing purpose with the limitations inherent in emerging adulthood. Is that self-reflection worth it?

DANIEL KAHNEMAN

A Nobel Prize–winner and veteran of the Israeli army, psychologist **Daniel Kahneman** is known for his work in the field of behavioral economics. He is currently a Senior Scholar; Eugene Higgins Professor of Psychology, Emeritus; and professor of psychology and public affairs, emeritus, at Princeton University's Woodrow Wilson School of Public and International Affairs. Kahneman is also a fellow of the Center for Rationality at the Hebrew

© Carsten Rehder/dpa/Corbis

University in Jerusalem, where he earned his B.A. in psychology and mathematics in 1954 before going on to receive his Ph.D. in psychology at the University of California–Berkeley in 1961.

Kahneman won the Nobel Prize in Economic Sciences in 2002, among other honors, including the Lifetime Contribution Award of the American Psychological Association in 2007 and the Presidential Medal of Freedom in 2013. His best-selling book on thinking and decision making, *Thinking, Fast and Slow*, won the National Academy of Sciences Best Book Award in 2012 and was named a best book of the year by the *New York Times Book Review*, the *Globe and Mail*, the *Economist*, and the *Wall Street Journal*.

"The Surety of Fools" was published in the *New York Times Magazine* in 2011, alongside articles on Japanese novelist Haruki Murakami, the consequences of arming and training Afghans, and Gotta Groove Records, one of the few plants in the United States still producing vinyl music albums. The essay draws from Kahneman's work in *Thinking, Fast and Slow*, in which he suggests that we have two modes of thinking—one that's very fast and instinctive and one that's slower and more deliberative. Kahneman looks at the consequences of these two systems of thinking to show that we place too much confidence in the judgments we make.

In this essay, Kahneman examines what he calls "illusions of validity"—false confidence based on "stories" individuals believe to be true, whether they are or not. Using examples from an Israeli Defense Forces obstacle field and from Wall Street, Kahneman substantiates his theory, ultimately asserting that "you should not take assertive and confident people at their own evaluation unless you have independent reason to believe that they know what they are talking about" (p. 220).

How important is confidence in decision making? How important, in light of Kahneman's theory, should it be?

▶ TAGS: *economics, judgment and decision-making, psychology*
▶ CONNECTIONS: *Gilbert, Ma, Padawer, Restak, Wood, Yang*

Questions for Critical Reading

1. Before reading, take a moment to reflect on the ways you make judgments and decisions. After you've outlined your methods, take notes on what Kahneman says about the process. Return to your own experiences: how do they reflect Kahneman's argument?

2. Kahneman is interested in *cognitive fallacy*. Using a dictionary or other resource, write a definition of this term. As you read, identify Kahneman's discussions of specific cognitive fallacies, especially WYSIATI, the "illusion of validity," and the "illusion of skill."

3. How can we avoid errors in making judgments? Identify places in the text where Kahneman offers us ways to avoid cognitive fallacies in our judgments.

The Surety of Fools

Many decades ago I spent what seemed like a great deal of time under a scorching sun, watching groups of sweaty soldiers as they solved a problem. I was doing my national service in the Israeli Army at the time. I had completed an undergraduate degree in psychology, and after a year as an infantry officer, I was assigned to the army's Psychology Branch, where one of my occasional duties was to help evaluate candidates for officer training. We used methods that were developed by the British Army in World War II.

One test, called the leaderless group challenge, was conducted on an obstacle field. Eight candidates, strangers to one another, with all insignia of rank removed and only numbered tags to identify them, were instructed to lift a long log from the ground and haul it to a wall about six feet high. There, they were told that the entire group had to get to the other side of the wall without the log touching either the ground or the wall, and without anyone touching the wall. If any of these things happened, they were to acknowledge it and start again.

A common solution was for several men to reach the other side by crawling along the log as the other men held it up at an angle, like a giant fishing rod. Then one man would climb onto another's shoulder and tip the log to the far side. The last two men would then have to jump up at the log, now suspended from the other side by those who had made it over, shinny their way along its length, and then leap down safely once they crossed the wall. Failure was common at this point, which required starting over.

As a colleague and I monitored the exercise, we made note of who took charge, who tried to lead but was rebuffed, how much each soldier contributed to the group effort. We saw who seemed to be stubborn, submissive, arrogant, patient, hot-tempered, persistent, or a quitter. We sometimes saw competitive spite when someone whose idea had been rejected by the group no longer worked very hard. And we saw reactions to crisis: who berated a comrade whose mistake caused the whole group to fail, who stepped forward to lead when the exhausted team had to start over. Under the stress of the event, we felt, each man's true nature revealed itself in sharp relief.

After watching the candidates go through several such tests, we had to summarize   5
our impressions of the soldiers' leadership abilities with a grade and determine who
would be eligible for officer training. We spent some time discussing each case and re-
viewing our impressions. The task was not difficult, because we had already seen each
of these soldiers' leadership skills. Some of the men looked like strong leaders, others
seemed like wimps or arrogant fools, others mediocre but not hopeless. Quite a few appeared to be so weak that we ruled them out as officer candidates. When our multiple
observations of each candidate converged on a coherent picture, we were completely
confident in our evaluations and believed that what we saw pointed directly to the
future. The soldier who took over when the group was in trouble and led the team over
the wall was a leader at that moment. The obvious best guess about how he would do
in training, or in combat, was that he would be as effective as he had been at the wall.
Any other prediction seemed inconsistent with what we saw.

Because our impressions of how well each soldier performed were generally coherent and clear, our formal predictions were just as definite. We rarely experienced doubt
or conflicting impressions. We were quite willing to declare: "This one will never make
it," "That fellow is rather mediocre, but should do OK," or "He will be a star." We felt no
need to question our forecasts, moderate them, or equivocate. If challenged, however,
we were fully prepared to admit, "But of course anything could happen."

We were willing to make that admission because, as it turned out, despite our
certainty about the potential of individual candidates, our forecasts were largely useless. The evidence was overwhelming. Every few months we had a feedback session in
which we could compare our evaluations of future cadets with the judgments of their
commanders at the officer-training school. The story was always the same: our ability to predict performance at the school was negligible. Our forecasts were better than
blind guesses, but not by much.

We were downcast for a while after receiving the discouraging news. But this was
the army. Useful or not, there was a routine to be followed, and there were orders to be
obeyed. Another batch of candidates would arrive the next day. We took them to the
obstacle field, we faced them with the wall, they lifted the log, and within a few minutes
we saw their true natures revealed, as clearly as ever. The dismal truth about the quality of our predictions had no effect whatsoever on how we evaluated new candidates
and very little effect on the confidence we had in our judgments and predictions.

I thought that what was happening to us was remarkable. The statistical evidence
of our failure should have shaken our confidence in our judgments of particular candidates, but it did not. It should also have caused us to moderate our predictions, but it
did not. We knew as a general fact that our predictions were little better than random
guesses, but we continued to feel and act as if each particular prediction was valid. I
was reminded of visual illusions, which remain compelling even when you know that
what you see is false. I was so struck by the analogy that I coined a term for our experience: the illusion of validity.

I had discovered my first cognitive fallacy.   10

Decades later, I can see many of the central themes of my thinking about judgment
in that old experience. One of these themes is that people who face a difficult question

often answer an easier one instead, without realizing it. We were required to predict a soldier's performance in officer training and in combat, but we did so by evaluating his behavior over one hour in an artificial situation. This was a perfect instance of a general rule that I call WYSIATI, "What you see is all there is." We had made up a story from the little we knew but had no way to allow for what we did not know about the individual's future, which was almost everything that would actually matter. When you know as little as we did, you should not make extreme predictions like "He will be a star." The stars we saw on the obstacle field were most likely accidental flickers, in which a coincidence of random events — like who was near the wall — largely determined who became a leader. Other events — some of them also random — would determine later success in training and combat.

You may be surprised by our failure: it is natural to expect the same leadership ability to manifest itself in various situations. But the exaggerated expectation of consistency is a common error. We are prone to think that the world is more regular and predictable than it really is, because our memory automatically and continuously maintains a story about what is going on, and because the rules of memory tend to make that story as coherent as possible and to suppress alternatives. Fast thinking is not prone to doubt.

The confidence we experience as we make a judgment is not a reasoned evaluation of the probability that it is right. Confidence is a feeling, one determined mostly by the coherence of the story and by the ease with which it comes to mind, even when the evidence for the story is sparse and unreliable. The bias toward coherence favors overconfidence. An individual who expresses high confidence probably has a good story, which may or may not be true.

I coined the term "illusion of validity" because the confidence we had in judgments about individual soldiers was not affected by a statistical fact we knew to be true — that our predictions were unrelated to the truth.

> **When a compelling impression of a particular event clashes with general knowledge, the impression commonly prevails.**

This is not an isolated observation. When a compelling impression of a particular event clashes with general knowledge, the impression commonly prevails. And this goes for you, too. The confidence you will experience in your future judgments will not be diminished by what you just read, even if you believe every word.

I first visited a Wall Street firm in 1984. I was there with my longtime collaborator Amos Tversky, who died in 1996, and our friend Richard Thaler, now a guru of behavioral economics. Our host, a senior investment manager, had invited us to discuss the role of judgment biases in investing. I knew so little about finance at the time that I had no idea what to ask him, but I remember one exchange. "When you sell a stock," I asked him, "who buys it?" He answered with a wave in the vague direction of the window, indicating that he expected the buyer to be someone else very much like him. That was odd: because most buyers and sellers know that they have the same information as one another, what made one person buy and the other sell? Buyers think the price is too low and likely to rise; sellers think the price is high and likely to drop. The puzzle is why buyers and sellers alike think that the current price is wrong.

Most people in the investment business have read Burton Malkiel's wonderful book *A Random Walk Down Wall Street.* Malkiel's central idea is that a stock's price incorporates all the available knowledge about the value of the company and the best predictions about the future of the stock. If some people believe that the price of a stock will be higher tomorrow, they will buy more of it today. This, in turn, will cause its price to rise. If all assets in a market are correctly priced, no one can expect either to gain or to lose by trading.

We now know, however, that the theory is not quite right. Many individual investors lose consistently by trading, an achievement that a dart-throwing chimp could not match. The first demonstration of this startling conclusion was put forward by Terry Odean, a former student of mine who is now a finance professor at the University of California, Berkeley.

Odean analyzed the trading records of 10,000 brokerage accounts of individual investors over a seven-year period, allowing him to identify all instances in which an investor sold one stock and soon afterward bought another stock. By these actions the investor revealed that he (most of the investors were men) had a definite idea about the future of two stocks: he expected the stock that he bought to do better than the one he sold.

To determine whether those appraisals were well founded, Odean compared the returns of the two stocks over the following year. The results were unequivocally bad. On average, the shares investors sold did better than those they bought, by a very substantial margin: 3.3 percentage points per year, in addition to the significant costs of executing the trades. Some individuals did much better, others did much worse, but the large majority of individual investors would have done better by taking a nap rather than by acting on their ideas. In a paper titled "Trading Is Hazardous to Your Wealth," Odean and his colleague Brad Barber showed that, on average, the most active traders had the poorest results, while those who traded the least earned the highest returns. In another paper, "Boys Will Be Boys," they reported that men act on their useless ideas significantly more often than women do, and that as a result women achieve better investment results than men.

Of course, there is always someone on the other side of a transaction; in general, it's a financial institution or professional investor, ready to take advantage of the mistakes that individual traders make. Further research by Barber and Odean has shed light on these mistakes. Individual investors like to lock in their gains; they sell "winners," stocks whose prices have gone up, and they hang on to their losers. Unfortunately for them, in the short run going forward recent winners tend to do better than recent losers, so individuals sell the wrong stocks. They also buy the wrong stocks. Individual investors predictably flock to stocks in companies that are in the news. Professional investors are more selective in responding to news. These findings provide some justification for the label of "smart money" that finance professionals apply to themselves.

Although professionals are able to extract a considerable amount of wealth from amateurs, few stock pickers, if any, have the skill needed to beat the market consistently, year after year. The diagnostic for the existence of any skill is the consistency of individual differences in achievement. The logic is simple: if individual differences in any one year are due entirely to luck, the ranking of investors and funds will vary erratically and the year-to-year correlation will be zero. Where there is skill, however, the rankings will be more stable. The persistence of individual differences is the measure by which we confirm the existence of skill among golfers, orthodontists, or speedy toll collectors on the turnpike.

Mutual funds are run by highly experienced and hard-working professionals who buy and sell stocks to achieve the best possible results for their clients. Nevertheless, the evidence from more than 50 years of research is conclusive: for a large majority of fund managers, the selection of stocks is more like rolling dice than like playing poker. At least two out of every three mutual funds underperform the overall market in any given year.

More important, the year-to-year correlation among the outcomes of mutual funds is very small, barely different from zero. The funds that were successful in any given year were mostly lucky; they had a good roll of the dice. There is general agreement among researchers that this is true for nearly all stock pickers, whether they know it or not — and most do not. The subjective experience of traders is that they are making sensible, educated guesses in a situation of great uncertainty. In highly efficient markets, however, educated guesses are not more accurate than blind guesses.

Some years after my introduction to the world of finance, I had an unusual opportunity to examine the illusion of skill up close. I was invited to speak to a group of investment advisers in a firm that provided financial advice and other services to very wealthy clients. I asked for some data to prepare my presentation and was granted a small treasure: a spreadsheet summarizing the investment outcomes of some 25 anonymous wealth advisers, for eight consecutive years. The advisers' scores for each year were the main determinant of their year-end bonuses. It was a simple matter to rank the advisers by their performance and to answer a question: Did the same advisers consistently achieve better returns for their clients year after year? Did some advisers consistently display more skill than others?

To find the answer, I computed the correlations between the rankings of advisers in different years, comparing Year 1 with Year 2, Year 1 with Year 3, and so on up through Year 7 with Year 8. That yielded 28 correlations, one for each pair of years. While I was prepared to find little year-to-year consistency, I was still surprised to find that the average of the 28 correlations was .01. In other words, zero. The stability that would indicate differences in skill was not to be found. The results resembled what you would expect from a dice-rolling contest, not a game of skill.

No one in the firm seemed to be aware of the nature of the game that its stock pickers were playing. The advisers themselves felt they were competent professionals performing a task that was difficult but not impossible, and their superiors agreed. On the evening before the seminar, Richard Thaler and I had dinner with some of the top executives of the firm, the people who decide on the size of bonuses. We asked them to guess the year-to-year correlation in the rankings of individual advisers. They thought they knew what was coming and smiled as they said, "not very high" or "performance certainly fluctuates." It quickly became clear, however, that no one expected the average correlation to be zero.

What we told the directors of the firm was that, at least when it came to building portfolios, the firm was rewarding luck as if it were skill. This should have been shocking news to them, but it was not. There was no sign that they disbelieved us.

How could they? After all, we had analyzed their own results, and they were certainly sophisticated enough to appreciate their implications, which we politely refrained from spelling out. We all went on calmly with our dinner, and I am quite sure that both our findings and their implications were quickly swept under the rug and that life in the firm went on just as before. The illusion of skill is not only an individual aberration; it is deeply ingrained in the culture of the industry. Facts that challenge such basic assumptions—and thereby threaten people's livelihood and self-esteem—are simply not absorbed. The mind does not digest them. This is particularly true of statistical studies of performance, which provide general facts that people will ignore if they conflict with their personal experience.

The next morning, we reported the findings to the advisers, and their response was equally bland. Their personal experience of exercising careful professional judgment on complex problems was far more compelling to them than an obscure statistical result. When we were done, one executive I dined with the previous evening drove me to the airport. He told me, with a trace of defensiveness, "I have done very well for the firm, and no one can take that away from me." I smiled and said nothing. But I thought, privately: Well, I took it away from you this morning. If your success was due mostly to chance, how much credit are you entitled to take for it?

We often interact with professionals who exercise their judgment with evident confidence, sometimes priding themselves on the power of their intuition. In a world rife with illusions of validity and skill, can we trust them? How do we distinguish the justified confidence of experts from the sincere overconfidence of professionals who do not know they are out of their depth? We can believe an expert who admits uncertainty but cannot take expressions of high confidence at face value. As I first learned on the obstacle field, people come up with coherent stories and confident predictions even when they know little or nothing. Overconfidence arises because people are often blind to their own blindness.

True intuitive expertise is learned from prolonged experience with good feedback   30
on mistakes. You are probably an expert in guessing your spouse's mood from one word on the telephone; chess players find a strong move in a single glance at a complex position; and true legends of instant diagnoses are common among physicians. To know whether you can trust a particular intuitive judgment, there are two questions you should ask: Is the environment in which the judgment is made sufficiently regular to enable predictions from the available evidence? The answer is yes for diagnosticians, no for stock pickers. Do the professionals have an adequate opportunity to learn the cues and the regularities? The answer here depends on the professionals' experience and on the quality and speed with which they discover their mistakes. Anesthesiologists have a better chance to develop intuitions than radiologists do. Many of the professionals we encounter easily pass both tests, and their off-the-cuff judgments deserve to be taken seriously. In general, however, you should not take assertive and confident people at their own evaluation unless you have independent reason to believe that they know what they are talking about. Unfortunately, this advice is difficult to follow: overconfident professionals sincerely believe they have expertise, act as experts, and look like experts. You will have to struggle to remind yourself that they may be in the grip of an illusion.

Exploring Context

1. Daniel Kahneman is a noted speaker. Learn more about his ideas by watching his TED talk at www.ted.com/talks/daniel_kahneman_the_riddle_of_experience_vs_memory. What common themes can you find in his work?

2. Visit the Securities and Exchange Commission's introduction to mutual funds at www.sec.gov/investor/pubs/inwsmf.htm. Does it suggest an illusion of validity or an illusion of skill? You might also search the Web more broadly for information about investing. Is the kind of randomness that Kahneman identifies acknowledged?

3. Tinder is a popular dating app. Explore its Web site at gotinder.com and trace the ways it relies on quick judgments. Based on Kahneman's argument, how useful would an app like this be?

Questions for Connecting

1. Daniel Gilbert, in "Reporting Live from Tomorrow" (p. 179), is similarly concerned with the problems of cognition — specifically our imagination's failure to predict what will make us happy. Synthesize Kahneman's and Gilbert's work in order to propose the best methods for us to make judgments that will make us happy. Might Gilbert's surrogates be a solution to the illusion of validity? Use your responses from Question 3 of Questions for Critical Reading and Question 1 of Exploring Context.

2. Does our poor aptitude for making judgments make the Dalai Lama's call for caution regarding genetic technologies in "Ethics and the New Genetics" (p. 63) more pressing? Incorporate Kahneman's ideas about judgment into the Dalai Lama's suggestion. Given our cognitive fallacies, is a moral compass more important than ever? You may want to use your work with cognitive fallacies from Question 2 of Questions for Critical Reading in supporting your response.

3. Given that art is closely connected to judgment, how does Kahneman's argument affect Rhys Southan's discussion of art and effective altruism in "Is Art a Waste of Time?" (p. 434)? Write a response in which you consider the potential of effective altruism given Kahneman's points.

Language Matters

1. Select a section of at least four paragraphs in Kahneman's essay. Find the topic sentence of each paragraph and then copy those sentences together to form a new paragraph. Does the paragraph made out of topic sentences make any sense? Does it reflect the flow of Kahneman's argument? How can you apply this exercise to your own writing?

2. Constellations help us make sense out of the stars — they give the stars meaning by grouping them into meaningful patterns. Examine how sentence structure does the same with words. Select a key quotation from Kahneman's essay and then create a map of its different parts. How did you choose to break up the sentence? What relationships

can you find among the parts? Are some connections more important than others? That is, if you took out certain parts of the sentence, would it still have the same meaning?

3. Citation is absolutely essential to academic writing, though it plays no role in Kahneman's essay. Why doesn't Kahneman use citation? Why is it so important in academic writing? Consider issues of audience and authority as you prepare your answer.

Assignments for Writing

1. What lessons can we learn from Kahneman? Write a paper in which you propose methods we can use to make more reliable judgments. Use your work from Questions 1–3 of Questions for Critical Reading to support your argument.

2. Kahneman's experience in the financial sector suggests that success is mostly a matter of chance. Evaluate and complicate Kahneman's argument by writing a paper in which you determine the relationship between skills and success. Is success a matter of perception or statistics? Consider drawing from your explorations in Question 2 of Exploring Context.

3. Kahneman's experiences in the Israeli army and on Wall Street suggest that people don't really care about the validity of judgments; in both cases nothing changed once the illusion of validity had been dispelled. Write a paper in which you consider the value of judgment. Should we always seek the most valid judgments? Do they make a difference? If so, how can we change behaviors that have relied on cognitive fallacies?

CHUCK KLOSTERMAN

Cultural critic and best-selling author **Chuck Klosterman** has written eight books: two novels, two nonfiction narratives, and four essay collections, including *Sex, Drugs, and Cocoa Puffs*; *Killing Yourself to Live*; and *Fargo Rock City*. Known for his oddball style and sharp, witty observations, Klosterman writes primarily about music, pop culture, and sports. He is "The Ethicist" for the *New York Times Magazine*, and his prolific writings have appeared in such publications as *GQ*, *Spin*, and *Esquire*. Klosterman graduated from the University of North Dakota with a degree in journalism in 1994. He served as the Picador Guest Professor for Literature at the University of Leipzig's Institute for American Studies in 2008.

© Seth Kushner/Retna Ltd./Corbis

"Electric Funeral" is taken from Klosterman's latest *New York Times* best-seller, *I Wear the Black Hat: Grappling with Villains (Real and Imagined)*. This 2013 essay collection examines the concept of villainy and the way so-called bad guys are perceived in modern culture, with essays on subjects such as the rock group the Eagles, the sitcom *Seinfeld*, Batman, folk hero and hijacker D. B. Cooper, and former president Bill Clinton. Reflecting Klosterman's work as "The Ethicist" for the *New York Times*, *I Wear the Black Hat* grapples with the larger question of good and evil, asking why we call some figures villains and others heroes.

In "Electric Funeral," Klosterman zooms in on technological innovation and the "villains" that champion it, profiling such figures as Perez Hilton, Julian Assange, and even the office IT guy. They have the power and they are the future, Klosterman posits, asserting that this position of power causes resentment, largely because it scares people. He argues that ultimately "the easiest way for any cutthroat person to succeed is to instinctively (and relentlessly) side with the technology of tomorrow, even if that technology is distasteful" (p. 225). From bloggers who matter because of how many followers they have to the founder of the controversial WikiLeaks Web site, Klosterman looks at the relationship between technological progress and our cultural concepts of villainy.

What do you think makes a villain? What is the nature of good and evil?

▶ TAGS: *culture, ethics, media, politics, science and technology, social change, social media*
▶ CONNECTIONS: *Appiah, Dalai Lama, Gilbert, Restak, Rosin, Singer, Wasik*

Questions for Critical Reading

1. How would you define *villainy*? What differentiates it from *evil*? Develop your own definition and then, as you read Klosterman's essay, note places where he supports or challenges your definition. What do you think villainy means to Klosterman?

2. What are the benefits and costs of technology? Locate passages where Klosterman discusses this issue.

3. Klosterman focuses quite a bit on the inevitability of progress. Mark passages where he suggests there is something problematic, if not villainous, about this position.

Electric Funeral

If you're reading [*I Wear the Black Hat*] in order, you've just finished a section about Bill Clinton, the forty-second president of the United States. Unless [*I Wear the Black Hat*] has survived far longer than I anticipate, most readers will picture Clinton as a living, breathing mammal. You remember where you were when he was elected in 1992 and the condition of your life during his two-term tenure. His time as POTUS might feel more recent than it actually is (and perhaps that makes you feel strange). But there's another chunk of readers who had a different experience when they read ["Arrested for Smoking," not included here] (and the size of that chunk will get progressively larger for the rest of eternity). Those in the second camp recall Clinton only vaguely, or not at all. You know he was once the president in the same way you know Woodrow Wilson was once the president. It feels like something that happened long ago. That makes you different from those in the first camp (and for a lot of different reasons). And there's one specific divergence that matters more than most people think: If you're in that first group, your parents worried about how you were affected by the media—and what they worried about was the *content* you were consuming. If you were born in 1960, your parents worried about Black Sabbath; if you were born in 1970, they worried about *Porky's*; if you were born in 1980, they worried about *Beavis and Butt-head*. Their fear was that you'd be changed by the images you saw and the messages you heard, and perhaps they believed that content needed to be regulated. Their concern was tethered to the message. But if you were born after 1990, this is not the case. Instead, your parents were (or are) primarily worried about the *medium* through which all of those things are accessed. The medium is far more problematic than the message. When a father looks at his typically unfocused four-year-old hypnotically immersed with an iPad for three straight hours, he thinks, "Somehow, I know this is bad." It does not matter that the four-year-old might be learning essential skills on that device; what matters is the way such an intense, insular, digital experience will irreparably alter the way he'll experience the non-simulated world. It's normalizing something that was once abnormal, and it's distancing the child from reality. It will transmogrify his brainstem into the opening credit sequence of Gaspar Noé's *Enter the Void*. And the worst part is that there is no other option. If a father stops his son from embracing the online universe, he's stopping him from becoming a competitive adult; it's like refusing to teach him how to drive a car or boil water. You may worry about all the ancillary consequences, but you can't take away the experience. Avoiding the Internet is akin to avoiding everything that matters. This is even true for adults. An author I know once explained why writing became so much more difficult in the twenty-first century: "The biggest problem in my life," he said, "is that my work machine is also my pornography delivery machine."

The future makes the rules.

The future makes the rules, so there's no point in being mad when the future wins. In fact, the easiest way for any cutthroat person to succeed is to instinctively (and relentlessly) side with the technology of tomorrow, even if that technology is distasteful. Time will eventually validate that position. The only downside is that—until that validation occurs—less competitive people will find you annoying and unlikable.

The future will retire undefeated, but it always makes a terrible argument for its own success. The argument is inevitably some version of this: "You might not like where we're going, and tomorrow might be worse than yesterday. But it's still going to happen, whether you like it or not. It's inevitable." And this is what people hate. They hate being *dragged* into the future, and they hate the technocrats who remind them that this is always, always, always happening. We tend to dislike cultural architects who seem *excited* that the world is changing, particularly when those architects don't seem

> **They know they will end up on the right side of history, because the future always wins.**

particularly concerned whether those changes make things worse. They know they will end up on the right side of history, because the future always wins. These are people who have the clearest understanding of what technology can do, but no emotional stake in how its application will change the lives of people who aren't exactly like them. [They know the most and care the least . . . and they kind of think that's funny.] Certainly, this brand of technophobia has always existed. As early as 1899, people like H. G. Wells were expressing apprehension about a future "ruled by an aristocracy of organizers, men who manage railroads and similar vast enterprises." But this is different. This is about the kind of person who will decide what that future is.

Early in the third season of *The Sopranos*, there's a two-episode subplot in which my favorite character (Christopher Moltisanti) sticks up a charity concert at Rutgers University (the musical headliner is Jewel). What's most interesting about this robbery is the person who hands over the money: The role of the terrified box office clerk is portrayed by an unknown actor named Mario Lavandeira. He has only two lines, but the scene—when viewed retroactively—is more culturally significant than everything else that happens in that particular episode. This is because Mario Lavandeira would soon rename himself Perez Hilton and become the first authentically famous blogger, which (of course) made him the most hated blogger of his generation.

[There are no famous bloggers who aren't hated.]

Perez Hilton once claimed that 8.82 million people read his website within a twenty-four-hour period in 2007. The magnitude of this number was disputed by competing gossip sources, but those critics came off like the type of person who wants to argue over the specific number of people killed during the Holocaust: They missed the point entirely. Even if Hilton was tripling his true traffic figures, the audience for what he was doing was massive. And what he was doing was terrible. It was objectively immoral. The crux of his publishing empire was based around defacing copyrighted photos of celebrities (often to imply they were addicted to cocaine). Other central pursuits included the outing of gay celebrities (Perez himself is homosexual) and publishing unauthorized photos of teen celebrities who may or may not be wearing underwear. The apex of his career was when he broke the news of Fidel Castro's death, a report mildly contradicted by Castro's unwillingness to stop living. Hilton was also a judge for the Miss USA Pageant, a referee for a WWE wrestling match, and the star of a VH1 reality show I never actually saw. [I realize Mr. Hilton would likely disagree with my overview of his career and insist that I failed to mention how he's also been involved with numerous sex-positive, pro-youth, anti-bullying initiatives. But I suspect he will totally agree with much of what I'm going to write next, mostly because it makes him look far less culpable than he probably is.]

Whenever you have an audience as large as Hilton's, there's obviously going to be a substantial swath of consumers who adore the person who built it. It would be wrong to say, "Everyone hates Perez Hilton," because that's just not true. But it's pretty hard to find an intelligent person who loves him. (Such individuals exist, but not in great numbers.) It's hard to find a thoughtful person who appreciates the way Hilton's appeal is so hyper-directed at the lowest common denominator. Even his decision to name himself after noted celebutard Paris Hilton perpetuates a desire to produce self-consciously vapid work. So this, it would seem, is why smart people hate him: Because of his blog's content. They find his ideas despicable (or so they would argue). Now, Perez would counter that accusation by charging his critics with jealousy. He (and his defenders) would claim that what people truly hate about Perez Hilton is not what he writes; it's the size of his audience and the scale of his reach. That argument is not invalid. For those who live on the Internet, the attention economy matters way more than making money or earning peer respect; there is a slice of the Web that would do *anything* to harvest Hilton's readership, even if it meant publishing photos of aborted celebrity fetuses while going bankrupt in the process. In other words, some people hate Perez for his ideas and some people hate Perez because they so desperately want to be like him. And as it turns out, both sides have a point. The reason Perez Hilton became a villain was the intersection of those two qualities: It wasn't just the content, and it wasn't just the success. It was the creeping fear that this type of content would become the *only* way any future person could be successful.

Necessity used to be the mother of invention, but then we ran out of things that were necessary. The postmodern mother of invention is desire; we don't really "need" anything new, so we only create what we *want*. This changes the nature of technological competition. Because the Internet is obsessed with its own version of non-monetary capitalism, it rewards the volume of response much more than the merits of whatever people are originally responding to. Moreover, there's no downside to creating something that repulses all those who exist outside your audience (in fact, a reasonable degree of outsider hatred usually helps). Intuitively understanding these rules, Hilton only went after the kind of pre-adult who simultaneously loved and loathed celebrity culture to an unhealthy degree; he knew that specific demographic was both expanding and underserved. It was a brilliant business model. It was like he opened a buffet restaurant that served wet garbage in a community where the population of garbage gluttons was much higher (and far more loyal) than anyone had ever realized. And this made all the normal food eaters hate him. Do they hate his product? Sure (although there are many things on the Internet far worse). Do they hate his success? Sure (although he's never been perceived as credible or particularly insightful, so the definition of his success is limited to pure populism). Do they simply think Hilton is a jerk? Yes (and perhaps he is—I have no idea). But none of those individual issues addresses the greater fear. The real reason Perez Hilton is vilified is the combination of a) what he does editorially, b) its level of public import, and c) the undeniable sense that all of this was somehow *inevitable*. Perez Hilton is a villain because he personifies the way desire-based technology drives mass culture toward primitive impulses. Any singular opinion of his work does not matter, the only thing that matters is the collective opinion, which can be dominated by a vocal, splintered minority who knows only that they want what they want. Everyone seems to understand this. And once everyone understands that this is how New Media works, it becomes normative. It becomes the main way we get information about everything (gossip or otherwise). There is no alternative option. By manipulating an audience that is complicit in the manipulation, Perez Hilton can force the rest of us to accept his version of the future.

Hilton is a technocrat, and technocrats inevitably share two unifying beliefs. The first is that they're already winning; the second is that they're going to push things forward, regardless of what that progress entails. Resistance to either principle is futile. Every day we grow closer to a full-on technocratic police state. "I don't care if you like me," Hilton has written. "I just care if you read my website." This is not exactly an original perspective; many writers feel like that, especially when they're young (Hilton was roughly twenty-four when he first experienced success). But the sentiment is disturbing when expressed by Perez. It seems like his entire objective. It's like he vividly sees the relationship between those two adversarial ideas, and everything else is built upon that foundation. And this would be totally fine, assuming we felt as if it was our decision to

> **At this point, we can't walk away from harmful technology. We've ceded control to the machines.**

agree or disagree. But we don't. At this point, we can't walk away from harmful technology. We've ceded control to the machines. The upside is that the machines still have masters. The downside is that we don't usually like who those masters are.

When Kim Dotcom was arrested during a 2012 police raid of his home, I had the same series of reactions as everyone else: There's a person literally named "Kim Dotcom"? And this person is a 350-pound, egocentric German multimillionaire who never went to college? And he got famous for being a computer hacker who refers to himself as Dr. Evil? And he lives in a mansion in New Zealand? And he participates in European road races and is the world's best *Modern Warfare 3* player? And he has a beautiful wife of unknown racial origin? And his twenty-four-acre, $30 million estate is populated with life-size statues of giraffes? And he likes to be photographed in his bathtub? Everything about his biography seemed like someone trying to make fun of a Roger Moore–era James Bond movie that was too dumb to exist. I could not believe that *this* was the person the FBI decided to go after in their ongoing dream of controlling the digital future. It seemed as if they were arbitrarily penalizing a cherubic foreigner for being wealthy and ostentatious, and New Zealand eventually deemed the raid illegal.

However, the arrest turned out to be far less arbitrary than I'd thought. Dotcom owned and operated the online service Megaupload. In an interview with Kiwi investigative reporter John Campbell, Dotcom (born Kim Schmitz in 1974) described Megaupload like this: "I basically created a server where I could upload a file and get a unique link, and then I would just e-mail that link to my friend so he would then get the file. And that's how Megaupload was started. It was just a solution to a problem that still exists today." In essence, Dotcom's argument was that he simply made it easier for people to exchange and store digital files that were too large for Gmail or AOL—and when described in this simplified manner, it seems like his motives were utilitarian. But this claim is such a profound distortion of reality that it almost qualifies as a lie, even though (I suppose) it's technically true. Megaupload was a place to steal music. There was no mystery about this; if you knew what Megaupload was, you knew it was a pirating service. There appeared to be dozens of other sites exactly like it. But what I did not realize was the scope of Dotcom's empire: The week after he was arrested, downloading illegal music became almost impossible (not *totally* impossible, but at least ten times more difficult than it had been in 2011). His arrest instantly changed the entire culture of recreational music theft. For most normal adults, ripping music from the Internet went from "a little too easy" to "a little too hard." Megaupload was more central to the process of stealing copyrighted material than every other file-sharing source combined. He really *was* the man. Kim Dotcom was not some goofy eccentric being persecuted for the sins of other people. He pretty much ran the Internet (or at least the part of the Internet that people with money actually care about). He denies this, as any wise man would. But even his denials suggest a secret dominance. Here's one exchange from his conversation with Campbell, the first TV interview he gave following his arrest . . .

> CAMPBELL: The FBI indictment against you alleges, and I quote, "Copyright infringement on a massive scale, with estimated harm to copyright holders well in excess of five hundred million U.S. dollars."
>
> DOTCOM: Well, that's complete nonsense. If you read the indictment and if you hear what the Prosecution has said in court, those $500 million of damage were just music files from a two-week time period. So they are actually talking about $13 billion U.S. damages within a year, just for music downloads. The entire U.S. music industry is less than $20 billion. So how can one website be responsible for this amount of damage? It's completely mind-boggling and unrealistic.

It *is* mind-boggling. But it isn't unrealistic. While I don't doubt the FBI is using an unusually high estimate, it doesn't seem implausible that $13 billion worth of music was flowing through Megaupload's channels (assuming we pretend a CD is still worth its fourteen-dollar retail price). Ripping music is not like buying music. It's not a meditative process. When you purchase music, you make a specific choice that (in your mind) justifies the exchange of currency. When you download music illegally, there's nothing to exchange; if you can simply *think* of a record's title and you can type it semi-correctly into a search engine, there's no reason not to drop it into your iTunes. That's pretty much the entire investment—the ability to type a band name into a search field. Megaupload made stealing simple (it was far better than the previous theft iteration, the Napster-like Limewire). The downloading process took (maybe) forty-five seconds per album, and—if you elected to never listen to those songs, even once—you lost nothing. People would download albums just because they were bored. Since the advent (and fall) of Napster in 1999, consumers' relationship to music as a commodity completely collapsed. Supply became unlimited, so demand became irrelevant. A better argument from Dotcom would have been that the $13 billion he was accused of "reappropriating" was not actually $13 billion, but merely the projected value of what such exchanges would have been worth in 1998 (and only if the world had become some kind of strange musical utopia where consumers immediately purchased every single album they were remotely intrigued by).

Weirder still is that the charge of music theft isn't even the main reason media conglomerates wanted Dotcom's arrest. Their real concern was the increasing potential for the pirating of feature-length films, which is only feasible through this kind of server (relative to the size of MP3 music clips, film files are massive). The movie industry makes the music industry look like a food co-op (in 2011, global film revenue was $87 billion). Kim Dotcom clearly understood this, which prompted him to make the kind of move usually reserved for the Joker: Despite being under arrest, he wrote an open letter to the *Hollywood Reporter*, mocking the film industry's inability to understand the future of its own vehicle. His twelve-paragraph letter opens like a Tweet: "Dear Hollywood: The Internet frightens you." And he just keeps going . . .

> (*paragraph 2*): "You get so comfortable with your ways of doing business that any change is perceived as a threat. The problem is, we as a society don't have a choice: The law of human nature is to communicate more efficiently."

> (*paragraph 4*): "My whole life is like a movie. I wouldn't be who I am if it wasn't for the mind-altering glimpse at the future in *Star Wars*. I am at the forefront of creating the cool stuff that will allow creative works to thrive in an Internet age. I have the solutions to your problems. I am not your enemy."

> (*paragraph 7*): "The people of the Internet will unite. They will help me. And they are stronger than you. We will prevail in the war for Internet freedom and innovation that you have launched. We have logic, human nature and the invisible hand on our side."

The document concludes with Dotcom's signature snark: "This open letter is free of copyright. Use it freely." Technically, he's trying to forward his opinion on how copyright law should be applied, based on the principle that the laws governing ownership over intellectual property are outdated and not designed for the machinations of the Internet age. But that's not what interests me. What interests me is his personality and his leverage—and in the case of Dotcom, those qualities are connected.   15

If you've ever worked in an office filled with computers (which, at this point, is the only kind of office that exists), you've undoubtedly had some kind of complicated, one-sided relationship with whoever worked in the IT department. "IT" stands for "information technology." [An easy illustration of the one-sidedness of this relationship can be quickly illustrated by asking random people what the "I" and "T" literally represent in that acronym. You may be surprised by the results.] Now, there are exceptions to every rule, and I don't want to unfairly stereotype anyone. But people fucking hate IT guys. They want to knife them in the throat and pour acid in their ears. They want to see them arrested for the possession of kiddie porn.

There are two reasons why this is.

The first is that workers typically encounter IT people only when something is already wrong with their desktop (there just aren't any situations where you *want* someone to be doing things to your computer that you can't do yourself). But the second reason is the one that matters more. Regardless of their station within the office hierarchy, there's never any debate over how much power the IT department has: It's borderline infinite. They control all, and they have access to everything. They can't fire you, but they could get you fired in twenty-four hours. You may have a despotic boss who insists he won't take no for an answer, but he'll take it from an IT guy. He'll eat shit from an IT guy, day after day after day.

Specialists in information technology are the new lawyers. Long ago, lawyers realized that they could make themselves culturally essential if they made the vernacular of contracts too complex for anyone to understand except themselves. They made the language of contracts unreadable on purpose. [Easy example: I can write a book, and my editor can edit a book . . . but neither one of us can read and understand the contract that allows those things to happen.] IT workers became similarly unstoppable the moment they realized virtually every machine powering the modern world is too complicated for the average person to fix or calibrate. And they know this. This is what makes an IT guy different from you. He might make less money, he might have less social prestige, and people might look at him in the cafeteria like he's a morlock—*but he can act however he wants.* He can be nice, but only if he feels like it. He can ignore the company dress code. He can lie for no reason whatsoever (because how would anyone understand what he's lying about?). He can smoke weed at lunch, because he'll still understand your iMac better than you. It doesn't matter how he behaves: The IT department dominates technology, and technology dominates the rest of us. And this state of being creates a new kind of personality. It creates someone like Kim Dotcom, a man who's essentially an IT guy for the entire planet.

"I'm an easy target," Mr. Dotcom claims in his defense. "My flamboyance, my history as a hacker. I'm not American, I'm living somewhere in New Zealand, around the world. I have funny number plates on my cars. I'm an easy target." (Kim Dotcom drives around in luxury vehicles with license plates that read GUILTY.) There is, certainly, something endearing about Kim Dotcom's attitude. He acts like a man who finds his own obesity hilarious. His relationship to pop culture gives him a childlike appeal. (He once made himself the main character in a seminal flash-animation film that centered on the cartoonish murder of Bill Gates. He named his animated alter ego Richard Kimball, the wrongly accused hero from *The Fugitive*.) Sometimes it seems like he can't possibly be serious. (After his arrest, he recorded an anti-copyright ABBA-like pop song titled "Mr. President" in which he directly compares himself to Martin Luther King.) In general, Americans enjoy the idea of computer hackers and prefer to imagine them as precocious elves. (Somehow, the touchstone for how hackers behave is still based on Matthew Broderick's performance in the 1983 film *WarGames*.) Dotcom is arrogant, but not unlikable; at the highest possible level, being an IT guy is vaguely cool. Yet his underlying message is troubling. He starts by arguing, "Change is good," which is only a semi-defensible position to begin with. But that evolves into "Change will happen whether you like it or not." He uses phrases like "*The law of human nature is to communicate more efficiently,*" which makes it seem like he's proposing something natural and obvious. But all he's really proposing is the business model for his own company (which might not be diabolical, but certainly isn't altruistic). He's trying to initiate an era when content is free and content providers make all the money, but he still wants to frame it like a more grassroots system ("*The people of the Internet will unite*"). Would his espoused structure actually be better? I don't think it's possible to know. But I do know

20

that any argument attacking Dotcom will come from a position of sad technological inferiority. It will seem unsophisticated and antediluvian. It's easier to just embrace Dotcom's viewpoint, even if it's self-serving and unfair; about a year after the initial raid, he launched another sharing service (this time simply called MEGA) that utilizes cloud technology. I suspect it will succeed. He is, in many ways, the most depressing kind of villain: the kind we *must* agree with in order to stay competitive. The only other option is being trampled.

> There is a view that one should never be permitted to be criticized for being — possibly, even in the future — engaged in a contributory act that might be immoral. And that type of arse covering is more important than saving people's lives. That it is better to let 1000 people die than risk going to save them and possibly running over someone on the way. And that is something I find philosophically repugnant.

These are the words of Julian Assange, the founder of the website WikiLeaks and the most archetypically villainlike villain of the Internet age. His appearance is so Aryan that it seems like he was engineered by the kind of scientist who ends up hiding in Argentina. I assume Assange can laugh, but I have no proof. He's truly a worldwide irritant: Assange has been accused of sexually assaulting two women in Sweden, applied for political asylum in Ecuador, and had a Canadian academic call for his assassination. His brilliance is impolite and self-defined. There is no one else like him; he is truly a New Thing.

If you know what WikiLeaks is, feel free to skip this paragraph. (I'm not going to outline anything you don't already know, nor am I going to take a strong position on its merits or flaws, nor have I seen the film *The Fifth Estate* starring sexy British weirdo Benedict Cumberbatch in the lead role.) If you don't know anything about it, here's a 230-word description: WikiLeaks is a website that publishes classified, present-tense documents from anonymous sources. The site's abiding premise is that the upside of absolute transparency is greater than the potential downside of publicly dumping sensitive information that might theoretically cause damage. The first noteworthy WikiLeaks release was some 2007 footage of a U.S. Apache helicopter killing an Iraqi journalist in Afghanistan (people generally viewed this release positively). The most discussed incident was an avalanche of "diplomatic cables" that went up in 2011; essentially, these were private correspondences American diplomats had exchanged among themselves. Most of these exchanges were more gossipy than meaningful, but it made some high-profile Americans seem crazy and facile. [It also created the impression that WikiLeaks cannot be controlled or regulated, which seemed scarier than the documents themselves.] That same year, WikiLeaks released seventy-five thousand U.S. military documents that came to be known as the Afghan War Diary. The Pentagon wasn't exactly stoked about this. Obviously, the details of all these fiascoes can be found more comprehensively elsewhere. But the takeaway is this: A very confident Australian (Assange) who's fixated on the problematic politics of one country (the United States) has created a way to publish information about that country that would have previously remained hidden (sometimes for valid reasons and sometimes due to corruption). It is journalism that attacks journalism, which is an extremely interesting topic to journalists.

Supporters of WikiLeaks believe it receives the same kind of unjust, reactionary criticism that was once lobbed at the Pentagon Papers (the Pentagon Papers were a classified overview of U.S. military involvement in the Vietnam War, published by the *New York Times* in 1971). Those who are against WikiLeaks counter this argument by noting that the Pentagon Papers were vetted by a news organization and only involved defunct military actions that were at least four years old (the study examined activities only through the year 1967). It's worth noting that the principal whistleblower in the Pentagon Papers (former U.S. military analyst Daniel Ellsberg) has requested a presidential pardon for the principal whistleblower in the WikiLeaks controversy, former U.S. soldier Bradley Manning. I have my own views on this topic, but they're contradictory and unimportant. What intrigues me more is Assange's quote at the top of this section: His statement either confronts (and obliterates) the problem I'm trying to describe, or it simply *is* the problem (described succinctly and expressed with monotone glee).

Assange comes at the media from a bottom-line, non-theoretical, the-ends-justify-the-means perspective that was (perhaps not so coincidentally) first described in Machiavelli's *The Prince*. He's arguing that people are too obsessed with the arcane ethics of print journalism, and he's willing to accept that an action that hurts one person is justified if it helps a hundred or a thousand or ten thousand others. It's an old problem. Perhaps the clearest metaphor for how much this disturbs people is the classic hypothetical of the runaway trolley car: Imagine you are operating a trolley car whose brakes have malfunctioned. You are flying down the tracks at an obscene speed. Up ahead, you see five workers on the track, unaware that this trolley is bearing down on them; if you continue on your current path, the trolley will kill them all. But then you notice an alternate track that will allow you to avoid colliding with the five workers. The only downside is that if you turn onto this alternate route, you will kill a different innocent person (but only one). Do you switch to the alternate track and kill one person in order to save five? [The folks usually credited with the creation and popularization of this dilemma are Philippa Foot and Judith Jarvis Thomson, but I'm roughly paraphrasing how it's described in Michael Sandel's wonderful book *Justice.*]

> **Assange comes at the media from a bottom-line, non-theoretical, the-ends-justify-the-means perspective.**

When you pose this question to any normal reader, they almost always say yes. It seems insane to kill five people instead of one. But that's not the true question; that's just the introduction. The real question is this: Let's say you're *not* operating the runaway trolley. Let's say you're not the conductor. Let's propose that you're just watching this event from a bridge above the track. You realize this runaway trolley is going to kill five people. You notice another person is watching this event alongside you — an extremely obese man. It dawns on you that if you push this man onto the track below, it will derail the trolley. Here again, you are killing one man in order to save five. Do you push the fat man off the bridge?

This second scenario always troubles people more: The most common answer tends to be, "I know these things are basically the same, but I could never push a man to his death." The reason people feel different is due to how the two scenarios position the decision maker. In the first problem, the decision maker is accepting the existing conditions and trying to choose whatever solution hurts the fewest individuals. In the second problem, the decision maker is injecting himself into the situation and taking on the responsibility of the outcome. The first scenario is a reaction. The second is a self-directed choice. What bothers people about WikiLeaks is that it creates a world in which the second scenario is happening constantly, and what bothers people about Assange is the way he makes that choice seem so stupidly self-evident.

Assange's belief is that everyone would be better off if all information was equally (and immediately) available. His critics say, "That's irresponsible. If you just release information—and particularly military information—without considering its sensitivity, someone will get killed." And that's probably true. If WikiLeaks continues in its current iteration, I'm sure it will (eventually) contribute to someone's death. But Assange makes us consider the larger value of that troubling possibility. What if the relentless release of classified information makes every nation less willing to conduct questionable military actions? Will this force all society to become more honest (and wouldn't that future reality be worth the loss of a hundred innocent people in the present)? Or would it actually make things worse? Will the fear of exposure simply prompt political figures to resist creating any paper trail at all? Will *everything* become hidden? I really have no idea. No one does, and that's the discomfort: We don't know if the old way is better (or worse) than the new way. But Assange does not let us choose. He possesses a sweeping technological advantage, and he knows that released information cannot be retracted. He can make us accept his philosophy against our will. Once a document is released, how we feel about the nature of its existence becomes meaningless; it's instantaneously absorbed into the media bloodstream as pure content. This is why Assange can make an argument that openly advocates actions that (in his words) "might be immoral." Those actions are going to happen anyway, so he doesn't have to pretend that they contradict the way we've always viewed morality. He doesn't have to convince us he's right, because our thoughts don't matter. His view of *everything* is like Perez Hilton's view of gossip or Kim Dotcom's view of entertainment: He believes everything longs to be free. And he will make that happen, because he knows how to do it and we don't know how to stop him. He's already beaten everybody. It was never close.

Exploring Context

1. Kim Dotcom's Web site is located at kim.com. In what ways does the site suggest that Dotcom has capitalized on his infamy? How does it reflect your work on the inevitability of technological progress from Question 3 of Questions for Critical Reading?

2. Visit Perez Hilton's blog at perezhilton.com. How does the site reinforce or challenge Klosterman's claims about Hilton and villainy?

3. WikiLeaks (wikileaks.org) remains quite an active Web site. Explore the site. Do you think the information contained there does good or harm?

Questions for Connecting

1. Peter Singer, in "Visible Man: Ethics in a World without Secrets" (p. 425), also examines WikiLeaks. Apply Klosterman's analysis to Singer's essay. Does Singer's discussion

confirm or complicate Klosterman's thoughts on the controversial Web site? Is sousveillance villainous? Use your work from Question 1 of Questions for Critical Reading and Question 3 of Exploring Context in composing your response.

2. In using social media to generate flash mobs, Bill Wasik, author of "My Crowd Experiment: The Mob Project" (p. 474), seems to be participating in some of the same aspects of technology as the figures Klosterman examines, such as Perez Hilton. Is Wasik a villain? Use your work from Questions 1 and 3 of Questions for Critical Reading to support your response.

3. Hanna Rosin's "Why Kids Sext" (p. 388) examines the disturbing rise of sexting among adolescents. To what extent do Klosterman's claims about technology and inevitability factor in this phenomenon? You might want to draw from your work in Question 3 of Questions for Critical Reading to support your argument.

Language Matters

1. Klosterman offers an analysis of Kim Dotcom's open letter to the *Hollywood Reporter*. Review this passage to see how Klosterman analyzes Dotcom's text. First evaluate Klosterman's analysis and then perform a similar analysis on a passage you feel is important in Klosterman's essay. How might you use these techniques to help you analyze and then improve your own writing?

2. Using Flickr (flickr.com), search for images that illustrate Klosterman's argument. Paste these images into a document to create a visual montage of this essay. What commonalities can you see in the images that weren't immediately apparent in the essay?

3. Drafting and revising are crucial components of the writing process. We often see a published piece of writing as perfect, but imagine earlier drafts of Klosterman's text. How do you think he started this piece? What areas do you think he revised the most? Where do you think you should do the most revision as you draft your own papers?

Assignments for Writing

1. What is villainy? Write a paper in which you develop a definition of *villainy* supported with quotations from Klosterman's text. You may want to draw from your work in Questions for Critical Reading and Exploring Context in developing your argument.

2. Klosterman's analysis of villainy in this essay is closely tied to the sense that the future of technology cannot and should not be stopped. Write a paper in which you examine the costs of technological progress. Use your answer to Question 2 of Questions for Critical Reading to support your argument.

3. None of the figures that Klosterman discusses seem particularly evil. Are any of them, then, villains? Select one of the cases that Klosterman uses and then provide your own analysis to determine whether or not that person is in fact a villain. You might find your work from Questions on Critical Reading useful as a starting point, and you may want to use your insights from Exploring Context to support your argument.

© Margaret Singer and Max Freedman

MARIA KONNIKOVA

Maria Konnikova was born in Moscow, Russia, and emigrated to the United States as a child. She studied psychology, creative writing, and government at Harvard University before receiving her Ph.D. in psychology from Columbia University. Konnikova's writing has appeared in popular publications such as the *Atlantic*, the *New York Times*, *Slate*, the *New Republic*, the *Wall Street Journal*, *Salon*, and *Scientific American*, and she currently writes a weekly column for the *New Yorker* online in which she focuses on psychology and science. Her *New York Times* best-selling book *Mastermind: How to Think Like Sherlock Holmes* was nominated for the Agatha Award and the Anthony Award for Best Nonfiction.

"The Limits of Friendship" was published October 7, 2014, in the online version of the *New Yorker*. The *New Yorker*, both in print and online, offers notable commentary on politics, global affairs, art and popular culture, and science and technology. It also publishes short fiction and poetry and is famous for its cartoons. The October 7, 2014, online edition also included articles on Ebola, New York's High Line green space, and the role of the Web site Reddit in Spanish politics.

In this essay, Konnikova explores the Dunbar number, the theoretical number of friends we can really have, and the ways in which social networking is affecting not only this number but also socialization itself. Along with anthropologist and psychologist Robin Dunbar, she questions whether increasingly pervasive virtual interaction will influence the friend groups and social skills of new generations. Asks Konnikova: "[W]hat happens if you're raised from a young age to see virtual interactions as akin to physical ones?" (p. 239).

Are virtual friends replacing actual friends? How many friends do you feel you have?

▶ TAGS: *community, culture, identity, media, social media, psychology, relationships, science and technology, social change*

▶ CONNECTIONS: *Appiah, Duhigg, Epstein, Friedman, Pollan, Restak, Rosin*

Questions for Critical Reading

1. As you read, mark passages where Konnikova defines the *Dunbar number* and the *rule of three*. Then explain these terms in your own words, referencing specific passages from Konnikova to support your response.

2. What do you think makes a good friend? List the qualities of close friendship. As you read, consider the effect of social media on friendship.

3. What's the role of biology in social organization? Examine closely those places where Konnikova draws from the research of Robin Dunbar and others. Does biology determine society?

The Limits of Friendship

Robin Dunbar came up with his eponymous number almost by accident. The University of Oxford anthropologist and psychologist (then at University College London) was trying to solve the problem of why primates devote so much time and effort to grooming. In the process of figuring out the solution, he chanced upon a potentially far more intriguing application for his research. At the time, in the nineteen-eighties, the Machiavellian Intelligence Hypothesis (now known as the Social Brain Hypothesis) had just been introduced into anthropological and primatology discourse.[1] It held that primates have large brains because they live in socially complex societies: the larger the group, the larger the brain. Thus, from the size of an animal's neocortex, the frontal lobe in particular, you could theoretically predict the group size for that animal.

Looking at his grooming data, Dunbar made the mental leap to humans. "We also had humans in our data set so it occurred to me to look to see what size group that relationship might predict for humans," he told me recently. Dunbar did the math, using a ratio of neocortical volume to total brain volume and mean group size, and came up with a number.[2] Judging from the size of an average human brain, the number of people the average person could have in her social group was a hundred and fifty. Anything beyond that would be too complicated to handle at optimal processing levels. For the last twenty-two years, Dunbar has been "unpacking and exploring" what that number actually means — and whether our ever-expanding social networks have done anything to change it.

The Dunbar number is actually a series of them. The best known, a hundred and fifty, is the number of people we call casual friends — the people, say, you'd invite to a large party. (In reality, it's a range: a hundred at the low end and two hundred for the more social of us.) From there, through qualitative interviews coupled with analysis of experimental and survey data, Dunbar discovered that the number grows and decreases according to a precise formula, roughly a "rule of three."[3] The next step down, fifty, is the number of people we call close friends — perhaps the people you'd invite to a group dinner. You see them often, but not so much that you consider them to be true intimates. Then there's the circle of fifteen: the friends that you can turn to for sympathy when you need it, the ones you can confide in about most things. The most intimate Dunbar number, five, is your close support group. These are your best friends (and often family members). On the flipside, groups can extend to five hundred, the acquaintance level, and to fifteen hundred, the absolute limit — the people for whom you can put a name to a face. While the group sizes are relatively stable, their composition can be fluid. Your five today may not be your five next week; people drift among layers and sometimes fall out of them altogether.

When Dunbar consulted the anthropological and historical record, he found remarkable consistency in support of his structure. The average group size among modern hunter-gatherer societies (where there was accurate census data) was 148.4 individuals. Company size in professional armies, Dunbar found, was also remarkably close to a hundred and fifty, from the Roman Empire to sixteenth-century Spain to the twentieth-century Soviet Union. Companies, in turn, tended to be broken down into smaller units of around fifty then further divided into sections of between ten and fifteen. At the opposite end, the companies formed battalions that ranged from five hundred and fifty to eight hundred, and even larger regiments.

Dunbar then decided to go beyond the existing evidence and into experimental methods. In one early study, the first empirical demonstration of the Dunbar number in action, he and the Durham University anthropologist Russell Hill examined the destinations of Christmas cards sent from households all over the UK — a socially pervasive practice, Dunbar explained to me, carried out by most typical households.[4] Dunbar and Hill had each household list its Christmas card recipients and rate them on several scales. "When you looked at the pattern, there was a sense that there were distinct subgroups in there," Dunbar said. If you considered the number of people in each sending household and each recipient household, each individual's network was composed of about a hundred and fifty people. And within that network, people fell into circles of relative closeness — family, friends, neighbors, and work colleagues. Those circles conformed to Dunbar's breakdown.

As constant use of social media has become the new normal, however, people have started challenging the continued relevance of Dunbar's number: Isn't it easier to have more friends when we have Facebook, Twitter, and Instagram to help us to cultivate and maintain them? Some, like the University of California, Berkeley, professor Morten Hansen, have pointed out that social media has facilitated more effective collaborations. Our real-world friends tend to know the same people that we do, but, in the online world, we can expand our networks strategically, leading to better business outcomes. Yet, when researchers tried to determine whether virtual networks increase our strong ties as well as our weak ones (the ones that Hansen had focused on), they found that, for now, the essential Dunbar number, a hundred and fifty, has remained constant. When Bruno Gonçalves and his colleagues at Indiana University at Bloomington looked at whether Twitter had changed the number of relationships that users could maintain over a six-month period, they found that, despite the relative ease of Twitter connections as opposed to face-to-face ones, the individuals that they followed could only manage between one and two hundred stable connections. When the Michigan State University researcher Nicole Ellison surveyed a random sample of undergraduates about their Facebook use, she found, that while their median number of Facebook friends was three hundred, they only counted an average of seventy-five as actual friends.[5]

There's no question, Dunbar agrees, that networks like Facebook are changing the nature of human interaction. "What Facebook does and why it's been so successful in so many ways is it allows you to keep track of people who would otherwise effectively disappear," he said. But one of the things that keeps face-to-face friendships strong is the nature of shared experience: you laugh together; you dance together; you gape at the hot-dog eaters on Coney Island together.[6] We do have a social-media equivalent — sharing, liking, knowing that all of your friends have looked at the same cat video on YouTube as you did — but it lacks the synchronicity of shared experience. It's like a comedy that you watch by yourself: you won't laugh as loudly or as often, even if you're fully aware that all your friends think it's hysterical. We've seen the same movie, but we can't bond over it in the same way.

With social media, we can easily keep up with the lives and interests of far more than a hundred and fifty people. But without investing the face-to-face time, we lack deeper connections to them, and the time we invest in superficial relationships comes at the expense of more profound ones. We may widen our network to two, three, or four hundred people that we see as friends, not just acquaintances, but keeping up an actual friendship requires resources. "The amount of social capital you have is pretty fixed," Dunbar said. "It involves time investment. If you garner connections with more people, you end up distributing your fixed amount of social capital more thinly so the average capital per person is lower." If we're busy putting in the effort, however minimal, to "like" and comment and interact with an ever-widening network, we have less time and capacity left for our closer groups. Traditionally, it's a sixty-forty split of attention: we spend sixty per cent of our time with our core groups of fifty, fifteen, and five, and forty with the larger spheres. Social networks may be growing our base, and, in the process, reversing that balance.

> **"The amount of social capital you have is pretty fixed."**

On an even deeper level, there may be a physiological aspect of friendship that virtual connections can never replace. This wouldn't surprise Dunbar, who discovered his number when he was studying the social bonding that occurs among primates through grooming. Over the past few years, Dunbar and his colleagues have been looking at the importance of touch in sparking the sort of neurological and physiological responses that, in turn, lead to bonding and friendship. "We underestimate how important touch is in the social world," he said. With a light brush on the shoulder, a pat, or a squeeze of the arm or hand, we can communicate a deeper bond than through speaking alone. "Words are easy. But the way someone touches you, even casually, tells you more about what they're thinking of you."

Dunbar already knew that in monkeys grooming activated the endorphin system.[7] Was the same true in humans? In a series of studies, Dunbar and his colleagues demonstrated that very light touch triggers a cascade of endorphins that, in turn, are important for creating personal relationships. Because measuring endorphin release directly is invasive — you either need to perform a spinal tap or a PET scan, and the latter, though considered safe, involves injecting a person with a radioactive tracer — they first looked at endorphin release indirectly. In one study, they examined pain thresholds: how long a person could keep her hand in a bucket of ice water (in a lab), or how long she could maintain a sitting position with no chair present (back against the wall, legs bent at a ninety degree angle) in the field.[8] When your body is flooded with endorphins, you're able to withstand pain for longer than you could before, so pain tolerance is often used as a proxy for endorphin levels. The longer you can stand the pain, the more endorphins have been released into your system. They found that a shared experience of laughter — a synchronous, face-to-face experience — prior to immersion, be it in the lab (watching a neutral or funny movie with others) or in a natural setting (theatre performances at the 2008 Edinburgh Fringe Festival) enabled people to hold their hands in ice or maintain the chair position significantly longer than they'd previously been able to.

Next, in an ongoing study, Dunbar and his colleagues looked at how endorphins were activated in the brain directly, through PET scans, a procedure that lets you look at how different neural receptors uptake endorphins. The researchers saw the same thing that happened with monkeys, and that had earlier been demonstrated with humans that were viewing positive emotional stimuli: when subjects in the scanner were lightly touched, their bodies released endorphins.[9] "We were nervous we wouldn't find anything because the touch was so light," Dunbar said. "Astonishingly, we saw a phenomenal response." In fact, this makes a great deal of sense and answers a lot of long-standing questions about our sensory receptors, he explained. Our skin has a set of neurons, common to all mammals, that respond to light stroking, but not to any other kind of touch. Unlike other touch receptors, which operate on a loop—you touch a hot stove, the nerves fire a signal to the brain, the brain registers pain and fires a signal back for you to withdraw your hand—these receptors are one-way. They talk to the brain, but the brain doesn't communicate back. "We think that's what they exist for, to trigger endorphin responses as a consequence of grooming," Dunbar said. Until social media can replicate that touch, it can't fully replicate social bonding.

But, the truth is, no one really knows how relevant the Dunbar number will remain in a world increasingly dominated by virtual interactions. The brain is incredibly plastic, and, from past research[10] on social interaction, we know that early childhood experience is crucial in developing those parts of the brain that are largely dedicated to social interaction, empathy, and other interpersonal concerns.[11] Deprive a child of interaction and touch early on, and those areas won't develop fully. Envelop her in a huge family or friend group, with plenty of holding and shared experience, and those areas grow bigger. So what happens if you're raised from a young age to see virtual interactions as akin to physical ones? "This is the big imponderable," Dunbar said. "We haven't yet seen an entire generation that's grown up with things like Facebook go through adulthood yet." Dunbar himself doesn't have a firm opinion one way or the other about whether virtual social networks will prove wonderful for friendships or ultimately diminish the number of satisfying interactions one has. "I don't think we have enough evidence to argue either way," he said.

One concern, though, is that some social skills may not develop as effectively when so many interactions exist online. We learn how we are and aren't supposed to act by observing others and then having opportunities to act out our observations ourselves. We aren't born with full social awareness, and Dunbar fears that too much virtual interaction may subvert that education. "In the sandpit of life, when somebody kicks sand in your face, you can't get out of the sandpit. You have to deal with it, learn, compromise," he said. "On the internet, you can pull the plug and walk away. There's no forcing mechanism that makes us have to learn." If you spend most of your time online, you may not get enough in-person group experience to learn how to properly interact on a large scale—a fear that, some early evidence suggests, may be materializing.[12] "It's quite conceivable that we might end up less social in the future, which would be a disaster because we need to be more social—our world has become so large," Dunbar said. The more our virtual friends replace our face-to-face ones, in fact, the more our Dunbar number may shrink.

NOTES

1. *MIT Encyclopedia of Cognitive Science*, s.v. "Machiavellian Intelligence Hypothesis," by Andrew Whiten, http://ai.ato.ms/MITECS/Entry/whiten.html.
2. R. I. M. Dunbar, "Coevolution of Neocortical Size, Group Size and Language in Humans," *Behavioral and Brain Sciences* 16 (1993): 681–735.

3. W.-X. Zhou et al., "Discrete Hierarchical Organization of Social Group Sizes," *Proceedings of the Royal Society B* 272 (2005): 439–44.

4. R. A. Hill and R. I. M. Dunbar, "Social Network Size in Humans," *Human Nature* 14, no. 1 (2003): 53–72.

5. Nicole B. Ellison et al., "Connection Strategies: Social Capital Implications of Facebook-Enabled Communication Practices," *New Media Society* 13 (2011): 873–92.

6. Curtis D. Hardin and Terri D. Conley, "A Relational Approach to Cognition: Shared Experience and Relationship Affirmation in Social Cognition," in *Cognitive Social Psychology: The Princeton Symposium on the Legacy and Future of Social Cognition*, ed. Gordon B. Moskowitz (Mahwah, NJ: Lawrence Erlbaum Associates Publishers, 2001), 3–17.

7. R. I. Dunbar, "The Social Role of Touch in Humans and Primates: Behavioural Function and Neurobiological Mechanisms," *Neuroscience and Biobehavioral Reviews* 34, no. 2 (2010): 260–68.

8. R. I. M. Dunbar et al., "Social Laughter Is Correlated with an Elevated Pain Threshold," *Proceedings of the Royal Society B* 279 (2012): 1161–67.

9. M. J. Koepp et al., "Evidence for Endogenous Opioid Release in the Amygdala during Positive Emotion," *NeuroImage* 44, no. 1 (2009): 252–56.

10. Jack P. Shonkoff and Deborah A. Phillips, eds., *From Neurons to Neighborhoods: The Science of Early Childhood Development* (Washington, DC: National Academy Press, 2000).

11. Charles A. Nelson, "Neural Plasticity and Human Development," *Current Directions in Psychological Science* 8, no. 2 (1999): 42–45.

12. Aimee L. Drolet and Michael W. Morris, "Rapport in Conflict Resolution: Accounting for How Face-to-Face Contact Fosters Mutual Cooperation in Mixed-Motive Conflicts," *Journal of Experimental Social Psychology* 36, no. 1 (2000): 26–50; Mitzi M. Montoya-Weiss et al., "Getting It Together: Temporal Coordination and Conflict Management in Global Virtual Teams," *Academy of Management Journal* 44, no. 6 (2001): 1251–62.

Exploring Context

1. Examine your list of friends on Facebook or another social media or online gaming site. How many of them are "real" friends? Try applying the rule of three to your list of friends. Does your experience confirm or challenge Konnikova's argument?

2. After you've examined your list of friends from Question 1 of Exploring Context, compare that list to the numbers you keep in your phone. Does the number of people you call relate to the Dunbar number? Does your phone reflect closer friendships than your social media presence?

3. Use a Web search engine to look for images of the Dunbar number. How do these visual representations help explain the concept?

Questions for Connecting

1. This essay seems to imply that extended connections through social media are less meaningful than the friendships at various levels of the "rule of three." Use the experiences of Dan Savage and Urvashi Vaid in "It Gets Better" (p. 406) and "Action Makes It Better" (p. 411) to evaluate Konnikova's thoughts about real and virtual connections. Given that both Savage and Vaid used social media to help LGBTQ youth, how might even tenuous connections have value?

2. Konnikova discusses brain research to support her exploration of friendships and social media. In "Attention Deficit: The Brain Syndrome of Our Era" (p. 373), Richard Restak also looks at the relationship between our behaviors and our brain. Synthesize the work of these two authors to consider the ways technology is changing our brains. How might "modern nerves" change our ability to relate to people in person? Could the rule of three mitigate our fragmented attention? You might also want to use your work from Question 3 of Questions for Critical Reading.

3. Given the ways in which connections can proliferate on social media, what are the risks of maintaining these connections? Consider the ways in which Konnikova's argument might help explain the phenomenon of sexting, as explained by Hanna Rosin in "Why Kids Sext" (p. 388). Is it easier to share photographs of others when they are not a part of your close circle? Work with your definitions of the terms from Konnikova's essay from Question 1 of Questions for Critical Reading.

Language Matters

1. Most often Konnikova spells out numbers, though occasionally she uses numerals instead. Using a grammar handbook or other reference resource, review the rules for writing numbers. When should they be spelled out, and when should numerals be used? Apply your findings to Konnikova's text. Does she follow these rules? How can you bring these insights to your own writing?

2. Quotations should always be integrated fluidly. Locate three instances where Konnikova includes quotations. What strategies does she use to integrate quotations into her own sentences? How can you apply these techniques to your own writing?

3. Editors often use correction symbols; your instructor might use them as well. Design symbols to represent some common errors you make. How are design and meaning related? Would your symbols make immediate sense to someone else?

Assignments for Writing

1. Write a paper in which you evaluate virtual friendships. Do they have advantages that Konnikova doesn't consider? You may want to use your work from Question 2 of Questions for Critical Reading and Question 1 of Questions for Connecting.

2. Robin Dunbar's research focuses on the relationship between the social and the biological. Write a paper in which you evaluate the ways in which culture is determined by biology. Are we limited by our biological impulses or can we transcend them? You may find your work from Question 3 of Questions for Critical Reading useful.

3. How does technology influence social and biological evolution? Write a paper in which you use Konnikova's work to consider the ways in which technology is affecting our development. Draw from your work in Question 3 of Questions for Critical Reading in making your response.

ARIEL LEVY

Ariel Levy, by permission

Ariel Levy, a staff writer at the *New Yorker*, has been called "feminism's newest and most provocative voice" by Malcolm Gladwell. While she has written many in-depth profiles on popular figures — Donatella Versace, Jude Law, and John Waters, to name a few — her work on gender and modern feminism has sparked the greatest interest from her readers. Her essays have appeared in publications as varied as the *New Yorker*, *Vogue*, and *Blender*. Levy received the National Magazine Award for Essays and Criticism for her piece "Thanksgiving in Mongolia," which appears in the 2014 *Best American Essays* anthology.

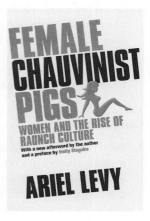

Levy's first book-length project, *Female Chauvinist Pigs: Women and the Rise of Raunch Culture* (2005), was inspired by a tag-along with the crew of the pornographic Girls Gone Wild series. Levy was bewildered that the girls participating in these videos, who take their clothes off for little more than attention and a GGW trucker cap, saw their participation as "liberating." This discovery led Levy to explore the ramifications of the "post-feminist" society that propagates this kind of thinking.

In the chapter included here, Levy identifies the subject of her work — Female Chauvinist Pigs (or *FCP*s for short). FCPs are seemingly educated women, many in positions of power, who participate in the very male-dominated culture of raunch and bawdiness that has plagued and exploited women for generations. When Levy connects the behavior she's noticing in popular culture to Harriet Beecher Stowe's *Uncle Tom's Cabin*, she ends up making a striking argument about gender politics and their effect on the oppressed — whoever those oppressed may be.

▶ TAGS: *community, culture, gender, identity, judgment and decision-making, media, politics*
▶ CONNECTIONS: *Gay, Padawer, Pozner, Serano*

Questions for Critical Reading

1. According to Levy, why is raunch appealing to some women? Mark passages where Levy uses her own language to describe why women engage in raunch culture, and passages where she uses other people's words/ideas to explore why raunch behavior is attractive. What differences can you find between Levy's explanations and the explanations of those she interviews?

2. What kinds of women does Levy use as examples to convey her points? What specific types of women does Levy define in her text, and how have these different definitions emerged?

3. What role, would Levy say, do men play in the production and perpetuation of not only raunch culture, but also definitions of gender and sex? Mark passages that support your position and pay particular attention to Levy's discussion of "Tomming," explaining its role in this process.

Female Chauvinist Pigs

On the first warm day of spring 2000, the organization New York Women in Film & Television threw a brunch to honor Sheila Nevins, a twenty-six-year veteran of HBO and their president of documentary and family programming. It was held in a grand, street-level room off Park Avenue, in which they'd assembled an impressive selection of stylish women, seasonal berries, and high-end teas. Through the windows you could see the passing streams of yellow taxis sparkling in the midtown sunlight.

But the vibe was more *Lifetime Intimate Portrait* than *Sex and the City*. "I was growing up in a society where women were quiet so I got to listen," Nevins reflected from the podium, where she sat lovely and serene in a pale pink shawl. "I like to laugh, I like to cry, the rest is paperwork."

Nevins is a big deal. She was once profiled as one of the "25 Smartest Women in America" along with Tina Brown, Susan Sontag, and Donna Brazile in *Mirabella*. *Crain's* has called Nevins "a revered player." Under her stewardship, HBO programs and documentary films have won seventy-one Emmy awards, thirteen Oscars, and twenty-two George Foster Peabody awards, including Nevins's own personal Peabody. In 2000, Nevins was inducted into the Broadcasting and Cable Hall of Fame, and she has received Lifetime Achievement Awards from the International Documentary Association and the Banff Television Festival. In 2002, Nevins was named the National Foundation for Jewish Culture's "Woman of Inspiration." She is an elegant blonde with a husband and a son and a glamorous, lucrative career that even involves an intimidating level of gravitas: She has overseen the making of films about the Holocaust, cancer, and war orphans.

At that breezy spring breakfast, all the women wore glazed, reverential expressions as they picked at their melon wedges and admired Nevins's sharp wit, keen intellect, and zebra-printed slides. "Who opened your career doors for you?" one wanted to know.

"Me," Nevins replied.

A tweedy gentleman with a bow tie started his question with, "I'm just the token guy . . ."

Nevins gave a little snort and said, "You're all tokens," and everyone had a good laugh.

But then a curly-haired woman in the back brought up *G-String Divas*, a late-night "docu-soap" Nevins executive produced, which treated audiences to extended showings of T & A sandwiched between interviews with strippers about tricks of the trade and their real-life sexual practices. "Why would a woman—a middle-aged woman with a child—make a show about strippers?" the woman asked. Everyone was stunned.

5

Nevins whipped around in her chair. "You're talking fifties talk! Get with the program!" she barked. "I love the sex stuff, I love it! What's the big deal?"

In fact, there *was* something vaguely anachronistic about this woman compared   10
to the rest with their blowouts and lip liner. She adjusted her eyeglasses, visibly shaken, but persisted. "Why is it still the case that if we're going to have a series about women on television, it has to be about their bodies and their sexuality?"

Nevins shook her head furiously. "Why is it that women will still go after women taking their clothes off and not after all the injustices in the workplace? I don't get it! As if women taking off their clothes is disgusting and degrading. Not being able to feed your kids, *that's* disgusting and degrading!"

"But . . ."

"Everyone has to bump and grind for what they want," Nevins interrupted. "Their bodies are their instruments and if I had that body I'd play it like a Stradivarius!"*

"But . . ."

"The women are beautiful and the men are fools! What's the problem?"   15

"But you're not really answering my question."

Of course not. Because part of the answer is that nobody wants to be the frump at the back of the room anymore, the ghost of women past. It's just not cool. What *is* cool is for women to take a guy's-eye view of pop culture in general and live, nude girls in particular. *You're worried about strippers?* Nevins seemed on the verge of hollering at her inquisitor, *Honey, they could teach you a thing or two about where it's at!* Nevins was threatening something she clearly considered far worse than being objectified: being out of touch.

If you are too busy or too old or too short to make a Stradivarius of yourself, then the least you can do is appreciate that achievement in others, or so we are told. If you still suffer from the (hopelessly passé) conviction that valuing a woman on the sole basis of her hotness is, if not disgusting and degrading, then at least dehumanizing, if you still cling to the (pathetically deluded) hope that a more abundant enjoyment of the "sex stuff" could come from a reexamination of old assumptions, then you are clearly stuck in the past (and you'd better get a clue, but quick).

If I told you that I'd met someone who executive produces a reality show about strippers, who becomes irritable and dismissive when faced with feminist debate, and who is a ferocious supporter of lap dances, you might reasonably assume I was talking about a man—the kind of man we used to call a Male Chauvinist Pig. But no. I'm talking about the Jewish Woman of Inspiration. I'm talking about an urbane, articulate, extremely successful woman who sits on a high perch in the middle of the mainstream, and I *could* be talking about any number of other women, because the ideas and emotions Nevins gave voice to are by no means uniquely her own: They are the status quo.

> **She is post-feminist. She is funny. She *gets it*.**

We decided long ago that the Male   20
Chauvinist Pig was an unenlightened rube, but the Female Chauvinist Pig (FCP) has risen to a kind of exalted status. She is post-feminist. She is funny. She *gets it*. She doesn't mind cartoonish stereotypes of female sexuality, and she doesn't mind a

---

*Stradivarius: Violin made in the workshop of Antonio Stradivari (1644–1737); a shorthand for excellence [Ed.].

cartoonishly macho response to them. The FCP asks: Why throw your boyfriend's *Playboy* in a freedom trash can when you could be partying at the Mansion? Why worry about *disgusting* or *degrading* when you could be giving—or getting—a lap dance yourself? Why try to beat them when you can join them?

There's a way in which a certain lewdness, a certain crass, casual manner that has at its core a me-Tarzan-you-Jane mentality can make people feel equal. It makes us feel that way because we are all Tarzan now, or at least we are all pretending to be. For a woman like Nevins, who "grew up in a society where women were quiet" and still managed to open all her career doors herself, this is nothing new. She has been functioning—with enormous success—in a man's world for decades. Somewhere along the line she had to figure out how to be one of the guys.

Nevins is (still) what used to be known as a "loophole woman," an exception in a male-dominated field whose presence supposedly proves its penetrability. (The phrase was coined by Caroline Bird in her book *Born Female: The High Cost of Keeping Women Down*, published in 1968.) Women in powerful positions in entertainment were a rare breed when Nevins started out, and they remain so today. In 2003, women held only 17 percent of the key roles—executive producers, producers, directors, writers, cinematographers, and editors—in making the top 250 domestic grossing films. (And progress is stalled: The percentage of women working on top films hasn't changed since 1998.) Meanwhile on television, men outnumbered women by approximately four to one in behind-the-scenes roles in the 2002–2003 prime-time season, which was also the case for the preceding four seasons. What the statistics indicate more clearly than the entertainment industry's permeability is a woman like Nevins's own vulnerability. To hang on to her position, she has to appear that much more confident, aggressive, and unconflicted about her choices—she has to do everything Fred Astaire* does, backward, in heels.

Women who've wanted to be perceived as powerful have long found it more efficient to identify with men than to try and elevate the entire female sex to their level. The writers Mary McCarthy and Elizabeth Hardwick were famously contemptuous of "women's libbers," for example, and were untroubled about striving to "write like a man." Some of the most glamorous and intriguing women in our history have been compared to men, either by admirers or detractors. One of poet Edna St. Vincent Millay's many lovers, the young editor John Bishop, wrote to her in a letter, "I think really that your desire works strangely like a man's." In an August 2001 article for *Vanity Fair*, Hillary Clinton's biographer Gail Sheehy commented that "from behind, the silhouette of the freshman senator from New York looks like that of a man." A high school classmate of Susan Sontag's told her biographers Carl Rollyson and Lisa Paddock that young "Sue" maintained a "masculine kind of independence." Judith Regan, the most feared and famous executive in publishing—and the woman who brought us Jenna Jameson's best-selling memoir—is fond of bragging, "I have the biggest cock in the building!" at editorial meetings (and referring to her detractors as "pussies"). There is a certain kind of woman—talented, powerful, unrepentant—whom we've always found difficult to describe without some version of the phrase "like a man," and

---

*Fred Astaire: Celebrated American actor and dancer (1899–1987); his most famous dance partner was Ginger Rogers (1911–1995), who was said to do everything that Astaire did, backwards, in high heels [Ed.].

plenty of those women have never had a problem with that. Not everyone cares that this doesn't do much for the sisterhood.

Raunch provides a special opportunity for a woman who wants to prove her mettle. It's in fashion, and it is something that has traditionally appealed exclusively to men and actively offended women, so producing it or participating in it is a way both to flaunt your coolness and to mark yourself as different, tougher, looser, funnier—a new sort of loophole woman who is "not like other women," who is instead "like a man." Or, more precisely, like a Female Chauvinist Pig.

Sherry, Anyssa, and Rachel are a trio of friends who share a taste for raunch: *Maxim*,   25
porn, Howard Stern, *Playboy*, you name it. All three are in their late twenties and, on the night we met, they had recently returned to New York City from a postcolle-giate spring break. Rachel, a registered nurse, a tough, compact girl with short red hair, had brought the others a memento: a postcard picturing a woman's tumescent breasts against a background of blue sky with the words *Breast wishes from Puerto Rico!* scrawled in loopy cursive across the top.

"When I first moved to New York, I couldn't get over Robin Byrd," said Rachel. She was talking about New York City's local-access television sex queen. Byrd has been on cable since 1977, hosting a show in which male and female performers strip and plug their upcoming appearances in clubs or magazines or porn movies. The finale of each show is Byrd—herself a former adult film performer—going around and licking or fondling each of her guest's breasts or genitals. "I wouldn't go out till I watched Robin Byrd, and when I did go out, I would talk about Robin Byrd," Rachel said. "Watching Robin Byrd doesn't turn me on, though. It's for humor."

"Yeah, it's all comical to me," Sherry agreed. Sherry had just completed her first day at a new job as an advertising account executive, and Rachel gave her a little congratu-latory gift: a thick red pencil with a rubber Farrah Fawcett head smiling on one end.

All three of them loved *Charlie's Angels* growing up, but more recently they had become "obsessed" with Nevins's show *G-String Divas*. "The other day we were on the subway and I wanted to dance on the pole in the middle," said Anyssa. "I could never be a stripper myself, but I think it would be so sexually liberating." Her looks were not holding her back. Anyssa was a Stradivarius . . . a built, beautiful young woman with milky skin and silky hair and a broad, lipsticked mouth. She aspired to be an actress, but in the meantime she was working at a bar near Union Square. "When I'm bartend-ing, I don't dress up though," she said. "Because I have to deal with enough assholes as it is. In college, Sherry and I, by day we would wear these guy outfits, and then at night we'd get dressed up, and people would be like, *Oh my God!* It's like a card . . . you pull out the hot card and let them look at you and it takes it to a whole different level." Anyssa smiled. "And maybe you get to *feel* like a stripper does."

Everyone was quiet for a moment, savoring that possibility.

I suggested there were reasons one might not want to feel like a stripper, that spin-   30
ning greasily around a pole wearing a facial expression not found in nature is more a parody of female sexual power than an expression of it. That did not go over well.

"I can't feel bad for these women," Sherry snapped. "I think they're asking for it."

Sherry considered herself a feminist. "I'm very pro-woman," she said. "I like to see women succeed, whether they're using their minds to do it or using their tits." But she didn't mind seeing women fail, either, if they weren't using both effectively. She liked the Howard Stern show, for example, because his is a realm in which fairness of a sort pervades: Women who are smart and funny like Sherry, or Stern's sidekick, the FCP Robin Quivers, get to laugh along with the boys. (Quivers has always been the mitigating presence that saves Stern's shows from being entirely frightening. His trademark shtick, getting female guests to take off their clothes so his staff can ogle or mock them, would seem a lot creepier if Quivers—a smart, articulate, fully clothed black woman—wasn't there to reassure the viewer or listener that there was a way out, an alternate role for a woman on the show. But then, Quivers is pretty much the only one who gets that option—the other women Stern invites into his universe are either hot or crazy or, his favorite, both.) The women who are pathetic enough to go on national television and strip down to their underwear in the hopes that Howard will buy them a boob job are punished with humiliation. Sherry and her friends found something about this routine reassuring. They seemed satisfied by what they experienced as justice being meted out; it was like the pleasure some people get watching the police throw the bad guys against the hood of their cars on *Cops*.

"Yeah, we're all women, but are we supposed to band together?" said Anyssa. "Hell, no. I don't trust women. Growing up, I hung out with all guys . . . these are the first girls I ever hung out with who had the same mentality as me and weren't going to starve themselves and paint their nails every fucking second. I've never been a girly-girl, and I've never wanted to compete in that world. I just didn't fit in."

Anyssa is not different from most FCPs: They want to be like men, and profess to disdain women who are overly focused on the appearance of femininity. But men seem to like those women, those girly-girls, or like to look at them, at least. So to *really* be like men, FCPs have to enjoy looking at those women, too. At the same time, they wouldn't mind being looked at a little bit themselves. The task then is to simultaneously show that you are not the same as the girly-girls in the videos and the Victoria's

> **But men seem to like those women, those girly-girls, or like to look at them, at least.**

Secret catalogs, but that you approve of men's appreciation for them, and that possibly you too have some of that same sexy energy and underwear underneath all your aggression and wit. A passion for raunch covers all the bases.

Twenty-two-year-old Erin Eisenberg, a city arts administrator, and her little sister Shaina, a student at Baruch College, kept a stack of men's magazines—*Playboy*, *Maxim*, *FHM*—on the floor of the bedroom they still shared in their parents' apartment. "A lot of times I say, Oh, she looks good, or check out that ass, but sometimes I'm also like, This is so airbrushed, or Oh, her tits are fake or whatever," said Erin. "I try not to be judgmental, but sometimes it's there."

"I pick up *Playboy* because I want to see who's on the cover," said Shaina. "The other day Shannen Doherty was on one and I just wanted to see what her breasts looked like."

The magazines and raunch culture in general piqued their curiosity and provided them with inspiration. Erin said, "There's countless times in my life where I know I've turned people on just by showing off." By putting on a little performance, making out with another girl, for instance. "It moved into Oh, this turns guys on if you do it in public. Having had that experience in a real-life setting, it was almost as if I was on *The Man Show* or something like that. But those times, it wasn't as sexy as in my fantasies."

Both Eisenberg sisters said they were "not easily offended," and Erin felt she had "a higher tolerance for sexual harassment" than most women.

"I went out with my friend a couple weeks ago and some guy touched her ass and she flipped out at him," said Shaina. "I was just like, Dude, he slapped your ass. To me that would be no big deal—if anything, I'd be flattered."

"You have to understand, a man is a man; it doesn't matter what position he's in," Erin said. "I have a lot of male friends. I feel conflicted being a woman, and I think I make up for it by trying to join the ranks of men. I don't think I have a lot of feminine qualities."   40

"You're not a girly-girl," Shaina cut in. "Like, her priority is not, *Am I gonna go get a manicure?*"

"Girly-girl" has become the term women use to describe exactly who they do not want to be: a prissy sissy. Girly-girls are people who "starve themselves and paint their nails every fucking second," as Anyssa put it; people who have nothing better to think about than the way they look. But while the FCP shuns girly-girls from her social life, she is fixated on them for her entertainment. Nobody has to wax as much as a porn star, and most strippers wouldn't be caught dead without a manicure. Weirdly, these are the women—the ultimate girly-girls—who FCPs spend their time thinking about.

Like Sherry, Erin Eisenberg professed an interest in feminism, and she showed me her copy of *The Feminine Mystique* to prove it. "But I don't try to espouse my ideas to everyone else," she said. "I'd rather observe and analyze on my own, and then do something else—further myself in other ways rather than start a debate. I gain strength by not exerting that energy."

"Gaining strength" is the key. FCPs have relinquished any sense of themselves as a collective group with a linked fate. Simply by being female and getting ahead, by being that strong woman we hear so much about, you are doing all you need to do, or so the story goes.

Carrie Gerlach, then an executive at Sony Pictures in Los Angeles, wrote in an e-mail in 2001:   45

> My best mentors and teachers have always been men. Why? Because I have great legs, great tits, and a huge smile that God gave to me. Because I want to make my first million before the age of thirty-five. So of course I am a female chauvinist pig. Do you think those male mentors wanted me telling them how to better their careers, marketing departments, increase demographics? Hell no, They wanted to play in my secret garden. But I applied the Chanel war paint, pried the door open with Gucci heels, worked, struggled and climbed the ladder. And made a difference!!! And I did it all in a short Prada suit.

Gerlach made no bones about wanting to "climb the ladder" so she could enjoy life's ultimate riches, namely Prada, Gucci, and Chanel. The ends justify the means, and the means are "great legs" and "great tits."

"Everyone wants to make money," said Erin Eisenberg, the daughter of a pair of erstwhile hippies. ("My dad claims he was a socialist," she said skeptically.) Where her parents had misgivings about the system, Erin has doubts only about its lower rungs. Gone is the sixties-style concern (and lip service) about society as a whole. FCPs don't bother to question the criteria on which women are judged, they are too busy judging other women themselves.

"Who doesn't want to be looked at as a sex symbol?" said Shaina. "I always tell people, if I had a twenty-three-inch waist and a great body, I would pose in *Playboy*. You know all those guys are sitting there staring at you, *awe-ing* at you. That must be power."

If we are to look for a precedent for this constellation of ideas and behaviors, we can find it in an unlikely place . . . a novel written before the Civil War. Published in 1852, Harriet Beecher Stowe's *Uncle Tom's Cabin* sold more copies than any book besides the Bible in the nineteenth century, and it is still widely considered to be the most historically significant novel ever written by an American author. Since it was first published, Stowe's book has been credited with having an enormous impact on the way Americans conceive of race. During Stowe's tour of Great Britain in 1853, the minister sent to greet her congratulated her by saying "that the voice which most effectively kindles enthusiasm in millions is the still small voice which comes forth from the sanctuary of a woman's breast." (Stowe proudly relayed his words in her travel book *Sunny Memories of Foreign Lands*.) These sentiments were echoed ten years later by Abraham Lincoln, who famously called Stowe the "little lady who made this big war" when he met her just after he issued the Emancipation Proclamation.

While Stowe inarguably advanced the cause of abolition (and intensified the ten- 50 sions over slavery that helped ignite the Civil War), she has also been blamed for exacerbating "the wrongheadedness, distortions and wishful thinkings about Negroes in general and American Negroes in particular that still plague us today," as the critic J. C. Furnas wrote in 1956. Stowe created various characters who "transcend" their race—which is to say that instead of acting "like a man" (or trying to), they "act white." One of Stowe's protagonists is a slave character, George Harris, who is light-skinned enough to pass as "a Spanish gentleman." But it is not just the skin Stowe gave him that allows George to move through her fictive society and her reader's imagination distinct from other slaves. In "Everybody's Protest Novel," an essay on *Uncle Tom's Cabin* published in the *Partisan Review* in 1949, James Baldwin* wrote that Stowe crafted George "in all other respects as white as she can make" him; Stowe created George "a race apart" from Tom and his fellow slaves.

The converse strategy for coping with race in Stowe's text is the one that has become notorious, and it is, of course, the one exhibited by Uncle Tom. Tom, remember, is a creation of Stowe's who so thoroughly accepts his oppression as a slave, he renders the standard appurtenances of enslavement unnecessary. When a slave trader transports him for sale, Tom can be left unshackled; there is no chance he will run away because he has so completely internalized the system of which he is a victim. He believes that he really *is* property, so to run away would be to rob his owner, a crime he wouldn't dream of committing.

---

*James Baldwin: Noted African American essayist, novelist, and playwright (1924–1987), who in reaction to the poor treatment of blacks and homosexuals, spent many of the later years of his life in Europe [Ed.].

Consequently, Tom is thought of by his masters—and by Stowe herself—as "steady," "honest," "sensible," and "pious." Not only does Tom submit to the system that oppresses him, he actively strives for the love of his oppressor, and loves him in return. George Shelby, the man Tom has served since his birth, is too ashamed to say good-bye to Tom after he literally sells him down the river, thus separating Tom from his wife, children, and home, and condemning him to a bleak and lethally brutal future. Yet Tom's wistful parting words as he is carted off to the auction block are, "Give my love to Mas'r George."

> **Not only does Tom submit to the system that oppresses him, he actively strives for the love of his oppressor, and loves him in return.**

Stowe wanted Tom to serve as a heartbreaking and representative example of the "soft, impressible nature of his kindly race, ever yearning toward the simple and childlike." In her book, this is simply the character's character. But the concept of an Uncle Tom has taken on a meaning very different from the one Stowe intended. An Uncle Tom is a person who deliberately upholds the stereotypes assigned to his or her marginalized group in the interest of getting ahead with the dominant group.

In a discussion of "Tom shows," the staged adaptations of *Uncle Tom's Cabin* that became wildly popular after the book's publication (and remained so into the 1930s), author Mary C. Henderson describes a "theatrical industry called 'Tomming,'" in which "Uncle Tom's original character was almost totally obliterated in the worst and cheapest dramatizations. Somewhere in tents set among the cornfields he lost his dignity and his persona and became the servile, obedient, sycophantic black man who gave the term 'Uncle Tom' its terrible taint."

Tomming, then, is conforming to someone else's—someone more powerful's—distorted notion of what you represent. In so doing, you may be getting ahead in some way—getting paid to dance in blackface in a Tom show, or gaining favor with Mas'r as Stowe's hero did in literature—but you are simultaneously reifying the system that traps you. 55

The notions of "acting white," as Stowe crafted George Harris to, and "acting black," as she decided Uncle Tom did (thus expressing the "nature of his kindly race"), are both predicated on the assumption that there is a fixed, unchanging essence of whiteness and another of blackness which can then be imitated. James Baldwin wrote, "We take our shape, it is true, within and against that cage of reality bequeathed us at our birth; and yet it is precisely through our dependence on this reality that we are most endlessly betrayed." The cage in which we "find ourselves bound, first without, then within," is the "nature of our categorization." We are defined and ultimately define ourselves, Baldwin argued, by the cultural meaning assigned to our broadest human details—blackness, whiteness, maleness, femaleness, and so on. In order to start Tomming, "acting black," we would necessarily have to first believe that there was such a thing as blackness to enact. And likewise, if we are going to act "like a man," there has to be an inherent manliness to which we can aspire.

It would be crazy to suggest that being a woman today (black or white) is anything remotely like being a slave (male or female) in antebellum America. There is obviously no comparison. But there are parallels in the ways we can think about the limits of what can be gained by "acting like" an exalted group or reifying the stereotypes attributed to a subordinate group. These are the two strategies an FCP uses to deal with her femaleness: either acting like a cartoon man—who drools over strippers, says things like "check out that ass," and brags about having the "biggest cock in the building"—or acting like a cartoon woman, who has big cartoon breasts, wears little cartoon outfits, and can only express her sexuality by spinning around a pole.

In a broader sense, both of these strategies have existed historically and continue to because to a certain extent they are unavoidable. Does a marginalized person—a female producer going to a job interview at an all-male film company, a Chinese attorney striving to make partner at an old-boy, white-shoe law firm,* a lesbian trying to fit in at a Big Ten keg party—need to act the way the people in charge expect in order to get what he or she wants? Without question. A certain amount of Tomming, of going along to get along, is part of life on planet Earth.

But Americans gave up the idea—or tried to, or pretended to—that there are certain characteristics and qualities that are essentially black and essentially white a long time ago. At the very least we can say that it would be considered wildly offensive and thoroughly idiotic to articulate ideas like that now. Yet somehow we don't think twice about wanting to be "like a man" or unlike a "girly-girl." As if those ideas even *mean* anything. Like which man? Iggy Pop? Nathan Lane? Jesse Jackson? Jesse Helms? It is a staggeringly unsophisticated way to think about being a human being, but smart people do it all the time.

The most obvious example in recent memory of someone intelligent espousing   60
such ideas publicly is the scholar Camille Paglia. Paglia notoriously proclaimed that "if civilization had been left in female hands, we would still be living in grass huts." That may be too puerile a provocation to bother with, but Paglia's more understated articulations of her beliefs about gender echo our still widely held cultural assumption that women are one way and men are another (and that there's nothing wrong with saying so). In an interview with *Spin* magazine (which Paglia liked enough to reprint in her book *Sex, Art, and American Culture*), Paglia defended her controversial views on date rape and assessed her critics:

> They have this stupid, pathetic, completely-removed-from-reality view of things that they've gotten from these academics who are totally off the wall, totally removed. Whereas my views on sex are coming from the fact that I am a football fan and I am a rock fan. Rock and football are revealing something true and permanent and eternal about male energy and sexuality. They are revealing the fact that women, in fact, *like* the idea of flaunting, strutting, wild masculine energy. The people who criticize me, these establishment feminists, these white upper-middle-class feminists in New York, especially, who think of themselves as so literate, the kind of music they like, is, like Suzanne Vega—you know, women's music.
> SPIN: *Yuck.*

---

*White-shoe law firm: Long-established, prestigious, and conservative firm run by Eastern elites [Ed.].

First off, one has to wonder if Paglia has ever heard of Patti Smith. Or Debbie Harry. Or Janis Joplin. Or Grace Jones. It seems as if she has temporarily forgotten even her idol, Madonna (the subject of two of Paglia's essays in that same book). Aren't these people women . . . who necessarily make women's music? Do these women not flaunt and strut and effuse the wild energy with which Paglia is so enthralled? Are they up-tight? Uncool?

Reducing "women's music" to something soft and neutered, something guaranteed to make her—female!—interviewer say "yuck," is a manipulative little move. It's a way for Paglia to separate herself from the human characteristics she finds most un-attractive—weakness, effeteness, pusillanimity—and to make these things "perma-nently and eternally" female. (Which, by the way, Paglia *is*.)

Paglia's equation of all things aggressive, arrogant, adventurous, and libidinous with masculinity, and her relegation of everything whiney, wimpy, needy, and com-placent to femininity, is, among other things, dopey. We have to wonder why a woman as crackling smart as Camille Paglia would be so unsophisticated in her conception of gender. We have to wonder why a woman as thoughtful as Sheila Nevins—a woman whose entire career is based on the intrepid exploration of complex stories—would have a knee-jerk reaction to a question that positioned her as a member of the female gender.

Instead of trying to reform other people's—or her own—perception of femininity, the Female Chauvinist Pig likes to position herself as something outside the normal bounds of womanhood. If defending her own little patch of turf requires denigrating other women—reducing them to "yuck" as Paglia does or airheads who prioritize manicures, or, Judith Regan's favorite, "pussies"—so be it.

It can be done very persuasively.   65

Mary Wells Lawrence was one of the first women in this country to start her own advertising agencies, certainly the most successful, and the first woman CEO of a company listed on the New York Stock Exchange. She stands out as one of the great giants of her industry, male or female. Wells Lawrence came up with the "I Love New York" campaign, which many people credit with resuscitating the city's image during the seventies; she also invented the weirdly unforgettable "Plop Plop Fizz Fizz" Alka-Seltzer ads.

One of her earliest successes was a colorful marketing strategy for Braniff Air-lines in the sixties that eventually prompted a transformation of the look of American airports. Wells Lawrence bucked the bland, military style of the times and had every Braniff plane painted a bright color. Then she hired Emilio Pucci to design riotous cos-tumes for the flight "hostesses." One of her ads featured what she called the "air strip," the process by which Braniff stewardesses pared down their Pucci flight uniforms little by little on the way to tropical destinations. Pucci "even made teeny-weeny bikinis for them, an inch of cloth," Wells Lawrence wrote in her memoir, *A Big Life (in Advertising)*. These ads, with their focus on pretty young women in escalating stages of undress, may have been what prompted Gloria Steinem to famously comment, "Mary Wells Uncle Tommed it to the top."

In her memoir, Wells Lawrence returned fire at Steinem. "What a silly woman," she wrote. "I wanted a big life. I worked as a man worked. I didn't preach it, I did it."

How scalding. How convincing. Who wouldn't pick action over nagging, succeed-ing over hand-wringing? Who doesn't want a big life?

There's just one thing: Even if you are a woman who achieves the ultimate and 70
becomes *like a man*, you will still always be like a woman. And as long as womanhood
is thought of as something to escape from, something less than manhood, you will be
thought less of, too.

There is a variety program on Comedy Central called *The Man Show*, which concludes
each episode with a segment of bouncing women appropriately called "Girls on Trampolines." The show's original hosts Jimmy Kimmel and Adam Carolla have left; Kimmel
now has his own network talk show, *Jimmy Kimmel Live*, on ABC, and both Kimmel and
Carolla executive produce *Crank Yankers* for Comedy Central. But when I went to visit
their set in L.A. in 2000, *The Man Show* was one of the top shows on cable, and it was
getting a lot of attention for its brand of self-described "chauvinistic fun." Thirty-eight
percent of *The Man Show's* viewers were female. It was co–executive produced by two
women.

Like Sheila Nevins, co–executive producer Jennifer Heftler was not who you'd expect to find as the wizard behind the curtain of a raunch operation. She was a big
woman who wore batik and had a tattoo of a dragonfly on her wrist and another of a
rose on her ankle. She described her program as "big, dumb, goofy fun."

"One of the perks to this job was that I wouldn't have to prove myself anymore,"
she said. "I could say, 'I worked at *The Man Show*' and no one would ever say 'Oh, that
prissy little woman' again." Heftler felt her female viewers' incentive for watching the
program was very much like her own for making it. "It's like a badge," she said. "Women
have always had to find ways to make guys comfortable with where we are, and this
is just another way of doing that. If you can show you're one of the guys, it's good."

The night I went to a taping, there wasn't enough space to fit all the guys who
had lined up outside the studio, and a team of heavy-limbed boys in matching green
T-shirts from Chico State were pumped to make it into the audience.

Don, the bald audience fluffer, seemed to be looking directly at them when he 75
yelled from the stage, "A few weeks ago we had trouble with guys touching the women
here. You can't just grab their asses—you don't do that in real life, do you? [Beat.]
Welllll . . . so do I!" The frat guys cheered, but not with the alarming gusto of the man
in front of them, a scrawny computer technician who resembled one of the P's in Peter,
Paul and Mary. "To the women," shouted Don, "today only, you're an honorary man!
Grab your dick!"

Abby, a brunette in tight white jeans, was called up to the stage for her big chance
to win a T-shirt. Honorary man status notwithstanding, she was asked to expose her
breasts. Abby declined, but agreed brightly to kiss another girl instead. A pert red-
head in her early twenties raced up from the audience to wrap her hands around
Abby's back and put her tongue in the stranger's mouth. "Yeah! Yeah! You're making me hard," shrieked Peter/Paul. He was nearly hit in the head by the Chico States-
man behind him, who pumped his fist in the air in front of his crotch, semaphoring
masturbation.

Soon after, the stage doors opened and out poured the Juggies, nine dancing girls
in coordinating pornographic nursery rhyme costumes: Little Red Riding Hood in
spike-heeled patent leather thighhighs, Bo Peep in a push-up bra so aggressive you
could almost see her nipples, and, of course, Puss 'n Boots.

They shimmied their way around the audience, and some did tricks on the poles like strippers. After the shouting died down, Adam Carolla and Jimmy Kimmel emerged from backstage, fresh as daisies in matching gingham shirts. "Who knows a good joke?" Carolla asked.

"How do you piss your girlfriend off when you're having sex?" a guy in the back volunteered. "Call her up and tell her."

Then they showed a pretaped spot about a mock clinic for wife evaluation, where 80
a prospective bride was assessed based on her grasp of football and her aptitude for administering fellatio to pornographer Ron Jeremy.

"There's a side to boydom that's fun," Jen Heftler declared. "They get to fart, they get to be loud — and I think now we're saying we can fart and curse and go to strip clubs and smoke cigars just as easily and just as well." As for the Juggies, we are supposed to experience them as kitsch. "In the sixties, Dean Martin had his Golddiggers, and they were basically Juggies," Heftler said, "but the audience wasn't in on the joke. It was just pretty girls because that's what a guy would have. Then it was, you can never have that, you can't show a woman as a sex object, that's terrible. Now we're back to having it, but it's kind of commenting on that as opposed to just being that. The girls are in on it, and the women watching it are in on it."

But after sitting in that audience, I have to wonder what exactly we are in on. That women are ditzy and jiggly? That men would like us to be?

"Listen," Heftler countered, "our generation has gone past the point where *The Man Show* is going to cause a guy to walk into a doctor's office and say, 'Oh, my God! A woman doctor!'"

Her co-executive producer, Lisa Page, a sweet, quiet woman, said, "It doesn't need to threaten us anymore."

The night after the taping, I had dinner with Carolla, Kimmel, and *The Man Show*'s 85
cocreator and executive producer, Daniel Kellison, at the restaurant inside the W Hotel in Westwood. I asked them why they supposed 38 percent of their viewers were women.

"We did a little research," said Carolla, "and it turns out 38 percent of all women have a sense of humor."

I laughed. I wanted to be one of those women. The women at the W were like another species: lush curves bursting off of impossibly thin frames and miles of hairless, sand-colored skin as far as the eye could see.

"It's a whole power thing that you take advantage of and career women take advantage of," Kellison offered. "If you read *Gear* or watch our show or Howard Stern or whatever, you have an overview of a cultural phenomenon, you have power. You take responsibility for your life and you don't walk around thinking, *I'm a victim of the press! I'm a victim of pop culture!* So you can laugh at girls on trampolines." He smiled warmly. "You get it."

For a moment I allowed myself to feel vaguely triumphant.

Kimmel sucked an oyster out of its shell and then snickered. "At TCA," the an- 90
nual Television Critics Association conference in Pasadena, "this woman asked, 'How does having a big-breasted woman in the Juggy dance squad differ from having black women in the darkie dance squad?' I said, 'First of all, that's the stupidest question I've ever heard.'"

"Then Adam said, 'Let me put your mind at ease: If we ever decide to put together a retarded dance squad, you'll be the first one in it,' " said Kellison, and all three of them laughed.

"What kind of women do you hang out with?" I asked them.

Kimmel looked at me like I was insane. "For the most part," he said, "*women* don't even want to hang out with their friends."

And there it is. The reason that being Robin Quivers or Jen Heftler or me, for that moment when I *got it*, is an ego boost but not a solution. It can be fun to feel exceptional—to be the loophole woman, to have a whole power thing, to be an honorary man. But if you are the exception that proves the rule, and the rule is that women are inferior, you haven't made any progress.

Exploring Context

1. Levy opens her essay by discussing HBO executive Sheila Nevins and, in particular, her decision to produce the show *G-String Divas*. Review Nevins's filmography at the Internet Movie Database (imdb.com/name/nm0627521). How much of her work reflects raunch culture? Is there any suggestion that she has changed since Levy wrote this essay?

2. What exactly is a *chauvinist*? What is the origin of the word? Use an online resource such as Wikipedia or Dictionary.com to define the term. How do its origins relate to the argument Levy is making?

3. The Bureau of Labor Statistics maintains data on earnings based on a variety of demographics (bls.gov/cps/earnings.htm#demographics). Explore this data. In economic terms, has raunch culture helped women generally? What other factors (age, race) affect economic success? Does Levy's discussion account for these factors?

Questions for Connecting

1. In "Preface" and "The New Civil Rights" (p. 539), Kenji Yoshino proposes that legal rulings are insufficient to address the social pressures that force individuals to "cover." Synthesize his discussion with Levy's concept of "Tomming." In what ways are Female Chauvinist Pigs "covering"? What social pressures might force them to do so?

2. How do issues of age and sexuality complicate Levy's argument? Consider the experiences of the young women in Hanna Rosin's "Why Kids Sext" (p. 388). How might young women negotiate the dangers of technology while also participating in raunch culture? Your responses to Questions 1 and 2 of Questions for Critical Reading might be helpful.

3. Consider the challenge that both Female Chauvinist Pigs and the transgender students of Wellesley College examined by Ruth Padawer in "Sisterhood Is Complicated" (p. 315) present to feminism. Synthesize the ideas of both authors to propose a definition of *feminism* that accounts for both groups.

Language Matters

1. Gender is a primary concern in this essay, and it is also an issue in writing. Writers use a variety of techniques to avoid sexist language, including alternating their use of *he* and *she* or employing the awkward construction *s/he*. Frequently, people use a plural pronoun with a singular antecedent to accomplish this goal — for example, "Someone who wants to avoid sexist language should watch their pronouns." Which method is best, leaving aside the rules of grammar? How might or must language change to accommodate nonsexist attitudes?

2. What is a hyphen? How is it used? Select a passage of this essay and revise it by adding hyphens. When would you use them in your own writing?

3. Raunch culture is closely related to class boundaries. What class boundaries exist in writing? Is slang an issue of class? Can you determine Levy's class from her writing? What class is reflected in academic writing? What level of class is reflected in the language used by the women Levy interviews?

Assignments for Writing

1. Levy discusses Female Chauvinist Pigs and raunch culture extensively. Write a paper in which you determine Levy's position on Female Chauvinist Pigs and raunch culture. Use specific quotations from her text that reveal her position.

2. Using Levy's ideas, write a paper in which you create a definition of *feminism*. Are Female Chauvinist Pigs feminists? Is feminism defined in opposition to Female Chauvinist Pigs? What are the goals of feminism? Incorporate your work on feminism from Question 3 of Questions for Connecting

3. Consider Levy's discussion of "Tomming." Extend her argument in that section by writing a paper in which you expand on the concept, providing additional examples that confirm or complicate her explanation of the concept.

YO-YO MA

© Lynn Goldsmith/Corbis

Cellist and songwriter **Yo-Yo Ma** began performing at five years old. In the more than half century since, he has won over seventeen Grammy Awards and has produced more than ninety albums. Ma has received numerous awards, including the World Economic Forum's Crystal Award (2008), the National Medal of Arts (2001), and the Presidential Medal of Freedom (2010); he was recognized as a Kennedy Center Honoree in 2011. He is a graduate of the Juilliard School and Harvard University.

"Necessary Edges: Arts, Empathy, and Education" was originally published on the *World-Post*, an online news and blog site created through a partnership between liberal news aggregator the *Huffington Post* and nonpartisan think tank the Berggruen Institute on Governance. The site was launched during the World Economic Forum in Davos, Switzerland, in January 2014, the same month as Ma's essay was published, and features high-profile contributors such as engineer and magnate Elon Musk, founder of electric car company Tesla; Tony Blair, the former prime minister of Great Britain; and Eric Schmidt, the executive chairman of Google.

In this essay, Ma considers the role of the arts in the world, arguing that the elements of empathy provided by artistic endeavors are essential to the kind of balanced thinking needed today. Ma thus advocates for STEAM education, which incorporates art into the science, technology, engineering, and mathematics curriculum. Together, art and science create an "edge effect" (p. 260) that promotes equilibrium and produces a global culture.

Does art have a role to play in the world? In education?

▶ TAGS: *art, collaboration, culture, education, empathy, globalism, science and technology*
▶ CONNECTIONS: *Appiah, DeGhett, Duhigg, Friedman, Fukuyama, Klosterman, Restak, Southan, Yang*

Questions for Critical Reading

1. What is the role of art? After writing your own thoughts in response to the question, read Ma's essay, paying attention to his thoughts about the benefits of art. Does his argument confirm or challenge your ideas?

2. Ma draws from neuroscience to make his argument. Note the places in the essay where he discusses empathy. How does empathy function in thinking and decision making?

3. As you read Ma's essay, look for his definitions of *necessary edges* and *edge effects*. How does he use these ideas to support his argument?

Necessary Edges: Arts, Empathy, and Education

In our highly interdependent global civilization, a lot of things are not working.

When I travel around the country and the world to perform, I pick up in my many conversations a growing sense that the first Enlightenment—which posited the rule of reason over emotion and feelings—is getting a little creaky, confining, and even counterproductive.

The neurobiologist Antonio Damasio has written about Descartes' error that, to put it in shorthand, "I think therefore I am." Damasio instead makes the compelling argument, empirically based in neurology, that feeling and emotions as expressed in art and music play a central role in high-level cognitive reasoning.

Advances in neurobiology now make it clear that we humans have dual neural pathways, one for critical thinking and one for empathetic thinking. Only one pathway can be activated at a time, so when one is on, the other is off. Yet we are also aware that wise and balanced judgment results from integrating the critical and empathetic, taking emotions as well as reason into account. While this can't be done in tandem, it does occur, we now know, through a loop-back process of layers of feedback.

These discoveries suggest that a new way of thinking is possible, a new conscious- 5
ness—perhaps a new Enlightenment—that brings the arts and science back together.

This new consciousness by which we purposely seek to bolster the integrative feedback loops of our dual neural pathways could provide a new energy for creativity in our weary civilization.

This integrative awareness is especially important today as our science-driven, technologically advanced world is breaking down into ever more compartments, specializations, and disciplines—even as the interdependence of globalization is creating more links with other cultures through which empathetic understanding is vital.

To be able to put oneself in another's shoes without prejudgment is an essential skill. Empathy comes when you understand something deeply through arts and literature and can thus make unexpected connections. These parallels bring you closer to things that would otherwise seem far away. Empathy is the ultimate quality that acknowledges our identity as members of one human family.

Visionaries like Elon Musk have spoken of the Internet and the planetary reach of the media as a "global thinking circuit." We need to be sure that this connecting circuit is about communication and not just information by fostering both empathetic and critical thinking.

From STEM to STEAM

Because the world economy is so hyper-competitive, much of the focus in education 10
these days from Singapore to Shanghai to American schools is on STEM—science, technology, engineering, and math. As important as that is, it is short-sighted. We need to add the empathetic reasoning of the arts to the mix—STEAM.

The values behind arts integration—collaboration, flexible thinking, and disciplined imagination—lead to the capacity to innovate. A pianist skilled to both read and improvise music is open to listening to what is around him but knows that, to reach excellence, he needs to filter the imagination through the discipline of knowledge. When he performs, you will know instantly if he has achieved that right balance and it works or not.

For me the most proficient way to teach the values of collaboration, flexibility, imagination, and innovation—all skill sets needed in today's world—is through the performing arts. If you have these tools, you can do well in any field from software engineering to the biosciences.

Empathy is the other key tool. Empathy and imagination, the artificial layering of different realities, are linked. Empathy is your capacity to imagine what someone else is going through; what they are thinking, feeling, and perceiving. That will not only give you an outlook on who they are—continually corrected by evidence—but also what your alternative possibilities are.

Empathetic thinking is something that is severely missing in education today that is only STEM oriented. Everyone wants innovation, recovering that inspired and innovative spirit of JFK talking about going to the moon. But you can't skim the top without the rest of it.

The arts teach us that there is something that connects us all and is bigger than each of us. In both places it is a matter of equilibrium, of centering the ego at the right point of balance between the individual and the community.   15

We are all addressing the same issues with different names attached to them.

STEAM will help us get there by resolving the education problem. Kids will then go to school because it is a passion and a privilege, not a requirement.

It's All about Equilibrium

Finding meaning and living—all of what we do as humans in society—occurs in that brain space between life and death. In our industrial societies there is a great deal of controversy these days over what life is and when it begins and how we approach the agony of death which, in industrial society, we try to avoid thinking about. Therefore we spend an unbelievable amount of money on medical care in those last few years before dying.

The arts help us cope with these issues by engaging, not avoiding, the deep emotions of intimate loss involved and retelling over and over again the story of the human condition and its limits. Only then can we can regain our spiritual balance and find meaning in more than trying to technically manage every aspect of our being from womb to tomb.

Necessary Edges

Equilibrium is what all life forms are seeking in order to survive. Evolution is the balance between stability and the changes necessary to cope with new challenges in the environment.   20

On this earth we can only survive within a very narrow bandwidth of conditions—oxygen, hydrogen, light, acidity, temperature.

Within that narrow bandwidth, most of what exists is concentrated in the middle. But, as we see in ecology, there are also "necessary edges." The "edge effect" in ecology occurs at the border where two ecosystems—for example the savannah and forest—meet. At that interface, where there is the least density and the greatest diversity of life forms, each living thing can draw from the core of the two ecosystems. That is where new life forms emerge.

In our advanced species, we also have these "necessary edges." The hard sciences are probing one far end of the bandwidth, searching for the origins of the universe or the secrets of the genome. People in the arts are probing the other far end of the bandwidth. Without the "necessary edges" that interface with a changing environment and find innovative response, the middle will go over the edge like lemmings. Those on the edge are, in effect, the scouts that say "there is a waterfall, there is a ledge, there is danger ahead. Stop. Don't go this way, go that way."

Equilibrium occurs when the information from the edges is available at the core.

Equilibrium occurs when the information from the edges is available at the core. Only when those meridians or pathways that connect the edges to the middle are open will a life-form survive, and even prosper. Only when science and the arts, critical and empathetic reasoning, are linked to the mainstream will we find a sustainable balance in society.

What is dangerous is when the center ignores the edges or the edges ignore the center—art for art's sake or science without a humanist and societal perspective. Then we are headed for doomsday without knowing it. 25

Globalization Creates Culture

My musical journeys have reinforced this point of view. What I've found is that the interactions brought about by globalization don't just destroy culture; they can create new culture and invigorate and spread traditions that have existed for ages precisely because of the "edge effect." Sometimes the most interesting things happen at the edge. The intersections there can reveal unexpected connections.

Culture is a fabric composed of gifts from every corner of the world. One way of discovering the world is by digging deeply into its traditions.

I have often used this example: At the core of any cellist's repertoire are the Cello Suites by Bach. At the heart of each suite is a dance movement called the sarabande.

The dance originated with music of the North African Berbers, where it was a slow, sensual dance. It next appeared in Spain, where it was banned because it was considered lewd and lascivious. Spaniards brought it to the Americas, but it also traveled on to France, where it became a courtly dance. In the 1720s, Bach incorporated the sarabande as a movement in his Cello Suites. Today, I play Bach, a Paris-born American musician of Chinese parentage. So who really owns the sarabande? Each culture has adopted the music, investing it with specific meaning, but each culture must share ownership: it belongs to us all.

In 1998, I founded the Silk Road Project to study the flow of ideas among the many cultures between the Mediterranean and the Pacific over several thousand years. When the Silk Road Ensemble performs, we try to bring much of the world together on one stage. Its members are a peer group of virtuosos, masters of living traditions, whether European, Arabic, Azeri, Armenian, Persian, Russian, Central Asian, Indian, Mongolian, Chinese, Korean, or Japanese. They all generously share their knowledge and are curious and eager to learn about other forms of expression.

Over the last several years, we have found that every tradition is the result of successful invention. One of the best ways to ensure the survival of traditions is by organic evolution, using all the tools available to us in the present day, from YouTube to the concert hall. 30

We Are More Than We Can Measure

We live in such a measuring society, people tend to put a person in a box they can put on their mental shelf. People think of me as a cellist because they can see my performances and take my measure as a musician. I think of my life as a musician as only the tip of an iceberg. That is only the audible part of my existence. Underneath the water is the life I'm leading, the thoughts I'm thinking, and the emotions that well up in me.

We all get into trouble if we think the universe only exists of the matter that we can see and measure, and not the anti-matter that is the counterpart that holds it all together.

Michelangelo famously said, "I liberate the statue from the marble." Similarly, my music emerges from the life all around me and the world we all share together. One is the condition of the other.

Exploring Context

1. According to Ma, "At the core of any cellist's repertoire are the Cello Suites by Bach" (p. 260). Using a search engine, look for videos of Ma playing Bach. Does his music reflect his argument in this essay? As you watch the entire video, do you observe elements that also support his ideas?

2. Apple is often cited as an example of a company that embodies STEAM education in its mix of technology and design. Explore Apple's Web site at apple.com, looking for elements that reflect Ma's argument. Does Apple reflect "necessary edges"? Use your work from Question 3 of Questions for Critical Reading in making your response.

3. Ma mentions his Silk Road Project. Explore the Web site for this endeavor at silkroadproject.org. How does this project reflect Ma's argument about the relationship between art, science, technology, and collaboration?

Questions for Connecting

1. Ma frequently discusses the importance of globalization and collaboration. These two elements are also central to Thomas L. Friedman's "The Dell Theory of Conflict Prevention" (p. 124). Synthesize the position of these two authors to consider the elements necessary for successful global collaboration. How does art function in global supply chains? Could empathy be used to combat terrorism? Consider using your work from Question 3 of Exploring Context.

2. Does Ma's argument change the answer to Rhys Southan's question in "Is Art a Waste of Time?" (p. 434). How does Ma's analysis change the relationship between art and effective altruism? Incorporate your answer from Question 1 of Questions for Critical Reading.

3. Synthesize Ma's essay with Graeme Wood's discussion of education in "Is College Doomed?" (p. 506). What role might technology play in the kind of education that Ma imagines? Does Minerva promote equilibrium?

Language Matters

1. How do the headings in Ma's essay contribute to your understanding of it? Devise new headings for this essay. Where would you make the divisions?

2. Ma uses a very clear organization to make his argument. Outline his essay and then consider how he uses organization to help prove his argument. How do the various sections build to a conclusion? How would the meaning of his essay change if it were rearranged? Apply what you learn to your own writing: How can you use organization to help prove your argument?

3. Ma uses acronyms in his essay, such as *STEM*. Review material on acronyms and abbreviations in a grammar handbook or other reliable resource. How well does Ma follow these rules? When should you use acronyms or abbreviations in your own writing? How should they be introduced?

Assignments for Writing

1. What role does empathy play in collaboration? Can collaboration function without it? Working with Ma's ideas about both practices, write a paper in which you examine the relationship between empathy and collaboration. You may want to use your work from Question 2 of Questions for Critical Reading and Question 1 of Questions for Connecting.

2. Consider your goals for your own education and then write a paper using Ma's ideas to argue for the proper aims of education. Should education be focused on career? Do we have an obligation to promote a broader education? Use your work from Question 3 of Questions for Connecting in supporting your argument.

3. Ma draws from ecological concepts in order to support his argument. Extend Ma's argument by writing a paper in which you consider other "edge effects" and "necessary edges." Can we locate these edges *within* the arts or *within* the sciences? Can we locate them *between* art, science, and other areas of human experience? What elements are necessary to reap the benefits of edge effects? Use your work from Question 3 of Questions for Critical Reading and Questions 1–3 of Exploring Context to support your argument. What other edges are used in the Silk Road Project?

RICHARD MANNING

Award-winning environmental journalist **Richard Manning** writes about critical global issues such as conservation, agriculture, and poverty, with a focus on the American West. His writing has appeared in *Harper's*, *Proceedings of the American Philosophical Society*, *Wired*, *Men's Journal*, and the *New York Times*. Manning has also published ten books, most recently *Go Wild: Free Your Body and Mind from the Afflictions of Civilization*, in which he, along with coauthor Dr. John J. Ratey, details the restorative health benefits of returning to lifestyle practices of the past. He has advised several organizations, including the McKnight Foundation and the Rockefeller Foundation, on issues of poverty, agriculture, and the environment, and from 1994 to 1995 he served as a John S. Knight Journalism Fellow at Stanford University.

Tracy Stone-Manning

"The Oil We Eat: Following the Food Chain Back to Iraq" was originally published in *Harper's* in 2004. *Harper's*, the second-oldest continuously-published monthly magazine in the United States, publishes essays on contemporary issues, including politics, finance, culture, and the arts. Manning's essay appeared alongside pieces on the over-fifty-years-old Centralia coal fire and excerpts from Cuban literacy textbooks.

In this essay, Manning reduces food to a basic measure of energy, allowing him to examine the relationship between agriculture and industry. Working from this base concept of energy, Manning is able to trace the history of agriculture and demonstrate its wastefulness in terms of total energy expenditure, in the process demonstrating why vegetarianism is not necessarily superior to other eating choices. The solution to this looming food-energy crisis, Manning suggests, is to eat minimally processed food low on the food chain.

How can we balance the world's need for food with our finite global energy resources?

▶ TAGS: *economics, energy, ethics, food and agriculture, health and medicine*
▶ CONNECTIONS: *Appiah, Dalai Lama, Friedman, Ma, Moalem, Pollan, Wallace*

Questions for Critical Reading

1. Take a moment to make a list of things you've eaten during the past day. As you read Manning's essay, evaluate your own impact on *primary productivity*. Be sure to note Manning's definition of this term and the ways in which he elaborates our individual impact on global resources. How does your own eating reflect Manning's argument?

2. How does energy circulate? Create a time line or map of energy production and consumption as you read, tracing the ways in which energy moves historically and locally.

3. Manning details many of the problems with food production today. But what is the solution? Identify any passages where Manning suggests a solution to the problems he discusses.

The Oil We Eat: Following the Food Chain Back to Iraq

> The secret of great wealth with no obvious source is some forgotten crime, forgotten because it was done neatly.
>
> —BALZAC

The journalist's rule says: follow the money. This rule, however, is not really axiomatic but derivative, in that money, as even our vice president will tell you, is really a way of tracking energy. We'll follow the energy.

We learn as children that there is no free lunch, that you don't get something from nothing, that what goes up must come down, and so on. The scientific version of these verities is only slightly more complex. As James Prescott Joule discovered in the nineteenth century, there is only so much energy. You can change it from motion to heat, from heat to light, but there will never be more of it and there will never be less of it. The conservation of energy is not an option, it is a fact. This is the first law of thermodynamics.

Special as we humans are, we get no exemptions from the rules. All animals eat plants or eat animals that eat plants. This is the food chain, and pulling it is the unique ability of plants to turn sunlight into stored energy in the form of carbohydrates, the basic fuel of all animals. Solar-powered photosynthesis is the only way to make this fuel. There is no alternative to plant energy, just as there is no alternative to oxygen. The results of taking away our plant energy may not be as sudden as cutting off oxygen, but they are as sure.

Scientists have a name for the total amount of plant mass created by Earth in a given year, the total budget for life. They call it the planet's "primary productivity." There have been two efforts to figure out how that productivity is spent, one by a group at Stanford University, the other an independent accounting by the biologist Stuart Pimm. Both conclude that we humans, a single species among millions, consume about 40 percent of Earth's primary productivity, 40 percent of all there is. This simple number may explain why the current extinction rate is 1,000 times that which existed before human domination of the planet. We 6 billion have simply stolen the food, the rich among us a lot more than others.

Energy cannot be created or canceled, but it can be concentrated. This is the larger and profoundly explanatory context of a national-security memo George Kennan wrote in 1948 as the head of a State Department planning committee, ostensibly about Asian policy but really about how the United States was to deal with its new-found role as the dominant force on Earth. "We have about 50 percent of the world's wealth but only 6.3 percent of its population," Kennan wrote. "In this situation, we cannot fail to be the object of envy and resentment. Our real task in the coming period 5 is to devise a pattern of relationships which will permit us to maintain this position of disparity without positive detriment to our national security. To do so, we will have to dispense with all sentimentality and day-dreaming; and our attention will have to be concentrated everywhere on our immediate national objectives. We need not deceive ourselves that we can afford today the luxury of altruism and world-benefaction."

"The day is not far off," Kennan concluded, "when we are going to have to deal in straight power concepts."

If you follow the energy, eventually you will end up in a field somewhere. Humans engage in a dizzying array of artifice and industry. Nonetheless, more than two thirds of humanity's cut of primary productivity results from agriculture, two thirds of which in turn consists of three plants: rice, wheat, and corn. In the 10,000 years since humans domesticated these grains, their status has remained undiminished, most likely because they are able to store solar energy in uniquely dense, transportable bundles of carbohydrates. They are to the plant world what a barrel of refined oil is to the hydrocarbon world. Indeed, aside from hydrocarbons they are the most concentrated form of true wealth—sun energy—to be found on the planet.

As Kennan recognized, however, the maintenance of such a concentration of wealth often requires violent action. Agriculture is a recent human experiment. For most of human history, we lived by gathering or killing a broad variety of nature's offerings. Why humans might have traded this approach for the complexities of agriculture is an interesting and long-debated question, especially because the skeletal evidence clearly indicates that early farmers were more poorly nourished, more disease-ridden and deformed, than their hunter-gatherer contemporaries. Farming did not improve most lives. The evidence that best points to the answer, I think, lies in the difference between early agricultural villages and their pre-agricultural counterparts—the presence not just of grain but of granaries and, more tellingly, of just a few houses significantly larger and more ornate than all the others attached to those granaries. Agriculture was not so much about food as it was about the accumulation of wealth. It benefited some humans, and those people have been in charge ever since.

Domestication was also a radical change in the distribution of wealth *within* the plant world. Plants can spend their solar income in several ways. The dominant and prudent strategy is to allocate most of it to building roots, stem, bark—a conservative portfolio of investments that allows the plant to better gather energy and survive the downturn years. Further, by living in diverse stands (a given chunk of native prairie contains maybe 200 species of plants), these perennials provide services for one another, such as retaining water, protecting one another from wind, and fixing free nitrogen from the air to use as fertilizer. Diversity allows a system to "sponsor its own fertility," to use visionary agronomist Wes Jackson's phrase. This is the plant world's norm.

There is a very narrow group of annuals, however, that grow in patches of a single 10 species and store almost all of their income as seed, a tight bundle of carbohydrates easily exploited by seed eaters such as ourselves. Under normal circumstances, this eggs-in-one-basket strategy is a dumb idea for a plant. But not during catastrophes such as floods, fires, and volcanic eruptions. Such catastrophes strip established plant communities and create opportunities for wind-scattered entrepreneurial seed bearers. It is no accident that no matter where agriculture sprouted on the globe, it always happened near rivers. You might assume, as many have, that this is because the plants needed the water or nutrients. Mostly this is not true. They needed the power of flooding, which scoured landscapes and stripped out competitors. Nor is it an accident, I think, that agriculture arose independently and simultaneously around the globe just as the last ice age ended, a time of enormous upheaval when glacial melt let loose sea-size lakes to create tidal waves of erosion. It was a time of catastrophe.

Corn, rice, and wheat are especially adapted to catastrophe. It is their niche. In the natural scheme of things, a catastrophe would create a blank slate, bare soil, that was good for them. Then, under normal circumstances, succession would quickly close that niche. The annuals would colonize. Their roots would stabilize the soil, accumulate organic matter, provide cover. Eventually the catastrophic niche would close. Farming is the process of ripping that niche open again and again. It is an annual artificial catastrophe, and it requires the equivalent of three or four tons of TNT per acre for a modern American farm. Iowa's fields require the energy of 4,000 Nagasaki bombs every year.

[Farming] is an annual artificial catastrophe, and it requires the equivalent of three or four tons of TNT per acre.

Iowa is almost all fields now. Little prairie remains, and if you can find what Iowans call a "postage stamp" remnant of some, it most likely will abut a cornfield. This allows an observation. Walk from the prairie to the field, and you probably will step down about six feet, as if the land had been stolen from beneath you. Settlers' accounts of the prairie conquest mention a sound, a series of pops, like pistol shots, the sound of stout grass roots breaking before a moldboard plow. A robbery was in progress.

When we say the soil is rich, it is not a metaphor. It is as rich in energy as an oil well. A prairie converts that energy to flowers and roots and stems, which in turn pass back into the ground as dead organic matter. The layers of topsoil build up into a rich repository of energy, a bank. A farm field appropriates that energy, puts it into seeds we can eat. Much of the energy moves from the earth to the rings of fat around our necks and waists. And much of the energy is simply wasted, a trail of dollars billowing from the burglar's satchel.

I've already mentioned that we humans take 40 percent of the globe's primary productivity every year. You might have assumed we and our livestock eat our way through that volume, but this is not the case. Part of that total—almost a third of it—is the *potential* plant mass lost when forests are cleared for farming or when tropical rain forests are cut for grazing or when plows destroy the deep mat of prairie roots that held the whole business together, triggering erosion. The Dust Bowl was no accident of nature. A functioning grassland prairie produces more biomass each year than does even the most technologically advanced wheat field. The problem is, it's mostly a form of grass and grass roots that humans can't eat. So we replace the prairie with our own preferred grass, wheat. Never mind that we feed most of our grain to livestock, and that livestock is perfectly content to eat native grass. And never mind that there likely were more bison produced naturally on the Great Plains before farming than all of beef farming raises in the same area today. Our ancestors found it preferable to pluck the energy from the ground and when it ran out move on.

Today we do the same, only now when the vault is empty we fill it again with new energy in the form of oil-rich fertilizers. Oil is annual primary productivity stored as hydrocarbons, a trust fund of sorts, built up over many thousands of years. On average, it takes 5.5 gallons of fossil energy to restore a year's worth of lost fertility to an acre of eroded land—in 1997 we burned through more than 400 years' worth of ancient fossilized productivity, most of it from someplace else. Even as the earth beneath Iowa shrinks, it is being globalized.

Six thousand years before sodbusters broke up Iowa, their Caucasian blood ancestors broke up the Hungarian plain, an area just northwest of the Caucasus Mountains. Archaeologists call this tribe the LBK, short for *linearbandkeramik*, the German word that describes the distinctive pottery remnants that mark their occupation of Europe. Anthropologists call them the wheat-beef people, a name that better connects those ancients along the Danube to my fellow Montanans on the Upper Missouri River. These proto-Europeans had a full set of domesticated plants and animals, but wheat and beef dominated. All the domesticates came from an area along what is now the Iraq-Syria-Turkey border at the edges of the Zagros Mountains. This is the center of domestication for the Western world's main crops and livestock, ground zero of catastrophic agriculture.

Two other types of catastrophic agriculture evolved at roughly the same time, one centered on rice in what is now China and India and one centered on corn and potatoes in Central and South America. Rice, though, is tropical and its expansion depends on water, so it developed only in floodplains, estuaries, and swamps. Corn agriculture was every bit as voracious as wheat; the Aztecs could be as brutal and imperialistic as Romans or Brits, but the corn cultures collapsed with the onslaught of Spanish conquest. Corn itself simply joined the wheat-beef people's coalition. Wheat was the empire builder; its bare botanical facts dictated the motion and violence that we know as imperialism.

The wheat-beef people swept across the western European plains in less than 300 years, a conquest some archaeologists refer to as a "blitzkrieg." A different race of humans, the Cro-Magnons—hunter-gatherers, not farmers—lived on those plains at the time. Their cave art at places such as Lascaux testifies to their sophistication and profound connection to wildlife. They probably did most of their hunting and gathering in uplands and river bottoms, places the wheat farmers didn't need, suggesting the possibility of coexistence. That's not what happened, however. Both genetic and linguistic evidence say that the farmers killed the hunters. The Basque people are probably the lone remnant descendants of Cro-Magnons, the only trace.

Hunter-gatherer archaeological sites of the period contain spear points that originally belonged to the farmers, and we can guess they weren't trade goods. One group of anthropologists concludes, "The evidence from the western extension of the LBK leaves little room for any other conclusion but that LBK-Mesolithic interactions were at best chilly and at worst hostile." The world's surviving Blackfeet, Assiniboine Sioux, Inca, and Maori probably have the best idea of the nature of these interactions.

Wheat is temperate and prefers plowed-up grasslands. The globe has a limited   20
stock of temperate grasslands, just as it has a limited stock of all other biomes. On average, about 10 percent of all other biomes remain in something like their native state
today. Only 1 percent of temperate grasslands remains undestroyed. Wheat takes what
it needs.

The supply of temperate grasslands lies in what are today the United States, Canada, the South American pampas, New Zealand, Australia, South Africa, Europe, and
the Asiatic extension of the European plain into the sub-Siberian steppes. This area
largely describes the First World, the developed world. Temperate grasslands make up
not only the habitat of wheat and beef but also the globe's islands of Caucasians, of European surnames and languages. In 2000 the countries of the temperate grasslands,
the neo-Europes, accounted for about 80 percent of all wheat exports in the world, and
about 86 percent of all corn. That is to say, the neo-Europes drive the world's agriculture. The dominance does not stop with grain.

These countries, plus the mothership—Europe—accounted for three fourths of
all agricultural exports of all crops in the world in 1999.

Plato wrote of his country's farmlands:

> What now remains of the formerly rich land is like the skeleton of a sick
> man. . . . Formerly, many of the mountains were arable. The plains that were
> full of rich soil are now marshes. Hills that were once covered with forests and
> produced abundant pasture now produce only food for bees. Once the land
> was enriched by yearly rains, which were not lost, as they are now, by flow-
> ing from the bare land into the sea. The soil was deep, it absorbed and kept the
> water in loamy soil, and the water that soaked into the hills fed springs and
> running streams everywhere. Now the abandoned shrines at spots where for-
> merly there were springs attest that our description of the land is true.

Plato's lament is rooted in wheat agriculture, which depleted his country's soil and
subsequently caused the series of declines that pushed centers of civilization to Rome,
Turkey, and western Europe. By the fifth century, though, wheat's strategy of depleting
and moving on ran up against the Atlantic Ocean. Fenced-in wheat agriculture is like
rice agriculture. It balances its equations with famine. In the millennium between 500
and 1500, Britain suffered a major "corrective" famine about every ten years; there
were seventy-five in France during the same period. The incidence, however, dropped
sharply when colonization brought an influx of new food to Europe.

The new lands had an even greater effect on the colonists themselves. Thomas Jef-   25
ferson, after enduring a lecture on the rustic nature by his hosts at a dinner party in
Paris, pointed out that all of the Americans present were a good head taller than all of
the French. Indeed, colonists in all of the neo-Europes enjoyed greater stature and longevity, as well as a lower infant-mortality rate—all indicators of the better nutrition
afforded by the onetime spend down of the accumulated capital of virgin soil.

The precolonial famines of Europe raised the question: What would happen when
the planet's supply of arable land ran out? We have a clear answer. In about 1960 expansion hit its limits and the supply of unfarmed, arable lands came to an end. There
was nothing left to plow. What happened was grain yields tripled.

The accepted term for this strange turn of events is the green revolution, though it would be more properly labeled the amber revolution, because it applied exclusively to grain—wheat, rice, and corn. Plant breeders tinkered with the architecture of these three grains so that they could be hypercharged with irrigation water and chemical fertilizers, especially nitrogen. This innovation meshed nicely with the increased "efficiency" of the industrialized factory-farm system. With the possible exception of the domestication of wheat, the green revolution is the worst thing that has ever happened to the planet.

For openers, it disrupted long-standing patterns of rural life worldwide, moving a lot of no-longer-needed people off the land and into the world's most severe poverty. The experience in population control in the developing world is by now clear: It is not that people make more people so much as it is that they make more poor people. In the forty-year period beginning about 1960, the world's population doubled, adding virtually the entire increase of 3 billion to the world's poorest classes, the most fecund classes. The way in which the green revolution raised that grain contributed hugely to the population boom, and it is the weight of the population that leaves humanity in its present untenable position.

Discussion of these, the most poor, however, is largely irrelevant to the American situation. We say we have poor people here, but almost no one in this country lives on less than one dollar a day, the global benchmark for poverty. It marks off a class of about 1.3 billion people, the hard core of the larger group of 2 billion chronically malnourished people—that is, one third of humanity. We may forget about them, as most Americans do.

More relevant here are the methods of the green revolution, which added orders of   30
magnitude to the devastation. By mining the iron for tractors, drilling the new oil to fuel them and to make nitrogen fertilizers, and by taking the water that rain and rivers had meant for other lands, farming had extended its boundaries, its dominion, to lands that were not farmable. At the same time, it extended its boundaries across time, tapping fossil energy, stripping past assets.

The common assumption these days is that we muster our weapons to secure oil, not food. There's a little joke in this. Ever since we ran out of arable land, food *is* oil. Every single calorie we eat is backed by at least a calorie of oil, more like ten. In 1940 the average farm in the United States produced 2.3 calories of food energy for every calorie of fossil energy it used. By 1974 (the last year in which anyone looked closely at this issue), that ratio was 1:1. And this understates the problem, because at the same time that there is more oil in our food there is less oil in our oil. A couple of generations ago we spent a lot less energy drilling, pumping, and distributing than we do now. In the 1940s we got about 100 barrels of oil back for every barrel of oil we spent getting it. Today each barrel invested in the process returns only ten, a calculation that no doubt fails to include the fuel burned by the Hummers and Blackhawks we use to maintain access to the oil in Iraq.

> **Ever since we ran out of arable land, food *is* oil. Every single calorie we eat is backed by at least a calorie of oil, more like ten.**

David Pimentel, an expert on food and energy at Cornell University, has estimated that if all of the world ate the way the United States eats, humanity would exhaust all known global fossil-fuel reserves in just over seven years. Pimentel has his detractors. Some have accused him of being off on other calculations by as much as 30 percent. Fine. Make it ten years.

Fertilizer makes a pretty fine bomb right off the shelf, a chemistry lesson Timothy McVeigh taught at Oklahoma City's Alfred P. Murrah Federal Building in 1995 — not a small matter, in that the green revolution has made nitrogen fertilizers ubiquitous in some of the more violent and desperate corners of the world. Still, there is more to contemplate in nitrogen's less sensational chemistry.

The chemophobia of modern times excludes fear of the simple elements of chemistry's periodic table. We circulate petitions, hold hearings, launch websites, and buy and sell legislators in regard to polysyllabic organic compounds — polychlorinated biphenyls, polyvinyls, DDT, 2-4d, that sort of thing — not simple carbon or nitrogen. Not that agriculture's use of the more ornate chemistry is benign — an infant born in a rural, wheat-producing county in the United States has about twice the chance of suffering birth defects as one born in a rural place that doesn't produce wheat, an effect researchers blame on chlorophenoxy herbicides. Focusing on pesticide pollution, though, misses the worst of the pollutants. Forget the polysyllabic organics. It is nitrogen — the wellspring of fertility relied upon by every Eden-obsessed backyard gardener and suburban groundskeeper — that we should fear most.

Those who model our planet as an organism do so on the basis that the earth appears to breathe — it thrives by converting a short list of basic elements from one compound into the next, just as our own bodies cycle oxygen into carbon dioxide and plants cycle carbon dioxide into oxygen. In fact, two of the planet's most fundamental humors are oxygen and carbon dioxide. Another is nitrogen.

Nitrogen can be released from its "fixed" state as a solid in the soil by natural processes that allow it to circulate freely in the atmosphere. This also can be done artificially. Indeed, humans now contribute more nitrogen to the nitrogen cycle than the planet itself does. That is, humans have doubled the amount of nitrogen in play.

This has led to an imbalance. It is easier to create nitrogen fertilizer than it is to apply it evenly to fields. When farmers dump nitrogen on a crop, much is wasted. It runs into the water and soil, where it either reacts chemically with its surroundings to form new compounds or flows off to fertilize something else, somewhere else.

That chemical reaction, called acidification, is noxious and contributes significantly to acid rain. One of the compounds produced by acidification is nitrous oxide, which aggravates the greenhouse effect. Green growing things normally offset global warming by sucking up carbon dioxide, but nitrogen on farm fields plus methane from decomposing vegetation make every farmed acre, like every acre of Los Angeles freeway, a net contributor to global warming. Fertilization is equally worrisome. Rainfall and irrigation water inevitably washes the nitrogen from fields to creeks and streams, which flows into rivers, which floods into the ocean. This explains why the Mississippi River, which drains the nation's Corn Belt, is an environmental catastrophe. The nitrogen fertilizes artificially large blooms of algae that in growing suck all the oxygen from the water, a condition biologists call anoxia, which means "oxygen-depleted." Here there's no need to calculate long-term effects, because life in such places has no long term: everything dies immediately. The Mississippi River's heavily fertilized effluvia has created a dead zone in the Gulf of Mexico the size of New Jersey.

America's biggest crop, grain corn, is completely unpalatable. It is raw material for an industry that manufactures food substitutes. Likewise, you can't eat unprocessed wheat. You certainly can't eat hay. You can eat unprocessed soybeans, but mostly we don't. These four crops cover 82 percent of American cropland. Agriculture in this country is not about food; it's about commodities that require the outlay of still more energy to *become* food.

About two thirds of U.S. grain corn is labeled "processed," meaning it is milled and   40 otherwise refined for food or industrial uses. More than 45 percent of that becomes sugar, especially high-fructose corn sweeteners, the keystone ingredient in three quarters of all processed foods, especially soft drinks, the food of America's poor and working classes. It is not a coincidence that the American pandemic of obesity tracks rather nicely with the fivefold increase in corn-syrup production since Archer Daniels Midland developed a high-fructose version of the stuff in the early seventies. Nor is it a coincidence that the plague selects the poor, who eat the most processed food.

It began with the industrialization of Victorian England. The empire was then flush with sugar from plantations in the colonies. Meantime the cities were flush with factory workers. There was no good way to feed them. And thus was born the after-noon tea break, the tea consisting primarily of warm water and sugar. If the workers were well off, they could also afford bread with heavily sugared jam — sugar-powered industrialization. There was a 500 percent increase in per capita sugar consumption in Britain between 1860 and 1890, around the time when the life expectancy of a male factory worker was seventeen years. By the end of the century the average Brit was getting about one sixth of his total nutrition from sugar, exactly the same percentage Americans get today — double what nutritionists recommend.

There is another energy matter to consider here, though. The grinding, milling, wetting, drying, and baking of a breakfast cereal requires about four calories of energy for every calorie of food energy it produces. A two-pound bag of breakfast cereal burns the energy of a half-gallon of gasoline in its making. All together the food-processing industry in the United States uses about ten calories of fossil-fuel energy for every calo-rie of food energy it produces.

That number does not include the fuel used in transporting the food from the fac-tory to a store near you, or the fuel used by millions of people driving to thousands of super discount stores on the edge of town, where the land is cheap. It appears, however, that the corn cycle is about to come full circle. If a bipartisan coalition of farm-state lawmakers has their way — and it appears they will — we will soon buy gasoline con-taining twice as much fuel alcohol as it does now. Fuel alcohol already ranks second as a use for processed corn in the United States, just behind corn sweeteners. According to one set of calculations, we spend more calories of fossil-fuel energy making ethanol than we gain from it. The Department of Agriculture says the ratio is closer to a gal-lon and a quart of ethanol for every gallon of fossil fuel we invest. The USDA calls this a bargain, because gasohol is a "clean fuel." This claim to cleanness is in dispute at the tailpipe level, and it certainly ignores the dead zone in the Gulf of Mexico, pesticide pollution, and the haze of global gases gathering over every farm field. Nor does this claim cover clean conscience; some still might be unsettled knowing that our SUVs' demands for fuel compete with the poor's demand for grain.

Green eaters, especially vegetarians, advocate eating low on the food chain, a simple matter of energy flow. Eating a carrot gives the diner all that carrot's energy, but feeding carrots to a chicken, then eating the chicken, reduces the energy by a factor of ten. The chicken wastes some energy, stores some as feathers, bones, and other inedibles, and uses most of it just to live long enough to be eaten. As a rough rule of thumb, that factor often applies to each level up the food chain, which is why some fish, such as tuna, can be a horror in all of this. Tuna is a secondary predator, meaning it not only doesn't eat plants but eats other fish that themselves eat other fish, adding a zero to the multiplier each notch up, easily a hundred times, more like a thousand times less efficient than eating a plant.

This is fine as far as it goes, but the vegetarian's case can break down on some details. On the moral issues, vegetarians claim their habits are kinder to animals, though it is difficult to see how wiping out 99 percent of wildlife's habitat, as farming has done in Iowa, is a kindness. In rural Michigan, for example, the potato farmers have a peculiar tactic for dealing with the predations of whitetail deer. They gut-shoot them with small-bore rifles, in hopes the deer will limp off to the woods and die where they won't stink up the potato fields.

Animal rights aside, vegetarians can lose the edge in the energy argument by eating processed food, with its ten calories of fossil energy for every calorie of food energy produced. The question, then, is: Does eating processed food such as soy burger or soy milk cancel the *energy* benefits of vegetarianism, which is to say, can I eat my lamb chops in peace? Maybe. If I've done my due diligence, I will have found out that the particular lamb I am eating was both local and grass-fed, two factors that of course greatly reduce the embedded energy in a meal. I know of ranches here in Montana, for instance, where sheep eat native grass under closely controlled circumstances—no farming, no plows, no corn, no nitrogen. Assets have not been stripped. I can't eat the grass directly. This can go on. There are little niches like this in the system. Each person's individual charge is to find such niches.

Chances are, though, any meat eater will come out on the short end of this argument, especially in the United States. Take the case of beef. Cattle are grazers, so in theory could live like the grass-fed lamb. Some cattle cultures—those of South America and Mexico, for example—have perfected wonderful cuisines based on grass-fed beef. This is not our habit in the United States, and it *is* simply a matter of habit. Eighty percent of the grain the United States produces goes to livestock. Seventy-eight percent of all of our beef comes from feed lots, where the cattle eat grain, mostly corn and wheat. So do most of our hogs and chickens. The cattle spend their adult lives packed shoulder to shoulder in a space not much bigger than their bodies, up to their knees in shit, being stuffed with grain and a constant stream of antibiotics to prevent the disease this sort of confinement invariably engenders. The manure is rich in nitrogen and once provided a farm's fertilizer. The feedlots, however, are now far removed from farm fields, so it is simply not "efficient" to haul it to cornfields. It is waste. It exhales methane, a global-warming gas. It pollutes streams. It takes thirty-five calories of fossil fuel to make a calorie of beef this way; sixty-eight to make one calorie of pork.

Still, these livestock do something we can't. They convert grain's carbohydrates to high-quality protein. All well and good, except that per capita protein production in the United States is about double what an average adult needs per day. Excess cannot be stored as protein in the human body but is simply converted to fat. This is the end result of a factory-farm system that appears as a living, continental-scale monument to Rube Goldberg, a black-mass remake of the loaves-and-fishes miracle. Prairie's productivity is lost for grain, grain's productivity is lost in livestock, livestock's protein is lost to human fat—all federally subsidized for about $15 billion a year, two thirds of which goes directly to only two crops, corn and wheat.

This explains why the energy expert David Pimentel is so worried that the rest of the world will adopt America's methods. He should be, because the rest of the world is. Mexico now feeds 45 percent of its grain to livestock, up from 5 percent in 1960. Egypt went from 3 percent to 31 percent in the same period, and China, with a sixth of the world's population, has gone from 8 percent to 26 percent. All of these places have poor people who could use the grain, but they can't afford it.

I live among elk and have learned to respect them. One moonlit night during the dead of last winter, I looked out my bedroom window to see about twenty of them grazing a plot of grass the size of a living room. Just that small patch among acres of other species of native prairie grass. Why that species and only that species of grass that night in the worst of winter when the threat to their survival was the greatest? What magic nutrient did this species alone contain? What does a wild animal know that we don't? I think we need this knowledge. 50

Food is politics. That being the case, I voted twice in 2002. The day after Election Day, in a truly dismal mood, I climbed the mountain behind my house and found a small herd of elk grazing native grasses in the morning sunlight. My respect for these creatures over the years has become great enough that on that morning I did not hesitate but went straight to my job, which was to rack a shell and drop one cow elk, my household's annual protein supply. I voted with my weapon of choice—an act not all that uncommon in this world, largely, I think, as a result of the way we grow food. I can see why it is catching on. Such a vote has a certain satisfying heft and finality about it. My particular bit of violence, though, is more satisfying, I think, than the rest of the globe's ordinary political mayhem. I used a rifle to opt out of an insane system. I killed, but then so did you when you bought that package of burger, even when you bought that package of tofu burger. I killed, then the rest of those elk went on, as did the grasses, the birds, the trees, the coyotes, mountain lions, and bugs, the fundamental productivity of an intact natural system, all of it went on.

Exploring Context

1. "Carbon footprint" is a concept that allows us to measure energy consumption through the production of greenhouse gases such as carbon dioxide. Calculate your own carbon footprint at nature.org/greenliving/carboncalculator. What role does eating play in our overall impact on the world?

2. Explore *National Geographic*'s interactive infographic on what the world eats at nationalgeographic.com/what-the-world-eats. How have food consumption patterns changed across time? Relate this information to Manning's argument.

3. Use a search engine to locate local resources for eating low on the food chain. Do you have options to avoid the kinds of agriculture that Manning criticizes? How realistic are those options for you? Connect your response to your work from Question 1 of Questions for Critical Reading.

Questions for Connecting

1. How does Manning's discussion of global agriculture change your understanding of David Foster Wallace's discussion of the ethics of eating lobster in "Consider the Lobster" (p. 459)? How can we balance the ethics of eating animals and the ethics of responsible food production?

2. Synthesize Manning's argument with Michael Pollan's discussion of organic farming in "The Animals: Practicing Complexity" (p. 344). Does Polyface represent a model solution to the problems that Manning explores? How realistic would this solution be on a global scale? What challenges would we need to overcome? Incorporate your research on global eating patterns from Question 2 of Exploring Context.

3. Manning documents a global problem. Might Thomas L. Friedman offer a solution in "The Dell Theory of Conflict Prevention" (p. 124)? Apply Friedman's discussion of global supply chains to Manning's argument. Can they be harnessed to address this issue or is the kind of global economy that Friedman describes part of the problem?

Language Matters

1. Indexes help you locate important information quickly. Create a simple index for Manning's essay. What terms or entries would you include? How often do they appear in the text?

2. Photocopy a couple of pages from Manning's essay and then cut out each individual paragraph with a pair of scissors. Trade these in small groups. Can everyone put the paragraphs back in the right order? How strong is Manning's organization? What elements of the paragraphs indicate their order within the piece?

3. Considering counterarguments is an important element in academic writing. Propose a series of counterarguments to Manning's points. How might he respond?

Assignments for Writing

1. Write a paper in which you propose solutions to the problems Manning delineates in food production. Can we change the way we eat to resolve this problem? Might new technologies help? Use your work from Question 3 of Questions for Critical Reading, Question 3 of Exploring Context, and Questions 2 and 3 of Questions for Connecting.

2. What are the ethics of eating? Using Manning's ideas, write a paper in which you propose an ethical model for the consumption of food. Consider using your work from Questions 1–3 of Exploring Context as well as your work from Question 1 of Questions for Connecting.

3. Manning's exploration of food includes both food itself and the industries that produce it. Based on his observations, write a paper in which you argue for the best balance between agriculture and industry. Use your work from Question 3 of Exploring Context and Question 2 of Questions for Connecting to support your argument.

SHARON MOALEM

Both a medical doctor and a doctor of philosophy, **Sharon Moalem** is a best-selling author whose works include *Survival of the Sickest* and *How Sex Works*. Moalem, whose research deals largely with genetics, is also an inventor and entrepreneur, having cofounded two biotechnology companies. Moalem and his research are often discussed in the mainstream media, from *The Daily Show with Jon Stewart* to the *New York Times*. He earned his Ph.D. in neurogenetics from the University of Toronto and his M.D. at New York's Mount Sinai School of Medicine.

Bloomberg/Getty Images

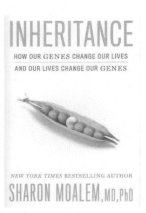

Moalem's most recent book, *Inheritance: How Our Genes Change Our Lives and Our Lives Change Our Genes*, explores the flexibility of genes. Far from being fixed at birth, our genetic inheritance is fluid. Moalem examines the ways in which environmental conditions and lifestyle choices can not only change the expression of our DNA but also alter it in ways that can be passed down for generations. Chapters cover rare genetic disorders, drugs used in athletic doping, and the ways in which insurance companies are using our genetic information.

In "Changing Our Genes: How Trauma, Bullying, and Royal Jelly Alter Our Genetic Destiny," a chapter from *Inheritance*, Moalem exposes the science of genetic inheritance, not only of physical attributes, but also of emotional traits. Based on studies of bees, mice, and humans, Moalem concludes that the effects of trauma, such as bullying, can change our genes and therefore also alter the genes of future generations.

What does this mean when it comes to the way society does, and should, treat post-traumatic stress?

▶ TAGS: *adolescence and adulthood, food and agriculture, genetics, health and medicine, science and technology, trauma and violence*

▶ CONNECTIONS: *Dalai Lama, DeGhett, Olson, Pollan, Pozner, Restak, Rosin, Savage/Vaid, Stillman*

Questions for Critical Reading

1. Moalem covers quite a bit of territory in this piece, moving from bees to the terrorist attacks of September 11, 2001. After you've read this essay, create a quick outline that traces Moalem's moves between these disparate examples, marking significant passages that link the examples together.

2. What factors can change genes? Pay close attention to places in the essay where Moalem discusses elements that can change our genetic information. Knowing that our DNA can be affected by what we do, how might we change our behaviors?

3. *Epigenetics* plays a significant role in Moalem's argument. Find passages where Moalem defines the term and then define it in your own words. Try to locate your own example of epigenetics.

Changing Our Genes: How Trauma, Bullying, and Royal Jelly Alter Our Genetic Destiny

Most people know about Mendel's* work with peas. Some have heard of his truncated work with mice. But what most people don't know is that Mendel also worked with honeybees—which he called "my dearest little animals."

Who can blame him for such adulation? Bees are endlessly fascinating and beautiful creatures—and they can tell us a lot about ourselves. For instance, have you ever been witness to the awesome and fearsome sight of an entire colony of bees swarming and on the move? Somewhere in the middle of that ethereal tornado is a queen bee that has left the hive.

Who is she to deserve such a grand parade?

Well, just look at her. For starters, just like human fashion models, queens have longer bodies and legs than their sister workers. They're more slender and have smooth, rather than furry, abdomens. Because they often need to protect themselves from entomological coups from younger royal upstarts, queen bees have stingers that can be reused on demand, unlike female worker bees, who die after using their stingers just once. Queen bees can live for years, though some of their workers live only a few weeks. They can also lay thousands of eggs in a day, while all their royal needs are tended to by sterile workers.[†]

So yeah, she's kind of a big deal.   5

Given the incredible differences between them, you could easily assume that queens differ genetically from the workers. That would make sense—after all, their physical traits differ considerably from their sister worker bees. But look deeper—DNA deeper—and a very different story emerges. The truth is that, genetically speaking, the queen is nobody special. A queen bee and her female workers can come from the same parents, and they can have completely identical DNA. Yet their behavioral, physiological, and anatomical differences are profound.

Why? Because larval queens eat better.

That's it. That's all. The food they eat changes their genetic expression—in this case through specific genes being turned off or on, a mechanism we call epigenetics. When the colony decides it's time for a new queen, they choose a few lucky larvae and bathe them in royal jelly, a protein- and amino acid–rich secretion produced by glands in the mouths of young worker bees. Initially, all larvae get a taste of royal jelly, but workers are quickly weaned. The little princesses, however, eat and eat and eat until

---

*Gregor Mendel: Austrian monk and scientist (1822–1884) whose garden experiments formed the foundation of modern understanding of genetics and heredity.

[†]Worker honeybees, at times, can lay eggs that will hatch into drones (male bees). But given the complexities of their reproductive genetics, worker bees are incapable of laying eggs that will become other female workers.

they emerge as a blue-blooded brood of elegant empresses. The one who murders all the rest of her royal sisters first gets to be queen.

Her genes are no different. But her genetic expression? Royal.[1]

Beekeepers have known for centuries—maybe longer—that larvae bathed in royal jelly will produce queens. But until the genome for the western honeybee, *Apis mellifera*, was sequenced in 2006, and the specific details of caste differentiation were worked out in 2011, no one knew exactly why.

Like every other creature on this planet, bees share a lot of genetic sequences with other animals—even us. And researchers quickly noticed that one of these shared codes was for DNA methyltransferase, or Dnmt3, which in mammals can change the expression of certain genes through epigenetic mechanisms.

When researchers used chemicals to shut down the Dnmt3 in hundreds of larvae, they got an entire brood of queens. When they turned it back on in another batch of larvae, they all grew to be workers. So rather than having something more than their workers, as might be expected, queens actually have a little less—the royal jelly the queens eat so much of, it appears, just turns down the volume on the gene that makes honeybees into workers.[2]

Our diet differs from that of bees, of course, but they (and the clever researchers who study them) have given us lots of amazing examples of how our genes express themselves to meet the demands of our lives.[3]

Like humans who fill a series of set roles during their lives—from students to workers to community elders—worker bees also follow a predictable pattern from birth to death. They start as housekeepers and undertakers, keeping the hive clean and, when necessary, disposing of their dead siblings to protect the colony from disease. Most then become nurses, working together to keep tabs on each larval member of the hive more than a thousand times a day. And then, right around the ripe old age of two weeks, they set off to forage for nectar.

A team of scientists from Johns Hopkins University and Arizona State University knew that sometimes, when more nurse bees are needed, foraging bees will go back to do that job. The scientists wanted to know why. So they looked for differences in gene expression, which can be found by searching for chemical "tags" that rest atop certain genes. And indeed, when they compared the nurses with the foragers, those markers were in different places on more than 150 genes.

So they played a little trick. When the foragers were off searching for nectar, the researchers removed the nurses. Not willing to permit their young ones to be neglected, upon their return the forager bees immediately reverted to nurse duties. And just as immediately, their genetic tagging pattern changed.[4]

Genes that weren't being expressed before, now were. Genes that were, now weren't. The foragers weren't just doing another job—they were fulfilling a different genetic destiny.

Now, we might not look like bees. And we might not feel like bees. But we share a striking number of genetic similarities with bees, including Dnmt3.[5]

And just like those bees, our lives can be momentously impacted by genetic expression, for better or for worse.

Take spinach, for instance. Its leaves are rich in a chemical compound called betaine. In nature or on a farm, betaine helps plants deal with environmental stress, such as low water, high salinity, or extreme temperatures. In your body, though, betaine can behave as a methyl donor—part of a chain of chemical events that leaves a mark on your genetic code. And researchers at Oregon State University have found that, in many people who eat spinach, the epigenetic changes can help influence how their cells fight back against genetic mutations caused by a carcinogen in cooked meat. In fact, in tests involving laboratory animals, researchers were able to cut the incidence of colon tumors nearly in half.[6]

In a very small but important way, compounds within spinach can instruct the cells within our bodies to behave differently—just like the royal jelly instructs bees to develop in different ways. So yes, eating spinach seems to be able to change the expression of your genes themselves.

Remember when [in Chapter 2: When Genes Misbehave, not included here] I told you that Mendel, if Bishop Schaffgotsch had not curtailed his work with mice, might have stumbled upon something even more revolutionary than his theory of inheritance? Well, now I'd like to tell you about how that idea finally came to light.

First of all, it took time. More than 90 years had passed since Mendel's death when, in 1975, geneticists Arthur Riggs and Robin Holliday, working separately in the United States and Great Britain, respectively, almost simultaneously came upon the idea that, while genes were indeed fixed, they could perhaps be expressed differently in response to an array of stimuli, thus producing a range of traits rather than the fixed characteristics commonly thought to be associated with genetic inheritance.

Suddenly, the idea that the way genes are inherited could only be changed by the epically slow process of mutation was thrown into immediate dispute. But just as Mendel's ideas had been roundly ignored, so too were the theories being offered by Riggs and Holliday. Once again, an idea about genetics that was ahead of its time failed to gain traction.

It would be another quarter century before these ideas—and their profound implications—would gain broader acceptance. And that came as the result of the striking work of a cherub-faced scientist named Randy Jirtle. Like Mendel, Jirtle suspected that there was more to inheritance than met the eye. And, like Mendel, Jirtle suspected the answers could be found in mice.

Experimenting with agouti mice, which carry a gene that renders them plump and bright orange like a Muppet, Jirtle and his associates at Duke University came upon a discovery that, at the time, was simply stunning. By doing nothing more than changing the diet of females by the addition of a few nutrients such as choline, vitamin B12, and folic acid, starting just before conception, their offspring would be smaller, mottled brown, and altogether more mouse-like in appearance. Researchers would later discover that these mice were less susceptible to cancer and diabetes as well.

Same exact DNA. Completely different creature. And the difference was simply a matter of expression. In essence, a change in the mother's diet tagged her offspring's genetic code with a signal to turn off the agouti gene, and that turned-off gene then became inherited and was passed down across generations.

But that's just the beginning. In the fast-paced world of twenty-first-century genetics, Jirtle's Muppets have already been relegated to syndicated reruns. Every day we're learning new ways to alter genetic expression—in the genes of mice and men. The question isn't whether we can intervene; that's now a given. Now we're examining how to do it with new drugs that are already approved for human use, in ways that will hopefully result in longer and healthier lives for ourselves and for our children. What Riggs and Holliday theorized about—and what Jirtle and his colleagues brought into popular acceptance—is now known as epigenetics. Broadly, epigenetics is the study of changes in gene expression that result from life conditions, such as those seen in honeybee larvae that are doused in royal jelly, without changes in the underlying DNA. One of the fastest growing and most exciting areas of epigenetic study is its heritability, the investigation of how these changes can impact the next generation, and every generation down the line.

One common way changes in genetic expression occur is through an epigenetic process called methylation. There are many different ways in which DNA can be modified without the underlying string of nucleotide letters being altered. Methylation works by the use of a chemical compound, in the shape of three-leaf clovers made up of hydrogen and carbon, that is attached to DNA that alters the genetic structure in such a way as to program our cells to be what they're supposed to be and to do what they're supposed to do—or what they've been told to do by previous generations. Methylation "tags" that turn genes on and off can give us cancer, diabetes, and birth defects. But don't despair—because they can also affect gene expression to give us better health and longevity.

And such epigenetic changes seem to have consequences in some unexpected places. For instance, at a summer weight-loss camp.   30

Genetic researchers decided to follow a group of 200 Spanish teens who were on a 10-week quest to battle the bulge. What geneticists discovered was that they could actually reverse engineer the campers' summer experience and predict which of the teens would lose the most weight depending on the pattern of methylation—the way their genes were turned off or on—in around five sites in their genome before summer camp even began.[7] Some kids were epigenetically primed to lose the bulge at summer camp while others were going to keep it on, despite diligent adherence to their counselors' dietary protocol.

We're now learning how to apply the knowledge gained from studies such as these to capitalize on our own unique epigenetic makeup. What the teenagers' methylation tags teach us is how critical it is to get to know our own distinctive epigenome in matters of weight loss, and so much else. Learning from these Spanish summer campers, we can start to mine our epigenome to find the information we need for the most optimal weight-loss strategies. For some of us that may mean saving on the exorbitant fees of a summer weight-loss adventure that is destined not to work.

But far from being static, our epigenome, along with the DNA that we've inherited, can also be impacted by what we do to our genes. We're quickly learning that epigenetic modifications, like methylation, are remarkably easy to impact. In recent years geneticists have devised a number of ways to study and even reprogram methylated genes—to turn them on and off, or to crank the volume up or down.

Changing the volume of our genetic expression can mean the difference between a benign growth and a raging malignancy.

These epigenetic changes can be caused by the pills we swallow, the cigarettes   35
we smoke, the drinks we consume, the exercise classes we attend, and the X-rays we undergo.

And we can also do it with stress.

Building on Jirtle's work on agouti mice, scientists in Zurich wanted to see whether early childhood trauma could impact gene expression, so they stole pup mice away from their mothers for three hours, then returned the blind, deaf, and furless little things to their mommies for the rest of the day. The next day, they did it again.

Then, after 14 consecutive days, they stopped. Eventually, as all mice do, the little ones gained sight and hearing, grew some fur, and became adults. But having suffered two weeks of torment, they grew up to become significantly maladjusted little rodents. In particular, they seemed to have trouble evaluating potentially risky places. When put in adverse situations, instead of fighting or figuring it out, they just gave up. And here's the amazing part: They transmitted these behaviors to their own pups—and then to the offspring of their offspring—even if they had no involvement whatsoever in the rearing.[8]

In other words, a trauma in one generation was genetically present two generations down the line. Incredible.

It's definitely worth noting here that the genome for a mouse is about 99 percent similar to ours. And the two genes impacted in the Zurich study—called *Mecp2* and *Crfr2*—are found in mice and people alike.

Of course, we can't be sure that what happens in mice will happen in humans until we do, in fact, see it. That can be challenging to do, because our relatively long lives make it hard to conduct tests that explore generational changes, and when it comes to humans, it's a lot harder to separate nature and nurture.

But that doesn't mean we haven't seen epigenetic changes related to stress in humans. We most certainly have.

Remember when [in the Introduction] I asked you to go back to the seventh grade? For some of us going back that far might evoke some rather unpleasant memories, events that, given a choice, we'd rather not recall. The real numbers are hard to come by, but it's thought that at least three quarters of all children have been bullied at some point in their lives, which means there's a good chance you were on the receiving end of such unfortunate experiences yourself while you were growing up. And as some of us have become parents since then, the concern for our children's own experiences and safety both at school and beyond has only grown.

Until very recently, we've been thinking and speaking about the serious and long-term ramifications of bullying in predominantly psychological terms. Everyone agrees that bullying can leave very significant mental scars. The immense psychic pain some children and teens experience can even lead them to consider and act on desires to physically harm themselves.

But what if our experiences of being bullied did a lot more than just saddle us with some serious psychological baggage? Well, to answer that question, a group of researchers from the UK and Canada decided to study sets of monozygotic "identical" twins from the age of five. Besides having identical DNA, each twin pair in the study, up until that point, had never been bullied.

You'll be glad to know that these researchers were not allowed to traumatize their subjects, unlike how the Swiss mice were handled. Instead, they let other children do their scientific dirty work.

After patiently waiting for a few years, the scientists revisited the twins where only one of the pair had been bullied. When they dropped back into their lives, they found the following: present now, at the age of 12, was a striking epigenetic difference that was not there when the children were five years old. The researchers found significant changes only in the twin who was bullied. This means, in no uncertain genetic terms, that bullying isn't just risky in terms of self-harming tendencies for youth and adolescents; it actually changes how our genes work and how they shape our lives, and likely what we pass along to future generations.

What does that change look like genetically? Well, on average, in the bullied twin a gene called *SERT* that codes for a protein that helps move the neurotransmitter serotonin into neurons had significantly more DNA methylation in its promoter region. This change is thought to dial down the amount of protein that can be made from the *SERT* gene—meaning the more it's methylated the more it's "turned off."

The reason these findings are significant is that these epigenetic changes are thought to be able to persist throughout our lives. This means that even if you can't remember the details of being bullied, your genes certainly do.

But that's not all these researchers found. They also wanted to see if there were any psychological changes between the twins to go along with the genetic ones that they observed. To test that, they subjected the twins to certain types of situational testing, which included public speaking and mental arithmetic—experiences most of us find stressful and would rather avoid. They discovered that one of the twins, the one with a history of being bullied (with a corresponding epigenetic change), had a much lower cortisol response when exposed to those unpleasant situations. Bullying not only turned those children's *SERT* gene to low, it also turned down their levels of cortisol when stressed.

At first this may sound counterintuitive. Cortisol is known as the "stress" hormone and is normally elevated in people under stress. Why, then, would it be blunted in the twin who had a history of being bullied? Wouldn't you think they would be *more* stressed in a heightened situation?

This gets a little complicated, but hang tight: As a response to the persistent bullying trauma, the *SERT* gene of the bullied twin can alter the hypothalamic-pituitary-adrenal (HPA) axis, which normally helps us cope with the stresses and tumbles of daily living. And according to the scientists' findings in the bullied twin, the greater the degree of methylation, the more the *SERT* gene is turned off. The more it's turned off, the more blunted the cortisol response. To understand the sheer depth of this genetic reaction, this type of blunted cortisol response is also often found in people with post-traumatic stress disorder (PTSD).

A spike of cortisol can help us through a tough situation. But having too much cortisol, for too long, can short-circuit our physiology pretty quickly. So, having a blunted cortisol response to stress was the twin's epigenetic reaction to be being bullied day after day. In other words, the twin's epigenome changed in response to protect them from too much sustained cortisol. This compromise is a beneficial epigenetic adaptation in these children that helps them survive persistent bullying. The implications of this are nothing short of staggering.

Many of our genetic responses to our lives work in such a fashion, favoring the short over the long term. Sure, it's easier in the short term to dull our response to persistent stress, but in the long run, epigenetic changes that cause long-term blunted cortisol responses can cause serious psychiatric conditions such as depression and alcoholism. And not to scare you too much, but those epigenetic changes are likely heritable from one generation to the next.

If we're finding such changes in individuals like the bullied twin, then what about traumatic events that affect large swaths of the population? 55

It all started, tragically, on a crisp and clear Tuesday morning in New York City. More than 2,600 people died in and around New York's World Trade Center on September 11, 2001. Many New Yorkers who were in direct proximity to the attacks were traumatized to the point of suffering from post-traumatic stress disorder in the months and years to come.

And for Rachel Yehuda, a professor of psychiatry and neuroscience at the Traumatic Stress Studies Division at the Mount Sinai Medical Center in New York, the terrible tragedy presented a unique scientific opportunity.

Yehuda had long known that people with PTSD often had lower levels of the stress hormone cortisol in their systems—she'd first seen that effect in combat veterans she studied in the late 1980s. So she knew where to start when she began looking at samples of saliva collected from women who were at or near the Twin Towers on 9/11, and who were pregnant at that time.

Indeed, the women who ultimately developed PTSD had significantly lower levels of cortisol. And so did their babies after birth—especially the ones who were in the third trimester of development when the attacks occurred.

Those babies are older now, and Yehuda and her colleagues are still investigating 60 how they've been impacted by the attacks. And they've already established that the children of the traumatized mothers are likely to become distressed more easily than others.[9]

What does all this mean? Taken together with the animal data we now have, it is safe to conclude that our genes do not forget our experiences, even long after we've sought therapy and feel that we've moved on. Our genes will still register and maintain that trauma.

> **Do we or do we not pass on the trauma we experience, be it bullying or 9/11, to the next generation?**

And so the compelling question remains: Do we or do we not pass on the trauma we experience, be it bullying or 9/11, to the next generation? We previously thought that almost all of these epigenetic marks or annotations that were made on our genetic code, like those made in the margins of a musical score, were wiped clean and removed before conception. As we prepare to leave Mendel behind, we are now learning that this is likely not the case.

It is also becoming apparent that there are actually windows of epigenetic susceptibility in embryonic development. Within these important time frames, environmental stressors such as poor nutrition affect whether certain genes become turned off and on and then affect our epigenome. That's right, our genetic inheritance becomes imprinted during pivotal moments of our fetal lives.

When exactly those moments occur no one yet knows precisely, so to be safe, moms now have a genetic motivation to watch their diets and stress levels consistently throughout gestation. Research is now even showing that factors such as a mother's obesity during pregnancy can cause a metabolic reprogramming in the baby, which puts the baby at risk for conditions such as diabetes.[10] This further buttresses the growing movement within obstetrics and maternal-fetal medicine that discourages pregnant woman from eating for two.

And, as in the example of the traumatized Swiss mice, we've already seen that many of these epigenetic changes can be passed on from one generation to the next. Which makes me think that the likelihood is rather high that in the coming years we'll have overwhelming evidence that humans are not immune from this type of epigenetic traumatic inheritance.

In the meantime, given the tremendous amount we've learned about what inheritance really means and what we can do to impact our genetic legacy—in good ways (spinach, perhaps) and bad (stress, it would appear)—you are far from helpless. While it may not always be possible to break completely free from your genetic inheritance, the more you learn, the more you will come to understand that the choices you make can result in a big difference in this generation, the next one, and possibly everyone else down the line.

Because what we do know is that we are the genetic culmination of our life experiences, as well as every event our parents and ancestors ever lived through and survived—from the most joyous to the most heartrending. By examining our capacity to change our genetic destiny through the choices we make and then pass those changes along through generations, we are now in the midst of fully challenging our cherished Mendelian beliefs regarding inheritance.

NOTES

1. This paper is cited by nearly a hundred others and stands out as a landmark: M. Kamakura (2011). Royalactin induces queen differentiation in honeybees. *Nature, 473:* 478. If you find bees as fascinating as I do, you might like to read this paper as well: A. Chittka and L. Chittka (2010). Epigenetics of royalty. *PLOS Biology, 8:* el000532.
2. F. Lyko et al. (2010). The honeybee epigenomes: Differential methylation of brain DNA in queens and workers. *PLOS Biology, 8:* el000506.
3. R. Kucharski et al. (2008). Nutritional control of reproductive status in honeybees via DNA methylation. *Science, 319:* 1827–1830.
4. B. Herb et al. (2012). Reversible switching between epigenetic states in honeybee behavioral subcastes. *Nature Neuroscience, 15:* 1371–1373.
5. Humans have two different versions, *DNMT3A* and *DNMT3B*, which have shared homology and similarity in the catalytic domain to the Dmnt3 gene found in *Apis mellifera*, the honeybee. If you'd like to read more about this, see the following paper: Y. Wang et al. (2006). Functional CpG methylation system in a social insect. *Science, 27:* 645–647.
6. M. Parasramka et al. (2012). MicroRNA profiling of carcinogen-induced rat colon tumors and the influence of dietary spinach. *Molecular Nutrition & Food Research, 56:* 1259–1269.
7. A. Moleres et al. (2013). Differential DNA methylation patterns between high and low responders to a weight loss intervention in overweight or obese adolescents: The EVASYON study. *FASEB Journal, 27:* 2504–2512.
8. T. Franklin et al. (2010). Epigenetic transmission of the impact of early stress across generations. *Biological Psychiatry, 68:* 408–415.

9. R. Yehuda et al. (2009). Gene expression patterns associated with posttraumatic stress disorder following exposure to the World Trade Center attacks. *Biological Psychiatry*, 66: 708–711; R. Yehuda et al. (2005). Transgenerational effects of posttraumatic stress disorder in babies of mothers exposed to the World Trade Center attacks during pregnancy. *Journal of Clinical Endocrinology & Metabolism*, 90: 4115–4118.

10. S. Sookoian et al. (2013). Fetal metabolic programming and epigenetic modifications: A systems biology approach. *Pediatric Research*, 73: 531–542.

Exploring Context

1. Learn more about epigenetics at the Learn Genetics Web site from the University of Utah at learn.genetics.utah.edu/content/epigenetics. How does this additional information change your understanding of Moalem's argument? Use the information you find to expand your response to Question 3 of Questions for Critical Reading.

2. Moalem is on the Medical and Scientific Advisory Board of Global Genes (globalgenes .org), a site dedicated to rare diseases, many of which are genetic. Visit the site to learn more about this advocacy group. How would a greater understanding of genetic flexibility help with such a project?

3. Sharon Moalem has a Tumblr blog, located at sharonmoalem.tumblr.com. Explore his blog. How do his current posts connect to his work in this essay?

Questions for Connecting

1. Sarah Stillman makes a very similar argument in "The Atomic Bomb and the Genetics of Trauma" (p. 443). Synthesize these two essays. What factors, cultural and biological, contribute to the persistence of trauma across generations?

2. Dan Savage, in "It Gets Better" (p. 406), and Urvashi Vaid, in "Action Makes It Better" (p. 411), discuss the consequences of the bullying of LGBTQ youth. Use Moalem's ideas to extend their argument. How does bullying become an even more pressing problem given what Moalem explains?

3. Moalem suggests that what we eat can have a tremendous epigenetic impact. Synthesize his work with Richard Manning's arguments in "The Oil We Eat: Following the Food Chain Back to Iraq" (p. 264). In what ways are agriculture and genetics connected?

Language Matters

1. Use the online mind-mapping tool bubbl.us (bubbl.us) to create a map of Moalem's essay. To what extent does his argument function like genes with multiple possible expressions?

2. Moalem uses endnotes to cite his sources. Research the systems of citation for various disciplines. Which ones promote the use of endnotes or footnotes? Given what you learn, can you determine Moalem's discipline? When might you use endnotes or footnotes, given the citation system you're using in this class?

3. Introductions do a lot of important work in your papers: They introduce the authors, the essays, and, most important, your position or argument. How does Moalem introduce this chapter? How effective is his introduction? Why would you want (or not want) to open your paper that way?

Assignments for Writing

1. Moalem examines the scientific relationship between the mind and body in his discussion of epigenetics. Extend his discussion to philosophy by writing a paper about the mind/body relationship. How does epigenetics change our understanding of the relationship between the two?

2. Write a paper about the persistence of trauma. How do traumatic events such as bullying affect victims? Extend Moalem's work on trauma to consider the larger ramifications of practices such as bullying. Use your work from Question 2 of Questions for Connecting.

3. Write a paper in which you use Moalem's ideas to propose an ethics of eating. How might the epigenetic impacts of food change the way we think about eating? Does the fact that the food changes our genetic code imply that there is a moral dimension to our food choices?

© Victor G. Jeffreys II

MAUREEN O'CONNOR

Maureen O'Connor is a columnist for both *New York* magazine and its fashion blog *The Cut*. Her writing has also appeared online on *Gawker* and the *Daily Beast*. Her writing focuses on issues of pop culture, lifestyle, and sex and relationships in the digital age.

"Race, Ethnicity, Surgery" was originally published in *New York* magazine. Founded in 1968, *New York* is a weekly magazine focusing on news, culture, politics, and entertainment. The July 28, 2014, issue of the magazine, from which this essay is taken, featured stories on the disruption of traditional cab service by Uber and Lyft and the proliferation of "hologram" performances by dead artists. "Race, Ethnicity, Surgery" served as the cover story, and the cover featured an image of face pieces from the popular children's toy Mr. Potato Head.

In "Race, Ethnicity, Surgery," O'Connor recounts the experience of being assessed in a plastic surgeon's office and having her Asian features treated like defects among her "nice" Caucasian ones. She then explores the world of "ethnic plastic surgery," a range of niche procedures available to non-Caucasians. O'Connor finds this field of medicine fraught with questions of beauty, vanity, and race and ethnicity. She considers whether these practices serve to further blur racial borders or instead act to enshrine white standards of beauty.

Have you ever considered surgery to change your features? Are these individual decisions or are they subtly promoted by our culture's standards?

▶ TAGS: *beauty, community, culture, economics, health and medicine, identity, judgment and decision-making, race and ethnicity*

▶ CONNECTIONS: *Gay, Levy, Olson, Pozner, Watters, Yang, Yoshino*

Questions for Critical Reading

1. O'Connor deals with many terms connected to questions of race. As you read pay particular attention to her definitions of *deracination, racial convergence, post-racial,* and *ethnic*.

2. What's the difference between race and ethnicity? Begin by writing out your own thoughts, and then, as you read the essay, mark passages where O'Connor uses these terms and discusses the difference between them. Synthesize her thoughts with your own.

3. Beauty is a central question for O'Connor. Pay close attention to the passages where she discusses standards of beauty. How is beauty measured?

Race, Ethnicity, Surgery

"You've got some nice Caucasian features," Dr. Edmund Kwan says, inspecting my face at his Upper East Side plastic-surgery practice, where the waiting room includes an ottoman larger than my kitchen table. "You're half-Asian mixed with what?" Chinese mom and white dad, I reply. "You inherited a Caucasian nose. Your nose is nice. Your eyes have a little bit of Asian mixed in." He proposes Asian blepharoplasty, a surgical procedure to create or enlarge the palpebral fold, the eyelid crease a few millimeters above the lashline that many Asians lack. "You've got nice big eyes," he admits, but eyelids more like my father's would make them look bigger.

To some, Kwan's assessment may seem offensive—an attempt to remove my mother's race from my face as though it were a pimple. But to others, it will seem as banal as a dietitian advising them to eat more leafy greens—advice having nothing to do with hiding one's race or mimicking another. Asian blepharoplasty belongs to a range of niche cosmetic procedures known colloquially as ethnic plastic surgery, the popularity of which has spiked in recent years—and is prone to heated arguments, major misunderstandings, alternating whiplashes of sympathy and disgust, and some intensely uncomfortable reckonings. (Including, perhaps, the ones in this article.) The issues at stake are loaded: ethnic identity, standards of beauty, the politics of diversity, what constitutes race, and whether exercises of vanity can reshape it.

From 2005 to 2013, the American Society of Plastic Surgeons estimates that the number of cosmetic procedures performed on Asian-Americans increased by 125 percent, Hispanics by 85 percent, and African-Americans by 56 percent. (Procedures on Caucasians increased just 35 percent.) This is, in part, simply a mark of rising purchasing power: Plastic surgery is nothing if not a sign that one has money to burn and status anxiety to spare.

And doctors comfortable advertising their expertise in ethnic plastic surgery are growing wealthy creasing Asian eyelids, pushing sloped foreheads forward, and pulling prominent mouths back. These are procedures outsiders generally view as deracinating processes, sharpening the stereotypically flat noses of Asians, blacks, and Latinos while flattening the stereotypically sharp noses of Arabs and Jews. Some are refinements of formerly rare procedures like the ones that deformed a generation of Jackson-family noses, while others arrived Stateside from the bone-breaking, muscle-shrinking, multi-procedure extremes of Korean and Japanese plastic surgery. And, in fact, many procedures under the "ethnic" umbrella have no Caucasian model at all, as the Asian women asking surgeons to reduce their cheekbones can attest.

And yet this new wave of such plastic surgeries has produced something of a principled outcry from people of all races and ethnicities. "Did I give in to the Man?" *The Talk* host and broadcast-news veteran Julie Chen asked last year, displaying photos from before and after the double-eyelid surgery she got after weathering workplace racism in the '90s. So many people replied "yes" that Chen took time to defend her choice the following week. Reports about Asians overseas getting surgery to resemble "pretty Western celebrities" have a tendency to go viral in Western outlets ranging from the *Daily Mail* to BuzzFeed to *This American Life*.

None of this should be too surprising: White standards still anchor our beauty culture, in part because white people still anchor our privileged classes. Procedures to

5

"white-ify" minorities are not altogether new, nor have their politics been resolved: Just this April, the U.S. Army banned many natural African-American hairstyles for women (an outcry produced only a promise of review). But walk down the street in New York, Miami, Chicago, or L.A.—or Macon, or Clovis, or Dearborn, or Kailua—and you'll see people exhibiting a vast array of personal and cultural aesthetics, some over-lapping, others starkly polarized. A tour of the cosmetic-medicine clinics shaping those bodies and faces paints a more complicated portrait of beauty, too—one that includes "white" ideals like thin noses and arched eyes, yes, but also alternative archetypes like childlike chins and exaggerated butts. The patients display an equally wide array of motivations.

As they traffic in all these modified body parts, even the most esteemed surgeons in the field can come across as almost blasphemously politically incorrect in casual conversation. (I had never thought *Mongoloid* was anything other than an insult until a black surgeon used it to praise a mouth, and even the term "ethnic plastic surgery" confuses most accepted distinctions between ethnicity, which is tied to culture and language, and race, which includes physical appearance.) These exchanges can be jar-ringly retro but also oddly refreshing—discussions of race with strangely post-racial specialists who choose to see beauty as something that can be built, à la carte, with features harvested from peoples all over the world. It feels like science fiction—but utopian or dystopian, I can't decide.

Because, as we all know, race is hugely more complicated than a handful of traits on a face. And many of these new procedures come with horror-show backstories, stretching from the ugly days of phrenology and eugenics to contemporary cultural flash points like hair-straightening and skin-lightening. Practitioners have long de-fended those treatments, too, as personal beauty choices and not deracination. But the stakes for ethnic plastic surgery are higher than those for a hairdo—most are alter-ations to the identity-giving part of the body, the face, and often permanent. Still, even as phrases like *nice Caucasian features* sneak into their language, the practitioners and recipients insist that ethnic plastic surgery isn't about looking white. To them, this new expanse of procedures is not a sign of ethnic self-loathing but proof that the loud-and-proud club of American narcissists has admitted a new set of members—and with them new ideas of what qualifies as beautiful. The people I interviewed differed in their aesthetics, politics, and medical preferences. But they passionately agreed on one thing: No matter what white people say, this isn't about them. Plastic surgery doesn't have to be a sign of deference to some master race, they told me. In fact, it could be the opposite.

> **No matter what white people say, this isn't about them.**

So why won't outsiders take them at their word? The most obvious answer is history. The first known Asian eyelid surgery was performed in 1896 in Japan, to create sym-metry in a woman born with one creased eyelid and one monolid. Thirty years later, it had reached the States. "Changes Racial Features: Young Japanese Wins American Bride by Resort to Plastic Surgery," the *New York Times* announced, in 1926, of a man named Shima Kito who fell in love with a white woman named Mildred. She agreed to marry him only after he "cut the eye corners so that the slant eye so characteristic of the Japanese race was gone. He lowered the skin and flesh of the nose so that the up-turned trait disappeared, and he tightened the pendulous lower lip." Then he changed his name to William White and got engaged to Mildred.

The modern history of double-eyelid surgery is short enough that it can be told 10 through the careers of two linked men — Edmund Kwan, the man who thinks my eyes need work, and his mentor, Dr. Robert Flowers, a white surgeon who began performing the operation in the 1960s.

Growing up in Fairfield County, Dr. Kwan heard about family friends who had their eyelids and noses "done." In medical school he gravitated first to surgery, then plastic surgery, thinking he'd one day serve Asian clientele. But in 1994, after training at Georgetown, Cornell, and Johns Hopkins's renowned facial-trauma surgery unit, he still hadn't performed a single Asian blepharoplasty. (Anti-aging eye lifts are also called blepharoplasties; the scars are similar but the procedures distinct.) Though the operation was known among Asians, and would grow more so in the decades ahead, it was less known in the general population, and thus in the corridors of medical schools and teaching hospitals. So Kwan moved to Hawaii to apprentice under Flowers. Flowers's technique, which requires sedation and an incision between the lashline and brow, is still predominant.

Flowers, who was raised in Tuscaloosa, Alabama, was a military surgeon when he first arrived in Hawaii in 1960. "I got over there just when we were stirring up a little mischief in Southeast Asia," he said through a southern drawl in a recent phone interview. An amateur artist, he found himself "fascinated by the Asian face! I think there was only one Asian family in the State of Alabama back then. When I got to Hawaii, it was so interesting and alien. I would draw pictures of what I considered to be lovely Asian faces and eyes, sketching and so forth. Sometimes a boyfriend would come up and I would get into a bit of trouble, just looking at and sketching Asian eyes," he said with a laugh.

"Everybody was a Flower," Kwan reminisces of those days. "Bob was truly an innovator. He didn't go to Hawaii with the intent of operating on Asian patients. He opened his practice and, just by the population out there, a lot of his patients were Asian."

"The general idea then — and I keep hearing it even today — was that Asians who have facial and eyelid surgery want to 'Westernize,'" says Flowers. "And that's even what Asian plastic surgeons thought they were doing then as well. But that's not what Asians want. They want to be beautiful Asians." Flowers advocated subtler surgeries, pointing out that naturally creased Asian eyelids — which he estimates occur in per-haps half of Asians — are not the same as Caucasian lids. Compared with Asian eyes, the white eye is more deeply set and the crease tends to run more parallel to the lash-line. Asian creases may be narrow or nonexistent at the inner eye — the goopy pink corner may be covered by downward-angled skin called an epicanthic fold — but flared up at the outer edge, creating an overall tilted eye shape.

Not that everyone understood or appreciated the subtlety, particularly at the be- 15 ginning. "I would say, 'Wow, those are big eyelid folds,'" Kwan says of meeting patients who had undergone earlier, cruder blepharoplasties. He grabs his own eyebrows and yanks them halfway to his hairline so that he resembles a startled cartoon character. "The patients from further back had high eyelid folds, but I noticed the lids were getting smaller and smaller over the years." Noticing how Asians' shallower brows and noses deemphasized the "beautiful Asian lid folds," Flowers began recommending brow-lifts and nose jobs to get the desired effect.

Kwan uses the term "ethnic nose" to describe a category of low-lying noses common to Asians, African-Americans, and Hispanics. "Caucasians usually have a high bridge, so their nose jobs are called 'reduction rhinoplasty and shaping.' We remove some bone, narrowing it and smoothing it out and making the tip a nicer shape," he explains. With "ethnic noses," "the bridge is flat and we have to add something," usually a hard silicone implant or cartilage grafted from the ear, rib, or septum. Similar implants can raise the profile of a sloping forehead or weak chin and cost several thousand dollars.

Blepharoplasty and rhinoplasty are among the first procedures that come to mind when thinking about ethnic plastic surgery, and both have charged histories. But this is not the case for other predominantly Asian procedures Kwan performs today, several of which fall under the literally bone-crushing category of "facial contouring." The first time Kwan broke and rearranged multiple bones in a patient's face, back in New York, it was by accident. He'd been filing down an Asian patient's cheekbones to narrow her face, which the patient believed was too wide and flat, when the delicate zygomatic bone snapped off in his hand. "I said, 'Oh my God! I broke the bone!'" he recalls. During his fellowship in the facial-trauma unit, he'd learned to reconstruct faces shattered in car accidents; this time he'd shattered one himself, but knew exactly what to do. "The patient came back and said, 'I love it!'"

Facial contouring is popular in Korea and includes procedures like V-line jaw shaving, which turns round faces into hearts in pursuit of an ideal more manga than *Playboy*, softening the angles of a square jaw and creating a daintier chin. "Double-jaw surgery" is a procedure sometimes used to treat severe underbites and other deformities, now being used for a cosmetic purpose, in which the jawbone is broken and pulled back while the maxilla (or palate) is broken and pulled forward, to yield a fetishized mini-chin.

To Westerners, facial contouring is among the most mysterious of Asian procedures. When I looked at before-and-after pictures of women with sharply jutting cheekbones who'd had their faces narrowed and smoothed via zygoma reduction, I inevitably thought they were prettier before. Without looking up from the pictures, Kwan replied, "Cheekbone reductions are just ethnic. Asians hate this kind of cheek." But white people never seem as fascinated with this surgery as they are with double eyelids, he added.

Maybe that's because the eyelid surgery provides a neat parable for those who believe race can be erased with a scalpel. Reality, of course, is rarely so neat. Monolids are mostly unique to Asians—but that means cosmetic alterations to them are a uniquely Asian cultural phenomenon, too. As has been the case for hair extensions, chemical straighteners, and wigs, beauty rituals that once seemed designed to oppress sometimes turn into symbols of group membership or the foundations of a new aesthetic. Adopted from Korea into a white family in Queens, Mee Young Mendler befriended Koreans at her school in Fresh Meadows; her brother, also adopted, had mostly white friends. To the extent that Mendler was self-conscious about race growing up, it was that she wanted to be more Asian so she could fit in with her friends. Imitating other girls, she sometimes taped her eyelids, a DIY crease-creating strategy akin to wearing false eyelashes. Mendler didn't fully understand blepharoplasty until she saw it on the news at age 19: "They were talking about the surgery and how sad it is that young girls wanted to change their identity. It may sound weird, but that's what made me go look into it." So she took a credit card and made her first big purchase: 20 minutes under the knife with Dr. Edmund Kwan. Her white adoptive mother did not support the choice—but plenty of her Asian friends did.

"I think we're kind of losing ethnic niches. I don't think there's going to be a black race or a white race or an Asian race," says Dr. Michael Jones, a plastic surgeon whose claim to fame is operating on Wendy Williams. ("He did my earlobes," she announces in a radio commercial.) "As we travel more, we have more interracial unions. Essentially, in 200 years, we're going to have one race. I see that even now, people just picking things they like from different ethnicities and calling that the ideal for the moment."

This fantasy of racial convergence, and post-racial or supra-racial beauty, is a common one, if sometimes insidious: a shortcut for imagining a sexy future beyond prejudice without any real effort, just some biracial boning. When *National Geographic* published a mixed-race portrait series called "The Changing Face of America," other websites raved about "the lovely faces" showing "how the 'average American' will look by the year 2050." ("Look at how beautiful it is to see everything diluted that we used to hate," *Hairpin* blogger Jia Tolentino groaned.) But even the work that Jones performs, on patients who are predominantly African-American, doesn't give a neat picture of racial convergence. "Our two big procedures are ethnic rhinoplasty, which tends to make an ethnic or African nose more Anglo—and butts! We are giving people larger derrières," Jones says. There, "they want more ethnicity." And unlike Asian cheekbone reduction, Jones points out that these "more ethnic" ideals have been adopted by the white mainstream, too. White women want "Kim Kardashian" butts and "a more full, Mongoloid- or African-looking lip," he says, sounding every bit the casually blasphemous plastic surgeon.

Fifteen years ago, Jones started his practice in the first floor of the Harlem brownstone he shared with his TV-anchor wife. He found himself revising bad surgeries from the 1990s that had left his black patients with significant scars or the dreaded L-shaped nasal implant, infamous for poking holes through the tips of patients' noses. Subtler implants have since come into style, and scarring is better understood, too. "It's almost a given that a person of color will exhibit some degree of hyperpigmentation to their scars or even a keloid behind the ear after face-lift surgery," Jones notes. "So we evolved our techniques." Jones estimates that 25 to 30 percent of his practice, now located at a midtown medical spa called House of Beauty, is dedicated to treating scars in patients of color.

A different kind of scar treatment brought Dr. Ferdinand Ofodile to plastic surgery. When Ofodile moved to the U.S. from Nigeria in the 1960s to study medicine, he planned to become a vascular surgeon. But a visit home during the Nigerian Civil War convinced him to pursue treatment for those deformed by traumatic injuries, congenital defects, and burns severe enough to impede locomotion, as when scar tissue fuses arms to the torso. Eventually, he returned to the U.S. and became Harlem Hospital's chief of plastic surgery—and an expert on African-American noses. He spent the early '90s measuring the noses of Harlem Hospital patients, employees, and grad students (and a few cadavers) and discovering that African-American nasal anatomy was more diverse than previously thought. Fewer than half were the shape "formerly called the Negroid nose," featuring a low or concave bridge and bulbous tip. Ofodile's signature "ethnic rhinoplasty" involves the insertion of a hard silicone implant. He has a trademarked design called the Ofodile nasal implant, an undulating arc of silicone "suited to satisfy Hispanic and African-American patient needs."

Name-brand nasal implants, it turns out, are a hallmark of the ethnic rhinoplasty 25 universe. "There is a lot of controversy. A lot of competition. People are just fighting for patients," explains Dr. Oleh Slupchynskyj, inventor of the proprietary SLUPimplant, a squared-off sliver of silicone not much larger than a matchstick. (He calls his mini-face-lift technique the SLUPlift.) Raised by Ukrainian immigrants in the Waterside Plaza towers in Kips Bay, Slupchynskyj has a New York accent, a flair for showmanship, and even less concern for political correctness than the other surgeons. During our interview, he spins in a swivel chair in his basement office, periodically dropping back his head to balance a SLUP implant on the bridge of his nose, followed by *Ta-da!* hand gestures.

As the visibly white owner of AfricanAmericanRhinoplasty.com, Slupchynskyj has been accused of racism. "Patients, they'll ask me the same question: 'How did you get into this?' I'll say, 'Well, people started coming to me, early in my practice, and they were getting turned away by other surgeons.' Nobody wanted to operate on these people. They didn't care, they had enough Caucasian rhinoplasty patients. But I saw a niche market." Ethnic rhinoplasty "requires a lot more surgery, a lot more technique" than "the Caucasian girl from Long Island coming to get a hump reduced." His rhinoplasties are priced in the ballpark of $10,000, plus a few thousand more if he's fixing someone else's work. He directs my attention to one of his YouTube videos, in which Slupchynskyj yanks another doctor's mangled nasal implant from the sliced-open face of a sedated black woman. Her facial expression is eerily peaceful.

Why do white people fixate on the "Westernizing" elements of ethnic plastic surgery? While working on this article, I found that people of all races had principled reservations about and passionate critiques of these practices. But the group that most consistently believed participants were deluding themselves about not trying to look white were, well, white people. Was that a symptom of in-group narcissism—white people assuming everyone wants to look like them? Or is it an issue of salience—white people

> **Regardless of whose face the patient idealizes, modern plastic surgery is often a matter of fitting in.**

only paying attention to aesthetics they already understand? Or is white horror at ethnic plastic surgery a cover for something uglier: a xenophobic fear of nonwhites "passing" as white, dressed up as free-to-be-you-and-me political correctness?

Regardless of whose face the patient idealizes, modern plastic surgery is often a matter of fitting in. First, each feature must "fit in" with the rest of the face; every surgeon I spoke to emphasized attention to proportions. Second, there's the matter of any one face "fitting in" with the rest of the population. But fitting in where, exactly? There is a term of art for the attraction to that which is average: *koinophilia*. In nature, averageness tends to be a sign of health, and studies consistently find that composite images of multiple faces are rated as more beautiful than the individual faces composing each image. Blend 50 and it becomes even better.

This phenomenon was first discovered by inventor and eugenicist Sir Francis Galton, who also happened to be Charles Darwin's cousin. In an attempt to determine which facial traits correlated with criminality, he created composites of mug shots—and discovered that the more mug shots he combined, the more attractive the criminals became. In the end, Galton failed completely at his stated goal of studying the criminal face, but he did make an elaborate map denoting towns in Great Britain where hotties could be found.

A modern map of composite hotties would probably show them floating, vaguely, in the oceans between continents, as the cult of mixed-race idealism promotes racially ambiguous stars like Jessica Alba and Kim Kardashian as avatars for post-racial beauty. In 2011, an *Allure* survey found that 85 percent of respondents believed increases in diversity had changed America's beauty standard; 64 percent considered mixed-race women "the epitome of beauty."   30

Though mixed-race couples still report rudeness and outright hostility from strangers—there are plenty of places in this country where they would be reasonably wary of walking in public hand in hand—I would wager that almost as many have experienced the bizarre enthusiasm of strangers who marvel, "Your babies will be so beautiful." You could be the ugliest man and woman in the world, but if you are from distinctly different races, Americans will chase you down the street to describe the color they imagine your babies will be, perhaps invoking the name of a creamy coffee drink or citing a beautiful cousin of a cousin who has slanted eyes that are *green*. Politically correct people who would never make normative statements about the beauty of one race over another nevertheless feel liberated to adjudicate physical supremacy when the subjects are composed of multiple socially constructed groups. "Asian and white is my favorite," a blonde soccer mom at my middle school told me once, as though my parents' decision to marry and have kids was an ingenuity akin to the creation of a Labradoodle. She meant well, of course, even as she fetishized a preteen directly to her face. Today, I would be tempted to respond, "Really? I kind of like Somali-Inuit-Peruvian better," though it may be worth noting that I'm a lot brattier about the subject when I'm talking to white people.

Some elements of beauty appear to be universal. Symmetry and unblemished skin, for instance, are attractive across cultures, likely as a measure of health. Some believe that eye-size preference has biological underpinnings, too; large eyes, particularly in women, are a mark of youthfulness and thus fertility. Still, when Japan sent a delegation of samurai to the United States in 1860 after centuries of isolation, *Survival of the Prettiest* author Nancy Etcoff reports that the warriors said it was "disheartening" to discover American women had "dogs' eyes." Which makes you think that, once you've reached the point where beauty ideals are shaped by social power, figuring out the origin of beauty may be beside the point. (Does the fact that hormonal changes at puberty tend to make women paler and men darker, which some use to explain preferences for lighter pigmentation, make discussions of skin color easier or harder?) And while it's tempting to see new multicultural beauty ideals as democratic in some way, we're still talking about the often cruel happenstance of being born into a body and a face that will be read as symbols, and the sometimes desperate ways people cope with that.

Around the same time that Kwan flew to Hawaii to learn blepharoplasty from Flowers, Dr. Michelle Yagoda flew to Japan's Otsuka Academy to learn an incision-less eyelid-creasing technique. A blue-eyed blonde whose last name means *berry* in Russian, Yagoda once dreamed of being a painter, but traded portraiture for plastic surgery. Her practice is across the street from the Metropolitan Museum of Art and includes "integrative beauty" treatments like homeopathy, stress management, and dietary supplements. "If you want it done right, she's the doctor *Ya-go-da!*" the staff likes to joke.

Incisionless blepharoplasty can be performed with local anesthesia and a needle in under an hour. The doctor flips the eyelid inside out ("everts" it) and connects one part of the eyelid to another. The upside is no incision or scarring; the downside is that the procedure tends to be less permanent.

When Euny Hong got incisionless blepharoplasty, her then-husband didn't even notice. She had it done while visiting family in Korea. "When I came back I kept waiting for him to say something. After a couple of days I said, 'You know what I did?' He almost didn't believe me, even after I explained and pointed. He's Caucasian, but even some of my Asian friends didn't notice." In the midst of Julie Chen's eyelid controversy, Hong, an American-born journalist who appeared frequently on television, wrote a column for the *Wall Street Journal* arguing that eyelid surgery isn't about looking white, to mixed response. "I felt that small eyes were just not adapted to TV technology," she said, characterizing hooded eyes as a televisual distraction on par with wearing eyeglasses. "It's kind of a race issue and definitely an explosive issue for some, but it doesn't indicate self-hatred." 35

Yagoda told me about a black man who had his lips reduced; an Asian family that pressured all female members to get blepharoplasty so their artificial faces would match; and a Latina who had "a nice nose with a small bump and very nice tip," but insisted on having it "scooped" into a ski-jump shape. Yagoda tried to persuade her to choose a less drastic surgery, but the woman replied that she wanted to look like her family — then displayed photos of a family of highly plastic women. "All had rhinoplasties. Bad ones, I think, overly scooped. But all looking pretty identical." Yagoda stalled, urging the woman to think carefully about the difficult-to-reverse procedure. After a year, the woman still wanted it. Yagoda performed the surgery, reasoning that it's not her job to dictate taste.

Dr. Steve Lee shares space with a chiropractor and a hand therapist in a neon-lit building in Flushing, Queens. This would seem to place him a world away from Kwan's office in the Upper East Side, but until recently, both had stock photos of the same Asian model with translucent skin and enormous eyes on the home pages of their websites. And both have made forays into controversial off-label procedures more commonly seen overseas. That off-label spectrum also includes, at its extremes, tabloid body-horror tales grouping elaborate Korean surgery with black-market scam artists who inject butts with cement and baffling fads like Japan's "bagelhead" phenomenon, inviting readers to gawk at faces unlike their own. (The reading experience is what I imagine attending a 19th-century freak show would have been like, conflating foreignness with deformity in the pursuit of titillation.)

But whereas Kwan slims faces by breaking and shaving bones, Lee will shoot 20 units of Botox straight into a patient's masseter jaw muscles to wither them temporarily: "I hate to use the word *side effect*, but if you use a higher dose of Botox, not only do you paralyze the muscle, but you can shrink the muscle," Lee explains, pointing to before-and-after pictures of a square-jawed woman whose lower face he narrowed. "It makes biting and chewing a little weaker. I tell people, 'If you want a good result, don't chew gum.'" The less you chew, the smaller your jaw.

The same tactic can be used to slim the muscles in a woman's legs, using "several times" the paralyzing agents necessary to slim a jaw. Kwan has experimented with permanent muscle-reduction techniques pioneered overseas, where there is less governmental oversight. "You actually cut the nerve to the muscle," he explains, displaying his leg and pointing to a spot below the inside of his knee. "There are some risks to it. There's a scar associated with it. And you could really cripple someone."

When blepharoplasty goes wrong, the result is usually correctable—a crease   40
that becomes uncreased, or droops a millimeter or two over time. When it goes really wrong, though, a patient may be permanently unable to close his eyes. "Technically it's not that they can't close their eyes, it's just that there's still a little gap when they do it," Lee explains. He performs a Google image search for blepharoplasty complications (never do this) and pulls up photos of a man trying and failing to fully blink.

To reduce costs and keep patients out of the surgery room, Lee often defaults to injectable solutions. He raises the bridge of the nose with fillers like Juvéderm, the squishy substance commonly used for plumping lips and filling wrinkles. He has also shot fillers into the earlobes of superstitious Chinese patients; large lobes signify luck. "Everybody wants something simple, easy, fast, cheap," he says. But some accept the price of blepharoplasty as the cost of doing business in America.

"One example was a bus driver," Lee recalls of a recent patient in his 30s. "He had droopy eyes. His supervisor jumped in: 'Are you sleeping on the job? Why is it every time I see you, you're sleeping on the job?' He was worried, and I felt bad because he's just a bus driver, not like he's a high-powered CEO or something. But he said, 'I want to look more awake so I don't lose my job,' and I said, 'Okay, let's do it.'" Lee's Asian blepharoplasties cost in the neighborhood of $2,500. He has since seen that patient driving his bus in the neighborhood. He says he looked alert.

But even if the idea of ethnic plastic surgery makes you queasy—even if plastic surgery, in general, makes you depressed—the more you talk to people who have actually undergone these procedures, the harder it becomes to view their choices as simple racial capitulations. (Still, I think I'll skip that blepharoplasty Kwan recommended.)

With Jamaican ancestry, a British upbringing, and a career that includes fashion journalism for *Essence* and *InStyle*, 47-year-old Zumba and fitness instructor Tina Redwood is something of a test case in multicultural aesthetics. "Growing up with pretty sisters and a beautiful mum, I was the one they called 'Noseybonk,'" she tells me at a coffee shop a few blocks from her home in Harlem. Following the birth of her daughter and the death of her father, Redwood went through a body-image reckoning that included a dramatic weight loss and a nose job. After ruling out a surgeon who created a digital composite that looked like a Caucasian nose pasted on a black face ("Yikes! Don't want that"), she chose Ofodile. He filed down part of her nose and inserted a modest implant, causing her brother to call her a "traitor" to the Redwood name. "I said, 'Hey, man, hallelujah. You can carry that look.'

"Older women have asked me if I wanted to look less black. Don't be ridiculous. Since landing in this country with a British accent, people always thought I was white." She gestures to the diverse crowd at the coffee shop: "I don't know what being black is anymore," she says. "I remember when I was fearful of the weave," she continues. "Because people were like, 'Oh, she's trying to be white with that Korean hair?'" Only later, listening to a recording of our interview, do I realize the irony of that accusation. "What's his name, my sweetheart, Al Sharpton? He said to judge a man by what's in his head, not on his head, back when he used to have that James Brown perm — we're finally defining ourselves individually rather than as a group. Because we are not a monolithic group," she says. "Mike Tyson, I was just watching his show on HBO, and he said, 'People keep asking me why I've got a tramp stamp on my face. If you don't like it, don't look! It's my face.' I was like, 'Amen.'"

Exploring Context

1. Use a Web search engine to find images of "ethnic plastic surgery." Who is represented and why? How do the images confirm or challenge O'Connor's argument? Analyze these images using your work from Question 3 of Questions for Critical Reading.

2. After completing Question 1, do a Web image search for "ethnic beauty." How do these images differ from the ones you found in Question 1? How do they reflect O'Connor's argument about standards of beauty?

3. Journalist Esther Honig, in her project "Before & After," asked Photoshop aficionados around the world to "make [her] beautiful." Explore the results of this project as well as a second similar project, "Before & After Part 2," at Honig's Web site, estherhonig .com. How is beauty perceived around the world? Do perceptions reflect particular ethnicities?

Questions for Connecting

1. Steve Olson, in "The End of Race: Hawaii and the Mixing of Peoples" (p. 300), also suggests that we are headed toward a post-racial future. Synthesize Olson's argument with O'Connor's. In what ways do race and ethnicity persist? You may want to use some of the terms you defined in Question 1 of Questions for Critical Reading.

2. How does culture enforce notions of beauty? Using both O'Connor's essay and Jennifer Pozner's "Ghetto Bitches, China Dolls, and Cha Cha Divas" (p. 359), examine the ways in which stereotypes of race and ethnicity intersect standards of beauty. Draw from your work in Exploring Context in making your argument.

3. Many ethnic surgery procedures are targeted toward Asians. Using Wesley Yang's "Paper Tigers" (p. 521), explore the ramifications of cultural stereotypes about Asians. Does Yang offer any solutions to the problems that O'Connor examines?

Language Matters

1. Varying your word choice adds interest for your reader, but it can be a particularly challenging task. Look back through O'Connor's essay. How does she vary her word choice to convey meaning? How many different words for *race* does she use? How does she handle the implications of these terms? How might you vary your word choice in your own writing?

2. Draw the argument of O'Connor's essay, either by hand or with a graphics program on your computer. How would the inclusion of this drawing affect O'Connor's text? What elements of visual argument do you use to convey O'Connor's meaning?

3. What is the difference between a dash and a hyphen? Use a grammar handbook or other reliable source to differentiate the two and review the rules on when to use each. Apply your findings to O'Connor's text. How does she use each? When might you use these punctuation marks in your own writing?

Assignments for Writing

1. In referring to the ways in which ethnic surgery can construct beauty, O'Connor states, "It feels like science fiction — but utopian or dystopian, I can't decide" (p. 289). Answer her question by writing a paper about the ethics of ethnic surgery. Does the availability of ethnic surgery allow us to change our notions of beauty or does it simply reinforce racial and ethnic stereotypes? Use your work from Questions for Critical Reading and Exploring Context to support your argument.

2. What is the future of race and ethnicity? Write a paper in which you project the trajectory of these concepts in our culture. Are we headed toward a post-racial future? Use your work from Questions for Critical Reading and Exploring Context as well as Question 1 of Questions for Connecting.

3. Ethnic surgeries are, ultimately, a matter of individual choice; however, O'Connor suggests that these choices affect larger groups. How does the body negotiate the relationship between individual and group identity? Write a paper in which you consider the role that the body and its appearance plays in group identities such as race and ethnicity.

STEVE OLSON

Journalist **Steve Olson**, who holds a B.S. in physics from Yale University, has reported for the *Atlantic*, *Science*, and *Scientific American* and has published multiple books, including *Mapping Human History: Genes, Race, and Our Common Origins* (2002), which was a finalist for the National Book Award, and *Count Down* (2004), about teens at the International Mathematical Olympiad.

In *Mapping Human History*, the source of the following selection, Olson studies the path of our species through genes and continents, tracking all of humanity back to a small group that lived in eastern Africa, debunking racial myths along the way. Regardless of what appear to be differences among us, suggests Olson, biologically we are all basically the same. Our group origins and differences, which were superficial to begin with, lose importance as time goes by.

AP Photo/Haraz N. Ghanbari

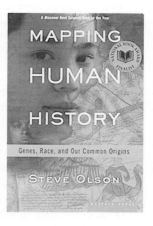

In "The End of Race: Hawaii and the Mixing of Peoples," Olson considers centuries of intermarriage between native and nonnative races in the Hawaiian islands. Although this extensive "mixing of peoples" has led some to propose Hawaii as an example of interracial harmony, Olson acknowledges that such claims are not entirely true. Though the majority of those born and raised in Hawaii come from a complex racial and ethnic makeup, social, political, and historical influences have contributed to deep cultural divides among the various island populations. Now, in the aftermath of European colonization, the preservation of Hawaiian culture and the definition of what it means to be a native Hawaiian are pressing questions with no easy genetic or biological answers. Thus Olson ultimately questions whether racial and cultural identity is rooted in biology or affiliation. The "end of race" is, perhaps, no end at all.

What defines *race*? And given how complicated such a definition must inevitably be, how can we end racism and promote racial harmony?

▶ TAGS: *community, culture, genetics, identity, judgment and decision-making, race and ethnicity, science and technology, social change, tradition*

▶ CONNECTIONS: *O'Connor, Watters, Yang, Yoshino*

Questions for Critical Reading

1. What is a *community of descent*? Develop a definition by reading Olson's text to locate quotations that define the concept. Offer, too, an example of a community of descent from your own experience.

2. As you read, ask yourself how Olson defines *race*. Create a definition and support it using quotations from Olson's essay. To do so, you will need to read his essay critically, paying close attention to what Olson has to say about the concept of race.

3. If race no longer has a biological basis, as Olson claims, why do ethnicities continue to function in society? Use Olson's text to propose reasons why race persists.

The End of Race: Hawaii and the Mixing of Peoples

> He loved everything, he was full of joyous love toward everything that he saw. And it seemed to him that was just why he was previously so ill—because he could love nothing and nobody.
>
> —HERMANN HESSE, *Siddhartha*

On the morning of November 26, 1778, the 100-foot-long, three-masted ship *Resolution*, captained by the fifty-year-old Englishman James Cook, sailed into view off the northeast coast of the Hawaiian island of Maui. The island's Polynesian inhabitants had never seen a European sailing ship before. The sight of the *Resolution* just beyond the fierce windward surf must have looked as strange to them as a spaceship from another planet. Yet they responded without hesitation. They boarded canoes and paddled to the ship. From atop the rolling swells they offered the sailors food, water, and, in the case of the women, themselves.

One can easily imagine the contrast: the European sailors—gaunt, dirty, many bearing the unmistakable signs of venereal disease—and the Polynesians, a people who abided by strict codes of personal hygiene, who washed every day and plucked the hair from their faces and underarms, whose women had bodies "moulded into the utmost perfection," in the words of one early admirer. At first Cook forbade his men to bring the women on board the ship "to prevent as much as possible the communicating [of the] fatal disease [gonorrhea] to a set of innocent people." In the weeks and months to come, as the *Resolution* lingered offshore, Cook was far less resolute. Toward the end of 1779, the first of what are today called *hapa haoles*—half European, half non-European—were born on the island of Maui.

The nineteenth-century stereotype of the South Pacific as a sexual paradise owes as much to the feverish imaginations of repressed Europeans as to the actions of the Polynesians. The young women who swam out to the ships in Hawaii, Tahiti, and other South Pacific islands were from the lower classes, not from the royalty, which carefully guarded its legitimacy. Many were training to be dancers in religious festivals. They would rise in status by exchanging their sexual favors for a tool, a piece of cloth, or an iron nail.

The Polynesians paid dearly for their openness. At least 300,000 people, and possibly as many as 800,000, lived on the Hawaiian islands when Captain Cook first sighted them (today the total population of the state is about 1.2 million). Over the course of the next century, diseases introduced by Europeans reduced the native population to fewer than 50,000. By the time the painter Paul Gauguin journeyed to the Pacific in 1891, the innocence that Europeans had perceived among the Polynesians was gone. "The natives, having nothing, nothing at all to do, think of one thing only, drinking," he wrote. "Day by day the race vanishes, decimated by the European diseases. . . . There is so much prostitution that it does not exist. . . . One only knows a thing by its contrary, and its contrary does not exist." The women in Gauguin's paintings are beautiful yet defeated, without hope, lost in a vision of the past.

Today visitors to Maui land on a runway just downwind from the shore where   5
Captain Cook battled the surf eleven generations ago. Once out of the airport, they encounter what is probably the most genetically mixed population in the world. To the genes of Captain Cook's sailors and the native Polynesians has been added the DNA of European missionaries, Mexican cowboys, African American soldiers, and plantation workers from throughout Asia and Europe. This intense mixing of DNA has produced a population of strikingly beautiful people. Miss Universe of 1997 and Miss America of 2001 were both from Hawaii. The former, Brook Mahealani Lee, is a classic Hawaiian blend. Her ancestors are Korean and Hawaiian, Chinese and European.

Bernie Adair—who was selling candles at a swap meet in Kahului, Maui's largest town, when I met her—told me that her family's history was typical. Adair, whose ancestors came to Hawaii from the Philippines, married a Portuguese man in the 1960s. In the 1980s their daughter Marlene married a man of mixed Hawaiian, Chinese, and Portuguese descent. Adair's granddaughter Carly, peeking shyly at me from under a folding table, therefore embodies four different ethnicities. "These children have grandparents with so many different nationalities you can't tell what they are," Adair said.

> **Hawaii's high rates of intermarriage have fascinated academics for decades.**

Almost half the people who live in Hawaii today are of "mixed" ancestry. What it means to be mixed is not at all obvious genetically, but for official purposes it means that a person's ancestors fall into more than one of the four "racial" categories identified on U.S. census forms: black, white, Native American, and Asian or Pacific Islander. Intermarriage is a cumulative process, so once an individual of mixed ancestry is born, all of that person's descendants also will be mixed. As intermarriage continues in Hawaii—and already almost half of all marriages are between couples of different or mixed ethnicities—the number of people who will be able to call themselves pure Japanese, or pure Hawaiian, or pure white (*haole* in Hawaiian), will steadily decline.

Hawaii's high rates of intermarriage have fascinated academics for decades. The University of Hawaii sociologist Romanzo Adams wrote an article titled "Hawai'i as a Racial Melting Pot" in 1926, and many scholars since then have extolled Hawaii as a model of ethnic and racial harmony. The researchers have always been a bit vague about the reasons for all this intermarriage; explanations have ranged from the benign climate to the "aloha spirit" of the Native Hawaiians. But their lack of analytic rigor hasn't damped their enthusiasm. One of the goals of the former Center for Research on Ethnic Relations at the University of Hawaii was "to determine why ethnic harmony exists in Hawai'i" and "to export principles of ethnic harmony to the mainland and the world."

The rest of the United States has a smaller percentage of mixed marriages than does Hawaii. But given recent trends, one might wonder if the country as a whole is headed down a road Hawaii took long ago. According to the 2000 census, one in twenty children under the age of eighteen in the United States is mixed, in that their parents fall into more than one racial category. Between the 1990 and 2000 censuses, the number of interracial couples quadrupled. This number—about 1.5 million of 55 million married couples—is not yet high, but because of kinship ties, American families are already much more mixed than they look. Demographer Joshua Goldstein of Princeton University has calculated that about 20 percent of Americans are already in extended families with someone from a different racial group—that is, they or their parents, uncles and aunts, siblings, or children have married someone classified as a member of a different race.

The rapid growth of interracial marriages in the United States and elsewhere marks a new phase in the genetic history of humanity. Since the appearance of modern humans in Africa more than 100,000 years ago, human groups have differentiated in appearance as they have expanded across the globe and have undergone some measure of reproductive isolation. This differentiation has always been limited by the recentness of our common ancestry and by the powerful tendency of groups to mix over time. Still, many human populations have remained sufficiently separate to develop and retain the distinctive physical characteristics we recognize today.

In Hawaii this process is occurring in reverse. It's as if a videotape of our species' history were being played backward at a fantastically rapid speed. Physical distinctions that took thousands of generations to produce are being wiped clean with a few generations of intermarriage.

The vision of the future conjured up by intermarriage in Hawaii can be seductive. When everyone is marrying everyone else, when the ethnic affiliation of most people can no longer be ascertained at a glance, one imagines that ethnic and racial tensions would diminish. But spending some time in Hawaii shows that the future will not be that simple. Despite the high rate of intermarriage here, ethnic and racial tensions haven't really disappeared. They have changed into something else, something less threatening, perhaps, but still divisive. Hawaii may well be a harbinger of a racially mixed future. But it won't be the future many people expect.

Many of the harshest conflicts in the world today are between people who are physically indistinguishable. If someone took a roomful of Palestinians and Israelis from the Middle East, or of Serbs and Albanians from the Balkans, or of Catholics and Protestants from Ireland, or of Muslims and Hindus from northern India, or of Dayaks and Madurese from Indonesia, gave them all identical outfits and haircuts, and forbade them to speak or gesture, no one could distinguish the members of the other group—at least not to the point of being willing to shoot them. The antagonists in these conflicts have different ethnicities, but they have been so closely linked biologically throughout history that they have not developed marked physical differences.

Yet one of the most perverse dimensions of ethnic thinking is the "racialization" of culture—the tendency to think of another people as not just culturally but genetically distinct. In the Yugoslavian war, the Croats caricatured their Serbian opponents as tall and blond, while the Serbs disparaged the darker hair and skin of the Croats—even though these traits are thoroughly intermixed between the two groups. During World

War II the countries of Europe fiercely stereotyped the physical attributes of their enemies, despite a history of intermarriage and migration that has scrambled physical characteristics throughout the continent. In Africa the warring Tutsis and Hutus often call attention to the physical differences of their antagonists, but most observers have trouble distinguishing individual members of the two groups solely on the basis of appearance.

The flip side of this biological stereotyping is the elevation of one's own ancestry.   15
The Nazis were the most notorious believers in the purity of their past, but many other groups have similar beliefs. They proclaim themselves to be descended from ancient tribes of noble warriors, or from prominent families in the distant past, or even from famous individuals.

Genetics research has revealed the flaw inherent in any such belief. Every group is a mixture of many previous groups, a fleeting collection of genetic variants drawn from a shared genetic legacy. The Polynesian colonizers of the Hawaiian archipelago are a good example. In 1795 the German anatomist J. F. Blumenbach proposed that the "Malays"—a collection of peoples, including the Polynesians, from southeastern Asia and Oceania—were one of the five races of humanity, in addition to Africans, Caucasians, Mongoloids, and Native Americans. But all of these groups (to the extent that they can be defined) are genetic composites of previous groups. In the case of the

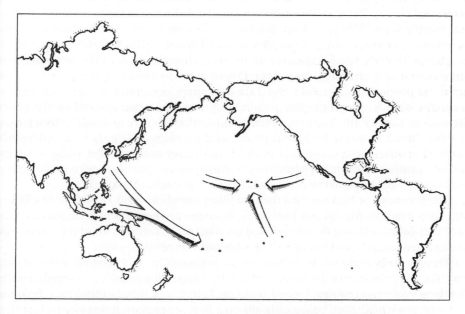

The Polynesian inhabitants of Hawaii are descended from people who lived both in southeastern Asia and in Melanesia, which includes New Guinea and nearby islands. The Polynesians migrated first to the South Pacific islands of Fiji, Tonga, and Samoa, with later migrations taking their descendants from the Marquesas islands to Hawaii. More recent migrants have included people from Asia, the Americas, and Europe.

Polynesians, this mixing was part of the spread of humans into the Pacific. The last major part of the world to be occupied by humans was Remote Oceania, the widely separated islands scattered in a broad crescent from Hawaii to New Zealand. Before that, humans had been living only in Near Oceania, which includes Australia, Papua New Guinea, and the Bismarck Archipelago. The humans who settled these regions were adept at short ocean crossings, but they never developed the kinds of boats or navigation skills needed to sail hundreds of miles to Fiji, Samoa, and beyond.

Then, about 6,000 years ago, rice and millet agriculture made the leap across the Formosa Strait from the mainland of southeastern Asia to Taiwan. From there, agriculture began to spread, island by island, to the south and southeast. With it came two important cultural innovations. The first was the Austronesian language family, which eventually spread halfway around the world, from Madagascar to Easter Island. The second was a suite of new technologies — pottery, woodworking implements, and eventually the outrigger canoe* and ways of using the stars to navigate across large expanses of open water. Archaeological evidence shows that people first reached the previously uninhabited island of Fiji about 3,000 years ago. They sailed to Easter Island, their farthest point east, in about AD 300 and to New Zealand, their farthest point south, in about 800.

One hypothesis, known as the express-train model of Polynesian origins, claims that both the knowledge of agriculture and Austronesian languages were carried into the Pacific by people descended almost exclusively from the first farmers who set sail from Taiwan. But genetic studies have revealed a much more complex picture. Mitochondrial and Y-chromosome haplotypes† among today's Polynesians show that there was extensive mixing of peoples in Near Oceania, which eventually produced the groups that set sail for the remote islands. Though many of the mitochondrial haplotypes and Y chromosomes of the Polynesians do seem to have come from the mainland of southeastern Asia and Taiwan, others originated in New Guinea and its nearby islands — a geographic region known as Melanesia (named for the generally dark skin of its inhabitants). Geneticists Manfred Kayser and Mark Stoneking of the Max Planck Institute for Evolutionary Anthropology in Leipzig have dubbed the resulting synthesis the "slow-boat model." According to this model, today's Polynesians can trace their ancestry both to the Austronesian speakers who moved out of southeastern Asia and to the people who already occupied Melanesia.

The Polynesians first reached the Hawaiian islands around AD 400, probably in a migration from the Marquesas islands. A subsequent wave of people migrated to Hawaii from Tahiti between the twelfth and the fourteenth century. Then the islands saw no more newcomers until Captain Cook's arrival four centuries later.

The discovery of Hawaii by Europeans did not result in an immediate influx of colonists. The early decades of the nineteenth century brought just a trickle of settlers to the islands — washed-up sailors, retired captains, British and Russian traders, missionaries. Large-scale migration began only after the first sugar plantations were established around the middle of the century. In 1852, three hundred Chinese men arrived to work the plantations. Over the next century nearly half a million more workers followed.

20

---

*Outrigger canoe: Canoe with a side floatation unit for increased stability [Ed.].

†Mitochondrial and Y-chromosome haplotypes: Genetic information that can be used to trace ancestry through the mother's and father's lineage [Ed.].

They came from China, Japan, Korea, Puerto Rico, Spain, Poland, Austria, Germany, Norway, and Russia. Some of these groups have long since disappeared, blending into the genetic background. Others still have a significant ethnic presence on the islands.

A few miles from the Honolulu airport is a vivid reminder of those times. Hawaii's Plantation Village is one of the few tourist attractions designed as much for the locals as for mainlanders. It meticulously recreates a camp town of the type that once dotted the islands, housing the workers who toiled each day in the sugar and pineapple fields. Each house along the main avenue reflects the ethnicity of the workers who lived there: A large bread oven sits next to the Portuguese house, rice cookers dominate the kitchen of the Chinese house, crucifixes adorn the walls of the Puerto Rican house. A Japanese shrine is a few doors away from the Chinese society building. Down the hill by the taro* fields is a *dohyo*, a sumo ring, where the workers wrestled every Sunday afternoon.

Mike Hama showed me around the day I was there. The descendant of Japanese, German, Hawaiian, and Irish grandparents, Hama grew up on a plantation camp in the 1940s. "Kids of all different nationalities played together in these camps," he told me. "We didn't know we were different." They communicated using a pidgin that combined words from many languages. The German kids taught the other kids to polka in the camp social halls. The Japanese kids taught their friends sumo wrestling. When the Japanese emperor visited Hawaii after World War II, according to a widely told if hard-to-verify story, he was so impressed to see wrestlers of all different nationalities in the *dohyo* that when he returned to Japan he opened the country's sumo rings to foreigners.

When Hama was eighteen, he joined the military and was stationed in California. "That was a real awakening for me," he recalls. "For the first time I saw the bigotry that was going on outside Hawaii." He moved back to Hawaii as soon as he could and married a woman of mixed ancestry. His four daughters think of themselves as nothing other than local Hawaiians.

The camp towns disappeared decades ago in Hawaii, yet they have left a remarkable legacy. Large-scale segregation in housing remains rare on the islands. People of all ethnic backgrounds live side by side, just as they did in the camp towns. The only people who live in ghettos are the soldiers on military bases and wealthy haoles who wall themselves off in gated communities. Because neighborhoods are integrated in Hawaii, so are most of the schools. Children of different ethnicities continue to grow up together and marry, just as they did in the camps.

Integrated neighborhoods, integrated schools, high rates of intermarriage—the islands sound as if they should be a racial paradise. But there's actually a fair amount of prejudice here. It pops up in novels, politics, the spiels of standup comics. And it's especially prominent in everyday conversation — "talk stink" is the pidgin term for disrespecting another group.

Some of the prejudice is directed toward haoles, who continue to occupy many of the positions of social and economic prominence on the islands (though their days as plantation overlords are long gone). Nonwhites label haoles as cold, self-serving, arrogant, meddling, loud, and even that old stereotype—smelly (because, it is held,

25

---

*Taro: Common name for several varieties of a root vegetable [Ed.].

they still do not bathe every day). White kids say they'll get beat up if they venture onto certain nonwhite beaches. Occasionally a rumor sweeps through a school about an upcoming "Kill a Haole" day. The rumors are a joke meant to shock the prevailing sensibilities. But one would not expect such a joke where racial tensions are low.

Other groups come in for similarly rough treatment. The Japanese are derided as clannish and power-hungry, the Filipinos as ignorant and underhanded, the Hawaiians as fat, lazy, and fun-loving. And, as is true of stereotypes everywhere, the objects of them have a tendency to reinforce them, either by too vigorously denying or too easily repeating them.

"Intermarriage may indicate tolerance," says Jonathan Okamura, an anthropologist at the University of Hawaii, "but it doesn't mean we have an egalitarian society on a larger scale." Though he calls his viewpoint a "minority position," Okamura holds that racial and ethnic prejudice is deeply ingrained in the institutional structures of everyday life in Hawaii. For example, the integration of the public schools is deceptive, he says. Well-off haoles, Chinese, and Japanese send their children to private schools, and the public schools are underfunded. "We've created a two-tiered system that makes inequality increasingly worse rather than better," says Okamura. Meanwhile the rapid growth of the tourism industry in Hawaii has shut off many traditional routes to economic betterment. Tourism produces mostly low-paying jobs in sales, service, and construction, Okamura points out, so people have few opportunities to move up career ladders.

Of course, talented and lucky individuals still get ahead. "Students with parents who didn't go to college come to the university and do well—that happens all the time," Okamura says. "But it doesn't happen enough to advance socioeconomically disadvantaged groups in society."

Several ethnic groups occupy the lower end of the socioeconomic scale, but one in particular stands out: the people descended from the island's original inhabitants. Native Hawaiians have the lowest incomes and highest unemployment rates of any ethnic group. They have the most health problems and the shortest life expectancy. They are the least likely to go to college and the most likely to be incarcerated.

Then again, applying statistics like these to a group as large and diverse as Native Hawaiians is inevitably misleading. Individuals with some Hawaiian ancestry make up a fifth of the population in Hawaii. Some are successful; some are not. Some are consumed by native issues; others pay them no mind. And Native Hawaiians are much less marginalized in Hawaii than are, for example, Native Americans in the rest of the United States. Hawaiian words, names, and outlooks have seeped into everyday life on the islands, producing a cultural amalgam that is one of the state's distinct attractions.

Native Hawaiians should not be seen as simply another ethnic group, the leaders of their community point out. Other cultures have roots elsewhere; people of Japanese, German, or Samoan ancestry can draw from the traditions of an ancestral homeland to sustain an ethnic heritage. If the culture of the Native Hawaiians disappears, it will be gone forever. Greater recognition of the value and fragility of this culture has led to a resurgence of interest in the Hawaiian past. Schools with Hawaiian language immersion programs have sprung up around the islands to supplement the English that children speak at home. Traditional forms of Hawaiian dance, music, canoeing, and religion all have undergone revivals.

This Hawaiian Renaissance also has had a political dimension. For the past several decades a sovereignty movement has been building among Native Hawaiians that seeks some measure of political autonomy and control over the lands that the U.S. government seized from the Hawaiian monarchy at the end of the nineteenth century. Reflecting the diversity of the native population, several sovereignty organizations have carried out a sometimes unseemly struggle over strategies and goals. One radical faction advocates the complete independence of the islands from the United States. More moderate groups have called for the establishment of a Native Hawaiian nation modeled on the Indian tribes on the mainland. Native Hawaiians would have their own government, but it would operate within existing federal and state frameworks, and its citizens would remain Americans.

Native Hawaiian sovereignty faces many hurdles, and it is premature to harp on exactly how it would work. But whenever the topic comes up in discussion, a question quickly surfaces: Exactly who is a Native Hawaiian? "Pure" Hawaiians with no non-Hawaiian ancestors probably number just a few thousand. Many Native Hawaiians undoubtedly have a preponderance of Hawaiian ancestors, but no clear line separates natives from nonnatives. Some people who call themselves Native Hawaiians probably have little DNA from Polynesian ancestors.

> **Exactly who is a Native Hawaiian?**

Past legislation has waffled on this issue. Some laws define Native Hawaiians as people who can trace at least half their ancestry to people living in Hawaii before the arrival of Captain Cook. Others define as Hawaiian anyone who has even a single precontact Hawaiian ancestor. These distinctions are highly contentious for political and economic as well as cultural reasons. Many state laws restrict housing subsidies, scholarships, economic development grants, and other benefits specifically to Native Hawaiians.

As the study of genetics and history has progressed, an obvious idea has arisen. Maybe science could resolve the issue. Maybe a genetic marker could be found that occurs only in people descended from the aboriginal inhabitants of Hawaii. Then anyone with that marker could be considered a Native Hawaiian.

No one is better qualified to judge this idea than Rebecca Cann, a professor of genetics at the University of Hawaii. Cann was the young graduate student at the University of California at Berkeley who, with Mark Stoneking, did much of the work that led to the unveiling of mitochondrial Eve.* She haunted hospital delivery rooms to obtain mitochondrion-rich placentas, which at that time was the only way to get enough mitochondrial DNA to sequence. She ran gels and compared nucleotides. Her faculty adviser, Allan Wilson, landed mitochondrial Eve on the cover of *Newsweek*, but Cann did the footwork.

She moved to Hawaii even before mitochondrial Eve made headlines, responding to an ad in *Science* magazine for a job. She's been here ever since, though her flat American accent still betrays a childhood spent in Iowa. She met me at the door of her office, in the foothills above Honolulu, dressed in sandals and a patterned Hawaiian

35

---

*Mitochondrial Eve: A term in genetics for the maternal ancestor of every human now alive. This woman is estimated to have lived about 200,000 years ago in East Africa [Ed.].

dress. "I think we correctly anticipated many of the applications and potential problems of this research," she said, "right down to people wanting to clone Elvis from a handkerchief he'd used to wipe his brow. What we didn't understand was the degree to which religious and cultural beliefs would dictate attitudes toward genetic materials. In Hawaii, for instance, there's a very strong belief in *mana*, in the power of the spirit, which is contained in the remains of a person's ancestors. The absolute disgust that many people have toward the desecration of a grave—that was a cultural eye-opener for me."

Despite the occasional cultural difficulties, Cann has continued her study of human genetics in Hawaii and has played an important role in piecing together the prehistory of the Pacific. By comparing the mitochondrial DNA sequences of people on various islands, she has traced the gradual eastward spread of modern humans from southeastern Asia and Melanesia. She has discovered that men and women had different migration patterns into the Pacific and has even detected tantalizing evidence, still unconfirmed, of genetic contacts between Pacific Islanders and South Americans. "I'm convinced that our history is written in our DNA," she told me.

Yet she cautioned against using genetics to determine ethnicity. "I get people   40
coming up to me all the time and saying, 'Can you prove that I'm a Hawaiian?'" She can't, she said, at least not with a high degree of certainty. A given individual might have a mitochondrial haplotype that is more common among Native Hawaiians. But the ancestors of the aboriginal Hawaiians also gave rise to other Pacific populations, so a mitochondrial sequence characteristic of Native Hawaiians could have come from a Samoan or Filipino ancestor.

Also, a person's mitochondrial DNA is not necessarily an accurate indication of ancestry. The only way for a person to have mitochondrial DNA from a woman who lived in Hawaii before the arrival of Captain Cook is for that person to have an unbroken line of grandmothers dating back to that woman. But because groups have mixed so much in Hawaii, mitochondrial lineages have become thoroughly tangled. People who think of themselves as Native Hawaiian could easily have had non-Hawaiian female ancestors sometime in the past eleven generations, which would have given them mitochondrial DNA from another part of the world.

These genetic exchanges are also common elsewhere in the world, even in populations that think of themselves as less mixed. Most native Europeans, for example, have mitochondrial DNA characteristic of that part of the world. But some have mitochondrial DNA from elsewhere—southern Africa, or eastern Asia, or even Polynesia—brought to Europe over the millennia by female immigrants. The British matron who has a mitochondrial haplotype found most often in southern Africans is not an African, just as the Native Hawaiian with mitochondrial DNA from a German great-great-grandmother does not automatically become German.

This confusion of genetic and cultural identities becomes even greater with the Y chromosome, given the ease with which that chromosome can insert itself into a genealogy. Most of the early migrants to Hawaii, for example, were males, especially the plantation workers. Those males mated with native women more often than native men mated with immigrant women, so nonnative Y chromosomes are now more common in mixed populations than nonnative mitochondrial DNA. In some populations in South America, virtually all the Y chromosomes are from Europe and all the mitochondrial DNA is from indigenous groups.

The mixing of genes can cause great consternation, but it is the inevitable consequence of our genetic history. Several years ago a geneticist in Washington, D.C., began offering to identify the homelands of the mitochondrial DNA and Y chromosomes of African Americans. The service foundered for several reasons, but one was that 30 percent of the Y chromosomes in African American males come from European ancestors.

Within a few years geneticists will be able to use DNA sequences from all the chromosomes to trace ancestry. But these histories will be just as convoluted as those of mitochondrial DNA and the Y. Granted, geneticists will be able to make statistical assessments. They will be able to say, for instance, that a given person has such and such a probability of descent from a Native Hawaiian population, and in some cases the probability will be very high. But probabilities don't convey the cold, hard certainties that people want in their genealogies.

Beyond the purely genetic considerations are the social ones. When children are adopted from one group into another, they become a member of that group socially, yet their haplotypes and those of their descendants can differ from the group norm. Rape is another way in which the genetic variants of groups mix. And sometimes people from one group make a conscious decision to join another and are gladly accepted, despite their different genetic histories.

"I get nervous when people start talking about using genetic markers to prove ethnicity," Cann told me. "I don't believe that biology is destiny. Allowing yourself to be defined personally by whatever your DNA sequence is, that's insane. But that's exactly what some people are going to be tempted to do."

When geneticists look at our DNA, they do not see a world of rigidly divided groups each going its own way. They see something much more fluid and ambiguous—something more like the social structures that have emerged in Hawaii as intermarriage has accelerated.

The most remarkable aspect of ethnicity in Hawaii is its loose relation to biology. Many people have considerable latitude in choosing their ethnic affiliations. Those of mixed ancestry can associate with the ethnicity of a parent, a grandparent, or a more distant ancestor. They can partition their ethnic affiliations: They can be Chinese with their Chinese relatives; Native Hawaiian with their native kin; and just plain local with their buddies. The community of descent that a person associates with has become more like a professional or religious affiliation, a connection over which a person has some measure of control.

People whose ancestors are from a single ethnic group have fewer options, but they, too, can partake of at least some of Hawaii's ethnic flexibility. Young whites, for example, sometimes try to pass themselves off as mixed by maintaining an especially dark tan. Among many young people, dating someone from a different ethnic group is a social asset rather than a liability, in part because of the doors it opens to other communities. Many prospective students at the University of Hawaii simply mark "mixed" in describing their ethnicity on application forms, even if both parents have the same ethnic background. "My students say they don't want to be pigeonholed," says Oka-mura. "That way they can identify with different groups."

Hawaii's high rates of intermarriage also contribute greatly to the islands' ethnic flux. Ethnicity is not defined just by who one's ancestors were. It also is defined pro-spectively — by the group into which one is expected to marry. For most young people in Hawaii, the pool of marriageable partners encompasses the entire population. Rela-tions among groups are inevitably less fractious when their members view each other as potential mates.

Of course, ethnic and even "racial" groups still exist in Hawaii, and they will for a long time. Despite the rapid growth of intermarriage in Hawaii and elsewhere, the mixing of peoples takes generations, not a few years or even decades. Most people around the world still choose marriage partners who would be classified as members of the same "race." In many parts of the world — the American Midwest, China, Ice-land — few other options are available. Five hundred years from now, unless human societies undergo drastic changes, Asians, Africans, and Europeans still will be physi-cally distinguishable.

But the social effects of intermarriage are much more immediate than are the bi-ological effects. Socially, intermarriage can quickly undermine the idea that culture has biological roots. When a substantial number of mixed individuals demonstrate, by their very existence, that choices are possible, that biology is not destiny, the barriers between groups become more permeable. Ethnicity in Hawaii, for example, seems far less stark and categorical than it does in the rest of the United States. The people of Ha-waii recognize overlaps and exceptions. They are more willing to accept the haole who claims to have non-European ancestors or the Native Hawaiian who affiliates with Filipinos. It's true that people talk about the differences among groups all the time, but even talking about these differences, rather than rigidly ignoring them, makes them seem less daunting. Expressions of social prejudice in Hawaii are more like a form of social banter, like a husband and wife picking at each other's faults.

The logical endpoint of this perspective is a world in which people are free to choose their ethnicity regardless of their ancestry. Ethnicity is not yet *entirely* volun-tary in Hawaii, but in many respects the islands are headed in that direction. State law, for example, is gradually coming to define a Native Hawaiian as anyone with a single Hawaiian ancestor. But at that point ethnicity becomes untethered from biology — it is instead a cultural, political, or historical distinction. People are no longer who they say they are because of some mysterious biological essence. They have chosen the group with which they want to affiliate.

Genetically, this view of ethnicity makes perfect sense. Our DNA is too tightly 55 interconnected to use biology to justify what are essentially social distinctions. Our preferences, character, and abilities are not determined by the biological history of our ancestors. They depend on our individual attributes, experiences, and choices. As this inescapable conclusion becomes more widely held, our genetic histories inevitably will become less and less important. When we look at another person, we won't think Asian, black, or white. We'll just think: person.

In his novel *Siddhartha*, Hermann Hesse tells the story of a young man in ancient India, a disciple of an inspired teacher, who sets out to find the reality beneath the world of appearance. After years of study and wandering, Siddhartha becomes a ferryman, learning from his predecessor how to listen to the voices in the passing river. One day a childhood friend named Govinda comes to the river. Siddhartha and Govinda have a long conversation about the interdependence of illusion and truth, about the existence of the past and future in the present, about the need not just to think about the world but to love it. Finally Govinda asks Siddhartha how he has achieved such peace in his life. Siddhartha replies, "Kiss me on the forehead, Govinda." Govinda is surprised by the request, but out of respect for his friend he complies. When he touches Siddhartha's forehead with his lips, he has a wondrous vision:

> He no longer saw the face of his friend Siddhartha. Instead he saw other faces, many faces, a long series, a continuous stream of faces—h ndreds, thousands, which all came and disappeared and yet all seemed to be there at the same time, which all continually changed and renewed themselves and which were all yet Siddhartha. . . . He saw the face of a newly born child, red and full of wrinkles, ready to cry. He saw the face of a murderer. . . . He saw the naked bodies of men and women in the postures and transports of passionate love. . . . Each one was mortal, a passionate, painful example of all that is transitory. Yet none of them died, they only changed, were always reborn, continually had a new face; only time stood between one face and another.

I began this book [*Mapping Human History*] by calling attention to the different appearances of human beings. I conclude it now by calling attention to the opposite. Throughout human history, groups have wondered how they are related to one another. The study of genetics has now revealed that we all are linked: the Bushmen hunting antelope, the mixed-race people of South Africa, the African Americans descended from slaves, the Samaritans on their mountain stronghold, the Jewish populations scattered around the world, the Han Chinese a billion strong, the descendants of European settlers who colonized the New World, the Native Hawaiians who look to a cherished past. We are members of a single human family, the products of genetic necessity and chance, borne ceaselessly into an unknown future.

Exploring Context

1. Read the U.S. Census Bureau's explanation of the racial categories used in the census taken every ten years at census.gov/topics/population/race.html. How do these categories relate to Olson's argument? Relate your response to your work on the persistence of race from Question 3 of Questions for Critical Reading.

2. Visit Hawaii's official state government Web site at hawaii.gov and then visit the official Hawaii tourism Web site at gohawaii.com. How is race represented on these sites? What races do you see in the images? Is the representation of race the same for residents and for tourists? Why might there be differences? Use the definition of *race* you developed in Question 2 of Questions for Critical Reading to support your position.

3. One place that race persists in Hawaii, according to Olson, is in schools. Locate Web sites for some schools in Hawaii. Do you find evidence to support Olson's argument or to complicate it?

Questions for Connecting

1. What is the relation between race and human dignity? Apply Francis Fukuyama's understanding of what it means to be human in "Human Dignity" (p. 143) to Olson's argument. Has intermarriage in Hawaii moved us toward a genetic equivalent of "Factor X"? How do communities of descent affect human dignity? Use your work from Question 1 of Questions for Critical Reading.

2. Apply your definition of the term *community of descent* from Question 1 of Questions for Critical Reading as well as Olson's other concepts to the question of gender as explored by Julia Serano in "Why Nice Guys Finish Last" (p. 415). Can gender have the same flexibility that race has in Hawaii? How might men align themselves differently based on particular social contexts?

3. Does Hawaii offer a model for the new civil rights that Kenji Yoshino advocates in "Preface" and "The New Civil Rights" (p. 539)? Given the end of race, should we pursue a liberty or an equality paradigm?

Language Matters

1. Choose a key quotation from Olson. Revise it to make it less effective but still grammatically correct. Would making it a question blunt its force? What about changing it to passive voice? Draw some general conclusions from this experiment. What makes a sentence effective?

2. Locate materials in a reference book or online on writing a résumé and then make a résumé for this essay. What would be this essay's "career objective"? What would be its "experience"? Whom would it list for references?

3. How would you "grade" Olson's essay? In small groups, develop a set of grading criteria and then apply those criteria to Olson's text. What does your group value in writing? What does this class value in writing?

Assignments for Writing

1. Can there be an end to race? Engage Olson's essay by writing a paper in which you examine the possibility of an end to race. Why does race persist? Can or should we move beyond concepts of race? Would something replace the idea of race or has something replaced it already? You may want to draw on your responses to the Questions for Critical Reading as well as your examination of the census from Question 1 of Exploring Context in making your argument. Also consider your work with human dignity and race from Question 1 of Questions for Connecting.

2. Olson's argument is based in part on advances in genetic technologies. Write a paper in which you evaluate the relationship between technology and race. Consider: Is race itself a kind of technology? Can technology move us beyond race? You may want to use the definition of *race* you developed in Question 2 of Questions for Critical Reading in making your argument.

3. Race is not the only factor in determining group identity; Olson discusses communities of descent as well. Using Olson's essay, write a paper in which you determine the relationship between race and cultural identity. Does the history of a particular race dictate its importance as a cultural identity? Can a particular race have ownership over its cultural aspects? Can an individual choose a racial or cultural identity? In making your argument, you may want to use the definition of *communities of descent* that you developed in Question 1 of Questions for Critical Reading.

RUTH PADAWER

Courtesy of Ruth Padawer, Photo by Tala Al-Ramahi

Ruth Padawer is an adjunct professor at Columbia University's Graduate School of Journalism, from which she received her M.S. degree. Her writing has appeared in *USA Today*, the *Guardian*, and the *New York Times Magazine* as well as the radio show *This American Life*. Her work often focuses on gender, health, and social issues.

The *New York Times Magazine* is a supplement included with every Sunday edition of the noted newspaper. It features articles that are longer and more in-depth, often by contributors of note, and is known for its fashion and style photography. "Sisterhood Is Complicated" appeared in the online version of the magazine on October 15, 2014. Four days later, it appeared in the print version, alongside articles about America's fascination with extreme fitness, the impact of music streaming on those who like obscure bands, and the role of money in politics. It also featured a column from Chuck Klosterman, another author featured in *Emerging*, about the ethics of telling a gorilla of a person's death.

"Sisterhood Is Complicated" deals with the experiences of female-to-male transgender individuals or "transmen" — those assigned female gender at birth but identifying as male — at one of America's few remaining all-women institutions of higher learning, Wellesley College. As Wellesley is not only traditionally but explicitly a school for female students, there are serious questions regarding how to handle students who were admitted as women but then became men. Padawer explores this complex issue by looking at the lives of trans students at Wellesley, the reactions of those around them, and the responses of the institution.

How should schools handle students who change their gender identity? How does *your* school handle these students?

▶ TAGS: *adolescence and adulthood, community, education, gender, identity, social change, tradition*

▶ CONNECTIONS: *Appiah, Gay, Levy, Savage/Vaid, Serano*

Questions for Critical Reading

1. Make a list of the issues facing Wellesley College. What solutions can you find in Padawer's essay?

2. Write a definition of *gender*. As you read the essay, mark passages where Padawer uses this or similar terms such as *genderqueer*. In what ways is the definition of *gender* changing?

3. How does gender affect education? As you read, note passages where Padawer discusses the relationship between gender and education at Wellesley College.

Sisterhood Is Complicated

Hundreds of young women streamed into Wellesley College on the last Monday of August, many of them trailed by parents lugging suitcases and bins filled with folded towels, decorative pillows, and Costco-size jugs of laundry detergent. The banner by the campus entranceway welcoming the Class of 2018 waved in the breeze, as if beckoning the newcomers to discover all that awaited them. All around the campus stood buildings named after women: the Margaret Clapp library, the Betsy Wood Knapp media and technology center, dorms, labs, academic halls, even the parking garage. The message that anything is possible for women was also evident at a fenced-in work site, which bore the sign "Elaine Construction," after a firm named for one woman and run by another.

It was the first day of orientation, and along the picturesque paths there were cheerful upper-class student leaders providing directions and encouragement. They wore pink T-shirts stamped with this year's orientation theme: "Free to Explore" — an enticement that could be interpreted myriad ways, perhaps far more than the college intended. One of those T-shirted helpers was a junior named Timothy Boatwright. Like every other matriculating student at Wellesley, which is just west of Boston, Timothy was raised a girl and checked "female" when he applied. Though he had told his

Timothy Boatwright (center), a trans man, with his Wellesley classmates.
© Martin Schoeller/AUGUST

high-school friends that he was transgender, he did not reveal that on his application, in part because his mother helped him with it, and he didn't want her to know. Besides, he told me, "it seemed awkward to write an application essay for a women's college on why you were not a woman." Like many trans students, he chose a women's college because it seemed safer physically and psychologically.

From the start, Timothy introduced himself as "masculine-of-center genderqueer." He asked everyone at Wellesley to use male pronouns and the name Timothy, which he'd chosen for himself.

For the most part, everyone respected his request. After all, he wasn't the only trans student on campus. Some two dozen other matriculating students at Wellesley don't identify as women. Of those, a half-dozen or so were trans men, people born female who identified as men, some of whom had begun taking testosterone to change their bodies. The rest said they were transgender or genderqueer, rejecting the idea of gender entirely or identifying somewhere between female and male; many, like Timothy, called themselves transmasculine. Though his gender identity differed from that of most of his classmates, he generally felt comfortable at his new school.

Last spring, as a sophomore, Timothy decided to run for a seat on the student-government cabinet, the highest position that an openly trans student had ever sought at Wellesley. The post he sought was multicultural affairs coordinator, or "MAC," responsible for promoting "a culture of diversity" among students and staff and faculty members. Along with Timothy, three women of color indicated their intent to run for the seat. But when they dropped out for various unrelated reasons before the race really began, he was alone on the ballot. An anonymous lobbying effort began on Facebook, pushing students to vote "abstain." Enough "abstains" would deny Timothy the minimum number of votes Wellesley required, forcing a new election for the seat and providing an opportunity for other candidates to come forward. The "Campaign to Abstain" argument was simple: Of all the people at a multiethnic women's college who could hold the school's "diversity" seat, the least fitting one was a *white man.*

"It wasn't about Timothy," the student behind the Abstain campaign told me. "I thought he'd do a perfectly fine job, but it just felt inappropriate to have a white man there. It's not just about that position either. Having men in elected leadership positions undermines the idea of this being a place where women are the leaders."

I asked Timothy what he thought about that argument, as we sat on a bench overlooking the tranquil lake on campus during orientation. He pointed out that he has important contributions to make to the MAC position. After all, at Wellesley, masculine-of-center students *are* cultural minorities; by numbers alone, they're about as minor as a minority can be. And yet Timothy said he felt conflicted about taking a leadership spot. "The patriarchy is alive and well," he said. "I don't want to perpetuate it."

In the 19th century, only men were admitted to most colleges and universities, so proponents of higher education for women had to build their own. The missions at these new schools both defied and reinforced the gender norms of the day. By offering women access to an education they'd previously been denied, the schools' very existence was radical, but most were nevertheless premised on traditional notions: College-educated women were considered more likely to be engaging wives and better mothers, who

5

would raise informed citizens. Over time, of course, women's colleges became more committed to preparing students for careers, but even in the early 1960s, Wellesley, for example, taught students how to get groceries into the back of a station wagon without exposing their thighs.

By the late 1960s, however, gender norms were under scrutiny. Amid the growing awareness of civil rights and women's liberation, academic separation based on gender, as with race, seemed increasingly outdated. As a vast majority of women opted for coed schools, enrollment at women's colleges tumbled. The number of women's colleges dropped to fewer than 50 today from nearly 300.

In response to shifting ideas about gender, many of the remaining women's colleges redefined themselves as an antidote to the sexism that feminists were increasingly identifying in society. Women's colleges argued that they offered a unique environment where every student leader was a woman, where female role models were abundant, where professors were far more likely to be women, and where the message of women's empowerment pervaded academic and campus life. All that seemed to foster students' confidence. Women's colleges say their undergrads are more likely to major in fields traditionally dominated by men. Wellesley alumnae in particular are awarded more science and engineering doctorates than female graduates of any other liberal-arts college in the nation, according to government data. Its alums have become two secretaries of state; a groundbreaking string theorist; a NASA astronaut; and Korea's first female ambassador.

As women's colleges challenged the conventions of womanhood, they drew a disproportionate number of students who identified as lesbian or bisexual. Today a small but increasing number of students at those schools do not identify as women, raising the question of what it means to be a "women's college." Trans students are pushing their schools to play down the women-centric message. At Wellesley, Smith, Mount Holyoke, and others, they and their many supporters have successfully lobbied to scrub all female references in student government constitutions, replacing them with gender-neutral language. At Wellesley, they have pressed administrators and fellow students to excise talk of sisterhood, arguing that that rhetoric, rather than being uplifting, excludes other gender minorities. At many schools, they have also taken leadership positions long filled by women: resident advisers on dorm floors, heads of student groups, and members of college government. At Wellesley, one transmasculine student was a dorm president. At Mills College, a women's school in California, even the president of student government identifies as male.

What's a women's college to do? Trans students point out that they're doing exactly what these schools encourage: breaking gender barriers, fulfilling their deepest yearnings, and forging ahead even when society tries to hold them back. But yielding to their request to dilute the focus on women would undercut the identity of a women's college. While women in coed schools generally outpace men in enrollment and performance, the equation shifts after college: Recent female graduates working full time earn far less than their male counterparts, and more experienced women are often still shut out of corporate and political leadership—all of which prompts women's-college advocates to conclude that a four-year, confidence-building workshop still has its place.

"Sisterhood is why I chose to go to Wellesley," said a physics major who graduated recently and asked not to be identified for fear she'd be denounced for her opinion.

"A women's college is a place to celebrate being a woman, surrounded by women. I felt empowered by that every day. You come here thinking that every single leadership position will be held by a woman: every member of the student government, every newspaper editor, every head of the Economics Council, every head of the Society of Physics. That's an incredible thing! This is what they advertise to students. But it's no longer true. And if all that is no longer true, the intrinsic value of a women's college no longer holds."

A few schools have formulated responses to this dilemma, albeit very different ones. Hollins University, a small women's college in Virginia, established a policy several years ago stating it would confer diplomas to only women. It also said that students who have surgery or begin hormone therapy to become men — or who legally take male names — will be "helped to transfer to another institution." Mount Holyoke and Mills College, on the other hand, recently decided they will not only continue to welcome students who become trans men while at school but will also admit those who identify on their applications as trans men, noting that welcoming the former and not the latter seemed unjustifiably arbitrary.

But most women's colleges, including Wellesley, consider only female applicants.   15
Once individuals have enrolled and announced that they are trans, the schools, more or less, leave it to the students to work out how trans classmates fit into a women's college. Two of those students hashed it out last fall after Kaden Mohamed, then a Wellesley senior who had been taking testosterone for seven months, watched a news program on WGBH-TV about the plummeting number of women's colleges. One guest was Laura Bruno, another Wellesley senior. The other guest was the president of Regis College, a women's school that went coed in 2007 to reverse its tanking enrollment. The interviewer asked Laura to describe her experience at an "all-female school" and to explain how that might be diminished "by having men there." Laura answered, "We look around and we see only women, only people like us, leading every organization on campus, contributing to every class discussion."

Kaden, a manager of the campus student cafe who knew Laura casually, was upset by her words. He emailed Laura and said her response was "extremely disrespectful." He continued: "I am not a woman. I am a trans man who is part of your graduating class, and you literally ignored my existence in your interview. . . . You had an opportunity to show people that Wellesley is a place that is complicating the meaning of being an 'all women's school,' and you chose instead to displace a bunch of your current and past Wellesley siblings."

Laura apologized, saying she hadn't meant to marginalize anyone and had actually vowed beforehand not to imply that all Wellesley students were women. But she said that under pressure, she found herself in a difficult spot: How could she maintain that women's colleges would lose something precious by including men, but at the same time argue that women's colleges should accommodate students who identify as men?

Although it may seem paradoxical, Jesse Austin said he chose to attend Wellesley because being female never felt right to him. "I figured if I was any kind of woman, I'd find it there. I knew Wellesley would have strong women. They produce a ton of strong women, strong in all sorts of ways."

When Jesse arrived on campus in the fall of 2009, his name was Sara. Eighteen years old, Sara wore form-fitting shirts and snug women's jeans, because growing up in a small, conservative town in Georgia, she learned that that's what girls were supposed to do—even though she never felt like a girl. As a child, Sara had always chosen to be male characters in pretend plays, and all her friends were boys. In middle school, those boys abandoned her because she was a social liability: not feminine enough to flirt with and not masculine enough to really be one of the guys. In high school, at the urging of well-intentioned female classmates, she started wearing her hair down instead of pulled back and began dressing like they did, even though people kept pointing out that she still acted and carried herself like a boy. "I had no idea that gender was something you could change," Jesse told me recently. "I just thought I needed to make myself fit into these fixed places: There are boys, and there are girls. I knew I didn't fit; I just didn't know what was wrong with me."

Around the middle of Sara's first year at Wellesley, she attended a presentation by trans alums, including one who was in the process of transitioning. As Sara listened, the gender dysphoria she'd always felt suddenly made sense. "It was all so clear to me," Jesse told me. "All I needed were the words." Sara spent the next two weeks scouring the Internet for videos and information on becoming a man. She learned that unlike previous generations, today's trans young adults don't consider physical transformation a prerequisite for identity. Some use hormones; some have their breasts removed in "top" surgery; some reject medical interventions altogether, as unnecessary invasions and expense. She discovered that sexual orientation is independent of gender: Some trans men are attracted to women, some to men, some to both. And she learned that trans men aren't necessarily determined to hide the fact they were raised as girls, or that they once attended a women's college. 20

Soon after, Sara cut her hair short and bought her first pair of men's jeans. Sara told friends she was a man. By second semester, he was using male pronouns and calling himself Jesse, the other name his mother had considered for her daughter. He also joined a tiny campus group for students who knew or suspected they were trans men. It was called Brothers, a counterweight to the otherwise ubiquitous message of sisterhood.

That summer, Jesse saw a gender therapist, and early in his sophomore year, he began injecting testosterone into his thigh every two weeks, making him one of the first students to medically transform into a man while at Wellesley. He became the administrator of Brothers. Though he felt supported, he also felt alone; all the other trans men on campus had graduated, and the other students in Brothers were not even sure they identified as men. Outside Brothers, everything at Wellesley was still sisterhood and female empowerment. Nevertheless, he said, "I thought of Wellesley as my home, my community. I felt fine there, like I totally belonged."

Jesse decided he wanted to have top surgery over winter break, and his parents agreed to pay for it. He returned for spring semester but only briefly, taking a sudden leave of absence to go home and help care for his ill father. When Jesse re-enrolled at Wellesley a year and a half later, in fall 2012, much had changed in Jesse and at school. Having been on testosterone for two years at that point, Jesse no longer looked like a woman trying to pass as a man. His voice was deep. His facial hair was thick, though he kept it trimmed to a stubble. His shoulders had become broad and muscular, his hips narrow, his arms and chest more defined.

Wellesley was different, too. By then, a whole crowd of people identified as trans—enough for two trans groups. Brothers had officially become Siblings and welcomed anyone anywhere on the gender spectrum except those who identified as women. Meanwhile, Jesse and some transmasculine students continued to meet unofficially as Brothers, though Jesse was the only one on testosterone.

Over all, campus life had a stronger trans presence than ever. At least four of the   25 school's 70 RAs did not identify as women. Student organizations increasingly began meetings by asking everyone to state preferred names and pronouns. Around campus, more and more students were replacing "sisterhood" with "siblinghood" in conversation. Even the school's oldest tradition, Flower Sunday—the 138-year-old ceremony that paired each incoming student with an upper-class Big Sister to support her—had become trans-inclusive. Though the school website still describes Flower Sunday as "a day of sisterhood," the department that runs the event yielded to trans students' request and started referring to each participant as a Big or Little "Sister/Sibling"—or simply as Bigs and Littles.

And yet even with the increased visibility of trans students on campus, Jesse stood out. When he swiped his Wellesley ID card to get into friends' dorms, the groundskeepers would stop him and say, "You can't go in there without a woman to escort you." Residential directors who spotted him in the dorm stairwells told him the same thing. In his own dorm, parents who were visiting their daughters would stop him to ask why he was there. Because bathrooms in the dorms are not labeled "women" or "men" but rather "Wellesley only" and "non-Wellesley," students who didn't know Jesse would call him out for using the "Wellesley only" bathroom instead of the one for visitors. When he tried to explain he *was* a Wellesley student, people sometimes thought he was lying.

"Everything felt very different than it had before," he said of that semester. "I felt so distinctly male, and I felt extremely awkward. I felt like an outsider. My voice was jarring—a male voice, which is so distinct in a classroom of women—so I felt weird saying much in class. I felt much more aware of Wellesley as a women's place, even though the college was starting to change."

Once spring semester ended, Jesse withdrew. "I still think of Wellesley as a women's place, and I still think that's a wonderful idea," he said. "It just didn't encompass me anymore. I felt it was a space I shouldn't tread in."

Some female students, meanwhile, said Wellesley wasn't female enough. They complained among themselves and to the administration that sisterhood had been hijacked. "Siblinghood," they argued, lacked the warm, pro-women connotation of "sisterhood," as well as its historic resonance. Others were upset that even at a women's college, women were still expected to accommodate men, ceding attention and leadership opportunities intended for women. Still others feared the changes were a step toward coeducation. Despite all that, many were uneasy: As a marginalized group fighting for respect and clout, how could women justify marginalizing others?

"I felt for the first time that something so stable about our school was about to   30 change, and it made me scared," said Beth, a junior that year, who asked to be identified

Clockwise from top: Jesse Austin, Alex Poon, and Kaden Mohamed, former Wellesley students.
© Martin Schoeller/AUGUST

by only her middle name because she was afraid of offending people she knew. "Chang-ing 'sister' to 'sibling' didn't feel like it was including more people; it felt like it was taking something away from sisterhood, transforming our safe space for the sake of someone else. At the same time, I felt guilty feeling that way." Beth went to Kris Nien-dorf, the director of residential life, who listened sympathetically and then asked: Why does "sibling" take away from your experience? After thinking about it, Beth concluded that she was connected to her classmates not because of gender but because of their shared experiences at Wellesley. "That year was an epiphany for me. I realized that if we excluded trans students, we'd be fighting on the wrong team. We'd be on the wrong side of history."

Exactly how Wellesley will resolve the trans question is still unclear. Trans students say that aside from making sure every academic building on campus has a unisex bathroom, Wellesley has not addressed what gender fluidity means for Wellesley's identity. Last spring, Alex Poon won Wellesley's 131-year-old hoop-rolling race, an an-nual spirit-building competition among seniors. Alex's mother was the hoop-rolling champion of the Class of '82 and had long ago taught her daughters the ways of the hoop, on the assumption that they would one day attend her alma mater. (One of Alex's older sisters was Wellesley Class of '11; another went to Bryn Mawr.) Alex was a former Girl Scout who attended an all-girls high school. But unknown to his mother, he was using Google to search for an explanation for his confusing feelings. By the time Alex applied to Wellesley, he secretly knew

> **"I realized that if we excluded trans students, we'd be fighting on the wrong team. We'd be on the wrong side of history."**

he was trans but was nonetheless certain Wellesley was a good fit. For one thing, going there was a family tradition; for another, it was a place where gender could be reimagined. In his sophomore year at Wellesley, he went public with his transgender status.

On hoop-rolling day, Alex — wearing a cap backward on his buzz-cut hair — broke through the finish-line streamer. President H. Kim Bottomly took a selfie with him, each with a wide smile. A small local newspaper covered the event, noting that for the first time in the school's history, the winner was a man. And yet the page on Wellesley's website devoted to school traditions continues to describe the race as if it involves only women. "Back in the day, it was proclaimed that whoever won the Hoop Roll would be the first to get married. In the status-seeking 1980s, she was the first to be C.E.O. Now we just say that the winner will be the first to achieve happiness and success, whatever that means to her." But Alex isn't a her, and he told me that his happiness and success includes being recognized for what he is: a man.

That page is not the only place on the site where Wellesley markets itself as a school of only female students. Elsewhere, it crows that "all the most courageous, most provocative, most accomplished people on campus are women." The student body, it says, is "2,300 smart, singular women feeling the power of 2,300 smart, singular women together" on a campus where "our common identity, spirit and pride as Wellesley women" are celebrated. Those sorts of messages, trans students say, make them feel invisible.

"I just wish the administration would at least acknowledge our existence," said Eli Cohen, a Wellesley senior who has been taking testosterone for nearly a year. "I'd be more OK with 'We're not going to cater to you, because men are catered to everywhere else in life,' rather than just pretending we don't exist."

Some staff and faculty members, however, are acknowledging the trans presence. 35 Women-and-gender-studies professors, and a handful of others, typically begin each semester asking students to indicate the names and pronouns they prefer for themselves. Kris Niendorf, director of campus and residential life, recruits trans students who want to be RAs, as she does with all minorities. Niendorf also initiated informational panels with trans students and alums. And before this school year began, at the urging of trans students, Niendorf required all 200 student leaders to attend a trans-sensitivity workshop focused on how to "create a more inclusive Wellesley College." For the last few years, orientation organizers have also included a trans student as one of the half-dozen upper-class students who stand before the incoming first-years and recount how they overcame a difficult personal challenge.

And yet many trans students feel that more needs to be done. They complain that too many professors assume all their students are women. Students provided numerous examples in courses across subject areas where they've been asked their viewpoint "as a woman." In a course on westerns two years ago, an essay assignment noted that western films and novels were aimed at male audiences and focused on masculinity. The professors asked students for their perspective "as a female reader or watcher" — wording that offended the three trans students in class. When a classmate pointed out the problematic wording to the professors, the instructors asked everyone instead "to explore how your own gender identity changes how you approach westerns."

At times, professors find themselves walking a fine line. Thomas Cushman, who has taught sociology at Wellesley for the last 25 years, first found out about Wellesley's trans population five years ago, after a student in one of his courses showed up at Cushman's office and introduced himself as a trans male. The student pointed out that every example Cushman gave in class referred to women, and every generic pronoun he used was female, as in "Ask your classmate if she. . . ." He told Cushman that Wellesley could no longer call itself a "women's college," given the presence of trans men, and he asked Cushman to use male pronouns and male examples more often, so trans students didn't feel excluded. Cushman said he would abide by whatever pronoun individual students requested for themselves, but he drew the line at changing his emphasis on women.

"All my life here," Cushman told me, "I've been compelled to use the female pronoun more generously to get away from the sexist 'he.' I think it's important to evoke the idea that women are part of humanity. That should be affirmed, especially after being denied for so long. Look, I teach at a women's college, so whenever I can make women's identity central to that experience, I try to do that. Being asked to change that is a bit ironic. I don't agree that this is a 'historically' women's college. It is still a *women's* college."

On the second day of orientation this fall, Eli Cohen arrived on campus in a muscle T and men's shorts, with a carabiner full of keys hanging from his belt loop. He was elated to be back to the place that felt most like home. It was the first time in four years that Eli had not been part of orientation—first as a newcomer and then two years as an RA. We hung out in the Lulu Chow Wang Campus Center, known affectionately as Lulu, and watched the excited first-years flutter by, clutching their orientation schedules and their newly purchased Wellesley wear.

Just 12 days earlier, Eli underwent top surgery, which he said gave him a new- 40 found self-assurance in his projection of manhood. It had been nine months since he started testosterone, and the effects had become particularly noticeable over the three-month summer break. His jaw line had begun to square, his limbs to thicken, and the hair on his arms and legs to darken. And of course now his chest was a flat wall. As his friends caught sight of him for the first time in months, they hugged him and gushed, "You look sooo good!"

Though Eli secretly suspected in high school that he was a boy, it wasn't until after he arrived at Wellesley that he could imagine he might one day declare himself a man. By his second year, he had buzz-cut his hair and started wearing men's clothes. He asked his friends to call him Beckett, which is similar to his female birth name, which he asked me not to mention. His parents live only 14 miles away and dropped by for short visits. He left his girl nameplate on his dorm door. His friends understood that whenever his parents arrived, everyone was to revert to his female name and its attendant pronouns. He was an RA at the time and decided not to reveal his male name to his first-year students, figuring it was too complicated to explain which name to use when.

Given how guarded he had to be, being Beckett was exhausting and anxiety-inducing. Demoralized, he eventually told his pals to just use his birth name. The summer after his sophomore year, he got an internship at a Boston health center serving the LGBT community, and many of his co-workers were trans. Their confidence gave him confidence. When the Wellesley office that coordinates internships sent out an email to all interns that began, "Good morning, ladies . . . ," he emailed back to say he did not identify as a woman. The coordinator apologized and explained that all the names on her paperwork from Wellesley were female.

By summer's end, he began introducing himself as Eli, a name utterly unlike his birth name. Eli mustered the courage to tell his parents. It took a little while for his mother to accept that her only daughter was actually a son, but she came around.

When I asked Eli if trans men belonged at Wellesley, he said he felt torn. "I don't necessarily think we have a right to women's spaces. But I'm not going to transfer, because this is a place I love, a community I love. I realize that may be a little selfish. It may be a lot selfish." Where, he wondered, should Wellesley draw a line, if a line should even be drawn? At trans men? At transmasculine students? What about students who are simply questioning their gender? Shouldn't students be "free to explore" without fearing their decision will make them unwelcome?

> **Shouldn't students be "free to explore" without fearing their decision will make them unwelcome?**

Other trans students have struggled with these questions, too. Last December, a transmasculine Wellesley student wrote an anonymous blog post that shook the school's trans community. The student wrote to apologize for "acting in the interest of preserving a hurtful system of privileging masculinity." He continued: "My feelings have changed: I do not think that trans men belong at Wellesley. . . . This doesn't mean that I think that all trans men should be kicked out of Wellesley or necessarily denied admission." He acknowledged he didn't know how Wellesley could best address the trans question, but urged fellow transmasculine classmates to "start talking, and thinking critically, about the space that we are given and occupying, and the space that we are taking from women."

The reactions were swift and strong. "A lot of trans people on campus felt emotionally unsafe," recalled Timothy, a sophomore that year. "A place that seemed welcoming suddenly wasn't. The difficulty was that because it was a trans person saying it, people who don't have enough of an understanding to appreciate the nuance of this can say, 'Well, even a trans person says there shouldn't be trans people at Wellesley, so it's OK for me to think the same thing, too.'"

Students and alums—queer and straight, trans and not—weighed in, sometimes in agreement but other times in anger. Some accused the blogger of speaking on behalf of women as if they were unable to speak for themselves. Others accused him of betraying transmasculine students. (He declined to comment for this article.) But other students, including several transmasculine ones, were glad he had the courage to start a public discussion about Wellesley's deeply conflicted identity. "It's a very important

₄₅

conversation to have," Eli said. "Why can't we have this conversation without feeling hurt or hated?"

In some ways, students are already having that conversation, though perhaps indirectly. Timothy ended up easily winning his seat on the student government last spring, capturing two-thirds of the votes. Given that 85 percent of the student body cast ballots in that race, his victory suggests most students think that transmasculine students—and transmasculine leaders—belong at Wellesley.

Another difficult conversation about trans students touches on the disproportionate attention they receive on campus. "The female-identified students somehow place more value on those students," said Rose Layton, a lesbian who said she views trans students as competitors in the campus dating scene. "They flirt with them, hook up with them. And it's not just the hetero women, but even people in the queer community. The trans men are always getting this extra bit of acknowledgment. Even though we're in a women's college, the fact is men and masculinity get more attention and more value in this social dynamic than women do."

Jesse Austin noticed the paradox when he returned to campus with a man's build and full swath of beard stubble after nearly two years on testosterone. "That was the first time in my life I was popular! People were clamoring to date me."   50

Trans bodies are seen as an in-between option, Timothy said. "So no matter your sexuality, a trans person becomes safe to flirt with, to explore with. But it's not really the person you're interested in, it's the novelty. For lesbians, there's the safety of 'I may be attracted to this person, but they're "really" a woman, so I'm not actually bi or straight.' And for straight people, it's 'I may be attracted to a woman's body, but he's a male, so I'm not really lesbian or bi.'"

Kaden Mohamed said he felt downright objectified when he returned from summer break last year, after five months of testosterone had lowered his voice, defined his arm muscles, and reshaped his torso. It was attention that he had never experienced before he transitioned. But as his body changed, students he didn't even know would run their hands over his biceps. Once at the school pub, an intoxicated Wellesley woman even grabbed his crotch and that of another trans man.

"It's this very bizarre reversal of what happens in the real world," Kaden said. "In the real world, it's women who get fetishized, catcalled, sexually harassed, grabbed. At Wellesley, it's trans men who do. If I were to go up to someone I just met and touch her body, I'd get grief from the entire Wellesley community, because they'd say it's assault—and it is. But for some reason, when it's done to trans men here, it doesn't get read the same way. It's like a free pass, that suddenly it's OK to talk about or touch someone's body as long as they're not a woman."

While trans men are allowed at most women's colleges if they identify as female when applying, trans women—people raised male who go on to identify as women—have found it nearly impossible to get through the campus gates. Arguably, a trans woman's identity is more compatible with a women's college than a trans man's is. But most women's colleges require that all of an applicant's documentation indicate the candidate is female. That's a high bar for a 17- or 18-year-old born and raised male, given that so few come out as trans in high school. (Admissions policies at private undergraduate schools are exempt from Title IX, which bans gender discrimination at schools receiving federal funds.) Two years ago, Calliope Wong, a high-school trans woman from Connecticut, applied to Smith College, but her application was returned because her federal aid form indicated she was male. She posted the rejection letter online, catalyzing a storm on the Internet and student rallies at Smith. Smith eventually agreed to require that the applicant be referred to as female only in the transcript and recommendation letters, but not on financial-aid documents; by then, however, Wong had decided to attend the University of Connecticut.

For its part, Wellesley has never admitted a trans woman, at least not knowingly.   55
Many Wellesley students, including some who are uncomfortable having trans men on campus, say that academically eligible trans women should be admitted, regardless of the gender on their application documents.

Others are wary of opening Wellesley's doors too quickly—including one of Wellesley's trans men, who asked not to be named because he knew how unpopular his stance would be. He said that Wellesley should accept only trans women who have begun sex-changing medical treatment or have legally changed their names or sex on their driver's licenses or birth certificates. "I know that's a lot to ask of an 18-year-old just applying to college," he said, "but at the same time, Wellesley needs to maintain its integrity as a safe space for women. What if someone who is male-bodied comes here genuinely identified as female, and then decides after a year or two that they identify as male—and wants to stay at Wellesley? How's that different from admitting a biological male who identifies as a man? Trans men are a different case; we were raised female, we know what it's like to be treated as females, and we have been discriminated against as females. We get what life has been like for women."

In May, Mills College became the first women's college to broaden its admissions policy to include self-identified trans women, even those who haven't legally or medically transitioned and even if their transcripts or recommendation letters refer to them as male. The new policy, which begins by affirming Mills's commitment to remaining a women's college, also welcomes biological females who identify anywhere on the gender spectrum, as long as they haven't become legally male. The change grew out of two years of study by a committee of faculty and staff, which noted that Mills has always fought gender-based oppression and concluded, "Trans inclusiveness represents not an erasure but an updating of this mission."

Mills also aims to educate students, staff, and faculty members to be more trans inclusive, said Brian O'Rourke, who oversees enrollment at the college and was the president's liaison to the committee. I asked O'Rourke if that included reducing the focus on women in the classroom. "I honestly don't know," he said. "We had a national speaker on trans issues join us on campus about a year ago, and one of the things she suggested is that we stop referring to Mills as a women's college, because that concept is exclusionary. In the auditorium, there was an audible gasp. We've had a lot of conversations about how to stress women's leadership and women's empowerment and at the same time, include people who may not identify as women. The answer is: We don't know yet."

Last month, Mount Holyoke College announced a more far-reaching policy: It would admit all academically qualified students regardless of their anatomy or self-proclaimed gender, except for those biologically male at birth who still identify as male.

In a list that reflects just how much traditional notions of gender have been upended, Mount Holyoke said eligible candidates now include anyone born biologically female, whether identified as woman, man, neither, or "other," and anyone born biologically male who identifies as a woman or "other." The school president, Lynn Pasquerella, said she and her officers made the decision after concluding it was an issue of civil rights.

But Pasquerella said accommodations for trans students will not include changing   60
the school's mission. "We're first and foremost committed to being a women's college," she told me. "I'm not going to stop using the language of sisterhood." She mentioned she taught a class in critical race theory two years ago and told her students, "When I use the term 'sisterhood,' I'm using it in a way that acknowledges the fact that not everybody here identifies as a woman. It is a rhetorical device . . . , but it is not intended to exclude anybody."

I said her explanation seemed like the one for using "he" as a generic pronoun for a male or female. She offered a different analogy, noting the parallel between women's colleges and historically black colleges and universities. "Isn't it still legitimate to speak of being a community of color even if you have half a dozen students who aren't individuals of color?" she asked. "The same might be said about women's colleges. Our mission was built upon education for women, and while we recognize that not everyone identifies this way, this is who we are and how we talk about things."

Meanwhile, Wellesley continues to struggle with its own identity. In August, Debra DeMeis, the dean of students, told me the administration had not yet worked out how to be a women's college at a time when gender is no longer considered binary. President H. Kim Bottomly and Jennifer C. Desjarlais, the dean of admissions, declined to talk to me. But a few days after Mount Holyoke's announcement, Bottomly released a statement saying that Wellesley would begin to think about how to address the trans question.

On the last Friday in May, some 5,000 parents, alumnae, and soon-to-be graduates streamed onto the rolling field near Severance Hall, named after Elisabeth Severance, a generous 1887 alumna. It was a gorgeous, temperate morning for Wellesley's 136th annual commencement, and once the last baccalaureate degree was conferred, the audience was asked to stand. As is the school's tradition, two graduates led an uplifting rendition of "America, the Beautiful." The lyrics, for those who needed them, were printed in the commencement program, including the chorus: "And crown thy good, with brotherhood, from sea to shining sea!"

Those words were penned by Katharine Lee Bates, an 1880 graduate of Wellesley who defied the expectations of her gender, and not just by becoming a professor, published author, and famous poet. A pastor's daughter, she never married, living instead for 25 years with Katharine Coman, founder of Wellesley's economics department, with whom she was deeply in love. When a colleague described "free-flying spinsters" as a "fringe on the garment of life," Bates, then 53, answered: "I always thought the fringe had the best of it."

As parents, professors, and graduates joined in the singing of Bates's most famous   65
poem, many felt an intense pride in their connection to the graduates and this remarkable college, which has sent forth so many women who leave impressive marks on the

world. As the hundreds of voices rounded the curve on "And crown thy good with . . . ," the unknowing parents continued to "brotherhood," the word that was always supposed to stand in for women too, but never really did. Wellesley women long ago learned that words matter, and for decades, this has been the point in the song when their harmonious choral singing abruptly becomes a bellow as they belt out "sisterhood," drowning out the word that long excluded them and replacing it with a demand for recognition. It's one of the most powerful moments of commencement, followed every year by cheers, applause, and tears, evoked by the rush of solidarity with women throughout time, and the thrill of claiming in one of the nation's most famous songs that women matter — even if the world they're about to enter doesn't always agree.

In the last few years, a handful of graduates have changed that word once again, having decided that "sisterhood," no matter how well intended, is exclusionary, and so they instead call out "siblinghood." A few trans men find even that insufficient, and in that instant, they roar the word that represents them best: "brotherhood," not as a sexist stand-in for all humankind, but as an appeal from a tiny minority struggling to be acknowledged.

In truth, it's difficult to distinguish in the cacophony each of the words shouted atop one another. What is clear is that whatever word each person is hollering is immensely significant as a proclamation of existence, even if it's hard to make out what anyone else is saying.

Exploring Context

1. Explore the Web site for Wellesley College at wellesley.edu. How does the site reflect the school's investment in women?

2. The National Center for Transgender Equality (transequality.org) is an organization dedicated to advocacy for transgender rights. Explore its Web site. Does it offer any resources that might be useful for Wellesley or its students?

3. Padawer also discusses admissions policy changes at Mills College (mills.edu) and Mount Holyoke College (mtholyoke.edu). Explore the Web sites for these schools. In what ways do they represent themselves, and how does that representation differ from Wellesley College's? Draw from your work in Question 1 of Exploring Context.

Questions for Connecting

1. Synthesize Wellesley College's educational mission with the vision of education explored by Graeme Wood in "Is College Doomed?" (p. 506). Does a single-gender school conform to outdated educational models? What might Wellesley learn, if anything, from Minerva's model? Use your work from Question 3 of Questions for Critical Reading and Questions 1 and 3 of Exploring Context.

2. Are the transgender students Padawer examines "good" feminists? Use Roxane Gay's understanding of feminism from "Bad Feminist." (p. 169) to evaluate the feminism of these students. Is feminism inherently related to gender? Can men, biological or transgender, be "good" feminists?

3. Julia Serano, a transgender woman, discusses rape culture in "Why Nice Guys Finish Last" (p. 415). Use her work and the comments of transgender students at Wellesley College to consider whether or not transgender people offer a unique perspective. Is there something to be gained by changing genders or having an outside perspective? What is gained, and what is lost? Use your work on gender from Question 2 of Questions for Critical Reading and your work on transgender advocacy from Question 2 of Exploring Context.

Language Matters

1. Many foreign languages are highly structured by questions of gender: Nouns, for example, might be masculine or feminine. How does the English language reflect gender? Use a grammar handbook or other reference source to explore the ways in which gender is built into English. Review Padawer's article. How does she handle issues of gender when talking about students at Wellesley College?

2. This article was originally published in a newspaper's magazine supplement. How does journalistic writing differ from academic writing? Locate one or more sentences from Padawer that seem especially to reflect journalism. Rewrite these as academic sentences. What changes? Word choice? Sentence structure? Tone?

3. This essay has two titles: "When Women Become Men at Wellesley" from the online version of the magazine and "Sisterhood Is Complicated" from the print edition. Which is more effective, and why? What role might titles play in your own writing?

Assignments for Writing

1. Padawer notes, "Exactly how Wellesley will resolve the trans question is still unclear" (p. 321). Write a paper in which you address this problem by suggesting principles Wellesley College can use to resolve this question. Should equality be the focus? Education? Or is there another principle that might guide this decision? Draw from your work in Question 1 of Questions for Critical Reading and Question 3 of Exploring Context.

2. How can schools like Wellesley promote the leadership and empowerment of women while accommodating the needs of trans students? Write a paper in which you propose strategies for balancing the needs of women with those of other students not only at schools like Wellesley but at other institutions of higher education as well.

3. Write a paper in which you assess the impact of evolving notions of gender. Are we headed toward a world with a greater range of gender options? What are the costs and benefits of diverse gender options? Consider using your work from Question 2 of Questions for Critical Reading and Question 2 of Exploring Context.

NICK PAUMGARTEN

Nick Paumgarten is a staff writer for the *New Yorker*, a position he has held since 2005. He still contributes to "The Talk of the Town," a regular feature of the *New Yorker* that he served as deputy editor of from 2000 to 2005. His work at the magazine often focuses on sports, music, and finance.

Thos Robinson/Getty Images

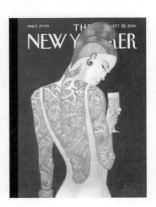

The *New Yorker*, published nearly weekly since 1925, is known for its highbrow reporting, criticism, cartoons, and literature. Regular contributors include high-profile writers and thinkers such as Malcolm Gladwell and James Surowiecki; Ariel Levy and Maria Konnikova, also featured in *Emerging*, regularly write for the magazine as well. The September 22, 2014, issue, from which this essay is taken, featured fiction from Victor Lodato as well as essays on a Wonder Woman museum, the inclusion of plus-size models at recent fashion shows, and Utah's attempt to solve homelessness by giving away homes.

In "We Are a Camera," Paumgarten explores the popularity of GoPro cameras, small, rugged personal video cameras most often mounted on a person and used to document some exciting, extraordinary event. Mountain climbers, bikers, divers, surfers, and others use them to share some of their most daring exploits. As these POV (point of view) videos produced by GoPro cameras become more and more popular, Paumgarten begins to consider the consequences of this technology. Tracing the history of the company and its technology, he examines the ways in which users come to value the footage of an experience more than the experience itself. Moreover, GoPro makes the pervasiveness of cameras feel benign when it may not be so at all.

Have you ever used a GoPro or seen footage? Do videos enhance our memories or replace them?

▶ TAGS: *art, culture, economics, empathy, media, photography and video, relationships*
▶ CONNECTIONS: *DeGhett, Klosterman, Ma, Restak, Rosin, Singer, Southan, Watters*

Questions for Critical Reading

1. As you read, keep a list of what Paumgarten believes are the problematic consequences of the GoPro camera. Do you feel these problems outweigh the benefits of the camera?

2. What cultural, economic, and technological factors contributed to the success of the GoPro? Note passages where Paumgarten discusses the elements that helped this camera thrive.

3. How do you measure the value of an experience? Record your own thoughts and then as you read the essay consider how Paumgarten feels we should value experiences. How do video cameras affect experience?

We Are a Camera

Late one fall afternoon two years ago, Aaron Chase, a professional mountain biker, was riding his bike in the Smoky Mountains, near Sun Valley, Idaho. He'd powered up to a high-altitude ridge and was gazing, less than eagerly, at the trail down toward the backcountry yurt where he and two fellow pro riders were camped for the week. He wasn't feeling well. He was tired, hungry, dehydrated, and a little woozy. In the argot, he was bonking.

He and the others, along with a professional photographer, had spent two days filming video footage of themselves hurtling down steep technical trails and executing tricks off natural features. They had brought along more than a dozen GoPros, the ubiquitous small digital point-of-view cameras.

Chase, who is sponsored by GoPro and is exceptionally adept at using GoPro cameras to make videos, likes to use a camera mount called the 360 Narwhal, after the species of whale with a tusk protruding from its jaw. The mount consists of a lightweight carbon rod affixed to the top of his helmet, like a helicopter rotor, to which he attaches a pair of GoPros, one at each end, a couple of feet from the center, in the manner of two buckets hanging from a carrying pole. The rod can rotate around its center, its movements determined by the cameras' weight and centrifugal momentum. Typically, Chase sets one camera a little farther out from his head than the other and, with subtle tilts of his head, exploits the asymmetry to manipulate the cameras' positions and movements as he rides. He is star athlete, director, and DP. He gives as much thought to getting the shot as he does to nailing the trick.

For two days in the Idaho mountains, Chase's cameras had been rolling virtually non-stop. Now, with his companions lagging behind, he started down the trail, which descended steeply into an alpine meadow. As he accelerated, he noticed, to his left, an elk galloping toward him from the ridge. He glanced at the trail, looked again to his left, and saw a herd, maybe thirty elk, running at full tilt alongside his bike, like a pod of dolphins chasing a boat. After a moment, they rumbled past him and crossed the trail, neither he nor the elk slowing, dust kicking up and glowing in the early-evening sun, amid a thundering of hooves. It was a magical sight. The light was perfect. And, as usual, Chase was wearing two GoPros. Here was his money shot—the stuff of TV ads and real bucks.

Trouble was, neither camera was rolling. What with his headache and the ample footage of the past days, he'd thought to hell with it, and had neglected, just this once, to turn his GoPros on. Now there was no point in riding with the elk. He slowed up and let them pass. "Idiot," he said to himself. "There goes my commercial."

Once the herd was gone, it was as though it'd never been there at all—Sasquatch, E.T., yeti. Pics or it didn't happen. Still, one doesn't often find oneself swept up in a stampede of wild animals. Might as well hope to wingsuit through a triple rainbow. So you'd think that, cameras or not, he'd remember the moment with some fondness. But no. "It was hell," Chase says now.

When the agony of missing the shot trumps the joy of the experience worth shooting, the adventure athlete (climber, surfer, extreme skier) reveals himself to be something else: a filmmaker, a brand, a vessel for the creation of content. He used to just do the thing—plan the killer trip or trick and then complete it, with panache. Maybe a photographer or film crew tagged along, and afterward there'd be a slide show at community centers and high-school gyms, or an article in a magazine. Now the purpose of the trip or trick is the record of it. Life is footage.

Chase's elk came to mind on the morning, in late June, of GoPro's initial public offering. When GoPro goes public, there is no chance of missing the shot. Before the opening bell, legions of GoPro executives, employees, family, and friends gathered on the ground floor of the NASDAQ building, in what is really just a TV studio, facing out onto Times Square. There's no trading floor at NASDAQ, so bell ringings are Potemkin affairs—in this case, not only for the usual phalanx of TV cameras but also for the fifty-odd GoPros the team had brought along, so everyone could chronicle the occasion from a variety of unconventional vantages.

The camera is a relatively simple device. High-tech guts in low-tech disguise—it's "cute and fancy," as the late Sony chairman Akio Morita is supposed to have said of the Walkman. A GoPro Hero 3+, the latest iteration (the tech rumor mill predicts that the Hero 4 will début next month), costs between three hundred and four hundred dollars. Once removed from its waterproof case—to the GoPro what armor was to the knight—it is small and spare. People say "matchbox-size" but it's more like two matchboxes. It has just three buttons and yet, somehow, dozens of settings.

The GoPro is defined as much by its limitations as by its advantages. It has no display, so you can't see what's in the frame. In a way, this doesn't matter, because the wide-angle lens takes in so broad a field (everything in focus, everything lit) that you need only point it in a general direction and you can expect to capture something good.   10

Both the indicator light and the control display are on the front of the camera, so this is where its operator must go to operate it, or to make sure that it is in fact operating. In unedited GoPro shots, the cameraman often appears in closeup in the frame, amid the muffled clatter of finger (or glove) brushing microphone; this routine parenthesis is the GoPro version of a director's slate. (You could cut an hour-long edit of these accidental selfies—a montage of scraped knuckles, double chins, and bloodshot eyes—and call it "Action!") The microphone picks up sound that is very close but misses sound farther away. GoPro shots are often characterized by one-sided conversation, the rattle of straps, or the beatbox fusillade of water and wind. This is one reason a polished GoPro edit is usually set to music. Still, the clarity of the picture, which renders trees, waves, seracs, clouds, and cliffs with a kind of lysergic radiance, flatters the natural world.

On the morning of the IPO, the company's founder, Nick Woodman, who devised a crude version of the camera twelve years ago to get photos of himself surfing, held GoPros, at different times, in his teeth, at arm's length, or on an array of mounts, filming himself and others, who in turn trained their cameras on him and on themselves. Woodman, in jeans and a dark-blue button-down shirt, tan and fit with white teeth and spiky dark hair, led them in impromptu banshee howls, the feral woo-hoos of joy-riders everywhere, and chants of "Go Pro! Go Pro! Go Pro!" and with his non-GoPro hand flashed the surfer's hang-loose shaka sign. He pointed a GoPro at himself and howled, "This is really happening!" The camera affirmed it.

Becoming a multibillionaire may not be as rare an occurrence these days as riding a mountain bike through a herd of elk, but it is nonetheless a feat worthy of documentation. GoPro's offering price, of twenty-four dollars a share, valued the company at around three billion dollars. Woodman's father, Dean Woodman, a hale gent of eighty-five who had himself once been a very successful entrepreneur, as a founder of the now defunct San Francisco investment bank Robertson Stephens, and who early on had lent his son two hundred thousand dollars to finance GoPro, came up to him and said, "You look like a rock star."

"I play one on TV," the son said. He is known as the Mad Billionaire, for his hyperactive antics and taste for adventure sports. But when it came time for him to talk, just before the opening, he teared up, presumably at this culmination of so much hard work — years of risks rewarded, doubts dashed, overpromises met, and paternal expectations exceeded. He recovered himself for the cameras. "I'm fired up!" he called out to his employees. "You fired up?"

After the bell, while the GoPro employees milled around and posed for photos, Brad Schmidt, GoPro's creative director, working on a laptop with GoPro editing software, quickly cut the footage into a packet to present to the TV producers who'd be interviewing Woodman and his fellow-executives throughout the day. As Schmidt has said, you don't hunt shots; you "capture" them. (This approach requires lots of work in the cutting room, or what *Surfing* called "a time-warping pain in the edit-ass.") Schmidt scrolled through dozens of vantages, many of them imbued with a kinetic intensity you don't usually see on the set of a stock-market show. "The button shot is amazing," he said; it had captured Woodman reaching down toward the camera to press a lit panel that would initiate the day's trading — the NASDAQ equivalent, perhaps, of getting tubed at Pipeline. 15

As he worked, half a dozen guests held their GoPros up to the window to film the Jumbotrons in Times Square, which NASDAQ had leased for the occasion in order to display GoPro videos. Among the cavalcade of images was an underwater shot of Woodman's toddler son learning to swim: a private event now magnified into mythology in the hall of mirrors that is our world of cameras and screens.

Woodman had the good fortune to invent a product that was well suited to a world he had not yet imagined. The ripening of the technology in his camera, after a half decade of tinkering, coincided with the fruition of broadband and the emergence of YouTube, Facebook, and other social-media platforms for the wide distribution of video. GoPro rode the wave. What might have been just another camcorder became a leading connector between what goes on in the real world and what goes out in the virtual one — a perfect instrument for the look-at-me age. Its charm lies perhaps in its sublimated conveyance of self, its sneaky tolerable narcissism. GoPro footage is related to the selfie, in its "Here I am" (or "was") ethos, and its wide view and variety of mounts often allow the filmmaker to include himself, or some part of himself, in the shot. But because it primarily points outward it's a record of what an experience looks like, rather than what the person who had the experience looked like when he stopped afterward and arranged his features into his pretested photo face. The result is not as much a selfie as a worldie. It's more like the story you'd tell about an adventure than the photo that would accompany it.

Though GoPro is known primarily for its connection to adventure sports, the camera is increasingly used in feature films and on TV, and by professionals of many stripes—musicians, surgeons, chefs. Many BMWs now come with an app to control a GoPro in the dash (in case you want to show the kids your commute). The company has

The result is not as much a selfie as a worldie.

been promoting its use in broadcasting traditional sports. An armada of GoPros greatly enhanced the coverage of last year's America's Cup, in San Francisco Bay, but perhaps they'd shed less light on the mysteries of an NFL line of scrimmage: one imagines indecipherable grunting and rustling, the filmic equivalent of a butt dial. The opposite of this, and the big thing these days, is the footage that comes from mounting GoPros on small quadcopter drones: sublime sweeping shots and heretofore unseen bird's-eye vantages, on the cheap.

As for its broadcast applications, we are still in a relatively primitive stage. A GoPro senior producer described to me the process he came up with last year to get POV footage of Shane Dorian surfing the giant waves at Mavericks, off the coast of Northern California, to use on a broadcast of a competition there. After Dorian had ridden a wave, a guy on a Jet Ski would zoom over, grab the camera, and then carry it in past the break to a paddleboarder, who'd maneuver through the swirling whitewash to the base of a cliff, over which a member of the broadcast team had lowered a basket. Up went the basket, and an assistant ran the camera over to the broadcast tent.

In going public, GoPro has tried to position itself not just as a camera-maker but as a media company—a producer and distributor of branded content. In this conception, it is hawking not only cameras and accessories (the source, up to now, of pretty much all of GoPro's revenue) but videos, too (a source, up to now, of pretty much no revenue). In the past five years, videos posted by GoPro have attracted half a billion views. On the GoPro channel on YouTube, videos average about half a million viewers each. The company thinks it can capitalize on the fact that thousands of people every day post videos online and, without prompting, tag them as GoPro.

Most of them are not the ones that come from their sponsored athletes (or "brand ambassadors"), like Aaron Chase, who are expected to submit footage. They are crowd-sourced—amateur-hour finds that turn pro. For the latter, GoPro pays very little—maybe some accessories or a camera, plus, say, a thousand dollars for the first million views. A cadre of editors at GoPro scours Facebook, YouTube, and Reddit and often reëdits the best and pushes them out on its own channels on YouTube, Pinterest, and other platforms. In the process, the company has nurtured a growing army of amateurs (eager providers of free content) and helped the GoPro name become shorthand not only for all POV cameras, including those made by other manufacturers, but for the genre of short video that has arguably become as much a feature of daily life as the three-minute pop song.

You can probably think of as many viral GoPro videos as you can recent hit singles. Have you seen the one that was shot from the beak of an airborne pelican? The one of the South African mountain biker being robbed by the gunman? The woman giving birth on the sidewalk? The fireman rescuing the kitten? The Lion Whisperer guy? "Toy Robot in Space"? The view from a car wheel or the inside of a fox's mouth or a drone soaring through a Fourth of July fireworks display? Of course you have, and if you haven't I'll send you the link.

The genre is characterized by point of view, by brevity, and by incident. The ones that go viral contain something extraordinary, be it unimaginable risk, uncharted beauty, unlikely encounter, or unexpected twist. The categories bleed. A common critique has been that the presence of the camera prods people to take greater risks as they aspire to virality—Kodak courage, which might now be more properly called GoPro guts. It may not be fair to say that it's the camera that causes people to attempt to brush the ground while flying past an outcrop in a wingsuit, but perhaps seeing it done on film inspires other people to try. Some have attributed this phenomenon to *Jackass*, the MTV program on which a band of pranksters subjected their bodies to clever, horrific abasements, but, really, people have attempted dangerous stunts for attention and money since the invention of the camera. Before there was Johnny Knoxville there was Buster Keaton. GoPro has been sensitive to the contention that their cameras play any role in getting people to do stupid, risky, dangerous, or unlawful things. It offers, with some plausibility, a kind of guns-don't-kill-people argument. Don't blame the camera. A spokesman cited Icarus.

A popular subgenre is the blooper, the so-called GoPro Fail. Sometimes the intention to Be a Hero causes one instead to Be the Schlemiel. There may be violence, but insofar as it ends well, you might call it comic. My favorite GoPro Fail, which first made the rounds in February, 2011, and still circles the Internet in a kind of ongoing viral orbit, was of, and by, a skier named Stefan Ager. The video is a minute and a half long and is shot from Ager's helmet mount. It begins with him and a friend atop a snow-clad peak in Austria, after a three-hour climb. The setting is a sheer ridge, with cliffs seemingly dropping off in all directions. After some giddy panorama shots, he holds his helmet out and turns the camera on himself, revealing a young shaggy dude. He dons the helmet and looks down to put on his skis, which he lays parallel in the snow, along the narrow ridge. He steps into his bindings, the skis drift backward a few inches, and—"Whoa!"—our man goes backward over the precipice. The camera tosses and clicks as Ager—"Aaaah!"—plummets more than a thousand vertical feet down a cliff, bouncing off rocks, before landing—"Oof!"—on the edge of a glacier. He moans a couple of times and then stands up (or so it looks from his shadow, which is topped by a silhouette of the GoPro). He looks around. Somehow, his survival makes the glacier all the more beautiful, even to the viewer. He glances back to where he came from, and then the video ends.

It's the mother of all pratfalls, and I've watched it more than a dozen times. It's had more than three million hits. Last month, when I tracked Ager down, via Facebook, I felt as though I'd found an e-mail address for, say, Lorde. He wrote back, "I am actually not interested in an interview regarding my fall. I am glad that nothing happened and I can keep skiing." 25

Every entrepreneurial success story hardens into legend, and the quickening often occurs around the time of the IPO. GoPro's is as follows: In 1999, during the dot-com boom, Woodman, a recent graduate of the University of California at San Diego and the son of a prominent Bay Area banker, started an online video-game company called Funbug. It failed two years later, amid the dot-com crash, and Woodman, embarrassed over having lost other people's money, decided to take six months off to surf and travel with his girlfriend. While in Indonesia, in 2002, he struck up a friendship with another surfer, named Brad Schmidt. They were both intrigued by the problem of how to get pictures of themselves riding waves. At this point, Woodman's innovation was a wrist wrap fashioned from the ankle end of his surfboard leash, to which, using rubber bands, he affixed a disposable Kodak camera in a waterproof case. He had a sense that the wristband could be marketable, but soon realized, after trying various cameras, that it would get complicated, with regard to licensing and legal permission. So he went to China to have a camera made to his specs.

By 2004, he had a prototype of the GoPro Hero, a clunky 35-mm. box that used film. In the next few years, with Schmidt testing it out on surfing trips and sending back astonishing images, Woodman made refinements, and started making money, too. He travelled around the country in a 1974 VW van he called Biscuit, to surf shops and trade shows (and did a couple of appearances on QVC); to raise extra funds he sold belts made of seashells he'd picked up in Bali. At surfing events, he handed out cameras to pros. One day, he attached a GoPro to the cockpit of a racecar, and everyone at the track became fascinated by both the device and the result. A light bulb: this thing wasn't just for surfers.

Schmidt, fresh out of film school, became the head of GoPro's media division, which distributed as many videos, from an ever-widening circle of sources, as it could—in part, as Schmidt has said, to convince the world that these videos were real. By the end of the decade, the GoPro was commonplace in the world of action sports. Every week seemed to bring a revelatory new vantage on some established exploit or trick. And then people began coming up with new moves and feats, to suit the camera.

The producers at GoPro are often athletes themselves, maybe with some film or photography experience. Woodman has always encouraged his employees to hire their friends. Zak Shelhamer, a photographer and former professional snowboarder, joined the company to help edit and produce snow-sport videos and now runs the adventure-sports division. He told me that he'd recently been talking to a pair of young Frenchmen who were planning to row a boat from Monterey to Hawaii. They'd submitted a proposal for a contest the company ran called How Will You GoPro? They didn't win, but Shelhamer gave them some cameras anyway and promised to take an interest in what they might come back with. In discussing the risks, he mentioned a guy who had tried rowing from Australia to New Zealand. "How'd he do?" one of the Frenchmen asked him.

"He drowned," Shelhamer said.

"How'd they figure that out?"

"They found his camera."

After the IPO, GoPro's stock price almost doubled and began to develop the characteristics of a so-called battleground stock. On one side were the believers, who, implicitly or not, endorsed the company's branded content aspirations. (One Wall Street analyst last week called GoPro a "movement.") On the other side were the skeptics who suspected that the stock's rise had as much to do with a love for the product as for its real

30

long-term prospects—cute and fancy winning out, for now, over hard and cold. They note that bigger companies are now making similar cameras (one can argue which are the best), and so they wonder how long GoPro can stay on top. The cautionary example, cited by doubters and by GoPro itself, is the Flip, the briefly ubiquitous digital camcorder, which got overtaken by smartphones and is now out of business.

The company wants to capitalize on the mass-market home-video urge, the camera's aptitude for capturing what GoPro's president, Tony Bates, calls "life's great moments," and yet retain its reputation as a kind of philosopher's stone, capable of transforming ordinary experience into magical footage. (Two tips: "Slow it down and you look like a pro." "The closer the better.") In some respects, the GoPro is like the Brownie and the Polaroid, devices that democratized photography and revolutionized the way we think about the past and even the way we fashion the present, with an eye to how it will look later, when we linger over photographs of it. But the analogy comes up short, because GoPro videos aspire to go viral. You're sharing the photos of your ski trip not just with your family and a few friends but, if you're any good, with thousands, if not millions, of people. The GoPro, by implication, asks its users to push a little harder, as both subjects and filmmakers. Be a Hero: The premise from the start has been that you, in every way an amateur, can go pro—on both sides of the lens. It's karaoke, but with the full Marshall stack.

The short video synonymous with GoPro is a kind of post-literate diary, a stop on the way to a future in which everything will be filmed from every point of view. Humans have always recorded their experiences, in an array of media and for a variety of reasons. Not until very recently, with the advent of digital photography and video, and unlimited storage and distribution capacity, has it been conceivable to film everything. As we now more than ever communicate through pictures, either still or moving, perhaps our lives come closer to Susan Sontag's imagined "anthology of images." An obvious example is the people who film concerts on their smartphones. Will they ever watch the video? And if they do will it measure up to the concert, which they half missed? Of course not. They film the concert to certify their attendance and convey their good fortune. The frame corroborates.

The computer scientist Gordon Bell, a former Digital Equipment Corporation engineer, an early developer of the Internet, and later a top researcher at Microsoft, spent several years as the main subject of a life-logging experiment called MyLifeBits, inspired by the work of the scientist Vannevar Bush, who, in 1945, wrote, "The camera hound of the future wears on his forehead a lump a little larger than a walnut." (To store all the images, and everything else, Bush envisioned a device called the "memex," short for memory extender.) Bell, in addition to digitizing every document, object, phone conversation, and transaction in his life, wore a Microsoft SenseCam around his neck. It snapped a photo every twenty seconds.

"What you're capturing is one thing," he told me. "The other is when are you going to use it." He'd recently gone to a conference on memory, sponsored by something called the Institute for the Future. Apparently, psychologists and neurologists have discovered that photos or video of an event are more effective than notes or conversation at helping people remember an experience.

Bell is amazed that a surfer in California cornered the market for what he calls go-everywhere cameras. "Where were the Japanese?" he said. "They totally ignored the fact that you could have a camera like this at this price point. But really it's not the camera—it's the Internet."

At any rate, he predicts that eventually GoPros and their ilk, as well as contrivances like Google Glass, will be supplanted by truly wearable cameras, with virtually no volume (a card, or a chip, or, one imagines, an implant in the retina). "Is there a time in the future where people will record everything they see and hear?" Bell asked. "Yes. It's at least a decade away." The difficulty arises in the sorting—a pain in the edit-ass of big-data proportions. "It requires an enormous amount of software."

By now, so much video is being produced that it's hard to imagine a fate for it other than obsolescence. Where does all this video go? If it's in the cloud, will it all come falling back to earth, in an apocalypse of pets, babies, head-cam porn, flight lessons, golf swings, and unicycle tricks?   40

Earlier this summer, I attended the GoPro Mountain Games, in Vail, Colorado, a competition-cum-festival featuring mountain bikers, rock climbers, and other outdoor athletes. Teeming with GoPros, the village, ersatz Alpine to begin with, felt a little like the set of a ski-town *Brigadoon*. One afternoon, I went whitewater kayaking down Gore Creek with Eric and Dane Jackson, father-and-son professional freestyle kayakers and GoPro ambassadors. The paddling wasn't hard, and yet the Jacksons, who routinely descend steep creeks and giant waterfalls, seemed intent on making my outing into an accomplishment worthy of recording and then foisting onto the world. Now and then, Dane paddled over, spat on his fingers, and rubbed saliva on the lens of the GoPro on the bow of my boat. We drifted past a man who was operating a quadcopter drone with a GoPro attached. It swooped over us and then receded upriver. Above the takeout, in town, a little girl with a GoPro on her forehead passed over us on a zip line. On bridges and banks: GoPros everywhere. We were mayflies, flashing through the frames of strangers.

When we were done, Eric Jackson, using GoPro's editing program, made a thirty-second video of our trip and posted it on his Facebook page. He scrolled down, interested only in how much attention his posts were getting, not in what others had to say. "I don't read any of this," he said. "I don't read Facebook. I don't watch the other videos. I don't want to read everyone else's diaries. I write a diary." He posts a video almost every day, in part to promote himself and his business (he also manufactures kayaks), but also out of some compulsion to leave a record of his exploits—to draw on the walls of the cave.

Two years ago, my son, then ten, won a GoPro in a school raffle. On a ski vacation that spring, he affixed it to the top of his helmet with the standard mount—Tinkywinky, we called him, after the Teletubby with the triangle on its head—and let it roll most of the day, five to fifteen minutes at a stretch. What struck me, while watching some of the footage on a laptop later, was the idiosyncratic ordinariness of it. As he skied, he whistled to himself, made odd sounds, looked around at the mountains, shouted to his brother and his cousin, cried out at the slightest hint of air, and now and then bent forward and filmed upside down through his legs. Even though the camera was turned outward, filled mainly by the sight of the terrain sliding past, it provided, more than anything, a glimpse into the mind of a dreamy and quiet boy—who, to my eyes, during the day, had been just a nose, his features and expressions otherwise hidden by helmet, neck gaiter, and goggles. I didn't need a camera to show me what he looked like to the world, but was delighted to find one that could show me what the world looked like to him. It captured him better than any camera pointed at him could. This was a proxy, of sorts.

This past spring, he again spent a few days skiing with the camera on his head—Tinkywinky at twelve. His best footage came from a powder morning, his first ever in the Rockies; the camera aimed just past the tips of his skis. Every civilian who skis powder with a GoPro on his head gets the same kind of shot, pole tips rhythmically appearing at the edges of the frame, ski tips porpoising in and out of the snow, the occasional whoop of joy. In my son's video, the whistling and whimsical attention of two years before had given way to a devoted concentration and perhaps an earnest attempt to record what he, in the manner of skiers everywhere, deemed a noteworthy experience. Later, he shot footage while following me through gaps in the trees. That night, I watched it—again in the manner of skiers everywhere—for glimpses of myself.

A month later, he had to make a presentation in class, and he decided to do his about the GoPro. Planning to demonstrate his handiwork, he edited the footage, but then, at the last moment, decided it was too commonplace. It wasn't awesome enough—or, anyway, he didn't want his classmates to think that he thought it was awesome. Instead, he featured, in his report, a famous video from the POV of a mountain biker named Kelly McGarry doing a backflip over a canyon gap in Virgin, Utah. My son had become a habitual consumer of GoPro videos. Even as a grommet, he had standards. He no longer thought of it as home video.

At many ski areas nowadays, you can rent a GoPro for the day. The slopes teem with Teletubbies. People have helmet mounts for POV cameras of every make, and even smartphones in waterproof shells. It's not just groms or pros. It's grampas and gapers, too ("gapers" being the shredder's term for hapless wannabes). A ski trip has become a kind of life-logging vacation. People who'd never film a minute of their ordinary lives deem a day riding chairlifts and creeping along groomed trails to be worthy of wall-to-wall coverage. The sense among many serious skiers is that the cameras have contributed to heedless, or at least distracted, behavior in the backcountry. Any attention given to getting the shot, or posing for it, is attention diverted from the task of staying safe. Of course, there is no data to support this, and it could well be mere curmudgeonly grumbling. It's just that there are so many videos of bad stuff happening to backcountry skiers. GoPros have made it possible to see, really for the first time, the way the snowpack jigsaws around you (a skier's version of a land mine's click) when an avalanche kicks off or how it looks and sounds to be buried when the slide comes to a stop.

When it ends badly, the camera can be a kind of black box. A fantasy of the film-everything movement is an end to forensic uncertainty. Wearable POV cameras are also coming into vogue as a tool for soldiers and police. The premise is that reviewability makes for greater accountability—that seeing is knowing. After the Michael Brown shooting, in Ferguson, many commentators, accustomed already to the ubiquity of cameras, were dismayed that there was no footage of the incident. In this instance, we may wish we had some, but a world in which the police film every interaction with

There are many things we'd rather not see or have seen.

the public is not all sweetness and light. You may catch some bad cops, but you'd also hamstring the good ones. By enforcing uninterpretable standards of exchange, a video record has the effect of a mandatory sentence. It deprives the police of discretion, and the public of leniency. There are many things we'd rather not see or have seen.

GoPro, like Google Glass, has the insidious effect of making the pervasiveness of cameras seem playful and benign when it may one day be anything but. The *Economist* called the film-everything culture "the people's panopticon"—the suggestion being that with all these nifty devices we might be unwittingly erecting a vast prison of self-administered surveillance.

Andrew Rossig started BASE jumping in 2004, under the tutelage of an Englishman who was a proponent of "bandit jumping"—that is, jumping off things you are not allowed to. He got his first GoPro in 2010. It was much lighter than existing wearable cameras, which typically involved the camera on one side of the helmet and a battery pack on the other, a strain and a threat to the neck. You might say that a BASE jump consists of two main ingredients: the jump itself and the record of it. The GoPro made feasible part two.

Rossig, a carpenter who works in New York City, building movie sets, began nurs- 50 ing an ambition to film himself leaping off all the city's iconic tall structures, but it eventually became clear to him that it wasn't very safe and that the authorities would never permit it. Still, a man could dabble. In 2012, he was arrested, with a fellow BASE jumper named James Brady, while attempting to jump off a thirty-three-story tower in Co-op City, in the Bronx. Not long afterward, they began planning a jump off One World Trade Center, which Brady, an ironworker, had helped to build. They talked about making a movie out of the whole thing or not filming any of it at all. They agreed that it was perhaps unwise and potentially incriminating, at least, to film their conversations and preparations. Still, isn't the point of jumping off an iconic building to create and share a record of the deed? Rossig felt they had to have footage, at least for the benefit one day of children and grandchildren.

One night last September, the two of them, with a third jumper and a lookout man, sneaked through a hole in the security fence at the construction site and walked up the hundred and four flights to the top of the tower. They wore GoPros on their helmets but opted not to turn them on, lest the red indicator lights give them away. Only once they were on top of the tower, at the edge, preparing to leap, did they start shooting.

Each of the three jumpers shot footage. The first jumper pulled his chute immediately and soared way out over the Hudson and then tacked back toward the towers. Brady was the second to go; his video would be the most widely distributed. Rossig went last, did a somersault in the air, and pulled his chute later in the plunge than the others. He actually passed Brady. Altogether, the three original videos have been viewed almost three and a half million times on YouTube. One is struck by the tranquillity and silence before the jump, the mixture of reverence and apprehension. Often GoPro undertakings have a frivolous air, but this one's no joke. Their silhouettes are backlit by a vast plain of city lights. One jumper coaxes another, with a gentleness uncommon to GoPro-land. Most striking of all is the vision, once the plummet begins, of the illuminated glass façade of the tower sliding past, the pace accelerating yet oddly slow, almost elegant, with no trace really of violence or terror. In 1878, "Sallie Gardner at a Gallop," in a sense history's first film, depicting a thoroughbred in profile, surprised many viewers who'd previously misconstrued the mechanics of a galloping horse. These days, the drift of One World Trade's lit windows has a similar effect. So this is free fall. The pace shifts abruptly when each jumper pulls his chute. They drift toward the pavement. At the end of each video, the jumper lands in abandoned streets and scurries toward the shadows and a getaway car.

That night, a passerby caught a glimpse of them and called 911. The police checked security footage from the Goldman Sachs building nearby. They noticed a suspicious car, and then, using footage from other cameras in the area, in an ever-widening radius (there are more than four thousand working security cameras and license-plate scanners below Canal Street), they identified the vehicle (apparently, the NYPD keeps a record of every vehicle that crosses into Lower Manhattan) and eventually, in part by subpoenaing cell-phone records, the jumpers themselves, who, in the immediate aftermath of the jump, had dispersed and refrained from calling each other. A month afterward, they got together with thumb drives to watch and share each other's footage of the jump. But once the cops had identified them, five months after the jump, they turned themselves in. It was only then that they posted their jump footage on YouTube, in the hope that the beauty and strangeness of it might persuade the public, if not prosecutors, that they meant no harm.

"The legal advice we got was that we should show we're not bad guys," Rossig said. "If we're going to get in trouble for it, maybe everyone should see how amazing it was. Who else is going to get that camera angle?"

After a week, the videos had attracted more than three million hits. Still, GoPro's   55
media staff did not reach out to them. "They didn't want to be associated with us," Rossig said.

He and the others now face numerous charges, including one felony, and as much as seven years in prison. The police have confiscated their cameras.

Exploring Context

1. Visit GoPro's Web site at gopro.com. How does the site represent the camera and its abilities? Relate what you find to Paumgarten's argument and to your response from Question 1 of Questions for Critical Reading.

2. Search YouTube for "GoPro" and "GoPro fail." What sorts of experiences do people record with this camera? How do these videos relate to Paumgarten's argument? You may want to incorporate your response from Question 3 of Questions for Critical Reading.

3. Paumgarten ends with the story of the three men who jumped off New York's One World Trade Center. Search YouTube for "NYC base jump" to view the footage of this jump.

Questions for Connecting

1. Peter Singer, in "Visible Man: Ethics in a World without Secrets" (p. 425), also discusses the consequences of a video-saturated culture. Synthesize Singer's and Paumgarten's arguments. What's the relationship between video culture and political power? Incorporate your work from Question 1 of Questions for Critical Reading.

2. Dan Savage's "It Gets Better" (p. 406) and Urvashi Vaid's "Action Makes It Better" (p. 411) both emerge from the It Gets Better video project. Use their texts to reconsider Paumgarten's argument. How might video technology be used to help others? How might records of experiences make things better for others?

3. Paumgarten examines the ramifications of this new technology. In "Why Kids Sext" (p. 388), Hanna Rosin also looks at the consequence of technology. Use both of their texts to propose ethical standards for the development and use of technology. What factors must we consider as technology continues to develop? Use your work from Questions 2 and 3 of Questions for Critical Reading as you make your response.

Language Matters

1. Use a handbook or other reliable resource to learn how to cite videos. Practice by completing a citation for one of the videos you looked at in Exploring Context.

2. Paumgarten includes personal anecdotes in his essay. What effect do these stories have on the reader? When is it appropriate to use personal anecdotes in academic writing?

3. Consider the relationship between form and content using the videos you looked at in Exploring Context. How do these videos' authors convey information in a video? How do they make arguments in a video? Apply your findings to the form of the academic paper. What kind of content does it allow? What kind of content doesn't "fit," given the space of the form?

Assignments for Writing

1. What has greater value: an experience or the memory of an experience? Write a paper in which you assess the role of memory in our lives. How does memory shape our beliefs and actions? How do we preserve it? Is such preservation more important than experiences themselves? Use your work in Question 3 of Questions for Critical Reading.

2. Paumgarten raises some of the problems surrounding a video-saturated culture. Write a paper in which you propose an ethics of video. In what situations should we promote the use of video? Are there areas where it is not appropriate and should be discouraged?

3. Paumgarten makes it clear that GoPro is as much a cultural phenomenon as a technological one. Write a paper in which you consider the ways in which technology shapes culture. Consider using your work in Exploring Context to support your response.

MICHAEL POLLAN

© James Leynse/Corbis

Michael Pollan is the Knight Professor of Science and Environmental Journalism at the University of California–Berkeley as well as the author of seven books, including: *The Omnivore's Dilemma: A Natural History of Four Meals* (2006), *In Defense of Food: An Eater's Manifesto* (2008), *Food Rules: An Eater's Manual* (2009), and *A Natural History of Transformation* (2013). A graduate of Bennington College and Columbia University, Pollan has won multiple journalism awards, and his writing has appeared in *The Norton Book of Nature Writing* (1990), *Best American Essays* (1990 and 2003), and *Best American Science Writing* (2004). Pollan's work can often be seen in the *New York Times*, where he is a contributing writer.

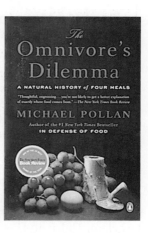

The *Omnivore's Dilemma*, declared by the *New York Times* to be one of 2006's best nonfiction books, traces three different food chains—the industrial, the pastoral, and the personal—from nature to table. Ultimately, the book is about the politics of eating: what we should eat, why we should eat it, and what impact our eating decisions have.

In "The Animals: Practicing Complexity" from *The Omnivore's Dilemma*, Pollan writes about an alternative to traditional agribusiness and profiles farmer Joel Salatin. With few outside raw materials, Salatin is able to run an incredibly productive farm that mimics a natural ecosystem in which nothing goes to waste. Pollan shows how order arises from the complex system of Salatin's farm, where everything plays a part, from a tree to a cow to the cow's manure, in a system—described as "holon" based—in which each element is simultaneously an individual whole and an active part in a complex system.

For Pollan, the omnivore's dilemma is one we face each day: what to have for dinner? This selection suggests that a healthy and sustainable answer to that question might come not from rejecting agribusiness entirely for an idealized agrarian past but from rethinking the intersection of business, farming, and food.

▶ TAGS: *collaboration, economics, education, food and agriculture*
▶ CONNECTIONS: *Dalai Lama, Manning, Wallace*

Questions for Critical Reading

1. What makes Polyface so successful? Locate passages where Pollan describes the key features of this farm, reading this essay critically to identify the key factors to the farm's success.

2. What is a *holon*? Use Pollan's text to define this term and to offer examples. Then apply the concept to another area by locating your own example of a holon.

3. Pollan subtitles this essay "Practicing Complexity." Use his text to explain what this means, referring to specific quotations or passages that show complexity in practice. You will need to read critically to determine your answer since Pollan never explains the relationship between this subtitle and his essay.

The Animals: Practicing Complexity

1. Tuesday Morning

It's not often I wake up at six in the morning to discover I've overslept, but by the time I had hauled my six-foot self out of the five-foot bed in Lucille's microscopic guest room, everyone was already gone and morning chores were nearly done. Shockingly, chores at Polyface commence as soon as the sun comes up (five-ish this time of year) and always before breakfast. Before coffee, that is, not that there was a drop of it to be had on this farm. I couldn't recall the last time I'd even attempted to do anything consequential before breakfast, or before caffeine at the very least.

When I stepped out of the trailer into the warm early morning mist, I could make out two figures — the interns, probably — moving around up on the broad shoulder of hill to the east, where a phalanx of portable chicken pens formed a checkerboard pattern on the grass. Among other things, morning chores consist of feeding and watering the broilers* and moving their pens one length down the hillside. I was supposed to be helping Galen and Peter do this, so I started up the path, somewhat groggily, hoping to get there before they finished.

As I stumbled up the hill, I was struck by how very beautiful the farm looked in the hazy early light. The thick June grass was silvered with dew, the sequence of bright pastures stepping up the hillside dramatically set off by broad expanses of blackish woods. Birdsong stitched the thick blanket of summer air, pierced now and again by the wood clap of chicken pen doors slamming shut. It was hard to believe this hillside had ever been the gullied wreck Joel had described at dinner, and even harder to believe that farming such a damaged landscape so intensively, rather than just letting it be, could restore it to health and yield this beauty. This is not the environmentalist's standard prescription. But Polyface is proof that people can sometimes do more for the health of a place by cultivating it rather than by leaving it alone.

By the time I reached the pasture Galen and Peter had finished moving the pens. Fortunately they were either too kind or too timid to give me a hard time for oversleeping. I grabbed a pair of water buckets, filled them from the big tub in the center of the pasture, and lugged them to the nearest pen. Fifty of these pens were spread out across the damp grass in a serrated formation that had been calibrated to cover every square foot of this meadow in the course of the fifty-six days it takes a broiler to reach slaughter weight; the pens moved ten feet each day, the length of one pen. Each

---

*Broilers: Chickens raised for their meat rather than for egg production [Ed.].

ten-by-twelve, two-foot-tall floorless pen houses seventy birds. A section of the roof is hinged to allow access, and a five-gallon bucket perched atop each unit fed a watering device suspended inside.

Directly behind each pen was a perfectly square patch of closely cropped grass re- 5 sembling a really awful Jackson Pollock painting, thickly spattered with chicken crap in pigments of white, brown, and green. It was amazing what a mess seventy chickens could make in a day. But that was the idea: Give them twenty-four hours to eat the grass and fertilize it with their manure, and then move them onto fresh ground.

Joel developed this novel method for raising broiler chickens in the 1980s and pop-ularized it in his 1993 book, *Pastured Poultry Profit$*, something of a cult classic among grass farmers. (Joel has self-published four other how-to books on farming, and all but one of them has a $ stepping in for an S somewhere in its title.) Left to their own devices, a confined flock of chickens will eventually destroy any patch of land, by pecking the grass down to its roots and poisoning the soil with their extremely "hot," or nitrog-enous, manure. This is why the typical free-range chicken yard quickly winds up bereft of plant life and hard as brick. Moving the birds daily keeps both the land and the birds healthy; the broilers escape their pathogens and the varied diet of greens supplies most of their vitamins and minerals. The birds also get a ration of corn, toasted soybeans, and kelp, which we scooped into long troughs in their pens, but Joel claims the fresh grass, along with the worms, grasshoppers, and crickets they peck out of the grass, provides as much as 20 percent of their diet—a significant savings to the farmer and a boon to the birds. Meanwhile, their manure fertilizes the grass, supplying all the ni-trogen it needs. The chief reason Polyface Farm is completely self-sufficient in nitrogen is that a chicken, defecating copiously, pays a visit to virtually every square foot of it at several points during the season. Apart from some greensand (a mineral supplement to replace calcium lost in the meadows), chicken feed is the only important input Joel buys, and the sole off-farm source of fertility. ("The way I look at it, I'm just returning some of the grain that's been extracted from this land over the last 150 years.") The chicken feed not only feeds the broilers but, transformed into chicken crap, feeds the grass that feeds the cows that, as I was about to see, feeds the pigs and the laying hens.

After we had finished watering and feeding the broilers, I headed up to the next pasture, where I could hear a tractor idling. Galen had told me Joel was moving the Eggmobile, an operation I'd been eager to watch. The Eggmobile, one of Joel's proudest innovations, is a ramshackle cross between a henhouse and a prairie schooner. Hous-ing four hundred laying hens, this rickety old covered wagon has hinged nesting boxes lined up like saddlebags on either side, allowing someone to retrieve eggs from the out-side. I'd first laid eyes on the Eggmobile the night before, parked a couple of paddocks away from the cattle herd. The hens had already climbed the little ramp into the safety of the coop for the night, and before we went down to dinner Joel had latched the trap-door behind them. Now it was time to move them into a fresh paddock, and Joel was bolting the Eggmobile to the hitch of his tractor. It wasn't quite 7:00 AM yet, but Joel seemed delighted to have someone to talk to, holding forth being one of his greatest pleasures.

"In nature you'll always find birds following herbivores," Joel explained, when I asked him for the theory behind the Eggmobile. "The egret perched on the rhino's nose, the pheasants and turkeys trailing after the bison—that's a symbiotic relationship we're trying to imitate." In each case the birds dine on the insects that would other-wise bother the herbivore; they also pick insect larvae and parasites out of the animal's droppings, breaking the cycle of infestation and disease. "To mimic this symbiosis on a domestic scale, we follow the cattle in their rotation with the Eggmobile. I call these gals our sanitation crew."

Joel climbed onto the tractor, threw it into gear, and slowly towed the rickety con-traption fifty yards or so across the meadow to a paddock the cattle had vacated three days earlier. It seems the chickens eschew fresh manure, so he waits three or four days before bringing them in—but not a day longer. That's because the fly larvae in the manure are on a four-day cycle, he explained. "Three days is ideal. That gives the grubs a chance to fatten up nicely, the way the hens like them, but not quite long enough to hatch into flies." The result is prodigious amounts of protein for the hens, the in-sects supplying as much as a third of their total diet—and making their eggs unusu-ally rich and tasty. By means of this simple

> I began to understand just how radically different this sort of farming is from the industrial models I'd observed before.

little management trick, Joel is able to use his cattle's waste to "grow" large quantities of high-protein chicken feed for free; he says this trims his cost of producing eggs by twenty-five cents per dozen. (Very much his accountant father's son, Joel can tell you the exact economic implication of every synergy on the farm.) The cows further oblige the chickens by shearing the grass; chickens can't navigate in grass more than about six inches tall.

After Joel had maneuvered the Eggmobile into position, he opened the trapdoor, and an eager, gossipy procession of Barred Rocks, Rhode Island Reds, and New Hamp-shire Whites filed down the little ramp, fanning out across the pasture. The hens picked at the grasses, especially the clover, but mainly they were all over the cowpats, doing this frantic backward-stepping break-dance with their claws to scratch apart the caked manure and expose the meaty morsels within. Unfolding here before us, I realized, was a most impressive form of alchemy: Cowpatties in the process of being transformed into exceptionally tasty eggs. 10

"I'm convinced an Eggmobile would be worth it even if the chickens never laid a single egg. These birds do a more effective job of sanitizing a pasture than anything human, mechanical, or chemical, and the chickens love doing it." Because of the Egg-mobile, Joel doesn't have to run his cattle through a headgate to slather Ivomectrin, a systemic parasiticide, on their hides or worm them with toxic chemicals. This is what Joel means when he says the animals do the real work around here. "I'm just the or-chestra conductor, making sure everybody's in the right place at the right time."

That day, my second on the farm, as Joel introduced me to each of his intricately lay-ered enterprises, I began to understand just how radically different this sort of farm-ing is from the industrial models I'd observed before, whether in an Iowa cornfield or an organic chicken farm in California. Indeed, it is so different that I found Polyface's system difficult to describe to myself in an orderly way. Industrial processes follow a clear, linear, hierarchical logic that is fairly easy to put into words, probably because words follow a similar logic: First this, then that; put this in here, and then out comes that. But the relationship between cows and chickens on this farm (leaving aside for the moment the other creatures and relationships present here) takes the form of a loop rather than a line, and that makes it hard to know where to start, or how to distinguish between causes and effects, subjects and objects.

Is what I'm looking at in this pasture a system for producing exceptionally tasty eggs? If so, then the cattle and their manure are a means to an end. Or is it a system for producing grass-fed beef without the use of any chemicals, in which case the chickens, by fertilizing and sanitizing the cow pastures, comprise the means to that end. So does that make their eggs a product or a by-product? And is manure—theirs or the cattle's—a waste product or a raw material? (And what should we call the fly larvae?) Depending on the point of view you take—that of the chicken, cow, or even the grass—the relationship between subject and object, cause and effect, flips.

Joel would say this is precisely the point, and precisely the distinction between a biological and industrial system. "In an ecological system like this everything's connected to everything else, so you can't change one thing without changing ten other things.

"Take the issue of scale. I could sell a whole lot more chickens and eggs than I do. They're my most profitable items, and the market is telling me to produce more of them. Operating under the industrial paradigm,* I could boost production however much I wanted—just buy more chicks and more feed, crank up that machine. But in a biological system you can never do just one thing, and I couldn't add many more chickens without messing up something else. 15

"Here's an example: This pasture can absorb four hundred units of nitrogen a year. That translates into four visits from the Eggmobile or two passes of a broiler pen. If I ran any more Eggmobiles or broiler pens over it, the chickens would put down more nitrogen than the grass could metabolize. Whatever the grass couldn't absorb would run off, and suddenly I have a pollution problem." Quality would suffer, too. Unless he added more cattle, to produce more grubs for the chickens and to keep the grass short enough for them to eat it, those chickens and eggs would not taste nearly as good as they do.

"It's all connected. This farm is more like an organism than a machine, and like any organism it has its proper scale. A mouse is the size of a mouse for a good reason, and a mouse that was the size of an elephant wouldn't do very well."

Joel likes to quote from an old agricultural textbook he dug out of the stacks at Virginia Tech many years ago. The book, which was published in 1941 by a Cornell Ag professor, offers a stark conclusion that, depending on your point of view, will sound either hopelessly quaint or arresting in its gnomic wisdom: "Farming is not adapted to large-scale operations because of the following reasons: Farming is concerned with plants and animals that live, grow, and die."

"Efficiency" is the term usually invoked to defend large-scale industrial farms, and it usually refers to the economies of scale that can be achieved by the application of technology and standardization. Yet Joel Salatin's farm makes the case for a very different sort of efficiency—the one found in natural systems, with their coevolutionary

---

*Paradigm: Pattern or model [Ed.].

relationships and reciprocal loops. For example, in nature there is no such thing as a waste problem, since one creature's waste becomes another creature's lunch. What could be more efficient than turning cow pies into eggs? Or running a half-dozen different production systems—cows, broilers, layers, pigs, turkeys—over the same piece of ground every year?

Most of the efficiencies in an industrial system are achieved through simplifica-   20
tion: doing lots of the same thing over and over. In agriculture, this usually means a monoculture of a single animal or crop. In fact, the whole history of agriculture is a progressive history of simplification, as humans reduced the biodiversity of their landscapes to a small handful of chosen species. (Wes Jackson calls our species "homo the homogenizer.") With the industrialization of agriculture, the simplifying process reached its logical extreme—in monoculture. This radical specialization permitted standardization and mechanization, leading to the leaps in efficiency claimed by industrial agriculture. Of course, how you choose to measure efficiency makes all the difference, and industrial agriculture measures it, simply, by the yield of one chosen species per acre of land or farmer.

By contrast, the efficiencies of natural systems flow from complexity and interdependence—by definition the very opposite of simplification. To achieve the efficiency represented by turning cow manure into chicken eggs and producing beef without chemicals you need at least two species (cows and chickens), but actually several more as well, including the larvae in the manure and the grasses in the pasture and the bacteria in the cows' rumens. To measure the efficiency of such a complex system you need to count not only all the products it produces (meat, chicken, eggs) but also all the costs it eliminates: antibiotics, wormers, parasiticides, and fertilizers.

Polyface Farm is built on the efficiencies that come from mimicking relationships found in nature, and layering one farm enterprise over another on the same base of land. In effect, Joel is farming in time as well as in space—in four dimensions rather than three. He calls this intricate layering "stacking" and points out that "it is exactly the model God used in building nature." The idea is not to slavishly imitate nature, but to model a natural ecosystem in all its diversity and interdependence, one where all the species "fully express their physiological distinctiveness." He takes advantage of each species' natural proclivities in a way that not only benefits that animal but other species as well. So instead of treating the chicken as a simple egg or protein machine, Polyface honors—and exploits—"the innate distinctive desires of a chicken," which include pecking in the grass and cleaning up after herbivores. The chickens get to do, and eat, what they evolved to do and eat, and in the process the farmer and his cattle both profit. What is the opposite of zero-sum?* I'm not sure, but this is it.

Joel calls each of his stacked farm enterprises a "holon," a word I'd never encountered before. He told me he picked it up from Allan Nation; when I asked Nation about it, he pointed me to Arthur Koestler, who coined the term in *The Ghost in the Machine.* Koestler felt English lacked a word to express the complex relationship of parts and wholes in a biological or social system. A holon (from the Greek *holos*, or whole, and the suffix *on*, as in proton, suggesting a particle) is an entity that from one perspective

---

*Zero-sum: Situation or system in which one side gains all and the other loses all [Ed.].

appears a self-contained whole, and from another a dependent part. A body organ like the liver is a holon; so is an Eggmobile.

At any given time, Polyface has a dozen or more holons up and running, and on my second day Joel and Daniel introduced me to a handful of them. I visited the Raken House, the former toolshed where Daniel has been raising rabbits for the restaurant trade since he was ten. ("Raken?" "Half rabbit, half chicken," Daniel explained.) When the rabbits aren't out on the pasture in portable hutches, they live in cages suspended over a deep bedding of woodchips, in which I watched several dozen hens avidly pecking away in search of earthworms. Daniel explained that the big problem in raising rabbits indoors is their powerful urine, which produces so much ammonia that it scars their lungs and leaves them vulnerable to infection. To cope with the problem most rabbit farmers add antibiotics to their feed. But the scratching of the hens turns the nitrogenous rabbit pee into the carbonaceous bedding, creating a rich compost teeming with earthworms that feed the hens. Drugs become unnecessary and, considering how many rabbits and chickens lived in it, the air in the Raken was, well, tolerable. "Believe me," Daniel said, "if it weren't for these chickens, you'd be gagging right about now, and your eyes would sting something awful."

Before lunch I helped Galen and Peter move the turkeys, another holon. Moving the turkeys, which happens every three days, means setting up a new "feathernet"—a paddock outlined by portable electric fencing so lightweight I could carry and lay out the entire thing by myself—and then wheeling into it the shademobile, called the Gobbledy-Go. The turkeys rest under the Gobbledy-Go by day and roost on top of it at night. They happily follow the contraption into the fresh pasture to feast on the grass, which they seemed to enjoy even more than the chickens do. A turkey consumes a long blade of grass by neatly folding it over and over again with its beak, as if making origami. Joel likes to run his turkeys in the orchard, where they eat the bugs, mow the grass, and fertilize the trees and vines. (Turkeys will eat much more grass than chickens, and they don't damage crops the way chickens can.) "If you run turkeys in a grape orchard," Joel explained, "you can afford to stock the birds at only seventy percent of normal density, and space the vines at seventy percent of what's standard, because you're getting two crops off the same land. And at seventy percent you get much healthier birds and grapevines than you would at 100 percent. That's the beauty of stacking." By industry standards, the turkey and grape holon are each less than 100 percent efficient; together, however, they produce more than either enterprise would yield if fully stocked, and they do so without fertilizer, weeding, or pesticide.

I had witnessed one of the most winning examples of stacking in the cattle barn during my first visit to Polyface back in March. The barn is an unfancy open-sided structure where the cattle spend three months during the winter, each day consuming twenty-five pounds of hay and producing fifty pounds of manure. (Water makes up the difference.) But instead of regularly mucking out the barn, Joel leaves the manure in place, every few days covering it with another layer of woodchips or straw. As this layer cake of manure, woodchips, and straw gradually rises beneath the cattle, Joel simply raises the adjustable feed gate from which they get their ration of hay; by winter's end the bedding, and the cattle, can be as much as three feet off the ground. There's one more secret ingredient Joel adds to each layer of this cake: a few bucketfuls of corn. All winter long the layered bedding composts, in the process generating heat to warm the barn (thus reducing the animals' feed requirements), and fermenting the corn. Joel calls it his cattle's electric blanket.

Why the corn? Because there's nothing a pig enjoys more than forty-proof corn, and there's nothing he's better equipped to do than root it out with his powerful snout and exquisite sense of smell. "I call them my pigaerators," Salatin said proudly as he showed me into the barn. As soon as the cows head out to pasture in the spring, several dozen pigs come in, proceeding systematically to turn and aerate the compost in their quest for kernels of alcoholic corn.

> **[T]hese were the happiest pigs I'd ever seen.**

What had been an anaerobic decomposition suddenly turns aerobic, which dramatically heats and speeds up the process, killing any pathogens. The result, after a few weeks of pigaerating, is a rich, cakey compost ready to use.

"This is the sort of farm machinery I like: never needs its oil changed, appreciates over time, and when you're done with it you eat it." We were sitting on the rail of a wooden paddock, watching the pigs do their thing—a thing, of course, we weren't having to do ourselves. The line about the pigaerators was obviously well-worn. But the cliché that kept banging around in my head was "happy as a pig in shit." Buried clear to their butts in composting manure, a bobbing sea of wriggling hams and corkscrew tails, these were the happiest pigs I'd ever seen.

I couldn't look at their spiraled tails, which cruised above the earthy mass like conning towers on submarines, without thinking about the fate of pigtails in industrial hog production. Simply put, there *are* no pigtails in industrial hog production. Farmers "dock," or snip off, the tails at birth, a practice that makes a certain twisted sense if you follow the logic of industrial efficiency on a hog farm. Piglets in these CAFOs* are weaned from their mothers ten days after birth (compared with thirteen weeks in nature) because they gain weight faster on their drug-fortified feed than on sow's milk. But this premature weaning leaves the pigs with a lifelong craving to suck and chew, a need they gratify in confinement by biting the tail of the animal in front of them. A normal pig would fight off his molester, but a demoralized pig has stopped caring. "Learned helplessness" is the psychological term, and it's not uncommon in CAFOs, where tens of thousands of hogs spend their entire lives ignorant of earth or straw or sunshine, crowded together beneath a metal roof standing on metal slats suspended over a septic tank. It's not surprising that an animal as intelligent as a pig would get depressed under these circumstances, and a depressed pig will allow his tail to be chewed on to the point of infection. Since treating sick pigs is not economically efficient, these underperforming production units are typically clubbed to death on the spot.

Tail docking is the USDA's recommended solution to the porcine "vice" of tail chewing. Using a pair of pliers and no anesthetic, most—but not quite all—of the tail is snipped off. Why leave the little stump? Because the whole point of the exercise is not to remove the object of tail biting so much as to render it even more sensitive. Now a bite to the tail is so painful that even the most demoralized pig will struggle to resist it. 30

---

*CAFOs: concentrated animal feeding operations [Ed.].

Horrible as it is to contemplate, it's not hard to see how the road to such a hog hell is smoothly paved with the logic of industrial efficiency.

A very different concept of efficiency sponsors the hog heaven on display here in Salatin's barn, one predicated on what he calls "the pigness of the pig." These pigs too were being exploited—in this case, tricked into making compost as well as pork. What distinguishes Salatin's system is that it is designed around the natural predilections of the pig rather than around the requirements of a production system to which the pigs are then conformed. Pig happiness is simply the by-product of treating pigs as pigs rather than as "a protein machine with flaws"—flaws such as pig tails and a tendency, when emiserated, to get stressed.

Salatin reached down deep where his pigs were happily rooting and brought a handful of fresh compost right up to my nose. What had been cow manure and wood-chips just a few weeks before now smelled as sweet and warm as the forest floor in summertime, a miracle of transubstantiation. As soon as the pigs complete their al-chemy, Joel will spread the compost on his pastures. There it will feed the grasses, so the grasses might again feed the cows, the cows the chickens, and so on until the snow falls, in one long, beautiful, and utterly convincing proof that in a world where grass can eat sunlight and food animals can eat grass, there is indeed a free lunch.

2.　Tuesday Afternoon

After our own quick lunch (ham salad and deviled eggs), Joel and I drove to town in his pickup to make a delivery and take care of a few errands. It felt sweet to be sitting down for a while, especially after a morning taken up with loading the hay we'd baled the day before into the hayloft. For me this rather harrowing operation involved at-tempting to catch fifty-pound bales that Galen tossed in my general direction from the top of the hay wagon. The ones that didn't completely knock me over I hoisted onto a conveyor belt that carried them to Daniel and Peter, stationed up in the hayloft. It was an assembly line, more or less, and as soon as I fell behind (or just fell, literally) the hay bales piled up fast at my station; I felt like Lucille Ball at the candy factory. I joked to Joel that, contrary to his claims that the animals did most of the real work on this farm, it seemed to me they'd left plenty of it for us.

On a farm, complexity sounds an awful lot like hard work, Joel's claims to the contrary notwithstanding. As much work as the animals do, that's still us humans out there moving the cattle every evening, dragging the broiler pens across the field before breakfast (something I'd pledged I'd wake up in time for the next day), and towing chicken coops hither and yon according to a schedule tied to the life cycle of fly larvae and the nitrogen load of chicken manure. My guess is that there aren't too many farmers today who are up for either the physical or mental challenge of this sort of farming, not when industrializing promises to simplify the job. Indeed, a large part of the appeal of industrial farming is its panoply of labor- and thought-saving devices: machines of every description to do the physical work, and chemicals to keep crops and animals free from pests with scarcely a thought from the farmer. George Naylor works his fields maybe fifty days out of the year; Joel and Daniel and two interns are out there every day sunrise to sunset for a good chunk of the year.

Yet Joel and Daniel plainly relish their work, partly because it is so varied from   35
day to day and even hour to hour, and partly because they find it endlessly interesting. Wendell Berry has written eloquently about the intellectual work that goes into
farming well, especially into solving the novel problems that inevitably crop up in a
natural system as complex as a farm. You don't see much of this sort of problem-solving
in agriculture today, not when so many solutions come ready-made in plastic bottles.
So much of the intelligence and local knowledge in agriculture has been removed from
the farm to the laboratory, and then returned to the farm in the form of a chemical or
machine. "Whose head is the farmer using?" Berry asks in one of his essays. "Whose
head is using the farmer?"

"Part of the problem is, you've got a lot of D students left on the farm today," Joel
said, as we drove around Staunton* running errands. "The guidance counselors encouraged all the A students to leave home and go to college. There's been a tremendous
brain drain in rural America. Of course that suits Wall Street just fine; Wall Street is
always trying to extract brainpower and capital from the countryside. First they take
the brightest bulbs off the farm and put them to work in Dilbert's cubicle, and then
they go after the capital of the dimmer ones who stayed behind, by selling them a
bunch of gee-whiz solutions to their problems." This isn't just the farmer's problem,
either. "It's a foolish culture that entrusts its food supply to simpletons."

It isn't hard to see why there isn't much institutional support for the sort of low-
capital, thought-intensive farming Joel Salatin practices: He buys next to nothing.
When a livestock farmer is willing to "practice complexity"—to choreograph the
symbiosis of several different animals, each of which has been allowed to behave and
eat as they evolved to—he will find he has little need for machinery, fertilizer, and,
most strikingly, chemicals. He finds he has no sanitation problem or any of the diseases
that result from raising a single animal in a crowded monoculture and then feeding it
things it wasn't designed to eat. This is perhaps the greatest efficiency of a farm treated
as a biological system: health.

I was struck by the fact that for Joel abjuring agrochemicals and pharmaceuticals
is not so much a goal of his farming, as it so often is in organic agriculture, as it is an indication that his farm is functioning well. "In nature health is the default," he pointed
out. "Most of the time pests and disease are just nature's way of telling the farmer he's
doing something wrong."

At Polyface no one ever told me not to touch the animals, or asked me to put on
a biohazard suit before going into the brooder house. The reason I had to wear one at
Petaluma Poultry is because that system—a monoculture of chickens raised in close
confinement—is inherently precarious, and the organic rules' prohibition on antibiotics puts it at a serious disadvantage. Maintaining a single-species animal farm on an
industrial scale isn't easy without pharmaceuticals and pesticides. Indeed, that's why
these chemicals were invented in the first place, to keep shaky monocultures from col-
lapsing. Sometimes the large-scale organic farmer looks like someone trying to practice industrial agriculture with one hand tied behind his back.

By the same token, a reliance on agrochemicals destroys the information feedback   40
loop on which an attentive farmer depends to improve his farming. "Meds just mask

---

*Staunton: Polyface Farm is located eight miles south of the city of Staunton, Virginia [Ed.].

genetic weaknesses," Joel explained one afternoon when we were moving the cattle. "My goal is always to improve the herd, adapt it to the local conditions by careful culling. To do this I need to know: Who has a propensity for pinkeye? For worms? You simply have no clue if you're giving meds all the time.

"So you tell me, who's really *in* this so-called information economy? Those who learn from what they observe on their farm, or those who rely on concoctions from the devil's pantry?"

Of course the simplest, most traditional measure of a farm's efficiency is how much food it produces per unit of land; by this yardstick too Polyface is impressively efficient. I asked Joel how much food Polyface produces in a season, and he rattled off the following figures:

30,000 dozen eggs
10,000 broilers
800 stewing hens
50 beeves (representing 25,000 pounds of beef)
250 hogs (25,000 pounds of pork)
1,000 turkeys
500 rabbits

This seemed to me a truly astonishing amount of food from one hundred acres of grass. But when I put it that way to Joel that afternoon—we were riding the ATV up to the very top of the hill to visit the hogs in their summer quarters—he questioned my accounting method. It was far too simple.

"Sure, you can write that we produced all that food from a hundred open acres, but if you really want to be accurate about it, then you've got to count the four hundred and fifty acres of woodlot too." I didn't get that at all. I knew the woodlot was an important source of farm income in the winter—Joel and Daniel operate a small sawmill from which they sell lumber and mill whatever wood they need to build sheds and barns (and Daniel's new house). But what in the world did the forest have to do with producing food?

Joel proceeded to count the ways. Most obviously, the farm's water supply depended on its forests to hold moisture and prevent erosion. Many of the farm's streams and ponds would simply dry up if not for the cover of trees. Nearly all of the farm's 550 acres had been deforested when the Salatins arrived; one of the first things Bill Salatin did was plant trees on all the north-facing slopes.

"Feel how cool it is in here." We were passing through a dense stand of oak and hickory. "Those deciduous trees work like an air conditioner. That reduces the stress on the animals in summer."

Suddenly we arrived at a patch of woodland that looked more like a savanna than a forest: The trees had been thinned and all around them grew thick grasses. This was one of the pig paddocks that Joel had carved out of the woods with the help of the pigs themselves. "All we do to make a new pig paddock is fence off a quarter acre of forest, thin out the saplings to let in some light, and then let the pigs do their thing." Their thing includes eating down the brush and rooting around in the stony ground, disturbing the soil in a way that induces the grass seed already present to germinate. Within several weeks, a lush stand of wild rye and foxtail emerges among the trees, and a savanna is born. Shady and cool, this looked like ideal habitat for the sunburn-prone pigs, who were avidly nosing through the tall grass and scratching their backs against the trees. There is something viscerally appealing about a savanna, with its pleasing balance of open grass and trees, and something profoundly heartening about the idea that, together, farmer and pigs could create such beauty here in the middle of a brushy second-growth forest.

But Joel wasn't through counting the benefits of woodland to a farm; idyllic pig habitat was the least of it.

"There's not a spreadsheet in the world that can measure the value of maintaining forest on the northern slopes of a farm. Start with those trees easing the swirling of the air in the pastures. That might not seem like a big deal, but it reduces evaporation in the fields — which means more water for the grass. Plus, a grass plant burns up fifteen percent of its calories just defying gravity, so if you can stop it from being wind whipped, you greatly reduce the energy it uses keeping its photovoltaic array pointed toward the sun. More grass for the cows. That's the efficiency of a hedgerow surrounding a small field, something every farmer used to understand before 'fencerow to fencerow' became USDA mantra."*

Then there is the water-holding capacity of trees, he explained, which on a north 50 slope literally pumps water uphill. Next was all the ways a forest multiplies a farm's biodiversity. More birds on a farm mean fewer insects, but most birds won't venture more than a couple hundred yards from the safety of cover. Like many species, their preferred habitat is the edge between forest and field. The biodiversity of the forest edge also helps control predators. As long as the weasels and coyotes have plenty of chipmunks and voles to eat, they're less likely to venture out and prey on the chickens.

There was more. On a steep northern slope trees will produce much more biomass than will grass. "We're growing carbon in the woods for the rest of the farm — not just the firewood to keep us warm in the winter, but also the woodchips that go into making our compost." Making good compost depends on the proper ratio of carbon to nitrogen; the carbon is needed to lock down the more volatile nitrogen. It takes a lot of woodchips to compost chicken or rabbit waste. So the carbon from the woodlots feeds the fields, finding its way into the grass and, from there, into the beef. Which it turns out is not only grass fed but tree fed as well.

These woods represented a whole other order of complexity that I had failed to take into account. I realized that Joel didn't look at this land the same way I did, or had before this afternoon: as a hundred acres of productive grassland patchworked into four hundred and fifty acres of unproductive forest. It was all of a biological piece, the trees and the grasses and the animals, the wild and the domestic, all part of a single ecological system. By any conventional accounting, the forests here represented a waste of land that could be put to productive use. But if Joel were to cut down the trees to graze more cattle, as any conventional accounting would recommend, the system would no longer be quite as whole or as healthy as it is. *You can't just do one thing.*

---

*USDA mantra: Policy of the United States Department of Agriculture [Ed.].

For some reason the image that stuck with me from that day was that slender blade of grass in a too big, wind-whipped pasture, burning all those calories just to stand up straight and keep its chloroplasts* aimed at the sun. I'd always thought of the trees and grasses as antagonists—another zero-sum deal in which the gain of the one entails the loss of the other. To a point, this is true: More grass means less forest; more forest less grass. But either-or is a construction more deeply woven into our culture than into nature, where even antagonists depend on one another and the liveliest places are the edges, the in-betweens or both-ands. So it is with the blade of grass and the adjacent forest as, indeed, with all the species sharing this most complicated farm. Relations are what matter most, and the health of the cultivated turns on the health of the wild. Before I came to Polyface I'd read a sentence of Joel's that in its diction had struck me as an awkward hybrid of the economic and the spiritual. I could see now how characteristic that mixing is, and that perhaps the sentence isn't so awkward after all: "One of the greatest assets of a farm is the sheer ecstasy of life."

Exploring Context

1. Learn more about Polyface Farm by visiting its Web site at polyfacefarms.com. Look under "Production" for pictures of the Eggmobile and the Gobbledy-Go. You can also learn more about the farm by clicking on "Principles" and "Our Story." How do you see the ideas that Pollan discusses at work in the farm's Web site? Use your work on the success of Polyface from Question 1 of Questions for Critical Reading in making your response.

2. Visit the Web site for the U.S. Department of Agriculture's National Organic Program at ams.usda.gov/nop. What differences can you locate between the philosophy of organic farming at Polyface and that of the U.S. government? Which seems like a better standard for *organic*, and why?

3. Spend some time at Michael Pollan's home page, michaelpollan.com. How does this essay fit into Pollan's other writing? What biases do you think he might have, based on the information you find on his site? Do these biases make a difference in this essay?

Questions for Connecting

1. Pollan's description of Polyface Farm reveals a complex economic and ecological system. In what ways is this system consistent with the global supply chains that Thomas L. Friedman explores in "The Dell Theory of Conflict Prevention" (p. 124)? Can local and global economic systems work together?

2. What role can organic farming play in the future of food? Synthesize the information in Sandra Allen's "A World Without Wine" (p. 34) with Pollan's observations about Polyface Farm. Connect your response to the work you did on Polyface and complexity in Questions 1 and 3 of Questions for Critical Reading.

---

*Chloroplasts: Specialized units in a plant cell responsible for photosynthesis [Ed.].

3. David Foster Wallace points to some of the ethical complications of food in "Consider the Lobster" (p. 459). How do the practices of Polyface that Pollan explores complicate Wallace's observation? Is organic farming more "ethical"?

Language Matters

1. Find a passage in Pollan's text that you think is central to his argument. Identify each of the verbs in your selected passage. What are the key verbs? What is the *action* of these sentences? Are there more verbs used in clauses rather than other parts or components of the sentence? What are the implications of each verb's location and the kind of verb used? How can you apply these insights to your own writing?

2. Understanding your audience is a crucial factor in the success of any piece of writing. Looking at Pollan's writing, identify the audience you think he has in mind. How do you know that? What audience should you keep in mind when writing in this class? How can you make sure that your writing reflects that audience?

3. Conjunctions are words that join nouns, phrases, or clauses. Find two quotations that seem to have some relation in Pollan's essay (or choose one from Pollan and one from another essay you've read for this class). Express the relationship between the two quotations using only one conjunction. When might you want to use this same conjunction in your own writing?

Assignments for Writing

1. Pollan reviews farmer Joel Salatin's alternative farming methods, in the process prompting us to question the very nature of farming. By attempting to simplify and sanitize farming, have we moved away from the health and efficiency inherent in a natural system? Can the benefits of biotechnology outweigh the benefits of symbiosis and nature? As biotechnology pushes science and food toward new frontiers, will we find that the old ways of farming are the better, more healthful ways, or is technologically engineered food simply a measurement of healthy progress, no different than progress in any other arena? Using Pollan's essay, formulate an argument on the relationship between food production methods and health. To support your position, consider the alternatives to Salatin's farming methods, the effect of farming practices on our health, and how the interdependence among the different parts of the farming process affects not only the farmer, the animals, and the farm's products but the consumer as well. Use your work with complexity from Question 3 of Questions for Critical Reading.

2. Using Pollan's essay, write a paper in which you evaluate the efficiency of nature-based farming methods versus the efficiency of biotechnology-based farming methods in food production. What does Pollan mean when he describes Salatin's methods as "holon" based? Why don't we all still farm in the traditional, interdependent manner practiced by Salatin? What are the benefits and disadvantages of "alternative" natural farming? What are the benefits and disadvantages of farming with biotechnology? Do complexity and multiculture lead to better efficiency? Are complexity and multiculture more or less efficient than simplicity and monoculture? Use your work with Pollan's essay from Questions for Critical Reading to support your argument.

3. As agribusiness continues to expand in a global economy, will we find that the old ways of farming are the more effective ways, or will we find that current monoculture practices are needed to keep up with the demands of an ever-expanding world population? Using Pollan's essay, write a paper in which you evaluate the advantages of monoculture-based farming methods versus multiculture-based farming methods in food production. What are the benefits and disadvantages of "alternative" natural farming, or what Pollan calls "coevolutionary relationships"? What are the benefits and disadvantages of farming with biotechnology in the form of vaccines, disease-resistant crop varieties, chemical fertilizers, and genetically modified seeds? Are complexity and multiculture necessary to feed the modern world? Are complexity and multiculture more or less efficient than simplicity and monoculture? Draw on your work on complexity from Question 3 of Questions for Critical Reading.

JENNIFER POZNER

Journalist **Jennifer Pozner** is the founder and executive director
of Women in Media & News, an organization devoted to media
literacy that also advocates for media reform. She has been published in *Bitch* magazine, the *Chicago Tribune*, *Newsday*, and the
Huffington Post. Pozner regularly speaks on college campuses
and provides commentary on television and radio shows, as well
as in the documentary *Miss Representation* (2011). *Reality Bites*
Back: The Troubling Truth about Guilty Pleasure TV (2010) is her first
book. In 2011, it was included on *Ms.* magazine's list of the "Top
100 Feminist Non-Fiction Books."

© Thomas Lascher

In *Reality Bites Back*, Pozner analyzes reality television's
messages through a feminist lens. Pozner locates and analyzes
a pattern in the portrayals of race, gender, class, sexuality, romance, and body image in reality television, claiming that most
series—from *The Bachelor* to *What Not to Wear*—perpetuate
negative and limiting ideals for women. She finds that the images promoted by these shows normalize domestic violence,
eating disorders, gossip, and the idea that romance and beauty
are the only things that can make women happy.

In "Ghetto Bitches, China Dolls, and Cha Cha Divas," a chapter from *Reality Bites Back*, Pozner examines the mixed messages
present in the long-running reality competition series *America's*
Next Top Model (ANTM). She argues that through selective casting
and heavy editing, *ANTM* perpetuates damaging racist stereotypes, while superficially claiming
to promote all types of individual beauty and to empower women. Ultimately, Pozner questions
the impact that such portrayals of race may have on how women of color view themselves.

▶ TAGS: *beauty, culture, gender, media, race and ethnicity*
▶ CONNECTIONS: *Gay, Levy, Padawer, Serano*

Questions for Critical Reading

1. How real do you think reality television is? Jot down notes about your own experiences
   with these television shows. As you read, pay attention to the ways in which Pozner
   indicates that these shows are actually highly scripted. Knowing that "reality" shows are
   mostly scripted, do you think that racial stereotyping on *America's Next Top Model* is as
   dangerous as Pozner implies?

2. Why do television show producers depict people in racially stereotyped roles? Do you
   think this is a positive or negative experience for viewers? How so? Look for evidence to
   support your position as you read Pozner.

358

3. In this selection, Pozner argues that shows such as *America's Next Top Model* should be taken off the air. Do you agree with her position? Locate passages that support your own position on this issue.

Ghetto Bitches, China Dolls, and Cha Cha Divas

It's my number one passion in my life to stretch the definition of beauty. I listen to many heartbreaking stories of women who thought they would be happier if they looked different. I want every girl to appreciate the skin she's in.

—TYRA BANKS, apologizing for making girls don blackface on *America's Next Top Model*[1]

As executive producer, Tyra Banks claims *America's Next Top Model* aims to expand beauty standards, as she herself did as the first Black solo cover model for *GQ*, *Victoria's Secret*, and *Sports Illustrated*'s swimsuit edition. Chapter 2 [not included here] documented how she fails at this lofty goal regarding weight, size, and eating disorders. Does she do any better at exploding race-based beauty biases?

Sometimes, yes. She exhorts *ANTM* contestants to be confident and love themselves, flaws and all. Her methods may be devised to break most models' spirits for our viewing pleasure, but there's something to be said for casting diverse young women and at least telling them that they're gorgeous. In a TV landscape that has typically depicted girls of color as ugly when not ignoring them entirely, sometimes a slightly positive mixed message is as good as it gets. Better yet, every once in a while a truly subversive, dare I say *feminist*, moment can be found among *ANTM*'s emotional and cultural wreckage. Model Anchal Joseph, who emigrated to the United States from New Delhi when she was six years old, wore blue contacts to her cycle 7 audition. When the judges asked her why, she said she'd always wanted different colored eyes:

TYRA: Do you think there's something culturally in America or even in your own country that is telling you that a lighter eye is prettier?*
ANCHAL: In India they do believe that lighter skin and lighter eyes are prettier. I actually want to beat that. Be like, "Hey, I'm dark, I'm beautiful, and I'm Indian, so I don't have to have light skin or have light-colored eyes to be beautiful."

After Anchal's baby browns were photographed au natural, the judges said she was so gorgeous she could be Miss World. Asked how she felt looking at her picture without the contacts, she replied:

ANCHAL: It makes me feel pretty.
TYRA: It does? Why's that?

---

*Asking Anchal to discuss beauty standards in the United States versus those from her "own country" is typical of *ANTM*. The show both normalizes and others immigrants, portraying them as an unmistakable part of the beauty that is America, while constantly implying that they are less authentically American than those born here. [All notes are Pozner's.]

ANCHAL: Because in a way I think I was hiding behind them. I'm glad. [At this, she
    broke down in tears of self-acceptance — and we got to watch her psychological
    breakthrough.]

TYRA [to judge Nigel Barker]: Nigel, you being Indian, how do you respond to that?*

NIGEL: You are beautiful the way you are. We are all unique in our own ways, and it's that
    uniqueness that makes people beautiful.

I'll never accuse Tyra Banks of having a tenth of Toni Morrison's wisdom. Still, I was impressed by the editing of Anchal's initial longing for societal affirmation, à la *The Bluest Eye*, followed by her eventual realization that her dark skin and brown eyes simply make her more authentically stunning.

China Dolls, Dragon Ladies, and Spicy Latinas

Such moments are exceptions on *ANTM*, which [. . .] set many of the templates for racial typecasting on network reality TV.

Of the 170 contestants cast by cycle 13, only five besides Anchal have been East or South Asian. The first, April Wilkner, half-Japanese and half-white, said that before she decided to model, "I never really thought about my ethnicity." *ANTM* made sure viewers could think of little else. They framed her as uncomfortable with her cultural identity, while confusing that identity by adorning her with symbols from a country unconnected to her heritage (Chinese lanterns placed on her head, a dragon painted on her chest).

Cut to the cycle 6 audition of Korean contestant Gina Choe, who said, "I think there's just not enough Asian models out there. I feel that I can break down that barrier, and I think it's my responsibility." Nice! You'd almost think the casting directors finally sought out an Asian American woman who was proud of her racial background.

Sadly, no. A moment later, she told us, "I'm not into Asian guys." From then until her elimination five weeks later, Gina was edited as if she was struggling with "an identity crisis," and stereotyped as an "exotic" fading flower who couldn't stand up for herself when attacked by her competitors. She was vilified on the show, on fan sites, and by culture critics as being a poor representative of her race for making statements such as "As a Korean person and as an American person, I'm just a little bit of both, and I don't know which one I am more of." What went unexplored was why *Top Model* thought it appropriate to make Gina feel she had to choose whether she was "more" tied to her ethnicity or her nationality — the subtext of which implies that a Korean American is not a "real" American, just as Anchal was asked about attitudes in her "own country."

Top Model has mixed and matched from various long-held stereotypes about Asian women in American movies, described in *The Asian Mystique* as including the cold and calculating "Dragon Lady" (traits assigned to ambivalent April) and the submissive

---

*Close, but no cigar. Fashion photographer and *ANTM* judge Nigel Barker (who passes for white) isn't Indian, he's British and Sri Lankan. Just another instance of *Top Model* playing the all-Asians-are-alike game, as many other reality shows do.

"Lotus Flower . . . China Doll" (docile Gina).[2] Cycle 11 finally cast a truly proud Asian American woman . . . then promptly reduced her to the clichéd "Vixen/Sex Nymph." When we were first introduced to Sheena Sakai, a half-Japanese, half-Korean go-go dancer with a large rack and an even bigger swagger, she announced, "I'm gonna show you, America. You ain't ready for this yellow fever. One time for the Asians!" Sheena was recruited by a casting director who saw her working as a stuntwoman for the movie *Tropic Thunder*—but as is often the case on reality television, producers revealed only those details that reinforced the frame they'd chosen for her character. Since they wanted her as that season's resident "hootchie," her stunt work wasn't discussed on the show or mentioned on her CW bio. Instead, she was criticized as too sexy in every episode. Early on a judge sneered, "You look like Victoria's Secretions." Later, during a challenge in Amsterdam's red light dis-

> **[S]he was criticized as too sexy in every episode.**

trict, where prostitutes pose in storefronts to entice customers, she was told she looked like she should be selling herself in that window, rather than modeling clothes.

Latina *Top Model* hopefuls have been consistently typecast as promiscuous sluts, "naturally" good dancers, or bursting with machisma and ready to throw down. Semi-finalist Angelea didn't make cycle 12's final cut after she got into a fight and was written off as hot-tempered, "ghettofied," and easily provoked to violence.

Cycle 8 winner Jaslene "Cha Cha Diva" Gonzalez, who spoke Spanish in her Cover-Girl commercial, was called "spicy" and portrayed as a cross between a "drag queen" and Carmen Miranda. High school dropout Felicia "Fo" Porter, half-Mexican and half-Black, was used to reinforce the "Latinos are lazy" trope: The unemployed model said she auditioned for the show to save herself "the busy hassle of putting your pictures out to agencies and hoping to get a call back."

Other Latina models throughout the series have been called "fiery" as a compliment and "hootchie" as an insult. Second-cycle winner Yoanna House, named one of *Latina* magazine's "It Girls," notably avoided such typecasting. Since she is fair-skinned enough to pass for white, the show chose to erase her ethnicity, playing into the standard Hollywood convention that positions Caucasians as the "default" American. Most viewers were unaware that she was half-Mexican. Instead, media outlets from NPR and *Time Out Chicago* to *International Cosmetic News* refer to Jaslene as "the first Latina" to win the series, an assumption echoed by *ANTM*'s fans.[3]

Entitled Divas and Ghetto Bitches

African Americans are pigeonholed into similar categories on *ANTM*, which introduced the Angry Black Woman to reality TV before Omarosa was a glint in the eye of *The Apprentice* producer Mark Burnett. Season 1 brought us self-indulgent, catty Camille, the Black model everyone loved to hate. By season 3, Tyra took to pretending she's not an executive producer who casts for type. She warned eventual winner "Eva the Diva" to act sweet, because "I don't want to cast another Black bitch." But of course she did cast and edit Eva as the bitch du jour—until week 8, when two white image consultants instructed her to doff the diva label by "showing your best possible manners."*

The Violent Ghetto Girl (or as one model was described, the "ghetto Black Barbie") also looms large. During her third-season tryout, low-income single mom Tiffany Richardson, who got kicked out of high school for acting like "the Devil," said she wanted to be on *ANTM* to "soften up" because "I don't want to fight no mo." Uh-oh. The semifinalists went out to a bar, where a local "skank" poured a drink over Tiffany's head. She freaked out, yelled, "Bitch poured beer on my weave!" and hurled a glass at her. Bottles started flying, and they hightailed it out of there. A white model condemned violence; Tiffany retorted, "That's great, Martin Luther King. But I'm with Malcolm." Violence is "all I know," she said, because "nobody ever taught me to handle my problems without fighting."

Though she was "trying to change for the better," she got sent home to "the hood"   15
by the end of the episode, calling herself a failure. But because she *always* wants to feature "another Black bitch" — especially of the ratings-generating "ghetto" variety — Banks brought Tiffany back for the fourth season, after she'd been through anger management classes.† She made it to the seventh episode, where she couldn't read from a teleprompter, grumbled, "This is humiliating more and more each week," and was eliminated. This time, instead of calling herself a failure, she smiled, hugged the other models, and told them she'd be okay. This didn't sit well with Tyra, who prefers self-flagellation and depression from rejectees, especially when they're poor and Black. So, she took it upon herself to remind the girl of her place: "This should be serious to you!" Tiffany replied that looks can be deceiving, but she was "sick of crying about stuff that I cannot change. I'm sick of being disappointed, I'm sick of all of it." Now apparently clairvoyant, Tyra yelled that Tiffany wasn't really sick of disappointment, because if she were, "you would stand up and take control of your destiny!"

Tyra continued to criticize her "defeatist attitude" until Tiffany got choked up, saying, "I don't have a bad attitude. Maybe I am angry inside, I've been through stuff, so I'm angry, but — " But she couldn't finish, because Tyra cut her off with a neck-rolling, finger-pointing, top-of-her-lungs tirade:

> Be quiet, Tiffany! BE QUIET! STOP IT! I have never in my life yelled at a girl like this! When my mother yells like this it's because she loves me. I was rooting for you, we were all rooting for you! How dare you! Learn something from this! When you go to bed at night, you lay there and you take responsibility for yourself, because nobody's going to take responsibility for you. You rollin' your eyes and you act like it's because you've heard it all before — you've heard

---

*Lighter-skinned African American and biracial girls such as cycle 4 winner Naima Mora and second-season finalist Mercedes Yvette have often escaped this frame. In this way, the show plays to intraracial beauty hierarchies in media, advertising, and political history positing that the darker a woman's complexion, the nastier her personality. Such hierarchies continue to cause pain within communities of color.[4]

†Tiffany never really had a chance of winning *ANTM*, lacking the "girl next door" image demanded by program sponsors CoverGirl and *Seventeen*, which use the winner in their ads. Producers raised her hopes for nothing; they only had her return because they knew she'd be a ratings draw. She was one of the most talked-about contestants on the third season, even though she lasted only one episode. "Bitch poured beer on my weave!" became an iconic quote, repeated on hundreds of fan sites and used as a *Vanity Fair* headline.[5]

it all before—you don't know where the hell I come from, you have no idea what I've been through. But I'm not a victim. I grow from it and I learn. Take responsibility for yourself!*

And with that, Tiffany was turned into *ANTM*'s symbol of the irresponsible ghetto chick who isn't willing to work hard to care for herself or her child. Such pop culture imagery builds on decades of inaccurate, scapegoating news reports dating back to the 1980s, which blamed so-called "welfare queens" (a phrase that became code for poor women of color, often young mothers) for the poverty, educational inequity, and violence that plagued their communities. According to this media mantra, these weren't systemic problems requiring institutional solutions, they simply stemmed from laziness, greed, and lack of discipline inherent among poor youth of color. (Black and Latina girls bore the added burden of being branded promiscuous and immoral, while young men of color were pathologized as "Super Predators.")† Tyra's hissy fit about Tiffany's supposed "victim" mentality and "defeatist attitude" was a revival of that sorry script. That she issued this verbal beatdown in the name of "love"—and treated the twenty-two-year-old as "ungrateful" for the chance to be used and shamed on national television—is deeply manipulative. That *Top Model* affects viewers' perceptions of young women of color is even worse. Parroting Tyra's rhetoric, a Television Without Pity commenter wrote, "Tiff *and others like her* can't be bothered to pick up a book? Read. Learn. Get good grades . . . Tyra was right. Get off your ass Tiff and accept responsibility for yourself. Her granmama put a roof over her head and food on the table and yet Tiff can't be bothered to study and get good grades and pull herself out of poverty? Slackers disgust me" (emphasis mine).[7]

Uppity Black Girls Need Humble Pie

Faced with a strong Black woman who couldn't be shoehorned as an ignorant, angry, ghetto bitch, Tyra had only one more card to play: "Bourgie Snob." Meet Yaya DaCosta, cycle 3's Ivy League runner-up. An African Studies and International Relations student at Brown University, she spoke Portuguese and French, auditioned with her hair

---

*Seems Tyra needed Tiffany's anger management course more than the model did. Faced with the privileged judge screaming in her face, Tiffany remained calm and in control. With an even voice, she told the cameras, "I'm not gonna break down for you or nobody else. You ain't did shit for me but bring me here and put me through hell." As the credits rolled, we heard her say she's glad that Tyra cares about her, and that will inspire her to be a better person. Two years later, Tiffany finally revealed her honest reaction to the incident on an *E! True Hollywood Story* exposé about *ANTM*. "Before, in all of my interviews . . . I would always tell people, 'Oh, Tyra loves me. I feel like the reason that she yelled at me was because she loved me.' That was bull. So let me tell you how I really felt. I feel like if she loved me, she wouldn't have showed it the way she showed it. Like my grandmother said, 'If you love someone, you won't humiliate them.'"

†To convince the public to roll back the social safety net for the poor, 1980s and 1990s conservatives waged a war in the media against poor women. In addition to the derogatory "welfare queen" said to be "popping out babies for checks," African Americans and Latinas in particular were labeled "immoral" "brood mares," and even called "public enemy number one" by ABC's Diane Sawyer. *Newsweek* senior editor Jonathan Alter went further, insisting that "every threat to the fabric of this country—from poverty to crime to homelessness—is connected to out-of-wedlock teen pregnancy." Riddled with inaccuracies, these reports nevertheless helped turn the tide of public opinion, enabling Democratic President Bill Clinton to pass a punitive welfare reform package in 1996 that resulted in hundreds of thousands of women and children falling deeper into poverty.[6]

in braids, and intended "to represent a beauty that is Black." She was elegant, intelligent, and poised. Tyra was initially "impressed" with Yaya's education and "her Afrocentric vibe," which may be why she was one of the only girls in *ANTM*'s history to be allowed to wear her hair in a natural 'fro, saying it showed her pride as a strong Black woman.

Alas, the sisterlove was short lived. Yaya looked like a stunning "chocolate Barbarella" in photos, but Tyra said she didn't seem "modelesque" in person. "Think . . . glamour, as opposed to natural," she instructed. A white stylist was brought on to tell her that her "Earth Mother" look would turn off advertisers: "If you go into a toothpaste ad, are you gonna go in a dashiki?" she sneered. "They'll see the big hair and they'll see the African print and it's like, oh my God!" Later, during judging, the stylist disparaged her "intensity to prove your sort of Africanness . . . , it's overbearing. It's just too much. It's sort of a layer on top of a layer." To her credit, the camera caught Tyra glaring, clearly pissed off. In contrast, Yaya wasn't allowed to be upset at this obviously racist swipe.* When she protested being stereotyped and turned into "a cliché," Tyra reprimanded her for "being very defensive, and it's not attractive," and made her apologize to a kente cloth hat. During evaluation, Tyra reiterated that "Yaya brings [a] superiority, condescending attitude" that is "so ugly."

From then on, they had their frame. Through the magic of editing, Yaya's education and elegance became pretentiousness; her eloquence was characterized as showing off. She took dazzling photographs and shined on the catwalk, yet for the rest of the competition Yaya was represented as an arrogant, Blacker-than-thou snob. She was chosen as fashion designers' favorite at client meetings, yet the judges condemned her as so stuck-up and hypersensitive that "no one will want to work with you." She made it to the finale, but lost because the judges didn't consider her "likable" enough. [20]

Viewers tend to believe that the caricatures they've seen on reality TV match (or at least resemble) participants' real-life personalities, regardless of the truth or falseness of that person's portrayal. Yaya is a case in point. The image foisted on her by *ANTM*'s producers clung to her for five years and numerous film and TV jobs later. In 2009, when *Entertainment Weekly* reported that she landed a role on ABC's *Ugly Betty*, readers said they "hate Yaya with a passion," called her "arrogant," "pretentious," and "nasty," and wrote that "she needs a big piece of humble pie!" When a smart, self-possessed African American woman is said to "need humble pie," the message is that this "uppity" Black person just doesn't know her place.[8]

Curious George, Work It Out!

Some of the above tropes, like Tyra's tirade against Tiffany, require some unpacking to realize how they connect to a long history of attacks on women of color in politics and the media. But deep-seated beauty biases were all too clear in the representation of

---

*Banks has regularly encouraged Black models to put up with blatant bigotry she herself would never stand for. For example, on an episode in Spain, a male model disparaged African American contestant Jaeda Young, saying he didn't like Black women and didn't want to kiss her in a commercial they had to film for Secret deodorant. Editing emphasized how shaken she was by his racism, which could have led to a denunciation of bias in the industry by the judges. Instead, they eliminated Jaeda for making "excuses" and having poor chemistry in her ad.

Kelle, an affluent African American gallery owner who called herself "a white girl with a really good tan." She came into the competition exuding confidence to the point of conceit, but a few weeks in Tyra's den of self-doubt changed all that.

Over numerous episodes, viewers were treated to multiple scenes in which Kelle sadly inspected herself in a mirror, pondering newly perceived flaws and telling the camera that she'd grown to believe the judges' appraisal of her. "I just see myself and I'm like, *Oh my God, I'm hideous!*" she sobbed. "I can't look at myself in the mirror anymore. . . . Every time I look in the mirror I'm crying." As one of her competitors explained, "Kelle came in this competition and she was like, 'Oh, oh, I'm beautiful!' and the judges have totally broke her!" After being told repeatedly that her face, and particularly her mouth, were not photogenic, she broke down in a fit of internalized racism. While Tyra made each girl reveal her deepest body insecurity, Kelle complained that she hated her profile. "It's like I have a protruding mouth. You know what I mean? I almost feel like I have a monkey mouth. I guess [it] can look like really, I don't know, primitive."

It's telling that the show chose to air that comment rather than leaving it on the cutting room floor with hundreds of not-ready-for-prime-time hours of tape. Yet such a statement could have been used as a teaching moment, to raise awareness of the historic dehumanization of Black women starting with imagery during slavery and progressing to contemporary ads that depict Black women as exotic, primal animals. So, did Tyra "I'm a proud, beautiful Black woman" Banks break it down for Kelle, and for the millions of young viewers who idolize the former Victoria's Secret supermodel? Did she tell Kelle to do some emotional work to reject the external messages she's gotten from a culture that tells Black women that they are low, ugly creatures? Or did she even spout one of her clichéd "Girl, your mouth is fierce!" Tyra-isms?

Fat chance. Rebuking racist imagery doesn't fly in advertiser-driven reality TV, and Banks's role as producer took precedence over any sense of social responsibility or ethnic solidarity. "We're gonna have to do some profile shots and analyze that . . . I'd be like, 'Go, Curious George, work it out!'" *Top Model*'s diva-in-chief replied. "I'm glad you guys are so honest, you know what I mean? That's what it's about, that everybody understands that you're not perfect. And that this is a business of smoke and mirrors, and fooling people into thinking you look like something else."

Let's unpack, shall we? A Black teenager thinks she's hot until *ANTM*'s judges convince her she's an ugly ape. To make her feel better, Tyra calls her Curious George* but assures her that with the "smoke and mirrors" of makeup, lighting, and camera angles she can "fool people" into thinking she's not so primitive after all. Kelle revealed what *ANTM* taught her in an episode titled, "The Girl Who Cries When She Looks in the Mirror":

> **A Black teenager thinks she's hot until *ANTM*'s judges convince her she's an ugly ape.**

25

---

*Curious George, the inquisitive monkey of children's book and PBS Kids fame, has been interpreted by literacy and culture scholars as a slave narrative. In the original story, The Man with the Big Yellow Hat kidnaps George from the African jungle and brings him to America, where he gets thrown in jail, escapes, and ends up behind bars in a zoo.[9]

I've realized what it was. It's this part of my mouth. It's like an extra layer of fat or something. So it's like a snout. . . . I was in denial about my snout. And now I know, and so it's just hard to work . . . [it makes me] very limited.

Black Models Gone "Wild"

Here's a phrase I wish I didn't have to say: At least Tyra didn't order Kelle to wear a monkey suit.

Remember the "sexy little animals" ad *ANTM* shot for Lubriderm as soon as they arrived in Cape Town, South Africa, mentioned in chapter 2 [not included here]? That shoot—like Kelle's "Curious George" instruction—fits into a lengthy and shameful history of racist imagery in advertising, media, and American politics.

The depiction of African Americans as animals and/or savages dates back to pre-abolition newspapers and magazines, where political cartoons and crude artwork accompanied editorial copy justifying the ownership of, and denial of basic human rights for, "the Negro race." At the same time, print ads sold all manner of products using such imagery to mock and dehumanize Black men, women, and children. Historically such media images functioned as visual propaganda, working to convince whites that Black people were not quite human—laying the groundwork for rationalizing slavery before abolition, segregation during Jim Crow, and contemporary proeugenics arguments.[10]

Such imagery is no longer considered appropriate in most mainstream news outlets.* But just as modern beauty advertisers discovered more sophisticated ways to package the same messages found in [. . .] early-twentieth-century Camay Soap and skin-whitening ads [. . .], the advertising industry continues to employ these themes, especially with female subjects.

Women's bodies have borne the brunt of this vile ideology in contemporary advertising, which continues to portray Black women as provocatively clothed, snarling-mouthed animals, in jungles, deserts, and safaris. "Tame and timid? That goes against my instincts," says a Black woman smoking a Virginia Slims cigarette in skintight leopard-print pants and matching halter top. "The hunting's always good at Daffy's," reads the caption of an ad featuring a Black model crouched on a beach next to a lion, her leg tucked under her in the same position as the cat's. "Gather your ammunition (cash, check, Mastercard, or Visa) and aim straight for Daffy's. It's the best hunting with the best bargains around." Are we hunting the feline, or the human? The ad draws no distinction—they're both wildcats.[12] In a September 2009 *Harper's Bazaar* spread headlined "Wild Things," supermodel Naomi Campbell skips rope with monkeys, rides an elephant and an alligator, and races a cheetah while her own spotted dress trails like a tail in the wind.[†]

30

---

*This is not to say it doesn't exist: During and after the 2008 election, media outlets such as Fox News, along with conservative news sites and blogs, circulated artwork, political cartoons, and protest imagery of President Barack Obama photoshopped as an African witch doctor with a bone through his nose, wearing a tribal headdress.[11]

†According to journalist Claire Sulmers, "The black-woman-in-the-African-wild theme . . . has been in vogue since the press pegged Somalian-born model Iman as a goat herder discovered in the jungle. She was, in fact, a university graduate and the daughter of a gynecologist and a diplomat."[13]

Like *ANTM's* "sexy little animals" photo shoot, Daffy's ad and *Harper's* spread tread old ground. In 1985, supermodel Iman was photographed next to a cheetah, her head tilted in the same position as the animal, her body turned in a catlike contortion, and her hair wrapped in a cheetah-print scarf. That same year, Iman stalked down a Thierry Mugler runway in safari garb with a live monkey hanging on her shoulder(!), while two buff Black men in loincloths trailed behind her carrying a giant umbrella.

Such images in advertising and fashion code women of color as "primitive," with untamed sexuality both fearful and seductive. Taken to its (il)logical conclusion, this fetishized depiction culminates in images of Black women as dangerous creatures who must be literally deprived of their freedom. Naomi Campbell's "Wild Things" pictorial was shot by world-famous fashion photographer Jean-Paul Goude. Nearly thirty years ago, Goude produced an infamous image of singer Grace Jones on all fours, naked, oiled up, and snarling inside a cage, surrounded by raw meat. Above her head, a zoolike plaque cautioned: Do Not Feed the Animal. (A similar caged photo of Jones graced the cover of Goude's 1981 book, *Jungle Fever*.) Locking her up is the only way to prevent her dangerous sexuality from overwhelming everyone in her wake, the picture suggests. This and several other now-iconic images of Jones posing behind bars, in chains, and with whips were replicated by biracial (Cape Verdian and Italian) model Amber Rose in the September 2009 issue of *Complex* magazine. As journalist Claire Sulmers notes, "Though the photos were taken decades apart, the message is the same. These women are so wild they must be caged—they're sultry, snarling sex beasts."[14]

By dressing a group of models up as "sexy" "native" creatures for a beauty ad as soon as they arrived in South Africa, *ANTM* wasn't engaging in a harmless homage to the land they were visiting. The Lubriderm photo shoot illustrates how the advertising industry's long-held racial essentialism influences the depiction of people of color in product-placement-driven reality TV.

I'm sure some may question whether the episode was actually racist, since white models were also featured as wildlife in the Lubriderm challenge. Yes, it was. The shoot built on a preestablished ad-industry precedent in which the mere *concept* of Africa and Black Africans is conjured to "represent white humans' own more primitive past," writes scholar Lisa Wade, on *Sociological Images*. Wade was describing a 2008–09 ad campaign by "Wild Africa Cream" liqueur, packaged in a leopard-print bottle with *ubuntu* beads around the neck. In the ads, a seductively clothed Black woman has grown a leopard's arm; another sports a cheetah's tail. White women and men in other ads in the series also have nonhuman features. The tagline? "Unleash your wild side." Each ad featured a smoldering male or female model, Black or white, each with a leopard's ear, hand, or arm. In an accompanying radio spot, a man speaks of following a sexy woman, wondering, "Did a leopard escape from the zoo?" while a female voice purrs that the liqueur can help everyone find "a little wild in them."[15]

Since fashion and beauty advertisers have worked with *ANTM's* producers to build the show's content around their products (and ideas), it's no surprise that *ANTM's* South African animals shoot shares the "Africa connects us to our animal natures" reasoning of Wild Africa Cream's marketing gambit. It's also why the show would see no problem devoting several episodes to the process of convincing a beautiful (and formerly confident) Black teenager that her "monkey" "snout" makes her ugly.

Dehumanizing African American women in advertising and media carries very real consequences for the self-esteem of Black girls and women, as well as for larger society. When an entire class of people are seen as animals, it becomes harder to prevent violence against them and easier to justify denying them equal social, economic, and political rights. If only Tyra Banks were equipped to realize the impact her programming choices can have.

Tyra Banks: Fashion Victim Turned Fashion Perpetrator

Tyra is a favorite punch line of *The Soup*'s Joel McHale and *The Dish*'s Danielle Fishel, who mock her increasingly cringe-worthy acting and odd insistence on inserting photos of herself into every episode. Culture analysts have wondered why a powerful Black model who seems to really want the best for young women of color would subject them to such demeaning double standards. "On camera, many of the black *ANTM* contestants talk about how thrilled they are to be in Tyra's presence; how her success as a black supermodel inspired them, helping them see themselves as beautiful for the first time," *Slate*'s J. E. Dahl writes, "but how does she repay their adoration? By trying to eradicate ethnic idiosyncrasies in their personality and appearance."[16]

Comics call her crazy, critics dismiss her as an opportunist, and her young fans fiercely defend her as the benevolent granter of young women's dreams. I have a different theory: I believe she has grown up mentally colonized by fashion and beauty advertisers, leaving her with something akin to Stockholm syndrome.*

Tyra Banks is many things. She's someone who believes she's an advocate for girls, especially girls of color. Four years before *ANTM* debuted she founded T-Zone, a summer camp program focused on self-esteem and leadership skills. Yet, she's also the ultimate capitalist beauty industry success story. She grew up without money, but used her nearly naked body, and an incredible parade of wigs, to become a media mogul. In addition to serving as host and executive producer of *ANTM*, she filled both those roles on her daytime chatfest, *The Tyra Banks Show*, for five seasons. This helped her earn an estimated $30 million in 2009 alone, more money than any other woman on prime-time TV. Her increasing fiscal power has drawn comparisons to Oprah Winfrey, despite the intellectual chasm between them.[17]

Most of the rest of us learn to navigate the everyday struggles of adolescence — body image insecurities, emerging sexuality, interpersonal relationships, and personal identity — from our friends, family, and community, at the same time as we are influenced by the media images surrounding us. But those images, and their makers, *were* Tyra's dominant community. From age fifteen on, Banks was raised by the fashion and beauty industry and its advertisers. In loco parentis, they gave her fame and fortune beyond her wildest dreams — but always while pitting her against other women, requiring her to hide her natural hair, and reminding her that her value depended on being young and thin.†

---

*Stockholm syndrome is popularly defined as a psychological condition in which kidnap or abuse victims form attachments to and identify with their captors.
†Banks quit high fashion for Victoria's Secret fame when she realized that curvy adulthood isn't welcome on couture catwalks.

And so the cycle continues. As a curvy Black model who achieved many firsts, Banks fought against unfair race and gender barriers throughout her career. But like so many dysfunctional patterns, Tyra grew up to become the ultimate perpetrator of the ideology of the fashion and beauty advertisers who stunted her intellectual development and shaped her self-image, psychology, and values. In that context, why is anyone surprised that she is simultaneously

- hilariously narcissistic, as well as compassionate;

- wracked with internalized racism and sexism, while renouncing the concept of discrimination; and

- concerned with girls' self-esteem, while profiting from a show that reinforces unhealthy body standards and racial stereotypes?

When she quit *The Tyra Banks Show* in 2010, she announced that her intention was to focus her Bankable Productions company on films that "can promote positive images of women."* I don't doubt Tyra's sincerity. But as *ANTM* illustrates, victims of advertiser-based Stockholm syndrome have an extremely skewed definition of what "positive" media imagery is and what it isn't.

The truth is, the best thing Tyra could do to help "more women and young girls" to "feel as fierce as we truly are" would be to take *ANTM* off the air—or drastically remodel its format.[18]

NOTES

1. "Tyra Banks Apologizes Over Bi-Racial Episode of 'ANTM,'" StyleList.com, Nov. 18, 2009. Oliver, Dana.
2. *The Asian Mystique: Dragon Ladies, Geisha Girls, & Our Fantasies of the Exotic Orient* (New York: PublicAffairs, 2006). Prasso, Sheridan, p. 87.
3. "Ethnic Magazine Editors Discuss Health, Hollywood Buzz," Sept. 12, 2007. National Public Radio. "Can She Stay on *Top?*" *Time Out Chicago*, no. 163: Apr. 10–16, 2008. Aeh, Kevin; "Hidden Potential; Reaching Consumers," *International Cosmetic News*, Mar. 1, 2008. Guilbault, Laure.
4. *Black Beauty: Aesthetics, Stylization, Politics* (Surrey, UK: Ashgate, 2009). Tate, Shirley Anne.
5. "Bitch Poured Beer on My Weave," *Vanity Fair* contributing editor James Wolcott's blog, Sept. 23, 2004.
6. *Extra!*, the magazine published by media watch organization Fairness & Accuracy in Reporting, produced some of the most well-documented debunking of 1980s and 1990s news coverage scapegoating "welfare queens" and criminalizing youth of color. See: "Five Media Myths about Welfare," *Extra!* May/June 1995; "Public Enemy Number One? Media's Welfare Debate Is a War on Poor Women," *Extra!* May/June 1995. Jackson, Janine, and Flanders, Laura; "Wild in Deceit: Why 'Teen Violence' Is Poverty Violence in Disguise," *Extra!* Mar./Apr. 1996. Males, Mike; "Superscapegoating: Teen 'Superpredators' Hype Set Stage for Draconian Legislation," *Extra!* Jan./Feb. 1998. Temple-

---

*She also signed a three-book deal to write a YA fantasy series about girls at a magic model school—sort of a *Harry Potter*-meets-*Top Model* franchise.

ton, Robin; "The Smell of Success: After 10 Years of 'Welfare Reform,' Ignoring the Human Impact," *Extra!* Nov./Dec. 2006. deMause, Neil.

7. "Eartha Quake," the avatar of a member of the TelevisionWithoutPity.com fan community, left this comment in the discussion forum devoted to Tiffany during *ANTM's* fourth season, Apr. 14, 2005.

8. "'Ugly Betty' Recast: 'Top Model' Is Willi's Daughter!" EW.com, Aug. 11, 2009. Ausiello, Michael.

9. "The Resisting Monkey: 'Curious George,' Slave Captivity Narratives, and the Postcolonial Condition," *Ariel: A Review of International English Literature* 28, no. 1 (Jan. 1997): 69–83. Cummins, June.

10. See: *Ethnic Notions*, 1987, directed by Marlon Riggs; and the Jim Crow Museum of Racist Memorabilia at Ferris State University.

11. "Obama as Witch Doctor: Racist or Satirical?" CNN.com, Sept. 18, 2009. Fantz, Ashley.

12. The Gender Ads Project. Lukas, Scott A., Ph.D. www.genderads.com/Gender_Ads .com.html.

13. "Naomi Campbell in Yet Another 'Out of Africa' Spread," *Black Voices' BV On Style* blog, Aug. 13, 2009.

14. "Caged Black Women: Grace Jones & Amber Rose," FashionBombDaily.com, Aug. 13, 2009. "Iman @ Thierry Mugler in 1985." MakeFetchHappen.blogspot.com, Aug. 22, 2008. Brigitte. "Why Photograph a Black Woman in a Cage?" Jezebel.com, Aug. 14, 2009. Jenna.

15. "Africa Is Wild, and You Can Be Too," SociologicalImages.blogspot.com, July 5, 2009. Wade, Lisa. Also see http://wildafricacream.blogspot.com/search/label/ADVERTISING.

16. "Is Tyra Banks Racist? The Peculiar Politics of 'America's Next Top Model,'" Slate.com, May 18, 2006. Dahl, J. E.

17. "Prime-Time's Top Earning Women," Forbes.com, Oct. 12, 2009. Rose, Lacey; "Who's the Next Oprah?" E! Online, Nov. 27, 2009. Gornstein, Leslie; "Tyra Banks on It," Forbes.com, July 3, 2006. Blakeley, Kiri.

18. "Tyra Banks to Leave Talk Show," Variety.com, Dec. 28, 2009; "Tyra Banks Says Goodbye to Talk Show," People.com, Dec. 28, 2009.

Exploring Context

1. Explore Pozner's tweets at twitter.com/jennpozner. In what ways do they suggest she continues to do the kind of critical work she does in this essay?

2. Visit the Web site for *America's Next Top Model* (cwtv.com/shows/americas-next-top-model). How do both the design and content of the site engage Pozner's argument?

3. The celebrity news and gossip Web site TMZ has a category devoted to reality television (tmz.com/category/reality-tv/). Look through recent posts to the site. Are the issues that Pozner explores limited to *America's Next Top Model*? Find evidence that either extends or complicates Pozner's analysis.

Questions for Connecting

1. Steve Olson argues in "The End of Race: Hawaii and the Mixing of Peoples" (p. 300) that although race no longer has any true genetic basis, ethnic divisions continue to persist. Extend Olson's argument by using Pozner's essay. What role do the media play in continuing our understanding of race?

2. Ariel Levy's essay "Female Chauvinist Pigs" (p. 243) examines the ways in which women participate in a raunch culture — a very different setting than the one Pozner examines in her analysis of *America's Next Top Model*. Synthesize these two essays in order to argue for a realistic and holistic understanding of women today. Is it possible to create such an image? Is "women" a category that can be easily described? How broad is it if it can contain both Female Chauvinist Pigs and Cha Cha Divas?

3. In "Paper Tigers" (p. 521), Wesley Yang also examines racial stereotypes. Synthesize his analysis with Pozner's argument. Do racial stereotypes operate in the same ways for men and women? Why or why not?

Language Matters

1. Listen to the latest podcast from Grammar Girl at grammar.quickanddirtytips.com. How might you apply what she's talking about in the podcast to this essay? How might you apply it to your writing instead?

2. Sometimes you can get the best feedback from peers by asking them to review a key section of your writing — something you know isn't quite there yet. If you were going to do a targeted peer revision session for Pozner, which section of her essay would you choose, and what feedback would you give?

3. Use a grammar handbook or other reference guide to review the rules for italicizing titles. Should television shows be in quotation marks or italicized? Why?

Assignments for Writing

1. Using Pozner's examples of specific "dehumanizing" racial stereotypes, write a paper in which you argue how shows such as *America's Next Top Model* may affect viewers' perceptions of race and ethnicity in modern-day America. Incorporate your work from Question 2 of Questions for Critical Reading and Question 2 of Exploring Context.

2. How can racial stereotypes be eradicated from reality TV? Write a paper in which you propose strategies for achieving this goal, using Pozner's essay as support. How might shows' ratings be affected? Use your work from Question 1 of Questions for Critical Reading and Question 1 of Questions for Connecting.

3. Write a paper in which you examine the role media and advertising play in the persistence of racial and ethnic divisions. Working from Pozner's analysis, consider as well the ways in which we support these divisions by viewing shows and participating in popular culture.

RICHARD RESTAK

Richard Restak received his M.D. from Georgetown University School of Medicine. He is a clinical professor of neurology at George Washington Hospital University School of Medicine and Health Sciences and is a former president of the American Neuropsychiatric Association. Known internationally as an expert on the brain, he has written close to twenty books on the human brain and has appeared on *Good Morning America, The Today Show,* and *All Things Considered.* Restak's expertise has led to multiple awards, articles in numerous national newspapers, and invitations to write entries for *Encyclopaedia Britannica, Compton's Encyclopedia,* and *World Book Encyclopedia.* His most recently published books are *Think Smart: A Neuroscientist's Prescription for Improving Your Brain's Performance* (2009) and *The Playful Brain: The Surprising Science of How Puzzles Improve Your Mind* (2012).

Courtesy of Carolyn Restak

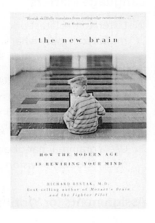

Restak's book *The New Brain: How the Modern Age Is Rewiring Your Mind* (2003) details research and technological advances that have provided new insights into the human brain. For example, technologies such as CAT and MRI scans can now prove such things as the harmful effects of television violence, and research on the brain can be leveraged to maximize our capabilities in areas ranging from academics to athletics. Restak suggests that research on the brain has yielded practical applications that we can use every day, from matching drugs to the disorders they can treat to identifying potentially violent individuals before they act out.

"Attention Deficit: The Brain Syndrome of Our Era," a chapter from *The New Brain,* deals with the effects of modern technology on "the plasticity of our brains." Here Restak examines the brain's ability to multitask and the consequences of multitasking — for example, the risks of talking on a cell phone while driving. Our tendency to juggle tasks, Restak warns, may be both unproductive and damaging to our brains. Diagnoses of disorders such as attention deficit disorder (ADD) and attention deficit hyperactivity disorder (ADHD) have become common in recent years, and Restak suggests that one of the reasons for this might be technology's effect on our evolution.

Multitasking forces our brains to process ever-increasing amounts of information at ever-increasing rates, which raises a question: Is the recent social and cultural trend toward multitasking actually rewiring our brains and causing such problems as ADD and ADHD?

▶ TAGS: *health and medicine, psychology, science and technology, social change*
▶ CONNECTIONS: *Henig, Klosterman, Konnikova, Paumgarten, Singer, Wasik*

Questions for Critical Reading

1. Do you think multitasking is possible? How does it function in your own life? According to Restak, what are the problems with multitasking? Locate passages where he discusses the impact of this practice.

2. How does culture affect biology? Perform a critical reading of Restak's text in order to describe the ways in which what we do can change what we are.

3. What are *modern nerves*? Define the term as it is used in Restak's essay and then provide examples from both his text and your own life.

Attention Deficit: The Brain Syndrome of Our Era

The plasticity of our brains, besides responding to the people and training to which we expose it, also responds, for good or for bad, to the technology all around us: television, movies, cell phones, e-mail, laptop computers, and the Internet. And by responding, I mean that our brain literally changes its organization and functioning to accommodate the abundance of stimulation forced on it by the modern world.

This technologically driven change in the brain is the biggest modification in the last 200,000 years (when the brain volume of *Homo sapiens* reached the modern level). But while biological and social factors, such as tool use, group hunting, and language, drove earlier brain changes, exposure to technology seems to be spurring the current alteration. One consequence of this change is that we face constant challenges to our ability to focus our attention.

For example, I was recently watching a televised interview with Laura Bush. While the interview progressed, the bottom of the screen was active with a "crawler" composed of a line of moving type that provided information on other news items.

Until recently, crawlers were used to provide early warning signs for hurricanes, tornados, and other impending threats. Because of their rarity and implied seriousness, crawlers grabbed our immediate attention no matter how engrossed we were in the television program playing out before our eyes. Crawlers, in short, were intended to capture our attention and forewarn us of the possible need for prompt action. But now, the crawler has become ubiquitous, forcing an ongoing split in our attention, a constant state of distraction and divided focus.

During the First Lady's interview I found my attention shifting back and forth from her remarks to the active stream of short phrases running below. From the crawler I learned that National Airport was expected to be opened in two days since its closure in the wake of the September 11 terrorist attacks; that this season's Super Bowl would be played in New Orleans one week later than usual; and that a home run record was about to be broken by Barry Bonds.

Despite my best efforts to concentrate on Laura Bush's words, I kept looking down at the crawler to find out what else might be happening that was perhaps even more interesting. As a result, at several points I lost the thread of the conversation between the

First Lady and the interviewer. Usually, I missed the question and was therefore forced to remain in the dark during the first sentence or so of her response.

On other occasions I've watched split-screen interviews, with each half of the screen displaying images or text of the topic under discussion while the crawler continues with short snippets about subjects totally divorced from the interview and accompanying video or text. In these instances I am being asked to split my visual attention into three components.

One can readily imagine future developments when attention must be divided into four or more components—perhaps an interview done entirely in the form of a voice-over, with the split-screen video illustrating two subjects unrelated to the subject of the interview and accompanied all the while by a crawler at the bottom of the screen dealing with a fourth topic.

Yet we shouldn't think of such developments as unanticipated or surprising. In 1916, prophets of the Futurist Cinema* lauded "cinematic simultaneity and interpenetrations of different times and places" and predicted "we shall project two or three different visual episodes at the same time, one next to the other." Yesterday's predictions have become today's reality. And in the course of that makeover we have become more frenetic, more distracted, more fragmented—in a word, more *hyperactive*.

How Many Ways Can Our Attention Be Divided?

Divisions of attention aren't new, of course. People have always been required to do more than one thing at a time or think of more than one thing at a time. But even when engaged in what we now call multitasking, most people maintained a strong sense of unity: They remained fully grounded in terms of what they were doing. Today the sense of unity has been replaced, I believe, by feelings of distraction and difficulty maintaining focus and attention. On a daily basis I encounter otherwise normal people in my neuropsychiatric practice who experience difficulty concentrating. "I no sooner begin thinking of one thing than my mind starts to wander off to another subject and before I know it I'm thinking of yet a third subject," is a typical complaint.

Certainly part of this shift from focus to distraction arises from the many and varied roles we all must now fulfill. But I think the process of personal *dis*-integration is also furthered by our constant exposure to the media, principally television. When watching TV, many of us now routinely flit from one program to another as quickly as our thumb can strike the remote control button. We watch a story for a few minutes and then switch over to a basketball game until we become bored with that, and then move on to Animal Planet. Feeling restless, we may then pick up the phone and talk to a co-worker about topics likely to come up at tomorrow's meeting while simultaneously directing our attention to a weather report on TV or flipping through our mail.

"The demands upon the human brain right now are increasing," according to Todd E. Feinberg, a neurologist at Beth Israel Medical Center in New York City. "For all we know, we're selecting for the capacity to multitask."

---

*Futurist Cinema: Italian Futurism was an influential movement in film in the early twentieth century. Futurism in the arts emphasized and glorified themes associated with contemporary concepts of the future, including youth, noise, new technologies, cities, violence, and speed [Ed.].

Feinberg's comment about "selecting" gets to the meat of the issue. At any given time evolution selects for adaptation and fitness to prevailing environmental conditions. And today the environment demands the capacity to do more than one thing at a time, divide one's attention, and juggle competing, often conflicting, interests. Adolescents have grown up in just such an environment. As a result, some of them can function reasonably efficiently under conditions of distraction. But this ability to multitask often comes at a price — Attention Deficit Disorder (ADD) or Attention Deficit Hyperactivity Disorder (ADHD).

Perhaps the best intuitive understanding of ADD/ADHD comes from the French philosopher Blaise Pascal who said, "Most of the evils in life arise from a man's being unable to sit still in a room." The fourth edition of the *Diagnostic and Statistical Manual of Mental Disorders* (DSM-IV) provides a more contemporary definition. Although ADD/ADHD affects adults as well as children, the DSM-IV describes symptoms as they affect three categories in children: motor control, impulsivity, and difficulties with organization and focus.

The motor patterns include:

15

   (a) often fidgets with hands or feet or squirms in seat

   (b) often leaves seat in classroom or in other situations in which remaining seated is expected

   (c) is often "on the go" or often acts as if driven by a motor

   (d) often runs about or expresses a subjective feeling of restlessness

   (e) often has difficulty playing or engaging in leisure activities quietly

   (f) often talks excessively

The impulsive difficulties include:

   (a) often experiences difficulty awaiting turn

   (b) interrupts or intrudes on others (e.g., butts into conversation or games)

   (c) often blurts out answers before questions have been completed

To earn the diagnosis of the "inattentive subtype" of ADD/ADHD, the child or adolescent shows any six of the following symptoms:

   (a) often does not follow through on instructions and fails to finish schoolwork, chores, or duties in the workplace

   (b) often fails to give close attention to details or makes careless mistakes in schoolwork, work, or other activities

   (c) often has difficulty sustaining attention in tasks or play activities

   (d) often does not seem to listen when spoken to directly

   (e) often avoids, dislikes, or is reluctant to engage in tasks that require sustained mental effort (such as schoolwork or homework)

   (f) often loses things necessary for tasks or activities

(g) is often easily distracted by extraneous stimuli

(h) is often forgetful in daily activities

For years doctors assured the parents of an ADD/ADHD child that the condition would disappear as their child grew older. But such reassurances have turned out to be overly optimistic. In the majority of cases, ADD/ADHD continues into adulthood, although the symptoms change.

In their best-selling book, *Driven to Distraction*, psychiatrists Edward Hallowell and John Ratey developed a list of criteria for the diagnosis of Adult Attention Deficit Disorder. Among the most common manifestations are:

1. A sense of underachievement, of not meeting one's goals

2. Difficulty getting organized

3. Chronic procrastination or trouble getting started

4. Many projects going simultaneously; trouble with follow-through

5. A tendency to say whatever comes to mind without necessarily considering the timing or appropriateness of the remark

6. A frequent search for high stimulation

7. Intolerance of boredom

8. Easy distractibility, trouble in focusing attention, a tendency to tune out or drift away in the middle of a page or conversation

9. Impatience; low frustration tolerance

10. A sense of insecurity

Other experts on adult attention disorder would add:

11. Low self-esteem and

12. Emotional lability: sudden and sometimes dramatic mood shifts

A Distinctive Type of Brain Organization

In many instances childhood and adult ADD/ADHD is inherited. Typically, the parents of a child diagnosed with the disorder will be found upon interview to exhibit many of the criteria for adult ADD/ADHD. But many cases of ADD/ADHD in both children and adults occur without any hereditary disposition, suggesting the probability of culturally induced ADD/ADHD.

As a result of increasing demands on our attention and focus, our brains try to adapt by rapidly shifting attention from one activity to another—a strategy that is now almost a requirement for survival. As a consequence, attention deficit disorder is becoming epidemic in both children and adults. This is unlikely to turn out to be a temporary condition. Indeed, some forms of ADD/ADHD have entered the mainstream of acceptable behavior. Many personality characteristics we formerly labeled as dysfunctional, such as hyperactivity, impulsiveness, and easy distractibility, are now almost the norm.

"With so many distracted people running around, we could be becoming the first society with Attention Deficit Disorder," writes Evan Schartz, a cyberspace critic in *Wired* magazine. In Schartz's opinion, ADHD may be "the official brain syndrome of the information age."

"Civilization is revving itself into a pathologically short attention span. The trend might be coming from the acceleration of technology, the short-horizon perspective of market-driven economies, the next-election perspective of democracies, or the distractions of personal multitasking. All are on the increase," according to Stewart Brand, a noted commentator on technology and social change. 20

As ADD expert Paul Wender puts it: "The attention span of the average adult is greatly exaggerated."

"It's important to note that neuroscientists and experts within the field are increasingly dissatisfied with ADHD being called a disorder," according to Sam Horn, author of *ConZentrate: Get Focused and Pay Attention—When Life Is Filled with Pressures, Distractions, and Multiple Priorities*, which lists forces in the modern world that "induce" ADD/ADHD. "They prefer to see ADHD as a distinctive type of brain organization."

Such an attitude change toward ADD/ADHD carries practical implications. When creating an optimum environment for learning, for instance, Horn suggests, "blocking out sounds can hurt. Today's younger generation has become accustomed to cacophony. Street sounds, the screeching of brakes, trucks changing gears, and the wails of ambulances are their norm. For these people silence can actually be disconcerting because it's so unusual."

To Horn's list of ADD/ADHD-inducing influences I would add time-compressed speech, which is now routinely used on radio and TV to inject the maximum amount of information per unit of time. As a result we have all become accustomed to rapid-fire motormouth commercials spoken at truly incomprehensible speeds. Think of the last car commercial you saw where all

> **"The attention span of the average adult is greatly exaggerated."**

the "fine print" of the latest deal was read with lightning speed, or the pharmaceutical pitch that names a dozen possible side effects in less than five seconds.

"The attitude seems to be one of pushing the limits on the listener as far as 'the market will bear' in terms of degrading the auditory signal and increasing the presentation rate of the spoken programming," according to Brandeis University psychologists Patricia A. Tun and Arthur Wingfield in their paper, "Slow But Sure in an Age of 'Make It Quick.'" 25

As these psychologists point out, laptop computers, cell phones, e-mail, and fax machines keep us in constant touch with the world while simultaneously exerting tremendous pressures on us to respond quickly and accurately. But speed and accuracy often operate at cross-purposes in the human brain.

In study after study both young and older listeners recall less from materials told to them at a rapid rate. A similar situation exists in the visual sphere. A television viewer's memory for information about the weather is actually poorer after viewing weather segments featuring colored charts and moving graphics than after viewing straightforward versions of the same information in which the weather is simply described.

As Tun and Wingfield put it: "The clutter, noise, and constant barrage of information that surround us daily contribute to the hectic pace of our modern lives, in which it is often difficult simply to remain mindful in the moment."

No Time to Listen

As the result of our "make it quick" culture, attention deficit is becoming the paradigmatic disorder of our times. Indeed, ADD/ADHD isn't so much a disorder as it is a cognitive style. In order to be successful in today's workplace you have to incorporate some elements of ADD/ADHD.

You must learn to rapidly process information, function amidst surroundings your parents would have described as "chaotic," always remain prepared to rapidly shift from one activity to another, and redirect your attention among competing tasks without becoming bogged down or losing time. Such facility in rapid information processing requires profound alterations in our brain. And such alterations come at a cost—a devaluation of the depth and quality of our relationships. 30

For example, a patient of mine who works as a subway driver was once unfortunate enough to witness a man commit suicide by throwing himself in front of her train. Her ensuing anguish and distress convinced her employers that she needed help, and they sent her to me. The hardest part of her ordeal, as she expressed it, was that no one would give her more than a few minutes to tell her story. They either interrupted her or, in her words, "gradually zoned out."

"I can't seem to talk fast enough about what happened to me," she told me. "Nobody has time to listen anymore."

The absence of the "time to listen" isn't simply the result of increased workloads (although this certainly plays a role) but from a reorganization of our brains. Sensory overload is the psychological term for the process, but you don't have to be a psychologist to understand it. Our brain is being forced to manage increasing amounts of information within shorter and shorter time intervals. Since not everyone is capable of making that transition, experiences like my patient's are becoming increasingly common.

"Don't tell me anything that is going to take more than 30 seconds for you to get out," as one of my adult friends with ADD/ADHD told his wife in response to what he considered her rambling. In fact, she was only taking the time required to explain a complicated matter in appropriate detail.

"The blistering pace of life today, driven by technology and the business imperative to improve efficiency, is something to behold," writes David Shenk in his influential book *Data Smog*. "We often feel life going by much, much faster than we wish, as we are carried forward from meeting to meeting, call to call, errand to errand. We have less time to ourselves, and we are expected to improve our performance and output year after year." 35

Regarding technology's influence on us, Jacques Barzun, in his best-seller, *From Dawn to Decadence*, comments, "The machine makes us its captive servants—by its rhythm, by its convenience, by the cost of stopping it or the drawbacks of not using it. As captives *we come to resemble it in its pace, rigidity, and uniform expectations*" [emphasis added].

Whether you agree that we're beginning to resemble machines, I'm certain you can readily bring to mind examples of the effect of communication technology on identity and behavior. For instance, cinematography provides us with many of our reference points and a vocabulary for describing and even experiencing our personal reality.

While driving to work in the morning we "fast-forward" a half-hour in our mind to the upcoming office meeting. We reenact in our imagination a series of "scenarios" that could potentially take place. A few minutes later, while entering the garage, we experience a "flashback" of the awkward "scene" that took place during last week's meeting and "dub in" a more pleasing "take."

Of course using the vocabulary of the latest technology in conversation isn't new. Soon after their introduction, railways, telegraphs, and telephone switchboards provided useful metaphors for describing everyday experiences: People spoke of someone "telegraphing" their intentions, or of a person being "plugged in" to the latest fashions.

Modern Nerves

In 1891 the Viennese critic Hermann Bahr predicted the arrival of what he called "new human beings," marked by an increased nervous energy. A person with "modern nerves" was "quick-witted, briskly efficient, rigorously scheduled, doing everything on the double," writes social critic Peter Conrad in *Modern Times, Modern Places.* 40

In the 1920s, indications of modern nerves were illustrated by both the silent films of the age, with their accelerated movement, and the change in drug use at the time, from sedating agents like opium to the newly synthesized cocaine—a shift that replaced languid immobility with frenetic hyperactivity and "mobility mania."

Josef Breuer, who coauthored *Studies on Hysteria* with Sigmund Freud, compared the modern nervous system to a telephone line made up of nerves in "tonic excitation." If the nerves were overburdened with too much "current," he claimed, the result would be sparks, frazzled insulation, scorched filaments, short circuits—in essence, a model for hysteria. The mind was thus a machine and could best be understood through the employment of machine metaphors. Athletes picked up on this theme and aimed at transforming their bodies into fine-tuned organisms capable, like machines, of instant responsiveness. "The neural pathways by which will is translated into physical movement are trained until they react to the slightest impulse," wrote a commentator in the 1920s on the "cult" of sports.

The Changing Rhythm of Life

In 1931 the historian James Truslow Adams commented, "As the number of sensations increase, the time which we have for reacting to and digesting them becomes less . . . the rhythm of our life becomes quicker, the wave lengths . . . of our mental life grow shorter. Such a life tends to become a mere search for more and more exciting sensations, undermining yet more our power of concentration in thought. Relief from fatigue and ennui is sought in mere excitation of our nerves, as in speeding cars or emotional movies."

In the 60 years since Adams's observation, speed has become an integral component of our lives. According to media critic Todd Gitlin, writing in *Media Unlimited*, "Speed is not incidental to the modern world—speed of production, speed of innovation, speed of investment, speed in the pace of life and the movement of images—but its essence. . . . Is speed a means or an end? If a means, it is so pervasive as to *become* an end."

In our contemporary society speed is the standard applied to almost everything   45
that we do. Media, especially television, is the most striking example of this acceleration. "It is the limitless media torrent that sharpens the sense that all of life is jetting forward—or through—some ultimate speed barrier," according to Gitlin. "The most widespread, most consequential speed-up of our time is the onrush in images—the speed at which they zip through the world, the speed at which they give way to more of the same, the tempo at which they move."

In response to this media torrent, the brain has had to make fundamental adjustments. The demarcation between here and elsewhere has become blurred. Thanks to technology, each of us exists simultaneously in not just one *here* but in several. While talking with a friend over coffee we're scanning e-mail on our Palm Pilot. At such times where are we *really?* In such instances no less is involved than a fundamental change in our concept of time and place.

> **Thanks to technology, each of us exists simultaneously in not just one *here* but in several.**

Where Is Where?

"Modernity is about the acceleration of time and the dispersal of places. The past is available for instant recall in the present," according to Peter Conrad. For example, I was recently sitting in a restaurant in Washington, D.C., while watching a soccer match take place several time zones away. During an interruption in play, the screen displayed action from another match played more than a decade ago. The commentator made a brief point about similarities and differences in the two matches and then returned to the action of the ongoing match. During all of this I was participating in a "present" comprised of two different time zones along with a "past" drawn from an event that occurred twelve years earlier. Such an experience is no longer unusual. Technology routinely places us in ambiguous time and place relationships.

As another example, while recently sitting on the beach at South Beach in Miami I was amazed at the number of people talking on cell phones while ostensibly spending the afternoon with the person who accompanied them to the beach. In this situation the *here* is at least partly influenced by the technology of the cell phone that both links (the caller and the unseen person on the other end of the cell phone) and isolates (the caller and the temporarily neglected person lying beside him or her on the beach blanket). Such technologies are forcing our brains to restructure themselves and accommodate to a world of multiple identity and presence.

Intellectually we have always known that the "reality" of the here and now before our eyes is only one among many. But we never directly experienced this multilevel reality until technology made it possible to reach from one end of the world to another and wipe out differences in time, space, and place. Starting with telephones we became able to experience the "reality" of people in widely dispersed areas of the world. With the cell phone, that process has become even more intimate. Time, distance, night, and day—the rules of the natural and physical world—cease to be limiting factors.

And while some of us may celebrate such experiences and thrive on constantly being connected, others feel the sensation of a giant electronic tentacle that will ensnare us at any moment. 50

My point here isn't to criticize technology but to emphasize the revolution that technology is causing in our brain's functioning. If, for example, through technology, anyone at any given moment is immediately available, "here" and "there" lose their distinctive meanings. We achieve that "acceleration of time and the dispersal of places" referred to by Peter Conrad.

And yet there is an ironic paradox in all this: As a result of technological advances we participate in many different and disparate "realities," yet as a result of our attention and focus problems we can't fully participate in them. We can shift back and forth from a phone conversation with someone in Hong Kong and someone directly in front of our eyes. Yet thanks to our sense of distraction we're not fully focused on either of them. What to do?

The Plastic on the Cheese

"If I can only learn to efficiently carry out several things simultaneously then my time pressures will disappear," we tell ourselves. And at first sight multitasking seems a sensible response to our compressed, overly committed schedules. Instead of limiting ourselves to only one activity, why not do several simultaneously? If you owe your mother a phone call, why not make that call while in the kitchen waiting for the spaghetti to come to a boil? And if Mom should call you first, why not talk to her while glancing down at today's crossword puzzle?

Actually, multitasking is not nearly as efficient as most of us have been led to believe. In fact, doing more than one thing at once or switching back and forth from one task to another involves time-consuming alterations in brain processing that reduce our effectiveness at accomplishing either one.

Whenever you attempt to do "two things at once," your attention at any given moment is directed to one or the other activity rather than to both at once. And, most important, these shifts decrease rather than increase your efficiency; they are time and energy depleting. 55

With each switch in attention, your frontal lobes—the executive control centers toward the front of your brain—must shift goals and activate new rules of operation. Talking on the phone and doing a crossword puzzle activate different parts of the brain, engage different muscles, and induce different sensory experiences.

In addition, the shift from one activity to another can take up to seven-tenths of a second. We know this because of the research of Joshua Rubinstein, a psychologist at the Federal Aviation Administration's William J. Hughes Technical Center in Atlantic City.

Rubinstein and his colleagues studied patterns of time loss that resulted when volunteers switched from activities of varying complexity and familiarity. Measurements showed that the volunteers lost time during these switches, especially when going from something familiar to something unfamiliar. Further, the time losses increased in direct proportion to the complexity of the tasks. To explain this finding the researchers postulate a "rule-activation" stage, when the prefrontal cortex "disables" or deactivates the rules used for the first activity and then "enables" the rules for the new activity. It's this process of rule deactivation followed by reactivation that takes more than half a second. Under certain circumstances this loss of time due to multitasking can prove not only inefficient but also dangerous.

For example, remember the speculation that cell phone–associated automobile accidents could be eliminated if drivers used hands-free devices? Well, that speculation isn't supported by brain research. The use of cell phones—hands-free or otherwise—divides a driver's attention and increases his or her sense of distraction.

In an important study carried out by psychologist Peter A. Hancock at the University of Central Florida in Orlando and two researchers from the Liberty Mutual Insurance Company, volunteers simulated using a hands-free cell phone while driving. The volunteers were instructed to respond to the ringing of a phone installed on the dashboard of their car. At the instant they heard the ring they had to compare whether the first digit of a number displayed on a computer screen on the dashboard corresponded to the first digit of a number they had previously memorized. If that first digit was the same, the driver was supposed to push a button. In the meantime, they were to obey all traffic rules and, in the test situation, bring the car to a full stop.

While the distracting ring had only a slight effect on the stopping distance of younger drivers (0.61 seconds rather than 0.5 seconds), it had a profound effect on the stopping distance of drivers between 55 and 65 years of age: 0.82 seconds rather than 0.61 seconds, according to the researchers. Distraction, in other words, reduces efficiency.

In another test of the cost of multitasking, volunteers at the Center for Cognitive Brain Imaging at Carnegie Mellon University in Pittsburgh underwent PET scans while simultaneously listening to sentences and mentally rotating pairs of three-dimensional figures. The researchers found a 29 percent reduction in brain activity generated by mental rotation if the subjects were also listening to the test sentences. This decrease in brain activity was linked to an overall decrease in efficiency: It took them longer to do each task.

A reduction in efficiency was also found when the researchers looked at the effect of mental rotation on reading. They discovered that brain activity generated when reading the sentences decreased by 53 percent if the subjects were also trying to mentally rotate the objects.

A similar loss of efficiency occurs when activities are alternated. For instance, David E. Meyer, a professor of mathematical psychology at the University of Michigan in Ann Arbor, recruited young adults to engage in an experiment where they would rapidly switch between working out math problems and identifying shapes. The volunteers took longer for both tasks, and their accuracy took a nosedive compared to their performance when they focused on each task separately.

"Not only the speed of performance, the accuracy of performance, but what I call the fluency of performance, the gracefulness of their performance, was negatively influenced by the overload of multitasking," according to Meyer.

All of which leads to this simple rule: Despite our subjective feelings to the contrary, actually our brain can work on only one thing at a time. Rather than allowing us to efficiently do two things at the same time, multitasking actually results in inefficient shifts in our attention. In short, the brain is designed to work most efficiently when it works on a single task and for sustained rather than intermittent and alternating periods of time. This doesn't mean that we can't perform a certain amount of multitasking. But we do so at decreased efficiency and accuracy.

But despite neuroscientific evidence to the contrary, we are being made to feel that we *must* multitask in order to keep our head above the rising flood of daily demands. Instead of "Be Here Now," we're encouraged to split our attention into several fragments and convinced that multitasking improves mental efficiency.

Instead, multitasking comes at a cost. And it's true that sometimes the cost is trivial, or even amusing, as with the following experience of a young mother: "I had to get dressed for my daughter's middle school choral program, get another child started on homework, and feed another who had to be ready to be driven to soccer practice. Of course, the phone kept ringing, too. I thought I had everything under control when the complaints about the grilled cheese started. Without getting too angry, I growled for her to just eat it so that I could finish getting dressed. What else could I do in such a rush? My daughter then said, 'I can't eat it, Mom. You left the plastic on the cheese.'"

Other times, the cost of multitasking can be much less amusing. Imagine yourself driving in light traffic on a clear day while chatting on a cell phone with a friend. You're having no problem handling your vehicle and also keeping up your end of the conversation. But over the next five minutes you encounter heavier traffic and the onset of a torrential rainstorm. Your impulse is to end the conversation and pay more attention to the road, but your friend on the other end of the line keeps talking. After all, he isn't encountering the same hazardous conditions from the comfort of his office or home. You continue to talk a bit longer, shifting your attention between your friend's patter and the rapidly deteriorating road conditions. As a result, you fail to notice that the tractor-trailer to your right is starting to slide in your direction. . . . Your survivors will never know that your divided attention, with its accompanying decrease in brain efficiency, set you up for that fatal accident.

In essence, the brain has certain limits that we must accept. While it's true that we can train our brain to multitask, our overall performance on each of the tasks is going to be less efficient than if we performed one thing at a time.

Cerebral Geography

Despite the inefficiency of multitasking, the brain is able to deal with more than one thing at a time. If that weren't true, we wouldn't be able to "walk and chew gum at the same time," as a critic once uncharitably described a former U.S. president. The trick is to avoid activities that interrupt the flow of the main activity.

For example, listening to music can actually enhance the efficiency among those who work with their hands. I first learned of this a year or so ago when a draftsman casually mentioned to me that he felt more relaxed and did better work while listening to background music. Many surgeons make similar claims. In a study aimed at testing such claims, researchers hooked up 50 male surgeons between the ages of 31 and 61 to machines that measured blood pressure and pulse. The surgeons then performed mental arithmetic exercises designed to mimic the stress a surgeon would be expected to experience in the operating room. They then repeated the exercise while the surgeons listened to musical selections of their own choosing. The performances improved when the surgeons were listening to the music.

In another study, listening to music enhanced the surgeons' alertness and concentration. What kind of music worked best? Of 50 instrumental tracks selected, 46 were concertos, with Vivaldi's *Four Seasons* as the top pick, followed by Beethoven's Violin Concerto op. 61, Bach's Brandenburg Concertos, and Wagner's "Ride of the Valkyries"—not exactly your standard "easy listening" repertoire.

But easy listening isn't the purpose, according to one of the surgeons interviewed. "In the O.R. it's very busy with lots of things going on, but if you have the music on you can operate. The music isn't a distraction but a way of blocking out all of the other distractions."

Music undoubtedly exerts its positive effects on surgical performance at least partially through its kinesthetic effects, an observation made by Socrates in Plato's *Republic*:* "More than anything else rhythm and harmony find their way to the inmost soul and take strongest hold upon it." Thanks to music, the surgeon is more concentrated, alert, technically efficient, and—most important—in the frame of mind most conducive to healing. "Take Puccini's *La Bohème*," says Blake Papsin, an ear, nose, and throat surgeon in Toronto. "It's an absolutely beautiful piece of music that compels the human spirit to perform, to care, to love—and that's what surgery is." [75]

Music and skilled manual activities activate different parts of the brain, so interference and competition are avoided. If the surgeon listened to an audiobook instead of a musical composition, however, there would likely be interference. Imagining a scene described by the narrator would interfere with the surgeon's spatial imaging. Listening to the audiobook would activate similar areas of the brain and cause competition between the attention needed to efficiently and accurately operate and to comprehend the images and story in the audiobook. We encounter here an example of the principle of *cerebral geography*: The brain works at its best with the activation of different, rather than identical, brain areas. That's why doodling while talking on the telephone isn't a problem for most people, since speaking and drawing use different brain areas. But writing a thank you note while on the phone results in mental strain because speaking and writing share some of the same brain circuitry.

---

*Socrates in Plato's *Republic*: Socrates was an Athenian Greek philosopher (469–399 BC). He is known chiefly through the writings of his students, notably Plato (c. 428 BC–c. 348 BC). In the *Republic*, one of the foundational texts of Western philosophy, Plato, himself an enormously influential philosopher, recounts dialogues Socrates holds as a means of discovering the truth (the "Socratic method") on such topics as justice [Ed.].

Thanks to new technology, especially procedures like functional MRI scans, neuroscientists will soon be able to compile lists of activities that can be done simultaneously with a minimal lapse in efficiency or accuracy. But, in general, it's wise to keep this in mind: A penalty is almost always paid when two activities are carried out simultaneously rather than separately.

Exploring Context

1. Take the ADD/ADHD test at psychcentral.com/addquiz.htm. How does your score reflect Restak's argument? Connect your response to your work on multitasking from Question 1 of Questions for Critical Reading.

2. Explore the Web site for Twitter at twitter.com. Is this abbreviated style of blogging a reflection of the problems that Restak explores? Or is staying hyperconnected to your friends a way of combating the demands on attention? Consider the relation between Twitter and your definition of *modern nerves* from Question 3 of Questions for Critical Reading.

3. Choose and play a multitasking game at multitaskgames.com. How does your performance in the game confirm or complicate Restak's argument? Connect your response to your work on multitasking from Question 1 of Questions for Critical Reading.

Questions for Connecting

1. Kwame Anthony Appiah, in "Making Conversation" and "The Primacy of Practice" (p. 44), explores the persistence of social practices and the possibilities of change. Can we use his ideas to address the problem that Restak describes? Does multitasking, as a practice, have a kind of primacy? Draw on your work in Questions for Critical Reading in making your argument.

2. In "Ethics and the New Genetics" (p. 63), the Dalai Lama asks us to consider the ethical implications of new technologies. But what are the ethical implications of existing technologies? Is multitasking an ethical issue? Synthesize these two texts to make a larger argument about the ethics of technology.

3. How do cultural processes shape biology? Consider not only Restak's argument but also Sharon Moalem's ideas in "Changing Our Genes: How Trauma, Bullying, and Royal Jelly Affect Our Genetic Destiny" (p. 277). You may want to draw on your work in Exploring Context in making your argument.

Language Matters

1. Create a series of presentation slides about this essay using PowerPoint or other software. Since such slides are most effective when they contain only a few key points per slide, you will have to locate the most important elements of Restak's argument; in designing the slides, you should also consider how visual elements like color, font, and alignment can enhance an argument.

2. Punctuation marks control the speed of speech: Commas ask us to pause and periods ask us to stop. Given Restak's argument, how can you use punctuation in your writing to guide your reader's attention and combat ADD/ADHD? Which marks might be most helpful, and which might you want to avoid?

3. What are the differences between editing, proofreading, and revising? What would you do to this essay if you were editing it? Revising it? How can you use these different skills in your own writing?

Assignments for Writing

1. Restak examines the way the human brain responds to modern technology, claiming that the changes made in the brain by technology are the biggest changes to that organ in thousands of years. Write an essay that examines the potential benefits of this change in the second decade of the twenty-first century. What is the role of television in the rewiring of the brain? What other technologies have similar effects? Is this change in brain function for the better? Is it possible that technological advances can move faster than is good for humankind? Consider using your work with Restak's concepts from Questions for Connecting in making your argument.

2. Restak looks closely at the role of modern media and communication devices in our daily lives. Write an essay in which you use Restak and your own experience to assess the ways in which current media has created a culture that demands a high-speed, high-efficiency lifestyle. Does media shape our attention? In what ways are we expected to speed up, and in what ways are we urged to slow down? Restak writes about the "crawler" on TV news. What other media features divide our attention?

3. Write an essay that examines the effectiveness of multitasking in the face of modern technologies, synthesizing Restak's text with your own experience. How does the brain multitask? What impedes our ability to multitask? Why is multitasking not as efficient as we may think? What role does modern technology play in our ability to multitask? Do we multitask more than we think? What demands do we place on ourselves when it comes to multitasking? Draw on your experience and your work with Exploring Context in making your argument.

HANNA ROSIN

Israeli-born **Hanna Rosin** has written for the *New Yorker*, *GQ*, and the *New Republic*; currently she is a senior editor and writes for the *Atlantic*. In 2009, she cofounded DoubleX, *Slate's* site for women. Rosin is the author of two books, *God's Harvard: A Christian College on a Mission to Save America* (2007) and *The End of Men: And the Rise of Women* (2012). She typically writes about religious, political, and gender issues.

Elizabeth Lippman/Contour/ Getty Images

"Why Kids Sext" was the cover story for the November 2014 issue of the *Atlantic*, a magazine with a focus on culture, politics, foreign affairs, and the economy. Recipient of the most National Magazine Awards of any monthly magazine, the *Atlantic* was founded in the middle of the nineteenth century and has a long and distinguished history. The November 2014 issue also included essays on flying drones, robot cars, and apps that help spouses cheat on one another.

In this essay, Rosin investigates the so-called sexting scandal that took place in Louisa County, Virginia. After a high school student's private nude photos showed up on an Instagram account, local police officers began conducting an investigation that left them thinking less that a "cabal" of students was hoarding these pictures and more that nearly every student at the school was sexting in some form. Rosin explores the larger context of contemporary teen culture and its relationship to sexting while also documenting the deep confusion over what, exactly, to do about teen sexting. This confusion extends to the legal realm. Currently, Rosin explains, the practice falls under child pornography laws in most states, meaning that teens who sext could be convicted as sex offenders.

How serious a problem is sexting? What, if anything, should we do about it?

▶ TAGS: *adolescence and adulthood, censorship, community, culture, education, ethics, gender, judgment and decision-making, law and justice, photography and video, relationships, sexuality, social media*

▶ CONNECTIONS: *DeGhett, Gay, Klosterman, Konnikova, Levy, O'Connor, Pozner*

Questions for Critical Reading

1. What is *sexting*? What is *self-production*? As you read, pay attention to Rosin's explanation of these terms. Why does the choice of terminology matter?

2. Rosin references several slang terms in this essay. As you read, note the definitions she provides of *slut*, *ghetto*, *thot*, and *vamping*. How are these terms connected to sexting?

3. Is sexting a problem? For whom? As you read, map out the various populations connected to sexting and their attitudes toward the practice.

Why Kids Sext

It was late on a school night, so Jennifer's kids were already asleep when she got a phone call from a friend of her 15-year-old daughter, Jasmine. "Jasmine is on a Web page and she's naked." Jennifer woke Jasmine, and throughout the night, the two of them kept getting texts from Jasmine's friends with screenshots of the Instagram account. It looked like a porn site—shot after shot of naked girls—only these were real teens, not grown women in pigtails. Jennifer recognized some of them from Jasmine's high school. And there, in the first row, was her daughter, "just standing there, with her arms down by her sides," Jennifer told me. "There were all these girls with their butts cocked, making pouty lips, pushing their boobs up, doing porny shots, and you're thinking, *Where did they pick this up?* And then there was Jasmine in a fuzzy picture looking awkward." (The names of all the kids and parents in this story have been changed to protect their privacy.) You couldn't easily identify her, because the picture was pretty dark, but the connection had been made anyway. "OMG no f-ing way that's Jasmine," someone had commented under her picture. "Down lo ho," someone else answered, meaning one who flies under the radar, because Jasmine was a straight-A student who played sports and worked and volunteered and was generally a "goody-goody two shoes," her mom said. She had long, silky hair and doe eyes and a sweet face that seemed destined for a Girl Scouts pamphlet, not an Instagram account where girls were called out as hos or thots (*thot* stands for "that ho over there").

That night, in March of this year, Jennifer tried to report the account to Instagram's privacy-and-safety center, hoping it would get taken down. She asked several friends to fill out the "report violations" page too, but after a few hours, the account was still up. (Instagram's help center recommends contacting local authorities in cases of serious abuse.) She considered calling 911, but this didn't seem like that kind of emergency. So she waited until first thing the next morning and called a local deputy sheriff who serves as the school resource officer, and he passed the message on to his superior, Major Donald Lowe. Over the years, Lowe had gotten calls from irate parents whose daughters' naked pictures had popped up on cellphones, usually sent around by an angry boyfriend after a breakup. But he immediately realized that this was a problem of a different order. Investigation into the Instagram account quickly revealed two other, similar accounts with slightly different names. Between them, the accounts included about 100 pictures, many of girls from the local high school, Louisa County High, in central Virginia. Some shots he later described to me as merely "inappropriate," meaning girls "scantily clad in a bra and panties, maybe in a suggestive pose." But some "really got us"—high-school girls masturbating, and then one picture showing a girl having sex with three boys at once.

Lowe has lived in Louisa County, or pretty close to it, for most of his life. The county is spread out and rural, but it is by no means small-town innocent. People there deal drugs and get caught up with gangs, and plenty of high-school girls end up pregnant. Usually Lowe can more or less classify types in his head—which kids from which families might end up in trouble after a drunken fight in the McDonald's parking lot. But this time the cast of characters was baffling. He knew many of the girls in the photos, knew their parents. A few were 14, from the local middle school. They came from "all across the board," Lowe says. "Every race, religion, social, and financial status in the town. Rich, poor, everyone. That's what was most glaring and blaring about the situation. If she was a teenager with a phone, she was on there." He knew some of the boys who had followed the Instagram accounts, too. Among them were kids with a lot to lose, including star athletes with scholarships to first-rate colleges.

It seemed to Lowe, in those early days, as if something had gone seriously wrong under his nose, and that's how the media reported it: "Deputies Bust Massive Teen Sexting Ring in Louisa County," one headline said. The word *ring* stuck out, as if an organized criminal gang had been pimping out girls at the school. The Instagram accounts were quickly taken down, and Louisa County High School was transformed into a crime scene, which it remained for the next month. Police cars sat parked at the school's entrance, and inside, a few deputies who reported to Lowe began interviewing kids—starting with girls they recognized in the pictures and boys who had followed the accounts. Jasmine, who was a sophomore, was one of the first to be called in. She told them she'd originally sent the picture to a boy in 11th grade she'd known for a couple of years and really liked. They asked her whether she knew of anyone else at school who had nude pictures on their phone, and she told them she did. For the most part, the kids were "more than cooperative," Lowe says. One person would give up 10 names. The next would give up five, and so on.

But pretty soon this got to be a problem. Within an hour, the deputies realized just   5
how common the sharing of nude pictures was at the school. "The boys kept telling us, 'It's nothing unusual. It happens all the time,'" Lowe recalls. Every time someone they were interviewing mentioned another kid who might have naked pictures on his or her phone, they had to call that kid in for an interview. After just a couple of days, the deputies had filled multiple evidence bins with phones, and they couldn't see an end to it. Fears of a cabal got replaced by a more mundane concern: what to do with "hundreds of damned phones. I told the deputies, 'We got to draw the line somewhere or we're going to end up talking to every teenager in the damned county!'" Nor did the problem stop at the county's borders. Several boys, in an effort to convince Lowe that they hadn't been doing anything rare or deviant, showed him that he could type the hashtag symbol (#) into Instagram followed by the name of pretty much any nearby county and then *thots*, and find a similar account.

Most of the girls on Instagram fell into the same category as Jasmine. They had sent a picture to their boyfriend, or to someone they wanted to be their boyfriend, and then he had sent it on to others. For the most part, they were embarrassed but not devastated, Lowe said. They felt betrayed, but few seemed all that surprised that their photos had been passed around. What seemed to mortify them most was having to talk about what they'd done with a "police officer outside their age group." In some he sensed low self-esteem—for example, the girl who'd sent her naked picture to a boy, unsolicited: "It just showed up! I guess she was hot after him?" A handful of senior girls became indignant during the course of the interview. "This is my life and my body and I can do whatever I want with it," or, "I don't see any problem with it. I'm proud of my body," Lowe remembers them saying. A few, as far as he could tell, had taken pictures especially for the Instagram accounts and had actively tried to get them posted. In the first couple of weeks of the investigation, Lowe's characterization of the girls on Instagram morphed from "victims" to "I guess I'll call them victims" to "they just fell into this category where they victimized themselves."

Lowe's team explained to both the kids pictured on Instagram and the ones with photos on their phones the serious legal consequences of their actions. Possessing or sending a nude photo of a minor—even if it's a photo of yourself—can be prosecuted as a felony under state child-porn laws. He explained that 10 years down the road they might be looking for a job or trying to join the military, or sitting with their families at church, and the pictures could wash back up; someone who had the pictures might even try to blackmail them. And yet the kids seemed strikingly blasé. "They're just sitting there thinking, *Wah, wah, wah,*" Lowe said, turning his hands into flapping lips. "It's not sinking in. Remember at that age, you think you're invincible, and you're going to do whatever the hell you want to do? We just couldn't get them past that."

After a week's immersive education on the subject, Donald Lowe found himself just where the rest of the nation's law-enforcement community—and much of the nation—is on the subject of teen sexting: totally confused. Were the girls being exploited? Or were they just experimenting? Was sexting harming the kids? And if so, why didn't they seem to care? An older man with whom Lowe was acquainted stopped him at the grocery store to tell him, "That's child porn, and you ought to lock those people up for a long time." But Lowe didn't want to charge kids "just for being stupid," he told me later. "We don't want to label them as child molesters."

> **Were the girls being exploited?**
> **Or were they just experimenting?**
> **Was sexting harming the kids?**
> **And if so, why didn't they seem to care?**

As soon as teenagers got cameraphones, they began using them to send nude selfies to one another, without thinking or caring that a naked picture of a minor, unleashed into the world, can set off explosions. And while adults send naked pictures too, of course, the speed with which teens have incorporated the practice into their mating rituals has taken society by surprise. I'd heard about the Louisa County sexting scandal in the news. It seemed like a good case study—the place is traditional but not isolated; it has annual beauty queens and football pageantry on a *Friday Night Lights* scale, and also many residents who work in Richmond, the state capital. I spent several weeks in and around the county this spring and summer talking to kids, parents, police officers, and lawmakers, trying to understand how officials sort through such a mess of a case. Maybe more important, I wanted to understand how teens themselves think about sexting—why they send naked pictures and what they hope to get in return; how much or how little sexting has to do with actual sex. My hope was to help figure out how parents and communities should respond. Because so often in sexting cases that go public, we adults inadvertently step into the role of Freddy Krueger, making teenage nightmares come true: We focus on all the wrong things; we overreact. Sometimes we create an even bigger disaster.

When I asked the kids from Louisa County High School, which has about 1,450 students, how many people they knew who had sexted, a lot of them answered "everyone." (Throughout this article, I will use *sexting* to mean the transmission of provocative selfies you wouldn't want your mother to see—not words, but pictures.) A few of the 30 or so kids I talked with said 80 percent or 60 percent, and no one said fewer than half. Kids, however, are known to exaggerate. Surveys on sexting have found pretty

10

consistently that among kids in their upper teens, about a third have sexted, making the practice neither "universal" nor "vanishingly rare," as Elizabeth Englander, a psychology professor at Bridgewater State University, writes, but common enough in a teenager's life to be familiar. A recent study of seven public high schools in East Texas, for example, found that 28 percent of sophomores and juniors had sent a naked picture of themselves by text or e-mail, and 31 percent had asked someone to send one.

The general public was first forced to contemplate teen sexting in 2009, when a scandal in rural Pennsylvania's Tunkhannock Area High School, similar to the school in Louisa County, made national news. By that point, the great majority of teens had cellphones—71 percent, almost the same percentage as adults. The National Campaign to Prevent Teen and Unplanned Pregnancy and CosmoGirl.com had just conducted the first public survey on sexting among teens and young adults, showing that, much to parents' chagrin, the practice was fairly common. In the Pennsylvania case, the local district attorney threatened to bring child-pornography charges against girls who showed up in the pictures, which was widely considered overkill. It "makes as much sense as charging a kid who brings a squirt gun to school with possession of an unlicensed firearm," wrote a columnist for the *Pittsburgh Post-Gazette*. Lawmakers around the country began searching for a better alternative.

"I really don't like the word *sexting*," says Michael Harmony, the commander of the southern-Virginia branch of the Internet Crimes Against Children Task Force, which covers Louisa County. The term he makes his investigators use is *self-production*, which is law-enforcement-speak for when minors produce pictures of themselves that qualify as child porn. But changing the term doesn't clarify much. Whether you call it self-production or sexting, it comes in too many forms to pin down. Harmony has dealt with a 13-year-old who posted her naked picture on MeetMe.com and had grown men show up at her house. He's investigated a 17-year-old boy who blackmailed a girl into sending him naked pictures, and another boy who threatened to send out the naked pictures a girl had given him if she didn't have sex with him. Lately, though, Harmony's office has been flooded with cases like the one in Louisa County, generating bins filled with cellphones that his investigators have to go through one by one.

Since 2009, state legislatures have tried to help guide law enforcement by passing laws specifically addressing sexting. At least 20 states have passed such laws, most of which establish a series of relatively light penalties. In Florida, for example, a minor who is guilty of transmitting or distributing a nude photograph or video must pay a fine, complete community service, or attend a class on sexting. A second offense is a misdemeanor and a third is a felony. Where they've been passed, the new laws have helpfully taken ordinary teen sexting out of the realm of child pornography and provided prosecutors with a gentler alternative. But they have also created deeper cultural confusion, by codifying into law the idea that *any* kind of sexting between minors is a crime. For the most part, the laws do not concern themselves with whether a sext was voluntarily shared between two people who had been dating for a year or was sent under pressure: a sext is a sext. So as it stands now, in most states it is perfectly legal for two 16-year-olds to have sex. But if they take pictures, it's a matter for the police.

Five years after the sexting scandal in Pennsylvania, cases still arise that betray shockingly little clarity about who should count as the perpetrator and who the victim. In another Pennsylvania case this year, two popular girls persuaded an autistic boy to share a picture of his penis with them, then forwarded the picture to a wide circle of schoolmates. The district attorney decided to go after the boy, according to Witold Walczak, the legal director of the ACLU of Pennsylvania, which intervened in the case. A recent study published in *Pediatrics* broke down how police departments handle "youth-produced sexual images." About two-thirds of the cases that have received police attention involved "aggravating circumstances," meaning an adult was involved, or one teen had blackmailed or sexually abused another, or had "recklessly circulated" the image without the person's consent. The remaining third were what the authors, who are associated with the Crimes Against Children Research Center, defined as having "no malicious elements"; those "may best be viewed as adolescent sexual experimentation." Nonetheless, in 18 percent of those cases, police departments reported making an arrest.

Virginia is not one of the states that has passed specific teen-sexting laws, and so Major Lowe was looking, potentially, at hundreds of felonies. Every boy who had a photo on his phone, every girl who'd snapped one of herself—all could be prosecuted as felons and sex offenders. If Lowe made an arrest, the case would land with Rusty McGuire, the main prosecutor for Louisa County. McGuire wouldn't talk with me about this situation specifically, but he expressed his concern more generally about nude pictures of minors landing in the wrong hands: "What do you do? Turn a blind eye? You're letting teenagers incite the prurient interest of predators around the country," fueling a demand that "can only be met by the actual abuse of real children." 15

McGuire has successfully prosecuted several actual pedophiles over the years, including a local man who had posed as a teenage girl on Facebook and solicited young boys for sex, and another man—a trusted teacher—who had been part of a ring whose members offered up their own children to other members for sex. When he talks about the awful details of these crimes, it's hard to get them out of your head. The Virginia legislature has long failed to pass a sexting law largely for fear of being soft on child porn, says Dave Albo, the chairman of the state Courts of Justice committee. Still, the absence of any obvious lesser alternative put Lowe in a difficult spot. "They're not violent criminals," he told me. "If these kids just made a dumb-ass mistake, we don't want to ruin their future."

"She's a whore. I've totally heard that she's a whore."

That comment came quickly, from a senior girl whose style was generally more refined. "She" was Briana, a sophomore softball player who, in school lore, was the one who'd started all the trouble.

"I have to show you something." Briana's friend had stopped her between classes one day and showed her a picture on Instagram, the same morning Jennifer, Jasmine's mom, contacted the police. It was a picture of a pair of breasts, and Briana, who is now a junior, recognized them as her own. Pretty much anyone at the high school would have. She was the only girl who had so many freckles going down her shoulders and arms, and it didn't take too much imagination to guess where else. Briana went to a young teacher she trusted. "I said, 'There's this picture of me up on Instagram.'" The teacher informed the principal, who eventually called the police. No one at school knew that Jennifer had already reported the account that morning.

While police were calling kids into a makeshift interview room at the high school, [20] one by one, a more unruly drama was unfolding in the hallways. Because the Instagram accounts had been up for only a short time, not everyone had seen them. Rumors spread about which girls had appeared in photos and what they'd been doing. One was supposedly making out with her sister (not true). Another was "messing with, like 10, 15 dudes" (also not true). A group of sociologists led by Elizabeth Armstrong has studied the class dynamics of the term *slut* as used by young college women. High-status women from affluent homes associate *slut* with women they call "trashy" and not "classy." To women from working-class families, upper-class women are "rich bitches in sororities"—whom they also commonly think of as sluts. The girl who called Briana a whore is a potential future sorority-chapter president. She and several other more affluent students described everyone associated with the Instagram accounts to me as "ghetto," which in this context had mild racial connotations but generally stands for "trashy" or "the lower crowd." The role of ultimate, quintessential slut fell to a "redneck" girl who appeared on Instagram. In the post-sexting-scandal lore, she "supposedly slept with her brother" (surely not true).

To the elite girls, the girls on Instagram were sluts not necessarily because they were sleeping around but because of what they looked like or how they acted. "Let's just say people have different body types," one girl told me. Others, speaking about girls in the photos, said, "You obviously have a little too much confidence," or just "Butter face" (as in: nice body, but her face . . .). In their college study, Armstrong and her team identify this brand of sniping as a way girls police one another and establish a sort of moral superiority without denying themselves actual sex, and something similar seemed to be happening here. Well-off, popular girls were most certainly in the Instagram photos, but none would admit as much unless I knew otherwise. Briana was, in many ways, on the opposite end of the spectrum—she lacked that kind of standing, and, because she had gone to the principal, she was the girl most widely associated with the accounts, and therefore the main character in the morality tale that was being stitched together between classes.

I met Briana in early June, just after school had ended. She was in a summer program for geometry remediation because she'd gotten a C in math. She told me that she had ADD and took Adderall, and that she loved history but hated math with a passion. "I don't know. I try hard. I'm just more into sports." On the day we met, she wore a purple tank top and not-too-tight shorts, and her long hair was down. She had a sunburn on her shoulders that was bothering her a little. She told me she ran track and played volleyball and softball. Mostly she seemed nervous and eager to please—"No, ma'am." "Yes, ma'am"—and to make me understand that she was not a bare-your-breasts kind of girl.

"Just let me see them, please?" She texted back, "No," she told me. He was a junior, one year ahead of her. She didn't consider him her boyfriend, just someone she talked with at school sometimes. Plus she felt "self-conscious." Briana is tall and fit but doesn't exude that sexy sheen some high-school girls do. He asked a dozen more times, in different ways, and one night the text came as she was getting out of the shower. "What are you doing?" he texted. "I just got out of the shower and I'm about to go to sleep." "Send me a picture, PLEASE." She caved. She sent it over Snapchat and said he had to let it erase right away. He said he did.

For days after the investigation began, Briana felt that people were staring at her, talking about her, blaming her for the fact that the high school seemed like a prison, or that they were being hauled into a police interview, or—worst of all—that they had to hide their phones or have them confiscated for God knows how long. "It was getting 10 times bigger," she told me. "As each day went by, more phones were being taken. It all went really, really fast—way faster than I expected." Sometimes her friends would tell her, "Hey, they were talking about you in second period."

Briana was prepared for part of the reaction: that everyone would think "if I show   25 my boobs then that means I would do anything." But the worst part was "everyone calling me a snitch. Everybody, like, hated me because they knew I had told. It was so bad that I didn't want to go to school."

Briana and Jasmine are friends, and the day after the police arrived, Jasmine also wanted to stay home from school. She had sobbed and thrown up when she saw her photo on Instagram. But Jennifer wouldn't let her stay home. In fact, she told her daughter she would be punished if she cried in school or showed in any way that she was upset: "They already got a piece of you," Jennifer told her. "Don't let them get any more." So Jasmine stayed stone-faced, and nobody said a thing to her. The future sorority girl told me she'd caught Jasmine's eye that first week and thought, "She must be thinking, *You've seen me naked*," but she also noted that Jasmine didn't betray anything. "She was just walking around the school as if nothing happened."

Briana was not so lucky. The incident always seemed to be there, at school and at home. When she and her mother were watching TV and a romantic or sexual scene came on, her mother would leave the room. During arguments she'd say, "You have no reason to have an attitude after everything you've done." One time, after her younger sister had misbehaved, her mom yelled, "Don't end up like your sister!" while Briana stood close by. (Her mother later apologized.) Briana told me she has tried to make amends. She cleans up the kitchen every night after dinner, cleans the bathrooms. "Some days we're okay, and some days I think it's all she thinks about. She sent me a note: 'I still think of you as my little girl.' I understand where she's coming from. But I'm not a little girl. I think she hasn't accepted the fact that I've grown up yet."

About a month after the investigation, Briana got into a fight with a boy on the bus. She was still "stressed out," she said, and he kept singing a song she found annoying, and she asked him to please stop. He told her, "Nobody even wants you here" and called her a bitch, and she said, "I'm gonna beat the effing crap out of you," and she hit him, and got suspended for three days. Those happened to be the days of softball tryouts, so she almost didn't make the team. Then, when the coach did let her join the team, a teammate accused Briana of putting her college scholarship in jeopardy because her phone had been confiscated and maybe the school would rescind its offer. Briana used to babysit for one of the teacher's kids, "but then his wife wouldn't have anything to do with me."

Studies on high-school kids' general attitudes about sexting turn up what you'd expect—that is, the practice inspires a maddening, ancient, crude double standard. Researchers from the University of Michigan recently surveyed a few dozen teenagers in urban areas. Boys reported receiving sexts from girls "I know I can get it from" and said that sexting is "common only for girls with slut reputations." But the boys also said that girls who don't sext are "stuck up" or "prude." The boys themselves, on the other hand, were largely immune from criticism, whether they sexted or not.

Sometimes in Louisa County, between interviews, I hung out with a group of 15-year-old boys who went to the library after school. They seemed like good kids who studied, played football, and occasionally got into fights, but no more than most boys. They'd watch videos of rappers from the area and talk about rumors in the rap world, like the one that the Chicago rapper Chief Keef, a rival of D.C.'s Shy Glizzy, had gotten a middle-school girl pregnant. They'd order and split a pizza to pass the time while waiting for their parents to leave work and pick them up. I started to think of them as the high school's Greek chorus because, while I recognized much of what they said as 15-year-old-boy swagger—designed to impress me and each other, and not necessarily true—they still channeled the local sentiment. This is how one of them described his game to me: "A lot of girls, they stubborn, so you gotta work on them. You say, 'I'm trying to get serious with you.' You call them beautiful. You say, 'You know I love you.' You think about it at night, and then you wake up in the morning and you got a picture in your phone."

"You wake up a happy man," his friend said.

"Yeah, a new man."

"Yeah, I'm the man."

How do you feel about the girl after she sends it?, I asked.

"Super thots."

"You can't love those thots!"

"That's right, you can't love those hos."

"Girls in Louisa are easy."

And thus it was with Briana and her seducer: "He was a jerk. He didn't talk to me anymore. And he just flirted with other girls."

Why do kids sext? One recent graduate told me that late at night, long after dinner and homework, her parents would watch TV and she would be in her room texting with her boyfriend. "You have a beautiful body," he'd write. "Can I see it?" She knew it would be hard for him to ever really see it. She had a strict curfew and no driver's license yet, and Louisa County is too spread out for kids to get anywhere on their own without a car.

"I live literally in the middle of nowhere," the girl told me. "And this boy I dated lived like 30 minutes away. I didn't have a car and my parents weren't going to drop me off, so we didn't have any alone time. Our only way of being alone was to do it over the phone. It was a way of kind of dating without getting in trouble. A way of being sexual without being sexual, you know? And it was his way of showing he liked me a lot and my way of saying I trusted him."

In the Texas high-school study, boys and girls were equally likely to have sent a sext, but girls were much more likely to have been asked to—68 percent had been. Plenty of girls just laugh off the requests. When a boy asked Olivia, who graduated last year from Louisa County High, "What are you wearing?," she told me she wrote back, "Stinky track shorts and my virginity rocks T-shirt." A boy asked another student for a picture, so she sent him a smiling selfie. "I didn't mean your face," he wrote back, so she sent him one of her foot. But boys can be persistent—like, 20-or-30-texts-in-a-row persistent. "If we were in a dark room, what would we do?" "I won't show it to anyone else." "You're only sending it to me." "I'll delete it right after."

When surveyed, by far the most common reason kids give for sexting is that their boyfriend or girlfriend wanted the picture, and my interviews in Louisa County support that. In a study of 18-year-olds by Elizabeth Englander, 77 percent said the picture they sent caused no problems for them. The most common outcome of a sext, says Englander, is "nothing": no loss, no gain. Most girls (70 percent) reported feeling some pressure to sext, but Englander singles out a distinct minority (12 percent) she calls the "pressured sexters," who say they sexted only because they felt pressure. These girls are more vulnerable. They tend to start sexting at a younger age, and to sext because they think they can get a boyfriend, as opposed to because they already have one. They have a fantasy that "if they sext, the popular people will see them as daring and self-confident, and they could get a boyfriend they wouldn't otherwise have gotten," Englander says. But generally that doesn't work out. Pressured sexters are much more apt to feel worse after sexting than other teens are—her interviews reveal them to be less self-confident about their bodies and less assured about their place in the social hierarchy after sending a sext.

> **Pressured sexters are much more apt to feel worse after sexting than other teens are.**

One recent study found that young adults who engaged in sexting were more likely to report recent substance abuse and high-risk sexual behavior, like unprotected sex or sex with multiple partners. Another found exactly the opposite, that "sexting is not related to sexual risk behavior or psychological well-being." In Englander's study, many of the worrisome behaviors associated with sexting showed up more in those who had been pressured. They were more likely, for example, to engage in a practice researchers call self-cyberbullying, a disturbing phenomenon in which teens post mean things about themselves on social-media sites, usually to get sympathy or attention. Pressured sexters were also more likely to have had problems with sexual violence in dating.

A consistent finding is that sexting is a pretty good indicator of actual sexual activity. This year, researchers in Los Angeles published a study of middle-schoolers showing that those who sent sexts were 3.2 times more likely to be sexually active than those who didn't. A story in the *Los Angeles Times* described the study as proof that "sexting is not a harmless activity." But in fact the findings seem a little obvious. Since most kids who sext report doing so in the context of a relationship, it makes sense that sex and sexting would go together. As Amy Hasinoff, the author of the forthcoming book *Sexting Panic: Rethinking Criminalization, Privacy, and Consent*, points out, "Sexting *is* a form of sexual activity," not a gateway to it.

But kids also sext, or ask for a sext, or gossip about sexting, for reasons only loosely related to sex. A recent *New York Times* story explored the practice of "vamping," or staying up after midnight to check in with friends online. The kids in Louisa County, like kids everywhere, are chronically overscheduled. They stay late at school to play sports or to take part in other after-school activities, then go home and do their homework. Nighttime is the only time teens get to have intimate conversations and freely navigate their social world, argues Danah Boyd, the author of *It's Complicated: The Social Lives of Networked Teens*. For the Louisa County kids, that means checking up

45

on the latest drama on Twitter—"Anyone still awake?" is a common post-midnight tweet—and filling up their Instagram accounts, or asking a girl for a pic.

In the vast majority of cases, the picture lands only where it was meant to. Surveys consistently show that very few recipients share explicit selfies—without the sender's consent. Englander's surveys show that pictures resulting from pressure are much more likely to be shared, and that rarely ends well. In the worst-case scenario, the girl is devastated, and in rare instances takes drastic action. In 2008, Jessica Logan committed suicide after her nude photo circulated around her Ohio town, and there have been several similar suicide cases since then. A few people in Louisa County recalled the time a popular, pretty girl at school sent a picture to her boyfriend that he then sent out to his friends, and "by second period," according to Olivia, "she was so upset that the guidance counselor had to send her home." But mostly, even a picture that's shared without consent travels between just two or three cellphones, and plays only a fleeting role in the drama of coming of age.

"The only reason to regret it is if you get caught," one girl told me. And while getting caught—by parents, teachers, future employers—is no joke, police departments would still do well to remember that. Whether a sext qualifies as relatively safe sexual experimentation or a disaster often depends on who finds out about it. Marsha Levick, a co-founder of the nonprofit Juvenile Law Center, sees many cases where the police investigation does much more harm than the incident itself. "The rush to prosecute always baffles me," she says. "It's the exponential humiliation of these boys, or more often girls, in an official setting, knowing their photos will be shown to police officers and judges and probation officers. And the reality is, a lot of these officials are going to be men. That process itself is what's traumatizing."

About a month into the investigation, Donald Lowe concluded that the wide phone-collection campaign had added up to one massive distraction. Yes, the girls who appeared on Instagram had done something technically illegal by sending naked photos of themselves. But charging them for that crime didn't make any sense. "They thought they were doing it privately," he told me, reaching much the same conclusion as Levick. "We're not helping them at all by labeling them at an early age." Lowe recalled to me a girl in his own high-school class who had developed a reputation as "the county slut, and it took her years and years to overcome that." These girls didn't need their names in the paper to boot.

By June, Lowe had made the decision to wipe the photos off most of the phones and 50 return them to the girls, and most of the boys, with a warning: "We don't want to put anything on your record, but the next time we come around, we're not going to be so nice about it." He held on to a few phones and got search warrants for a few more, and began to focus on what seemed more like the actual crime: the posting of explicit photos without consent on Instagram.

Within the first day or two of the investigation, Lowe had developed a pretty good suspicion of who was behind that. A few of the boys he talked to—and a couple of girls as well—had told him they'd sent photos directly to boys who they thought had set up the accounts. A few others had sent them to a go-between, but still had a decent idea of who was setting up the accounts. The organizers had apparently spent weeks gathering photos. They said they would open the accounts only when they had a lot of pictures in hand, and that anyone who sent one in would be guaranteed access. Lowe wasn't sure whether it was just a couple of boys working together or with a slightly larger group of accomplices. His investigators subpoenaed Instagram for the IP address of the accounts' originating computer, but because of a technical aberration, that turned out to be inconclusive. He continued to search for other, solid evidence.

Lowe would not confirm to me the identity of the main suspects in the investigation, but according to some of the kids and parents, they are two brothers—one a student at the school, one a recent graduate. One was a troublemaker known for hitting people on the bus, and the other a popular kid. One was under 18 and the other over, meaning that if they were charged, they could be subject to very different legal treatment. The key would be to figure out their intent—were the boys trying to make porn available to adults, or was it a "me and my buddies want to collect a bunch of pictures" kind of deal?

Lowe strongly suspected the latter, that this was about "raging hormones and bragging." Kids, after all, described the accounts to him, and to me, as "funny," "just something to laugh at," "just a bunch of friends sitting around having a laugh." If that were true, at least for any minors involved, a child-porn charge seemed too "Big Brother" to Lowe, and he and the local prosecutor might want to come up with a lesser charge or even no charge at all, especially because the account had been closed down so quickly and had been seen by relatively few people, limiting potential harm. But largely because of community pressures, he had to consider the possibility that he'd just discovered "the tip of an iceberg of some organized-crime thing."

In late July, rumors were spreading among parents that the boys who had set up the Instagram accounts might be part of a gang. There had been some prominent gang activity in the area lately, and one local crew had been involved in the shooting of a cop. Maybe these gangs were also involved in child trafficking; maybe they would use the young girls' pictures as an advertisement to lure johns. There was no evidence at all that whoever was behind the accounts was part of a gang, or that local gangs were involved in sex trafficking. In fact the theory seemed pretty far-fetched. But the mere mention of it was enough for Lowe to say—or feel pressured to say—that he couldn't "rule it out." At the time of this writing, in mid-September, the investigation was ongoing.

Many teen-sexting cases are aggravated by vague fears of predation and pedophilia, at times creating irresistible momentum. But "the conjecture that the Internet or sexting has increased the number of molesters or their motivation to offend has not really been supported by the evidence," says David Finkelhor, who runs the Crimes Against Children Research Center. In fact, all of the evidence suggests that child molesting and sex offenses in general have declined over the period in which sexting has become popular, Finkelhor says. His group analyzed seven major sources of data about violence against children and found large declines in sexual abuse of children since the early 1990s. From 2003 to 2011, a span that coincides almost exactly with the rise of sexting, sexual-victimization rates of minors declined by 25 percent. Finkelhor cites a handful of possible factors but, ironically, one is that kids have started to do their "risk taking" and "independence testing" online, which could minimize their exposure to actual violence and physical harm.

Cases that turn up genuine signs of child pornography should of course be investigated and prosecuted to the full extent of the law. But child-porn laws are designed explicitly to protect children from adults. Cases involving only minors fall into a different category, and deserve entirely different labels and punishments—or no punishments. Getting these standards right is important, because the investigation itself causes its own trauma, because not every law-enforcement officer is as considered as Donald Lowe, and because something that a third of older teenagers do routinely shouldn't remain a crime, much less a crime on the order of child porn.

> **[S]omething that a third of older teenagers do routinely shouldn't remain a crime, much less a crime on the order of child porn.**

Many legal-reform advocates say the key is to distinguish between voluntarily sharing a photo and having it shared without your consent. "We should draw the line between my daughter stupidly sending a photo of herself to her boyfriend and her boyfriend sending it to all his friends to humiliate her," Levick, of the Juvenile Law Center, told *Slate* last year. "The first is stupid. The second is more troubling and should be criminal." Levick's group has been trying for years to get states to recognize the difference between sexting that's part of normal sexual exploration and sexting that's coercive or violates privacy.

And yet few lawmakers are willing to concede that naked pictures of teenagers, even if voluntarily shared, are in any way acceptable. As Levick says, "I think this is coming from grown-ups who fear that their kids are doing things they don't understand. The technology is both hyper-visible and invisible, and parents are spooked by it. So kids are finding what's a normal part of adolescent experimentation being criminalized."

In cases involving only minors, the poles at either end of the continuum of all that a sext can represent seem pretty clear. Uploading another minor's naked picture to the Web, where anyone might eventually find it, should be a criminal act, though not one that should necessarily be prosecuted as child porn. Taking a selfie and sending it to someone who might be receptive to it, or receiving a selfie and keeping it, should not be criminal at all. What's in between—such as forwarding a selfie to one or 10 friends without consent—is more difficult. In Louisa County, the deputies gave an especially stern lecture to the boys they sensed had solicited pictures so they could forward them on to friends, taking advantage of the vulnerability of certain girls. The nonconsensual sharing of pictures, even among just a few people, should probably count as a criminal act, as long as there is prosecutorial discretion. But even in these instances, the policing should, if possible, be left to teachers and parents, not to the actual police. Or in some cases to no one, because since when was any version of adolescent sexuality fair and free of pain?

Shortly before the police got involved in Louisa County, Ryan, a quiet junior known as   60
a math whiz, received the picture of Briana's breasts from a friend at the beginning of lunch. "Guess who ??? wht do u think?" Throughout the whole afternoon, he could not get the photo out of his head: the size and shape of the breasts—which he described, improbably, as floating "like the Nerf ball I once threw too far into the waves"—and

also all the freckles, suggesting summer and romantic surprises. Ryan had only one other similar photo, which a generous friend had sent his way. But being out of that game, as he saw it, had its advantages. He was free of the never-ending status competition at school—who had a new picture, who had the most, who had one no one else could get—and could just let his imagination wander.

He waited until late at night, when his mom was watching TV, to look at the photo again. Seated on his bed, he pulled out his phone. The first thing he noticed was that his battery bar was red. Now there was the problem of finding the power cord, and stretching it as far as the center of the bed. He noticed a text from his coach—had he forgotten a practice? Was there some piece of equipment he had to remember to bring in the next day? Finally he pulled up the picture. He knew Briana; he'd helped her with math once. And he couldn't get the image of the girl sitting in class, puzzling over a problem, out of his head. He suddenly felt guilty, and also—because he'd heard about some boys collecting photos for an Instagram account—a little afraid. He hesitated, and then deleted the picture and got up to retrieve his laptop. He opened the first free porn site that popped into his head and typed in *milf*. Immediately, dozens of images flirted for his attention. He considered one in the second row, but then scrolled down a little further to find a curvier type, although a few weeks later, when he was recounting the moment to me, he couldn't remember any other details beyond "long brown hair" and "big boobs."

Briana's parents—and Briana herself—would probably be creeped out if they knew how this scene had played out. And most parents would be upset if they learned that a naked picture of their daughter had showed up on a boy's phone, even if he did delete it. But that such a photo should come to light doesn't mean the girl and the boy are having sex, or that the boy is a stalker, or that the photo is going to show up on the Web.

Outside of actual romantic relationships, sexts usually seem to play a very minimal role in anyone's sex life. In *Thy Neighbor's Wife*, Gay Talese's 1981 book about the sexual revolution, a teenage boy spends hours looking at his favorite picture in a photographic-art magazine, treating the image with an archivist's care. But the high-school boys I spoke with barely glance at the sexts they receive. They gloat inwardly or brag to friends; they store them in special apps or count them. But actual fantasies come from porn, freely and widely available on the Internet. "Guys would pile them up," one girl who had graduated a year earlier told me, referring to sexts they'd gotten. "It was more of a baseball-card, showing-off kind of thing." Olivia described it as "like when they were little boys, playing with Pokémon cards."

So how should parents think about sexting, especially when their daughters are involved? The research suggests that if your child is sexting but not yet in high school, you should worry more. And that you should do the same if your daughter has no real relationship with the boy she's sending sexts to, but is pursuing a relationship, or just responding to repeated requests for a photo. Sexts don't create sexual dynamics; they reveal them. Parents should use the opportunity to find out what those dynamics are, lest they accidentally make things worse.

What bothered Jennifer, Jasmine's mother, about her daughter's picture was not that her little girl was all grown up. It was the awkwardness of her daughter's pose, the fact that she had to be really talked into sending that photo. Jennifer fits no one's image of a perfect mother. As a kid, she had done drugs and gotten into fights and had a baby at 15. But life experience has made her a very perceptive parent. Another one of her daughters, who is two years younger than Jasmine, "is rebellious as hell. If she sent a picture, it's because she damn well wanted to. She'd be like, *snap, snap,* 'This is me,' all over the place. If she didn't want to, she'd send a picture of a cat and say, 'That's the only pussy you're gonna get!' But this one"—meaning Jasmine—"she's a pushover. She would do anything for anybody. Even with stupid things, like her sister asks her to fold the laundry even though she folded the last 20 loads, and she'll say, 'Sure.' It *infuriates* me. Girl, stand up for yourself! You should do something because you want to do it, not because somebody pushed you into it."

Danah Boyd, the author of *It's Complicated*, often talks about social media as a window into the teenage world. A parent who reacts purely by scaling up the restrictions is missing a chance to know what's actually going on with their child, to know things that in previous eras would have stayed hidden from them. In her talks, Boyd advises parents not to, for example, shut down accounts. Kids will just find ways to open new ones under names that have nothing to do with their real ones, that their parents could never track, or they will migrate to new platforms. (Many of the kids I met in Louisa County used inventive, inscrutable names for their Instagram accounts, names only their peers knew about.) Instead, parents should take a deep breath—even in the most uncomfortable scenarios—and ask questions. Kids can have a million motivations to send a naked picture of themselves, and unless you ask, you won't know whether the one that was in their head seems more like reasonable experimentation or something else.

A recent review of 10 official sexting-education campaigns concluded that all of them erred on the side of what the researchers called "abstinence"—that is, advising teens not to sext at all. These tend to link sexting tightly to ruinous consequences, but that's a problem, because ruination doesn't normally follow the sending of a sext. "If we present it as inevitable, then we've lost our audience," says Elizabeth Englander, who leads groups about sexting in middle and high schools, "because they know very well that in the vast majority of cases it doesn't happen." If you say otherwise, "then the kids know immediately that you don't know anything."

In the vast majority of cases, the picture lands only where it was meant to. But pictures sent as a result of pressure are much more likely to be shared, and that rarely ends well.

Instead, Englander eases kids into the dangers slowly. She usually starts out by talking about how in life, it's sensible to avoid risk. You wear a seat belt even though the chances of a fatal crash are slim. This way, she says, the kids understand that she knows the risks of a picture getting out are rare, but they also understand that if it does get out, the effects on their social life and future could be catastrophic. She gets the kids talking about why they send the pictures, so she can narrow in on the more risky situations she has identified from her research—namely, ones involving lots of pressure and very little trust.

Teens in Louisa County, like teens everywhere, hear a lot about sex, but really know only a little about it. Briana's Twitter feed is a mix of little-girl cute and grown-woman sexy: a fuzzy kitten, inspirational quotes from Athletes for Christ, an ass in a bow thong. Any senior at Louisa County High School can tick off the names of girls who got pregnant in the past year. But the kids in Louisa County are also part of a 70 generation that's seen teen pregnancy decline to a record low. Teens are waiting longer to have sex than they did in the recent past. The majority now report that their first sexual experience was with a steady partner. Given how inundated and unfazed they are by sexual imagery, perhaps the best hope is that one day, in the distant future, a naked picture of a girl might simply lose its power to humiliate.

In late August, about two weeks after the new school year started, Rusty McGuire, the Louisa County prosecutor, gave an evening community presentation at the middle school about sexting. He cited statistics showing how popular it was and explained that under Virginia's child-porn laws, it was a serious crime. However, he acknowledged that sternly explaining to kids that it's illegal or has long-term consequences "isn't working." As an alternative, he suggested humor, and showed a campaign called "Give It a Ponder," run by LG. The series involves the actor James Lipton pinning a beard on kids who are about to sext, so they pause for a sober second thought, and it is, indeed, pretty funny. But only about a dozen parents and kids were there to see it.

Instead, the entire community seemed to be outside on the vast fields near the high school and middle school, seduced by the Thursday-night pause before the first home football game of the season, which would take place the next night. The sun was dropping and taking the worst of the August heat. Little kids were kicking up dirt on the baseball field or practicing their cheerleading ("Time to get loud! Time to represent!"). Parents were leaning against their bumpers drinking water or soda, and teenagers were using their bodies in ways the parents could admire: slamming into tackling dummies at the final pregame practice, doing sumo squats, running around the track.

Briana was there; her volleyball team had just won its game in three sets. "New me, new life, gotta get my shit together," she'd retweeted before the start of school. Her profile picture showed her in a bikini, but she was staying clear of trouble. So far she'd earned all A's. Her mom was trusting her to get her learner's permit and even asked her why she'd decided to go to homecoming with a friend instead of a boyfriend. ("That's the last thing on my mind," she'd replied.) Coming out of the gym after the game, she and her friends were as loud and boisterous as the football players who were psyching themselves up for the following night's game. A mom came up and pinched her butt: "Good job, Bri!" Nearby, a boy and a girl from school were enacting an airport-worthy goodbye.

Briana and two teammates leaned into each other and took a picture. "Photobomb!" a boy yelled behind them, but they barely paid him any attention. It was just another picture, and this one was theirs.

Exploring Context

1. Instagram (instagram.com) is the app used in the sexting scandal at the center of Rosin's essay. Explore the app or its Web site. You might want to visit the site's support and privacy pages in particular. How does Instagram respond to abuse? How does the app's design and function lend itself to the kinds of abuse noted by Rosin?

2. Use the Web to research teen sexting laws for your state. Are there laws that specifically address this issue? Do they distinguish between teen and adult sexting? What would happen in your state if there were an incident like the one in Louisa County?

3. Briana sent a sext using the app Snapchat (snapchat.com). Explore the Web site for this app. Does it reflect an awareness of the ways in which the app can be abused?

Questions for Connecting

1. In "From Civil Rights to Megachurches" (p. 86), Charles Duhigg suggests that peer pressure and both strong and weak ties are important tools for social change. But might these same forces be destructive? Apply Rosin's analysis to Duhigg's argument. How did peer pressure and strong and weak ties contribute to the Louisa Country sexting incident? Consider using your work from Question 3 of Questions for Critical Reading.

2. Kwame Anthony Appiah, in "Making Conversation" and "The Primacy of Practice" (p. 40), discusses some ways in which cultural practices change. Using his ideas and examples, propose solutions we might pursue for the problem of teen sexting culture. How might we encourage this practice to change? What social forces would be needed for it to change? Your work in Question 3 of Questions for Critical Reading might help.

3. Technology plays a significant role in Rosin's essay. Using Chuck Klosterman's discussion of technology and villainy in "Electric Funeral" (p. 224), examine the ways in which attitudes toward technology contribute to the sexting problem that Rosin examines.

Language Matters

1. Locate a key passage from Rosin's text and then revise the quotation you've selected using more informal language or slang. How does this revision change the meaning of the quotation? What audience would be most receptive to your revision? Why did Rosin choose the tone she used in this essay, and what tone might you choose in your own writing for this class?

2. *Sexting* is a relatively new word. Using a grammar handbook, reference source, or the Web, research neologisms. How are new words created? When might you want to create terms in your own writing? What cultural forces enable new or slang words to enter common use?

3. Pictures of the girls in this essay were tagged on Instagram with a hashtag (#). What purpose do hashtags serve? How to they function? Develop a series of hashtags for this essay.

Assignments for Writing

1. Rosin notes the confusion caused by current laws governing teen sexting. How can we resolve this confusion? Write a paper in which you propose principles we could use to resolve the confusion around teen sexting. What role should law play? How might we shape cultural expectations around this practice? Is privacy a critical principle? Consent? Consider using your work from Question 3 of Questions for Critical Reading and Question 1 of Questions for Connecting.

2. Write a paper in which you trace the ways that technology shapes sexuality. Does sexting emerge from the technology that enables it or does that aspect of sexuality exist

independently of the technology? Draw from your work in Question 3 of Questions for Connecting.

3. Age has much to do with this texting controversy. Working from Rosin's discussion, write a paper in which you determine the key factors of adulthood. What makes an adult? How might that definition emerge from, resolve, or complicate a situation like the scandal in Louisa County?

DAN SAVAGE AND URVASHI VAID

Dan Savage is the cofounder of the It Gets Better Project, which focuses on preventing suicide among adolescents in the LGBT community. He is also the author of a weekly relationship and sex advice column titled "Savage Love" and the editorial director of the *Stranger*, a weekly Seattle newspaper. Savage is a frequent contributor to *This American Life*, *Out* magazine, and HBO's *Real Time with Bill Maher*. He is also the author of *Savage Love: Straight Answers from America's Most Popular Sex Columnist* (1998), *The Kid: What Happened after My Boyfriend and I Decided to Go Get Pregnant* (2000), *Skipping Towards Gomorrah* (2003), *The Commitment: Love, Sex, Marriage, and My Family* (2006), and *American Savage: Insights, Slights, and Fights on Faith, Sex, Love, and Politics* (2013). He and his husband, Terry Miller, edited a collection of essays titled *It Gets Better: Coming Out, Overcoming Bullying, and Creating a Life Worth Living* (2011).

Urvashi Vaid received her law degree from Northeastern University School of Law and is now an attorney, community activist, and writer. She directs the Engaging Tradition Project, located at the Center for Gender and Sexuality Law at Columbia University. Vaid is also the author of *Virtual Equality: The Mainstreaming of Gay & Lesbian Liberation* (1996) and *Irresistible Revolution* (2012), and she is coeditor of *Creating Change: Sexuality, Public Policy, and Civil Rights* (2000).

"A masterstroke…revolutionary."
—Armistead Maupin, author of *Tales of the City*

IT GETS BETTER

Coming Out, Overcoming Bullying, and Creating a Life Worth Living

Edited by DAN SAVAGE and TERRY MILLER

The It Gets Better Project was started in September of 2010 after the suicides of two teenagers who had been bullied because of their sexual orientation. The essays in *It Gets Better: Coming Out, Overcoming Bullying, and Creating a Life Worth Living* are inspired by the project and send messages of hope and encouragement to teenagers within the LGBT community who struggle to overcome bullying. Contributors to the collection include young adults who have overcome this struggle, civil rights activists, and even President Obama.

In his introduction to the book, retitled here "It Gets Better," Savage introduces the tragic deaths that spurred the project. He investigates the heart of the issue of bullying and the difficulties of putting an end to the problem. Perhaps most importantly, he addresses social activism and how it is crucial to making any progress in such a heartbreaking and complex issue. In her contribution to the collection, "Action Makes It Better," Vaid focuses on action and the ways in which advocating for change helps make lives better.

▶ TAGS: *adolescence and adulthood, civil rights, community, conversation, identity, photography and video, relationships, sexuality, social change, social media, trauma and violence*

▶ CONNECTIONS: *Fukuyama, Moalem, Rosin*

Questions for Critical Reading

1. Use both Savage's and Vaid's experiences to explain the claim "it gets better." What gets better? How? Mark passages that support your answer as you read the text.

2. What can be done about bullying? Locate strategies suggested by both Savage and Vaid. Is sending a video message the best response? What other options might we explore?

3. How do Savage's and Vaid's positions differ when it comes to making things better? As you read, locate passages that suggest those differences. Whose position offers a better option? Support your response with quotations from the text.

It Gets Better

One hundred videos.

That was the goal, and it seemed ambitious: one hundred videos—best-case scenario: two hundred videos—made by lesbian, gay, bisexual, and transgender adults for lesbian, gay, bisexual, and transgender youth.

I was sitting in a hotel room in Bloomington, Indiana, when I began to suspect that we were going to see a lot more than one hundred videos. The video that I had made with my husband, Terry, a week earlier, the very first It Gets Better video, had been live on YouTube for just a few hours when e-mails and likes and friend requests started coming in so fast that my computer crashed. The second It Gets Better video arrived within twenty-four hours. Three days later we hit one hundred videos. Before the end of the first week, we hit one thousand videos.

Terry and I were relieved to learn that we weren't the only people out there who wanted to reach out to LGBT kids in crisis.

Justin Aaberg was just fifteen when he killed himself in the summer of 2010. He came   5 out at thirteen, and endured years of bullying at the hands of classmates in a suburban Minnesota high school. Justin hanged himself in his bedroom; his mother found his body.

Billy Lucas, also fifteen, wasn't gay-identified but he was perceived to be gay by his classmates in Greensburg, Indiana. His tormentors threatened him, called him a fag, and urged him to kill himself. Billy hanged himself in a barn on his grandmother's property in early September of 2010. His mother found his body.

Reading about Justin and Billy was emotionally crushing—I was particularly outraged to learn that "Christian" parents were blocking efforts to address the rampant anti-gay bullying at Justin's school, claiming that doing so would somehow infringe upon the "religious freedom" of their straight children—and I began to think about the problem of anti-gay bullying.

I was aware of anti-gay bullying, of course. I had been bullied in the Catholic schools my parents sent me to; my husband endured years of much more intense bullying—it's amazing he survived—at the public high school he attended; I knew that many of my LGBT friends had been bullied. But it wasn't something we talked about or dwelt on.

I was stewing in my anger about what had been done to Justin and Billy when I read this comment, left on a blog post I wrote about Billy: "My heart breaks for the pain and torment you went through, Billy Lucas. I wish I could have told you that things get better."

What a simple and powerful truth. Things get better—things *have* gotten better, things *keep* getting better—for lesbian, gay, bisexual, and transgender people.

I knew that to be true because things had certainly gotten better for me.

I came to fully understand that I was gay—that I had always been gay—when I was a thirteen-year-old boy being bullied at a Catholic school on the north side of Chicago. I became increasingly estranged from my parents at a time when I needed them most because I was working so hard to hide who I was from them. Five years later, I found the courage to start coming out. Coming out is a long process, not a single event, and I tested the waters by telling my eldest brother, Billy, before telling my mom or dad.

> **"My heart breaks for the pain and torment you went through, Billy Lucas. I wish I could have told you that things get better."**

Billy was supportive and it helped me decide to tell my mother, which would be the hardest thing I had yet done in my life. Because coming out in 1982 didn't just mean telling my mother that I was gay. It meant telling her that I would never get married, that I would never be a parent, that my professional life would be forever limited by my sexuality.

Eight years after coming out, I would stumble into a rewarding and unlikely career as a sex-advice columnist, of all things, and somehow leverage that into a side gig as a potty-mouthed political pundit. And fifteen years after coming out, I would adopt a son with the love of my life—the man I would marry—and, with him at my side, present my parents with a new grandchild, my siblings with a new nephew.

Things didn't just get better for me. All of the gay, lesbian, bisexual, and transgender adults I knew were leading rich and rewarding lives. We weren't the same people and we didn't have or want the same things—gay or straight, not everyone wants kids or marriage; people pursue happiness in different ways—but we all had so much to be thankful for, and so much to look forward to. Our lives weren't perfect; there was pain, heartbreak, and struggle. But our lives were better. Our lives were joyful.

What was to be gained by looking backward? Why dwell on the past?

There wasn't anything we could do about the bullying we had endured in school and, for too many of us, at the hands of our families. And it didn't seem like there was anything we could do about or for all the LGBT kids who were currently being bullied.

A bullied gay teenager who ends his life is saying that he can't picture a future with enough joy in it to compensate for the pain he's in now. Justin and Billy—and, as that terrible September ground on, Seth and Asher and Tyler and Raymond and Cody—couldn't see how their own lives might get better. Without gay role models to mentor and support them, without the examples our lives represent, they couldn't see how they might get from bullied gay teenager to safe and happy gay adult. And the people gay teenagers need most—their own parents—often believe that they can somehow prevent their children from growing up to be gay—or from ever coming out—by depriving them of information, resources, support, and positive role models. (Justin Aaberg's parents knew he was gay, and were supportive.)

That fall, as I thought about Justin and Billy, I reflected on how frequently I'm invited to speak at colleges and universities. I address audiences of gay and straight students, and I frequently talk about homophobia and gay rights and tolerance. But I don't get invited to speak at high schools or middle schools, the places where homophobia does the most damage. Gay kids trapped in middle and high schools would benefit from hearing from LGBT adults—lives could be saved—but very few middle or high schools would ever invite gay adults to address their student bodies. Acknowledging the existence of LGBT people, even in sex-ed curriculums, is hugely controversial. A school administrator who invited a gay adult to address an assembly before there was a crisis—before a bullied gay teenager took his own life—would quickly find herself in the crosshairs of homophobic parents and bigoted "Christian" organizations.

It couldn't happen—schools would never invite gay adults to talk to kids; we would never get permission.

I was riding a train to JFK Airport when it occurred to me that I was waiting for 20 permission that I no longer needed. In the era of social media—in a world with YouTube and Twitter and Facebook—I could speak directly to LGBT kids right now. I didn't need permission from parents or an invitation from a school. I could look into a camera, share my story, and let LGBT kids know that it got better for me and it would get better for them too. I could give 'em hope.

But I didn't want to do it alone. I called Terry from the airport and tentatively explained my idea for a video outreach campaign. I wanted to encourage other LGBT adults to make videos for LGBT kids and post them to YouTube. I wanted to call it: The It Gets Better Project. And I wanted us to make the first video together, to talk about our lives together, to share our joy.

This was a big ask. Terry doesn't do interviews, he doesn't allow cameras in our home, he has no desire to go on television. But he said yes. My husband was the first person to recognize the power of this idea.

The second person to recognize it was our good friend Kelly O, a straight friend and a supremely talented photographer and filmmaker. She had just one question after I explained what we wanted to do: "When can we shoot it?"

We did two takes. The first was a long, depressing video that we shot against a bare wall in our dining room. It looked like a hostage video and we both talked too much about the bullying we'd endured in high school. We watched the video and shook our heads. Kids who are currently being bullied don't need to be told what bullying looks and feels like. Kelly packed up her camera and we went to a friend's bar and tried again. This time Kelly peppered us with questions: Share a happy memory. How did you two meet? What would you tell your teenage self? Are you happy to be alive?

Kelly edited the video, created a YouTube account, and called me when it was live. 25

Four weeks later I got a call from the White House. They wanted me to know that the President's It Gets Better video had just been uploaded to YouTube.

My computer crashed a second time.

The It Gets Better Project didn't just crash my computer. It brought the old order crashing down. By giving ourselves permission to speak directly to LGBT youth, Terry and I gave permission to all LGBT adults everywhere to speak to LGBT youth. It forced straight people—politicians, teachers, preachers, and parents—to decide whose side they were on. Were they going to come to the defense of bullied LGBT teenagers? Or were they going to remain silent and, by so doing, give aid and comfort to the young anti-gay bullies who attack LGBT children in schools and the adult anti-gay bullies at conservative "family" organizations who attack LGBT people for a living?

The culture used to offer this deal to lesbian, gay, bisexual, and transgender people: You're ours to torture until you're eighteen. You will be bullied and tormented at school, at home, at church—until you're eighteen. Then, you can do what you want. You can come out, you can move away, and maybe, if the damage we've done isn't too severe, you can recover and build a life for yourself. There's just one thing you can't do after you turn eighteen: You can't talk to the kids we're still torturing, the LGBT teenagers being assaulted emotionally, physically, and spiritually in the same cities, schools, and churches you escaped from. And, if you do attempt to talk to the kids we're still torturing, we'll impugn your motives, we'll accuse you of being a pedophile or pederast, we'll claim you're trying to recruit children into "the gay lifestyle."

That was the old order and it fell apart when the It Gets Better Project went viral. 30 Suddenly gay, lesbian, bisexual, and transgender adults all over the country—*all over the world*—were speaking to LGBT youth. We weren't waiting for anyone's permission anymore. We found our voices. And LGBT adults who made videos for the project weren't just talking *at* LGBT youth. The kids who watched videos sent e-mails, via YouTube, to the adults posting them. Thousands of LGBT adults who thought they were just going to contribute a video found themselves talking with LGBT youth, offering them not just hope but advice, insight, and something too many LGBT youth lack: the ear of a supportive adult who understands what they're going through.

Soon straight people—politicians and celebrities—were talking to LGBT youth, too, delivering the same message: It gets better, there's nothing wrong with you, and we're working to make it better. LGBT kids could see that the world was full of people like our friend Kelly—loving, supportive, progressive straight people. And as a capstone—living proof—that things were indeed getting better, Don't Ask/Don't Tell was finally repealed. Days later Joe Biden, who also made an It Gets Better video, would go on television and describe marriage equality—marriage rights for lesbian and gay couples—as an inevitability.

Things are getting better before our very eyes.

I do want to acknowledge what the It Gets Better Project can't do, though.

It can't do the impossible. It won't solve the problem of anti-gay bullying, everywhere, all at once, forever, overnight. The point of the project is to give despairing LGBT kids *hope*. The point is to let them know that things *do* get better, using the examples of our own lives. For some people things get better once they get out of high school, for others things get better while they're still in high school. And there are brave, out LGBT kids in high schools and middle schools all over the country who are helping to make things better—for themselves and their peers—in their schools today.

Nothing about letting LGBT kids know that it gets better excuses or precludes us 35 from pressing for the passage of the Student Non-Discrimination Act; demanding anti-bullying programs in all schools; confronting bigots who are making things worse for all kinds of kids; and supporting the work of the Trevor Project, GLSEN, and the American Civil Liberties Union's LGBT Project's Youth & Schools program. (Indeed, the It

Gets Better Project has raised tens of thousands of dollars for these organizations.) But we're not going to get legislation passed this instant and it will be years before we get anti-bullying programs and GSAs (Gay-Straight Alliances) into all public schools, and we may never get them into the private evangelical schools where they're needed most.

In the meantime, while we work to make our schools safer, we can and should use the tools we have at our disposal right now—social media and YouTube and digital video and this book—to get messages of hope to kids who are suffering *right now* in schools that do not have GSAs and to kids whose parents bully and reject them for being lesbian, gay, bisexual, or transgender. There's nothing about the It Gets Better Project—nothing about making a video or sharing one—that prevents people from doing more. Indeed, we've heard from thousands of people who were inspired to do more after making or watching a video.

A few weeks after we launched the It Gets Better Project, this letter arrived for me and my husband:

> Thank you for the It Gets Better Project. My son is 14 and a sophomore in high school in rural Kentucky. He isn't athletic. He isn't religious. He isn't in ROTC. He is constantly being called "gay" or "faggot," oftentimes by the people he thought were his friends. . . . So far, it hasn't gone beyond name-calling, but I worry. I showed him your site the day it went live. He sat down and watched the video that you and Terry put up. Since then, I have seen him checking the site out on his own. I don't know if he is gay, but I do know that your message has touched him. Although he does confide that four years is still a long time to wait for things to get better. I think that seeing so many other people say the same thing holds much more weight than having his mother tell him. So thank you again for sharing.

Four years *is* a long time to wait. So let's all commit to making things better right now, let's all do what we can to create a world where no child, gay or straight, is bullied for being different.

We don't live in that world yet. There are children out there who are being bullied every day, and while gay, lesbian, bisexual, or transgender children aren't the only kids dealing with this harassment, they are often more isolated, more alone, and more at risk.

Nine out of ten LGBT students report experiencing bullying in their schools; LGBT teenagers are four to seven times likelier to attempt suicide. LGBT children who are rejected by their families are eight times likelier to attempt suicide and at much higher risk of winding up homeless and living on the streets. 40

If you know a child who's being bullied for being gay or perceived to be gay— particularly if you know a child who isn't lucky enough to have a mother like the one who wrote to us—you can help that child find hope by helping them find their way to this book and the It Gets Better Project's website (itgetsbetter.org), with more than ten thousand videos and counting.

Do your part. Give 'em hope.

Action Makes It Better

Despite the title of this book, there is nothing inevitable about change for the better. The only reason big changes happen is when people like you and me decide to fight for things to change, when we take action to make things different.

Gandhi organized for decades in India to get rid of the British. In 1947 (only sixty-four years ago!), the movement he created overthrew one of the biggest colonial empires using nonviolent resistance.

Your grandmothers and great-grandmothers could not vote in the United States — it only changed in 1921 (ninety years ago!).

Black people did not have full voting rights in this country until 1965 (forty-six years ago!).

And lesbian, gay, bisexual, and transgender people did not have the right to have sexual relationships without violating criminal laws until 2003 (only eight years ago!). Or think about India: The LGBT movement just got a court to overturn the laws criminalizing same-sex/same-gender behavior in 2009 (two years ago!).

All of these changes — for women, for African Americans, for LGBT folks — took a massive social movement to make happen.

This is my story of how it's gotten better for me. I'm Indian American, born there, and grew up here since I was eight. Like all Asian kids, my family's expectations — their dreams for me, their demands on me — weighed heavily on me, and never heavier than when I realized I was a lesbian.

But you know what? Activism saved my life. I got involved with a feminist group (of men and women working to really transform gender roles and patriarchy into a more just system). I got involved with a movement trying to end the racist Apartheid system in South Africa (you guys, it only ended in 1994!). I got involved with queer activism, with lefty groups, with all the rabble-rousers and radicals working to end the AIDS epidemic, to create a fairer economy, to win rights for immigrants, to end wars, and make the world more fun and sexy!

What I found in social movements was a whole life that has given me hope, inspiration, friendships, and my lover, Kate (of twenty-three years), whom I met at a queer conference. Social activism is all about optimism, even when you lose. The process of doing something about it all generates lots of adrenaline and serotonin that just make you feel better, like a sweaty dance to music you love.

> **Social activism is all about optimism, even when you lose.**

But truthfully, social change is not always fun — just like life. There's a lot of wacky people, nut-bucket opponents, and powerful forces that want to maintain things just the way they are — so defeat, occasional despair, loss, and discomfort are all part of the process of social action.

What keeps me going, though, is a combination of stubbornness (I'll be damned if they are going to knock me around and get away with it), cold-blooded anger (don't get mad, get even), faith (social-justice activism is an act of belief in the possibility of something you do not know will ever happen), and pleasure (in the people I have met along the way, the incredible change I have been a small part of making, and the massive amounts of fun I have had along the way).

The great news is that there is a global queer movement today. And it is full of young and old people fighting to make space for us to live and love and breathe and be who we are and create the lives we imagine. You can join it; in fact you can lead it. It's all being made right before your eyes.

So make it better — get active.

Exploring Context

1. Savage's and Vaid's essays emerge out of the It Gets Better Project. Visit the project's Web site at itgetsbetter.org and watch some of the videos there. What are some common themes in these videos? How do they resonate with Savage's and Vaid's discussions?

2. Visit the U.S. government's official anti-bullying Web site (stopbullying.gov). Given the extent of this problem and its sometimes severe consequences, does the site offer any realistic solutions to the problem?

3. The Trevor Project (thetrevorproject.org) is also focused on helping LGBT youth — specifically in preventing suicide. Explore the site. What can each of us do to help prevent these suicides?

Questions for Connecting

1. In "Preface" and "The New Civil Rights" (p. 539), Kenji Yoshino discusses both "covering" — a way of downplaying aspects of one's identity to fit in — and a new model of civil rights based on basic liberties available to all. How can you use the selections from Savage and Vaid to support Yoshino's claims? Would a liberty paradigm of civil rights solve the kinds of problems that spurred the It Gets Better Project?

2. What effect does bullying have on human dignity? Use Francis Fukuyama's discussion of the concept in "Human Dignity" (p. 143) to analyze the experiences of Savage and Vaid.

3. How do Savage and Vaid function as surrogates? Use Daniel Gilbert's definition of the term from "Reporting Live from Tomorrow" (p. 179) to consider how Savage's and Vaid's essays might offer youth a glimpse of a future that includes happiness.

Language Matters

1. These essays use a number of acronyms, primarily *LGBT*. Using the Web or some other reference source, locate the rules for introducing and using acronyms. Examine these rules in the context of these essays. Do the authors introduce acronyms properly? How and when should you use acronyms in your own writing?

2. Review the rules for pronouns and their antecedents using a grammar handbook or other reference resource. In these same sources, review any material on gender-neutral language. How does maintaining gender-neutral language complicate pronoun usage? How do Savage and Vaid handle this problem? How should you handle pronouns in a gender-neutral way in your own writing? Alternating *he* and *she*? Using *he/she*?

3. Vaid's essay is quite short. Outline the essay to trace the argument. How does Vaid manage to make an argument in so little space? What key moves are necessary to make an argument in a short essay? How can you apply these techniques in your own writing?

Assignments for Writing

1. "Action Makes It Better," claims Vaid. Write a paper in which you explore the relationship between social activism and change, using ideas from both Savage and Vaid to support your position.

2. How has technology changed social activism? Consider the It Gets Better Project, using it to form an argument about the ways in which technology and social media facilitate (or hamper) social change.

3. Using your own experience, write a paper about how things get better, addressed to a specific audience — bullied teenagers or LGBT youth. Connect your experiences to Savage and Vaid in making your argument for how things can get better.

JULIA SERANO

Julia Serano, who holds a Ph.D. in biochemistry and molecular biophysics from Columbia University, is a writer, spoken-word performer, and activist. Serano is a frequent speaker on transgender and queer issues and is the author of *Whipping Girl: A Transsexual Woman on Sexism and the Scapegoating of Femininity* (2007) and *Excluded: Making Feminist and Queer Movements More Inclusive* (2013). She has been anthologized in *Trans/Love: Radical Sex, Love & Relationships beyond the Gender Binary* (2011) and *Yes Means Yes!: Visions of Female Sexual Power & a World without Rape* (2008), where the following essay originally appeared.

Courtesy of Julia Serano

Yes Means Yes!: Visions of Female Sexual Power & a World without Rape, edited by Jaclyn Friedman and Jessica Valenti, is a feminist anthology that addresses issues of rape and sexuality by arguing that consent requires affirmative declaration—yes means yes. The editors contend that rather than only declaring what they do not want, women should also actively discover what they *do* want. Essays in the collection focus on body image and self-esteem, incest, rape culture, mass media, pornography, and more. Ultimately, *Yes Means Yes!* seeks to deconstruct the rape culture in which we live and foster understanding and respect for female sexual pleasure.

Julia Serano's contribution to the anthology, "Why Nice Guys Finish Last," explores her own somewhat unique perspective on rape culture from her identity as a transgendered woman who transitioned relatively late in life. She notes that rape culture is perpetuated not only by our preconceptions about women (that they are passive "prey") but also by our preconceptions about men (that they are "predators"). Serano attempts to explain why women tend to prefer "assholes" over "nice guys" and how that preference is a symptom of rape culture, and in the process she also illustrates how gendered stereotypes are detrimental to both women and men.

How do you think cultural expectations shape both men and women? How have they shaped you?

▶ TAGS: *culture, empathy, gender, identity, media, race and ethnicity, relationships, sexuality, social change, trauma and violence*

▶ CONNECTIONS: *Appiah, Gay, Levy, O'Connor, Padawer, Pozner, Rosin, Yang*

Questions for Critical Reading

1. Serano introduces a number of terms in making her argument. As you read, take note as she defines *cisgender*, *unilateral sexism*, the *predator/prey mindset*, *virgin/whore*, and *internalized/externalized misogyny*.

2. *Rape culture* figures prominently in Serano's essay, though she never explicitly defines it. Using what she does say about rape culture, formulate a definition of the term.

3. Take a moment to think about the cultural expectations of men. As you read, take note of the ways that Serano claims the socialization of men contributes to rape culture. Do your thoughts confirm her argument?

Why Nice Guys Finish Last

Sexualization and intimidation haunt all of us who move through the world as women. I have had men talk over me, speak down to me, and shout angrily at me when I've tried to deflect their unwanted passes. Strange men have hurled catcalls and sexual innuendos at me, and have graphically described what they'd like to do with me as I pass by them on city streets. I've also survived an attempted date rape. And frankly, I consider myself lucky that nothing more serious than that has happened to me. Needless to say, like all women, I have a great interest in bringing an end to rape culture.

Having said that, being transsexual—having had the experience of navigating my way through the world as male prior to my transition to female—has given me a somewhat different take on rape culture than the view that is often taken for granted among many cisgender (i.e., non-transgender) women. From my perspective, much of the existing rhetoric used to describe and theorize sexual harassment, abuse, and rape is, unfortunately, mired in the concept of "unilateral sexism"—that is, the belief that men are the oppressors and women are the oppressed, end of story.

Some of those who buy into unilateral sexism believe that men are inherently oppressive, dominating, and violent. Others believe that the problem is rooted in patriarchy and male socialization conspiring to condition men to become sexual predators. While there is certainly some truth to the idea that men are socialized to be sexually aggressive, even predatory, this is not the only force at work in their lives. Male children and teenagers are also regularly and explicitly reminded that they should be respectful of girls and women, and are often punished severely for picking on or "playing rough" with, their female peers. Further, the men-are-just-socialized-that-way argument fails to explain the countless men who never sexually abuse or harass women in their lifetime.

The truth is that rape culture is a mindset that affects each and every one of us, shaping how we view and respond to the

> **[R]ape culture is a mindset that affects each and every one of us.**

world, and creating double binds for both women and men. I call this phenomenon the predator/prey mindset, and within it, men can only ever be viewed as sexual aggressors and women as sexual objects.

The predator/prey mindset creates many of the double standards that exist in how we view female versus male sexuality. For example, on numerous occasions I've heard heterosexual female friends of mine ogle some man and make comments about how he has a nice ass. While one could certainly make the case that such discussions are "objectifying" or "sexualizing," what strikes me is that they don't *feel* that way. But if I were to overhear a group of men make the exact same comments about a woman, they would *feel* very different. They would *feel* sexualizing.

Similarly, if a male high school teacher were to have sex with one of his female teenage students, we would all be appalled. The incident would clearly *feel* like statutory rape to us. However, when the roles are reversed—when the adult teacher is female and the teenage student is male—it generally *feels* like a completely different thing to us. While it still fits the definition of statutory rape, we often have problems mustering up the *feeling* that the boy has been violated or abused. In fact, after one recent high-profile case, comedian Bill Maher joked that such teenage boys are "lucky," and the audience broke into laughter.

What these anecdotes reveal is that the predator/prey mindset essentially ensures that men cannot be viewed as legitimate sexual objects, nor can women be viewed as legitimate sexual aggressors. This has the effect of rendering invisible instances of man-on-man and woman-on-woman sexual harassment and abuse, and it makes the idea of woman-on-man rape utterly inconceivable. It's also why women cannot simply "turn the tables" and begin sexualizing men. After all, if a woman were to shout catcalls at a man, or were to pinch a guy's ass as he walked by, her actions wouldn't mean the same thing as they would if the roles were reversed. Her actions would likely be seen as suggestive and slutty, rather than intimidating and predatory.

Because of the predator/prey mindset, when a woman does act in a sexually active or aggressive way, she is generally not viewed as a sexual aggressor, but rather as opening herself up to being sexually objectified by others. This is why rape trials have historically dwelled on whether the woman in question was dressed in a revealing or provocative fashion, or whether she met with the man privately, and so on. If she did any of these things, others are likely to view her as inviting her own sexualization, as "asking for it." The underlying assumption is that women should simply know better—they should recognize that they are prey and men are predators, and they should act "appropriately."

What should be becoming increasingly clear is that the predator/prey mindset enables the virgin/whore double bind that feminists have long been rallying against. Women, as prey, are expected to play down their sexuality—to hide or repress it. Good girls, after all, are supposed to be "virgins." Women who do not downplay or repress their sexualities—that is, who do not act like prey—are viewed stereotypically as "whores." As stereotypes, both "virgin" and "whore" are disempowering, because they both frame female sexuality in terms of the predator/prey mindset. This is why reclaiming their sexuality has been such a double-edged sword for women. If a woman embraces her sexuality, it may be personally empowering for her, but she still has to deal with the fact that others will project the "whore" stereotype onto her and assume that she's inviting male sexualization. In other words, a woman may be personally empowered, but she is not seen as being sexually powerful and autonomous in the culture at large. In order for that to happen, we as individuals must begin to challenge our own (as well as other people's) perceptions and interpretations of gender. We must all move beyond viewing the world through the predator/prey mindset.

To do that, we must examine an issue that has traditionally received far less attention: the ways in which the predator/prey mindset complicates the lives of men. Trans perspectives (those of trans women, trans men, and other transgender-spectrum people) can be really vital in this regard, as many of us have had the experience of

10

moving through the world as both women and men at different points in our lives, and thus can consider the male position without undermining or dismissing female perspectives (and vice versa). In thinking about these issues, I draw heavily on my own experiences being raised as a boy, and as a young adult who was viewed by others as a heterosexual man (as I am primarily attracted to women). It is not my intention to speak on behalf of all men, both because I never fully identified as male at the time, and also because I had a very specific and privileged male existence (for example, I am white and middle-class). It will take the experiences of other trans folks and cisgender men to fill in the whole picture.

Just as it is difficult for women to navigate their way through the world, given the fact that they are nonconsensually viewed as prey, it is often difficult for men to move through a world in which they are nonconsensually viewed as predators. When I was male-bodied, it was not uncommon for women to cross the street if I was walking behind them at night, or to have female strangers misinterpret innocent things that I said as unsolicited sexual advances. It is telling, I think, that I had to deal with the predator stereotype despite the fact that my appearance was about as unthreatening as it gets: I was a very small and unmasculine/androgynous man. Bigger and more masculine-appearing men have to deal with this stereotype much more than I ever did. Perhaps no issue exacerbates the male predator stereotype more than race. I have heard several trans men of color say that they feel that the male privilege they have gained since transitioning has been very much offset by the increased visibility and the societal stereotypes of black men as predators that others are constantly projecting onto them.

While the predator stereotype affects men's interactions with women, it probably has an even greater impact on their interactions with children. When I was male-bodied, I found that if I were to interact enthusiastically with children, women would often give me dirty looks. A trans male acquaintance of mine recently told me that the greatest loss he experienced upon transitioning from female to male was his ability to interact freely and enthusiastically with children. He teaches young children and has found that he's had to modify his whole approach — for example, keeping more distance and not being as effusive or affectionate with his students as before — in order to avoid other adults' viewing him as creepy or suspect.

Obviously, men make up the overwhelming majority of sexual predators. But that does not mean that *all* men are necessarily sexual predators. It is important for us to keep in mind that the men-as-predator stereotype is exactly that — a stereotype — and it creates obstacles that all men must navigate, whether they are predators or not. This is especially true for those men who are additionally marginalized with regard to race and class. Given how destructive and injuring sexual abuse and violence are to those who experience them, I wouldn't dare suggest that it is the (potential or actual) victim's fault for propagating these stereotypes. At the same time, the truth is that we cannot begin to have an honest discussion about how to dismantle rape culture unless we are willing to acknowledge the negative impact that this stereotype has on those men who are not predatory.

The predator stereotype also complicates and constrains male sexuality. While many feminists have discussed how the sexual object/prey stereotype creates a double bind for women in which they can only ever be viewed as either "virgins" or "whores," not enough have considered how the sexual aggressor/predator stereotype might create a similar double bind for men. Having experienced this dilemma myself firsthand, I have come to refer to it (for reasons that will be clear in a moment) as the assholes / nice guys double bind. "Assholes" are men who fulfill the men-as-sexual-aggressors stereotype; "nice guys" are the ones who refuse or eschew it.

Just as women receive mixed messages in our culture — some encouraging them to be "virgins," others encouraging them to be "whores" — men receive similar mixed messages. As I alluded to earlier, male children often receive lots of explicit encouragement to be respectful of women. Even in adulthood, men who make blatantly sexist comments, or who suggest (in mixed company, at least) that women are "only good for one thing" will often be looked down upon or taken to task for it. So when it comes to their formal socialization, boys/men receive plenty of encouragement to be "nice guys." 15

The problem is that boys/men receive conflicting messages from society at large. This informal socialization comes mostly from the meanings and expectations that are regularly projected onto women and men, especially in the media and within the context of heterosexual relationships. Just as women are expected to fulfill the stereotype of being sexual objects in order to gain male attention, men are expected to fulfill the sexual aggressor stereotype in order to gain female attention. In other words, they have to act like "assholes." Granted, this isn't true in *all* situations. For example, in the progressive, artsy, and/or queer circles I inhabit nowadays, men who act like "assholes" don't get very far. But in the heterosexual mainstream culture, men who unapologetically act like "assholes" tend to thrive.

This really confused me in my late teens and young adulthood. I had lots of close female friends back then, and it always used to bum me out when they would completely fall for a guy doing the "asshole" routine: acting confident to the point of being cocky, being sexually forward if not downright pushy, and relentlessly teasing girls in a junior high school–esque way with the expectation that they would smile and giggle in response. It always seemed really contrived to me. I suppose I was privy to insider information: I had the experience of interacting regularly with many of those same men *as a man* (not a woman), and in those situations they did not act nearly as cocky or presumptive or dismissive toward me as they did around women they were interested in.

Anyway, time and time again, my female friends would fall for an "asshole" and then be crushed because he never called her the next day, as he'd promised, or because he started bragging to his guy friends about his "sexual conquest," or because he tried to push things along faster and farther sexually than she was willing to go. Sometimes after being hurt by some "asshole," my female friends would come to me for advice or to be consoled. They came to me because I was a "nice guy." In their eyes, I was safe. Respectful. Harmless. Sometimes during these post-"asshole" conversations, my friends would go on a tirade about how all men are jerks and cannot be trusted, or they'd ask, "Why can't I find a guy who will treat me with respect?" Whenever they did this, I would point out that there are lots of guys who are not jerks, who are respectful of women. I'd even name a few. Upon hearing the names I suggested, my friends would invariably say something like "I don't find him attractive" or "I think of him more as a friend."

Just as women who refuse to play the role of sexual object often fail to attract male attention, "nice guys" who refuse to play the role of sexual aggressor typically fail to attract female attention. (Note that I'm not speaking here of the type of man referred to in the feminist blogosphere as a Nice Guy, who is the sort of man who argues that being a "nice guy" entitles him to sex with whomever he wants, thus revealing himself to be merely a closeted "asshole.") In high school and college, I had several male friends who, apparently concerned with the lack of action I was getting, literally told me that women like it when guys act like "assholes." For them, it was just something one did to attract women. And as much as I hate to admit it, it generally seemed to be true.

> **"[N]ice guys" who refuse to play the role of sexual aggressor typically fail to attract female attention.**

During my college years, I watched a number of "nice guys" transform into "assholes." And when they did, women suddenly became interested in them. The most stunning transformation I witnessed was in this guy who lived in my dorm, whom I'll call Eric. Freshman and sophomore years, he was a super-sweet and respectful guy. Despite the fact that he was fairly good-looking, women were not generally interested in him. Somewhere around junior year, he suddenly began acting like an "asshole" (around women, at least). Instead of engaging women in conversations (as he used to), he would instead relentlessly tease them. The things he would say sounded really dismissive to me, but often the intended recipient would just giggle in response. Suddenly he was picking women up at parties, and I'd occasionally overhear women who never knew Eric back when he was a "nice guy" discussing how cute they thought he was.

The last time I saw Eric was about two years after college. We had both moved to New York City, and a mutual friend came up to visit and suggested that we all go out together. The bar that we went to was really crowded, and at one point, Eric started talking about how in situations like this, he would sometimes fold his arms across his chest and subtly grope women as they walked by. Between the fact that the bar was so crowded and the way he held his arms to obscure his hands, women weren't able to figure out that it was Eric. Upon hearing this, I walked out of the bar, appalled.

The reason I tell this story is that it complicates many of the existing presumptions regarding the origins of rape culture. Some have suggested that men are biologically programmed to be sexual predators. The existence of Eric (and others like him) challenges that argument because, after all, he was a "nice guy" for most of his life until about the age of twenty—well after his sex drive kicked in. Eric challenges overly simplistic men-are-socialized-to-be-that-way arguments for the same reason: He made it to early adulthood—well beyond his formative childhood and teenage years—before becoming an "asshole." It would be really hard to make the case that Eric became a sexual predator because he was influenced by media imagery or pornography, or because his male peers egged him on. Like I said, I lived in the same dorm as he did, and I never once saw any guys teasing him for being a "nice guy" or coercing him into being an "asshole." I would argue that the primary reason Eric became sexually aggressive was that he was interested in attracting women. And, as with many men, once Eric began disrespecting women on a regular basis, the lines between flirting and harassment, between sex and violation, between consensual and nonconsensual, became blurred or unimportant to him.

Not to sound corny, but we all want the same things in life: to gain other people's attention, to be adored, to be sexually desired, to be intimate with people we

20

find attractive, and to have great sex. In a culture where women are generally viewed as sexual objects, some women will take on that role in order to gain attention and to feel desirable. By the same token, in a world where men are only ever viewed as sexual aggressors, some men will take on that role in order to gain attention and to feel desirable. So long as the predator/prey mindset predominates and a demand remains for women and men to fulfill those stereotypes, a large percentage of people will continue to gravitate toward them.

This is why single-tact solutions to abolish rape culture will always fail. For instance, many people in both the political/religious Right, as well as many anti-pornography feminists, seem to take what I call the "virgin" approach. Their line of reasoning goes something like this: Because men are predators, we should desexualize women in the culture by, for example, banning pornography and discouraging representations of women (whether media imagery or actual women) that others can interpret as sexually arousing or objectifying. This approach not only is sexually repressive and disempowering for many women, but it also reinforces the idea that men are predators and women are prey. In other words, it reaffirms the very system that it hopes to dismantle.

I also get frustrated by people who think that it's simply up to male allies to call out those men who are sexist or disrespectful of women. While this approach can have some positive effect, I believe that many cisgender women overestimate its potential. First off, it essentially makes the "nice guys" responsible for policing the "assholes." This overlooks the fact that in the heterosexual mainstream, "assholes" are seen as being higher up in the social pecking order than "nice guys." As a result, a "nice guy" calling out an "asshole" about how he needs to be more respectful of women tends to have as much societal clout as if the geeky girl in class were to lecture the cheerleaders about how they shouldn't play dumb and giggle at every joke that the popular boys make. Such comments, when they are made, are often ignored or outright dismissed. Furthermore, I've experienced a number of situations in my life (e.g., high school locker rooms) where I honestly did not feel safe enough to protest the sexist comments that some boys and men make. After all, one of the ways in which the hierarchical status quo is maintained in male circles is through the threat of physical intimidation and violence.

Any attempts to critique men for being sexually aggressive, or to critique women for fulfilling the role of sexual object, will have a very limited effect. These tactics, after all, fail to address the crucial issue of demand. So long as heterosexual women are attracted to men who act like aggressors, and heterosexual men are attracted to women who act like objects, people will continue to fulfill those roles. In contrast, critiques that challenge why individuals desire stereotypical "sex objects" and "sexual aggressors" seem to me to get closer to the root of the problem. 25

I have heard many feminists critique men who prefer women that fulfill the sexual object stereotype. Many of these critiques (rightfully, I think) suggest that the man in question must be somewhat shallow or insecure if he's willing to settle for someone whom he does not view as his intellectual and emotional equal. What I have seen far less of are critiques of women who are attracted to sexually aggressive men. Perhaps this stems in part from the belief that such comments might be misinterpreted as blaming women for enabling the sexual abuse they receive at the hands of men. While I can understand this reluctance, I nevertheless feel that it is a mistake to ignore this issue, given the fact that many men become sexual aggressors primarily, if not solely, to attract the attention of women. In fact, if heterosexual women suddenly decided en masse that "nice guys" are far sexier than "assholes," it would create a huge shift in the predator/prey dynamic. While I wouldn't suggest that such a change would completely eliminate rape or sexual abuse (because there are clearly other societal forces at work here), I do believe that it would greatly reduce the number of men who harass and disrespect women on a daily basis.

Those feminists who have critiqued the tendency of women to be attracted to sexually aggressive men often refer to the phenomenon as "internalized misogyny." In other words, they presume that because women have been socialized to take shit from men, they have become conditioned to continually seek out men who will treat them like shit. Personally, I find this explanation unsatisfying. I don't think that women are attracted to sexual aggressors because they believe that those men will treat them like shit. Rather, they tend to be attracted to other aspects of sexual aggressors, and only later become disappointed by the way they are treated.

This phenomenon is more accurately viewed as a form of "externalized misogyny." There are a lot of subliminal meanings built into the predator/prey mindset: that men are aggressive and women are passive, that men are strong and women are weak, that men are rebellious and women are harmless, and so on. It is no accident that the meanings associated with women are typically viewed as inferior to, or lamer than, those associated with men. Given this context, I would argue that "nice guys" are generally read as emasculated or effeminized men in our culture. In a world where calling a man "sensitive" is viewed as a pejorative, the very act of showing respect for women often disqualifies a male from being seen as a "real man." I believe that this is a major reason why many heterosexual women are not sexually interested in "nice guys."

I think that women who are attracted to sexual aggressors are primarily drawn to the rebellious, bad-boy image they project—an image that is essentially built into our cultural ideal of maleness. The odd thing is that for many men, fulfilling the aggressor role represents the path of least resistance. How rebellious can it be to fulfill a stereotype? "Nice guys," on the other hand, *are* rebellious, at least in one sense: They buck the system and refuse to reduce themselves to the predator stereotype. It is time that we begin to recognize and celebrate this rebellion.

Lots of women I know want to create a world in which women are allowed and encouraged to be sexual without having to be nonconsensually sexualized. This is a laudable goal. But having been on the other side of the gender divide, I would argue that for this to happen, we will also have to work to simultaneously ensure that men can be respectful of women without being *desexualized*. One cannot happen without the other. I think that a lot of men would be eager to work with women to create such a world. A movement that refuses to render invisible and desexualize men who are not predators, and that attempts to debunk both the virgin/whore *and* the asshole/nice guy double binds, would excite and attract many male allies.

Perhaps most important, understanding the predator/prey mindset can help us to recognize that rape culture is reinforced both by people's actions *and* by their perceptions. The system will not be dismantled until all (or at least most) of us learn not to project the predator stereotype onto men and the prey stereotype onto women. Just as we must learn to debunk the many racist, sexist, classist, homophobic, and ageist cultural stereotypes we've absorbed over the course of a lifetime, we must also learn to move beyond predator/prey stereotypes. Honestly, I find this the most personally challenging aspect of this work. Moving through the world as a woman, and having to deal with being harassed by men on a regular basis, makes me wary of letting my guard down in any way. Viewing all men as predators is a convenient self-defense mechanism, but it ignores the countless men who are respectful of women. I am not suggesting that we, as women, ignore the important issue of safety — to do so at this moment in time would be beyond unwise. What I am suggesting is that we won't get to where we want to be until the men-as–predator / sexual aggressor assumption no longer dominates our thinking. It's difficult to imagine getting there from here, but we're going to have to try.

Exploring Context

1. Visit the blog for *Yes Means Yes!* at yesmeansyesblog.wordpress.com. Read through several entries. How does the blog continue or complement Serano's project?

2. FORCE: Upsetting Rape Culture (upsettingrapeculture.com) is a Web site dedicated to fighting rape culture. Explore the site to learn more about this concept and the ways in which it can be fought. How does the site change your definition of *rape culture* from Question 2 of Questions for Critical Reading?

3. The "friendzone" is a popular expression to describe the fate of "nice guys." Using the Web, do an image search for "friendzone." In what ways does this concept reflect Serano's argument? Relate your findings to your answer about cultural expectations of men from Question 3 of Questions for Critical Reading.

Questions for Connecting

1. Part of Serano's argument concerns the power of stereotypes. Synthesize her position with Jennifer Pozner's argument in "Ghetto Bitches, China Dolls, and Cha Cha Divas" (p. 359). How do stereotypes of race, class, and gender shape both men and women? Incorporate your work from Question 3 of Questions for Critical Reading and Question 3 of Exploring Context.

2. Using Ariel Levy's "Female Chauvinist Pigs" (p. 243), assess the relationship between raunch culture and rape culture. Where would Female Chauvinist Pigs fall on the virgin/whore spectrum? Does raunch culture feed or fight rape culture? Draw from your work on rape culture from Question 2 of Questions for Critical Reading and Question 2 of Exploring Context.

3. Serano acknowledges the difficulties in changing our thinking about men and women. Use Kwame Anthony Appiah's ideas from "Making Conversation" and "The Primacy of Practice" (p. 44) to propose strategies to pursue Serano's vision. Can cosmopolitanism help men and women? How does the persistence of rape culture reveal the primacy of practice, and how can we shift that practice?

Language Matters

1. Sentences can be written in either active or passive voice. If you're not sure what these terms mean, look up *active voice* and *passive voice* in a grammar handbook or reference guide. Then select a quotation from Serano's essay that you think is key to her argument. Identify whether it is written in active or passive voice, noting how you know this to be the case. Then rewrite the sentence in the opposite voice. Is the argument weaker in passive voice or in active voice? Are concepts clearer in one voice or the other? Why or why not? Why might you choose active or passive voice in your own writing?

2. What's the relationship between point of view and authority? Serano suggests that her position as a transgendered woman provides a unique perspective on the issues of the essay. Is that a legitimate basis for authority? How do you find your authority to speak when doing academic writing?

3. Serano uses a number of specialized terms. Note how she defines these terms in her text. How well does context function to help a reader define terms? When should you look up a word in the dictionary, and when is it sufficient to determine a word's meaning from the context of its use?

Assignments for Writing

1. Serano works with a number of binaries (virgin / whore, nice guy / asshole). Write a paper in which you propose a solution to the problem of rape culture that avoids binary positions. Is it possible to locate positions for men and women that don't rely on these binaries? What options does Serano suggest that could lead to such a solution? You may want to work with the definitions you developed in Questions 1 and 2 of Questions for Critical Reading as well as your work on cultural expectations of men from Question 3 of Questions for Critical Reading.

2. Serano draws from her experience in order to argue that nice guys finish last. Write a paper in which you synthesize your own experience with Serano's argument, treating your experiences as evidence to be connected to Serano's. Does your experience confirm or complicate Serano's observations?

3. How can we mitigate the power of stereotypes? Using Serano's ideas, write a paper in which you suggest strategies for dismantling stereotypes in culture. You may want to use your work from Question 3 of Questions for Critical Reading and Question 1 of Questions for Connecting.

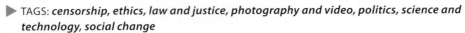

PETER SINGER

Peter Singer is the Ira W. DeCamp Professor of Bioethics at Princeton University as well as the Laureate Professor at the Centre for Applied Philosophy and Public Ethics at the University of Melbourne. He founded the Centre for Human Bioethics at Monash University, and the Council of Australian Humanist Societies recognized him as Humanist of the Year in 2004. Singer has published dozens of books and essays, but among the most well-known books are *Animal Liberation: A New Ethics for Our Treatment of Animals* (1975), *Practical Ethics* (1979), *How Are We to Live? Ethics in an Age of Self-Interest* (1993), and *The Life You Can Save: Acting Now to End World Poverty* (2009). Most recently, he has published *The Most Good You Can Do: How Effective Altruism Is Changing Ideas about Living Ethically* (2015).

Princeton University, Office of Communications

Singer's essay "Visible Man: Ethics in a World without Secrets" was published in the August 2011 edition of *Harper's Magazine*. This issue was published as the country neared the tenth anniversary of the 9/11 tragedy, so accompanying articles were on the FBI's attempt to find internal terrorists as well as the limits of remembrance since the terrorist attacks. The issue also included a series of watercolor images by Steve Mumford, produced while embedded with American troops in Afghanistan.

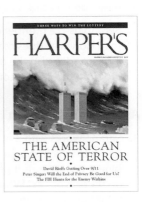

"Visible Man: Ethics in a World without Secrets" focuses on the concepts of transparency and personal privacy. With a focus on the controversial Web site WikiLeaks (wikileaks.org), Singer discusses the modern-day changes in surveillance technology and how these changes might alter our government as well as our society. While Singer seemingly argues in favor of this transparency, he also makes note of the possibility that information collected by these technologies might be misused. By arguing that surveillance work should both aid and expose government, Singer is encouraging readers to question current views on privacy and examine how new technologies have the ability to affect the future.

▶ TAGS: *censorship, ethics, law and justice, photography and video, politics, science and technology, social change*

▶ CONNECTIONS: *Henig, Klosterman, Konnikova, Paumgarten, Restak, Wasik*

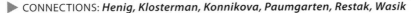

Questions for Critical Reading

1. What is *privacy*? Write your own definition of this term. As you read Singer's essay, mark passages where he explains privacy — especially where he considers how the concept of privacy changes. Can you reconcile your definition with Singer's? What factors cause concepts such as privacy to change meaning?

2. As you read Singer's text, look for the term *sousveillance*. What does this term mean? Does it support or undermine democracy? Locate quotations from Singer that support your position.

3. How can we balance the rights of the individual with the need for security? Consider this question as you read Singer's text. What is his position on this question?

Visible Man: Ethics in a World without Secrets

In 1787, the philosopher Jeremy Bentham proposed the construction of a "Panopticon," a circular building with cells along the outer walls and, at the center, a watchtower or "inspector's lodge" from which all the cells could be seen but no one would know, at any given moment, due to a system of blinds and partitions, whether he was actually being observed. Bentham thought this design would be particularly suited to prisons but suggested it could also be applied to factories, hospitals, mental asylums, and schools. Not only would prisoners, workers, the ill, the insane, and students be subject to observation, but also—if the person in charge of the facility visited the inspector's area—the warders, supervisors, caregivers, and teachers. The gradual adoption of this "inspection principle" would, Bentham predicted, create "a new scene of things," transforming the world into a place with "morals reformed, health preserved, industry invigorated, instruction diffused, public burdens lightened."

The modern Panopticon is not a physical building, and it doesn't require the threat of an inspector's presence to be effective. Technological breakthroughs have made it easy to collect, store, and disseminate data on individuals, corporations, and even the government. With surveillance technology like closed-circuit television cameras and digital cameras now linked to the Internet, we have the means to implement Bentham's inspection principle on a much vaster scale. What's more, we have helped construct this new Panopticon, voluntarily giving up troves of personal information. We blog, tweet, and post what we are doing, thinking, and feeling. We allow friends and contacts, and even strangers, to know where we are at any time. We sign away our privacy in exchange for the conveniences of modern living, giving corporations access to information about our financial circumstances and our spending habits, which will then be used to target us for ads or to analyze our consumer habits.

Then there is the information collected without our consent. Since 2001, the number of U.S. government organizations involved in spying on our own citizens, both at home and abroad, has grown rapidly. Every day, the National Security Agency intercepts 1.7 billion emails, phone calls, instant messages, bulletin-board postings, and other communications. This system houses information on thousands of U.S. citizens, many of them not accused of any wrongdoing. Not long ago, when traffic police stopped a driver they had to radio the station and wait while someone checked records. Now, handheld devices instantly call up a person's Social Security number and license status, records of outstanding warrants, and even mug shots. The FBI can also cross-check your fingerprints against its digital archive of 96 million sets.

Yet the guarded have also struck back, in a sense, against their guardians, using organizations like WikiLeaks, which, according to its founder Julian Assange, has released more classified documents than the rest of the world's media combined, to keep tabs on governments and corporations. When Assange gave the *Guardian* 250,000 confidential cables, he did so on a USB drive the size of your little finger. Efforts to close down the WikiLeaks website have proven futile, because the files are mirrored on hundreds of other sites. And in any case, WikiLeaks isn't the only site revealing private information. An array of groups are able to release information anonymously. Governments, corporations, and other organizations interested in protecting privacy will strive to increase security, but they will also have to reckon with the likelihood that such measures are sometimes going to fail.

New technology has made greater openness possible, but has this openness made us better off? For those who think privacy is an inalienable right, the modern surveillance culture is a means of controlling behavior and stifling dissent. But perhaps the inspection principle, universally applied, could also be the perfection of democracy, the device that allows us to know what our governments are really doing, that keeps tabs on corporate abuses, and that protects our individual freedoms just as it subjects our personal lives to public scrutiny. In other words, will this technology be a form of tyranny or will it free us from tyranny? Will it upend democracy or strengthen it?

> **New technology has made greater openness possible, but has this openness made us better off?**

The standards of what we want to keep private and what we want to make public are constantly evolving. Over the course of Western history, we've developed a desire for more privacy, quite possibly as a status symbol, since an impoverished peasant could not afford a house with separate rooms. Today's affluent Americans display their status not only by having a bedroom for each member of the family, plus one for guests, but also by having a bathroom for every bedroom, plus one for visitors so that they do not have to see the family's personal effects. It wasn't always this way. A seventeenth-century Japanese *shunga* depicts a man making love with his wife while their daughter kneels on the floor nearby, practicing calligraphy. The people of Tikopia, a Pacific island inhabited by Polynesians, "find it good to sleep side by side crowding each other, next to their children or their parents or their brothers and sisters, mixing sexes and generations," according to the anthropologist Dorothy Lee. "[A]nd if a widow finds herself alone in her one-room house, she may adopt a child or a brother to allay her intolerable privacy." The Gebusi people in New Guinea live in communal longhouses and are said to "shun privacy," even showing reluctance to look at photos in which they are on their own.

With some social standards, the more people do something, the less risky it becomes for each individual. The first women to wear dresses that did not reach their knees were no doubt looked upon with disapproval, and may have risked unwanted sexual attention; but once many women were revealing more of their legs, the risks dissipated. So too with privacy: when millions of people are prepared to post personal information, doing so becomes less risky for everyone. And those collective, large-scale forfeitures of personal privacy have other benefits as well, as tens of thousands of

Egyptians showed when they openly became fans of the Facebook page "We are all Khaled Said," named after a young man who was beaten to death by police in Alexandria. The page became the online hub for the protests that forced the ouster of President Hosni Mubarak.

Whether Facebook and similar sites are reflecting a change in social norms about privacy or are actually driving that change, that half a billion are now on Facebook suggests that people believe the benefits of connecting with others, sharing information, networking, self-promoting, flirting, and bragging outweigh breaches of privacy that accompany such behavior.

More difficult questions arise when the loss of privacy is not in any sense a choice. Bentham's Panopticon has become a symbol of totalitarian intrusion. Michel Foucault* described it as "the perfection of power." We all know that the police can obtain phone records when seeking evidence of involvement in a crime, but most of us would be surprised by the frequency of such requests. Verizon alone receives 90,000 demands for information from law-enforcement agencies annually. Abuses have undoubtedly accompanied the recent increase in government surveillance. One glaring example is the case of Brandon Mayfield, an Oregon attorney and convert to Islam who was jailed on suspicion of involvement in the 2004 Madrid train bombings. After his arrest, Mayfield sued the government and persuaded a federal judge to declare the provision of the Patriot Act that the FBI used in investigating him unconstitutional. But as with most excesses of state power, the cause is not so much the investigative authority of the state as the state's erroneous interpretation of the information it uncovers and the unwarranted detentions that come about as a result. If those same powers were used to foil another 9/11, most Americans would likely applaud.

There is always a danger that the information collected will be misused — whether by regimes seeking to silence opposition or by corporations seeking to profit from more detailed knowledge of their potential customers. The scale and technological sophistication of this data-gathering enterprise allow the government to intercept and store far more information than was possible for secret police of even the most totalitarian states of an earlier era, and the large number of people who have access to sensitive information increases the potential for misuse.† As with any large-scale human activity, if enough people are involved eventually someone will do something corrupt or malicious. That's a drawback to having more data gathered, but one that may well be outweighed by the benefits. We don't really know how many terrorist plots have been foiled because of all this data-gathering.‡ We have even less idea how many innocent Americans were initially suspected of terrorism but *not* arrested because the enhanced data-gathering permitted under the Patriot Act convinced law-enforcement agents of their innocence.

The degree to which a government is repressive does not turn on the methods by which it acquires information about its citizens, or the amount of data it retains. When

10

---

*Michel Foucault: Influential French philosopher and historian (1926–1984), known for his writings on the nature of being, knowledge, and power [Ed.].

†Including those involved in international operations relating to homeland security and intelligence, 854,000 people currently hold top-secret security clearances, according to the *Washington Post*.

‡In 2003, FBI director Robert Mueller claimed that the number of thwarted plots was more than one hundred.

regimes want to harass their opponents or suppress opposition, they find ways to do it, with or without electronic data. Under President Nixon, the administration used tax audits to harass those on his "enemies list." That was mild compared with how "enemies" were handled during the dirty wars in Argentina, Guatemala, and Chile, and by the Stasi in East Germany. These repressive governments "disappeared" tens of thousands of dissidents, and they targeted their political enemies with what now seem impossibly cumbersome methods of collecting, storing, and sorting data. If such forms of abuse are rare in the United States, it is not because we have prevented the state from gathering electronic data about us. The crucial step in preventing a repressive government from misusing information is to have alert and well-informed citizens with a strong sense of right and wrong who work to keep the government democratic, open, just, and under the rule of law. The technological innovations used by governments and corporations to monitor citizens must be harnessed to monitor those very governments and corporations.

One of the first victories for citizen surveillance came in 1991, when George Holliday videotaped Los Angeles police officers beating Rodney King. Without that video, yet another LAPD assault on a black man would have passed unnoticed. Instead, racism and violence in police departments became a national issue, two officers went to prison, and King received $3.8 million in civil damages. Since then, videos and photographs, many of them taken on mobile phones, have captured innumerable crimes and injustices. Inverse surveillance—what Steve Mann, professor of computer engineering and proponent of wearing imaging devices, terms "sousveillance"—has become an effective way of informing the world of abuses of power.

We have seen the usefulness of sousveillance again this year in the Middle East, where the disclosure of thousands of diplomatic cables by WikiLeaks helped encourage the Tunisian and Egyptian revolutions, as well as the protest movements that spread to neighboring countries. Yet most government officials vehemently condemned the disclosure of state secrets. Secretary of State Hillary Clinton claimed that WikiLeaks' revelations "tear at the fabric of the proper function of responsible government." In February of this year, at George Washington University, she went further, saying that WikiLeaks had endangered human rights activists who had been in contact with U.S. diplomats, and rejecting the view that governments should conduct their work in full view of their citizens. As a counterexample, she pointed to U.S. efforts to secure nuclear material in the former Soviet states. Here, she claimed, confidentiality was necessary in order to avoid making it easier for terrorists or criminals to find the materials and steal them.

Clinton is right that it is not a good idea to make public the location of insecurely stored nuclear materials, but how much of diplomacy is like that? There may be some justifiable state secrets, but they certainly are few. For nearly all other dealings between nations, openness should be the norm. In any case, Clinton's claim that WikiLeaks releases documents "without regard for the consequences" is, if not deliberately misleading, woefully ignorant. Assange and his colleagues have consistently stated that they are motivated by a belief that a more transparent government will bring better consequences for all, and that leaking information has an inherent tendency toward greater justice, a view Assange laid out on his blog in December 2006, the month in which WikiLeaks published its first document:

> The more secretive or unjust an organization is, the more leaks induce fear and paranoia in its leadership and planning coterie. . . . Since unjust systems, by their nature induce opponents, and in many places barely have the upper hand, leaking leaves them exquisitely vulnerable to those who seek to replace them with more open forms of governance.*

Assange could now claim that WikiLeaks' disclosures have confirmed his theory. For instance, in 2007, months before a national election, WikiLeaks posted a report on corruption commissioned but not released by the Kenyan government. According to Assange, a Kenyan intelligence official found that the leaked report changed the minds of 10 percent of Kenyan voters, enough to shift the outcome of the election.

Two years later, in the aftermath of the global financial crisis, WikiLeaks released documents on dealings by Iceland's Kaupthing Bank, showing that the institution made multibillion-dollar loans, in some cases unsecured, to its major shareholders shortly before it collapsed. Kaupthing's successor, then known as New Kaupthing, obtained an injunction to prevent Iceland's national television network from reporting on the leaked documents but failed to prevent their dissemination. WikiLeaks' revelations stirred an uproar in the Icelandic parliament, which then voted unanimously to strengthen free speech and establish an international prize for freedom of expression. Senior officials of the bank are now facing criminal charges.

And of course, in April 2010, WikiLeaks released thirty-eight minutes of classified cockpit-video footage of two U.S. Army helicopters over a Baghdad suburb. The video showed the helicopter crews engaging in an attack on civilians that killed eighteen people, including two Reuters journalists, and wounded two children. Ever since the attack took place, in 2007, Reuters had unsuccessfully sought a U.S. military inquiry into the deaths of its two employees, as well as access to the cockpit video under the Freedom of Information Act. The United States had claimed that the two journalists were killed during a firefight. Although no action has been taken against the soldiers involved, if the military is ever going to exercise greater restraint when civilian lives are at risk, it will have been compelled to do so through the release of material like this.

Months before the Arab Spring began, Assange was asked whether he would release the trove of secret diplomatic cables that he was rumored to have obtained. Assange said he would, and gave this reason: "These sort of things reveal what the true state of, say, Arab governments are like, the true human rights abuses in those governments." As one young Tunisian wrote to the *Guardian*, his countrymen had known for many years that their leaders were corrupt, but that was not the same as reading the full details of particular incidents, rounded off with statements by American diplomats that corruption was keeping domestic investment low and unemployment high. The success of Tunisia's revolution undoubtedly influenced the rest of the Arab

15

---

*Robert Manne, a professor of politics at Australia's La Trobe University and the author of a detailed examination of Assange's writings that appeared recently in *The Monthly*, comments: "There are few original ideas in politics. In the creation of WikiLeaks, Julian Assange was responsible for one."

world, putting U.S. diplomats in an uncomfortable predicament. A mere three months after condemning WikiLeaks for releasing stolen documents "without regard to the consequences," Secretary Clinton found herself speaking warmly about one of those outcomes: the movement for reform in the Middle East.

WikiLeaks' revelations have had profound ramifications, but as with any event of this scale, it is not easy to judge whether those consequences are, on the whole, desirable. Assange himself admitted to the *Guardian* that as a result of the leaked corruption report in Kenya, and the violence that swept the country during its elections, 1,300 people were killed and 350,000 displaced; but, he added, 40,000 Kenyan children die every year from malaria, and these and many more are dying because of the role corruption plays in keeping Kenyans poor.* The Kenyan people, Assange believes, had a right to the information in the leaked report because "decision-making that is based upon lies or ignorance can't lead to a good conclusion."

In making that claim, Assange aligned himself with a widely held view in demo-   20
cratic theory, and a standard argument for freedom of speech: elections can express the will of the people only if the people are reasonably well informed about the issues on which they base their votes. That does not mean that decision-making based on the truth always leads to better outcomes than decision-making based on ignorance. There is no reason for Assange to be committed to that claim, any more than a supporter of democracy must be committed to the claim that democratic forms of government always reach better decisions than authoritarian regimes. Nor does a belief in the benefits of transparency imply that people must know the truth about everything; but it does suggest that more information is generally better, and so provides grounds for a presumption against withholding the truth.

What of Clinton's claims that the leaks have endangered human rights activists who gave information to American diplomats? When WikiLeaks released 70,000 documents about the war in Afghanistan, in July 2010, Admiral Mike Mullen, chairman of the Joint Chiefs of Staff, said that Assange had blood on his hands, yet no casualties resulting from the leaks have been reported — unless you count the ambassadors forced to step down due to embarrassing revelations. Four months after the documents were released, a senior NATO official told CNN that there had not been a single case of an Afghan needing protection because of the leaks. Of course, that may have been "just pure luck," as Daniel Domscheit-Berg, a WikiLeaks defector, told the *New York Times* in February. Assange himself has admitted that he cannot guarantee that the leaks will not cost lives, but in his view the likelihood that they will save lives justifies the risk.

WikiLeaks has never released the kind of information that Clinton pointed to in defending the need for secrecy. Still, there are other groups out there, such as the Russian anti-corruption site Rospil.info, the European Union site BrusselsLeaks, the Czech PirateLeaks, Anonymous, and so on, that release leaked materials with less scrupulousness. It is entirely possible that there will be leaks that everyone will regret. Yet given that the leaked materials on the wars in Afghanistan and Iraq show tens of thousands

---

*The United Nations claimed that as many as 600,000 Kenyans were displaced after the election.

of civilian lives lost due to the needless, reckless, and even callous actions of members of the U.S. military, it is impossible to listen to U.S. leaders blame WikiLeaks for endangering innocent lives without hearing the tinkle of shattering glass houses.

In the Panopticon, of course, transparency would not be limited to governments. Animal rights advocates have long said that if slaughterhouses had glass walls, more people would become vegetarian, and seeing the factory farms in which most of the meat, eggs, and milk we consume are produced would be more shocking even than the slaughterhouses. And why should restaurant customers have to rely on occasional visits by health inspectors? Webcams in food-preparation areas could provide additional opportunities for checking on the sanitary conditions of the food we are about to eat.

Bentham may have been right when he suggested that if we all knew that we were, at any time, liable to be observed, our morals would be reformed. Melissa Bateson and her colleagues at England's Newcastle University tested this theory when they put a poster with a pair of eyes above a canteen honesty box. People taking a hot drink put almost three times as much money in the box with the eyes present as they did when the eyes were replaced by a poster of flowers. The mere suggestion that someone was watching encouraged greater honesty. (Assuming that the eyes did not lead people to overpay, the study also implies a disturbing level of routine dishonesty.)

We might also become more altruistic. Dale Miller, a professor of organizational behavior at Stanford University, has pointed out that Americans assume a "norm of self-interest" that makes acting altruistically seem odd or even irrational. Yet Americans perform altruistic acts all the time, and bringing those acts to light might break down the norm that curtails our generosity. Consistent with that hypothesis, researchers at the University of Pennsylvania found that people are likely to give more to listener-sponsored radio stations when they are told that other callers are giving above-average donations. Similarly, when utility companies send customers a comparison of their energy use with the average in their neighborhood, customers with above-average use reduce their consumption.

The world before WikiLeaks and Facebook may have seemed a more secure place, but to say whether it was a better world is much more difficult. Will fewer children ultimately die from poverty in Kenya because WikiLeaks released the report on corruption? Will life in the Middle East improve as a result of the revolutions to which WikiLeaks and social media contributed? As the Chinese communist leader Zhou Enlai responded when asked his opinion of the French Revolution of 1789, it is too soon to say. The way we answer the question will depend on whether we share Assange's belief that decision-making leads to better outcomes when based on the truth than when based on lies and ignorance.

Exploring Context

1. Locate and then review the privacy policy at Facebook or some other site you frequently use. How does the content of that policy relate to Singer's arguments about our willingness to disclose information about ourselves? Given Singer's examples, do you think any privacy policy can protect you? Use your response to Question 1 of Questions for Critical Reading in forming your answer.

2. Explore the Web site for WikiLeaks (wikileaks.org). Use what you find there to argue whether or not the site threatens or supports democracy. Incorporate your work from Question 3 of Questions for Critical Reading.

3. Some people have been arrested for recording or taking pictures of police on duty — the kind of "sousveillance" that Singer suggests keeps governments honest. Visit the Web site Privacy & Technology, maintained by the American Civil Liberties Union (aclu.org/issues/privacy-technology). How does the information you find there change your understanding of Singer's argument? Does it change your response to Question 2 of Questions for Critical Reading?

Questions for Connecting

1. Kwame Anthony Appiah explores how practices change in societies in his essays "Making Conversation" and "The Primacy of Practice" (p. 44). Apply Appiah's ideas to Singer's analysis of the evolution of privacy. What drives recent changes to our understanding of privacy: values or practices? Incorporate your work from Question 1 of Questions for Critical Reading in making your response.

2. Tomas van Houtryve, in "From the Eyes of a Drone" (p. 449), considers the military uses of surveillance drones, expressing his concerns at this "weaponization" of photography. Apply Singer's argument to van Houtryve to consider the ways that drones might be used in sousveillance. Does the public potential of this technology mitigate its military uses? How do Van Houtryve's own photographs relate to sousveillance? Use your thoughts on sousveillance from Question 2 of Questions for Critical Reading.

3. In his essays "Preface" and "The New Civil Rights" (p. 539), Kenji Yoshino argues both that we have a tendency to "cover" or downplay parts of our identity and that we need to move to a new model of civil rights, one based on basic rights and freedoms for all individuals. How does the kind of society Singer describes complicate Yoshino's argument? Is it as easy to cover in a society of surveillance with less concern about privacy? Is Yoshino's "liberty paradigm" for civil rights realistic, given social technologies and their impact on privacy?

Language Matters

1. Audience is a primary concern for all writers. Consider the difference between private and public audiences, using Singer's ideas about privacy. How does your writing change based on notions of privacy? What level of privacy, and thus what audience, is reflected in academic writing?

2. Consider how you write for social media — places like Facebook or Twitter. What are the conventions of writing in these arenas, and how do they differ from those of writing in an academic setting? How important is context to writing?

3. The Swedish furniture maker Ikea uses simplistic pictorial instructions to help people assemble furniture. Go to Ikea's Web site (ikea.com/us/en/), look up a furniture product, and click on the link for "Assembly Instructions" in the Product Information section.

Using these instructions as a model, create a pictorial guide to Singer's argument, a set of instructions for understanding his essay.

Assignments for Writing

1. What is the role of privacy in a democracy? Write a paper in which you address this question using ideas from Singer's essay. Should democracies protect privacy? Is transparency necessary for democracy? Use your work from Questions for Critical Reading in making your response.

2. Write a paper in which you determine the ethics of privacy. When, if ever, is it ethical to violate privacy? What ethical standards should we use in determining and protecting privacy? Use Singer's discussion to support your position as well as your work in Questions for Critical Reading. Consider, too, the subtitle of Singer's essay, "Ethics in a World without Secrets."

3. Using Singer's discussion, write a paper in which you trace the evolution and implications of notions of privacy. What forces shape our understanding of privacy? How has privacy changed? What can we do to shape its future?

RHYS SOUTHAN

Rhys Southan is a freelance writer who maintains his own blog, *Let Them Eat Meat*, about veganism from his ex-vegan perspective. His writing has appeared in the *New Inquiry*, the *New York Times*, and *Aeon Magazine*.

Aeon Magazine is an online-only publication founded in 2012 by Paul and Brigid Hains that specializes in publishing original essays almost every day, on topics ranging from science and philosophy to modern society. "Is Art a Waste of Time?" appeared in *Aeon Magazine* on March 20, 2014. In it, Southan explains that an activism movement called "Effective Altruism" has been embraced by a growing group of people who "want to reduce suffering and increase lifespan and happiness" (p. 436) across the world. This seems well and good, but the movement is also caught up in the core concept of replaceability, which suggests that because people who spend their available time creating art are not feeding the homeless, art (and thus all artistic expression) is not worth pursuing.

Does art have a place in our world? What is its function?

▶ TAGS: *art, community, economics, empathy, ethics, globalism, judgment and decision-making, social change*

▶ CONNECTIONS: *Appiah, Dalai Lama, DeGhett, Klosterman, Ma, Pollan, Savage/Vaid, Wallace, Watters*

Questions for Critical Reading

1. How important do you feel it is to relieve suffering in the world? What are you willing to do to contribute to that goal? As you read, pay close attention to the definition and practice of *Effective Altruism*. Do you support this philosophy? What do you do that you think is consistent with the practice?

2. According to Effective Altruists, when *is* it OK to make art? Mark the passages where Southan explains justifiable reasons to make art when acting from Effective Altruism.

3. Central to Effective Altruism is the notion of *replaceability*. Note Southan's definition of this term. In what ways does it function within the Effective Altruism movement?

Is Art a Waste of Time?

With less than a week to finish my screenplay for the last round of a big screenwriting competition, I stepped on a train with two members of a growing activism movement called Effective Altruism. Holly Morgan was the managing director for The Life You Can Save, an organization that encourages privileged Westerners to help reduce global poverty. Sam Hilton had organized the London pub meet-up where I'd first heard about the movement (known as "EA" for short; its members are EAs). The pair of them were heading to East Devon with a few others for a cottage retreat, where they were going to relax among sheep and alpacas, visit a ruined abbey, and get some altruism-related writing done. I decided to join them because I liked the idea of finishing my script (a very dark comedy) in the idyllic English countryside, and because I wanted to learn more about the EA goal of doing as much good as you possibly can with your life. We were already halfway there when my second reason for going threatened to undermine my first.

Around Basingstoke, I asked Hilton what EAs thought about using art to improve the world. In the back of my mind I had my own screenplay, and possibly also Steven Soderbergh's 2001 Oscar acceptance speech for best director, which I'd once found inspiring:

> I want to thank anyone who spends a part of their day creating. I don't care if it's a book, a film, a painting, a dance, a piece of theater, a piece of music. Anybody who spends part of their day sharing their experience with us. I think this world would be unlivable without art.

It turns out that this is not a speech that would have resonated with many Effective Altruists. The idea that someone's book, film, painting, or dance could be their way to reduce the world's suffering struck Hilton as bizarre, almost to the point of incoherence. As I watched his furrowing brow struggle to make sense of my question, I started to doubt whether this retreat was an appropriate venue for my screenwriting ambitions after all.

In 1972, the Australian moral philosopher Peter Singer published an essay called "Famine, Affluence, and Morality," which contained the following thought experiment. Suppose you saw a child drowning in a pond: would you jump in and rescue her, even if you hadn't pushed her in? Even if it meant ruining your clothes? It would be highly controversial to say "no" — and yet most of us manage to ignore those dying of poverty and preventable disease all over the world, though we could easily help them. Singer argues that this inconsistency is unjustifiable. The EAs agree, and have dedicated their lives to living out the radical implications of this philosophy. If distance is morally irrelevant, then devastating poverty and preventable disease surround us. Any break we take from working to reduce suffering throughout the world is like having a leisurely nap beside a lake where thousands of children are screaming for our help.

The EA movement started coalescing in Oxford in 2009 when the philosophers Toby Ord and William MacAskill came together with around 20 others to work out how to make radical altruism mainstream. MacAskill told me that they went by the jokey moniker "Super Hardcore Do-Gooders," until they came up with "Effective Altruism" in 2011. Along with various other EA-affiliated organizations, Ord and MacAskill co-founded Giving What We Can, which suggests a baseline donation of 10 percent of your income to effective charities.

This is often what EA comes down to: working hard to earn money and then giving as much of it as you can to the needy. Good deeds come in many forms, of course, and there are other ways of making a difference. But the gauntlet that EA throws down is simply this: does your preferred good deed make as much of a difference as simply handing over the money? If not, how good a deed is it really?

Once we'd settled in at the cottage, Hilton and I stepped out for a walk through the bits of forest that hadn't been razed for pasture, and he asked if my script would be one of the best scripts ever written. At the time I thought he was trolling me. I obviously couldn't say "yes," but "no" would somehow feel like an admission of failure. It was only after talking to other EAs that I came to understand what he was getting at. As EAs see it, writing scripts and making movies demands resources that, in the right hands, could have saved lives. If the movie in question is clearly frivolous, this seems impossible to justify ethically. If, on the other hand, you're making the best movie of all time . . . well, it could almost start to be worthwhile. But I told Hilton "no," and felt a lingering sense of futility as we tramped on through the stinging nettles around the cottage.

I did manage to finish the script that weekend, despite Hilton's crushing anti-pep talk. I felt good about it—but something about the movement had captured my interest, and over the following weeks I kept talking to EAs. Like Hilton, most of them seemed doubtful that art had much power to alter the world for the better. And somewhere between submitting my script in September and receiving the regret-to-inform in December, I started to feel like they might have a point.

The central premise of Effective Altruism is alluringly intuitive. Simply put, EAs want to reduce suffering and increase lifespan and happiness. That's it; nothing else matters. As Morgan explained in an email to me:

> I find that most of us seem to ultimately care about something close to the concept of "wellbeing"—we want everyone to be happy and fulfilled, and we promote anything that leads to humans and animals feeling happy and fulfilled. I rarely meet Effective Altruists who care about, say, beauty, knowledge, life or the environment for their own sake—rather, they tend to find that they care about these things only insofar as they contribute to wellbeing.

From this point of view, the importance of most individual works of art would have to be negligible compared with, say, deworming 1,000 children. An idea often paraphrased in EA circles is that it doesn't matter who does something—what matters is that it gets done. And though artists often pride themselves on the uniqueness of their individuality, it doesn't follow that they have something uniquely valuable to offer society. On the contrary, says Diego Caleiro, director of the Brazil-based Institute for Ethics, Rationality, and the Future of Humanity, most of them are "counterfactually replaceable": one artist is as pretty much as useful as the next. And of course, the supply is plentiful.

Replaceability is a core concept in EA. The idea is that the only good that counts is what you accomplish over and above what the next person would have done in your place. In equation form, Your Apparent Good Achieved minus the Good Your Counterfactual Replacement Would Have Achieved equals Your Actual Good Achieved. This is a disconcerting calculation, because even if you think you've been doing great work, your final score could be small or negative. While it might seem as though working for a charity makes a major positive impact, you have to remember the other eager applicants who would have worked just as hard if they'd been hired instead. Is the world in which you got the job really better than the world in which the other person did? Maybe not.

It is in the interests of becoming irreplaceable that a lot of EAs promote "earning to give" — getting a well-paid job and donating carefully. If you score a lucrative programming job and then give away half your income, most of your competition probably wouldn't have donated as much money. As far as the great universal calculation of utility is concerned, you have made yourself hard to replace. Artists, meanwhile, paint the beautiful landscape in front of them while the rest of the world burns.

Artists, meanwhile, paint the beautiful landscape in front of them while the rest of the world burns.

Ozzie Gooen, a programmer for the UK-based ethical careers website 80,000 Hours, told me about a satirical superhero he invented to spoof creative people in rich countries who care more about making cool art than helping needy people, yet feel good about themselves because it's better than nothing. "I make the joke of 'Net-Positive Man,'" Gooen said. "He has all the resources and advantages and money, and he goes around the world doing net-positive things. Like he'll see someone drowning in a well, and he's like, 'But don't worry, I'm here. Net positive! Here's a YouTube Video! It's net positive!'"

If, despite all this, you remain committed to a career in the arts, is there any hope for you? In fact, yes: two routes to the praiseworthy life remain open. If you happen to be successful already, you can always earn to give. And if you aren't, perhaps you can use your talent to attract new EA recruits and spread altruistic ideas.

"We're actually very stacked out with people who have good mathematic skills, good philosophy skills," Robert Wiblin, executive director of the Centre for Effective Altruism, told me. "I would really love to have some artists. We really need visual designers. It would be great to have people think about how Effective Altruism could be promoted through art." Aesthetic mavericks who anticipate long wilderness years of rejection and struggle, however, would seem to have little to contribute to the cause. Perhaps they should think about ditching their dreams for what Caleiro calls "an area with higher expected returns."

For an aspiring screenwriter like me, this is a disappointing message. Brian Tomasik, the American writer of the website Essays on Reducing Suffering, told me that artists who abandon their craft to help others should take solace in the theory that all possible artwork already exists somewhere in the quantum multiverse. As he put it: "With reducing suffering, we care about decreasing the quantity that exists, but with artwork, it seems you'd only care about existence or not in a binary fashion. So if all art already exists within some measure, isn't that good enough?"

I actually do find that mildly comforting, if it's true, but I'm not convinced that it will win many supporters to the EA cause. The problem, ironically, might actually be an aesthetic one.

Effective Altruism is part subversive, part conformist: subversive in its radical egalitarianism and its critique of complacent privilege; conformist in that it's another force channeling us towards the traditional success model. The altruistic Übermensch is a hard-working money mover, a clean-cut advocate, or a brilliant innovator of utility-improving devices or ideas. As usual, creative types are ignored if their ideas aren't lucrative or if they don't support a favored ideology. Crass materialism and ethical anti-materialism now seem to share identical means: earning money or rephrasing the ideas of others. But there are plenty of people drawn to the media and the arts who care about making the world better. For them to accept the EA position will often require that they give up what they love to do most. What do EAs say to that? For the most part, they say "tough."

"What's implied by utilitarianism," explained Michael Bitton, a once-aspiring Canadian filmmaker turned EA, "is that nothing is sacred. Everything that exists is subject to utilitarian calculations. So there's no such thing as, 'Oh, this is art, or, oh, this is my religion, therefore it's exempt from ethical considerations.'" Wiblin has a similar view. "It is true that Effective Altruism would sometimes say that the thing you most enjoy isn't the most moral thing to do," he told me. "And yeah, some people wanted to be writers, but actually instead they should go into development aid or go into activism or something else."

> **"Effective Altruism would sometimes say that the thing you most enjoy isn't the most moral thing to do."**

Still, disappointed arts types might be able to console themselves with the thought that not even science is exempt from EA's remorseless logic. "I myself was extremely interested in evolutionary biology," Wiblin said, "and I would have liked to become an academic in that area. But I couldn't really justify it on the effects that it has on helping other people, even though I found it fascinating."

The iron logic of replaceability leaves many dreams dead on the ground, to be sure. But is this a problem with EA as an ideology, or a problem with reality? It would be great if the arts and humanities were hugely beneficial to the world, because they tend to be personally satisfying. Still, if they're not in fact helping much, artists might be operating on some questionable values. Is your self-expression more important than human lives and suffering? Would you rather contribute to the culture of rich societies than work to reduce the suffering of the poor, or of future generations? Is it not arbitrary to fill the world with your own personal spin on things, simply because it's yours?

Here's a simple test to determine if you're creating art for yourself or for the world. If you discovered that someone else had independently come up with a project idea that you'd also had, but they produced and distributed their work first, would you be upset? Or would you be thrilled that this vitally important stuff was out there, altering perspectives and making everything better in a real, quantifiable way—even though it wouldn't increase your social status?

"I think that there's sort of a mass delusion among artists and writers that just because there's almost nothing that confers more privilege and prestige and symbolic capital than art, just because it's high-status, people think it's of a high importance," said the Australian writer Chris Rodley. "And I think that's wrong. Which is probably a weird, contradictory position for someone who wants to do art to take."

Rodley is one of the two EAs I talked to with a media and arts background. The other was Michael Bitton, who is a postgraduate in media production in Toronto. "I wanted to be a filmmaker, and then I thought, 'Well what good does this do?'" he told me. "So I kind of stopped wanting to be a filmmaker."

Despite their reservations, both Rodley and Bitton are investigating the kinds of creative projects with potential to do the most good, on the assumption that it could sometimes make sense for EAs to influence culture through arts and media. For Bitton, this means questioning whether "the traditional criteria of artistic greatness, like the profundity of ideas, or the emotional impact, or originality or timelessness or popularity," automatically translates into good consequences. "The concept of artistic integrity is inherently in opposition to the concept of Effective Altruism," he told me. "I don't think you could go all the way Effective Altruist as an artist without compromising your 'artistic integrity.'" In theory, Bitton suggests, "you could have an artist who's making stuff that he or she has no interest in whatsoever, doesn't like, doesn't find interesting or funny, doesn't know the point of, but that's the optimal work of art according to our magic consequences calculator . . ."

Rodley suggests that EA artists could have something to learn from the medieval period, when social value and impact were the goals of art, before the "art for art's sake mythology" shifted the focus to intrinsic merit. Take the Christian mystery plays: "They were proto-utilitarian art works. A lot of them were trying to save the audience's souls. And what greater utilitarian deed could you accomplish than averting infinite suffering?"

> **"[W]hat greater utilitarian deed could you accomplish than averting infinite suffering?"**

Of course, most EAs don't believe in souls, much less eternal damnation, so a return to passion plays and Last Supper paintings isn't what they're suggesting. They're more interested in how we could use art to reduce the suffering of humans, animals, and future beings—including AI computers and emulated minds. I talked to Bitton and Rodley separately, but they converged on some general guidelines for the utilitarian-minded artist.

Firstly, the entertainment value of a project is fleeting, so what really matters is how it influences political or social behavior. That's why narrative, or at least some way of expressing concrete ideas, is essential. "It's hard to see how a vase or something would really impact culture in any one way, because what does it teach you about life?" Bitton said. He suggests that it might be useful to sneak good memes such as "racism is bad" or "sexism is bad" into mainstream fictional works, especially if you can avoid the heavy-handed "very special episode" feel.

Rodley, meanwhile, pointed to experimental sound design as an anti-utilitarian dead end. In general, the avant-garde is suspect because art's impact grows by reaching larger audiences, which gives the advantage to books, films, lyrical songs, video games, and smartphone apps that make altruistic ideas palatable. "Look at Singer's shallow-pond analogy," Rodley said. "In a way, that's sort of an artistic, fictional parable. It's quite striking and has many of the features of a creative work."

Still, if we were to consult our magic utilitarian consequences calculator, how often would it tell us to bother making art at all? Persuasive, progressive art might be better than nothing, but that doesn't make it an optimal use of time and resources. Even if a socially minded piece of media gets enough attention to make a positive impact (rare enough in itself), its noticeable effects are often mixed. 30

Rodley pointed out that the U.S. TV series *Will & Grace* might have made some Americans more accepting of gay people, but it also arguably imposed "homonormative" expectations on how gay people are supposed to act. Similarly, Harriet Beecher Stowe's novel *Uncle Tom's Cabin* (1852) apparently turned many white Americans against slavery while also perpetuating damaging stereotypes. The U.S. documentary

Searching for Sugar Man (2012) claims that the music of Sixto Rodriguez helped to inspire anti-apartheid protestors in South Africa, but presents this as an accidental and serendipitous side-effect rather than something Rodriguez could have consciously set out to do. Famous artists have a lot of influence and money to give away to good causes. But, said Rodley: "By definition, most artists are mediocre, and their art doesn't really please many people, if any."

If what you want to do is make the world better, the impact of paying to treat many people with curable diseases might seem a little humdrum compared with the revolution in human consciousness that will surely come when you publish your novel. But if donating to charity feels a bit generic, the lives it saves are not. All of which is to say, when I thought that writing a movie was the best way for me to contribute to the world, I was almost certainly kidding myself. Then again, to some extent, we all do.

"If you accept the shallow-pond analogy, everyone is morally horrific," said Rodley. "Even Peter Singer himself. Everyone can be doing more than they currently are."

For now, that will have to be my justification. I'm not ready to give up writing. I'm not ready to take up some high-paid job that I'd hate in order to reduce the world's suffering. Maybe that will change. For now, call me Net-Positive Man.

Exploring Context

1. Visit the Web site for the Centre for Effective Altruism at centreforeffectivealtruism.org. Explore the site to learn more about Effective Altruism. How does the site echo Southan's characterization of this movement?

2. Southan mentions the Web site 80,000 Hours (80000hours.org). What does the site have to say about your intended career? What techniques does the site use to try to persuade you to make the most of your career in terms of its social impact?

3. The Life You Can Save is another Effective Altruism organization that Southan discusses. Visit its Web site at thelifeyoucansave.org. Based on the content and design, what audience do you think the site imagines? Does its audience include you?

Questions for Connecting

1. One of the goals of Effective Altruism is to promote the well-being of animals as well as people. Apply Southan's understanding of Effective Altruism to the problem of eating lobsters as detailed by David Foster Wallace in "Consider the Lobster" (p. 459). How might Effective Altruism offer a solution to the challenge of animal suffering? How can we balance well-being with eating? Draw from your work in Question 1 of Questions for Critical Reading as well as your exploration of Effective Altruism in Exploring Context.

2. Judgment is central to Effective Altruism since one must make decisions about how to maximize contributions to the well-being of others. Are these judgments subject to the "illusion of validity" discussed by Daniel Kahneman in "The Surety of Fools" (p. 215)? How does Kahneman's argument challenge the practice of Effective Altruism? How can we resolve any possible contradiction?

3. Apply Effective Altruism's standards for art to the war photograph at the center of Torie Rose DeGhett's "The War Photo No One Would Publish" (p. 74). Would Effective Altruism support the publication of this photograph? Is that image "replaceable"? What good might it have done in the world? Use your work on the value of art and the concept of replaceability from Questions 2 and 3 of Questions for Critical Reading.

Language Matters

1. Southan often uses colons in his writing. Locate several examples of sentences where he uses a colon. Then, using a grammar handbook or other reliable resource, review the rules for colons. Does Southan's usage follow these rules? When might you use colons in your own writing?

2. The television series *Will & Grace* and the novel *Uncle Tom's Cabin* both appear as examples in Southan's essay. Review the rules for using italics for titles using a grammar handbook or other reliable reference source. Would the title of Southan's own essay be italicized?

3. Select a section of the essay and then locate and remove the topic sentence of each paragraph in that section. What strategies did you use to find the topic sentences? How does removing a paragraph's topic sentence affect the meaning of the paragraph?

Assignments for Writing

1. According to Southan, Effective Altruism is "conformist in that it's another force channeling us towards the traditional success model" (p. 437). Write a paper in which you challenge the model of success at the core of Effective Altruism. Does Effective Altruism guide people to high-paying jobs despite their interests? Is money central to success? Use your explorations of Effective Altruism organizations in Exploring Context to support your argument.

2. Which careers are ethical? Using Southan's ideas, write a paper in which you propose standards for working ethically. Is there a way to pursue a career consistent with ethical principles that doesn't involve heavily donating income? Is it more ethical to be true to yourself in your choice of career or to dedicate your work to helping others?

3. The concept of replaceability helps Effective Altruists measure one's contributions to the world. Write a paper in which you analyze the implications of replaceability. What happens if you extend this idea to other areas of life? Does uniqueness exist? Does it hold inherent value? Use your work from Question 3 of Questions for Critical Reading in your response.

SARAH STILLMAN

Courtesy of Sarah Stillman

Sarah Stillman is a staff writer for the *New Yorker* and has served as a visiting scholar at the Arthur L. Carter Journalism Institute at New York University. Her work has also been published in the *Washington Post*, the *Nation*, and the *Atlantic*, and she has received the Hillman Prize, the George Polk Award, and the National Magazine Award.

On August 12, 2014, Stillman's "Hiroshima and the Inheritance of Trauma" was published in the online version of the *New Yorker*, alongside articles documenting the civil unrest in Ferguson, Missouri, and remembering the then recently deceased Robin Williams. Like its print counterpart, the online edition of the *New Yorker* includes thoughtful essays (including those that appear in the print issues), but it also features daily contributions from *New Yorker* writers and artists as well as podcasts, videos, and interactive graphics.

In "Hiroshima and the Inheritance of Trauma," Stillman not only explores the lingering effects of trauma on the person who experiences it (here through the lens of a *hibakusha*, one who survived the atomic bombs in Hiroshima and Nagasaki) but also examines how that trauma becomes "trans-generational" and affects people in the survivor's family and community who have not experienced the trauma directly themselves. Though we often think of trauma as an experience that affects the individual who survives it, Stillman suggests that it is instead a contagious disease, one that can spread across both families and generations. For Shoji, the *hibakusha* at the center of Stillman's essay, part of her recovery from this disease involves telling her story of survival in the aftermath of an atomic bomb.

▶ TAGS: *genetics, health and medicine, psychology, trauma and violence, war and conflict*
▶ CONNECTIONS: *DeGhett, Epstein, Gilbert, Moalem, Paumgarten, Restak, Serano*

Questions for Critical Reading

1. Write some notes on your understanding of how a communicable disease like the flu works. As you read, pay attention to the ways in which Stillman argues that trauma functions like this kind of disease. Does her description of the effects of the Hiroshima bombing match your own understanding of how diseases work? How do they differ? How does your disease model challenge or complicate Stillman?

2. What role does shame play in trauma? As you read, note places where Stillman discusses shame and its effects. What does the role of shame suggest about the link between the body and the mind?

3. Does knowing that trauma can be inherited change our moral obligations in relation to war? Consider how our decisions regarding war might change with a different understanding of trauma, supporting your points with passages from Stillman.

Hiroshima and the Inheritance of Trauma

Sixty-nine years ago last week, a slender woman named Tomiko Shoji was struck and sent aloft by a bright white light. She'd just arrived at her secretarial job, at a tobacco factory, and was standing by the door when the flash occurred; the light's source had a nickname, Little Boy, but it meant nothing to her at the time. She flew backward under the crushing force of the office door, passed out, and awoke with shards of glass in her head and an expanse of bodies around her—some dead, some alive but dazed, and many more, she soon found, floating "like charcoal" in nearby rivers. The nineteen-year-old climbed up and out of the shell of her younger self; she had survived the U.S. atomic bombing of Hiroshima. Nearly seven decades later, Keni Sabath, Shoji's youngest granddaughter, started to wonder: Had the bombing's aftermath reshaped not just the psyche of her *bachan* (grandmother) but also, in ways both culturally and historically particular, her own?

In recent years, a public-health hypothesis has emerged that one of the world's most poorly understood pandemics isn't a conventional virus—like H1N1, say, or some hemorrhagic fever. This hypothesis suggests that untended wartime trauma can move vertically and horizontally through individuals and families, morphing across years, decades, or even centuries. Sabath began considering the prospect as early as high school, after certain overpowering symptoms emerged on a family visit to Hiroshima when she was six. It was Sabath who had arranged for me to visit her *bachan* at her aunt's home in Hilliard, Ohio, where Shoji agreed to share her first full account of the bombing and the family mysteries that followed.

On my way to Hilliard, I carried my copy of John Hersey's *Hiroshima*. (My 1989 edition bears the cover endorsement "Everyone able to read should read it," and I agree.) Its text first appeared as an entire issue of this magazine, on the one-year anniversary of the bombing, and followed the fates of six civilians in the aftermath. Even now, on a more distant anniversary, Hersey's granular rendering gives an urgency to these stories: of a young clerk, Shoji's age, who found herself crushed beneath a pile of books; of a Methodist pastor who charged his way back into the city to help, passing victims whose eyebrows had been singed off and women with the flower patterns of kimonos burned into their skin.

As I entered Shoji's home, on a quiet cul-de-sac, she swept my hand into hers and pressed her cool forehead against mine by way of welcome. Her eldest daughter, Minori, gave me a pair of slippers to wear inside; as the three of us shuffled into the kitchen, where fresh berries and tea cakes awaited, we paused to examine photographs of the Reverend Kiyoshi Tanimoto, the same pastor who weaves his way through Hersey's narrative, and who also, apparently, stood at the center of Shoji's. She first came across him preaching in an open-air bazaar in Hiroshima not long after the bombing; he gave her a piece of paper with information about his church, and she soon converted to Christianity. (He later baptized her grandson, Isao, who served as my translator well into the early evening.) Some of the first words Shoji spoke to me in Japanese were about the Reverend: "He would say, 'Tomiko, why don't we go all over the world together and tell them of our experiences with the bomb?'"

Tanimoto made a second career out of his own suggestion; on the fortieth anniversary of the bombing, Hersey wrote a follow-up story for the magazine, "Hiroshima: The Aftermath," in which he described the pastor's extensive U.S. speaking tour to promote peace. But Shoji wasn't ready to speak freely at the time. This past July, the last surviving crew member of the *Enola Gay*, the plane that dropped Little Boy, died in Stone Mountain, Georgia, having given many interviews. By then, Shoji had made up her mind that, in her eighty-eighth year, she would share her own account of what happened on the other side of the bomb. So we began right there, with the flash.

"Radiation! Heat! The wind from the bomb!" When Shoji began to describe her recollections from August 6, 1945, she took on a staccato pattern of speech, gesticulating rapidly. A tiny woman with pixie-gray hair and a sweet, flushed face, she slapped her small hands together and pummelled her head with pinched fingers, as if to imitate flying debris from the blast. At one point, she pretended to fling burned skin across the room like zucchini peels. Then she closed her eyes and went into a deep repose, resurfacing with a sudden phrase: "I'm scared to meet people," she said, speaking in the present tense of her teen-age self, who might also be herself at eighty-eight. "Something could just blow up. I've seen it before."

On the morning of the bombing—it was 8:15, the start of the workday—Shoji recalls briefly losing consciousness at the Bureau of Tobacco. "When I got up, I ran down to the first floor, down to the bomb shelter," she said. "All over was smoke; the entire city was covered with smoke. I saw people coming across the bridge just completely black—covered by blood, coming towards us. . . . The whole city was a sea of fire. And then, at night, it rained black rain."

Collecting herself, she began walking with colleagues across the city's many bridges, toward the sea. She caught a train in Hiroshima's west hoping to find her sister, to no avail; en route were whole trolley cars that had been blown off their tracks, filled with singed corpses. After spending the night, she returned home to find a note from the same sister, which read, "You can find me at the school." The two stayed in the school turned shelter for some time thereafter, living in a true dystopia. "There were tens of thousands of flies from the dead bodies," she recalled. "Our greetings to each other became: are you having diarrhea?"

For all those who perished in the bombing, many more survived, day by day. Only later would some, like Shoji, come to discover that the most devastating aftereffects were like ghosts: coming and going on a whim, wreaking forms of havoc often incomprehensible to outsiders and, sometimes, even to those who suffered it.

> **[T]he most devastating aftereffects were like ghosts: coming and going on a whim, wreaking forms of havoc often incomprehensible to outsiders.**

I'd always assumed, in ignorance, that to survive the atomic bomb—to be a *hibakusha*, or "explosion-affected person"—was to have conferred upon you a certain esteem or deference, not unlike that afforded to the bearer of a Purple Heart. Shoji's family wasted no time correcting me. To be a *hibakusha*, they explained, was not an honorific but a source of shame, a secret to be closely held. Even grandchildren have often feared telling romantic partners of their grandparents' experience, worried that their genetic material would be perceived as spoiled goods.

Eventually, Shoji's family planned for her to enter an arranged marriage with a prominent policeman in Taiwan, where she relocated in her early twenties. They kept her *hibakusha* status hushed, and refused to allow the two to talk before the ceremony, so as to better seal the secret. "My hands were shaking, holding my bouquet," Shoji recalled. When her husband learned the news afterward, he spiralled into a rage that never lifted. For the rest of the marriage, Shoji's daughter Minori said, "He felt he'd been cheated."

The next several decades brought a parade of physical ailments that were easily traceable to the bomb: Shoji's eyes and ears gave up early; her insides felt perpetually cold; her teeth fell out, requiring dentures in her forties. But perhaps most debilitating were the psychological symptoms that she didn't think she could attribute to the radiation. "For thirty or forty years, I was so afraid of thunder and lightening," she told me, as one of many examples. "It would just crush me. I just lost control." Raising four daughters was a challenge of another scale. "Nobody understood me; I was like a beggar," she said, recalling that when her children were young she faced almost daily bouts of overwhelming panic. At night, in dreams, she shouted, "The Earth—the Earth is going to fall!" "At the time, I didn't know what was affecting me so badly," Shoji said. "I couldn't talk about it. Even before I opened my mouth, I would collapse with fear."

Minori chimed in, gently stroking her mother's shoulder: "When we would go into her bedroom in the morning, we would see her get so angry—she would throw things. When we were young, I never saw her laugh—she was quiet, and weak." Back then, neither Shoji nor her children spoke openly about this behavior as tied to the bomb. Remarkably, Shoji says that the idea didn't come easily to her. She was unfamiliar with the concept of post-traumatic stress disorder, or shell shock, or its classic presentation (nightmares, flashbacks, hypervigilance); these traits seemed unrelated to her experience. "Every year I have these crazy episodes—my family is so good to me, but I have these outbursts, these moments when I lose control," she said. Years ago, she insists, it all seemed completely inexplicable.

Still, somewhere within her, she began to trace a clear line between her inner state and the events of her nineteenth year. "After I got married, the family would yell at me, and even when I'm beaten, I can't respond, and I don't know why. But deep inside, I remember, oh, that's what it is: the bomb, the aftereffects of the bomb. It's worse than the day of the bomb."

Shoji's granddaughter Keni Sabath grew up in Hawaii and Texas, the child of a New Jersey–born Navy JAG officer and a fashionable Taiwan-born language tutor. Like her older sister Zena, Keni often spent her days with her *bachan*, who lived in their home for years before joining Keni's aunt Minori in Ohio. In the summers, the family would travel back to Japan. "I first became aware of my grandmother's experience in a very disturbing way, when I was six years old," Keni Sabath told me after my Ohio visit. "I went to the Peace Park in Hiroshima with my grandmother and my mom. We walked by the river and my mom would translate, 'This river here was turned into a blood river, and people would jump into it and their skin would burn off.' " The family proceeded to the local memorial museum, where life-size wax statues depicted local children fleeing the bombing site, their skin melting and their clothing singed. "The children were my height!" Sabath said. "It was so hard for me to reconcile that hell with the current city. I couldn't understand: How were people over it?"

Sabath's crying became incessant thereafter. She couldn't sleep; each time she saw a plane in the air, she panicked, just as her grandmother continued to do. "My mother ended up taking me to a witch doctor," she told me. "They thought I was haunted by the ghosts of Hiroshima" (called *yurie*, or faint spirits). For years, the *yurie* resurfaced in Sabath each summer, making her anxious, watchful, her eyes skyward.

> **[E]ach time she saw a plane in the air, she panicked, just as her grandmother continued to do.**

In recent years, a growing body of scholarship has sought to better understand accounts like Shoji's and Sabath's through the framework of "trans-generational trauma," which traces experiences of catastrophic loss across the span of a family or a community. A wide range of studies have examined evidence of "secondary trauma" in the children of Holocaust survivors, the wives of Vietnam veterans, and, more informally, in the families of U.S. veterans who've faced PTSD after deployments to Iraq and Afghanistan. In 2007, a study on the wives of fifty-six traumatized war veterans in Croatia found that more than a third of the veterans' wives met the criteria for secondary traumatic stress; often, this meant symptoms "similar to those present in directly traumatized persons: nightmares about the person who was directly traumatized, insomnia, loss of interest, irritability, chronic fatigue, and changes in self-perception, perception of one's own life, and of other people." More recently, speaking to Mac McClelland for an article on trauma in the families of Iraq and Afghanistan war veterans, the clinical psychologist Robert Motta said, "Trauma is really not something that happens to an individual." Instead, he proposed, "Trauma is a contagious disease; it affects everyone that has close contact with a traumatized person."

But even metaphors of trauma as contagion feel inadequate, or even potentially counterproductive; for one thing, they can get mixed up with questions of shame and stigma, seeming to assign blame or stir up anxieties about contamination where the antidote to both is needed. And stigma, too, gets internalized. As a small child, Sabath said, when she began to fear a plane above, "I would think, how could I let the plane know that I was American?" She would beg her father to come along to Japan during the summers, thinking, "My white military dad—a Navy JAG officer—he signalled my identity, my patriotic Americanness." Only in his presence could she feel, as the mixed-race grandchild of a *hibakusha*, that "there is no way you would ever harm us."

When she reached high school, Sabath became a debating champion and made nuclear proliferation her focus. She went on to college at Yale and visited the White House as a student leader for Global Zero, the international nuclear-disarmament group, for which she recently authored a personal essay on her *bachan*'s "scenes of living hell." "I hope you will remember my grandmother's message and act upon it," she wrote.

In the late nineteen-fifties, the Japanese government began issuing certificates to *hibakusha*, entitling them to certain health benefits, and Shoji became the first survivor living abroad to travel back to Japan to reap the benefits. Over the course of those treatments, Shoji gathered for the first time with other survivors, at healing hot springs. It was in that community that she got her first glimpse of psychological relief, and perhaps began to decipher some of her experiences and speak of them to others. Last fall, she traveled to Yale to say to her granddaughter's classmates, "I want with every breath, with all my strength, to tell people" about the bomb.

In the final pages of Hersey's *Hiroshima*, he observed that many people he met there were often reticent to speak or even think about the ethics of the bomb; instead, they would offer approximations of "*Shikata ga nai*," a Japanese expression that he translated as "It can't be helped. Oh well. Too bad."

At eighty-eight, Shoji seems to have thrown off that cosmic shrug. When we finished in the dining room, her daughter gave me a bundle of pastries and fruit, and we all shuffled to the foyer. The whole family stood in the doorway and waved goodbye. Shoji's cheeks looked pink, and, as I drove off, it was easy to imagine how she might have appeared on her way to work at nineteen, looking up at the August sky.

Exploring Context

1. Hibakusha Stories (hibakushastories.org) is a site dedicated to sharing the stories of *hibakusha* in order to promote disarmament. Explore the site to learn more about other survivors of the nuclear blasts. How do they reflect the kinds of trauma that Stillman examines?

2. Visit the Web site for the Hiroshima Peace Memorial Museum at www.pcf.city .hiroshima.jp/index_e2.html. Expand your work from Question 1 by looking for additional representations of trauma in relation to Hiroshima. Relate what you find to Stillman's arguments.

3. The National Institute of Mental Health has a site about post-traumatic stress disorder at nimh.nih.gov/health/topics/post-traumatic-stress-disorder-ptsd. Does its representation reflect the idea that trauma can be contagious? How does it represent this disorder? How does it confirm or challenge Stillman's argument? Relate your findings to your work from Question 1 of Questions for Critical Reading.

Questions for Connecting

1. In "Reporting Live From Tomorrow" (p. 179), Daniel Gilbert suggests that we use surrogates to predict our future happiness. Might we use this same method to learn other things? Use Gilbert's ideas to consider the ways in which Shoji serves as a surrogate. In what other ways can surrogates be useful? Use your work from Questions 1 and 2 of Exploring Context to support your response, considering how other survivors act as surrogates.

2. Torie Rose DeGhett also considers the horrors of war in "The War Photo No One Would Publish" (p. 74). Synthesize DeGhett and Stillman to consider the relationship between war and remembrance. How should war shape our memories? If our memories are shaped in this way, how might our decisions about war change? Use your response to expand your answer to Question 3 of Questions for Critical Reading.

3. What's the relationship between shame and trauma? Is shame itself a kind of trauma? Does shame affect one's ability to heal? Use Dan Savage's "It Gets Better" (p. 406) and Urvashi Vaid's "Action Makes It Better" (p. 411) as well as Stillman to explore the relationship between shame and trauma. Incorporate your work on shame from Question 2 of Questions for Critical Reading.

Language Matters

1. Stillman's essay contains a number of foreign words and phrases, including *hibakusha*. Use a grammar handbook or other reference resource to review the rules for including words from other languages. How well does Stillman conform to these rules? How should you demarcate foreign words in your own writing?

2. At times Stillman uses parentheses to set off information; other times she uses dashes. Review the rules for both of these punctuation marks in a grammar handbook or other reference resource. When should you use one or the other to set off information that is not the main point of your sentence?

3. Stillman uses a translator when she visits Shoji. What special concerns might bilingual speakers have when it comes to academic writing? How does speaking more than one language complicate the process of composition? Consult a grammar handbook or reference source. Does it provide specific resources for writers who speak other languages? What kind of support is included, and why?

Assignments for Writing

1. Stillman suggests that trauma is a contagious disease. Write a paper in which you explore the effects of personal trauma on families. Is trauma a disease? What is the cure? How can families support healing from trauma? Use your work from Questions 1 and 3 from Questions for Connecting in making your argument.

2. Shoji struggles with shame. Using Stillman's ideas, write a paper about the power of shame. Is shame, like trauma, a disease? What does shame cost individuals and families? Use your work from Question 2 of Questions for Critical Reading and Question 3 of Questions for Connecting to make your argument.

3. Embedded in Stillman's argument is the question of ethics in relation to war. Write a paper in which you shape an ethics for war, using Stillman's ideas. Given the nature of trauma, when is war justified? What responsibilities do governments have to those who survive?

TOMAS VAN HOUTRYVE

© Sebastien Van Malleghem/
VII Photo Agency

Tomas van Houtryve is a photojournalist and writer, who worked with the Associated Press in Latin America before working freelance on his own artistic and critical projects around the world. His photography has appeared in *Harper's Magazine*, the *Atlantic*, the *New York Times Magazine*, and *National Geographic*.

National Geographic has been published continuously since 1888 and has come to be known for its extensive use of photography in documenting the cultures and natural geography of places all over the world. Van Houtryve's "From the Eyes of a Drone" was published in *Proof*, the online photography journal of *National Geographic*, on August 15, 2014. *Proof* offers a look at the processes of visual storytelling while presenting the work of emerging photographers in order to create conversations about journalism, art, and photography.

In "From the Eyes of a Drone," van Houtryve juxtaposes stunning aerial photography captured by drones with some of the more questionable and nefarious uses of those very same drones. He hopes that we can use the power and mobility of these photography drones for art's sake but wonders about the military uses of photographic drones.

▶ TAGS: *ethics, photography and video, science and technology, war and conflict*
▶ CONNECTIONS: *DeGhett, Paumgarten, Stillman*

Questions for Critical Reading

1. As you read, consider closely the relationship between van Houtryve's text and his photographs. How do these images support his argument? In what ways is van Houtryve making a visual argument?

2. What problems does van Houtryve see with the military use of drones? As you read, make a list of these issues. Are van Houtryve's concerns justified?

3. Define for yourself the word *weaponized*. What does this term mean for van Houtryve? Mark passages where he discusses the process and its consequences.

From the Eyes of a Drone

For the past 15 years I've worked as a professional photojournalist, inspired by the camera's ability to connect human beings, document news, and capture beauty. But there is a darker side to how photography is used in our world today. Cameras are increasingly deployed for surveillance, spying, or targeting. I often wonder whether these uses have already eclipsed traditional ones, such as portraiture and fine art. Are we at a point in the evolution of photography where the medium has become weaponized?

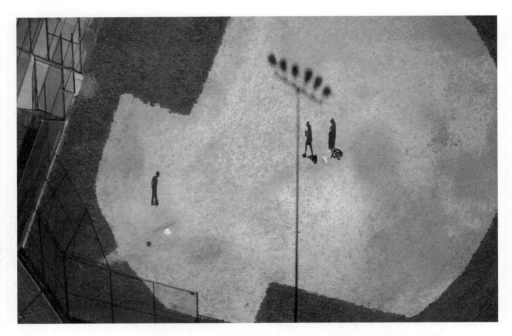

Baseball practice in Montgomery County, Maryland. The FAA issued 1,428 domestic drone permits between 2007 and early 2013. According to records obtained from the agency, the National Institute of Standards and Technology and the U.S. Navy have applied for drone authorization in Montgomery County.

© Tomas van Houtryve/VII Photo Agency

Nothing symbolizes this trend better than the rise of drones, robotic aircraft pioneered by the military which rely on their cameras to link remote operators to their targets.

Last year, I started to explore photography's dark side, hoping to engage in the debate about how imaging technology is changing the nature of personal privacy, surveillance, and contemporary warfare.

I started by buying my own consumer drone, and I was surprised by how easy it was to acquire. Hobby shops and online retailers sell small drones equipped with GPS receivers for a few hundred dollars. With a bit of tinkering, I was able to add a high-resolution camera and a system for transmitting live video back to the ground—a greatly simplified version of the system that American pilots use to guide military drones like Reaper and Predator over foreign airspace.

Drones have been used for air strikes over Pakistan for the past decade, marking   5 a significant shift in how America fights wars. Pilots based in Nevada and New Mexico track and record human activity via an infrared video feed. They never leave the ground or cross over hostile territory. Although a huge amount of footage has been collected, the program is classified, and few people have ever seen images of the drone war and its casualties. This seems like a paradox in our thoroughly media-connected

Residential homes surrounding a circular park are seen from above in Montgomery County, Maryland.
© Tomas van Houtryve/VII Photo Agency

age. How can America be involved in a decade-long war where the sky is buzzing with cameras, and yet the public remains totally in the dark?

To learn more about the drone war, I looked up reports compiled by investigative journalists and human rights groups. I found the details of many of the strikes startling. A Human Rights Watch report about a drone attack on a wedding in Yemen stated:

"The December 12 attack killed 12 men and wounded at least 15 other people, including the bride."[1]

But the testimony of one particular Pakistani boy named Zubair Rehman jarred me the most. In October 2012, Rehman's 67-year-old grandmother was killed by a drone strike while she was picking vegetables outside her home. "I no longer love blue skies," said Rehman. "In fact, I now prefer gray skies. The drones do not fly when the skies are gray."[2]

In the past few years, drone use has spread from foreign conflicts to America's domestic airspace. Often, unarmed versions of military aircraft are used, such as the fleet of Predator drones operated by U.S. Customs and Border Protection. Initially, the fleet was meant for border surveillance, but records indicate that drones were lent out hundreds of times to other government entities—including the DEA, the FBI, the Texas Rangers, and local sheriff's departments.[3] The trend of drones used by government security forces is only likely to increase, and some companies such as Amazon are lobbying to put drones to commercial use too.

A wedding in central Philadelphia. In December 2013, a U.S. drone reportedly struck a wedding in Radda, in central Yemen, killing twelve people and injuring fifteen.

© Tomas van Houtryve/VII Photo Agency

A playground seen from above in Sacramento County, California. The London-based Bureau of Investigative Journalism estimates that over 200 children were killed in drone strikes in Pakistan, Yemen, and Somalia between 2004 and 2013.

© Tomas van Houtryve/VII Photo Agency

"Tent City" jail in Maricopa County, Arizona. Sheriff Joe Arpaio announced in 2013 that he planned to purchase two surveillance drones for the facility, which is already outfitted with perimeter stun fences, four watchtowers, and a facial-recognition system.

© Tomas van Houtryve/VII Photo Agency

As drones fill the skies above America, how is the public likely to react? Will the sight of them eventually be as ordinary as seeing an airplane or bird, or will people start wishing for gray skies like the traumatized young Zubair Rehman? 10

I got a full range of reactions when I flew my own drone in public places earlier this year. Often I would purposely fly my camera over the same type of situations listed in those foreign drone strike reports, such as weddings, funerals, and people entering or leaving religious schools. At other times, I used my drone to look down from the sky over the same areas where the government does aerial surveillance, like along the U.S.-Mexico border.

While flying in a park in Maryland, a small girl saw my drone hovering in the sky and asked her mother what it was. I heard the mother answer, "It's a drone, and if you don't do your homework, it's going to go after you!"

On another occasion flying in rural Northern California, a man watched my drone for a long while before approaching me to ask for a look at the control screen. He told me he'd worked as an engineer for a military contractor during the Iraq war, assigned to a team flying the Global Hawk, a large high-altitude surveillance drone. He told me that he worried the technology he had seen as a contractor was moving in a spooky direction, and that the newest weapons systems could decide when to fire or not based on algorithms and lightning-fast calculations, eliminating human will—and judgment—from the battlefield.

A U.S. Border Patrol vehicle in San Diego County, California. U.S. Customs and Border Protection has been using Predator drones since 2005. A Freedom of Information Act lawsuit filed in 2012 revealed that the Customs and Border Protection lent its fleet of drones to other government entities — including the DEA, the FBI, the Texas Rangers, and local sheriff's departments — nearly 700 times between 2010 and 2012.
© Tomas van Houtryve/VII Photo Agency

A national war cemetery is seen from above in Philadelphia. In the nearby suburbs, the Horsham Air Guard Base is a drone command center for foreign strikes and surveillance.
© Tomas van Houtryve/VII Photo Agency

A fire truck and crew respond to a car fire in the Gila River Indian Community in Maricopa County, Arizona. U.S. drone operators are known to engage in "double-tap" strikes, in which consecutive rounds of missiles are fired on the same target, with the second round intended to kill those who respond to the first. The London-based Bureau of Investigative Journalism documented at least five such strikes in Pakistan in 2012.

© Tomas van Houtryve/VII Photo Agency

And I recently read that graduate students at MIT are experimenting with drones which automatically adapt studio lighting for portraits.[4]

Not everyone I met spoke about the sinister capabilities of drones. Flying near Silicon Valley, a man offered me his business card after I landed in a grassy clearing. He said he was working on a startup company which would manufacture drones to take selfies.

It seems clear that when the next chapter in the evolution of photography is written, drones will have a very prominent role. As more and more cameras take to the skies, my sincere hope is that drones which use photography to celebrate and inspire the best of human values outnumber those designed for darker aims.

15

NOTES

1. Human Rights Watch, "A Wedding That Became a Funeral: US Drone Attack on Marriage Procession in Yemen," *Human Rights Watch*, February 20, 2014.
2. Tomas van Houtryve, "Blue Sky Days," *Harper's*, April 2014, 37.

3. Jennifer Lynch, "Drone Loans: Customs and Border Protection Records 500 Predator Flights for Other Agencies," Electronic Frontier Foundation, September 27, 2013, https://www.eff.org/deeplinks/2013/09/500-cbp-drone-flights-other-agencies.

4. Larry Hardesty, "Drone Lighting: Autonomous Vehicles Could Automatically Assume the Right Positions for Photographic Lighting," *MIT News*, July 11, 2014, http://newsoffice.mit.edu/2014/drone-lighting-0711.

Exploring Context

1. Visit van Houtryve's Web site at tomasvh.com. How is this essay consistent with van Houtryve's larger body of work?

2. The Predator and Reaper drones that van Houtryve mentions are made by General Atomics Aeronautical (ga-asi.com). Visit this company's Web site. How does it represent these drones? How does its visual representation of the drones confirm or complicate van Houtryve's argument? Use your findings to expand your answer to Question 2 of Questions for Critical Reading.

3. Parrot (parrot.com) manufactures consumer drones like the one van Houtryve uses to capture his photographs. Explore its Web site, noting the ways Parrot presents and markets its drones. Compare this to the work you did on General Atomics Aeronautical in Question 2.

Questions for Connecting

1. Van Houtryve notes that at some point drones could decide when to fire on their own, removing human judgment; he also notes times when human judgment with military drones led to the loss of innocent lives. Use Daniel Kahneman's ideas about human judgment from "The Surety of Fools" (p. 215) to evaluate the role of drones in the military. Might self-firing drones be a good idea based on the failures of human judgment? Or is it a bad idea to remove humans from these decisions?

2. Nick Paumgarten, in "We Are a Camera" (p. 331), looks at another innovation in photographic technology — the GoPro video camera. Synthesize these two essays in order to specify the power of the image today. Do photographs enhance or replace experience? How do new points of view, as conveyed by the GoPro or drones, change our perspective?

3. The Dalai Lama suggests that technology moves faster than ethics in "Ethics and the New Genetics" (p. 63). Apply his ideas to van Houtryve's discussion of drones. Has this particular technology evolved faster than our ethical frameworks? Do we need a moral compass in order to guide the use and development of drones? Use your work from Questions 2 and 3 of Questions for Critical Reading in making your response.

Language Matters

1. Given the visual nature of this selection, citation is a particular challenge. How should you properly cite van Houtryve's images? Review information on citation in a grammar

handbook or other reference resource. Is there a specific format you should use? How would you cite the images, and how would you cite textual quotations from this essay?

2. A complete sentence has a subject and a verb. What is the visual equivalent of a sentence? Consider van Houtryve's photographs as sentences. How can you identify the subject and verb? Consider, for starters, the difference between *subject* in its grammatical sense and the *subject* of a piece of art or writing.

3. Punctuation marks delineate boundaries between words. What is the visual equivalent? Using van Houtryve's photographs, consider what elements act as "punctuation marks." Is the border of a photograph a period? Can the arrangement of elements in an image act as a question mark?

Assignments for Writing

1. Van Houtryve expresses concern about the "weaponization" of drones. Write a paper in which you explore the relationship of technology and war. What role should technology play in combat? Does it save lives or make it easier to take lives? Use your work from Questions 2 and 3 of Questions for Critical Reading and Question 3 of Exploring Context to support your argument.

2. Photographs play an important role in van Houtryve's essay. Write a paper in which you analyze van Houtryve's photographs as a visual argument. What argument does he make with these images? How do the images support that argument? You may want to review the material on analyzing images in Part One (pp. 8–9); also consider using your work from Question 1 of Questions for Critical Reading.

3. Van Houtryve flies his drones through a number of public spaces. Write a paper in which you examine how space determines meaning. How does the setting for van Houtryve's photography influence the meaning of the images? How do people react to the drone based on space? Do different spaces create different meanings for drones and their images?

© Gary Hannbarger/Corbis

DAVID FOSTER WALLACE

Novelist and essayist **David Foster Wallace** was the Roy E. Disney Professor of Creative Writing at Pomona College until his death in 2008. Highly respected during his lifetime, he was a recipient of the MacArthur fellowship (colloquially known as the "genius grant") from 1997 to 2002, as well as a winner of the Salon Book Award and the Lannan Literary Award for fiction. His significant publications include the novels *The Broom of the System* (1987) and *Infinite Jest* (1996) as well as *Brief Interviews with Hideous Men* (1999), a collection of short stories. Wallace was also a noted essayist, writing for publications such as *Rolling Stone*, *Harper's Magazine*, and the *Atlantic*. Wallace's *The Pale King* (2011), an unfinished novel, was published three years after his death.

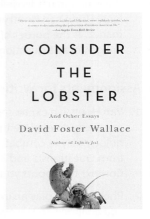

In *Consider the Lobster and Other Essays* (2005), the collection from which this selection is taken, Wallace explores a broad range of topics, including the adult film industry's Adult Video News Awards, the criticisms of novelist John Updike, Kafka's wit, the political underbelly of dictionary publications, Senator John McCain, and the seductive and disappointing paradox of sports athlete memoirs. While these topics appear to be unrelated, Wallace's versatility exemplifies his common concern with current concepts of morality. This notion of morality is strikingly clear in the title essay "Consider the Lobster," originally published in *Gourmet* magazine.

Wallace finds it curious that lobster is the one creature that is usually cooked while still alive. Though many people find this practice unproblematic, believing that lobsters cannot feel pain, Wallace observes that lobsters can at least exhibit a preference for not being lowered into a pot of boiling water. This observation leads Wallace to question our justifications for eating lobster, and indeed, our eating of animals altogether. Ultimately, "Consider the Lobster" raises many questions about the practices we engage in as a species, our definitions of pain and suffering, and our understanding of the world around us.

▶ TAGS: *empathy, ethics, food and agriculture, judgment and decision-making*
▶ CONNECTIONS: *Allen, Dalai Lama, Manning, Pollan*

Questions for Critical Reading

1. How does Wallace feel about eating lobsters? As you read, mark passages that reveal his position on the issue. Does it shift through the essay?

2. Wallace asks, "Is it all right to boil a sentient creature alive just for our gustatory pleasure?" (p. 464). Answer this question for yourself, and then as you read Wallace's essay, locate quotations that support your position.

3. Near the end of his essay, Wallace turns to a discussion of *preference*. Read this section closely. What does Wallace mean by *preference*? What role does it play in his overall argument?

Consider the Lobster

The enormous, pungent, and extremely well-marketed Maine Lobster Festival is held every late July in the state's midcoast region, meaning the western side of Penobscot Bay, the nerve stem of Maine's lobster industry. What's called the midcoast runs from Owl's Head and Thomaston in the south to Belfast in the north. (Actually, it might extend all the way up to Bucksport, but we were never able to get farther north than Belfast on Route 1, whose summer traffic is, as you can imagine, unimaginable.) The region's two main communities are Camden, with its very old money and yachty harbor and five-star restaurants and phenomenal B&Bs, and Rockland, a serious old fishing town that hosts the festival every summer in historic Harbor Park, right along the water.[1]

Tourism and lobster are the midcoast region's two main industries, and they're both warm-weather enterprises, and the Maine Lobster Festival represents less an intersection of the industries than a deliberate collision, joyful and lucrative and loud. The assigned subject of this *Gourmet* article is the 56th Annual MLF, 30 July–3 August 2003, whose official theme this year was "Lighthouses, Laughter, and Lobster." Total paid attendance was over 100,000, due partly to a national CNN spot in June during which a senior editor of *Food & Wine* magazine hailed the MLF as one of the best food-themed galas in the world. 2003 festival highlights: concerts by Lee Ann Womack and Orleans, annual Maine Sea Goddess beauty pageant, Saturday's big parade, Sunday's William G. Atwood Memorial Crate Race, annual Amateur Cooking Competition, carnival rides and midway attractions and food booths, and the MLF's Main Eating Tent, where something over 25,000 pounds of fresh-caught Maine lobster is consumed after preparation in the World's Largest Lobster Cooker near the grounds' north entrance. Also available are lobster rolls, lobster turnovers, lobster sauté, Down East lobster salad, lobster bisque, lobster ravioli, and deep-fried lobster dumplings. Lobster thermidor is obtainable at a sit-down restaurant called the Black Pearl on Harbor Park's northwest wharf. A large all-pine booth sponsored by the Maine Lobster Promotion Council has free pamphlets with recipes, eating tips, and Lobster Fun Facts. The winner of Friday's Amateur Cooking Competition prepares Saffron Lobster Ramekins, the recipe for which is now available for public downloading at www.mainelobster festival.com. There are lobster T-shirts and lobster bobblehead dolls and inflatable lobster pool toys and clamp-on lobster hats with big scarlet claws that wobble on springs. Your assigned correspondent saw it all, accompanied by one girlfriend and both his own parents — one of which parents was actually born and raised in Maine, albeit in

---

[1]There's a comprehensive native apothegm: "Camden by the sea, Rockland by the smell." [All notes are Wallace's.]

the extreme northern inland part, which is potato country and a world away from the touristic midcoast.[2]

For practical purposes, everyone knows what a lobster is. As usual, though, there's much more to know than most of us care about — it's all a matter of what your interests are. Taxonomically speaking, a lobster is a marine crustacean of the family Homaridae, characterized by five pairs of jointed legs, the first pair terminating in large pincerish claws used for subduing prey. Like many other species of benthic carnivore, lobsters are both hunters and scavengers. They have stalked eyes, gills on their legs, and antennae. There are a dozen or so different kinds worldwide, of which the relevant species here is the Maine lobster, *Homarus americanus*. The name "lobster" comes from the Old English *loppestre*, which is thought to be a corrupt form of the Latin word for locust combined with the Old English *loppe*, which meant spider.

Moreover, a crustacean is an aquatic arthropod of the class Crustacea, which comprises crabs, shrimp, barnacles, lobsters, and freshwater crayfish. All this is right there in the encyclopedia. And arthropods are members of the phylum Arthropoda, which phylum covers insects, spiders, crustaceans, and centipedes/millipedes, all of whose main commonality, besides the absence of a centralized brain-spine assembly, is a chitinous exoskeleton composed of segments, to which appendages are articulated in pairs.

The point is that lobsters are basically giant sea insects.[3] Like most arthropods, they date from the Jurassic period, biologically so much older than mammalia that they might as well be from another planet. And they are — particularly in their natural brown-green state, brandishing their claws like weapons and with thick antennae awhip — not nice to look at. And it's true that they are garbagemen of the sea, eaters of dead stuff,[4] although they'll also eat some live shellfish, certain kinds of injured fish, and sometimes one another.

The point is that lobsters are basically giant sea insects.

But they are themselves good eating. Or so we think now. Up until sometime in the 1800s, though, lobster was literally low-class food, eaten only by the poor and institutionalized. Even in the harsh penal environment of early America, some colonies had laws against feeding lobsters to inmates more than once a week because it was thought to be cruel and unusual, like making people eat rats. One reason for their low status was how plentiful lobsters were in old New England. "Unbelievable abundance" is how one source describes the situation, including accounts of Plymouth Pilgrims wading out and capturing all they wanted by hand, and of early Boston's seashore being littered with lobsters after hard storms — these latter were treated as a smelly nuisance and ground up for fertilizer. There is also the fact that premodern lobster was cooked dead and then preserved, usually packed in salt or crude hermetic containers.

---

[2]N.B. All personally connected parties have made it clear from the start that they do not want to be talked about in this article.

[3]Midcoasters' native term for a lobster is, in fact, "bug," as in "Come around on Sunday and we'll cook up some bugs."

[4]Factoid: Lobster traps are usually baited with dead herring.

Maine's earliest lobster industry was based around a dozen such seaside canneries in the 1840s, from which lobster was shipped as far away as California, in demand only because it was cheap and high in protein, basically chewable fuel.

Now, of course, lobster is posh, a delicacy, only a step or two down from caviar. The meat is richer and more substantial than most fish, its taste subtle compared to the marine-gaminess of mussels and clams. In the U.S. pop-food imagination, lobster is now the seafood analog to steak, with which it's so often twinned as Surf 'n' Turf on the really expensive part of the chain steakhouse menu.

In fact, one obvious project of the MLF, and of its omnipresently sponsorial Maine Lobster Promotion Council, is to counter the idea that lobster is unusually luxe or un-healthy or expensive, suitable only for effete palates or the occasional blow-the-diet treat. It is emphasized over and over in presentations and pamphlets at the festival that lobster meat has fewer calories, less cholesterol, and less saturated fat than chicken.[5] And in the Main Eating Tent, you can get a "quarter" (industry shorthand for a 1¼-pound lobster), a four-ounce cup of melted butter, a bag of chips, and a soft roll w/ butter-pat for around $12.00, which is only slightly more expensive than supper at McDonald's.

Be apprised, though, that the Maine Lobster Festival's democratization of lobster comes with all the massed inconvenience and aesthetic compromise of real democracy. See, for example, the aforementioned Main Eating Tent, for which there is a constant Disneyland-grade queue, and which turns out to be a square quarter mile of awning-shaded cafeteria lines and rows of long institutional tables at which friend and stranger alike sit cheek by jowl, cracking and chewing and dribbling. It's hot, and the sagged roof traps the steam and the smells, which latter are strong and only partly food-related. It is also loud, and a good percentage of the total noise is masticatory. The sup-pers come in styrofoam trays, and the soft drinks are iceless and flat, and the coffee is convenience-store coffee in more styrofoam, and the utensils are plastic (there are none of the special long skinny forks for pushing out the tail meat, though a few savvy diners bring their own). Nor do they give you near enough napkins considering how messy lobster is to eat, especially when you're squeezed onto benches alongside children of various ages and vastly different levels of fine-motor development — not to mention the people who've somehow smuggled in their own beer in enormous aisle-blocking cool-ers, or who all of a sudden produce their own plastic tablecloths and spread them over large portions of tables to try to reserve them (the tables) for their own little groups. And so on. Any one example is no more than a petty inconvenience, of course, but the MLF turns out to be full of irksome little downers like this — see for instance the Main Stage's headliner shows, where it turns out that you have to pay $20 extra for a folding chair if you want to sit down; or the North Tent's mad scramble for the Nyquil-cup-sized samples of finalists' entries handed out after the Cooking Competition; or the much-touted Maine Sea Goddess pageant finals, which turn out to be excruciat-ingly long and to consist mainly of endless thanks and tributes to local sponsors. Let's not even talk about the grossly inadequate Port-A-San facilities or the fact that there's

---

[5]Of course, the common practice of dipping the lobster meat in melted butter torpedoes all these happy fat-specs, which none of the council's promotional stuff ever mentions, any more than potato industry PR talks about sour cream and bacon bits.

nowhere to wash your hands before or after eating. What the Maine Lobster Festival really is is a midlevel county fair with a culinary hook, and in this respect it's not unlike Tidewater crab festivals, Midwest corn festivals, Texas chili festivals, etc., and shares with these venues the core paradox of all teeming commercial demotic events: It's not for everyone.[6] Nothing against the euphoric senior editor of *Food & Wine*, but I'd be surprised if she'd ever actually been here in Harbor Park, amid crowds of people slapping canal-zone mosquitoes as they eat deep-fried Twinkies and watch Professor Paddywhack, on six-foot stilts in a raincoat with plastic lobsters protruding from all directions on springs, terrify their children.

Lobster is essentially a summer food. This is because we now prefer our lobsters fresh, which means they have to be recently caught, which for both tactical and economic reasons takes place at depths less than 25 fathoms. Lobsters tend to be hungriest and most active (i.e., most trappable) at summer water temperatures of 45–50 degrees. In the autumn, most Maine lobsters migrate out into deeper water, either for warmth or to avoid the heavy waves that pound New England's coast all winter. Some burrow into the bottom. They might hibernate; nobody's sure. Summer is also lobsters' molting season — specifically early- to mid-July. Chitinous arthropods grow by molting, rather the way people have to buy bigger clothes as they age and gain weight. Since lobsters can live to be over 100, they can also get to be quite large, as in 30 pounds or more — though truly senior lobsters are rare now because New England's waters are so heavily trapped.[7] Anyway, hence the culinary distinction between hard- and soft-shell lobsters, the latter sometimes a.k.a. shedders. A soft-shell lobster is one that has

10

---

[6]In truth, there's a great deal to be said about the differences between working-class Rockland and the heavily populist flavor of its festival versus comfortable and elitist Camden with its expensive view and shops given entirely over to $200 sweaters and great rows of Victorian homes converted to upscale B&Bs. And about these differences as two sides of the great coin that is U.S. tourism. Very little of which will be said here, except to amplify the above-mentioned paradox and to reveal your assigned correspondent's own preferences. I confess that I have never understood why so many people's idea of a fun vacation is to don flip-flops and sunglasses and crawl through maddening traffic to loud, hot, crowded tourist venues in order to sample a "local flavor" that is by definition ruined by the presence of tourists. This may (as my festival companions keep pointing out) all be a matter of personality and hardwired taste: the fact that I do not like tourist venues means that I'll never understand their appeal and so am probably not the one to talk about it (the supposed appeal). But, since this FN will almost surely not survive magazine-editing anyway, here goes:

As I see it, it probably really is good for the soul to be a tourist, even if it's only once in a while. Not good for the soul in a refreshing or enlivening way, though, but rather in a grim, steely-eyed, let's-look-honestly-at-the-facts-and-find-some-way-to-deal-with-them way. My personal experience has not been that traveling around the country is broadening or relaxing, or that radical changes in place and context have a salutary effect, but rather that intranational tourism is radically constricting, and humbling in the hardest way — hostile to my fantasy of being a true individual, of living somehow outside and above it all. (Coming up is the part that my companions find especially unhappy and repellent, a sure way to spoil the fun of vacation travel.) To be a mass tourist, for me, is to become a pure late-date American: alien, ignorant, greedy for something you cannot ever have, disappointed in a way you can never admit. It is to spoil, by way of sheer ontology, the very unspoiledness you are there to experience. It is to impose yourself on places that in all non-economic ways would be better, realer, without you. It is, in lines and gridlock and transaction after transaction, to confront a dimension of yourself that is as inescapable as it is painful: As a tourist, you become economically significant but existentially loathsome, an insect on a dead thing.

[7]Datum: In a good year, the U.S. industry produces around 80,000,000 pounds of lobster, and Maine accounts for more than half that total.

recently molted. In midcoast restaurants, the summer menu often offers both kinds, with shedders being slightly cheaper even though they're easier to dismantle and the meat is allegedly sweeter. The reason for the discount is that a molting lobster uses a layer of seawater for insulation while its new shell is hardening, so there's slightly less actual meat when you crack open a shedder, plus a redolent gout of water that gets all over everything and can sometimes jet out lemonlike and catch a tablemate right in the eye. If it's winter or you're buying lobster someplace far from New England, on the other hand, you can almost bet that the lobster is a hard-shell, which for obvious reasons travel better.

As an à la carte entrée, lobster can be baked, broiled, steamed, grilled, sautéed, stir-fried, or microwaved. The most common method, though, is boiling. If you're someone who enjoys having lobster at home, this is probably the way you do it, since boiling is so easy. You need a large kettle w/ cover, which you fill about half full with water (the standard advice is that you want 2.5 quarts of water per lobster). Seawater is optimal, or you can add two tbsp salt per quart from the tap. It also helps to know how much your lobsters weigh. You get the water boiling, put in the lobsters one at a time, cover the kettle, and bring it back up to a boil. Then you bank the heat and let the kettle simmer — ten minutes for the first pound of lobster, then three minutes for each pound after that. (This is assuming you've got hard-shell lobsters, which, again, if you don't live between Boston and Halifax is probably what you've got. For shedders, you're supposed to subtract three minutes from the total.) The reason the kettle's lobsters turn scarlet is that boiling somehow suppresses every pigment in their chitin but one. If you want an easy test of whether the lobsters are done, you try pulling on one of their antennae — if it comes out of the head with minimal effort, you're ready to eat.

A detail so obvious that most recipes don't even bother to mention it is that each lobster is supposed to be alive when you put it in the kettle. This is part of lobster's modern appeal — it's the freshest food there is. There's no decomposition between harvesting and eating. And not only do lobsters require no cleaning or dressing or plucking, they're relatively easy for vendors to keep alive. They come up alive in the traps, are placed in containers of seawater, and can — so long as the water's aerated and the animals' claws are pegged or banded to keep them from tearing one another up under the stresses of captivity[8] — survive right up until they're boiled. Most of us have been in supermarkets or restaurants that feature tanks of live lobsters, from which you can pick out your supper while it watches you point. And part of the overall spectacle of the Maine Lobster Festival is that you can see actual lobstermen's vessels docking at the wharves along the northeast grounds and unloading fresh-caught product, which is transferred by hand or cart 150 yards to the great clear tanks stacked up around the

---

[8]N.B. Similar reasoning underlies the practice of what's termed "debeaking" broiler chickens and brood hens in modern factory farms. Maximum commercial efficiency requires that enormous poultry populations be confined in unnaturally close quarters, under which conditions many birds go crazy and peck one another to death. As a purely observational side-note, be apprised that debeaking is usually an automated process and that the chickens receive no anesthetic. It's not clear to me whether most *Gourmet* readers know about debeaking, or about related practices like dehorning cattle in commercial feed lots, cropping swine's tails in factory hog farms to keep psychotically bored neighbors from chewing them off, and so forth. It so happens that your assigned correspondent knew almost nothing about standard meat-industry operations before starting work on this article.

festival's cooker — which is, as mentioned, billed as the World's Largest Lobster Cooker and can process over 100 lobsters at a time for the Main Eating Tent.

So then here is a question that's all but unavoidable at the World's Largest Lobster Cooker, and may arise in kitchens across the U.S.: Is it all right to boil a sentient creature alive just for our gustatory pleasure? A related set of concerns: Is the previous question irksomely PC or sentimental? What does "all right" even mean in this context? Is the whole thing just a matter of personal choice?

As you may or may not know, a certain well-known group called People for the Ethical Treatment of Animals thinks that the morality of lobster-boiling is not just a matter of individual conscience. In fact, one of the very first things we hear about the MLF . . . well, to set the scene: We're coming in by cab from the almost indescribably odd and rustic Knox County Airport[9] very late on the night before the festival opens, sharing the cab with a wealthy political consultant who lives on Vinalhaven Island in the bay half the year (he's headed for the island ferry in Rockland). The consultant and cabdriver are responding to informal journalistic probes about how people who live in the midcoast region actually view the MLF, as in is the festival just a big-dollar tourist thing or is it something local residents look forward to attending, take genuine civic pride in, etc. The cabdriver (who's in his seventies, one of apparently a whole platoon of retirees the cab company puts on to help with the summer rush, and wears a U.S.-flag lapel pin, and drives in what can only be called a very *deliberate* way) assures us that locals do endorse and enjoy the MLF, although he himself hasn't gone in years, and now come to think of it no one he and his wife know has, either. However, the demilocal consultant's been to recent festivals a couple times (one gets the impression it was at his wife's behest), of which his most vivid impression was that "you have to line up for an ungodly long time to get your lobsters, and meanwhile there are all these ex–flower children coming up and down along the line handing out pamphlets that say the lobsters die in terrible pain and you shouldn't eat them."

And it turns out that the post-hippies of the consultant's recollection were activ-   15 ists from PETA. There were no PETA people in obvious view at the 2003 MLF,[10] but they've been conspicuous at many of the recent festivals. Since at least the mid-1990s, articles in everything from the *Camden Herald* to the *New York Times* have described

---

[9]The terminal used to be somebody's house, for example, and the lost-luggage-reporting room was clearly once a pantry.

[10]It turned out that one Mr. William R. Rivas-Rivas, a high-ranking PETA official out of the group's Virginia headquarters, was indeed there this year, albeit solo, working the festival's main and side entrances on Saturday, 2 August, handing out pamphlets and adhesive stickers emblazoned with "Being Boiled Hurts," which is the tagline in most of PETA's published material about lobsters. I learned that he'd been there only later, when speaking with Mr. Rivas-Rivas on the phone. I'm not sure how we missed seeing him *in situ* at the festival, and I can't see much to do except apologize for the oversight — although it's also true that Saturday was the day of the big MLF parade through Rockland, which basic journalistic responsibility seemed to require going to (and which, with all due respect, meant that Saturday was maybe not the best day for PETA to work the Harbor Park grounds, especially if it was going to be just one person for one day, since a lot of diehard MLF partisans were off-site watching the parade [which, again with no offense intended, was in truth kind of cheesy and boring, consisting mostly of slow homemade floats and various midcoast people waving at one another, and with an extremely annoying man dressed as Blackbeard ranging up and down the length of the crowd saying, "Arrr" over and over and brandishing a plastic sword at people, etc.; plus it rained]).

PETA urging boycotts of the Maine Lobster Festival, often deploying celebrity spokesmen like Mary Tyler Moore for open letters and ads saying stuff like "Lobsters are extraordinarily sensitive" and "To me, eating a lobster is out of the question." More concrete is the oral testimony of Dick, our florid and extremely gregarious rental-car liaison,[11] to the effect that PETA's been around so much during recent years that a kind of brittlely tolerant homeostasis now obtains between the activists and the festival's locals, e.g.: "We had some incidents a couple years ago. One lady took most of her clothes off and painted herself like a lobster, almost got herself arrested. But for the most part they're let alone. [Rapid series of small ambiguous laughs, which with Dick happens a lot.] They do their thing and we do our thing."

This whole interchange takes place on Route 1, 30 July, during a four-mile, 50-minute ride from the airport[12] to the dealership to sign car-rental papers. Several irreproducible segues down the road from the PETA anecdotes, Dick — whose son-in-law happens to be a professional lobsterman and one of the Main Eating Tent's regular suppliers — explains what he and his family feel is the crucial mitigating factor in the whole morality-of-boiling-lobsters-alive issue: "There's a part of the brain in people and animals that lets us feel pain, and lobsters' brains don't have this part."

Besides the fact that it's incorrect in about nine different ways, the main reason Dick's statement is interesting is that its thesis is more or less echoed by the festival's own pronouncement on lobsters and pain, which is part of a Test Your Lobster IQ quiz that appears in the 2003 MLF program courtesy of the Maine Lobster Promotion Council:

> The nervous system of a lobster is very simple, and is in fact most similar to the nervous system of the grasshopper. It is decentralized with no brain. There is no cerebral cortex, which in humans is the area of the brain that gives the experience of pain.

Though it sounds more sophisticated, a lot of the neurology in this latter claim is still either false or fuzzy. The human cerebral cortex is the brain-part that deals with higher faculties like reason, metaphysical self-awareness, language, etc. Pain reception is known to be part of a much older and more primitive system of nociceptors and prostaglandins that are managed by the brain stem and thalamus.[13] On the other hand, it is true that the cerebral cortex is involved in what's variously called suffering, distress, or the emotional experience of pain — i.e., experiencing painful stimuli as unpleasant, very unpleasant, unbearable, and so on.

---

[11]By profession, Dick is actually a car salesman; the midcoast region's National Car Rental franchise operates out of a Chevy dealership in Thomaston.

[12]The short version regarding why we were back at the airport after already arriving the previous night involves lost luggage and a miscommunication about where and what the midcoast's National franchise was —Dick came out personally to the airport and got us, out of no evident motive but kindness. (He also talked nonstop the entire way, with a very distinctive speaking style that can be described only as manically laconic; the truth is that I now know more about this man than I do about some members of my own family.)

[13]To elaborate by way of example: The common experience of accidentally touching a hot stove and yanking your hand back before you're even aware that anything's going on is explained by the fact that many of the processes by which we detect and avoid painful stimuli do not involve the cortex. In the case of the hand and stove, the brain is bypassed altogether; all the important neurochemical action takes place in the spine.

Before we go any further, let's acknowledge that the questions of whether and how different kinds of animals feel pain, and of whether and why it might be justifiable to inflict pain on them in order to eat them, turn out to be extremely complex and difficult. And comparative neuroanatomy is only part of the problem. Since pain is a totally subjective mental experience, we do not have direct access to anyone or anything's pain but our own; and even just the principles by which we can infer that other human beings experience pain and have a legitimate interest in not feeling pain involve hardcore philosophy — metaphysics, epistemology, value theory, ethics. The fact that even the most highly evolved nonhuman mammals can't use language to communicate with us about their subjective mental experience is only the first layer of additional complication in trying to extend our reasoning about pain and morality to animals. And everything gets progressively more abstract and convoluted as we move farther and farther out from the higher-type mammals into cattle and swine and dogs and cats and rodents, and then birds and fish, and finally invertebrates like lobsters.

The more important point here, though, is that the whole animal-cruelty-and-   20
eating issue is not just complex, it's also uncomfortable. It is, at any rate, uncomfortable for me, and for just about everyone I know who enjoys a variety of foods and yet does not want to see herself as cruel or unfeeling. As far as I can tell, my own main way of dealing with this conflict has been to avoid thinking about the whole unpleasant thing. I should add that it appears to me unlikely that many readers of *Gourmet* wish to think about it, either, or to be queried about the morality of their eating habits in the pages of a culinary monthly. Since, however, the assigned subject of this article is what it was like to attend the 2003 MLF, and thus to spend several days in the midst of a great mass of Americans all eating lobster, and thus to be more or less impelled to think hard about lobster and the experience of buying and eating lobster, it turns out that there is no honest way to avoid certain moral questions.

There are several reasons for this. For one thing, it's not just that lobsters get boiled alive, it's that you do it yourself — or at least it's done specifically for you, on-site.[14] As mentioned, the World's Largest Lobster Cooker, which is highlighted as an attraction in the festival's program, is right out there on the MLF's north grounds for everyone to see. Try to imagine a Nebraska Beef Festival[15] at which part of the festivities is

---

[14]Morality-wise, let's concede that this cuts both ways. Lobster-eating is at least not abetted by the system of corporate factory farms that produces most beef, pork, and chicken. Because, if nothing else, of the way they're marketed and packaged for sale, we eat these latter meats without having to consider that they were once conscious, sentient creatures to whom horrible things were done. (N.B. "Horrible" here meaning really, really horrible. Write off to PETA or peta.org for their free "Meet Your Meat" video, narrated by Mr. Alec Baldwin, if you want to see just about everything meat-related you don't want to see or think about. [N.B.₂ Not that PETA's any sort of font of unspun truth. Like many partisans in complex moral disputes, the PETA people are fanatics, and a lot of their rhetoric seems simplistic and self-righteous. But this particular video, replete with actual factory-farm and corporate-slaughterhouse footage, is both credible and traumatizing.])

[15]Is it significant that "lobster," "fish," and "chicken" are our culture's words for both the animal and the meat, whereas most mammals seem to require euphemisms like "beef" and "pork" that help us separate the meat we eat from the living creature the meat once was? Is this evidence that some kind of deep unease about eating higher animals is endemic enough to show up in English usage, but that the unease diminishes as we move out of the mammalian order? (And is "lamb"/"lamb" the counterexample that sinks the whole theory, or are there special, biblico-historical reasons for that equivalence?)

watching trucks pull up and the live cattle get driven down the ramp and slaughtered right there on the World's Largest Killing Floor or something — there's no way.

The intimacy of the whole thing is maximized at home, which of course is where most lobster gets prepared and eaten (although note already the semiconscious euphemism "prepared," which in the case of lobsters really means killing them right there in our kitchens). The basic scenario is that we come in from the store and make our little preparations like getting the kettle filled and boiling, and then we lift the lobsters out of the bag or whatever retail container they came home in . . . whereupon some uncomfortable things start to happen. However stuporous a lobster is from the trip home, for instance, it tends to come alarmingly to life when placed in boiling water. If you're tilting it from a container into the steaming kettle, the lobster will sometimes try to cling to the container's sides or even to hook its claws over the kettle's rim like a person trying to keep from going over the edge of a

> **The lobster . . . behaves very much as you or I would behave if we were plunged into boiling water (with the obvious exception of screaming).**

roof. And worse is when the lobster's fully immersed. Even if you cover the kettle and turn away, you can usually hear the cover rattling and clanking as the lobster tries to push it off. Or the creature's claws scraping the sides of the kettle as it thrashes around. The lobster, in other words, behaves very much as you or I would behave if we were plunged into boiling water (with the obvious exception of screaming[16]). A blunter way to say this is that the lobster acts as if it's in terrible pain, causing some cooks to leave the kitchen altogether and to take one of those little lightweight plastic oven-timers with them into another room and wait until the whole process is over.

There happen to be two main criteria that most ethicists agree on for determining whether a living creature has the capacity to suffer and so has genuine interests that it may or may not be our moral duty to consider.[17] One is how much of the neurological hardware required for pain-experience the animal comes equipped with — nociceptors, prostaglandins, neuronal opioid receptors, etc. The other criterion is whether the animal demonstrates behavior associated with pain. And it takes a lot of intellectual gymnastics and behaviorist hairsplitting not to see struggling, thrashing, and lid-clattering as just such pain-behavior. According to marine zoologists, it usually takes

---

[16]There's a relevant populist myth about the high-pitched whistling sound that sometimes issues from a pot of boiling lobster. The sound is really vented steam from the layer of seawater between the lobster's flesh and its carapace (this is why shedders whistle more than hard-shells), but the pop version has it that the sound is the lobster's rabbit-like death-scream. Lobsters communicate via pheromones in their urine and don't have anything close to the vocal equipment for screaming, but the myth's very persistent — which might, once again, point to a low-level cultural unease about the boiling thing.

[17]"Interests" basically means strong and legitimate preferences, which obviously require some degree of consciousness, responsiveness to stimuli, etc. See, for instance, the utilitarian philosopher Peter Singer, whose 1974 *Animal Liberation* is more or less the bible of the modern animal-rights movement:

> It would be nonsense to say that it was not in the interests of a stone to be kicked along the road by a schoolboy. A stone does not have interests because it cannot suffer. Nothing that we can do to it could possibly make any difference to its welfare. A mouse, on the other hand, does have an interest in not being kicked along the road, because it will suffer if it is.

lobsters between 35 and 45 seconds to die in boiling water. (No source I could find talks about how long it takes them to die in superheated steam; one rather hopes it's faster.)

There are, of course, other ways to kill your lobster on-site and so achieve maximum freshness. Some cooks' practice is to drive a sharp heavy knife point-first into a spot just above the midpoint between the lobster's eyestalks (more or less where the Third Eye is in human foreheads). This is alleged either to kill the lobster instantly or to render it insensate, and is said at least to eliminate some of the cowardice involved in throwing a creature into boiling water and then fleeing the room. As far as I can tell from talking to proponents of the knife-in-head method, the idea is that it's more violent but ultimately more merciful, plus that a willingness to exert personal agency and accept responsibility for stabbing the lobster's head honors the lobster somehow and entitles one to eat it (there's often a vague sort of Native American spirituality-of-the-hunt flavor to pro-knife arguments). But the problem with the knife method is basic biology: Lobsters' nervous systems operate off not one but several ganglia, a.k.a. nerve bundles, which are sort of wired in series and distributed all along the lobster's underside, from stem to stern. And disabling only the frontal ganglion does not normally result in quick death or unconsciousness.

Another alternative is to put the lobster in cold saltwater and then very slowly   25
bring it up to a full boil. Cooks who advocate this method are going on the analogy to a frog, which can supposedly be kept from jumping out of a boiling pot by heating the water incrementally. In order to save a lot of research-summarizing, I'll simply assure you that the analogy between frogs and lobsters turns out not to hold—plus, if the kettle's water isn't aerated seawater, the immersed lobster suffers from slow suffocation, although usually not decisive enough suffocation to keep it from still thrashing and clattering when the water gets hot enough to kill it. In fact, lobsters boiled incrementally often display a whole bonus set of gruesome, convulsionlike reactions that you don't see in regular boiling.

Ultimately, the only certain virtues of the home-lobotomy and slow-heating methods are comparative, because there are even worse/crueler ways people prepare lobster. Time-thrifty cooks sometimes microwave them alive (usually after poking several vent-holes in the carapace, which is a precaution most shellfish-microwavers learn about the hard way). Live dismemberment, on the other hand, is big in Europe—some chefs cut the lobster in half before cooking; others like to tear off the claws and tail and toss only these parts into the pot.

And there's more unhappy news respecting suffering-criterion number one. Lobsters don't have much in the way of eyesight or hearing, but they do have an exquisite tactile sense, one facilitated by hundreds of thousands of tiny hairs that protrude through their carapace. "Thus it is," in the words of T. M. Prudden's industry classic *About Lobster*, "that although encased in what seems a solid, impenetrable armor, the lobster can receive stimuli and impressions from without as readily as if it possessed a soft and delicate skin." And lobsters do have nociceptors,[18] as well as invertebrate

---

[18]This is the neurological term for special pain-receptors that are "sensitive to potentially damaging extremes of temperature, to mechanical forces, and to chemical substances which are released when body tissues are damaged."

versions of the prostaglandins and major neurotransmitters via which our own brains register pain.

Lobsters do not, on the other hand, appear to have the equipment for making or absorbing natural opioids like endorphins and enkephalins, which are what more advanced nervous systems use to try to handle intense pain. From this fact, though, one could conclude either that lobsters are maybe even *more* vulnerable to pain, since they lack mammalian nervous systems' built-in analgesia, or, instead, that the absence of natural opioids implies an absence of the really intense pain-sensations that natural opioids are designed to mitigate. I for one can detect a marked upswing in mood as I contemplate this latter possibility. It could be that their lack of endorphin/enkephalin hardware means that lobsters' raw subjective experience of pain is so radically different from mammals' that it may not even deserve the term "pain." Perhaps lobsters are more like those frontal-lobotomy patients one reads about who report experiencing pain in a totally different way than you and I. These patients evidently do feel physical pain, neurologically speaking, but don't dislike it —though neither do they like it; it's more that they feel it but don't feel anything *about* it—the point being that the pain is not distressing to them or something they want to get away from. Maybe lobsters, who are also without frontal lobes, are detached from the neurological-registration-of-injury-or-hazard we call pain in just the same way. There is, after all, a difference between (1) pain as a purely neurological event, and (2) actual suffering, which seems crucially to involve an emotional component, an awareness of pain as unpleasant, as something to fear/dislike/want to avoid.

Still, after all the abstract intellection, there remain the facts of the frantically clanking lid, the pathetic clinging to the edge of the pot. Standing at the stove, it is hard to deny in any meaningful way that this is a living creature experiencing pain and wishing to avoid/escape the painful experience. To my lay mind, the lobster's behavior in the kettle appears to be the expression of a *preference*; and it may well be that an ability to form preferences is the decisive criterion for real suffering.[19] The logic of this (preference → suffering) relation may be easiest to see in the negative case. If you cut certain kinds of worms in half, the halves will often keep crawling around and going about their vermiform business as if nothing had happened. When we assert, based on their post-op behavior, that these worms appear not to be suffering, what we're really saying is that there's no sign the worms know anything bad has happened or would *prefer* not to have gotten cut in half.

Lobsters, though, are known to exhibit preferences. Experiments have shown that they can detect changes of only a degree or two in water temperature; one reason for their complex migratory cycles (which can often cover 100-plus miles a year) is to pursue the temperatures they like best.[20] And, as mentioned, they're bottom-dwellers and

30

---

[19]"Preference" is maybe roughly synonymous with "interests," but it is a better term for our purposes because it's less abstractly philosophical— "preference" seems more personal, and it's the whole idea of a living creature's personal experience that's at issue.

[20]Of course, the most common sort of counterargument here would begin by objecting that "like best" is really just a metaphor, and a misleadingly anthropomorphic one at that. The counterarguer would posit that the lobster seeks to maintain a certain optimal ambient temperature out of nothing but unconscious instinct (with a similar explanation for the low-light affinities upcoming in the main text). The thrust of such a counterargument will be that the lobster's thrashings and clankings in the kettle express not unpreferred pain

do not like bright light — if a tank of food-lobsters is out in the sunlight or a store's fluorescence, the lobsters will always congregate in whatever part is darkest. Fairly solitary in the ocean, they also clearly dislike the crowding that's part of their captivity in tanks, since (as also mentioned) one reason why lobsters' claws are banded on capture is to keep them from attacking one another under the stress of close-quarter storage.

In any event, at the MLF, standing by the bubbling tanks outside the World's Largest Lobster Cooker, watching the fresh-caught lobsters pile over one another, wave their hobbled claws impotently, huddle in the rear corners, or scrabble frantically back from the glass as you approach, it is difficult not to sense that they're unhappy, or frightened, even if it's some rudimentary version of these feelings . . . and, again, why does rudimentariness even enter into it? Why is a primitive, inarticulate form of suffering less urgent or uncomfortable for the person who's helping to inflict it by paying for the food it results in? I'm not trying to give you a PETA-like screed here — at least I don't think so. I'm trying, rather, to work out and articulate some of the troubling questions that arise amid all the laughter and saltation and community pride of the Maine Lobster Festival. The truth is that if you, the festival attendee, permit yourself to think that lobsters can suffer and would rather not, the MLF begins to take on the aspect of something like a Roman circus or medieval torture-fest.

Does that comparison seem a bit much? If so, exactly why? Or what about this one: Is it possible that future generations will regard our present agribusiness and eating practices in much the same way we now view Nero's entertainments or Mengele's experiments? My own initial reaction is that such a comparison is hysterical, extreme — and yet the reason it seems extreme to me appears to be that I believe animals are less morally important than human beings;[21] and when it comes to defending such a belief, even to myself, I have to acknowledge that (a) I have an obvious selfish interest in this belief, since I like to eat certain kinds of animals and want to be able to keep doing it, and (b) I haven't succeeded in working out any sort of personal ethical system in which the belief is truly defensible instead of just selfishly convenient.

Given this article's venue and my own lack of culinary sophistication, I'm curious about whether the reader can identify with any of these reactions and acknowledgments and discomforts. I'm also concerned not to come off as shrill or preachy when what I really am is more like confused. For those *Gourmet* readers who enjoy

---

but involuntary reflexes, like your leg shooting out when the doctor hits your knee. Be advised that there are professional scientists, including many researchers who use animals in experiments, who hold to the view that nonhuman creatures have no real feelings at all, merely "behaviors." Be further advised that this view has a long history that goes all the way back to Descartes, although its modern support comes mostly from behaviorist psychology.

To these what-looks-like-pain-is-really-just-reflexes counterarguments, however, there happen to be all sorts of scientific and pro-animal rights counter-counterarguments. And then further attempted rebuttals and redirects, and so on. Suffice it to say that both the scientific and the philosophical arguments on either side of the animal-suffering issue are involved, abstruse, technical, often informed by self-interest or ideology, and in the end so totally inconclusive that as a practical matter, in the kitchen or restaurant, it all still seems to come down to individual conscience, going with (no pun) your gut.

[21]Meaning *a lot* less important, apparently, since the moral comparison here is not the value of one human's life vs. the value of one animal's life, but rather the value of one animal's life vs. the value of one human's taste for a particular kind of protein. Even the most diehard carniphile will acknowledge that it's possible to live and eat well without consuming animals.

well-prepared and -presented meals involving beef, veal, lamb, pork, chicken, lobster, etc.: Do you think much about the (possible) moral status and (probable) suffering of the animals involved? If you do, what ethical convictions have you worked out that permit you not just to eat but to savor and enjoy flesh-based viands (since of course refined *enjoyment*, rather than mere ingestion, is the whole point of gastronomy)? If, on the other hand, you'll have no truck with confusions or convictions and regard stuff like the previous paragraph as just so much fatuous navel-gazing, what makes it feel truly okay, inside, to just dismiss the whole thing out of hand? That is, is your refusal to think about any of this the product of actual thought, or is it just that you don't want to think about it? And if the latter, then why not? Do you ever think, even idly, about the possible reasons for your reluctance to think about it? I am not trying t bait anyone here — I'm genuinely curious. After all, isn't being extra aware and atte. tive and thoughtful about one's food and its overall context part of what distinguishes a real gourmet? Or is all the gourmet's extra attention and sensibility just supposed to be sensuous? Is it really all just a matter of taste and presentation?

These last few queries, though, while sincere, obviously involve much larger and more abstract questions about the connections (if any) between aesthetics and moral-ity — about what the adjective in a phrase like "The Magazine of Good Living" is really supposed to mean — and these questions lead straightaway into such deep and treach-erous waters that it's probably best to stop the public discussion right here. There are limits to what even interested persons can ask of each other.

Exploring Context

1. Explore the Web site for the Maine Lobster Festival (mainelobsterfestival.com). How do both the design and content of the site reflect Wallace's experience attending the festival? Is there anything on the site that addresses the ethical concerns that Wallace raises? Why would the organizers of the festival include or omit such information? Why do you think Wallace raises these concerns?

2. Watch the YouTube video "How to Boil a Live Maine Lobster" by Dan "The Lobster Man" of Lobster Gram. How does Wallace's essay change your reaction to this video? In what ways does the video address Wallace's points about lobsters? Incorporate your response to Question 2 of Questions for Critical Reading.

3. Wallace's essay was originally published in *Gourmet* magazine. Visit Epicurious (epicurious.com), a Web site with a similar audience. Based on what you find there, how do you think Wallace's original audience reacted to his essay? Why might he have written the essay with this style, focus, and content for such a magazine?

Questions for Connecting

1. In "Ethics and the New Genetics" (p. 63), the Dalai Lama calls for a "moral compass" to guide us through the rapid advances of science and technology. How can you syn-thesize the Dalai Lama's position on ethics with Wallace's discussion of lobsters? Pay particular attention to Wallace's suggestion that lobsters have clear "preferences." Is preference sufficient for a moral compass? Use your analysis of "preference" from Ques-tion 3 of Questions for Critical Reading.

2. Considering the information that Sandra Allen presents in "A World Without Wine" (p. 34), to what extent are Wallace's musings a moral luxury? That is, given the complex changes required to continue feeding the world can we afford to consider the kinds of ethical questions Wallace raises about lobsters?

3. Using ideas from Yo-Yo Ma's "Necessary Edges: Arts, Empathy, and Education" (p. 258), discuss the role that empathy plays in decisions about what we eat. What mode of thinking determines our choice of food? Would more empathetic thinking change our approach to eating?

Language Matters

1. Wallace's writing makes frequent use of footnotes. How do they function in his text? When should you use footnotes in your own writing? In considering your response, also review the proper format for footnotes using a grammar handbook or other reliable reference resource.

2. Narrowing one's topic can be a challenge, even for writers like Wallace. Imagine a "research pyramid" for this essay, with the broadest category at the bottom and the most ridiculously specific one at the top point of the pyramid. How many different levels can you find for this essay? Would the essay have been as strong if it were less or more specific? Why did Wallace choose this level of the pyramid for his work?

3. Imagine you could invite Wallace into the discussion in your classroom. What questions would you want to ask him about this essay? Use that experience to think about larger issues. What are the limits of written discourse? How might you anticipate your audience's questions when you write?

Assignments for Writing

1. Wallace asks, "Is it possible that future generations will regard our present agribusiness and eating practices in much the same way we now view Nero's entertainments or Mengele's experiments?" (p. 470). Write a paper in which you address Wallace's query. Rather than answering Wallace's admittedly extreme future with a *yes* or *no*, consider instead the implications of his scenario as you build an argument that articulates how we might define an ethics of creature-based food.

2. Using Wallace for support, take the point of view of either a committed meat eater or a committed vegetarian, arguing your position by drawing on food-related issues such as health, hunger, and treatment of animals. Locate support for your position in Wallace's essay.

3. Wallace suggests an ethics built on "preference" — lobsters, that is, clearly would prefer not to be boiled alive. Evaluate the possibility of a preference-based ethics by locating your own example and connecting it to Wallace's discussion of suffering in animals. Is preference sufficient to make moral and ethical decisions? Can it be expanded to other ethical situations or is it limited to questions of food? You may also want to draw on your work in Questions 1 and 2 of Questions for Connecting.

BILL WASIK

Bill Wasik is a senior editor at *Wired* magazine. Prior to his work there, he was an editor at *Harper's Magazine* and the *Weekly Week*. Wasik is the author of *And Then There's This: How Stories Live and Die in Viral Culture* (2009) and the coauthor of *Rabid: A Cultural History of the World's Most Diabolical Virus* (2012), as well as the editor of *Submersion Journalism: Reporting in the Radical First Person from Harper's Magazine* (2008), a collection of essays from *Harper's*. Wasik is perhaps best known for inventing the flash mob, which he created as a social experiment in 2003.

Brad Barket/Getty Images

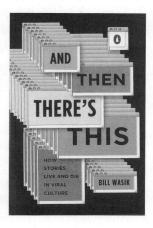

The book from which this selection is taken, *And Then There's This*, investigates our current media culture and the surges of interest that spread throughout our society. He defines these moments of intense, short-lived interest in an event or a person as a "nanostory." Throughout the book, Wasik investigates the people, the culture, the media, and the politics that create our current interest in these nanostories.

In the chapter titled "My Crowd Experiment: The Mob Project," Wasik describes the beginning of the flash mob as a social experiment to satiate his thirst for something new and interesting; simply, he was bored. Yet while the flash mob began as a prank Wasik initiated for the sake of entertainment and curiosity, it quickly took on a life of its own, becoming a "meme" (p. 479) and coming to hold a recognized place in our culture. In looking at the flash mob as a meme, Wasik explores the social forces that enabled the spread of this idea as well as the biological reasoning for our desire to jump on the bandwagon and be part of something big.

Have you ever participated in a flash mob? What memes have you helped spread through e-mail or social media like Facebook?

▶ TAGS: *collaboration, community, culture, psychology, social media*
▶ CONNECTIONS: *Henig, Klosterman, Konnikova, Paumgarten, Restak, Singer*

Questions for Critical Reading

1. Write your own definition of a *flash mob*. As you read, mark those places in the text where Wasik defines the term. What makes a flash mob? What are its essential components?

2. Find an example of an Internet meme from your own experience or by researching online. How does Wasik define *meme*? What role do memes play in our culture today?

3. What purpose, if any, do flash mobs serve? Are they useful forms of social organization, disruptive gatherings, or nothing more than entertainment? As you read Wasik's text, look for passages that support your position.

My Crowd Experiment: The Mob Project
Boredom

I started the Mob Project because I was bored . . . and perhaps that explanation seems simple enough. But before we proceed to the rise and fall of my peculiar social experiment, I think that boredom is worth interrogating in some detail. The first recorded use of the term, per the *OED*, did not take place until 1852, in Charles Dickens's *Bleak House*, Chapter 12. It is deployed by way of describing Lady Dedlock, a woman with whose habits of mind I often find myself in sympathy:

> Concert, assembly, opera, theatre, drive, nothing is new to my Lady, under the worn-out heavens. Only last Sunday, when poor wretches were gay — . . . encompassing Paris with dancing, lovemaking, wine-drinking, tobacco-smoking, tomb-visiting, billiard, card and domino playing, quack-doctoring, and much murderous refuse, animate and inanimate — only last Sunday, my Lady, in the desolation of Boredom and the clutch of Giant Despair, almost hated her own maid for being in spirits.

Psychologists have been trying to elucidate the nature of boredom since at least Sigmund Freud, who identified a "lassitude" in young women that he attributed to penis envy. In 1951, Otto Fenichel described boredom as a state where the "drive-tension" is present but the "drive-aim" is absent, a state of mind that he said could be "schematically formulated" in this enigmatic but undeniably evocative way: "I am excited. If I allow this excitation to continue I shall get anxious. Therefore I tell myself, I am not at all excited, I don't want to do anything. Simultaneously, however, I feel I do want to do something; but I have forgotten my original goal and do not know what I want to do. The external world must do something to relieve me of my tension without making me anxious."

In the 1970s, researchers developed various tests designed, in part to assess the boredom-plagued, from the Imaginal Processes Inventor (Singer and Antrobus, 1970) to the Sensation Seeking Scale (Zuckerman, Eysenck & Eysenck, 1978). But it was not until 1986, with the unveiling of the Boredom Proneness Scale (BPS), that the propensity toward boredom in the individual could be comprehensively measured and reckoned with. The test was created by Richard Farmer and Norman Sundberg, both of the University of Oregon, and it has allowed researchers in the two decades since to tally up boredom's grim wages. The boredom-prone, we have discovered, display higher rates of procrastination, inattention, narcissism, poor work performance, and "solitary sexual behaviors" including both onanism and the resort to pornography.

The BPS test consists of twenty-eight statements to which respondents answer true or false, with a point assessed for each boredom-aligned choice, e.g.:

1. *It is easy for me to concentrate on my activities.* [*+1 for False.*]

5. *I am often trapped in situations where I have to do meaningless things.* [+1 *for True.*]

25. *Unless I am doing something exciting, even dangerous, I feel half-dead and dull.* [+1 *for True.*]

Farmer and Sundberg found the average score to be roughly 10. My own score is 16, and indeed when I peruse the list of correct answers I feel as if I am scanning a psychological diagnosis of myself. I *do* find it hard to concentrate; I *do* find myself constantly trapped doing meaningless things; and half-dead or dull does not begin to describe how I feel when I lack a project that is adequately transgressive or, worse, find myself exiled somewhere among the slow-witted. I worry about other matters while I work (#2), and I find that time passes slowly (#3). I am bad at waiting patiently (#15), and in fact when I am forced to wait in line, I get restless (#17). Even for those questions to which I give the allegedly nonbored answer, I tend to feel I am forfeiting the points on some technicality. Yes, I do have "projects in mind, all the time" (#7)—so many that few of them ever get acted upon, precisely because my desperate craving for variety means that I am rarely satisfied for very long with even projects that are hypothetical. Yes, others do tend to say that I am a "creative or imaginative person" (#22), but honestly I think this is due to declining standards.

And no, I do not often find myself "at loose ends" (#4), sitting around doing nothing (#14), with "time on my hands" (#16), without "something to do or see to keep me interested" (#13). But such has been true for me only since the start of this viral decade, when my idle stretches have been erased by the grace of the Internet, with its soothingly fast and infinitely available distractions, engaging me for hours on end without assuaging my fundamental boredom in any way. In fact, I would advance the prediction that answers to these latter four questions have become meaningless in recent years, when all of our interactive technologies—video games and mobile devices as well as the web—have kept those of us most boredom-prone from generally thinking, as we might while watching TV, that we are "doing nothing," even if in every practical sense we are doing precisely that. I fear I am ahead of the science, however, because I have been unable to find any study that either supports or undercuts this conjecture. I put the question to Richard Farmer, the lead author of the Boredom Proneness Scale, only to find that he had not done boredom research in many years. He had moved on to other topics. I did not ask him why, though I have the glimmer of a notion.

Experiment: The Mob Project

That May my boredom was especially acute, but none of the projects crowding around in my mind seemed feasible. I wanted to use e-mail to get people to come to some sort of show, where something surprising would happen, perhaps involving a fight; or an entire fake arts scene, maybe, some tight-knit band of fictitious young artists and writers who all lived together in a loft, and we would reel in journalists and would-be admirers eager to congratulate themselves for having discovered the next big thing. Both of these ideas seemed far too difficult. It was while ruminating on these two ideas, in the shower, that I realized I needed to make my idea *lazier*. I could use e-mail to gather an audience for a show, yes, but the point of the show should be no show at all: the e-mail would be straightforward about exactly what people would see, namely nothing but *themselves*, coming together for no reason at all. Such a project would work, I reflected, because it was *meta*, i.e., it was a self-conscious idea for a self-conscious culture, a promise to create something out of nothing. It was the perfect project for me.

During the week between the first MOB e-mail and the appointed day, I found myself anxious, not knowing what to expect. MOB's only goal was to attract a crowd, but as an event it had none of the typical draws: no name of any artist or performer, no endorsement by any noted tastemaker. All it had was its own ironically wild, unsupportable claims — that "tons" of people would be there, that they would constitute a "mob." The subject heading of the e-mail had read *MOB #1*, so as to imply that it was the first in what would be an ongoing series of gatherings. (In fact, I was unsure whether there would be a MOB #2.) As I was gathering my things to head north the seven blocks from my office to the mob site, I received a call from my friend Eugene, a stand-up comedian whose attitude toward daily living I have long admired. Once, on a slow day

> **[T]he point of the show would be no show at all.**

while he was working at an ice-cream store, he slid a shovel through the inside handles of the store's plate-glass front doors, along with a note that read CLOSED DUE TO SHOVEL.

"Is the mob supposed to be at Claire's Accessories?" Eugene asked.

Yes, I said.

"There's six cops standing guard in front of it," he said. "And a paddywagon."

This was not the mob I had been anticipating. If anyone was to land in that paddywagon, I thought, it ought to be me, and so I hastened to the site. The cops, thankfully, did not seem to be in an arresting mood. But they would not allow anyone to enter the store, even when we told them (not unpersuasively, I thought) that we were desperate accessories shoppers. I scanned the faces of passersby, hoping to divine how many had come to mob — quite a few, I judged, based on their excited yet wry expressions, but seeing the police they understandably hurried past. Still others lingered around, filming with handheld video cameras or snapping digital pictures. A radio crew lurked with a boom mike. Despite the police, my single e-mail had generated enough steam to power a respectable spectacle.

The underlying science of the Mob Project seemed sound, and so I readied plans for MOB #2, which would be held two weeks later, on June 17. I found four ill-frequented bars near the intended site and had the participants gather at those beforehand, again split by the month of their birth. Ten minutes before the appointed time of 7:27 PM, slips of paper bearing the final destination were distributed at the bars. The site was the Macy's rugs department, which in that tremendous store is a mysterious and inaccessible kingdom, the farthest reach of the ninth and uppermost floor, accessed by a seemingly endless series of ancient escalators that grind past women's apparel and outerwear and furs and fine china and the in-store Starbucks and Au Bon Pain. By quarter past seven waves of mobbers were sweeping through the dimly illuminated furniture department, glancing sidelong toward the rugs room as they pretended to shop for loveseats and bureaus; but all at once, in a giant rush, two hundred people wandered over to the carpet in the back left corner and, as instructed, informed clerks that they all lived together in a Long Island City commune and were looking for a "love rug."

"E-mail Mob Takes Manhattan" read the headline two days later on *Wired News*, an online technology-news site. More media took note, and interview requests began to filter in to my anonymous webmail account: on June 18, from *New York* magazine;

10

on June 20, from the *New York Observer*, NPR's *All Things Considered*, the BBC World Service, the Italian daily *Corriere della Serra*. By MOB #3, which was held two weeks after the previous one, I had gotten fifteen requests in total. Would-be mobbers in other cities had heard the call as well, and soon I received e-mails from San Francisco, Minneapolis, Boston, Austin, announcing their own local chapters. Some asked for advice, which I very gladly gave. ("Before you send out the instructions, visit the spot at the same time and on the same day of the week, and figure out how long it will take people to get to the mob spot, etc.," I wrote to Minneapolis.)

Perhaps most important, the Mob Project was almost immediately taken up by 15 blogs. A blog called Cheesebikini, run by a thirty-one-year-old graduate student in Berkeley named Sean Savage, gave the concept its name—"flash mobs"—as an homage to a 1973 science-fiction short story called "Flash Crowd," by Larry Niven. The story is a warning about the unexpected downside of cheap teleportation technology: packs of thrill seekers can beam themselves in whenever something exciting is going down. The protagonist, Jerryberry Jensen, is a TV journalist who broadcasts a fight in a shopping mall, which soon, thanks to teleportation booths, grows into a multiday riot, with miscreants beaming in from around the world. Jensen is blamed, and his bosses threaten to fire him, but eventually he clears his name by showing how the technology was to blame. Since the mid-1990s, the term "flash crowd" had been invoked from time to time as a metaphor for the sudden and debilitating traffic surges that can occur when a small website is linked to by a very popular one. This is more commonly known as the "Slashdot effect," after the popular tech-head site Slashdot.org, which was—and still is—known to choke the sites on which it bestows links.

With its meteorological resonance, its evocation of a "flash flood" of people mobbing a place or a site or a thing all at once and then dispersing, the term "flash mob" was utterly perfect. The phenomenon it described, now properly named, could venture out into the universe and begin swiftly, stylishly, assuredly to multiply.

Hypothesis

The logic behind the Mob Project ran, roughly, as follows.

1. At any given time in New York—or in any other city where culture is actively made—the vast majority of events (concerts, plays, readings, comedy nights, and gallery shows, but also protests, charities, association meetings) are summarily ignored, while a small subset of events attracts enormous audiences and, soon, media attention.

2. For most of these latter events, the beneficiaries of that ineffable boon known as *buzz*, one can, after the fact, point out nominal reasons for their sudden popularity: high quality, for example; or perception of high quality due to general acclamation, or at least an assumption of general acclamation, or the participation of some well-liked figure, or the presence, or rumored presence, of same; etc.

3. *But*: so often does popularity, even among the highest of brow, bear no relationship to merit, that an experiment might be devised to determine just how far one might take the former while neglecting the latter entirely; that is, how much buzz one could create about an event whose only point was buzz, a show whose audience

was itself the only show. Given all culture in New York was demonstrably commingled with *scenesterism*, my thinking ran, it should theoretically be possible to create an art project consisting of *pure scene*—meaning the scene would be the entire point of the work, and indeed would itself constitute the work.

At its best, the Mob Project brought to this task a sort of formal unity, as can be illustrated in MOB #3, which took place fifteen days after #2. To get the slips with the destination, invitees were required to roam the downstairs food court of Grand Central Station, looking for Mob Project representatives reading the *New York Review of Books*. The secret location was a hotel adjacent to the station on Forty-second Street, the Grand Hyatt, which has a block-long lobby with fixtures in the high '80s style: gold-chrome railings and sepia-mirror walls and a fountain in marblish stone and a mezzanine overhead, ringed around. Mob time was set for 7:07 PM, the tail end of the evening rush hour; the train station next door was thick with commuters and so (visible through the hotel's tinted-glass facade) was the sidewalk outside, but the lobby was nearly empty: only a few besuited types, guests presumably, sunk here and there into armchairs.

Starting five minutes beforehand the mob members slipped in, in twos and threes and tens, milling around in the lobby and making stylish small talk. Then all at once, they rode the elevators and escalators up to the mezzanine and wordlessly lined the banister, like so:

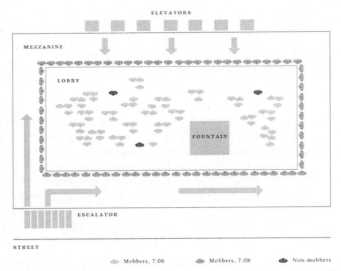

Graphics from *And Then There's This* by Bill Wasik. Copyright © 2009 by Bill Wasik. Used by permission of Viking Penguin, a division of Penguin Group (USA) Inc.

The handful of hotel guests were still there, alone again, except now they were confronted with a hundreds-strong armada of mobbers overhead, arrayed shoulder to shoulder, staring silently down. Intimidation was not the point; we were staring down at *where we had just been*, and also across at one another, two hundred artist-spectators commandeering an atrium on Forty-second Street as a coliseum-style theater of self-regard. After five minutes of staring, the ring erupted into precisely fifteen seconds of tumultuous applause—for itself—after which it scattered back downstairs and out the door, just as the police cruisers were rolling up, flashers on.

The Meme, Supreme

From the moment flash mobs first began to spread, there was a term applied to them by both boosters and detractors, and that term was *meme*. "The Flash Mob meme is #1 with a bullet," wrote the author Howard Rheingold on his blog. Three days later, on MetaFilter, one commenter wrote, "I was going to take the time to savage this wretched warmed-over meme, but am delighted to see that so many of you have already done so"; countered the next commenter, "I happen to think the meme is a bit silly, but the backlash even more so." In September, when the comic strip *Doonesbury* had one of its characters create flash mobs for Howard Dean, one blogger named Eric enthused, "Trust Gary [*sic*] Trudeau to combine the hottest memes of the summer," adding as an aside: "Yes, I fully realize that [I] just called Dr Dean a meme."

Readers will be excused for their ignorance of this term, though in 1998 it did enter the Merriam-Webster dictionary, which defines it as "an idea, behavior, style, or usage that spreads from person to person within a culture." The operative word here is "spreads," for this simple monosyllabic noun has buried within it a particular vision of culture and how it evolves. In a meme's-eye view of the world, any idea—from a religious belief or a political affiliation to a new style of jeans or a catchy tune—can be seen as a sort of independent agent loosed into the population, where it travels from mind to mind, burrowing into each, colonizing all as widely and ruthlessly as it can. Some brains are more susceptible than others to certain memes, but by and large memes spread by virtue of their own inherent contagiousness. The meme idea, that is, sees cultural entities as being similar to genes, or better, to *viruses*, and in fact the term "viral" is often used to express the same idea.

If we consider the meme idea itself as a meme, we see that its virulence in the Internet era has been impressive. The term was coined in 1976 by the biologist Richard Dawkins in his first book, *The Selfish Gene*, in which he persuasively argues that genes are the operative subjects of evolutionary selection: that is, individuals struggle first and foremost to perpetuate their genes, and insofar as evolution is driven by the "survival of the fittest," it is the fitness of our genes, not of us, that is the relevant factor. He puts forward a unified vision of history in which replication is king: in Dawkins's view, from that very first day when, somewhere in the murk, there emerged the first genes—molecules with the ability to create copies of themselves—these selfish replicators have been orchestrating the whole shebang. After extending out this argument to explain the evolution of species, Dawkins turns to the question of human culture. If replication, over long periods of time, explains why we exist, then might it not serve also to explain what inhabits our minds? Dawkins writes, with characteristic flourish,

> I think that a new kind of replicator has recently emerged on this very planet. It is staring us in the face. It is still in its infancy, still drifting clumsily about in its primeval soup. . . . The new soup is the soup of human culture. We need a name for the new replicator, a noun that conveys the idea of a unit of cultural transmission, or a unit of imitation. "Mimeme" [Greek for "that which is imitated"] comes from a suitable Greek root, but I want a monosyllable that

sounds a bit like gene. I hope my classicist friends will forgive me if I abbreviate mimeme to *meme*.

Although Dawkins clearly intends the meme to be analogous first and foremost to the gene—which spreads itself only through successive generations, through the reproduction of its host—on the very same page he invokes the more apt biological metaphor of the virus. "When you plant a fertile meme in my mind you literally parasitize my brain," he wrote, "turning it into a vehicle for the meme's propagation in just the way that a virus may parasitize the genetic mechanism of a host cell."

Why has the meme meme spread? Why has the viral become so viral? *The Selfish* 25 *Gene* was a bestselling book thirty years ago, but it was not until the mid-1990s that the meme and viral ideas became epidemics of their own. I would hazard two reasons for this chronology, one psychological and one technological. The psychological reason is the rise of market consciousness, in a culture where stock ownership increased during the 1990s from just under a quarter to more than half. After all, the meme vision of culture—where ideas compete for brain space, unburdened by history or context— really resembles nothing so much as an economist's dream of the free market. We are asked to admire the marvelous theoretical efficiencies (no barriers to entry, unfettered competition, persistence of the fittest) but to ignore the factual inequalities: the fact, for example, that so many of our most persistent memes succeed only through elaborate sponsorship (what would be a genetic analogy here? factory-farm breeding, perhaps?), while other, fitter memes wither.

The other, technological reason for the rise of the meme/viral idea is perhaps more obvious: the Internet. But it is worth teasing out just *what* about the Internet has conjured up these memes all around us. Yes, the Internet allows us to communicate instantaneously with others around the world, but that has been possible since the telegraph. Yes, the Internet allows us to find others with similar interests and chat among ourselves; but this is just an online analogue of what we always have been able to do in person, even if perhaps not on such a large scale. What the Internet has done to change culture—to create a new, viral culture—is to *archive* trillions of our communications, to make them linkable, trackable, searchable, quantifiable, so they can serve as ready grist for yet more conversation. In an offline age, we might have had a vague notion that a slang phrase or a song or a perception of a product or an enthusiasm for a candidate was spreading through social groups; but lacking any hard data about *how* it was spreading, why would any of us (aside from marketers and sundry social scientists) really care? Today, though, in the Internet, we have a trillion-terabyte answer that in turn has influenced our questions. We can see how we are embedded in numerical currents, how we precede or lag curves, how we are enmeshed in so-called social networks, and how our networks compare to the networks of others. The Internet has given us not just new ways of communicating but new ways of measuring ourselves.

Propagation

To spread the Mob Project, I endeavored to devise a *media strategy* on the project's own terms. The mob was all about the herd instinct, I reasoned, about the desire not to be left out of the latest fad; logically, then, it should grow as quickly as possible, and eventually—this seemed obvious—to buckle under the weight of its own popularity. I developed a simple maxim for myself, as custodian of the mob: "Anything that grows the mob is pro-mob." And in accordance with this principle, I gave interviews to all reporters who asked. In the six weeks following MOB #3 I did perhaps thirty different interviews, not only with local newspapers (the *Post* and the *Daily News*, though not yet the *Times*—more on that later) but also with *Time*, *Time Out New York*, the *Christian Science Monitor*, the *San Francisco Chronicle*, the *Chicago Tribune*, the Associated Press, Reuters, Agence France-Presse, and countless websites.

There was also the matter of how I would be identified. My original preference had been to remain entirely anonymous, but I had only half succeeded; at the first, aborted mob, a radio reporter had discovered my first name and broadcast it, and so I was forced to be Bill—or, more often, "Bill"—in my dealings with the media thereafter. "[L]ike Cher and Madonna, prefers to use only his first name," wrote the *Chicago Daily Herald*. (To those who asked my occupation, I replied simply that I worked in the "culture industry.") Usually a flash-mob story would invoke me roughly three quarters of the way

There were dark questions as to my intentions.

down, as the "shadowy figure" at the center of the project. There were dark questions as to my intentions. "Bill, who denies he is on a power-trip, declined to be identified," intoned Britain's *Daily Mirror*. Here is an exchange from Fox News's *On the Record with Greta Van Susteren*:

> ANCHOR: Now, the guy who came up with the Mob Project is a mystery man named Bill. Do either of you know who he is?
> MOBBER ONE: Nope.
> MOBBER TWO: Well, I've—I've e-mailed him. That's about it.
> MOBBER ONE: Oh, you have . . . ?
> ANCHOR: What—what—who is this Bill? Do you know anything about him?
> MOBBER TWO: Well, from what I've read, he's a—he works in the culture industry, and that's—that's about as specific as we've gotten with him.

As the media frenzy over the mobs grew, so did the mobs themselves. For MOB #4, I sent the mob to a shoe store in SoHo, a spacious plate-glassed corner boutique whose high ceilings and walls made of undulating mosaic gave it an almost aquatic feel, and I was astonished to see the mob assemble: as I marched with one strand streaming down Lafayette, we saw another mounting a pincers movement around Prince Street from the east, pouring in through the glass doors past the agape mouths of the attendants, perhaps three hundred bodies, packing the space and then, once no one else could enter, crowding around the sidewalk, everyone gawking, taking pictures with cameras, calling friends on cell phones (as the instructions for this mob had ordered), each pretending to be a tourist, all feigning awe—an awe I myself truly felt—to be not merely in New York but so close to the center of something so big.

Outside New York, too, the mob was multiplying in dizzying ways, far past the point that I could correspond with the leaders or even keep up with all the different new cities: not only all across the United States but London, Vienna, twenty-one different municipalities in Germany. In July, soon after New York's MOB #4, Rome held its first two flash mobs; in the first, three hundred mobbers strode into a bookstore

30

and demanded nonexistent titles (e.g., *Pinocchio 2: The Revenge*), while the second (which, based on descriptions I read later, is perhaps my favorite flash mob of any ever assembled) was held right in the Piazza dell'Esquilino, in a crosswalk just in front of the glorious Basilica di Santa Maria Maggiore, where the crowd broke into two and balletically crossed back and forth and met each other multiple times, first hugging, then fighting, and then asking for the time: "*CHE ORE SONO?*" yelled one semi-mob, and the other replied, "*LE SETTE E QUARANTA*," — "It's 7:40" —which, in fact, it was exactly.

Up: The Bandwagon Effect

When a British art magazine asked me who, among artists past or present, had most influenced the flash-mob project, I named Stanley Milgram—i.e., the social psychologist best known for his authority experiments in which he induced average Americans to give seemingly fatal shocks to strangers. As it happens, I later discovered that Milgram also did a project much like a flash mob, in which a "stimulus crowd" of his confederates, varying in number from one to fifteen, stopped on a busy Manhattan sidewalk and all at once looked up to the same sixth-floor window. The results, in a chart from his paper "Notes on the Drawing Power of Crowds of Different Size":

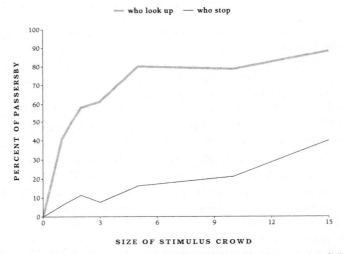

Graphics from *And Then There's This* by Bill Wasik. Copyright © 2009 by Bill Wasik. Used by permission of Viking Penguin, a division of Penguin Group (USA) Inc.

In this single chart, Milgram elegantly documented the essence of herd behavior, what economists call a "bandwagon effect": the instinctive tendency of the human animal to rely on the actions of others in choosing its own course of action. We get interested in the things we see others getting interested in. *Homo sapiens* has been jumping on bandwagons, as the expression goes, since long before the vogue for such vehicles in the late nineteenth century (when less popular American politicians would clamor to be seen aboard the bandwagon of a more popular candidate for another office, hence the meaning we have today); since long before, even, the invention of the wheel.

The bandwagon effect is especially pronounced in Internet culture-making, however, because popularity can immediately be factored into how choices are presented to us. If in our nonwired lives we jump on a bandwagon once a day, in our postwired existence we hop whole fleets of them—often without even knowing it. Start, for example, where most of us start online, with Google: when we search for a phrase, Google's sophisticated engine delivers our results in an order determined (at least in part) by how many searchers before us eventually clicked on the pages in question. Whenever we click on a top-ten Google result, we are jumping on an invisible bandwagon. Similarly with retailers such as Amazon, whose front-page offerings, tailored to each customer, are based on what other customers have bought: another invisible bandwagon. Then there are the countless visible bandwagons, in the form of the ubiquitous lists: most bought, most downloaded, most e-mailed, most linked-to. Even the august *New York Times*, through its "most e-mailed" list, has turned the news into a popularity contest, whose winners in turn get more attention among Internet readers who have only a limited amount of attention to give. Thus do the attention-rich invariably get richer.

In some cases, our bandwagons—online or off—do us a service, by weeding out extraneous or undesirable information through the "wisdom of crowds" (as a bestselling book by James Surowiecki put it). Moreover, in the case of culture, what is already popular in some respect has more intrinsic value: we read news, or watch television, or listen to music in part so we can have discussions with other people who have done the same. But it is a severe mistake to assume, as the economically minded often do, that the bandwagon effect manages to select for intrinsic worth, or even to give individuals what they actually want. This was demonstrated ingeniously a few years ago in an experiment run by Matthew Salganik, a sociologist who was then at Columbia University. Fourteen thousand participants were invited to join a music network where they could listen to songs, rate them, and, if they wanted, download the songs for free. A fifth of the volunteers—the "independent" group—were left entirely to their own tastes, unable to see what their fellows were downloading. The other four-fifths were split up into eight different networks—the "influence" groups—all of which saw the same songs, but listed in rank order based on how often they had been downloaded in that particular group. The songs were by almost entirely unknown bands, to avoid having songs get popular based on preexisting associations with the band's name.

What Salganik and his colleagues found was that the "independent" group chose songs that differed significantly from those chosen in the "influence" groups, which in turn differed significantly from one another. In their paper, the sociologists call the eight different networks "worlds," and they mean this in the philosophical sense of possible worlds: each network began from the same starting point with the same universe of songs, but each of these independent evolutionary environments yielded very different outcomes. A band called 52metro, for example, was #1 in one world but didn't even rate the top ten in five of the other seven worlds. Similarly, a band called Silent Film topped one chart but was #3, #4, #7, or #8 (twice) on five of the charts, and was entirely left off the other two. "Quality"—if we define that to mean the independent group's choices—did not seem to be entirely irrelevant: the top-rated song on their list,

35

by a group called Parker Theory, made all eight of the "influence" lists and topped five of them. But of the other nine acts on the independent list, one was entirely shut out of the influence lists, and three made only two lists. On average, the top ten bands for the independent group made only four of the eight influence lists. Apparently they were drowned out, in the other worlds, by noise from the bandwagons.

The Mob Project was a *self-conscious* bandwagon—advertised itself as a bandwagon, as a joke about conformity, and it lampooned bandwagons in doing so. But curiously, this seemed not to diminish its actual bandwagonesque properties. Indeed, if anything, the self-consciousness made it even more viral. The e-mails poured in: "I WANT IN." "Request to mob, sir." "Girls can keep secrets!" "Want to get my mob on." In Boston's first flash mob, entitled "Ode to Bill," hundreds packed the greeting-card aisles of a Harvard Square department store, telling bystanders who inquired that they were looking for a card for their "friend Bill in New York." By making a halfhearted, jesting attempt to elevate me to celebrity status, Boston had given the flash-mob genre an appropriately sly turn.

Peak and Backlash

The best attended of all the New York gatherings was MOB #6, which for a few beautiful minutes stifled what has to be the most ostentatious chain store in the entire city: the Times Square Toys "Я" Us, whose excesses are too many to catalog here but include, in the store's foyer, an actual operational Ferris wheel some sixty feet in diameter. Up until the appointed time of 7:18 PM, the mobbers loitered on the upper level, among the GI Joes and the Nintendos and up inside the glittering pink of the two-floor Barbie palace. But then all at once the mob, five hundred strong, crowded around the floor's centerpiece, a life-size animatronic Tyrannosaurus rex that growls and feints with a Hollywood-class lifelikeness. "Fill in all around it," the mob slip had instructed. "It is like a terrible god to you."

> **"Fill in all around it," the mob slip had instructed. "It is like a terrible god to you."**

Two minutes later, the mob dropped to its knees, moaning and cowering at the beast behind outstretched hands; in doing so we repaid this spectacle, which clearly was the product of not only untold expenditure but many man-months of *imagineering*, with an en masse enactment of the very emotions—visceral fright and infantile fealty—that it obviously had been designed to evoke. MOB #6 was, as many bloggers pointed out pejoratively, "cute," but the cuteness had been massed, refracted, and focused to such a bright point that it became a physical menace. For six minutes the upper level was paralyzed; the cash registers were cocooned behind the moaning, kneeling bodies pressed together; customers were trapped; business could not be done. The terror-stricken personnel tried in vain to force the crowd out. "Is anyone making a purchase?" one was heard to call out weakly. As the mob dispersed down the escalators and out into the street, the police were downstairs, telling us to leave, but we had already accomplished the task, had delivered what was in effect a warning.

Almost unanimously, though, the bloggers panned MOB #6. "Another Mob Botched" was the verdict on the blog Fancy Robot: "[I]nstead of setting the Flash Mob out in public on Times Square itself, as everyone had hoped, The Flash Master decided to set it in Toys "Я" Us, with apparently dismal results." SatansLaundromat.com (a photo-blog that contains the most complete visual record of the New York project) concurred — "not public enough," the blogger wrote, without enough "spectators to bewilder" — as did Chris from the CCE Blog: "I think the common feeling among these blogger reviews is: where does the idea go from here? . . . After seeing hundreds of people show up for no good reason, it's obvious that there's some kind of potential for artistic or political expression here."

The idea seemed to be that flash mobs could be made to convey a message, but for a number of reasons this dream was destined to run aground. First, as outlined above, flash mobs were gatherings of *insiders*, and as such could hardly communicate to those who did not already belong. They were intramural play; they drew their energies not from impressing outsiders or freaking them out but from showing them utter disregard, from using the outside world as merely a terrain for private games. Second, in terms of time, flash mobs were by definition *transitory*, ten minutes or fewer, and thereby not exactly suited to standing their ground and testifying. Third, in terms of physical space, flash mobs relied on *constraints* to create an illusion of superior strength. I never held mobs in the open, the bloggers complained, in view of enough onlookers, but this was entirely purposeful on my part, for like Colin Powell I hewed to a doctrine of overwhelming force. Only in enclosed spaces could the mob generate the necessary self-awe; to allow the mob to feel small would have been to destroy it.

The following week, the interview request from the *New York Times* finally arrived. On the phone the reporter, Amy Harmon, made it clear to me that the *Times* knew it was behind on the story. The paper would be remedying this, she told me, by running a prominent piece on flash mobs in its Sunday Week in Review section. What the *Times* did, in fascinating fashion, was not just to run the backlash story (which I had been expecting in three to five more weeks) but to do so preemptively — i.e., before there was actually a backlash. Harmon's piece bore the headline "Guess Some People Don't Have Anything Better to Do," and its nut sentence ran: "[T]he flash mob juggernaut has now run into a flash mob backlash that may be spreading faster than the fad itself." As evidence, she mustered the following:

> E-mail lists like "antimob" and "slashmob" have sprung up, as did a Web site warning that "flashmuggers" are bound to show up "wherever there's groups of young, naïve, wealthy, bored fashionistas to be found." And a new definition was circulated last week on several Web sites: "flash mob, noun: An impromptu gathering, organized by means of electronic communication, of the unemployed."

Two e-mail lists, a website, and a forwarded definition hardly constituted a "backlash" against this still-growing, intercontinental fad, but what I think Harmon and the *Times* rightly understood was that a backlash was the only avenue by which they could advance the story, i.e., find a new narrative. Whether through direct causation or mere journalistic intuition, the *Times* timed its backlash story (8/17/03) with remarkable accuracy:

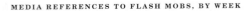

MEDIA REFERENCES TO FLASH MOBS, BY WEEK

WEEK BEGINNING

Permutations

Whether the backlash was real or not, it almost didn't matter: there was no way for the flash mob to keep growing, and since the entire logic of the mob was to grow, the mob was destined to die. It couldn't become political, or even make any statement at all, within the prescribed confines of a ten-minute burst. After six mobs, even conceiving of new enough crowd permutations started to feel like a challenge. We had done consumers collaborating (MOB #2) and consumers not collaborating (MOB #4). We had done an ecstatic, moaning throng (MOB #6) and a more sedate, absurdist one (MOB #5, in which the mob hid in some Central Park woods and simulated animal noises). In MOB #3, we had formed an inward-facing ring, and the idea of another geometrical mob appealed to me. I decided that MOB #7, set for late August, should be a queue.

Scouting locations had become in many ways the most pleasant task of the experiment. Roughly a week before each appointed day, having chosen the neighborhood in advance, I would stroll nonchalantly around the streets, looking at parks and stairways and stores, imagining a few hundred people descending at once upon each: How would such a mob arrive? How would it array itself? What would it do? Could it be beautiful? For MOB #7 I had picked Midtown, the commercial heart of the city, and so one Thursday in the late afternoon I took the subway uptown from my office to envision a crowd. I started on Fiftieth Street at Eighth Avenue and walked east, slipping through the milling Broadway tourists: too much real crowd for a fake crowd to stand out successfully. At Sixth Avenue I eyed Radio City Music Hall—an inviting target, to be sure, but the sidewalk in front was too narrow, too trafficked, for a mob comfortably to do its work. At Rockefeller Center, I eyed the Christmas tree spot, which was empty that August; but there was far too much security lurking about.

When I arrived at Fifth Avenue, though, and looked up at the spires of Saint   45
Patrick's Cathedral, I realized I had found just the place. A paramount Manhattan

landmark with not much milling out front (since tourists were generally allowed inside); a sacred site, moreover, all the better for profaning with a disposable crowd. Crossing Fifth, I started around the structure from the north, following it to Madison and coming around the south side back to Fifth Avenue. I wanted a line, but it would be too risky to have it start at the front doors, since the cathedral staff that stood near the door might disperse it before it could fully form. But on each side of the cathedral, I noticed, was a small wooden door, not open to the public. If a line began at one of these doors, it could wind around the grand structure but keep staff confused long enough to last for the allotted five minutes. I stood at the corner of Fiftieth and Fifth, pondering what should happen after that. Flash mobbers were mostly people like me, downtown and Brooklyn kids, a demographic seldom seen in either Midtown or church. I loved the idea that Saint Patrick's might somehow have inexplicably become cool, a place where if one lined up at the side door, one might stand a chance of getting in for — *what?* Tickets to see some stupidly cool band, I thought; and in the summer of 2003 the right band to make fun of was the Strokes, a band that had been clearly manufactured, Monkees-like, precisely for our delectation. It was settled, then: the mob would line up from the small door on the north side, wind around the front and down the south side. When passersby asked why they were lining up, mobbers were to say they "heard they're selling Strokes tickets."

Having settled the script that Thursday afternoon, I started back down Fiftieth, only to see a man walk out of the side door. He was a short man with curly hair tight to his head, and he wore a knit blue tie over a white patterned button-down shirt. Without acknowledging me in any way, he walked to the curb and then stood still, staring up at the sky. Back at Madison, I saw that since I last was at the corner, the stoplight had gone dark: an uncommon city sight. As I headed south down Madison, weaving through accumulating traffic crowding crosswalks, more people began to trickle out of the office buildings, looking dazed, rubbing their eyes in the sunlight. A woman dressed as Nefertiti was fanning herself. Customers lined up at bodegas to buy bottles of water. I thought I would walk south until I got out of the blackout zone; by Union Square I realized that the blackout zone was very large indeed, though it was not until I got back to work, walking the eleven flights up, that I was told the zone was not just all of New York City but most of the northeastern United States. Having spent my last half hour envisioning my own absurdist mob, I had suddenly stepped into a citywide flash mob planned by no one, born not of a will to metaspectacle but of basic human need. The power returned within the week, and MOB #7 went on exactly as planned; but to gather a crowd on New York's streets never felt quite the same, and I knew my days making mobs were dwindling fast.

Down: Boredom Redux

I wrote of boredom as inspiring the mob's birth; but I suspect that boredom helped to hasten its death, as well—the boredom, that is, of the constantly distracted mind. This paradoxical relationship between boredom and distraction was demonstrated elegantly in 1989, by psychologists at Clark University in Worcester, Massachusetts. Ninety-one undergraduates, broken up into small groups, were played a tape-recorded reading of fifteen minutes in length, but during the playback for some of the students a modest distraction was introduced: the sound of a TV soap opera, playing at a "just no-ticeable" level. Afterward, when the students were asked if their minds had wandered during the recording, the results were as to be expected. Seventy percent of the inten-tionally distracted listeners said their minds had wandered, as opposed to 55 percent of the control group. What was far more surprising, however, were the reasons they gave: among those whose minds wandered, 76 percent of the distracted listeners said this was because the tape was "boring," versus only 41 percent of their nondistracted counterparts. We tend to think of boredom as a response to having too few external stimuli, but here boredom was perceived more keenly at the precise time that more stimuli were present.

The experiment's authors, Robin Damrad-Frye and James Laird, argue that the results make sense in the context of "self-perception theory": the notion that we de-termine our internal states in large part by observing our own behavior. Other stud-ies have supported this general idea. Subjects asked to mimic a certain emotion will then report feeling that emotion. Subjects made to argue in favor of a statement, either through a speech or an essay, will afterward attest to believing it. Subjects forced to gaze into each other's eyes will later profess sexual attraction for each other. In the case of boredom, the authors write, "The reason people know they are bored is, at least in part, that they find they cannot keep their attention focused where it should be." That is, they ascribe their own inattention to a deficiency not in themselves, or in their sur-roundings, but in that to which they are supposed to be attending.

Today, in the advanced stages of our information age, with our e-mail in-boxes and phones and instant messages all chirping for our attention, it is as if we are conducting Damrad-Frye and Laird's experiment on a society-wide scale. Gloria Mark, a profes-sor at the University of California at Irvine, has found that white-collar officework-ers can work for only eleven minutes, on average, without being interrupted. Among the young, permanent distraction is a way of life: the majority of seventh- to twelfth-graders in the United States say that they "multitask" — using other media — some or even most of the time they are reading or using the computer. The writer and software expert Linda Stone has called this lifestyle one of "continuous partial attention," an elegant phrase to describe the endless wave of electronic distraction that so many of us ride. There is ample evidence that all this distraction impairs our ability to do things well: a psychologist at the University of Michigan found that multitasking subjects made more errors in each task and took from 50 to 100 percent more time to finish. But far more intriguing, I think, is how our constant distraction may be feeding back into our perception of the world—the effect observed among those Clark undergraduates, writ large; the sense, that is, that nothing we attend to is adequate, precisely because nothing can escape the roiling scorn of our distraction.

This, finally, is what kills nanostories, I think, and what surely killed the flash   50 mob, not only in the media but in my own mind: this always-encroaching boredom, this need to tell ever *new stories* about our society and ourselves, even when there are no new stories to be told. This impulse itself is far from new, of course; it is a species of what Neil Postman meant in 1984 when he decried the culture of news as entertain-ment, and indeed of what Daniel Boorstin meant in 1961 when he railed against our "extravagant expectations" for the world of human events. What viral culture adds is, in part, just pure acceleration—the speed born of more data sources, more frequent updates, more churn—but far more crucially it adds interactivity, and with it a perverse kind of market democracy. As more of us take on the media mantle ourselves, telling our own stories rather than allowing others to tell them for us, it is we who can act to assuage our own boredom, our inadequacy, our despair by projecting them out through how we describe the world.

Dispersal

I announced that MOB #8, in early September, would be the last. The invitation e-mail's subject was *MOB #8: The end*, and the text began with a FAQ:

> **Q. The end?**
> A. Yes.
>
> **Q. Why?**
> A. It can't be explained. Like the individual mobs, the Mob Project appeared for no reason, and like the mobs it must disperse.
>
> **Q. Will the Mob Project ever reappear?**
> A. It might. But don't expect it.

The site was a concrete alcove right on Forty-second Street, just across from the Condé Nast building. Participants had been told to follow the instructions blaring from a cheap boom box I had set up beforehand atop a brick ledge. I had prerecorded a tape of myself, barking out commands. I envisioned my hundreds of mobbers, following the dictates of what was effectively a loudspeaker on a pole. It was hard to get more straightforward than that, I thought.

But the cheering of the hundreds grew so great that it drowned out the speakers. The mob soon became unmoored. All of a sudden a man in a toque, apparently some sort of opportunistic art shaman, opened his briefcase to reveal a glowing neon sign, and the crowd bent to his will. He held up two fingers, and to my horror the mob began chanting "Peace!" In retrospect, I saw it as a fitting end for an experiment about bandwagons and conformity, about inattention and media hype. My crowd had ultimately been hijacked by a figure more mysterious, more enigmatic than even the semianonymous "Bill"—by a better story, that is, than me.

Of all my experiments in viral culture, the Mob Project was by far the most impressive in its spread; and indeed this spread spurred much of my ensuing interest in the subject. In starting the project, my major interest had been in the intersection of the virtual and the physical—I had seen the mob as a way for online connections to manifest themselves visually, corporeally, disruptively in the sidewalks and spaces of urban life. But as the mob grew beyond my most optimistic projections, and then collapsed, I became less fixated on the mobs themselves and more focused on the *storytelling* about them. The arc of a mob, of the Mob Project, of flash mobs as a general phenomenon, of the media narrative *about* the phenomenon—all were strangely congruent in the rapid rise and fall, and I desperately wanted to understand the storytelling that made these spikes operate.

Chapter 2 [not included here] is an exploration of the most basic breeding ground 55 for spikes, and the stories—i.e., the nanostories—that fuel them: the *niche*, or *subculture*, which the Internet as a medium has both invigorated and transformed.

Exploring Context

1. Explore the Web site for Improv Everywhere (improveverywhere.com), "a New York City–based prank collective that causes scenes of chaos and joy in public places." How does this group use flash mobs? While exploring the site, look for additional evidence to support your answer to Question 3 of Questions for Critical Reading.

2. Flash Mob America (flashmobamerica.com) claims to be the "#1 Flash Mob Company in the World." Explore its site, paying special attention to the section on how to hire this company. Does the meaning of a flash mob change when it's commercialized? Use your findings to extend your answer to Question 1 of Questions for Critical Reading.

3. Visit the Internet Meme Database (knowyourmeme.com). Working with the information on the site, can you determine how memes are created? How does the site confirm or complicate your work from Question 2 of Questions for Critical Reading?

Questions for Connecting

1. How does social media enable phenomena like flash mobs? Use Maria Konnikova's discussion of the Dunbar number in "The Limits of Friendship" (p. 236) to examine the ways in which social media allows memes to spread. How does the rule of three enable viral ideas? Do the limitations of the Dunbar number represent a limitation on viral culture as well?

2. Wasik isn't only discussing the origin of flash mobs; he's also describing contemporary culture. Apply his ideas to Nick Paumgarten's "We Are a Camera" (p. 331) in order to explore the ways in which contemporary culture has fueled the rise of the GoPro. What role does boredom play in the impulse to record experiences? How might the bandwagon effect be in play in the spread of the GoPro?

3. Wasik ends by discussing the death of the "nanostory" and the return of boredom. Use Richard Restak's discussion of technology's impact on brain biology in "Attention Deficit: The Brain Syndrome of Our Era" (p. 373) to extend Wasik's discussion. Does multitasking necessarily result in an increase of boredom? What is the best way to address this problem?

Language Matters

1. Ellipses and brackets are useful punctuation marks when using quotations. Select a long passage from Wasik's essay that represents an important part of his essay. How would you use these punctuation marks to incorporate the quotation into your own writing? How might they be instead used, even unintentionally, to misrepresent the

meaning of the quotation? How can you be sure you're using these punctuation marks correctly?

2. The most solid transitions come from a statement that directly ties together two paragraphs. Select two paragraphs from Wasik's essay. Write a one-sentence summary of the first paragraph and then another one-sentence summary of the second paragraph. Then combine these two sentences into one to form a new transition between the paragraphs. How does your sentence differ from Wasik's transition? How can you use this skill in your own writing?

3. Section headings can help a reader understand the organization of your writing. Make a list of Wasik's headings. How do they provide insight into the structure of his essay? In what situations might you use headings in your own writing?

Assignments for Writing

1. Wasik begins his flash mob project out of boredom. Write a paper in which you assess the role of boredom in our culture today. Does technology produce boredom? Does choice? How do we cope with boredom? Is there a boredom "epidemic"? How might Wasik's essay offer strategies to deal with boredom? Consider using your work from Question 3 of Questions for Critical Reading or Question 2 of Questions for Connecting.

2. How do memes function? Write a paper in which you determine the role that memes play in digital society. Use your work from Questions for Critical Reading, Exploring Context, and Questions for Connecting. Why do memes spread so quickly in our culture? Are memes harmless? Can they be used for social change? Locate your own example of a meme and analyze it using Wasik's ideas.

3. Although Wasik ended his own flash mob experiment, the phenomenon continues to be a part of our culture today. Write a paper in which you trace the continuing role that flash mobs play in our culture. Use your work from Questions for Critical Reading, Exploring Context, and Questions for Connecting. Do flash mobs function as remedies to boredom? Are they simply driven by memes? Are they a kind of performance art? Locate another example of a flash mob and use it to extend or complicate Wasik's observations.

ETHAN WATTERS

Photo by Chris Hardy

Journalist **Ethan Watters** is the author of *Urban Tribes: A Genera-tion Redefines Friendship, Family, and Commitment* (2003); *Crazy Like Us: The Globalization of the American Psyche* (2010); and, with Richard Ofshe, *Therapy's Delusions: The Myth of the Unconscious and the Exploitation of Today's Walking Worried* (1999). His writing has appeared in such varied magazines as the *New York Times Magazine, Wired, Details, Spin,* and *Pacific Standard.*

Pacific Standard magazine was first published in 2008 under the name *Miller-McCune* for its publisher, the nonprofit Miller-McCune Center for Research, Media, and Public Policy. In keeping with its new name, the magazine seeks to cover stories from a West Coast perspective. Subtitled *The Science of Society,* the magazine covers topics as diverse as politics, health, nature, technology, and culture. On February 25, 2013, the online edition of the magazine published "Being WEIRD: How Culture Shapes the Mind," a featured culture article.

In "Being WEIRD: How Culture Shapes the Mind," Watters looks at the work of anthropologist Joe Henrich, whose work with the "ultimatum game" experiment in isolated small-scale communities around the world revealed that much of what social scientists, economists, and psychologists assumed to be "universal" human behavior was in fact a reflection of a distinctly Western psyche. Henrich and his colleagues use this work and other research to argue that Westerners are *WEIRD*: Western, educated, industrialized, rich, and democratic. Far from serving as examples of the universal, Americans (who form the subjects of many experiments in fields such as psychology) are the "weirdest" of all, with responses indicating that they are the outliers among the outliers. Watters examines the implications of these claims, which threaten the foundation of many disciplines.

Are there universal traits to the human mind? How can we discover them?

▶ TAGS: *community, culture, economics, education, globalism, psychology*
▶ CONNECTIONS: *Appiah, Dalai Lama, Friedman, Fukuyama, Gilbert, Konnikova, Pozner, Restak, Wallace*

Questions for Critical Reading

1. According to Watters, why are Americans "weird"? Locate the definition of *WEIRD* in this context and then note the ways in which Americans are "weird."

2. How does culture shape the human mind? As you read, note specific examples that show how culture affects cognition.

3. How do Western and Eastern notions of the self differ? Pay attention to Watters's discussion of this distinction. How do these different notions of the self contribute to the problems that Watters traces?

Being WEIRD: How Culture Shapes the Mind

In the summer of 1995, a young graduate student in anthropology at UCLA named Joe Henrich traveled to Peru to carry out some fieldwork among the Machiguenga, an indigenous people who live north of Machu Picchu in the Amazon basin. The Machiguenga had traditionally been horticulturalists who lived in single-family, thatch-roofed houses in small hamlets composed of clusters of extended families. For sustenance, they relied on local game and produce from small-scale farming. They shared with their kin but rarely traded with outside groups.

While the setting was fairly typical for an anthropologist, Henrich's research was not. Rather than practice traditional ethnography, he decided to run a behavioral experiment that had been developed by economists. Henrich used a "game"—along the lines of the famous prisoner's dilemma—to see whether isolated cultures shared with the West the same basic instinct for fairness.[1] In doing so, Henrich expected to confirm one of the foundational assumptions underlying such experiments, and indeed underpinning the entire fields of economics and psychology: that humans all share the same cognitive machinery—the same evolved rational and psychological hardwiring.

The test that Henrich introduced to the Machiguenga was called the ultimatum game. The rules are simple: in each game there are two players who remain anonymous to each other. The first player is given an amount of money, say $100, and told that he has to offer some of the cash, in an amount of his choosing, to the other subject. The second player can accept or refuse the split. But there's a hitch: players know that if the recipient refuses the offer, both leave empty-handed. North Americans, who are the most common subjects for such experiments, usually offer a 50-50 split when on the giving end. When on the receiving end, they show an eagerness to punish the other player for uneven splits at their own expense. In short, Americans show the tendency to be equitable with strangers—and to punish those who are not.

Among the Machiguenga, word quickly spread of the young, square-jawed visitor from America giving away money. The stakes Henrich used in the game with the Machiguenga were not insubstantial—roughly equivalent to the few days' wages they sometimes earned from episodic work with logging or oil companies. So Henrich had no problem finding volunteers. What he had great difficulty with, however, was explaining the rules, as the game struck the Machiguenga as deeply odd.

When he began to run the game it became immediately clear that Machiguengan behavior was dramatically different from that of the average North American. To begin with, the offers from the first player were much lower. In addition, when on the receiving end of the game, the Machiguenga rarely refused even the lowest possible amount. "It just seemed ridiculous to the Machiguenga that you would reject an offer of free money," says Henrich. "They just didn't understand why anyone would sacrifice money to punish someone who had the good luck of getting to play the other role in the game."

The potential implications of the unexpected results were quickly apparent to Henrich. He knew that a vast amount of scholarly literature in the social sciences—particularly in economics and psychology—relied on the ultimatum game and similar experiments. At the heart of most of that research was the implicit assumption that the results revealed evolved psychological traits common to all humans, never mind that

5

the test subjects were nearly always from the industrialized West. Henrich realized that if the Machiguenga results stood up, and if similar differences could be measured across other populations, this assumption of universality would have to be challenged.

Henrich had thought he would be adding a small branch to an established tree of knowledge. It turned out he was sawing at the very trunk. He began to wonder: What other certainties about "human nature" in social science research would need to be reconsidered when tested across diverse populations?

Henrich soon landed a grant from the MacArthur Foundation to take his fairness games on the road. With the help of a dozen other colleagues he led a study of 14 other small-scale societies, in locales from Tanzania to Indonesia. Differences abounded in the behavior of both players in the ultimatum game. In no society did he find people who were purely selfish (that is, who always offered the lowest amount, and never refused a split), but average offers from place to place varied widely and, in some societies—ones where gift-giving is heavily used to curry favor or gain allegiance—the first player would often make overly generous offers in excess of 60 percent, and the second player would often reject them, behaviors almost never observed among Americans.

The research established Henrich as an up-and-coming scholar. In 2004, he was given the U.S. Presidential Early Career Award for young scientists at the White House. But his work also made him a controversial figure. When he presented his research to the anthropology department at the University of British Columbia during a job interview a year later, he recalls a hostile reception. Anthropology is the social science most interested in cultural differences, but the young scholar's methods of using games and statistics to test and compare cultures with the West seemed heavy-handed and invasive to some. "Professors from the anthropology department suggested it was a bad thing that I was doing," Henrich remembers. "The word 'unethical' came up."

So instead of toeing the line, he switched teams. A few well-placed people at the   10
University of British Columbia saw great promise in Henrich's work and created a position for him, split between the economics department and the psychology department. It was in the psychology department that he found two kindred spirits in Steven Heine and Ara Norenzayan. Together the three set about writing a paper that they hoped would fundamentally challenge the way social scientists thought about human behavior, cognition, and culture.

A modern liberal arts education gives lots of lip service to the idea of cultural diversity. It's generally agreed that all of us see the world in ways that are sometimes socially and culturally constructed, that pluralism is good, and that ethnocentrism is bad. But beyond that the ideas get muddy. That we should welcome and celebrate people of all backgrounds seems obvious, but the implied corollary—that people from different ethno-cultural origins have particular attributes that add spice to the body politic—becomes more problematic. To avoid stereotyping, it is rarely stated bluntly just exactly what those culturally derived qualities might be. Challenge liberal arts graduates on their appreciation of cultural diversity and you'll often find them retreating to the anodyne notion that under the skin everyone is really alike.

If you take a broad look at the social science curriculum of the last few decades, it becomes a little more clear why modern graduates are so unmoored. The last generation or two of undergraduates have largely been taught by a cohort of social scientists busily doing penance for the racism and Eurocentrism of their predecessors, albeit in different ways. Many anthropologists took to the navel gazing of postmodernism and swore off attempts at rationality and science, which were disparaged as weapons of cultural imperialism.

Economists and psychologists, for their part, did an end run around the issue with the convenient assumption that their job was to study the human mind stripped of culture. The human brain is genetically comparable around the globe, it was agreed, so human hardwiring for much behavior, perception, and cognition should be similarly universal. No need, in that case, to look beyond the convenient population of undergraduates for test subjects. A 2008 survey of the top six psychology journals dramatically shows how common that assumption was: more than 96 percent of the subjects tested in psychological studies from 2003 to 2007 were Westerners—with nearly 70 percent from the United States alone. Put another way: 96 percent of human subjects in these studies came from countries that represent only 12 percent of the world's population.

Henrich's work with the ultimatum game was an example of a small but growing countertrend in the social sciences, one in which researchers look straight at the question of how deeply culture shapes human cognition. His new colleagues in the psychology department, Heine and Norenzayan, were also part of this trend. Heine focused on the different ways people in Western and Eastern cultures perceived the world, reasoned, and understood themselves in relationship to others. Norenzayan's research focused on the ways religious belief influenced bonding and behavior. The three began to compile examples of cross-cultural research that, like Henrich's work with the Machiguenga, challenged long-held assumptions of human psychological universality.

Some of that research went back a generation. It was in the 1960s, for instance, that researchers discovered that aspects of visual perception were different from place to place. One of the classics of the literature, the Müller-Lyer illusion, showed that where you grew up would determine to what degree you would fall prey to the illusion that [the] two lines [in the figure on p. 496] are different in length:[2]

15

Researchers found that Americans perceive the line with the ends feathered outward (B) as being longer than the line with the arrow tips (A). San foragers of the Kalahari, on the other hand, were more likely to see the lines as they are: equal in length. Subjects from more than a dozen cultures were tested, and Americans were at the far end of the distribution—seeing the illusion more dramatically than all others.

More recently psychologists had challenged the universality of research done in the 1950s by pioneering social psychologist Solomon Asch. Asch had discovered that test subjects were often willing to make incorrect judgments on simple perception tests to conform with group pressure. When the test was performed across 17 societies, however, it turned out that group pressure had a range of influence. Americans were again at the far end of the scale, in this case showing the least tendency to conform to group belief.

As Heine, Norenzayan, and Henrich furthered their search, they began to find research suggesting wide cultural differences almost everywhere they looked: in spatial

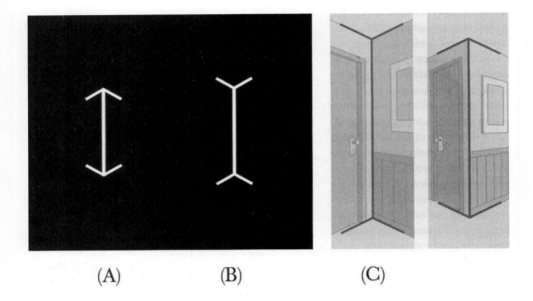

(A)   (B)   (C)

reasoning, the way we infer the motivations of others, categorization, moral reason-ing, the boundaries between the self and others, and other arenas. These differences, they believed, were not genetic. The distinct ways Americans and Machiguengans played the ultimatum game, for instance, wasn't because they had differently evolved brains. Rather, Americans, without fully realizing it, were manifesting a psychological tendency shared with people in other industrialized countries that had been refined and handed down through thousands of generations in ever more complex market economies. When people are constantly doing business with strangers, it helps when they have the desire to go out of their way (with a lawsuit, a call to the Better Business Bureau, or a bad Yelp review) when they feel cheated. Because Machiguengan culture had a different history, their gut feeling about what was fair was distinctly their own. In the small-scale societies with a strong culture of gift-giving, yet another concep-tion of fairness prevailed. There, generous financial offers were turned down because people's minds had been shaped by a cultural norm that taught them that the accep-tance of generous gifts brought burdensome obligations. Our economies hadn't been shaped by our sense of fairness; it was the other way around.

The growing body of cross-cultural research that the three researchers were com-piling suggested that the mind's capacity to mold itself to cultural and environmen-tal settings was far greater than had been assumed. The most interesting thing about cultures may not be in the observable things they do—the rituals, eating preferences, codes of behavior, and the like—but in the way they mold our most fundamental con-scious and unconscious thinking and perception.

For instance, the different ways people perceive the Müller-Lyer illusion likely re-   20
flects lifetimes spent in different physical environments. American children, for the most part, grow up in box-shaped rooms of varying dimensions. Surrounded by car-pentered corners, visual perception adapts to this strange new environment (strange

and new in terms of human history, that is) by learning to perceive converging lines in three dimensions.

When unconsciously translated in three dimensions, the line with the outward-feathered ends (C) appears farther away and the brain therefore judges it to be longer. The more time one spends in natural environments, where there are no carpentered corners, the less one sees the illusion.

As the three continued their work, they noticed something else that was remarkable: again and again one group of people appeared to be particularly unusual when compared to other populations—with perceptions, behaviors, and motivations that were almost always sliding down one end of the human bell curve.

In the end they titled their paper "The Weirdest People in the World?"[3] By "weird" they meant both unusual and Western, Educated, Industrialized, Rich, and Democratic. It is not just our Western habits and cultural preferences that are different from the rest of the world, it appears. The very way we think about ourselves and others—and even the way we perceive reality—makes us distinct from other humans on the planet, not to mention from the vast majority of our ancestors. Among Westerners, the data showed that Americans were often the most unusual, leading the researchers to conclude that "American participants are exceptional even within the unusual population of Westerners—outliers among outliers."

Given the data, they concluded that social scientists could not possibly have picked a worse population from which to draw broad generalizations. Researchers had been doing the equivalent of studying penguins while believing that they were learning insights applicable to all birds.

Not long ago I met Henrich, Heine, and Norenzayan for dinner at a small French restaurant in Vancouver, British Columbia, to hear about the reception of their weird paper, which was published in the prestigious journal *Behavioral and Brain Sciences* in 2010. The trio of researchers are young—as professors go—good-humored family men. They recalled that they were nervous as the publication time approached. The paper basically suggested that much of what social scientists thought they knew about fundamental aspects of human cognition was likely only true of one small slice of humanity. They were making such a broadside challenge to whole libraries of research that they steeled themselves to the possibility of becoming outcasts in their own fields.

"We were scared," admitted Henrich. "We were warned that a lot of people were going to be upset."

"We were told we were going to get spit on," interjected Norenzayan.

"Yes," Henrich said. "That we'd go to conferences and no one was going to sit next to us at lunchtime."

Interestingly, they seemed much less concerned that they had used the pejorative acronym WEIRD to describe a significant slice of humanity, although they did admit that they could only have done so to describe their own group. "Really," said Henrich, "the only people we could have called weird are represented right here at this table."

Still, I had to wonder whether describing the Western mind, and the American mind in particular, as weird suggested that our cognition is not just different but somehow malformed or twisted. In their paper the trio pointed out cross-cultural studies that suggest that the "weird" Western mind is the most self-aggrandizing and egotistical on the planet: we are more likely to promote ourselves as individuals versus advancing as a group. WEIRD minds are also more analytic, possessing the tendency to telescope in on an object of interest rather than understanding that object in the context of what is around it.

The WEIRD mind also appears to be unique in terms of how it comes to understand and interact with the natural world. Studies show that Western urban children grow up so closed off in man-made environments that their brains never form a deep or complex connection to the natural world. While studying children from the U.S., researchers have suggested a developmental timeline for what is called "folkbiological reasoning." These studies posit that it is not until children are around 7 years old that they stop projecting human qualities onto animals and begin to understand that humans are one animal among many. Compared to Yucatec Maya communities in Mexico, however, Western urban children appear to be developmentally delayed in this regard. Children who grow up constantly interacting with the natural world are much less likely to anthropomorphize other living things into late childhood.

Given that people living in WEIRD societies don't routinely encounter or interact with animals other than humans or pets, it's not surprising that they end up with a rather cartoonish understanding of the natural world. "Indeed," the report concluded, "studying the cognitive development of folkbiology in urban children would seem the equivalent of studying 'normal' physical growth in malnourished children."

During our dinner, I admitted to Heine, Henrich, and Norenzayan that the idea that I can only perceive reality through a distorted cultural lens was unnerving. For me the notion raised all sorts of metaphysical questions: Is my thinking so strange that I have little hope of understanding people from other cultures? Can I mold my own psyche or the psyches of my children to be less WEIRD and more able to think like the rest of the world? If I did, would I be happier?

Henrich reacted with mild concern that I was taking this research so personally. He had not intended, he told me, for his work to be read as postmodern self-help advice. "I think we're really interested in these questions for the questions' sake," he said.

The three insisted that their goal was not to say that one culturally shaped psychology was better or worse than another—only that we'll never truly understand human behavior and cognition until we expand the sample pool beyond its current small slice of humanity. Despite these assurances, however, I found it hard not to read a message between the lines of their research. When they write, for example, that weird children develop their understanding of the natural world in a "culturally and experientially impoverished environment" and that they are in this way the equivalent of "malnourished children," it's difficult to see this as a good thing.

The turn that Henrich, Heine, and Norenzayan are asking social scientists to make is not an easy one: accounting for the influence of culture on cognition will be a herculean task. Cultures are not monolithic; they can be endlessly parsed. Ethnic backgrounds, religious beliefs, economic status, parenting styles, rural upbringing versus urban or suburban—there are hundreds of cultural differences that individually and in endless combinations influence our conceptions of fairness, how we categorize things, our method of judging and decision making, and our deeply held beliefs about the nature of the self, among other aspects of our psychological makeup.

We are just at the beginning of learning how these fine-grained cultural differences affect our thinking. Recent research has shown that people in "tight" cultures, those with strong norms and low tolerance for deviant behavior (think India, Malaysia, and Pakistan), develop higher impulse control and more self-monitoring abilities than those from other places. Men raised in the honor culture of the American South

> **[A]ccounting for the influence of culture on cognition will be a herculean task.**

have been shown to experience much larger surges of testosterone after insults than do Northerners. Research published late last year suggested psychological differences at the city level too. Compared to San Franciscans, Bostonians' internal sense of self-worth is more dependent on community status and financial and educational achievement. "A cultural difference doesn't have to be big to be important," Norenzayan said. "We're not just talking about comparing New York yuppies to the Dani tribesmen of Papua New Guinea."

As Norenzayan sees it, the last few generations of psychologists have suffered from "physics envy," and they need to get over it. The job, experimental psychologists often assumed, was to push past the content of people's thoughts and see the underlying universal hardware at work. "This is a deeply flawed way of studying human nature," Norenzayan told me, "because the content of our thoughts and their process are intertwined." In other words, if human cognition is shaped by cultural ideas and behavior, it can't be studied without taking into account what those ideas and behaviors are and how they are different from place to place.

This new approach suggests the possibility of reverse-engineering psychological research: look at cultural content first; cognition and behavior second. Norenzayan's recent work on religious belief is perhaps the best example of the intellectual landscape that is now open for study. When Norenzayan became a student of psychology in 1994, four years after his family had moved from Lebanon to America, he was excited to study the effect of religion on human psychology. "I remember opening textbook after textbook and turning to the index and looking for the word 'religion,'" he told me, "Again and again the very word wouldn't be listed. This was shocking. How could psychology be the science of human behavior and have nothing to say about religion? Where I grew up you'd have to be in a coma not to notice the importance of religion on how people perceive themselves and the world around them."

Norenzayan became interested in how certain religious beliefs, handed down through generations, may have shaped human psychology to make possible the creation of large-scale societies. He has suggested that there may be a connection between the growth of religions that believe in "morally concerned deities"—that is, a god or gods who care if people are good or bad—and the evolution of large cities and nations. To be cooperative in large groups of relative strangers, in other words, might have required the shared belief that an all-powerful being was forever watching over your shoulder.

If religion was necessary in the development of large-scale societies, can large-scale societies survive without religion? Norenzayan points to parts of Scandinavia with atheist majorities that seem to be doing just fine. They may have climbed the ladder of religion and effectively kicked it away. Or perhaps, after a thousand years of religious belief, the idea of an unseen entity always watching your behavior remains in our culturally shaped thinking even after the belief in God dissipates or disappears.

Why, I asked Norenzayan, if religion might have been so central to human psychology, have researchers not delved into the topic? "Experimental psychologists are the weirdest of the weird," said Norenzayan. "They are almost the least religious academics, next to biologists. And because academics mostly talk amongst themselves, they could look around and say, 'No one who is important to me is religious, so this must not be very important.' " Indeed, almost every major theorist on human behavior in the last 100 years predicted that it was just a matter of time before religion was a vestige of the past. But the world persists in being a very religious place.

Henrich, Heine, and Norenzayan's fear of being ostracized after the publication of the WEIRD paper turned out to be misplaced. Response to the paper, both published and otherwise, has been nearly universally positive, with more than a few of their colleagues suggesting that the work will spark fundamental changes. "I have no doubt that this paper is going to change the social sciences," said Richard Nisbett, an eminent psychologist at the University of Michigan. "It just puts it all in one place and makes such a bold statement."

More remarkable still, after reading the paper, academics from other disciplines began to come forward with their own mea culpas. Commenting on the paper, two brain researchers from Northwestern University argued that the nascent field of neuroimaging had made the same mistake as psychologists, noting that 90 percent of neuroimaging studies were performed in Western countries.[4] Researchers in motor development similarly suggested that their discipline's body of research ignored how different child-rearing practices around the world can dramatically influence states of development.[5] Two psycholinguistics professors suggested that their colleagues had also made the same mistake: blithely assuming human homogeneity while focusing their research primarily on one rather small slice of humanity.[6]

At its heart, the challenge of the WEIRD paper is not simply to the field of experimental human research (do more cross-cultural studies!); it is a challenge to our Western conception of human nature. For some time now, the most widely accepted answer to the question of why humans, among all animals, have so successfully adapted to environments across the globe is that we have big brains with the ability to learn, improvise, and problem-solve.

Henrich has challenged this "cognitive niche" hypothesis with the "cultural niche" hypothesis. He notes that the amount of knowledge in any culture is far greater than the capacity of individuals to learn or figure it all out on their own. He suggests that individuals tap that cultural storehouse of knowledge simply by mimicking (often unconsciously) the behavior and ways of thinking of those around them. We shape a tool in a certain manner, adhere to a food taboo, or think about fairness in a particular way, not because we individually have figured out that behavior's adaptive value, but because we instinctively trust our culture to show us the way. When Henrich asked Fijian women why they avoided certain potentially toxic fish during pregnancy and breastfeeding, he found that many didn't know or had fanciful reasons. Regardless of their personal understanding, by mimicking this culturally adaptive

> **[O]ur big brains are evolved to let local culture lead us in life's dance.**

45

behavior they were protecting their offspring. The unique trick of human psychology, these researchers suggest, might be this: our big brains are evolved to let local culture lead us in life's dance.

The applications of this new way of looking at the human mind are still in the offing. Henrich suggests that his research about fairness might first be applied to anyone working in international relations or development. People are not "plug and play," as he puts it, and you cannot expect to drop a Western court system or form of government into another culture and expect it to work as it does back home. Those trying to use economic incentives to encourage sustainable land use will similarly need to understand local notions of fairness to have any chance of influencing behavior in predictable ways.

Because of our peculiarly Western way of thinking of ourselves as independent of others, this idea of the culturally shaped mind doesn't go down very easily. Perhaps the richest and most established vein of cultural psychology—that which compares Western and Eastern concepts of the self—goes to the heart of this problem. Heine has spent much of his career following the lead of a seminal paper published in 1991 by Hazel Rose Markus, of Stanford University, and Shinobu Kitayama, who is now at the University of Michigan.[7] Markus and Kitayama suggested that different cultures foster strikingly different views of the self, particularly along one axis: some cultures regard the self as independent from others; others see the self as interdependent. The interdependent self—which is more the norm in East Asian countries, including Japan and China—connects itself with others in a social group and favors social harmony over self-expression. The independent self—which is most prominent in America—focuses on individual attributes and preferences and thinks of the self as existing apart from the group.

That we in the West develop brains that are wired to see ourselves as separate from others may also be connected to differences in how we reason, Heine argues. Unlike the vast majority of the world, Westerners (and Americans in particular) tend to reason analytically as opposed to holistically. That is, the American mind strives to figure out the world by taking it apart and examining its pieces. Show a Japanese and an American the same cartoon of an aquarium, and the American will remember details mostly about the moving fish while the Japanese observer will likely later be able to describe the seaweed, the bubbles, and other objects in the background. Shown another way, in a different test analytic Americans will do better on something called the "rod and frame" task, where one has to judge whether a line is vertical even though the frame around it is skewed. Americans see the line as apart from the frame, just as they see themselves as apart from the group.

Heine and others suggest that such differences may be the echoes of cultural activities and trends going back thousands of years. Whether you think of yourself as interdependent or independent may depend on whether your distant ancestors farmed rice (which required a great deal of shared labor and group cooperation) or herded animals (which rewarded individualism and aggression). Heine points to Nisbett at Michigan, who has argued that the analytic/holistic dichotomy in reasoning styles can be clearly seen, respectively, in Greek and Chinese philosophical writing dating back 2,500 years.[8] These psychological trends and tendencies may echo down generations, hundreds of years after the activity or situation that brought them into existence has disappeared or fundamentally changed.

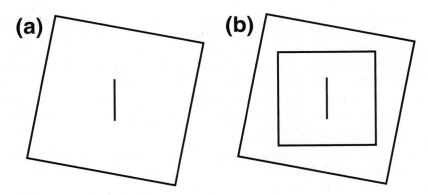

The classic "rod and frame" task: Is the line in the center vertical?

And here is the rub: the culturally shaped analytic/individualistic mind-sets may partly explain why Western researchers have so dramatically failed to take into account the interplay between culture and cognition. In the end, the goal of boiling down human psychology to hardwiring is not surprising given the type of mind that has been designing the studies. Taking an object (in this case the human mind) out of its context is, after all, what distinguishes the analytic reasoning style prevalent in the West. Similarly, we may have underestimated the impact of culture because the very ideas of being subject to the will of larger historical currents and of unconsciously mimicking the cognition of those around us challenges our Western conception of the self as independent and self-determined. The historical missteps of Western researchers, in other words, have been the predictable consequences of the WEIRD mind doing the thinking.

NOTES

1. *Stanford Encyclopedia of Philosophy*, s.v. "Prisoner's Dilemma," revised August 29, 2014, http://plato.stanford.edu/entries/prisoner-dilemma/.
2. "The Muller-Lyer Illusion," Rochester Institute of Technology, http://www.rit.edu/cla/gssp400/muller/muller.html.
3. Joseph Henrich, Steven J. Heine, and Ara Norenzayan, "The Weirdest People in the World?" *Behavioral and Brain Sciences* 33, no. 2–3 (June 2010): 61–83.
4. Joan Y. Chiao and Bobby K. Cheon, "The Weirdest Brains in the World," (Department of Psychology, Northwestern University), http://culturalneuro.psych.northwestern.edu/ChiaoCheon_BBS_inpress.pdf.
5. Lana B. Karasik et al., "WEIRD Walking: Cross-Cultural Research on Motor Development," *Behavioral and Brain Sciences* 33, no. 2–3 (June 2010): 95–96.
6. Asifa Majid and Stephen C. Levinson, "WEIRD Languages Have Misled Us, Too," *Behavioral and Brain Sciences* 33, no. 2–3 (June 2010): 103.
7. Hazel Rose Markus and Shinobu Kitayama, "Culture and the Self: Implications for Cognition, Emotion, and Motivation," *Psychological Review* 98 (1991): 224–253.
8. Richard E. Nisbett et al., "Culture and Systems of Thought: Holistic vs. Analytic Cognition," http://www-personal.umich.edu/~nisbett/images/cultureThought.pdf.

Exploring Context

1. Visit Joe Henrich's Web site at www2.psych.ubc.ca/~henrich. How has he continued his work on the cultural dependence of seemingly universal traits? Connect the information you find there to Watters's argument.

2. Play the prisoner's dilemma game at serendip.brynmawr.edu/playground/pd.html. Do you feel your choices are shaped by your culture? How might the communities that Henrich studies play the game instead?

3. Using a search engine, find images of "cultural diversity." Do these images confirm Watters's claim that in education notions of cultural diversity rely on the idea that we're all the same underneath the skin?

Questions for Connecting

1. Is emerging adulthood "weird"? Apply Watters's analysis to Robin Marantz Henig's argument in "What Is It About 20-Somethings?" (p. 199). Is this life stage unique to the West? How might the shape of other cultures change the development of individuals? Use your work in Questions for Critical Reading in making your response.

2. In "Human Dignity" (p. 143), Francis Fukuyama claims that humans universally possess "Factor X." Assess his claim using Watters's argument. Does it rely on aspects of the mind that are "weird"? Is it possible to identify universal elements of the human mind?

3. How might Watters's insights be useful in fighting the spread of HIV/AIDS in Africa? Use his ideas about culture and cognition to consider campaigns against the disease as explained by Helen Epstein in "AIDS, Inc." (p. 110). You may want to use your work from Question 3 of Questions for Critical Reading in making your response.

Language Matters

1. How does culture shape language? Consider one aspect of language use in English and make an argument about how it reflects Western notions of the mind and self. How might this aspect of language be different in other cultures?

2. Why doesn't Watters use periods between the letters in the acronym *WEIRD*? Using a grammar handbook or other reliable reference resource, review the rules for acronyms. When should you use periods?

3. The choice of genre often controls the way in which content is presented. Create a summary of Watters's essay as a text message, as a tweet, and as an e-mail. In what ways does form control content?

Assignments for Writing

1. Watters notes that Henrich's findings challenge the notion of diversity as currently practiced in liberal education. Write a paper in which you propose a new model of cultural diversity that takes Henrich's argument into account. What role would

Americans play in such a model? How can we promote cultural diversity in ways that aren't "weird"? Use your work from Question 3 of Exploring Context to support your argument.

2. Write a paper in which you examine the ways in which culture shapes thinking. How do cultural practices influence the way we see the world? Use your work from Question 2 of Questions for Critical Reading to help you make your argument.

3. Watters ends with a discussion of Eastern and Western notions of the self. Write a paper in which you synthesize these concepts to create a holistic notion of selfhood. Is the self ultimately independent, interdependent, or a combination of the two? Is it possible to define the self apart from culture? If so, what kind of culture could emerge from blending East and West?

GRAEME WOOD

A lecturer in the Department of Political Science at Yale University, **Graeme Wood** is also an accomplished reporter, screenwriter, and editor. His work has appeared in *Pacific Standard*, the *New Republic*, and the *Atlantic*, and he has received fellowships from the Social Sciences Research Council, the South Asian Journalists Association, the East-West Center, and the U.S. Holocaust Memorial Museum's Center for the Prevention of Genocide.

© Copyright 2015 by Graeme Wood, used by permission of The Wylie Agency, LLC

The September 2014 issue of the *Atlantic*, from which this essay is taken, featured articles on Haruki Murakami's novels and the sudden renewed popularity of rye whiskey, as well as several other articles about education, including one on the poor job prospects of law school graduates and another on the value of getting an online education. "Is College Doomed?" served as the cover story.

In "Is College Doomed?" Wood investigates the Minerva Schools at KGI, a new four-year university in the United States founded by Ben Nelson, the former president of Snapfish — an online photo sharing site now owned by Hewlett-Packard. Nelson's vision of the new undergraduate education is explicitly for-profit and lacks the campuses we associate with modern universities. All courses are conducted online through a proprietary platform, so teachers can reside anywhere in the country, and there are no

lectures to speak of. Minerva thus represents a new concept of higher learning in terms of its approach to teaching, its technology, and its (reasonable) cost.

Why did you choose the school you attend? Would you consider an innovative online university?

▶ TAGS: *economics, education, science and technology, tradition*
▶ CONNECTIONS: *Friedman, Henig, Ma, Padawer, Pollan, Restak, Yang*

Questions for Critical Reading

1. What are the goals of education? Take a moment to write down what you feel an education should offer an individual. As you read, note places where Wood discusses Minerva's goals. Are they the same as your vision for education? How do they differ?

2. What's the relationship between education and technology? Pay attention to the passages where Wood discusses different technologies used in education. How is technology changing the methods and goals of education?

3. Considering the cost of college tuition, it's not surprising that education and economics are closely linked. As you read, note places where Wood discusses the relationship between education and economics. How is Minerva changing that relationship?

Is College Doomed?

On a Friday morning in April, I strapped on a headset, leaned into a microphone, and experienced what had been described to me as a type of time travel to the future of higher education. I was on the ninth floor of a building in downtown San Francisco, in a neighborhood whose streets are heavily populated with winos and vagrants, and whose buildings host hip new businesses, many of them tech start-ups. In a small room, I was flanked by a publicist and a tech manager from an educational venture called the Minerva Project, whose founder and CEO, the 39-year-old entrepreneur Ben Nelson, aims to replace (or, when he is feeling less aggressive, "reform") the modern liberal-arts college.

Minerva is an accredited university with administrative offices and a dorm in San Francisco, and it plans to open locations in at least six other major world cities. But the key to Minerva, what sets it apart most jarringly from traditional universities, is a proprietary online platform developed to apply pedagogical practices that have been studied and vetted by one of the world's foremost psychologists, a former Harvard dean named Stephen M. Kosslyn, who joined Minerva in 2012.

Nelson and Kosslyn had invited me to sit in on a test run of the platform, and at first it reminded me of the opening credits of *The Brady Bunch*: a grid of images of the professor and eight "students" (the others were all Minerva employees) appeared on the screen before me, and we introduced ourselves. For a college seminar, it felt impersonal, and though we were all sitting on the same floor of Minerva's offices, my fellow students seemed oddly distant, as if piped in from the International Space Station. I half expected a packet of astronaut ice cream to float by someone's face.

Within a few minutes, though, the experience got more intense. The subject of the class—one in a series during which the instructor, a French physicist named Eric Bonabeau, was trying out his course material—was inductive reasoning. Bonabeau began by polling us on our understanding of the reading, a *Nature* article about the sudden depletion of North Atlantic cod in the early 1990s. He asked us which of four possible interpretations of the article was the most accurate. In an ordinary undergraduate seminar, this might have been an occasion for timid silence, until the class's biggest loudmouth or most caffeinated student ventured a guess. But the Minerva class extended no refuge for the timid, nor privilege for the garrulous. Within seconds, every student had to provide an answer, and Bonabeau displayed our choices so that we could be called upon to defend them.

Bonabeau led the class like a benevolent dictator, subjecting us to pop quizzes, cold calls, and pedagogical tactics that during an in-the-flesh seminar would have taken precious minutes of class time to arrange. He split us into groups to defend opposite propositions—that the cod had disappeared because of overfishing, or that other factors were to blame. No one needed to shuffle seats; Bonabeau just pushed a button, and the students in the other group vanished from my screen, leaving my three fellow debaters and me to plan, using a shared bulletin board on which we could record our ideas. Bonabeau bounced between the two groups to offer advice as we worked. After a representative from each group gave a brief presentation, Bonabeau ended by showing a short video about the evils of overfishing. ("Propaganda," he snorted, adding that

5

we'd talk about logical fallacies in the next session.) The computer screen blinked off after 45 minutes of class.

The system had bugs—it crashed once, and some of the video lagged—but overall it worked well, and felt decidedly unlike a normal classroom. For one thing, it was exhausting: a continuous period of forced engagement, with no relief in the form of time when my attention could flag or I could doodle in a notebook undetected. Instead, my focus was directed relentlessly by the platform, and because it looked like my professor and fellow edu-nauts were staring at me, I was reluctant to ever let my gaze stray from the screen. Even in moments when I wanted to think about aspects of the material that weren't currently under discussion—to me these seemed like moments of creative space, but perhaps they were just daydreams—I felt my attention snapped back to the narrow issue at hand, because I had to answer a quiz question or articulate a position. I was forced, in effect, to learn. If this was the education of the future, it seemed vaguely fascistic. Good, but fascistic.

> **If this was the education of the future, it seemed vaguely fascistic. Good, but fascistic.**

Minerva, which operates for profit, started teaching its inaugural class of 33 students this month. To seed this first class with talent, Minerva gave every admitted student a full-tuition scholarship of $10,000 a year for four years, plus free housing in San Francisco for the first year. Next year's class is expected to have 200 to 300 students, and Minerva hopes future classes will double in size roughly every year for a few years after that.

Those future students will pay about $28,000 a year, including room and board, a $30,000 savings over the sticker price of many of the schools—the Ivies, plus other hyperselective colleges like Pomona and Williams—with which Minerva hopes to compete. (Most American students at these colleges do not pay full price, of course; Minerva will offer financial aid and target middle-class students whose bills at the other schools would still be tens of thousands of dollars more per year.) If Minerva grows to 2,500 students a class, that would mean an annual revenue of up to $280 million. A partnership with the Keck Graduate Institute in Claremont, California, allowed Minerva to fast-track its accreditation, and its advisory board has included Larry Summers, the former U.S. Treasury secretary and Harvard president, and Bob Kerrey, the former Democratic senator from Nebraska, who also served as the president of the New School, in New York City.

Nelson's long-term goal for Minerva is to radically remake one of the most sclerotic sectors of the U.S. economy, one so shielded from the need for improvement that its biggest innovation in the past 30 years has been to double its costs and hire more administrators at higher salaries.

The paradox of undergraduate education in the United States is that it is the envy of the world, but also tremendously beleaguered. In that way it resembles the U.S. health-care sector. Both carry price tags that shock the conscience of citizens of other developed countries. They're both tied up inextricably with government, through student loans and federal research funding or through Medicare. But if you can afford the Mayo Clinic, the United States is the best place in the world to get sick. And if you get a scholarship to Stanford, you should take it, and turn down offers from even the best   10 universities in Europe, Australia, or Japan. (Most likely, though, you won't get that scholarship. The average U.S. college graduate in 2014 carried $33,000 of debt.)

Financial dysfunction is only the most obvious way in which higher education is troubled. In the past half millennium, the technology of learning has hardly budged. The easiest way to picture what a university looked like 500 years ago is to go to any large university today, walk into a lecture hall, and imagine the professor speaking Latin and wearing a monk's cowl. The most common class format is still a professor standing in front of a group of students and talking. And even though we've subjected students to lectures for hundreds of years, we have no evidence that they are a good way to teach. (One educational psychologist, Ludy Benjamin, likens lectures to Velveeta cheese—something lots of people consume but no one considers either delicious or nourishing.)

In recent years, other innovations in higher education have preceded Minerva, most famously massive open online courses, known by the unfortunate acronym MOOCs. Among the most prominent MOOC purveyors are Khan Academy, the brainchild of the entrepreneur Salman Khan, and Coursera, headed by the Stanford computer scientists Andrew Ng and Daphne Koller. Khan Academy began as a way to tutor children in math, but it has grown to include a dazzling array of tutorials, some very effective, many on technical subjects. Coursera offers college-level classes for free (you can pay for premium services, like actual college credit). There can be hundreds of thousands of students in a single course, and millions are enrolled altogether. At their most basic, these courses consist of standard university lectures, caught on video.

But Minerva is not a MOOC provider. Its courses are not massive (they're capped at 19 students), open (Minerva is overtly elitist and selective), or online, at least not in the same way Coursera's are. Lectures are banned. All Minerva classes take the form of seminars conducted on the platform I tested. The first students will by now have moved into Minerva's dorm on the fifth floor of a building in San Francisco's Nob Hill neighborhood and begun attending class on Apple laptops they were required to supply themselves.

Each year, according to Minerva's plan, they'll attend university in a different place, so that after four years they'll have the kind of international experience that other universities advertise but can rarely deliver. By 2016, Berlin and Buenos Aires campuses will have opened. Likely future cities include Mumbai, Hong Kong, New York, and London. Students will live in dorms with two-person rooms and a communal kitchen. They'll also take part in field trips organized by Minerva, such as a tour of Alcatraz with a prison psychologist. Minerva will maintain almost no facilities other than the dorm itself—no library, no dining hall, no gym—and students will use city parks and recreation centers, as well as other local cultural resources, for their extracurricular activities.

The professors can live anywhere, as long as they have an Internet connection.   15
Given that many academics are coastal-elite types who refuse to live in places like Evansville, Indiana, geographic freedom is a vital part of Minerva's faculty recruitment.

The student body could become truly global, in part because Minerva's policy is to admit students without regard to national origin, thus catering to the unmet demand of, say, prosperous Chinese and Indians and Brazilians for American-style liberal-arts education.

The Minerva boast is that it will strip the university experience down to the aspects that are shown to contribute directly to student learning. Lectures, gone. Tenure, gone. Gothic architecture, football, ivy crawling up the walls—gone, gone, gone. What's left will be leaner and cheaper. (Minerva has already attracted $25 million in capital from investors who think it can undercut the incumbents.) And Minerva officials claim that their methods will be tested against scientifically determined best practices, unlike the methods used at other universities and assumed to be sound just because the schools themselves are old and expensive. Yet because classes have only just begun, we have little clue as to whether the process of stripping down the university removes something essential to what has made America's best colleges the greatest in the world.

Minerva will, after all, look very little like a university—and not merely because it won't be accessorized in useless and expensive ways. The teaching methods may well be optimized, but universities, as currently constituted, are only partly about classroom time. Can a school that has no faculty offices, research labs, community spaces for students, or professors paid to do scholarly work still be called a university?

If Minerva fails, it will lay off its staff and sell its office furniture and never be heard from again. If it succeeds, it could inspire a legion of entrepreneurs, and a whole category of legacy institutions might have to liquidate. One imagines tumbleweeds rolling through abandoned quads and wrecking balls smashing through the windows of classrooms left empty by students who have plugged into new online platforms.

The decor in the lobby of the Minerva office building nods to the classical roots of education: enormous Roman statues dominate. (Minerva is the Roman goddess of wisdom.) But where Minerva's employees work, on the ninth floor, the atmosphere is pure business, in a California-casual sort of way. Everyone, including the top officers of the university, works at open-plan stations. I associate scholars' offices with chalk dust, strewn papers, and books stacked haphazardly in contravention of fire codes. But here, I found tidiness. 20

One of the Minerva employees least scholarly in demeanor is its founder, chief executive, and principal evangelist. Ben Nelson attended the University of Pennsylvania's Wharton School as an undergraduate in the late 1990s and then had no further contact with academia before he began incubating Minerva, in 2010. His résumé's main entry is his 10-year stint as an executive at Snapfish, an online photo service that allows users to print pictures on postcards and in books.

Nelson is curly-haired and bespectacled, and when I met him he wore a casual button-down shirt with no tie or jacket. His ambition to reform academia was born of his own undergraduate experience. At Wharton, he was dissatisfied with what he perceived as a random barrage of business instruction, with no coordination to ensure that he learned bedrock skills like critical thinking. "My entire critique of higher education started with curricular reform at Penn," he says. "General education is nonexistent. It's effectively a buffet, and when you have a noncurated academic experience, you effectively don't get educated. You get a random collection of information. Liberal-arts education is about developing the intellectual capacity of the individual, and learning to be a productive member of society. And you cannot do that without a curriculum."

Students begin their Minerva education by taking the same four "Cornerstone Courses," which introduce core concepts and ways of thinking that cut across the sciences and humanities. These are not 101 classes, meant to impart freshman-level knowledge of subjects. ("The freshman year [as taught at traditional schools] should not exist," Nelson says, suggesting that MOOCs can teach the basics. "Do your freshman year at home.") Instead, Minerva's first-year classes are designed to inculcate what Nelson calls "habits of mind" and "foundational concepts," which are the basis for all sound systematic thought. In a science class, for example, students should develop a deep understanding of the need for controlled experiments. In a humanities class, they need to learn the classical techniques of rhetoric and develop basic persuasive skills. The curriculum then builds from that foundation.

Nelson compares this level of direction favorably with what he found at Penn (curricular disorder), and with what one finds at Brown (very few requirements) or Columbia (a "great books" core curriculum). As Minerva students advance, they choose one of five majors: arts and humanities, social sciences, computational sciences, natural sciences, or business.

Snapfish sold for $300 million to Hewlett-Packard in 2005, and Nelson made enough to fund two years of planning for his dream project. He is prone to bombastic pronouncements about Minerva, making broad claims about the state of higher education that are at times insightful and at times speculative at best. He speaks at many conferences, unsettling academic administrators less radical than he is by blithely dismissing long-standing practices. "Your cash cow is the lecture, and the lecture is over," he told a gathering of deans. "The lecture model . . . will be obliterated." 25

In academic circles, where overt competition between institutions is a serious breach of etiquette, Nelson is a bracing presence. (Imagine the president of Columbia telling the assembled presidents of other Ivy League schools, as Nelson sometimes tells his competitors, "Our goal is not to put you out of business; it is to lead you. It is to show you that there is a better way to do what you are doing, and for you to follow us.")

The other taboo Nelson ignores is acknowledgment of profit motive. "*For-profit* in higher education equates to evil," Nelson told me, noting that most for-profit colleges are indeed the sort of disreputable degree mills that wallpaper the Web with banner ads. "As if nonprofits aren't money-driven!" he howled. "They're just corporations that dodge their taxes."

Minerva is built to make money, but Nelson insists that its motives will align with student interests. As evidence, Nelson points to the fact that the school will eschew all federal funding, to which he attributes much of the runaway cost of universities. The compliance cost of taking federal financial aid is about $1,000 per student—a tenth of Minerva's tuition—and the aid wouldn't be of any use to the majority of Minerva's students, who will likely come from overseas.

> **Minerva is built to make money, but Nelson insists that its motives will align with student interests.**

Subsidies, Nelson says, encourage universities to enroll even students who aren't likely to thrive, and to raise tuition, since federal money is pegged to costs. These effects pervade higher education, he says, but they have nothing to do with teaching students. He believes Minerva would end up hungering after federal money, too, if it ever allowed itself to be tempted. Instead, like Ulysses, it will tie itself to the mast and work with private-sector funding only. "If you put a drug" —federal funds— "into a system, the system changes itself to fit the drug. If [Minerva] took money from the government, in 20 years we'd be majority American, with substantially higher tuition. And as much as you try to create barriers, if you don't structure it to be mission-oriented, that's the way it will evolve."

When talking about Minerva's future, Nelson says he thinks in terms of the life spans 30 of universities — hundreds of years as opposed to the decades of typical corporate time horizons. Minerva's very founding is a rare event. "We are now building an institution that has not been attempted in over 100 years, since the founding of Rice" — the last four-year liberal-arts-based research institution founded in this country. It opened in 1912 and now charges $53,966 a year.

So far, Minerva has hired its deans, who will teach all the courses for this inaugural class. It will hire rank-and-file faculty later in the year. One of Minerva's main strategies is to lure a few prominent scholars from existing institutions. Other "new" universities, especially fantastically wealthy ones like King Abdullah University of Science and Technology, in Saudi Arabia, have attempted a similar strategy — at times with an almost cargocult-like confidence that filling their labs and offices with big-shot professors will turn the institutions themselves into important players.

Among the bigger shots hired by Minerva is Eric Bonabeau, the dean of computational sciences, who taught the seminar I participated in. Bonabeau, a physicist who has worked in academia and in business, studies the mathematics of swarming behavior (of bees, fish, robots), and his research helped inspire Michael Crichton's terrible thriller *Prey*. Diane Halpern, a prominent psychologist, signed on this year as the dean of social sciences.

Minerva's first major hire, Stephen M. Kosslyn, is a man I met in the fall of 1999, when I went to have my head examined. Kosslyn taught cognitive psychology and neuroscience for 32 years at Harvard, and during my undergraduate years I visited his lab and earned a few dollars here and there as one of his guinea pigs. The studies usually involved sticking my head in an fMRI machine so he and his researchers could record activity in my brain and observe which parts fired when.

Around that time, Kosslyn's lab made news because it began to show how "mental imagery" — the experience of seeing things in your mind's eye — really works. (One study involved putting volunteers into fMRI machines and asking them to hold an image of a cat in their head for as long as possible. You can try this exercise now. If you're especially good at concentrating, the cat might vanish in a matter of a few seconds, as soon as your brain — distractible as a puppy — comes up with another object of attention.) Kosslyn served as Harvard's dean of social sciences from 2008 to 2010, then spent two years at Stanford as the director of its Center for Advanced Study in the Behavioral Sciences. In 2013, after a few months of contract work for Minerva, he resigned from Stanford and joined Minerva as its founding dean.

Kosslyn speaks softly and slowly, with little emotional affect. Bald and bearded, he 35 has an owlish stare, and at times during my recent conversations with him, he seemed to be scanning my brain with his eyes. For purposes of illustration (and perhaps also amusement), he will ask you to perform some cognitive task, then wait patiently while you do it — explain a concept, say, or come up with an argument — before telling you matter-of-factly what your mind just did. When talking with him, you often feel as though your brain is a machine, and his job is to know how it works better than it knows itself.

He spent much of his first year at Minerva surveying the literature on education and the psychology of learning. "We have numerous sound, reproducible experiments that tell us how people learn, and what teachers can do to improve learning." Some of the studies are ancient, by the standards of scientific research—and yet their lessons are almost wholly ignored.

For example, he points to a 1972 study by Fergus I. M. Craik and Robert S. Lockhart in *The Journal of Verbal Learning and Verbal Behavior,* which shows that memory of material is enhanced by "deep" cognitive tasks. In an educational context, such tasks would include working with material, applying it, arguing about it (rote memorization is insufficient). The finding is hardly revolutionary, but applying it systematically in the classroom is. Similarly, research shows that having a pop quiz at the beginning of a class and (if the students are warned in advance) another one at a random moment later in the class greatly increases the durability of what is learned. Likewise, if you ask a student to explain a concept she has been studying, the very act of articulating it seems to lodge it in her memory. Forcing students to guess the answer to a problem, and to discuss their answers in small groups, seems to make them understand the problem better—even if they guess wrong.

Kosslyn has begun publishing his research on the science of learning. His most recent co-authored article, in *Psychological Science in the Public Interest,* argues (against conventional wisdom) that the traditional concept of "cognitive styles"—visual versus aural learners, those who learn by doing versus those who learn by studying—is muddled and wrong.

The pedagogical best practices Kosslyn has identified have been programmed into the Minerva platform so that they are easy for professors to apply. They are not only easy, in fact, but also compulsory, and professors will be trained intensively in how to use the platform.

This approach does have its efficiencies. In a normal class, a pop quiz might involve   40
taking out paper and pencils, not to mention eye-rolls from students. On the Minerva platform, quizzes—often a single multiple-choice question—are over and done in a matter of seconds, with students' answers immediately logged and analyzed. Professors are able to sort students instantly, and by many metrics, for small-group work—perhaps pairing poets with business majors, to expose students who are weak in a particular class to the thought processes of their stronger peers. Some claim that education is an art and a science. Nelson has disputed this: "It's a science and a science."

Nelson likes to compare this approach to traditional seminars. He says he spoke to a prominent university president—he wouldn't say which one—early in the planning of Minerva, and he found the man's view of education, in a word, faith-based. "He said the reason elite university education was so great was because you take an expert in the subject, plus a bunch of smart kids, you put them in a room and apply pressure—and *magic* happens," Nelson told me, leaning portentously on that word. "That was his analysis. They're trying to sell magic! Something that happens by accident! It sure didn't happen when I was an undergrad."

To Kosslyn, building effective teaching techniques directly into the platform gives Minerva a huge advantage. "Typically, the way a professor learns to teach is completely haphazard," he says. "One day the person is a graduate student, and the next day, a professor standing up giving a lecture, with almost no training." Lectures, Kosslyn says, are pedagogically unsound, although for universities looking to trim budgets they are at least cost-effective, with one employee for dozens or hundreds of tuition-paying students. "A great way to teach," Kosslyn says drily, "but a terrible way to learn."

I asked him whether, at Harvard and Stanford, he attempted to apply any of the lessons of psychology in the classroom. He told me he could have alerted colleagues to best practices, but they most likely would have ignored them. "The classroom time is theirs, and it is sacrosanct," he says. The very thought that he might be able to impose his own order on it was laughable. Professors, especially tenured ones at places like Harvard, answer to nobody.

It occurred to me that Kosslyn was living the dream of every university administrator who has watched professors mulishly defy even the most reasonable directives. Kosslyn had powers literally no one at Harvard—even the president—had. He could tell people what to do, and they had to do it.

There were moments, during my various conversations with Kosslyn and Nelson, when I found I couldn't wait for Minerva's wrecking ball to demolish the ivory tower. The American college system is a frustrating thing—and I say this as someone who was a satisfied customer of two undergraduate institutions, Deep Springs College (an obscure but selective college in the high desert of California) and Harvard. At Deep Springs, my classes rarely exceeded five students. At Harvard, I went to many excellent lectures and took only one class with fewer than 10 students. I didn't sleepwalk or drink my way through either school, and the education I received was well worth the $16,000 a year my parents paid, after scholarships. 45

But the Minerva seminar did bring back memories of many a pointless, formless discussion or lecture, and it began to seem obvious that if Harvard had approached teaching with a little more care, it could have improved the seminars and replaced the worst lectures with something else.

When Eric Bonabeau assigned the reading for his class on induction, he barely bothered to tell us what induction was, or how it related to North Atlantic cod. When I asked him afterward about his decision not to spend a session introducing the concept, he said the Web had plenty of tutorials about induction, and any Minerva student ought to be able to learn the basics on her own time, in her own way. Seminars are for advanced discussion. And, of course, he was right.

Minerva's model, Nelson says, will flourish in part because it will exploit free online content, rather than trying to compete with it, as traditional universities do. A student who wants an introductory economics course can turn to Coursera or Khan Academy. "We are a university, and a MOOC is a version of publishing," Nelson explains. "The reason we can get away with the pedagogical model we have is because MOOCs exist. The MOOCs will eventually make lectures obsolete."

Indeed, the more I looked into Minerva and its operations, the more I started to think that certain functions of universities have simply become less relevant as information has become more ubiquitous. Just as learning to read in Latin was essential before books became widely available in other languages, gathering students in places where they could attend lectures in person was once a necessary part of higher education. But by now books are abundant, and so are serviceable online lectures by knowledgeable experts.

On the other hand, no one yet knows whether reducing a university to a smooth-running pedagogical machine will continue to allow scholarship to thrive—or whether it will simply put universities out of business, replace scholar-teachers with just teachers, and retard a whole generation of research. At any great university, there are faculty who are terrible at teaching but whose work drives their field forward with greater momentum than the research of their classroom-competent colleagues. Will there be a place for such people at Minerva—or anywhere, if Minerva succeeds? 50

> **[C]ertain functions of universities have simply become less relevant as information has become more ubiquitous.**

Last spring, when universities began mailing out acceptance letters and parents all over the country shuddered as the reality of tuition bills became more concrete, Minerva sent 69 offers. Thirty-three students decided to enroll, a typical percentage for a liberal-arts school. Nelson told me Minerva would admit students without regard for diversity or balance of gender.

Applicants to Minerva take a battery of online quizzes, including spatial-reasoning tests of the sort one might find on an IQ test. SATs are not considered, because affluent students can boost their scores by hiring tutors. ("They're a good way of determining how rich a student is," Nelson says.) If students perform well enough, Minerva interviews them over Skype and makes them write a short essay during the interview, to ensure that they aren't paying a ghost writer. "The top 30 applicants get in," he told me back in February, slicing his hand through the air to mark the cutoff point. For more than three years, he had been proselytizing worldwide, speaking to high school students in California and Qatar and Brazil. In May, he and the Minerva deans made the final chop.

Of the students who enrolled, slightly less than 20 percent are American—a percentage much higher than anticipated. (Nelson ultimately expects as many as 90 percent of the students to come from overseas.) Perhaps not surprisingly, the students come disproportionately from unconventional backgrounds—nearly one-tenth are from United World Colleges, the chain of cosmopolitan hippie high schools that brings together students from around the globe in places like Wales, Singapore, and New Mexico.

In an oddly controlling move for a university, Minerva asked admitted students to run requests for media interviews by its public-relations department. But the university gave me the names of three students willing to speak.

When I got through to Ian Van Buskirk of Marietta, Georgia, he was eager to tell me about a dugout canoe that he had recently carved out of a two-ton oak log, using only an ax, an adze, and a chisel, and that he planned to take on a maiden voyage in the hour after our conversation. He told me he would have attended Duke University if Minerva hadn't come calling, but he said it wasn't a particularly difficult decision, even though Minerva lacks the prestige and 176-year history of Duke. "There's no reputation out there," he told me. "But that means we get to make the reputation ourselves. I'm creating it now, while I'm talking to you." 55

Minerva had let him try out the same online platform I did, and Van Buskirk singled out the "level of interaction and intensity" as a reason for attending. "It took deep concentration," he said. "It's not some lecture class where you can just click 'record' on your tape." He said the focus required was similar to the mind-set he'd needed when he made his first hacks into his oak log, which could have cracked, rendering it useless.

Another student, Shane Dabor, of the small city of Brantford, Ontario, had planned to attend Canada's University of Waterloo or the University of Toronto. But his experiences with online learning and a series of internships had led him to conclude that traditional universities were not for him. "I already had lots of friends at university who weren't learning anything," he says. "Both options seemed like a wager, and I chose this one."

A young Palestinian woman, Rana Abu Diab, of Silwan, in East Jerusalem, described how she had learned English through movies and books (a translation of the Norwegian philosophical novel *Sophie's World* was a particular favorite). "If I had relied on my school, I would not be able to have a two-minute conversation," she told me in fluent English. During a year studying media at Birzeit University, in Ramallah, she heard about Minerva and decided to scrap her other academic plans and focus on applying there. For her, the ability to study overseas on multiple continents, and get an American-style liberal-arts education in the process, was irresistible. "I want to explore everything and learn everything," she says. "And that's what Minerva is offering: an experience that lets you live multiple lives and learn not just your concentration but how to think." Minerva admitted her, and, like a third of her classmates in the founding class, she received a supplemental scholarship, which she could use to pay for her computer and health insurance.

Two students told me that they had felt a little trepidation, and a need to convince themselves or their parents that Minerva wasn't just a moneymaking scheme. Minerva had an open house weekend for admitted students, and (perhaps ironically) the in-person interactions with Minerva faculty and staff helped assure them that the university was legit. The students all now say they're confident in Minerva—although of course they can leave whenever they like, with little lost but time.

Some people consider universities sacred places, and they might even see professors' freedom to be the fallible sovereigns of their own classrooms as a necessary part of what makes a university special. To these romantics, universities are havens from a world dominated by orthodoxy, money, and quotidian concerns. Professors get to think independently, and students come away molded by the total experience—classes, social life, extracurriculars—that the university provides. We spend the rest of our lives chasing mates, money, and jobs, but at university we enjoy the liberty to indulge aimless curiosity in subjects we know nothing about, for purposes unrelated to efficiency or practicality.

Minerva is too young to have attracted zealous naysayers, but it's safe to assume that the people with this disposition toward the university experience are least likely to be enthusiastic about Minerva and other attempts to revolutionize education through technical innovation. MOOCs are beloved by those too poor for a traditional university, as well as those who like to dabble, and those who like to learn in their pajamas. And MOOCs are not to be knocked: for a precocious Malawian peasant girl who learns math through free lessons from Khan Academy, the new Web resources can change her life. But the dropout rate for online classes is about 95 percent, and they skew strongly toward quantitative disciplines, particularly computer science, and toward privileged male students. As Nelson is fond of pointing out, however, MOOCs will continue to get better, until eventually no one will pay Duke or Johns Hopkins for the possibility of a good lecture, when Coursera offers a reliably great one, with hundreds of thousands of five-star ratings, for free.

The question remains as to whether Minerva can provide what traditional universities offer now. Kosslyn's project of efficiently cramming learning into students' brains is preferable to failing to cram in anything at all. And it is designed to convey not just information, as most MOOCs seem to, but whole mental tool kits that help students become more thoughtful citizens. But defenders of the traditional university see efficiency as a false idol.

"Like other things that are going on now in higher ed, Minerva brings us back to first principles," says Harry R. Lewis, a computer-science professor who was the dean of Harvard's undergraduate college from 1995 to 2003. What, he asks, does it mean to be educated? Perhaps the process of education is a profound one, involving all sorts of leaps in maturity that do not show up on a Kosslyn-style test of pedagogical efficiency. "I'm sure there's a market for people who want to be more efficiently educated," Lewis says. "But how do you improve the efficiency of growing up?"

He warns that online-education innovations tend to be oversold. "They seem to want to re-create the School of Athens in every little hamlet on the prairie—and maybe they'll do that," he told me. "But part of the process of education happens not just through good pedagogy but by having students in places where they see the scholars working and plying their trades."

> **"Plutarch said the mind is not a vessel to be filled but a fire to be lit."**

He calls the "hydraulic metaphor" of education—the idea that the main task of education is to increase the flow of knowledge into the student—an "old fallacy." As Lewis explains, "Plutarch said the mind is not a vessel to be filled but a fire to be lit. Part of my worry about these Internet start-ups is that it's not clear they'll be any good at the fire-lighting part."

In February, at a university-administrator conference at a Hyatt in downtown San Francisco, Ben Nelson spoke to a plenary session of business-school deans from around the world. Daphne Koller of Coursera sat opposite him onstage, and they calmly but assuredly described what sounded to me like the destruction of the very schools where their audience members worked. Nelson wore a bored smirk while an introductory video played, advertising the next year's version of the same conference. To a pair of educational entrepreneurs boasting the low price of their new projects, the slickly produced video must have looked like just another expensive barnacle on the hull of higher education.

"Content is about to become free and ubiquitous," Koller said, an especially worrying comment for deans who still thought the job of their universities was to teach "content." The institutions "that are going to survive are the ones that reimagine themselves in this new world."

Nelson ticked off the advantages he had over legacy institutions: the spryness of a well-funded start-up, a student body from all over the world, and deals for faculty (they get to keep their own intellectual property, rather than having to hand over lucrative patents to, say, Stanford) that are likely to make Minerva attractive.

Yet in some ways, the worst possible outcome would be for U.S. higher education to accept Minerva as its model and dismantle the old universities before anyone can really be sure that it offers a satisfactory replacement. During my conversations with the three Minerva students, I wanted to ask whether they were confident Minerva would give them all the wonderful intangibles and productive diversions that Harry Lewis found so important. But then I remembered what I was like as a teenager headed off to college, so ignorant of what college was and what it could be, and so reliant on the college itself to provide what I'd need in order to get a good education. These three young students were more resourceful than I was, and probably more deliberate in their choice of college. But they were newcomers to higher education, and asking them whether their fledgling alma mater could provide these things seemed akin to asking the passengers on the *Mayflower* how they liked America as soon as their feet touched Plymouth Rock.

Lewis is certainly right when he says that Minerva challenges the field to return to   70 first principles. But of course the conclusions one reaches might not be flattering to traditional colleges. One possibility is that Minerva will fail because a college degree, for all the high-minded talk of liberal education—of lighting fires and raising thoughtful citizens—is really just a credential, or an entry point to an old-boys network that gets you your first job and your first lunch with the machers at your alumni club. Minerva has no alumni club, and if it fails for this reason, it will look naive and idealistic, a bet on the inherent value of education in a world where cynicism gets better odds.

In another sense, it's difficult to imagine Minerva failing altogether: it will offer something that resembles a liberal education to large segments of the Earth's population who currently have to choose between the long-shot possibility of getting into a traditional U.S. school, and the more narrowly career-oriented education available in their home country. That population might give Minerva a steady flow of tuition-paying warm bodies even if U.S. higher education ignores it completely. It could plausibly become the Amherst of the world beyond the borders of the United States.

These are not, however, the terms by which Ben Nelson defines success. To him, the brass ring is for Minerva to force itself on the consciousness of the Yales and Swarthmores and "lead" American universities into a new era. More modestly, we can expect Minerva to force some universities to justify what previously could be waved off with mentions of "magic" and a puff of smoke. Its seminar platform will challenge professors to stop thinking they're using technology just because they lecture with PowerPoint.

It seems only remotely possible that in 20 years Minerva could have more students enrolled than Ohio State will. But it is almost a certainty that the classrooms of elite universities will in that time have come to look more and more like Minerva classrooms, with professors and students increasingly separated geographically, mediated through technology that alters the nature of the student-teacher relationship. Even if Minerva turns out not to be the venture that upends American higher education, other innovators will crop up in its wake to address the exact weaknesses Nelson now attacks. The idea that college will in two decades look exactly as it does today increasingly sounds like the forlorn, fingers-crossed hope of a higher-education dinosaur that retirement comes before extinction.

At the university-administrator conference where Nelson spoke in February, I sat at a table with an affable bunch of deans from Australia and the United States. They listened attentively, first with interest and then with growing alarm. Toward the end of the conversation, the sponsoring organization's president asked the panelists what they expected to be said at a similar event in 2017, on the same topic of innovative online education. ("Assuming we're still in business," a dean near me whispered to no one in particular.)

Daphne Koller said she expected Coursera to have grown in offerings into a uni-   75
versity the size of a large state school—after having started from scratch in 2012. Even before Nelson gave his answer, I noticed some audience members uncomfortably shifting their weight. The stench of fear made him bold.

"I predict that in three years, four or five or seven or eight of you will be onstage here, presenting your preliminary findings of your first year of a radical new conception of your undergraduate [or] graduate program . . . And the rest of you will look at two or three of those versions and say, 'Uh-oh.'" This was meant as a joke, but hardly anyone laughed.

Exploring Context

1. Explore Minerva's Web site at minerva.kgi.edu. How does it reflect Wood's argument in its content and design?

2. Minerva contrasts itself to massive open online courses (MOOCs). Visit MOOC List, a compendium of such courses, at mooc-list.com. How do these courses contribute to Minerva's model of education? Expand your response to Question 1 by comparing this site to Minerva's.

3. Visit the Web site for your school. How does it attract students through its design and content? What vision of education does it offer? Incorporate your responses to Questions 1 and 2 in order to assess the model of education for your school.

Questions for Connecting

1. Minerva attracts many international students. Use Thomas L. Friedman's essay "The Dell Theory of Conflict Prevention" (p. 124) to examine the connections between globalization and education. Does Minerva use global supply chains? What role does collaboration play in education? Use your work from Questions for Critical Reading and Exploring Context to support your response.

2. Chuck Klosterman, in "Electric Funeral" (p. 224), suggests that technological change is often driven by a sense of inevitability. Apply his arguments to Wood to answer Wood's questions about reinventing college. Is Minerva's model of education inevitable? Is it villainous? Use your work from Question 2 of Questions for Critical Reading and Questions 1 and 2 from Exploring Context.

3. What role might Minerva play in the world? Consider Kwame Anthony Appiah's arguments in "Making Conversation" and "The Primacy of Practice" (p. 44). In what ways

does Minerva reflect cosmopolitanism? How might the current practice of education resist change, and how might Minerva fail or succeed?

Language Matters

1. Technology is at the heart of Minerva. Using your own experience with these tools, develop your own methods of using technology to address issues of language and grammar. Are there Web sites that are particularly useful? How can apps or software help us become better writers?

2. Group work plays an important role at Minerva. Working in small groups in class, debate a common grammatical issue or error, such as the run-on sentence. Should it be considered an error? How important is that error or any one type of error? How does your discussion reflect Wood's ideas about learning?

3. Wood occasionally uses ellipses in his writing. Using a grammar handbook or other reliable reference resource, review the rules for using ellipses. Does Wood follow these rules? When might you want to use these in your writing?

Assignments for Writing

1. What is reinventing college? Write a paper in which you use Wood's ideas to formulate a model for education. What role should technology play? How can education's cost be controlled? What should students be learning? Use your work from Questions 1 and 3 of Questions for Critical Reading and Question 3 of Questions for Connecting to support your argument.

2. Wood quotes Minerva's founder, Ben Nelson, as saying education is "a science and a science" (p. 512). Write a paper in which you examine the relationship between technology and education. What role does art play in the delivery of education? Is teaching a science? What technologies are best used in education, and where might technology fail? Consider using your work on technology and education from Question 2 of Questions for Critical Reading and Question 2 of Questions for Connecting.

3. Minerva does not shy from its for-profit nature. But what role should economics play in education? Write a paper in which you define the best relationship between economics and education. Should we control the cost of education? How? What economic privileges enable one to get an education, and how might we allow more people to achieve those privileges? Should government play a role? Use your work from Question 3 of Questions for Critical Reading.

WESLEY YANG

. . . .

Wesley Yang is a contributing editor at both *Tablet* and *New York* magazines, with more than ten of his essays appearing in both the print and online editions of the latter. His varied articles on race, sexuality, and politics have also been published in noted magazines such as *Salon*, the *New York Observer*, and the *National*.

Courtesy of Wesley Yang

The May 16, 2011, issue of *New York* magazine, from which this selection was taken, was enveloped in the then-recent killing of Osama bin Laden, which had taken place just over two weeks prior, with blurbs about the event on the cover alongside feature pieces on Lady Gaga. But the cover image, one of Wesley Yang himself in stark closeup fading to white with his own words superimposed over the photo, signified that "Paper Tigers" was indeed the centerpiece of the issue.

In "Paper Tigers," Wesley Yang discusses his own experiences as an Asian American, tying them into the larger picture of Asians functioning in American society. Yang argues that while Asian Americans are indeed the most "successful" ethnic group in the country in terms of education and accumulation of wealth (often trumping the majority demographic — whites), there is a perception in popular culture that Asian Americans are "the products of a timid culture, easily pushed around by more assertive people" (p. 522). Yang asks us to consider the implications of stereotypes — even positive ones — and how they affect not only the viewing of other peoples, but the way those very people being stereotyped integrate into society.

What stereotypes have been applied to you? Is it possible for us to discard stereotypes altogether, especially in the face of continual evidence of their tendency toward misrepresentation?

▶ TAGS: *adolescence and adulthood, civil rights, community, culture, economics, education, identity, race and ethnicity*

▶ CONNECTIONS: *Gilbert, Kahneman, Ma, O'Connor, Olson, Padawer, Watters, Wood, Yoshino*

. . . .

Questions for Critical Reading

1. We've all heard about the *American Dream*. Before you read this essay, write a brief definition of what this term means to you. As you read, pay attention to how Yang defines the term. What does it mean to him, and how does he apply it to minorities? Is the "American Dream" the same for all Americans?

2. Look up the meaning of the word *estrangement*. How does Yang define this term? While reading, take note of places where he discusses estrangement. How does it relate to the argument he wants to make?

3. Yang discusses the "Bamboo Ceiling" (p. 526). Do you agree with his analysis and use of the concept? What other "ceilings" might there be for other classes of people? You might begin your response by looking into the "glass ceiling" faced by women in the workplace.

Paper Tigers

Sometimes I'll glimpse my reflection in a window and feel astonished by what I see. Jet-black hair. Slanted eyes. A pancake-flat surface of yellow-and-green-toned skin. An expression that is nearly reptilian in its impassivity. I've contrived to think of this face as the equal in beauty to any other. But what I feel in these moments is its strangeness to me. It's my face. I can't disclaim it. But what does it have to do with me?

Millions of Americans must feel estranged from their own faces. But every self-estranged individual is estranged in his own way. I, for instance, am the child of Korean immigrants, but I do not speak my parents' native tongue. I have never called my elders by the proper honorific, "big brother" or "big sister." I have never dated a Korean woman. I don't have a Korean friend. Though I am an immigrant, I have never wanted to strive like one.

You could say that I am, in the gently derisive parlance of Asian-Americans, a banana or a Twinkie (yellow on the outside, white on the inside). But while I don't believe our roots necessarily define us, I do believe there are racially inflected assumptions wired into our neural circuitry that we use to sort through the sea of faces we confront. And although I am in most respects devoid of Asian characteristics, I do have an Asian face.

Here is what I sometimes suspect my face signifies to other Americans: an invisible person, barely distinguishable from a mass of faces that resemble it. A conspicuous person standing apart from the crowd and yet devoid of any individuality. An icon of so much that the culture pretends to honor but that it in fact patronizes and exploits. Not just people "who are good at math" and play the violin, but a mass of stifled, repressed, abused, conformist quasi-robots who simply do not matter, socially or culturally.

I've always been of two minds about this sequence of stereotypes. On the one hand, it offends me greatly that anyone would think to apply them to me, or to anyone else, simply on the basis of facial characteristics. On the other hand, it also seems to me that there are a lot of Asian people to whom they apply.   5

Let me summarize my feelings toward Asian values: Fuck filial piety. Fuck grade-grubbing. Fuck Ivy League mania. Fuck deference to authority. Fuck humility and hard work. Fuck harmonious relations. Fuck sacrificing for the future. Fuck earnest, striving middle-class servility.

I understand the reasons Asian parents have raised a generation of children this way. Doctor, lawyer, accountant, engineer: These are good jobs open to whoever works hard enough. What could be wrong with that pursuit? Asians graduate from college at a rate higher than any other ethnic group in America, including whites. They earn a higher median family income than any other ethnic group in America, including whites. This is a stage in a triumphal narrative, and it is a narrative that is much shorter than many remember. Two thirds of the roughly 14 million Asian-Americans are foreign-born. There were less than 39,000 people of Korean descent living in America in 1970, when my elder brother was born. There are around 1 million today.

Asian-American success is typically taken to ratify the American Dream and to prove that minorities can make it in this country without handouts. Still, an undercurrent of racial panic always accompanies the consideration of Asians, and all the more so as China becomes the destination for our industrial base and the banker controlling our burgeoning debt. But if the armies of Chinese factory workers who make our fast fashion and iPads terrify us, and if the collective mass of high-achieving Asian-American students arouse an anxiety about the laxity of American parenting, what of the Asian-American who obeyed everything his parents told him? Does this person really scare anyone?

Earlier this year, the publication of Amy Chua's *Battle Hymn of the Tiger Mother* incited a collective airing out of many varieties of race-based hysteria. But absent from the millions of words written in response to the book was any serious consideration of whether Asian-Americans were in fact taking over this country. If it is true that they are collectively dominating in elite high schools and universities, is it also true that Asian-Americans are dominating in the real world? My strong suspicion was that this was not so, and that the reasons would not be hard to find. If we are a collective juggernaut that inspires such awe and fear, why does it seem that so many Asians are so readily perceived to be, as I myself have felt most of my life, the products of a timid culture, easily pushed around by more assertive people, and thus basically invisible?

A few months ago, I received an e-mail from a young man named Jefferson Mao, who   10
after attending Stuyvesant High School had recently graduated from the University of Chicago. He wanted my advice about "being an Asian writer." This is how he described himself: "I got good grades and I love literature and I want to be a writer and an intellectual; at the same time, I'm the first person in my family to go to college, my parents don't speak English very well, and we don't own the apartment in Flushing that we live in. I mean, I'm proud of my parents and my neighborhood and what I perceive to be my artistic potential or whatever, but sometimes I feel like I'm jumping the gun a generation or two too early."

One bright, cold Sunday afternoon, I ride the 7 train to its last stop in Flushing, where the storefront signs are all written in Chinese and the sidewalks are a slow-moving river of impassive faces. Mao is waiting for me at the entrance of the Main Street subway station, and together we walk to a nearby Vietnamese restaurant.

Mao has a round face, with eyes behind rectangular wire-frame glasses. Since graduating, he has been living with his parents, who emigrated from China when Mao was 8 years old. His mother is a manicurist; his father is a physical therapist's aide. Lately, Mao has been making the familiar hour-and-a-half ride from Flushing to downtown Manhattan to tutor a white Stuyvesant freshman who lives in Tribeca. And what he feels, sometimes, in the presence of that amiable young man is a pang of regret. Now he understands better what he ought to have done back when he was a Stuyvesant freshman: "Worked half as hard and been twenty times more successful."

Entrance to Stuyvesant, one of the most competitive public high schools in the country, is determined solely by performance on a test: The top 3.7 percent of all New York City students who take the Specialized High Schools Admissions Test hoping to go to Stuyvesant are accepted. There are no set-asides for the underprivileged or, conversely, for alumni or other privileged groups. There is no formula to encourage "diversity" or any nebulous concept of "well-roundedness" or "character." Here we have something like pure meritocracy. This is what it looks like: Asian-Americans, who make up 12.6 percent of New York City, make up 72 percent of the high school.

This year, 569 Asian-Americans scored high enough to earn a slot at Stuyvesant, along with 179 whites, 13 Hispanics, and 12 blacks. Such dramatic overrepresentation, and what it may be read to imply about the intelligence of different groups of New Yorkers, has a way of making people uneasy. But intrinsic intelligence, of course, is precisely what Asians don't believe in. They believe — and have proved — that the constant practice of test-taking will improve the scores of whoever commits to it. All throughout Flushing, as well as in Bayside, one can find "cram schools," or storefront academies, that drill students in test preparation after school, on weekends, and during summer break. "Learning math is not about learning math," an instructor at one called Ivy Prep was quoted in the *New York Times* as saying. "It's about weightlifting. You are pumping the iron of math." Mao puts it more specifically: "You learn quite simply to nail any standardized test you take."

And so there is an additional concern accompanying the rise of the Tiger Children, one focused more on the narrowness of the educational experience a non-Asian child might receive in the company of fanatically preprofessional Asian students. Jenny Tsai, a student who was elected president of her class at the equally competitive New York public school Hunter College High School, remembers frequently hearing that "the school was becoming too Asian, that they would be the downfall of our school." A couple of years ago, she revisited this issue in her senior thesis at Harvard, where she interviewed graduates of elite public schools and found that the white students regarded the Asian students with wariness. (She quotes a music teacher at Stuyvesant describing the dominance of Asians: "They were mediocre kids, but they got in because they were coached.") In 2005, the *Wall Street Journal* reported on "white flight" from a high school in Cupertino, California, that began soon after the children of Asian software engineers had made the place so brutally competitive that a B average could place you in the bottom third of the class.

Colleges have a way of correcting for this imbalance: The Princeton sociologist Thomas Espenshade has calculated that an Asian applicant must, in practice, score 140 points higher on the SAT than a comparable white applicant to have the same chance of admission. This is obviously unfair to the many qualified Asian individuals who are punished for the success of others with similar faces. Upper-middle-class white kids, after all, have their own elite private schools, and their own private tutors, far more expensive than the cram schools, to help them game the education system.

You could frame it, as some aggrieved Asian-Americans do, as a simple issue of equality and press for race-blind quantitative admissions standards. In 2006, a decade after California passed a voter initiative outlawing any racial engineering at the public universities, Asians composed 46 percent of UC–Berkeley's entering class; one could imagine a similar demographic reshuffling in the Ivy League, where Asian-Americans currently make up about 17 percent of undergraduates. But the Ivies, as we all know, have their own private institutional interests at stake in their admissions choices, including some that are arguably defensible. Who can seriously claim that a Harvard University that was 72 percent Asian would deliver the same grooming for elite status its students had gone there to receive?

Somewhere near the middle of his time at Stuyvesant, a vague sense of discontent started to emerge within Mao. He had always felt himself a part of a mob of "nameless, faceless Asian kids," who were "like a part of the décor of the place." He had been content to keep his head down and work toward the goal shared by everyone at Stuyvesant: Harvard. But around the beginning of his senior year, he began to wonder whether this march toward academic success was the only, or best, path.

"You can't help but feel like there must be another way," he explains over a bowl of phô. "It's like, we're being pitted against each other while there are kids out there in the Midwest who can do way less work and be in a garage band or something—and if they're decently intelligent and work decently hard in school . . ."

Mao began to study the racially inflected social hierarchies at Stuyvesant, where, 20 in a survey undertaken by the student newspaper this year, slightly more than half of the respondents reported that their friends came from within their own ethnic group. His attention focused on the mostly white (and Manhattan-dwelling) group whose members seemed able to manage the crushing workload while still remaining socially active. "The general gist of most high-school movies is that the pretty cheerleader gets with the big dumb jock, and the nerd is left to bide his time in loneliness. But at some point in the future," he says, "the nerd is going to rule the world, and the dumb jock is going to work in a carwash.

"At Stuy, it's completely different: If you looked at the pinnacle, the girls and the guys are not only good-looking and socially affable, they also get the best grades and star in the school plays and win election to student government. It all converges at the top. It's like training for high society. It was jarring for us Chinese kids. You got the sense that you had to study hard, but it wasn't enough."

Mao was becoming clued in to the fact that there was another hierarchy behind the official one that explained why others were getting what he never had—"a high-school sweetheart" figured prominently on this list—and that this mysterious hierarchy was going to determine what happened to him in life. "You realize there are things you really don't understand about courtship or just acting in a certain way. Things that somehow come naturally to people who go to school in the suburbs and have parents who are culturally assimilated." I pressed him for specifics, and he mentioned that he had visited his white girlfriend's parents' house the past Christmas, where the family had "sat around cooking together and playing Scrabble." This ordinary vision of suburban-American domesticity lingered with Mao: Here, at last, was the setting in which all that implicit knowledge "about social norms and propriety" had been transmitted. There was no cram school that taught these lessons.

Before having heard from Mao, I had considered myself at worst lightly singed by the last embers of Asian alienation. Indeed, given all the incredibly hip Asian artists and fashion designers and so forth you can find in New York, it seemed that this feeling was destined to die out altogether. And yet here it was in a New Yorker more than a dozen years my junior. While it may be true that sections of the Asian-American world are devoid of alienation, there are large swaths where it is as alive as it has ever been.

A few weeks after we meet, Mao puts me in touch with Daniel Chu, his close friend from Stuyvesant. Chu graduated from Williams College last year, having won a creative-writing award for his poetry. He had spent a portion of the $18,000 prize on a trip to China, but now he is back living with his parents in Brooklyn Chinatown.

Chu remembers that during his first semester at Williams, his junior adviser would periodically take him aside. Was he feeling all right? Was something the matter? "I was acclimating myself to the place," he says. "I wasn't totally happy, but I wasn't depressed." But then his new white friends made similar remarks. "They would say, 'Dan, it's kind of hard, sometimes, to tell what you're thinking.'" 25

Chu has a pleasant face, but it would not be wrong to characterize his demeanor as reserved. He speaks in a quiet, unemphatic voice. He doesn't move his features much. He attributes these traits to the atmosphere in his household. "When you grow up in a Chinese home," he says, "you don't talk. You shut up and listen to what your parents tell you to do."

At Stuyvesant, he had hung out in an exclusively Asian world in which friends were determined by which subway lines you traveled. But when he arrived at Williams, Chu slowly became aware of something strange: The white people in the New England wilderness walked around smiling at each other. "When you're in a place like that, everyone is friendly."

He made a point to start smiling more. "It was something that I had to actively practice," he says. "Like, when you have a transaction at a business, you hand over the money—and then you smile." He says that he's made some progress but that there's still plenty of work that remains. "I'm trying to undo eighteen years of a Chinese upbringing. Four years at Williams helps, but only so much." He is conscious of how his father, an IT manager, is treated at work. "He's the best programmer at his office," he says, "but because he doesn't speak English well, he is always passed over."

Though Chu is not merely fluent in English but is officially the most distinguished poet of his class at Williams, he still worries that other aspects of his demeanor might attract the same kind of treatment his father received. "I'm really glad we're having this conversation," he says at one point—it is helpful to be remembering these lessons in self-presentation just as he prepares for job interviews.

"I guess what I would like is to become so good at something that my social deficiencies no longer matter," he tells me. Chu is a bright, diligent, impeccably credentialed young man born in the United States. He is optimistic about his ability to earn respect in the world. But he doubts he will ever feel the same comfort in his skin that he glimpsed in the people he met at Williams. That kind of comfort, he says— "I think it's generations away." 30

While he was still an electrical-engineering student at Berkeley in the nineties, James Hong visited the IBM campus for a series of interviews. An older Asian researcher looked over Hong's résumé and asked him some standard questions. Then he got up without saying a word and closed the door to his office.

"Listen," he told Hong, "I'm going to be honest with you. My generation came to this country because we wanted better for you kids. We did the best we could, leaving our homes and going to graduate school not speaking much English. If you take this job, you are just going to hit the same ceiling we did. They just see me as an Asian Ph.D., never management potential. You are going to get a job offer, but don't take it. Your generation has to go farther than we did, otherwise we did everything for nothing."

The researcher was talking about what some refer to as the "Bamboo Ceiling"—an invisible barrier that maintains a pyramidal racial structure throughout corporate America, with lots of Asians at junior levels, quite a few in middle management, and virtually none in the higher reaches of leadership.

> **[I]t is a part of the bitter undercurrent of Asian-American life that so many graduates of elite universities find that meritocracy as they have understood it comes to an abrupt end after graduation.**

The failure of Asian-Americans to become leaders in the white-collar workplace does not qualify as one of the burning social issues of our time. But it is a part of the bitter undercurrent of Asian-American life that so many Asian graduates of elite universities find that meritocracy as they have understood it comes to an abrupt end after graduation. If between 15 and 20 percent of every Ivy League class is Asian, and if the Ivy Leagues are incubators for the country's leaders, it would stand to reason that Asians would make up some corresponding portion of the leadership class.

And yet the numbers tell a different story. According to a recent study, Asian-Americans represent roughly 5 percent of the population but only 0.3 percent of corporate officers, less than 1 percent of corporate board members, and around 2 percent of college presidents. There are nine Asian-American CEOs in the Fortune 500. In specific fields where Asian-Americans are heavily represented, there is a similar asymmetry. A third of all software engineers in Silicon Valley are Asian, and yet they make up only 6 percent of board members and about 10 percent of corporate officers of the Bay Area's 25 largest companies. At the National Institutes of Health, where 21.5 percent of tenure-track scientists are Asians, only 4.7 percent of the lab or branch directors are, according to a study conducted in 2005. One succinct evocation of the situation appeared in the comments section of a website called Yellowworld: "If you're East Asian, you need to attend a top-tier university to land a good high-paying gig. Even if you land that good high-paying gig, the white guy with the pedigree from a mediocre state university will somehow move ahead of you in the ranks simply because he's white."

Jennifer W. Allyn, a managing director for diversity at PricewaterhouseCoopers, works to ensure that "all of the groups feel welcomed and supported and able to thrive and to go as far as their talents will take them." I posed to her the following definition of parity in the corporate workforce: If the current crop of associates is 17 percent Asian, then in fourteen years, when they have all been up for partner review, 17 percent of those who are offered partner will be Asian. Allyn conceded that Pricewaterhouse-Coopers was not close to reaching that benchmark anytime soon—and that "nobody else is either."

Part of the insidious nature of the Bamboo Ceiling is that it does not seem to be caused by overt racism. A survey of Asian-Pacific-American employees of Fortune 500 companies found that 80 percent reported they were judged not as Asians but as individuals. But only 51 percent reported the existence of Asians in key positions, and only 55 percent agreed that their firms were fully capitalizing on the talents and perspectives of Asians.

More likely, the discrepancy in these numbers is a matter of unconscious bias. Nobody would affirm the proposition that tall men are intrinsically better leaders, for instance. And yet while only 15 percent of the male population is at least six feet tall, 58 percent of all corporate CEOs are. Similarly, nobody would say that Asian people are unfit to be leaders. But subjects in a recently published psychological experiment consistently rated hypothetical employees with Caucasian-sounding names higher in leadership potential than identical ones with Asian names.

Maybe it is simply the case that a traditionally Asian upbringing is the problem. As Allyn points out, in order to be a leader, you must have followers. Associates at PricewaterhouseCoopers are initially judged on how well they do the work they are assigned. "You have to be a doer," as she puts it. They are expected to distinguish themselves with their diligence, at which point they become "super-doers." But being a leader requires different skill sets. "The traits that got you to where you are won't necessarily take you to the next level," says the diversity consultant Jane Hyun, who wrote a book called *Breaking the Bamboo Ceiling.* To become a leader requires taking personal initiative and thinking about how an organization can work differently. It also requires networking, self-promotion, and self-assertion. It's racist to think that any given Asian individual is unlikely to be creative or risk-taking. It's simple cultural observation to say that a group whose education has historically focused on rote memorization and "pumping the iron of math" is, on aggregate, unlikely to yield many people inclined to challenge authority or break with inherited ways of doing things.

Sach Takayasu had been one of the fastest-rising members of her cohort in the marketing department at IBM in New York. But about seven years ago, she felt her progress begin to slow. "I had gotten to the point where I was overdelivering, working really long hours, and where doing more of the same wasn't getting me anywhere," she says. It was around this time that she attended a seminar being offered by an organization called Leadership Education for Asian Pacifics.

LEAP has parsed the complicated social dynamics responsible for the dearth of Asian-American leaders and has designed training programs that flatter Asian people even as it teaches them to change their behavior to suit white-American expectations. Asians who enter a LEAP program are constantly assured that they will be able to "keep your values, while acquiring new skills," along the way to becoming "culturally competent leaders."

In a presentation to 1,500 Asian-American employees of Microsoft, LEAP president and CEO J. D. Hokoyama laid out his grand synthesis of the Asian predicament in the workplace. "Sometimes people have perceptions about us and our communities which may or may not be true," Hokoyama told the audience. "But they put those perceptions onto us, and then they do something that can be very devastating: They make decisions about us not based on the truth but based on those perceptions." Hokoyama argued that it was not sufficient to rail at these unjust perceptions. In the end, Asian people themselves would have to assume responsibility for unmaking them. This was both a practical matter, he argued, and, in its own way, fair.

Aspiring Asian leaders had to become aware of "the relationship between values, behaviors, and perceptions." He offered the example of Asians who don't speak up at meetings. "So let's say I go to meetings with you and I notice you never say anything. And I ask myself, 'Hmm, I wonder why you're not saying anything. Maybe it's because you don't know what we're talking about. That would be a good reason for not saying anything. Or maybe it's because you're not even interested in the subject matter. Or maybe you think the conversation is beneath you.' So here I'm thinking, because you never say anything at meetings, that you're either dumb, you don't care, or you're arrogant. When maybe it's because you were taught when you were growing up that when the boss is talking, what are you supposed to be doing? Listening."

Takayasu took the weeklong course in 2006. One of the first exercises she encountered involved the group instructor asking for a list of some qualities that they identify with Asians. The students responded: upholding family honor, filial piety, self-restraint. Then the instructor solicited a list of the qualities the members identify with leadership, and invited the students to notice how little overlap there is between the two lists.

At first, Takayasu didn't relate to the others in attendance, who were listing typi-   45
cal Asian values their parents had taught them. "They were all saying things like 'Study hard,' 'Become a doctor or lawyer,' blah, blah, blah. That's not how my parents were. They would worry if they saw me working too hard." Takayasu had spent her childhood shuttling between New York and Tokyo. Her father was an executive at Mitsubishi; her mother was a concert pianist. She was highly assimilated into American culture, fluent in English, poised and confident. "But the more we got into it, as we moved away from the obvious things to the deeper, more fundamental values, I began to see that my upbringing had been very Asian after all. My parents would say, 'Don't create problems. Don't trouble other people.' How Asian is that? It helped to explain why I don't reach out to other people for help." It occurred to Takayasu that she was a little bit "heads down" after all. She was willing to take on difficult assignments without seeking credit for herself. She was reluctant to "toot her own horn."

Takayasu has put her new self-awareness to work at IBM, and she now exhibits a newfound ability for horn tooting. "The things I could write on my résumé as my team's accomplishments: They're really impressive," she says.

The law professor and writer Tim Wu grew up in Canada with a white mother and a Taiwanese father, which allows him an interesting perspective on how whites and Asians perceive each other. After graduating from law school, he took a series of clerkships, and he remembers the subtle ways in which hierarchies were developed among the other young lawyers. "There is this automatic assumption in any legal environment that Asians will have a particular talent for bitter labor," he says, and then goes on to define the word *coolie*, a Chinese term for "bitter labor." "There was this weird self-selection where the Asians would migrate toward the most brutal part of the labor."

By contrast, the white lawyers he encountered had a knack for portraying themselves as above all that. "White people have this instinct that is really important: to give off the impression that they're only going to do the really important work. You're a quarterback. It's a kind of arrogance that Asians are trained not to have. Someone told me not long after I moved to New York that in order to succeed, you have to understand which rules you're supposed to break. If you break the wrong rules, you're finished. And so the easiest thing to do is follow all the rules. But then you consign yourself to a lower status. The real trick is understanding what rules are not meant for you."

This idea of a kind of rule-governed rule-breaking—where the rule book was unwritten but passed along in an innate cultural sense—is perhaps the best explanation I have heard of how the Bamboo Ceiling functions in practice. LEAP appears to be very good at helping Asian workers who are already culturally competent become more self-aware of how their culture and appearance impose barriers to advancement. But I am not sure that a LEAP course is going to be enough to get Jefferson Mao or Daniel

Chu the respect and success they crave. The issue is more fundamental, the social dynamics at work more deeply embedded, and the remedial work required may be at a more basic level of comportment.

What if you missed out on the lessons in masculinity taught in the gyms and locker rooms of America's high schools? What if life has failed to make you a socially dominant alpha male who runs the American boardroom and prevails in the American bedroom? What if no one ever taught you how to greet white people and make them comfortable? What if, despite these deficiencies, you no longer possess an immigrant's dutiful forbearance for a secondary position in the American narrative and want to be a player in the scrimmage of American appetite right now, in the present?

How do you undo eighteen years of a Chinese upbringing?

This is the implicit question that J. T. Tran has posed to a roomful of Yale undergraduates at a master's tea at Silliman College. His answer is typically Asian: practice. Tran is a pickup artist who goes by the handle Asian Playboy. He travels the globe running "boot camps," mostly for Asian male students, in the art of attraction. Today, he has been invited to Yale by the Asian-American Students Alliance.

"Creepy can be fixed," Tran explains to the standing-room-only crowd. "Many guys just don't realize how to project themselves." These are the people whom Tran spends his days with, a new batch in a new city every week: nice guys, intelligent guys, motivated guys, who never figured out how to be successful with women. Their mothers had kept them at home to study rather than let them date or socialize. Now Tran's company, ABCs of Attraction, offers a remedial education that consists of three four-hour seminars, followed by a supervised night out "in the field," in which J. T., his assistant Gareth Jones, and a tall blonde wing-girl named Sarah force them to approach women. Tuition costs $1,450.

"One of the big things I see with Asian students is what I call the Asian poker face—the lack of range when it comes to facial expressions," Tran says. "How many times has this happened to you?" he asks the crowd. "You'll be out at a party with your white friends, and they will be like—'Dude, are you angry?'" Laughter fills the room. Part of it is psychological, he explains. He recalls one Korean-American student he was teaching. The student was a very dedicated schoolteacher who cared a lot about his students. But none of this was visible. "Sarah was trying to help him, and she was like, 'C'mon, smile, smile,' and he was like . . ."

> **"Sarah was trying to help him, and she was like, 'C'mon, smile, smile,' and he was like . . ." And here Tran mimes the unbearable tension of a face trying to contort itself into a simulacrum of mirth.**

And here Tran mimes the unbearable tension of a face trying to contort itself into a simulacrum of mirth. "He was so completely unpracticed at smiling that he literally could not do it." Eventually, though, the student fought through it, "and when he finally got to smiling he was, like, really cool."

Tran continues to lay out a story of Asian-American male distress that must be relevant to the lives of at least some of those who have packed Master Krauss's living room. The story he tells is one of Asian-American disadvantage in the sexual marketplace, a disadvantage that he has devoted his life to overturning. Yes, it is about picking up women. Yes, it is about picking up white women. Yes, it is about attracting those women whose hair is the color of the midday sun and eyes are the color of the ocean, and it is about having sex with them. He is not going to apologize for the images of blonde women plastered all over his website. This is what he prefers, what he stands for, and what he is selling: the courage to pursue anyone you want, and the skills to make the person you desire desire you back. White guys do what they want; he is going to do the same.

But it is about much more than this, too. It is about altering the perceptions of Asian men—perceptions that are rooted in the way they behave, which are in turn rooted in the way they were raised—through a course of behavior modification intended to teach them how to be the socially dominant figures that they are not perceived to be. It is a program of, as he puts it to me later, "social change through pickup."

Tran offers his own story as an exemplary Asian underdog. Short, not good-looking, socially inept, sexually null. "If I got a B, I would be whipped," he remembers of his childhood. After college, he worked as an aerospace engineer at Boeing and Raytheon, but internal politics disfavored him. Five years into his career, his entire white cohort had been promoted above him. "I knew I needed to learn about social dynamics, because just working hard wasn't cutting it."

His efforts at dating were likewise "a miserable failure." It was then that he turned to "the seduction community," a group of men on Internet message boards like alt .seduction.fast. It began as a "support group for losers" and later turned into a program of self-improvement. Was charisma something you could teach? Could confidence be reduced to a formula? Was it merely something that you either possessed or did not possess, as a function of the experiences you had been through in life, or did it emerge from specific forms of behavior? The members of the group turned their computer-science and engineering brains to the question. They wrote long accounts of their dates and subjected them to collective scrutiny. They searched for patterns in the raw material and filtered these experiences through social-psychological research. They eventually built a model.

This past Valentine's Day, during a weekend boot camp in New York City sponsored by ABCs of Attraction, the model is being played out. Tran and Jones are teaching their students how an alpha male stands (shoulders thrown back, neck fully extended, legs planted slightly wider than the shoulders). "This is going to feel very strange to you if you're used to slouching, but this is actually right," Jones says. They explain how an alpha male walks (no shuffling; pick your feet up entirely off the ground; a slight sway i the shoulders). They identify the proper distance to stand from "targets" (a slightly b nt arm's length). They explain the importance of "kino escalation." (You must touch h r. You must not be afraid to do this.) They are teaching the importance of sub-communication: what you convey about yourself before a single word has been spoken. They explain the importance of intonation. They explain what intonation is. "Your voice moves up and down in pitch to convey a variety of different emotions."

All of this is taught through a series of exercises. "This is going to feel completely artificial," says Jones on the first day of training. "But I need you to do the biggest shit-eating grin you've ever made in your life." Sarah is standing in the corner with her back to the students—three Indian guys, including one in a turban, three Chinese guys,   60 and one Cambodian. The students have to cross the room, walking as an alpha male walks, and then place their hands on her shoulder—firmly but gently—and turn her around. Big smile. Bigger than you've ever smiled before. Raise your glass in a toast. Make eye contact and hold it. Speak loudly and clearly. Take up space without apology. This is what an alpha male does.

Before each student crosses the floor of that bare white cubicle in midtown, Tran asks him a question. "What is good in life?" Tran shouts.

The student then replies, in the loudest, most emphatic voice he can muster: "To crush my enemies, see them driven before me, and to hear the lamentation of their women—in my bed!"

For the intonation exercise, students repeat the phrase "I do what I want" with a variety of different moods.

"Say it like you're happy!" Jones shouts. ("I do what I want.") Say it like you're sad! ("I do what I want." The intonation utterly unchanged.) Like you're sad! ("I . . . do what I want.") Say it like you've just won $5 million! ("I do what I want.")

Raj, a 26-year-old Indian virgin, can barely get his voice to alter during intona- 65 tion exercise. But on Sunday night, on the last evening of the boot camp, I watch him cold-approach a set of women at the Hotel Gansevoort and engage them in conversation for a half-hour. He does not manage to "number close" or "kiss close." But he had done something that not very many people can do.

Of the dozens of Asian-Americans I spoke with for this story, many were success-ful artists and scientists; or good-looking and socially integrated leaders; or tough, brassy, risk-taking, street-smart entrepreneurs. Of course, there are lots of such people around—do I even have to point that out? They are no more morally worthy than any other kind of Asian person. But they have figured out some useful things.

The lesson about the Bamboo Ceiling that James Hong learned from his inter-viewer at IBM stuck, and after working for a few years at Hewlett-Packard, he decided to strike off on his own. His first attempts at entrepreneurialism failed, but he finally struck pay dirt with a simple, not terribly refined idea that had a strong primal appeal: hotornot.com. Hong and his co-founder eventually sold the site for roughly $20 million.

Hong ran hotornot.com partly as a kind of incubator to seed in his employees the habits that had served him well. "We used to hire engineers from Berkeley—almost all Asian—who were on the cusp of being entrepreneurial but were instead headed toward jobs at big companies," he says. "We would train them in how to take risk, how to run things themselves. I remember encouraging one employee to read *The Game*—the infamous pickup-artist textbook—"because I figured growing the *cojones* to take risk was applicable to being an entrepreneur."

If the Bamboo Ceiling is ever going to break, it's probably going to have less to do with any form of behavior assimilation than with the emergence of risk-takers whose success obviates the need for Asians to meet someone else's behavioral standard. People like Steve Chen, who was one of the creators of YouTube, or Kai and Charles Huang, who created Guitar Hero. Or Tony Hsieh, the founder of Zappos.com, the on-line shoe retailer that he sold to Amazon for about a billion dollars in 2009. Hsieh is a short Asian man who speaks tersely and is devoid of obvious charisma. One cannot imagine him being promoted in an American corporation. And yet he has proved that an awkward Asian guy can be a formidable CEO and the unlikeliest of management gurus.

Hsieh didn't have to conform to Western standards of comportment because he adopted early on the Western value of risk-taking. Growing up, he would play recordings of himself in the morning practicing the violin, in lieu of actually practicing. He credits the experience he had running a pizza business at Harvard as more important than anything he learned in class. He had an instinctive sense of what the real world would require of him, and he knew that nothing his parents were teaching him would get him there. 70

You don't, by the way, have to be a Silicon Valley hotshot to break through the Bamboo Ceiling. You can also be a chef like Eddie Huang, whose little restaurant on the Lower East Side, BaoHaus, sells delicious pork buns. Huang grew up in Orlando with a hard-core Tiger Mom and a disciplinarian father. "As a kid, psychologically, my day was all about not getting my ass kicked," he says. He gravitated toward the black kids at school, who also knew something about corporal punishment. He was the smallest member of his football team, but his coach named him MVP in the seventh grade. "I was defensive tackle and right guard because I was just mean. I was nasty. I had this mentality where I was like, 'You're going to accept me or I'm going to fuck you up.'"

Huang had a rough twenties, bumping repeatedly against the Bamboo Ceiling. In college, editors at the Orlando *Sentinel* invited him to write about sports for the paper. But when he visited the offices, "the editor came in and goes, 'Oh, no.' And his exact words: 'You can't write with that face.'" Later, in film class at Columbia, he wrote a script about an Asian-American hot-dog vendor obsessed with his small penis. "The screenwriting teacher was like, 'I love this. You have a lot of Woody Allen in you. But do you think you could change it to Jewish characters?'" Still later, after graduating from Cardozo School of Law, he took a corporate job, where other associates would frequently say, "You have a lot of opinions for an Asian guy."

Finally, Huang decided to open a restaurant. Selling food was precisely the fate his parents wanted their son to avoid, and they didn't talk to him for months after he quit lawyering. But Huang understood instinctively that he couldn't make it work in the professional world his parents wanted him to join. "I've realized that food is one of the only places in America where we are the top dogs," he says. "Guys like David Chang or me—we can hang. There's a younger generation that grew up eating Chinese fast food. They respect our food. They may not respect anything else, but they respect our food."

Rather than strive to make himself acceptable to the world, Huang has chosen to buy his way back in, on his own terms. "What I've learned is that America is about money, and if you can make your culture commodifiable, then you're relevant," he says. "I don't believe anybody agrees with what I say or supports what I do because they truly want to love Asian people. They like my fucking pork buns, and I don't get it twisted."

Sometime during the hundreds of hours he spent among the mostly untouched English-language novels at the Flushing branch of the public library, Jefferson Mao discovered literature's special power of transcendence, a freedom of imagination that can 75 send you beyond the world's hierarchies. He had written to me seeking permission to swerve off the traditional path of professional striving—to devote himself to becoming an artist—but he was unsure of what risks he was willing to take. My answer was highly ambivalent. I recognized in him something of my own youthful ambition. And I knew where that had taken me.

Unlike Mao, I was not a poor, first-generation immigrant. I finished school alienated both from Asian culture (which, in my hometown, was barely visible) and the manners and mores of my white peers. But like Mao, I wanted to be an individual. I had refused both cultures as an act of self-assertion. An education spent dutifully acquiring credentials through relentless drilling seemed to me an obscenity. So did adopting the manipulative cheeriness that seemed to secure the popularity of white Americans.

Instead, I set about contriving to live beyond both poles. I wanted what James Baldwin sought as a writer—"a power which outlasts kingdoms." Anything short of that seemed a humiliating compromise. I would become an aristocrat of the spirit, who prides himself on his incompetence in the middling tasks that are the world's business. Who does not seek after material gain. Who is his own law.

This, of course, was madness. A child of Asian immigrants born into the suburbs of New Jersey and educated at Rutgers cannot be a law unto himself. The only way to approximate this is to refuse employment, because you will not be bossed around by people beneath you, and shave your expenses to the bone, because you cannot afford more, and move into a decaying Victorian mansion in Jersey City, so that your sense of eccentric distinction can be preserved in the midst of poverty, and cut yourself free of every form of bourgeois discipline, because these are precisely the habits that will keep you chained to the mediocre fate you consider worse than death.

Throughout my twenties, I proudly turned away from one institution of American life after another (for instance, a steady job), though they had already long since turned away from me. Academe seemed another kind of death—but then again, I had a transcript marred by as many F's as A's. I had come from a culture that was the middle path incarnate. And yet for some people, there can be no middle path, only transcendence or descent into the abyss.

I was descending into the abyss.

80

All this was well deserved. No one had any reason to think I was anything or anyone. And yet I felt entitled to demand this recognition. I knew this was wrong and impermissible; therefore I had to double down on it. The world brings low such people. It brought me low. I haven't had health insurance in ten years. I didn't earn more than $12,000 for eight consecutive years. I went three years in the prime of my adulthood without touching a woman. I did not produce a masterpiece.

I recall one of the strangest conversations I had in the city. A woman came up to me at a party and said she had been moved by a piece of writing I had published. She confessed that prior to reading it, she had never wanted to talk to me, and had always been sure, on the basis of what she could see from across the room that I was nobody worth talking to, that I was in fact someone to avoid.

But she had been wrong about this, she told me: It was now plain to her that I was a person with great reserves of feeling and insight. She did not ask my forgiveness for this brutal misjudgment. Instead, what she wanted to know was—why had I kept that person she had glimpsed in my essay so well hidden? She confessed something of her own hidden sorrow: She had never been beautiful and had decided, early on, that it therefore fell to her to "love the world twice as hard." Why hadn't I done that?

Here was a drunk white lady speaking what so many others over the years must have been insufficiently drunk to tell me. It was the key to many things that had, and had not, happened. I understood this encounter better after learning about LEAP, and visiting Asian Playboy's boot camp. If you are a woman who isn't beautiful, it is a social reality that you will have to work twice as hard to hold anyone's attention. You can either linger on the unfairness of this or you can get with the program. If you are an Asian person who holds himself proudly aloof, nobody will respect that, or find it intriguing, or wonder if that challenging façade hides someone worth getting to know. They will simply write you off as someone not worth the trouble of talking to.

Having glimpsed just how unacceptable the world judges my demeanor, could I too strive to make up for my shortcomings? Practice a shit-eating grin until it becomes natural? Love the world twice as hard? 85

I see the appeal of getting with the program. But this is not my choice. Striving to meet others' expectations may be a necessary cost of assimilation, but I am not going to do it.

Often I think my defiance is just delusional, self-glorifying bullshit that artists have always told themselves to compensate for their poverty and powerlessness. But sometimes I think it's the only thing that has preserved me intact, and that what has been preserved is not just haughty caprice but in fact the meaning of my life. So this is what I told Mao: In lieu of loving the world twice as hard, I care, in the end, about expressing my obdurate singularity at any cost. I love this hard and unyielding part of myself more than any other reward the world has to offer a newly brightened and ingratiating demeanor, and I will bear any costs associated with it.

The first step toward self-reform is to admit your deficiencies. Though my early adulthood has been a protracted education in them, I do not admit mine. I'm fine. It's the rest of you who have a problem. Fuck all y'all.

Amy Chua returned to Yale from a long, exhausting book tour in which one television interviewer had led off by noting that Internet commenters were calling her a monster. By that point, she had become practiced at the special kind of self-presentation required of a person under public siege. "I do not think that Chinese parents are superior," she declared at the annual gathering of the Asian-American Students Alliance. "I think there are many ways to be a good parent."

Much of her talk to the students, and indeed much of the conversation surrounding the book, was focused on her own parenting decisions. But just as interesting is how her parents parented her. Chua was plainly the product of a brute-force Chinese education. *Battle Hymn of the Tiger Mother* includes many lessons she was taught by her parents—lessons any LEAP student would recognize. "Be modest, be humble, be simple," her mother told her. "Never complain or make excuses," her father instructed. "If something seems unfair at school, just prove yourself by working twice as hard and being twice as good." 90

In the book, Chua portrays her distaste for corporate law, which she practiced before going into academe. "My entire three years at the firm, I always felt like I was playacting, ridiculous in my suit," she writes. This malaise extended even earlier, to her time as a student. "I didn't care about the rights of criminals the way others did, and I froze whenever a professor called on me. I also wasn't naturally skeptical and questioning; I just wanted to write down everything the professor said and memorize it."

At the AASA gathering at Yale, Chua made the connection between her upbringing and her adult dissatisfaction. "My parents didn't sit around talking about politics and philosophy at the dinner table," she told the students. Even after she had escaped from corporate law and made it onto a law faculty, "I was kind of lost. I just didn't feel the passion." Eventually, she made a name for herself as the author of popular books about foreign policy and became an award-winning teacher. But it's plain that she was no better prepared for legal scholarship than she had been for corporate law. "It took me a long, long time," she said. "And I went through lots and lots of rejection." She recalled her extended search for an academic post, in which she was "just not able to do a good interview, just not able to present myself well."

In other words, *Battle Hymn* provides all the material needed to refute the very cultural polemic for which it was made to stand. Chua's Chinese education had gotten her through an elite schooling, but it left her unprepared for the real world. She does not hide any of this. She had set out, she explained, to write a memoir that was "defiantly self-incriminating"—and the result was a messy jumble of conflicting impulses, part provocation, part self-critique. Western readers rode roughshod over this paradox and made of Chua a kind of Asian minstrel figure. But more than anything else, *Battle Hymn* is a very American project—one no traditional Chinese person would think to undertake. "Even if you hate the book," Chua pointed out, "the one thing it is not is meek."

"The loudest duck gets shot" is a Chinese proverb. "The nail that sticks out gets hammered down" is a Japanese one. Its Western correlative: "The squeaky wheel gets the grease." Chua had told her story and been hammered down. Yet here she was, fresh from her hammering, completely unbowed.

There is something salutary in that proud defiance. And though the debate she sparked about Asian-American life has been of questionable value, we will need more people with the same kind of defiance, willing to push themselves into the spotlight and to make some noise, to beat people up, to seduce women, to make mistakes, to become entrepreneurs, to stop doggedly pursuing official paper emblems attesting to their worthiness, to stop thinking those scraps of paper will secure anyone's happiness, and to dare to be interesting. 95

Exploring Context

1. The popular TV show *Glee* had an episode called "Asian F." Watch a clip of this episode on YouTube and read the comments left in response. How do this clip and viewer reactions reflect the issues that Yang discusses in his essay?

2. In some ways, Yang's essay is a response to Amy Chua's book *Battle Hymn of the Tiger Mother*, in which she discusses a set of culturally inflected parenting techniques that are packed into the term *Tiger Mom*. Visit Tiger Mom Says (tigermomsays.tumblr.com). How do the images there reflect the themes of Yang's essay?

3. Review the Ivy League college acceptance rates as represented by Bradshaw College Consulting, a company that specializes in helping students get into universities (bradshawcollegeconsulting.com/college_acceptance_rate.html). How do these

acceptance rates confirm or complicate Yang's argument? What does the existence of companies such as Bradshaw College Consulting suggest about the claims Yang makes?

Questions for Connecting

1. In "The End of Race: Hawaii and the Mixing of Peoples" (p. 300), Steve Olson suggests that race no longer has any genetic basis even though the notion of race (and the ramifications of it) continues to exist. How does Yang contribute to Olson's argument? Synthesize both authors to consider why race is persistent. Can it ever be possible for us to move beyond the idea of race? Use both authors to support your position.

2. Kenji Yoshino, an Asian American himself, talks about the ways we tend to downplay part of our identity—a process he calls "covering" in "Preface" and "The New Civil Rights" (p. 539). What response does Yang offer to Yoshino's concept of covering? Given Yang's argument, what are the possibilities of achieving Yoshino's goals for civil rights?

3. In part, Yang is concerned with exploring the realities behind the stereotypes of Asian Americans. Jennifer Pozner's "Ghetto Bitches, China Dolls, and Cha Cha Divas" (p. 359) examines how racial stereotypes play out in popular media, specifically the television show *America's Next Top Model*. In what ways does Yang confirm Pozner's argument? Synthesize the arguments of both authors to form a statement about the impact of racial stereotypes on individuals and on society.

Language Matters

1. At the start of this selection, Yang uses several sentence fragments (see if you can find them). Why does Yang use these? In what situations might a sentence fragment be acceptable? In what ways does intentional use of sentence fragments rely on an understanding of context and audience? When, if ever, should fragments be used in academic writing?

2. Quotations in academic writing must be of appropriate length. Find a significant passage from the essay and choose the shortest and longest useful quotations from the passage. How short is too short? How long is too long? How might you use quotations of different lengths for different ends?

3. The classic rhetorical triangle is composed of receiver, sender, and message. Using this essay, design a new shape to explain its rhetorical situation: What additional elements should be considered? Would the inclusion of style make a rhetorical square? What elements would be included in a rhetorical hexagon?

Assignments for Writing

1. Yang's essay is centrally concerned with the relationship between stereotypes and the realities behind them. Write a paper on the impact of stereotypes on individuals. In what ways are stereotypes enabling? Can there be positive stereotypes? Is it possible to get rid of stereotypes?

2. How can Asian Americans break through the "Bamboo Ceiling"? Write a paper in which you propose strategies for overcoming this limitation, building on the strategies discussed in Yang's essay and incorporating your work from Question 3 of Questions for Critical Reading.

3. Both education and upbringing play important roles in the lives of the people Yang discusses in his essay. How do these factors interact to shape a person's future? Write a paper in which you discuss the roles of education and parenting in the shaping of an individual. Is it possible to escape these influences? To what end? How does Yang challenge either or both?

KENJI YOSHINO

Kenji Yoshino is the Chief Justice Earl Warren Professor of Constitutional Law at New York University. Previously, Yoshino was
a professor of law and the deputy dean of intellectual life at Yale
Law School, where he earned a J.D. after graduating from Harvard and Oxford Universities. His articles have appeared in various law journals as well as the *New York Times*, the *Village Voice*,
the *Boston Globe*, and the *Nation*. He is the author of *Covering: The
Hidden Assault on Our Civil Rights* (2006), *A Thousand Times More
Fair: What Shakespeare's Plays Teach Us about Justice* (2011), and
Speak Now: Marriage Equality on Trial (2015).

Courtesy of Kenji Yoshino,
photo by Chris Macke

Covering offers a unique perspective on the familiar concepts of assimilation and passing, utilizing Yoshino's background
experience as both a law scholar and a gay Asian American.
Yoshino combines personal narrative and legal argument to lay
out a new definition of civil rights. The term *covering*, as Yoshino
uses it, means "to tone down a disfavored identity to fit into the
mainstream" (p. 539), and Yoshino argues that though Americans
value the idea of the melting pot as a model for our culture, that
ideal can have unintended negative consequences. Despite our
avowed appreciation for multiculturalism, the unstated public
expectation is still for people of all genders, sexual orientations,
and races to conform to rigid expectations.

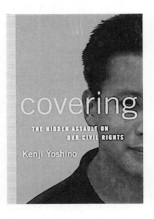

The selections here, "Preface" and "The New Civil Rights," form something close to a set
of bookends for Yoshino's argument in *Covering*. After defining the concept of covering and
the problems caused by it in the "Preface" and investigating the issue of a distinct "True Self"
and "False Self" in the second excerpt, Yoshino moves on to propose a new paradigm for civil
rights. Questioning the idea of legislating civil rights, Yoshino suggests that the next step may
have to occur in bars, restaurants, and Internet chat rooms; he also suggests that in order to
accommodate an increasingly diverse population, the model of civil rights itself must change.
Yoshino points the way by helping us to rethink our model of civil rights and the mechanisms
used to bring those rights into existence.

The United States is more diverse than ever. How can we balance the rights of diverse
groups with the demands of individuals and the nation?

▶ TAGS: *civil rights, community, conversation, identity, law and justice, politics, race and
ethnicity, social change*

▶ CONNECTIONS: *Appiah, Duhigg, Epstein, O'Connor, Olson, Southan, Watters, Yang*

Questions for Critical Reading

1. What does Yoshino mean by the *"new" civil rights?* Define the term as you read by locating passages from his text. What makes it new? How does it differ from "old" civil rights? Use Yoshino's text to define *liberty* and *equality paradigms* as part of your response.

2. What is *covering*? Define the concept using Yoshino's text and then offer your own example.

3. How does Yoshino think we can achieve the new civil rights? Identify passages that show his position, and then respond to it. Do you think his vision is possible? Is it something we should strive for? To prepare for your response, read Yoshino's text critically to locate points of connection between his position and yours.

Preface

Everyone covers. To cover is to tone down a disfavored identity to fit into the mainstream. In our increasingly diverse society, all of us are outside the mainstream in some way. Nonetheless, being deemed mainstream is still often a necessity of social life. For this reason, every reader of this book has covered, whether consciously or not, and sometimes at significant personal cost.

Famous examples of covering abound. Ramón Estévez covered his ethnicity when he changed his name to Martin Sheen, as did Krishna Bhanji when he changed his name to Ben Kingsley. Margaret Thatcher covered her status as a woman when she trained with a voice coach to lower the timbre of her voice. Long after they came out as lesbians, Rosie O'Donnell and Mary Cheney still covered, keeping their same-sex partners out of the public eye. Issur Danielovitch Demsky covered his Judaism when he became Kirk Douglas, as did Joseph Levitch when he became Jerry Lewis. Franklin Delano Roosevelt covered his disability by ensuring his wheelchair was always hidden behind a desk before his Cabinet entered.

I doubt any of these people covered willingly. I suspect they were all bowing to an unjust reality that required them to tone down their stigmatized identities to get along in life. Sheen says he needed to "get a name people could pronounce and connect with" if he "wanted to work commercially." Yet he now regrets having done so, and has exhorted his sons—Emilio and Charlie—to use the family name. One of them has not done so, signaling the enduring force of the covering demand.

In a supposedly enlightened age, the persistence of the covering demand presents a puzzle. Today, race, national origin, sex, religion, and disability are all protected by federal civil rights laws. An increasing number of states and localities include sexual orientation in civil rights laws as well. Albeit with varying degrees of conviction, Americans have come to a consensus that people should not be penalized for being different along these dimensions. That consensus, however, does not protect individuals against demands that they mute those differences. We need an explanation for why the civil rights revolution has stalled on covering.

Covering has enjoyed such a robust and stubborn life because it is a form of as-   5
similation. At least since Hector St. John de Crèvecoeur's 1782 *Letters from an American
Farmer,* this country has touted assimilation as the way Americans of different backgrounds would be "melted into a new race of men." By the time Israel Zangwill's play
of that name was performed in 1908, the "melting pot" had acquired the burnish of
an American ideal. Only with the civil rights movement of the 1960s was this ideal
challenged in any systematic way, with calls to move "beyond the melting pot" and to
"celebrate diversity." And notwithstanding that challenge, assimilation has never lost
its hold on the American imagination. Indeed, as our country grows more pluralistic,
we have seen a renaissance of the melting pot ideal. Fearful that we are spinning apart
into balkanized groups, even liberals like Arthur Schlesinger have called for a recom-
mitment to that ethic. In the United States, as in other industrialized democracies, we
are seeing the "return of assimilation."

I recognize the value of assimilation, which is often necessary to fluid social interaction, to peaceful coexistence, and even to the dialogue through which difference is valued.
For that reason, this is no simple screed against conformity. What I urge here is that we
approach the renaissance of assimilation in this country critically. We must be willing to
see the dark side of assimilation, and specifically of covering, which is the most widespread
form of assimilation required of us today.

Covering is a hidden assault on our civil rights. We have not been able to see it as
such because it has swaddled itself in the benign language of assimilation. But if we look
closely, we will see that covering is the way many groups are being held back today. The
reason racial minorities are pressured to "act white" is because of white supremacy.
The reason women are told to downplay their child-care responsibilities in the workplace is because of patriarchy. And the reason gays are asked not to "flaunt" is because
of homophobia. So long as such covering demands persist, American civil rights will
not have completed its work.

Unfortunately, the law has yet to perceive covering as a threat. Contemporary civil
rights law generally only protects traits that individuals cannot change, like their skin
color, chromosomes, or innate sexual orientations. This means that current law will
not protect us against most covering demands, because such demands direct themselves at the behavioral aspects of our personhood. This is so despite the fact that covering imposes costs on us all.

The universality of the covering demand, however, is also a potential boon for civil
rights advocates. I, too, worry about our current practice of fracturing into groups,
each clamoring for state and social solici-
tude. For this reason, I do not think we can   **We must instead build a new**
move forward by focusing on old-fashioned   **civil rights paradigm on what**
group-based identity politics. We must in-   **draws us together rather than**
stead build a new civil rights paradigm on   **on what drives us apart.**
what draws us together rather than on what
drives us apart. Because covering applies to us all, it provides an issue around which we
can make common cause. This is the desire for authenticity, our common human wish
to express ourselves without being impeded by unreasoning demands for conformity.

I thought I would make this argument in purely political terms. As a law professor,   10
I have become accustomed to the tones of legal impersonality. But I came to see that I

could not compose an argument about the importance of human authenticity without risking such authenticity myself. So I have written this . . . in a more intimate voice, blending memoir with argument. In trying to make the stakes of assimilation vivid, I draw on my attempts to elaborate my identity as a gay man, and, to a lesser extent, my identity as an Asian-American.

Yet this is not a standard "coming out" narrative or racial memoir. I follow the Romantics here in their belief that if a human life is described with enough particularity, the universal will begin to speak through it. What interests me about my story, and the stories of others, is how similar they are in revealing the bones of our common human endeavor, the yearning for human emancipation that stirs within us all.

The New Civil Rights

To describe the new civil rights, I return to the source of my argument. What most excited me about gay civil rights was its universal resonance. Unlike other civil rights groups, gays must articulate invisible selves without the initial support of our immediate communities. That makes the gay project of self-elaboration emblematic of the search for authenticity all of us engage in as human beings. It is work each of us must do for ourselves, and it is the most important work we can do.

In looking for a vocabulary for this quest for authenticity, I found psychoanalysts more helpful than lawyers. The object-relations theorist D. W. Winnicott makes a distinction between a True Self and a False Self that usefully tracks the distinction between the uncovered and covered selves. The True Self is the self that gives an individual the feeling of being real, which is "more than existing; it is finding a way to exist as oneself, and to relate to objects as oneself, and to have a self into which to retreat for relaxation." The True Self is associated with human spontaneity and authenticity: "Only the True Self can be creative and only the True Self can feel real." The False Self, in contrast, gives an individual a sense of being unreal, a sense of futility. It mediates the relationship between the True Self and the world.

What I love about Winnicott is that he does not demonize the False Self. To the contrary, Winnicott believes the False Self protects the True Self: "The False Self has one positive and very important function: to hide the True Self, which it does by compliance with environmental demands." Like a king castling behind a rook in chess, the more valuable but less powerful piece retreats behind the less valuable but more powerful one. Because the relationship between the True Self and the False Self is symbiotic, Winnicott believes both selves will exist even in the healthy individual.

Nonetheless, Winnicott defines health according to the degree of ascendancy the True Self gains over the False one. At the negative extreme, the False Self completely obscures the True Self, perhaps even from the individual herself. In a less extreme case, the False Self permits the True Self "a secret life." The individual approaches health only when the False Self has "as its main concern a search for conditions which will make it possible for the True Self to come into its own." Finally, in the healthy individual, the False Self is reduced to a "polite and mannered social attitude," a tool available to the fully realized True Self.

15

This paradigm captures my coming-out experience. My gay self, the True Self, was hidden behind an ostensibly straight False Self. Yet it would be wrong to cast the closeted self as purely inimical to the gay one. In my adolescence, this False Self protected the True Self until its survival was assured. Only at this point did the False Self switch from being a help to being a hindrance. And even after I came out, the False Self never disappeared. It was reduced to the minimum necessary to regulate relations between the True Self and the world.

I could slot other civil rights identities into Winnicott's paradigm. The importance of the paradigm, however, lies in its self-conscious universality. Winnicott posits that each of us has a True Self that must be expressed for us to have the feeling of being switched on, of being alive. And if the True Self embodies the importance of authenticity, the False Self embodies our ambivalence about assimilation, which is both necessary to survival and obstructive of life. The goal is not to eliminate assimilation altogether, but to reduce it to the necessary minimum. This is what the reason-forcing conversation seeks to do.

When I describe the uncovered self in Winnicott's terms, many people respond immediately with stories that attest to the concept's universality. Most of these have little to do with conventional civil rights categories. They often pertain to choices about people's careers or personal lives, like the woman who left a career in law to write plays, or the man who left his fiancée at the altar to pursue his first childhood love. I nonetheless hear the same themes threading through these stories as I do through the traditional civil rights cases. These individuals cannot articulate what authenticity is, but know an existence lived outside its imperative would be a substitute for life.

Parents often respond to the concept of the True Self by speaking of their children. Based on extensive clinical research, psychologist Carol Gilligan argues that children have an authentic voice they lose as they mature, with girls retaining it longer than boys. (The breaking of this emotional voice mirrors the breaking of the physical voice, as the voices of boys break earlier and more dramatically than those of girls.) Gilligan's work is replete with instances of parents awed by the directness and realness of their children. These parents suggest that one of the most agonizing dilemmas of parenting is how much they should require their children to cover in the world.

This psychological discourse about authentic selves sounds distant from current 20 civil rights discourse. We must close that gap. The new civil rights must harness this universal impulse toward authenticity. That impulse should press us toward thinking of civil rights less in terms of groups than in terms of our common humanity.

Two recent cases show that the Supreme Court is sympathetic to that shift. In the 2003 case of *Lawrence v. Texas* . . . the Supreme Court struck down a Texas statute that criminalized same-sex sodomy. Many assumed the Court would use this case to decide whether to give gays the judicial protections currently accorded to racial minorities and women. But while the Court struck down the statute (and overruled *Bowers v. Hardwick* in the process), it did not do so based on the equality rights of gays. Rather, it held that the statute violated the fundamental right of all persons—straight, gay, or otherwise—to control our intimate sexual relations.

Similarly, in the 2004 case of *Tennessee v. Lane*, the Supreme Court considered the question of whether two paraplegic individuals could sue Tennessee for failing to make its courthouses wheelchair accessible. (One plaintiff was forced to crawl up the courthouse steps to answer criminal charges against him; the other, a certified court reporter, alleged she had lost job opportunities because some county courthouses were inaccessible.) Again, the Court ruled in favor of the minority group without framing its ruling in group-based equality rhetoric. Rather, it held that all persons—disabled or otherwise—have a "right of access to the courts," which had been denied in this case.

In an era when the Supreme Court has closed many civil rights doors, it has left this one wide open. It is much more sympathetic to "liberty" claims about freedoms we all hold than to "equality" claims asserted by a subset of the population. It is easy to see why. Equality claims—such as group-based accommodation claims—inevitably involve the Court in picking favorites among groups. In an increasingly pluralistic society, the Court understandably wishes to steer clear of that enterprise. Liberty claims, on the other hand, emphasize what all Americans (or more precisely, all persons within the jurisdiction of the United States) have in common. The claim that we all have a right to sexual intimacy, or that we all have a right to access the courts, will hold no matter how many new groups proliferate in this country.

The Supreme Court's shift toward a more universal register can also be seen in its nascent acceptance of human rights. I worked on a friend-of-the-court brief in the *Lawrence* case produced by a team centered at Yale Law School. With the former President of Ireland and U.N. High Commissioner Mary Robinson as our client, we argued that decisions by international tribunals and courts in other Western democracies had recognized the fundamentality of the right to adult consensual sexual intimacy. We knew this argument would be resisted by some justices on the Court, who do not take kindly to arguments that decisions outside the United States should guide their jurisprudence. But to our surprise, the majority opinion cited our brief for the proposition that *Bowers* violated "values we share with a wider civilization."

At the end of their lives, both Martin Luther King Jr. and Malcolm X argued for   25
this transition from civil rights to human rights. Both believed that civil rights unduly focused on what distinguished individuals from one another, rather than emphasizing what they had in common. As Stewart Burns, one of the editors of the King papers at Stanford, observes, King "grasped that 'civil rights' carried too much baggage of the dominant tradition of American individualism and not enough counterweight from a tradition of communitarian impulses, collective striving, and common good." Similarly, Malcolm X exhorted Americans to "expand the civil-rights struggle to the level of human rights," so that the "jurisdiction of Uncle Sam" would not prevent us from allying with our "brothers" of other nations.

The universal rights of persons will probably be the way the Court will protect difference in the future. I predict that if the Court ever recognizes language rights, it will protect them as a liberty to which we are all entitled, rather than as an equality right attached to a particular national-origin group. And if the Court recognizes rights to grooming, such as the right to wear cornrows or not to wear makeup, I believe it will do so under something more akin to the German Constitution's right to personality rather than as a right attached to groups like racial minorities or women.

One of the great benefits of analyzing civil rights in terms of universal liberty rather than in terms of group-based equality is that it avoids making assumptions about group cultures. I've touched on the problem that the covering concept might assume too quickly that individuals behaving in "mainstream" ways are hiding some true identity, when in fact they might just be "being themselves." A female colleague of mine gave me a powerful version of this critique: "Here is what I dislike about your project. When I do something stereotypically masculine—like fixing my bike—your project makes it more likely people will think I'm putting on a gender performance rather than accepting the most straightforward explanation for what I'm doing. I don't fix my bike because I'm trying to downplay the fact that I'm a woman. I fix it because it's broken."

She gave another example: "When I was in graduate school, there was an African-American man who studied German Romantic poetry. Under your model, I could easily see someone saying he was 'covering' his African-American identity by studying something so esoteric and highbrow. But it was clear to me he was studying Romantic poetry because he was seized by it. And if someone had assumed he was studying it to 'act white,' they would have diminished him as a human being."

The coup de grâce: "Your commitment is to help people 'be themselves'—to resist demands to conform that take away their ability to be the individuals they are. But the covering idea could perpetuate the stereotypes you want to eliminate. One way minorities break stereotypes is by acting against them. If every time they do so, people assume they are 'covering' some essential stereotypical identity, the stereotypes will never go away."

I have literally lost sleep over this criticism. But in my waking hours, I take it more 30 as a caution than as a wholesale indictment. I agree that we must not assume that individuals behaving in "mainstream" ways are necessarily covering. My ultimate commitment is to autonomy as a means of achieving authenticity, rather than to a fixed conception of what authenticity might be. (Here I follow Winnicott, who observes the

> **I have literally lost sleep over this criticism.**

True Self is not susceptible to specific definition, as its nature differs for each of us.) In talking about classic civil rights groups, I have focused on the demand to conform to the mainstream because I think that for most groups (except women) these are the demands that most threaten our authenticity. But I am equally opposed to demands that individuals reverse cover, because such demands are also impingements on our autonomy, and therefore on our authenticity.

In practice, I expect the liberty paradigm to protect the authentic self better than the equality paradigm. While it need not do so, the equality paradigm is prone to essentializing the identities it protects. Under an equality paradigm, if a woman who wore a lot of makeup were protected by a court because makeup is an "essential" part of being a woman, this could reinforce the stereotype that women wear makeup. But if the same woman were given the liberty right to elaborate her own gender identity in ways that did not impinge on her job performance, she would be protected from demands to be either more "masculine" or more "feminine." Marsha Wislocki-Goin would be protected for wearing "too much makeup" and Darlene Jespersen would be protected for not wearing it at all. Each woman would then have the full panoply of options from which she could fashion her gender identity. And in protecting that range, the law would not articulate any presupposition about what an "authentic" or "essential" woman would look like. Authenticity would be something these women, and not the state or employer, would find for themselves.

Group-based identity politics is not dead. As I have argued, I still believe in a group-based accommodation model for existing civil rights groups. This is in part because I believe we have made a commitment to those groups to protect them from such covering demands. The statutory language of the Civil Rights Act and the Americans with Disabilities Act already protects racial minorities, religious minorities, women, and individuals with disabilities *as groups* against covering demands. It has been the courts that have erroneously limited the ambit of those protections. Such a group-based equality paradigm is completely consistent with the individual liberty paradigm. In fact, the equality and liberty strands of antidiscrimination law are inextricably intertwined.

Moreover, even if we shift the focus of civil rights law away from equality to liberty, identity politics will still be crucial. If it weren't for the gay rights movement, or the disability rights movement, cases like *Lawrence* or *Lane* would never have made it to the Court. But I'm sympathetic to the Court's desire to frame these cases not as "gay" or "disability" cases, but as cases touching on rights that, like a rising tide, will lift the boat of every person in America. Ironically, it may be the explosion of diversity in this country that will finally make us realize what we have in common. Multiculturalism has forced us to vary and vary the human being in the imagination until we discover what is invariable about her.

While I have great hopes for this new legal paradigm, I also believe law will be a relatively trivial part of the new civil rights. A doctor friend told me that in his first year of medical school, his dean described how doctors were powerless to cure the vast majority of human ills. People would get better, or they would not, but it would not be doctors who would cure them. Part of becoming a doctor, the dean said, was to surrender a layperson's awe for medical authority. I wished then that someone would give an analogous lecture to law students, and to Americans at large. My education in law has been in part an education in its limitations.

For starters, many covering demands are made by actors the law does not — and in my view should not — hold accountable, such as friends, family, neighbors, or people themselves. When I hesitate before engaging in a public display of same-sex affection, I am not thinking of the state or my employer, but of the strangers around me and my own internal censor. And while I am often tempted to sue myself, this is not my healthiest impulse.

Law is also an incomplete solution to coerced assimilation because it has yet to recognize the myriad groups subjected to covering demands outside traditional civil rights classifications like race, sex, orientation, religion, and disability. Whenever I speak about covering, I receive new instances of identities that can be covered. This is Winnicott's point — each one of us has a False Self that hides a True one. The law may someday move to protect some of these identities. But it will never protect them all.

Most important, law is incomplete in the qualitative remedies it provides. I confronted this recently when I became a plaintiff in a lawsuit against the Department of Defense. Under a congressional statute called the Solomon Amendment, the department threatened to cut off $350 million of federal funding from Yale University if the law school did not exempt the military from the law school's policy of protecting gays against discrimination by employers. Our suit argues that the statute is unconstitutional. I believe in this lawsuit, and was heartened that the vast majority of my law school colleagues signed on as plaintiffs. I was also elated when the district court judge, Judge Janet Hall, granted summary judgment in our favor. (As the government has taken

35

an appeal, the case is still pending.) But there is nothing like being a plaintiff to realize that lawsuits occur between people who have no better way of talking to each other.

When I think about the elaboration of my gay identity, I am grateful to see litigation has had little to do with it. The department is the only entity I have ever wanted to sue. Even when I encountered demands for assimilation, my best response was to draw my interlocutor into a conversation. Just as important, framing the project of self-elaboration in purely legal—and therefore adversarial—terms would fail to honor all those who were not adversaries. I have described in these pages many individuals who helped me toward myself. But there were many more. I think here of my law professor Charles Reich, who wrote a memoir about coming out in 1976, when it was an act of real courage to do so, and who let me write the essay that begins this book in his class, though its relationship to the law was then entirely unclear. I think of the chair of my midtenure review committee, who sat me down when I was the only untenured member of the faculty and, unsurprisingly, a mass of nerves, to give me the verdict of the committee. He told me his only advice for the coming years was that I should be more myself, that instead of reasoning within the law as it existed, I should speak my truth and make the law shape itself around me. And I think of my parents, whose response to this manuscript was to say, with calm and conviction, that they were proud of the man I have become.

For these reasons, I am troubled that Americans seem increasingly to turn toward the law to do the work of civil rights precisely when they should be turning away from it. The real solution lies in all of us as citizens, not in the tiny subset of us who are lawyers. People who are not lawyers should have reason-forcing conversations outside the law. They should pull Goffman's term "covering" out of academic obscurity and press it into the popular lexicon, so that it has the same currency as terms like "passing" or "the closet." People confronted with demands to cover should feel emboldened to seek a reason for that demand, even if the law does not reach the actors making the demand, or recognize the group burdened by it. These reason-forcing conversations should happen outside courtrooms—in workplaces and restaurants, schools and playgrounds, chat rooms and living rooms, public squares and bars. They should occur informally and intimately, where tolerance is made and unmade.

What will constitute a good enough reason to justify assimilation will obviously   40
be controversial. But I want to underscore that we have come to some consensus that certain reasons are illegitimate—like white supremacy, patriarchy, homophobia, religious intolerance, and animus toward the disabled. I ask us to be true to the commitments we have made by never accepting such biases as legitimate grounds for covering demands. Beyond that, I have sought to engender a series of conversations, rather than a series of results—what reasons count, and for what purposes, will be for us to decide by facing one another as individuals. My personal inclination is always to privilege the claims of the individual against countervailing interests like "neatness" or "workplace harmony." But we should have that conversation.

Such conversations are the best—and perhaps the only—way to give both assimilation and authenticity their proper due. These conversations will help us chart and stay the course between the monocultural America suggested by conservative alarmists and the balkanized America suggested by the radical multiculturalists. They will reveal the true dimension of civil rights. The aspiration of civil rights has always been to permit people to pursue their human flourishing without limitations based on bias. Focusing on law prevents us from seeing the revolutionary breadth of that aspiration, as law has limited civil rights to particular groups. I am not faulting that limitation, as I think prioritization is necessary, and that the law's priorities are correct. But civil rights, which has always extended far beyond the law, may now need to do so more than ever. It is only when we leave the law that civil rights suddenly stops being about particular groups and starts to become a project of human flourishing in which we all have a stake.

We must use the relative freedom of adulthood to integrate the many selves we hold. This includes uncovering the selves we buried long ago because they were inconvenient, impractical, or even hated. Because they must pass the test of survival, most of the selves we hold, like most of our lives, are ordinary. Yet sometimes, what is consequential in us begins to shine.

Exploring Context

1. Explore the Web site for the U.S. Commission on Civil Rights (usccr.gov). Which paradigm does it reflect, *liberty* or *equality*? Use your definition of these terms from Question 1 of Questions for Critical Reading.

2. Yoshino uses recent Supreme Court decisions to make his argument. Visit the Web site for the Supreme Court at supremecourtus.gov. What recent cases have concerned civil rights? What impact do these cases (or the lack of such cases) have on Yoshino's argument?

3. According to Yoshino, changes in civil rights should come not from legislation but through conversation. Search Internet blogs and forums for "civil rights" and related terms. Are people talking about these issues online? What does this say about Yoshino's argument? Connect your exploration to your response to Question 3 of Questions for Critical Reading.

Questions for Connecting

1. Kwame Anthony Appiah also extols the power of conversation in "Making Conversation" and "The Primacy of Practice" (p. 44). Place his ideas in conversation with Yoshino's essay, synthesizing the authors' ideas about the power of conversation. Is Yoshino also calling for cosmopolitanism? How do civil rights function like other social practices?

2. Yoshino discusses some of the social costs of covering but how do the pressures of cultural assimilation contribute to other forms of trauma? Expand Yoshino's ideas about covering using Sarah Stillman's "Hiroshima and the Inheritance of Trauma" (p. 443). What role does covering play in Shoji's trauma, both within her culture and within a larger American context? Your work with covering in Question 2 of Questions for Critical Reading might be a good place to start.

3. Francis Fukuyama argues for the necessity of a concept of human dignity in his essay of the same name (p. 143). What role might human dignity play in civil rights? Is Factor X an essential component of a new civil rights? Synthesize the ideas of Fukuyama and Yoshino into an argument about human rights.

Language Matters

1. Every part of speech and every punctuation mark has certain "rights"; for example, the period has the right to end a sentence and the comma does not. How can we describe the rules of grammar using Yoshino's ideas of liberty and equality paradigms?

2. Defining terms is an important part of academic writing. Locate a passage where Yoshino defines a term. What strategies does he use? Does he offer a dictionary definition? An example? An authority? How should you define terms in your own text?

3. Is there a form of covering that takes place in peer revision? Are people tempted to tone down unfavorable comments? How does Yoshino's discussion of covering offer advice for more effective peer revision?

Assignments for Writing

1. Yoshino discusses the concept of groups and individuals covering in order to conform to the mainstream. Locate your own example of covering and then write an essay that extends or complicates Yoshino's argument through your example. Does your example reinforce or refute Yoshino's ideas about covering? Are any civil rights at stake in your example? What relation is there between covering and civil rights? You will want to use your definition of the term *covering* from Question 2 of Questions for Critical Reading.

2. Yoshino discusses the challenges to civil rights posed by the proliferation of groups engendered by a diverse society; he offers his own vision of how to transform civil rights to account for these groups. Write a paper in which you suggest what changes we should make to civil rights and how we might achieve those changes. Draw on your work in Questions for Critical Reading and Questions for Connecting in making your argument. Consider, too: Should we use a liberty paradigm or an equality paradigm? Would you propose a different paradigm of your own? Is legislation the best way to achieve your vision for civil rights? Is conversation?

3. In response to Question 3 of Exploring Context, you examined current online conversations about civil rights. Yoshino suggests that such conversations are the best means of achieving a new civil rights. Write a paper in which you argue for the role of conversation in social change. Is talking about an issue enough to engender change? Does it matter who is doing the talking? How does change happen in society?

....

SEQUENCE 1

How Is Technology Changing Us?

MARIA KONNIKOVA

ROBIN MARANTZ HENIG

BILL WASIK

NICK PAUMGARTEN

RICHARD RESTAK

CHUCK KLOSTERMAN

PETER SINGER

In this sequence, you will consider the ways in which technology such as social media is changing who we are and how we relate to one another. You'll begin by reading Maria Konnikova to examine the quality of relationships in the age of social media. Then, using Robin Marantz Henig, you will relate these changes to our growth and development as human beings. Nick Paumgarten will help you examine the psychological impact of these changes and then, using Chuck Klosterman, you will determine whether or not these changes are beneficial or detrimental. Alternate assignments ask you to expand on the biological, emotional, and ethical dimensions of these changes using Bill Wasik, Richard Restak, and Peter Singer.

Assignment 1. Analyze: KONNIKOVA

How does social media change the nature of relationships such as friendships? Write a paper in which you evaluate the quality of relationships in the digital age, drawing from the work of Maria Konnikova. In making your argument, you may want to use your work on the qualities of friendship from Question 2 of Questions for Critical Reading (p. 235), your reflections on your own experiences from Exploring Context (p. 240), and your work on the impact of virtual friendships from Question 1 of Assignments for Writing (p. 241).

To help you begin your critical thinking on this assignment, consider these questions: Does the Dunbar number remain relevant in the digital age? How does technology enable us to sustain relationships? What is lost when we use technology to do so? How does your own experience confirm or complicate Konnikova's argument?

Assignment 2. Connect: KONNIKOVA AND HENIG

Robin Marantz Henig examines the complicated life stage of "emerging adulthood." Is the emergence of this life stage connected to the rise of technologies such as social media? Write a paper in which you determine the relationship between social media and social development, using ideas from both Henig and Maria Konnikova. You might begin by working with the definition of *adulthood* you developed in Question 2 of Questions for Critical Reading for Henig (p. 198).

To help you begin your critical thinking on this assignment, reflect on these questions: How do our friendships and other relationships relate to our own development as human beings? What role does connection play in our ability to act as adults? Does technology shape our experience of emerging adulthood or does emerging adulthood predispose individuals to certain uses of technology?

Alternate Assignment 2. Connect: KONNIKOVA AND WASIK

Bill Wasik begins and ends his essay about flash mobs, "My Crowd Experiment: The Mob Project," with boredom. His experience in between suggests that our emotions are closely related to our use of social media and other technologies. Write a paper in which you determine the emotional impact of technology using ideas from both Wasik and Maria Konnikova. You may wish to develop your work from Question 1 of Assignments for Writing for Wasik (p. 491).

What role does emotion play in our use of technology? Does social media support or hinder our emotional development? What impact do memes or the bandwagon effect have on the ways in which we use technology? Do you turn to social media when you are bored? Does our ability to connect to others rely on emotions?

Assignment 3. Synthesize: KONNIKOVA AND PAUMGARTEN

Both Maria Konnikova and Nick Paumgarten are interested in the ways we connect to others as well as to ourselves. Both, too, examine the ways in which technology changes these connections. Using both Konnikova and Paumgarten to support your argument, write a paper in which you assess the impact of technology on our abilities to connect.

To help you begin your critical thinking on this assignment, ask yourself these questions: Does the GoPro help or hinder our ability to connect to others in ways that reflect Konnikova's argument? What is the value of experience, and how are real-world interactions vital to experience? Can technology allow us to connect in different (if not better) ways? What role does memory play in both essays, and how do memories affect our connections?

Alternate Assignment 3. Synthesize: KONNIKOVA, PAUMGARTEN, AND RESTAK

Both Konnikova and Restak examine the relationship between digital cultures and the brain; in examining the GoPro, Paumgarten also considers the ways in which technology shapes and imitates the brain — in this instance the capacity for point of view and memory. Write a paper synthesizing the ideas of these authors in which you determine the extent to which technologies are changing biologies.

You will probably want to start your work on this question by expanding your answer from Question 2 of Questions for Connecting (p. 241) that you may have completed after reading Konnikova's essay. Questions 2 and 3 from the Assignments for Writing (p. 241) following Konnikova's essay might also be useful. Consider also these questions: What general conclusions can you reach about the effects of connection and fragmentation on biological processes like the brain? How does technology *enable* the study of the brain? How do we balance those advances against virtual friendships and "modern nerves"? In what ways does technology try — and fail — to replicate biological functions such as friendship, attention, or memory?

Assignment 4. Emerge: KLOSTERMAN AND ONE OTHER

Chuck Klosterman uses the figures of Kim Dotcom and Julian Assange to consider the villainy of each man. And yet while he does identify a cultural narrative promoting the inevitability of the future, Klosterman doesn't seem to address the larger question of whether or not technological progress itself is villainous. Using the ideas of Klosterman and one of the other authors from this sequence, write a paper in which you determine the villainy and virtue of technological progress. You will want to use your work from the Questions for Critical Reading (p. 223) that accompany Klosterman's essay as well as Questions 1 and 2 of Assignments for Writing (p. 234).

Think also about these questions: How does the persistence of the Dunbar number complicate Klosterman's claims about the inevitability of technology? Is villainy a matter of ethics or emotions? How does technology's impact on our brains and emotions confirm or challenge Klosterman?

Alternate Assignment 4. Emerge: SINGER AND ONE OTHER

Although Peter Singer fears an erosion of privacy in the age of digital technology and social media, he also uncovers the ways in which these tools can be used to empower people and hold governments accountable. Using Singer's ideas and one other author from this sequence, write a paper in which you expand Singer's argument to identify the ways in which technology promotes social change.

Consider: How do virtual friendships empower collaborative action? What qualities of emerging adults might make them inclined to use technology for social change? Is the GoPro a kind of sousveillance?

SEQUENCE 2

Why Does Race Still Matter?

STEVE OLSON

WESLEY YANG

MAUREEN O'CONNOR

ETHAN WATTERS

KENJI YOSHINO

This sequence asks you to examine the lingering significance of race and ethnicity: Why do we continue to place so much (fraught) meaning in these categories? The first assignment, using Steve Olson, asks you to consider the mechanisms that enable racial categories to persist despite having no real biological basis. You will then extend this understanding by looking at the intersection of race, ethnicity, and economic and cultural factors using Wesley Yang's discussion of Asian American identity. Building on that understanding, you will use Maureen O'Connor in the third assignment to look at the relationship between these concepts and beauty by considering the impact of plastic surgery on race. The last assignment uses Ethan Watters to question the universality of sociological understandings of race and ethnicity. An alternate assignment uses Kenji Yoshino to consider the future of civil rights in light of all you've discovered about race and ethnicity.

Assignment 1. Analyze: OLSON

According to Steve Olson, Hawaii demonstrates the fact that there is no biological basis for race; regardless, notions of race and ethnicity persist in that state and elsewhere. Write a paper in which you determine the mechanisms that allow race to continue to operate. You will want to start with your analysis from Question 3 of Questions for Critical Reading (p. 300) as well as Questions 1 and 3 of Assignments for Writing (p. 312).

Also consider these questions: What institutions reinforce race? What new mechanisms are emerging for grouping people? How are communities of descent different from racial categories? What role does education play in race? What about marriage?

Assignment 2. Connect: OLSON AND YANG

Wesley Yang looks at the multiple impacts of race and ethnicity on communities and individuals, and in some ways, he offers an insider view of the kinds of effects that Olson discusses. Using Olson and Yang, write a paper in which you explore the socioeconomic dimensions of race and ethnicity. Consider using your responses to Questions 1 and 3 of Questions for Critical Reading (p. 520) and Question 1 of Questions for Connecting (p. 536) for Yang.

Also ask yourself these questions: How do race and ethnicity limit an individual's economic potential? What does race *cost*? What relationship is there between race, ethnicity, and social class? What advantages do they offer an individual, and how do they preserve community? How do race and ethnicity offer advantages or disadvantages for individuals?

Assignment 3. Synthesize: OLSON, YANG, AND O'CONNOR

Maureen O'Connor's discussion of ethnic plastic surgery suggests a significant intersection between race and ethnicity and cultural notions of beauty. At the same time, the surgical practices she describes seem to further challenge the notion of stable racial and ethnic categories. Synthesize these authors to write a paper in which you determine the impact of cultural standards of beauty on race and ethnicity. Draw from your work in Questions for Critical Reading (p. 287), Questions 1 and 3 of Questions for Connecting (p. 297), and Question 2 of Assignments for Writing for O'Connor (p. 298).

Also think about: Is ethnic plastic surgery creating a "post-racial" world? How does beauty function in Yang's essay? Does beauty, as something universal, transcend and thus erode notions of race? Or does it instead enforce a specifically racialized notion of value based on the looks of one particular race?

Assignment 4. Emerge: WATTERS AND ONE OTHER

Ethan Watters's argument seems to suggest that the entire controversy about race and ethnicity could be a purely Western phenomenon. Bound as we are by our cultural perspective, is it possible that our categorization of people by race and ethnicity reflects "WEIRD" notions of the self? Write a paper using Watters and one of the other authors from this sequence in which you determine the limitations of racial and ethnic categories. Consider using your work on diversity from Question 1 of Assignments for Writing for Watters (p. 503).

Consider: Based on Watters's argument, might we consider Western identity itself as an ethnic category? If so, how might the insights about race and ethnicity from the other authors be applied to the concept of WEIRD? Are the categories universal or uniquely Western? How might other cultures encode human variety? Does WEIRD transcend race and ethnicity? To what extent does it reinforce those categories instead?

Alternate Assignment 4. Emerge: YOSHINO AND ONE OTHER

Civil rights are centrally connected to our understanding of race and ethnicity. Kenji Yoshino considers the challenge presented by proliferating groups claiming rights and offers a model that can account for all peoples. Using Yoshino and one other author, identify the challenges to the progress of civil rights and propose strategies we can use to overcome those challenges.

You might start by asking yourself: Does the persistence of racial categories in Hawaii suggest the challenge of civil rights? Which model of civil rights might account for communities of descent? Can legal protections ever mitigate the damage caused by stereotypes? How? Should economic rights be considered as well as civil rights? Could such rights dismantle the "Bamboo Ceiling"?

....

SEQUENCE 3

How Does Gender Shape Us, and How Do We Shape Gender?

JULIA SERANO

ROXANE GAY

ARIEL LEVY

RUTH PADAWER

JENNIFER POZNER

In this sequence, you will explore the consequences of our current system of gender. You will begin by using Julia Serano to look at the ways in which gender shapes men in relation to sexuality and rape culture. Roxane Gay will then help you articulate the relationship between women and representations of feminism. Using Ariel Levy, you will synthesize these authors to articulate a set of tools we can all use to understand gender and its impact on our lives. The final series of assignments and alternate assignments asks you to consider the role of gender in education (Ruth Padawer) and media (Jennifer Pozner).

Assignment 1. Analyze: SERANO

According to Julia Serano, when it comes to sex nice guys finish last, a result of a powerful set of cultural assumptions that shape both men and women in relation to rape culture. Write a paper in which you extend Serano's analysis to suggest strategies we can use to mitigate the stereotypes that influence men in our culture. You will want to start with your analysis from Question 3 of Questions for Critical Reading (p. 415) as well as Questions 2 and 3 of Assignments for Writing (p. 423).

  Also consider these questions: Who is responsible for rape culture? How do our cultural understandings of gender victimize both men and women? How can we change gender-based stereotypes? What role might the media play? How can our personal behaviors contribute to this effort? Is there a strategy that will allow nice guys to finish first? What would it look like? Or are gendered expectations so entrenched that there is no solution?

Assignment 2. Connect: SERANO AND GAY

While Serano considers the impact of stereotypes on men, Roxane Gay looks instead at her personal relationship to the expectations that come with the term *feminist*. Using both of these authors, write a paper in which you determine how categories related to gender limit our abilities to act personally and politically. Use your work from Questions for Critical Reading (p. 414) as well as Question 3 of Assignments for Writing for Serano (p. 423).

You might also use these questions to help you think about your response: How does Serano's use of binaries relate to Gay's understanding of a good or bad feminist? What kind of feminist — "good" or "bad" or something else — might work with men to dismantle gendered stereotypes? Does essential feminism empower people to act? Which people? How might individuals take action while avoiding the kinds of labels that come with stereotypes?

Assignment 3. Synthesize: SERANO, GAY, AND LEVY

One might say that the Female Chauvinist Pigs that Ariel Levy examines operate from notions that relate both to cultural expectations of men (the ones that cause nice guys to finish last) and very particular notions of feminism. Synthesizing all three authors, write a paper in which you propose strategies and practices that can move us toward gender equality. You may find your work from Question 3 of Questions for Critical Reading (p. 243) useful as well as your work from Question 2 of Assignments for Writing for Levy (p. 256).

Consider, too: How is power — cultural, social, and economic — related to gender, and what would it take to change that relationship? What sort of politics could benefit everyone in relation to gender? What kind of feminism discussed by these authors has the most potential for changing our system of gender?

Assignment 4. Emerge: PADAWER AND ONE OTHER

The transgender students of Wellesley College in Ruth Padawer's essay offer a complex problem to the school. How can the school reconcile its mission relating to women and education with the needs of these students? Using Padawer and one of the other authors in this sequence, write a paper in which you determine the relationship between gender and education in order to suggest possible answers to the question of transgender students at Wellesley. You may find your responses to Questions for Critical Reading (p. 314) and Assignments for Writing for Padawer (p. 329) helpful. If you are working with Gay, also consider using your work from Question 2 of Questions for Connecting (p. 328); if working with Serano, you may want to use your work from Question 3 of Questions for Connecting (p. 329).

Also think about these questions: Does being transgender men expose these students to the problems other men face in rape culture? Does it expose them to the pitfalls of raunch culture? How does Gay's experience of feminism offer strategies for accommodating transgender students at the school? Which strand of feminism discussed by these authors offers the best solution?

Alternate Assignment 4. Emerge: Pozner and One Other

Jennifer Pozner looks at the intersection of race and gender in her discussion of *America's Next Top Model*. Using her essay and one other author from this sequence, write a paper in which you determine the ways in which media shape our notions of race and gender.

Consider: How does the question of gender become more complex when race is also considered? What role do media like television play in shaping our expectations of others and their behavior? Do racial and gendered stereotypes operate in the same way?

SEQUENCE 4

What Does Ethical Conflict Look Like in a Global Economy?

Thomas L. Friedman

Torie Rose DeGhett

Tomas van Houtryve

Sarah Stillman

Kwame Anthony Appiah

In this sequence, you will consider the complexities of war and conflict within our deeply connected world. Thomas L. Friedman will introduce you to the relationship between war and economics and suggest the ways in which a global economic system works to prevent conflict. Then, using either Torie Rose DeGhett or Tomas van Houtryve, you will consider the ethics of conflicts when they occur, particularly in relation to economic systems of media and technology. Sarah Stillman will help you further articulate these ethical questions, while Kwame Anthony Appiah will offer you tools we might use to resolve the problems of conflict in a global economy.

Assignment 1. Analyze: Friedman

Thomas L. Friedman argues that countries participating in global supply chains become economically interdependent and are thus less likely to be involved in political conflicts. At the same time, he warns that terrorists are using similar supply chains to spread violence around the world. How can we mitigate terrorist supply chains? Write a paper in which you assess whether or not the tools that Friedman describes could be used to combat global terrorism. Draw from your work in Questions 1 and 3 of Questions for Critical Reading (p. 124).

Also consider these questions: How can we use collaboration to combat terrorism? Are economic incentives and growth a possible solution or part of the problem? Could other kinds of supply chains work against terrorism?

Assignment 2. Connect: Friedman and DeGhett or van Houtryve

Torie Rose DeGhett and Tomas van Houtryve each explore the role of the image in modern conflict. These images are not only connected to the technologies that captured them but also embedded in global economic systems, whether the system of publication at play in DeGhett's essay or the system that allows van Houtryve to buy a drone of his own. Connect one of these two essays to Friedman's essay in order to write a paper in which you propose ethical standards for military products in global economic systems. What questions should we ask, and what standards should we use in making decisions about technologies or products when it comes to war? You may wish to use your work from Assignments for Writing (p. 84) for DeGhett or Question 3 of Questions for Critical Reading (p. 449) and Question 1 of Assignments for Writing (p. 457) for van Houtryve.

You might also use these questions to help you think about your response: Do global supply chains have an ethical obligation to mitigate conflict? Do they have an ethical obligation to display the consequences of conflict? Who makes decisions about conflict, technology, and media in these essays? What ethical considerations, if any, seem to govern their decisions?

Assignment 3. Synthesize: STILLMAN AND ONE OTHER

The consequences of conflict, Sarah Stillman suggests, ripple across generations. Given the biological impact of trauma, how can we conduct conflict ethically? Write a paper in which you synthesize Stillman and one of the other authors in this sequence to determine how the long-term consequences of war could shape our decisions regarding conflict. It might be helpful to start with your responses to Question 3 of Questions for Critical Reading (p. 442), Question 2 of Questions for Connecting (p. 447), and Question 3 of Assignments for Writing for Stillman (p. 448).

You may also find these questions helpful: How would considering trauma a disease and viewing images of war change the way we make decisions about armed conflict? Might global supply chains be used to disseminate information in a way that mitigates conflict? What role does shame play in the global economy? How are mutant supply chains like a disease?

Assignment 4. Emerge: APPIAH AND ONE OTHER

Kwame Anthony Appiah states that cosmopolitanism names the problem as much as the solution, suggesting that the challenge facing us is how to get along in a crowded and interdependent world. Using his ideas and those of one other author in this sequence, write a paper in which you propose strategies for ending and avoiding armed conflicts.

You may find these questions helpful: Can practices of economic interdependence enhance peace in the world? What role do both collaboration and conversation have in this process? How might images of war change our values and practices in relation to conflict? Do remote technologies like drones make it easier to wage war? How might the lingering impact of trauma be used to change conversations about conflict?

How Can You Make a Difference in the World?

CHARLES DUHIGG

RHYS SOUTHAN

KENJI YOSHINO

KWAME ANTHONY APPIAH

HELEN EPSTEIN

What tools can you use to change the world around you? In this sequence, you will examine ideas that will help you advocate for social change. Charles Duhigg's examination of the power of peer pressure in the civil rights movement will help you think about the ways in which you can use the relationships you have to make a difference in the world. Rhys Southan then offers a very different and very stark approach to change by looking at Effective Altruism. You will then synthesize these approaches with ideas about civil rights from Kenji Yoshino. Ultimately, using Helen Epstein's ideas, you will test your facility with these tools for social change by looking at ways to halt the spread of HIV. An alternate assignment continues your work in this areas using Kwame Anthony Appiah.

Assignment 1. Analyze: DUHIGG

Charles Duhigg looks at some of the elements that powered both the Montgomery bus boycott and the explosive growth of Saddleback Church. In particular, he considers the potential for relationships to create change. Write a paper in which you evaluate Duhigg's ideas as tools for changing the world. In order to do so, you will first need to identify these tools; then you will need to *assess* how effective they are; and finally you will need to *predict* their potential usefulness in other contexts of change. Your work with Question 3 of Questions for Critical Reading (p. 86) and Question 1 of Assignments for Writing (p. 107) might be good starting places.

Consider also these questions: How do relationships create change? How can we use that knowledge to shape the changes we want to see? What are the drawbacks of these methods? What is the most powerful tool Duhigg examines, and what makes it so powerful?

Assignment 2. Connect: DUHIGG AND SOUTHAN

Rhys Southan also writes about changing the world, examining in his essay the potential (and potential problems) of Effective Altruism. While Duhigg's analysis focuses largely on the potential of relationships, Southan's analysis of Effective Altruism seems to depend much more on individuals alone. Write a paper in which you determine the power of the individual in producing social change.

You might want to think about these questions to help you get started: Does change start with individuals or in our relationships with the world around us? Do weak and strong ties play a part in Effective Altruism? How do friendships and other relationships complicate the notion of replaceability? Are individuals more important than Effective Altruism suggests? Does Effective Altruism rely on a kind of peer pressure? If you want to make a difference in the world, how would you use the tools offered by these authors?

Assignment 3. Synthesize: DUHIGG, SOUTHAN, AND YOSHINO

What is the best way to use law to protect the rights of all individuals? You might locate an answer to that question by synthesizing Kenji Yoshino's discussion of civil rights with the ideas of Duhigg and Southan. Write a paper in which you identify an effective approach to protecting the rights of all individuals through civil rights and other legislation. Your work from Question 2 of Assignments for Writing for Yoshino (p. 548) might be a particularly good place to begin this work.

Also consider: How can the conversations that Yoshino calls for leverage the power of strong and weak ties? How does peer pressure contribute to the liberty paradigm, and how might it be used instead in service of the equality paradigm? Can Effective Altruism's economic focus be applied to civil rights?

Alternate Assignment 3. Synthesize: DUHIGG, SOUTHAN, AND APPIAH

Kwame Anthony Appiah looks at cultural practices that *have* changed as a way of considering the mechanisms that allow social change to happen. Write a paper in which you synthesize the ideas of Appiah, Duhigg, and Southan in order to evaluate the most effective means of generating social change. Your work from Question 2 of Assignments for Writing for Appiah (p. 61) might be a useful start.

You might also find these questions helpful: What causes practices to shift? How do groups, cultures, and organizations play a role in making change happen? What role does peer pressure play in the changes Appiah examines? Does Effective Altruism rely on values or practices? Does it rely on individual effort? What role might it play in cosmopolitanism?

Assignment 4. Emerge: EPSTEIN AND ONE OTHER

Helen Epstein examines the HIV epidemic in Africa, considering some reasons why certain prevention programs work better than others. Her examination of this disease offers a useful case study for you to continue to explore ideas about how to promote change. Using Epstein and one other author in this sequence, write a paper in which you propose strategies for effectively combating the spread of HIV not only in Africa but globally as well. You may want to start with your response to Question 3 of Questions for Critical Reading (p. 110); your work in Assignments for Writing (p. 122) for Epstein might also inform your response.

Consider, too: What role does peer pressure play in the spread of HIV in Africa, and how might we shift that role in order to slow the spread of the disease? How might we harness Effective Altruism? What role can conversation play in disease prevention?

SEQUENCE 6

What Should Be the Goal of an Education?

Yo-Yo Ma

Graeme Wood

Ruth Padawer

Wesley Yang

Daniel Gilbert

Daniel Kahneman

Is education only about getting a job or should it have other goals as well? In this sequence of assignments, you will explore the goals of education, a topic that may be particularly relevant to your life today. To start, you will use Yo-Yo Ma to consider the role that different disciplines can play in education and in the world. You will then develop that understanding by looking at Graeme Wood's discussion of the future of education. Using either Ruth Padawer's examination of the plight of transgender students at Wellesley College or Wesley Yang's discussion of Asian Americans, you will test your developing ideas against specific, challenging situations. Then, using either Daniel Gilbert or Daniel Kahneman, you will consider the role that education plays in our judgment and future happiness.

Assignment 1. Analyze: MA

Yo-Yo Ma argues for the value of the "necessary edges" found at the intersection of different kinds of thinking and learning; in doing so, he also argues for the value of the arts in education. Using Ma's ideas, write a paper in which you evaluate the value of a liberal arts education in a world driven by science and technology. Your work with Questions 1 and 3 of Questions for Critical Reading (p. 257) and Questions 2 and 3 of Assignments for Writing (p. 262) may be useful.

You might also find these questions helpful: What does an education in the liberal arts add to understandings of science and technology? How does education relate to empathy? Is empathy something we learn? What role does education play in collaboration?

Assignment 2. Connect: MA AND WOOD

Minerva, Graeme Wood suggests, represents a new direction in education, not only in the technology it uses but also in the way it imagines the curriculum students should pursue. And much like Ma, Wood has a lot to say about education. Using the ideas of both of these authors, write a paper in which you evaluate the general education or core curriculum at your school. Your responses to Questions 1 and 2 of Questions for Critical Reading for Wood (p. 505) might be useful places to start; consider also using your work in Question 1 of Assignments for Writing for Wood (p. 519).

Also think about these questions: Does your school promote "necessary edges"? How does the list of courses you're required to take reflect Ma's points about education? What does your school assume you've already learned or can learn on your own? What values does Minerva reflect when it comes to education, and what values does your school reflect, based on the courses you're required to take?

Assignment 3. Synthesize: Ma, Wood, and Padawer or Yang

Both Ruth Padawer and Wesley Yang examine some of the problems particular populations confront in relation to education, whether transgender students at Wellesley College or Asian Americans. Using either Padawer or Yang as well as both Ma and Wood, write a paper in which you determine what responsibility, if any, educational institutions have to student populations. Your work from Question 2 of Assignments for Writing for Padawer (p. 329) might be a particularly good place to begin this work.

Also consider: What kinds of responsibilities do educational institutions have to students? Do they have a responsibility to keep students safe? To offer them intellectual challenges or a certain kind of environment? How much of education is the responsibility of schools, and how much is the responsibility of students?

Assignment 4. Emerge: Gilbert or Kahneman and One Other

Both Daniel Gilbert and Daniel Kahneman illustrate the difficulties we have when we try to make decisions toward our future goals. Given that the choices we make in our education are particularly important to our future happiness, use either Gilbert or Kahneman and one other author in this sequence to write a paper in which you determine the methods you should use in making decisions about your education that provide the best chance for your future happiness. Whether using Gilbert or Kahneman, you may find Questions 1 and 2 of Assignments for Writing (p. 197 or p. 222) useful.

Also consider: Do authors like Ma act as surrogates? Can working within necessary edges help us avoid the illusion of validity? Based on Wood's analysis, is all of education merely a super-replicator? Can an education such as the one offered at Minerva help us to make better judgments? How do Yang's and Padawer's essays act as surrogates? Can we find reliable ways to make decisions about our education?

....

SEQUENCE 7

What Do We Do about Bullying?

FRANCIS FUKUYAMA

SHARON MOALEM

HANNA ROSIN

DAN SAVAGE AND URVASHI VAID

Bullying is an epidemic that results in emotional trauma and, more seriously, disturbing rates of suicide. In this sequence, you will first work with readings that help you think about this problem and then move into your own research to consider possible solutions. You will begin by considering the nature of human dignity using Francis Fukuyama. Sharon Moalem's work with epigenetics will then help you consider the biological effects of bullying. Hanna Rosin or the selections from Dan Savage and Urvashi Vaid will provide specific case studies and possible solutions to the problem. Having worked with these sources, you will end this sequence by locating your own sources to help you address bullying.

Assignment 1. Analyze: FUKUYAMA

Francis Fukuyama considers the nature of human dignity and what it means to be human while also considering the ways in which biotechnology threatens both. Yet bullying would also seem to deny a person's human dignity. Write a paper in which you propose essential measures we must take to preserve human dignity. Your responses to Questions for Critical Reading (p. 143) might be useful as you compose your response.

You might also think about these questions: What are the consequences when human dignity is violated? What role does Factor X play in maintaining human dignity? How can we promote the preservation of dignity? Law? Cultural norms?

Assignment 2. Connect: FUKUYAMA AND MOALEM

Both Sharon Moalem and Francis Fukuyama suggest that questions of ethics, morality, and philosophy are closely bound with issues of biology. Our traumatic experiences such as bullying thus have extended ramifications not only on our psyche but on our bodies as well. Using the insights of both of these authors, write a paper in which you determine the consequences of bullying. Your response to Question 2 of Assignments for Writing for Moalem (p. 286) may be useful.

Also think about these questions: What are the epigenetic consequences of bullying? How does bullying affect human dignity? How long do the effects of bullying last? Does bullying people diminish their humanity?

Assignment 3. Synthesize: Fukuyama, Moalem, and Rosin or Savage and Vaid

The essays by Hanna Rosin and Dan Savage and Urvashi Vaid contain examples of bullying and its effects on people. They thus offer useful cases for exploring the impact of bullying while also suggesting some further solutions to the problem. Using ideas from both Fukuyama and Moalem, write a paper in which you suggest solutions to the kinds of bullying that take place in either Rosin or Savage and Vaid. If you are working with Rosin, you might want to use your response to Question 1 of Assignments for Writing (p. 403); if you are using Savage and Vaid, you may want to use your work from Question 2 of Questions for Critical Reading (p. 406).

Also consider: Across all of these essays, what can we do to help things get better? Can laws be useful, as Rosin suggests? What actions should we take? What role does technology play in making a difference?

Assignment 4. Emerge: Research Project

So far, you've considered the problem of bullying using much larger ideas, ranging from the notion of human dignity to epigenetics. These ideas have offered you a broad context for considering this issue, and you've used them to look at specific instances of bullying. For your research project, locate two academic sources with specific ideas and theories about how to reduce and prevent bullying. Then, using these two sources and one of the other authors you've read in this sequence, write a paper in which you determine the most effective approach to solving the problem of bullying by applying ideas from your sources or synthesizing your sources to propose an idea of your own.

SEQUENCE 8

Will We Have Enough to Eat?

SANDRA ALLEN

RICHARD MANNING

MICHAEL POLLAN

THE DALAI LAMA

DAVID FOSTER WALLACE

In this country, we are usually surrounded by food so much that we don't think much about it. Globally, however, hunger remains a serious issue. More locally, many have questioned the ethics of how and what we eat. In this sequence, you will explore the many issues surrounding food. You will start by looking at the consequences of modern agricultural practices using either Richard Manning or Sandra Allen. Then, using Michael Pollan, you will consider the potential of alternative approaches to growing the food we need, and doing so ethically. Then you will consider larger ethical questions surrounding food by using either the Dalai Lama or David Foster Wallace. Finally, you will conduct your own research on a food issue that means something to you.

Assignment 1. Analyze: MANNING

Richard Manning presents a powerful critique of modern agriculture; nevertheless, we live in a hungry world that requires significant food production. Write a paper in which you balance Manning's concerns with the need for global food production. You may want to draw from your work from Question 3 of Questions for Critical Reading (p. 264) and Questions 1 and 3 from Assignments for Writing (p. 274).

Consider, too: Does our need for sufficient food supplies justify our current agricultural energy expenditures? What alternatives might we explore to reduce energy consumption while maintaining food production? How do we weigh the ethics of energy versus the ethics of feeding the world? Does energy matter in the face of famine?

Alternate Assignment 1. Analyze: ALLEN

Sandra Allen uses wine as a touch point for a larger discussion about the future of agriculture. Write a paper in which you evaluate the challenges to agriculture presented by climate change. You may want to draw from your work from Questions 1 and 3 of Questions for Critical Reading (p. 33) and Questions 1 and 3 from Assignments for Writing (p. 42).

Consider, too: Are we prepared to feed a hungry world? Does a focus on "luxury" products such as wine distract us from larger issues or does it help draw attention to the problem? Is climate change a problem? How must agriculture respond to it?

Assignment 2. Connect: MANNING AND POLLAN

Michael Pollan, like Richard Manning, is concerned about our current agricultural systems. His exploration of Polyface Farm might offer new solutions to the problems they both explore. Using ideas from both of these authors, evaluate the potential of organic farming to meet our food production needs. Your work with Question 1 of Questions for Critical Reading (p. 343) for Pollan and Questions 2 and 3 of Assignments for Writing for Pollan (p. 356) might be useful.

Also think about these questions: How does energy work in the system used by Polyface Farm? Does it offer a solution to the problems that Manning sees? What factors might stop other farmers from adopting this approach? Given the scope of the problem described by Manning, what solutions are workable?

Assignment 3. Synthesize: MANNING, POLLAN, AND THE DALAI LAMA OR WALLACE

Making enough food is part of the problem, but all of these authors ask us to consider the many ethical questions surrounding our food. The Dalai Lama calls for a moral compass in relation to all genetic technologies; David Foster Wallace considers the lobster and the ethics of what we eat. Using the ideas of one of these authors as well as the ideas of both Manning and Pollan, write a paper in which you develop an ethics of food. Whether working with the Dalai Lama or with Wallace, you might find your work with Questions for Critical Reading (p. 62 or p. 458) useful.

You might also find these questions helpful: What would a moral compass look like in farming? Is the need for food pressing enough to justify the use of genetic technologies? How might the model of agribusiness that Manning reveals subvert genetic technologies? What role should they play in a possible moral compass? What role might holons play? Does that fact that lobsters express a "preference" justify an ethical framework for eating? What would that framework look like if it were to avoid the problems that Manning describes? Does the food produced by Polyface meet that framework?

Assignment 4. Emerge: RESEARCH PROJECT

So far, you have explored only very limited areas of the much larger questions surrounding food production and consumption. For this research project, you will draft a specific question of interest to you and then locate two academic sources with specific ideas and theories that help you answer your research question. Write a paper using these two sources and one of the other authors you've read in this sequence to make an argument that responds to your own research question.

Acknowledgments (continued from page iv)

Sandra Allen, "How Climate Change Will End Wine As We Know It" in Buzzfeed Inc., Nov. 20, 2014. Reprinted by permission of the publisher. http://www.buzzfeed.com/sandraeallen/how-climate-change-will-end-wine-as-we-know-it#.gcDq4keXV

Kwame Anthony Appiah, from *Cosmopolitanism: Ethics in a World of Strangers*, copyright © 2006 by Kwame Anthony Appiah. Used by permission of W.W. Norton & Company, Inc.

The Dalai Lama, from *The Universe in a Single Atom: The Convergence of Science and Spirituality*. Copyright © 2005 The Dalai Lama. Used by permission of Morgan Road Books, an imprint of Penguin Random House LLC. All rights reserved. Any third party use of this material, outside of this publication, is prohibited. Interested parties must apply directly to Penguin Random House LLC for permission.

Torie Rose DeGhett, "The War Photo No One Would Publish" from *The Atlantic*, Aug. 8, 2014, is reprinted by permission of the author.

Charles Duhigg, Chapter 8, "Saddleback Church and the Montgomery Bus Boycott: How Movements Happen" from *The Power of Habit: Why We Do What We Do in Life and Business*, copyright © 2012 by Charles Duhigg. Used by permission of Random House, an imprint and division of Penguin Random House LLC. All rights reserved. Any third party use of this material, outside of this publication, is prohibited. Interested parties must apply directly to Penguin Random House LLC for permission.

Helen Epstein, "AIDS, Inc." from *The Invisible Cure: Why We Are Losing the Fight Against AIDS in Africa*. Copyright © 2007 by Helen Epstein. Reprinted by permission of Farrar, Straus and Giroux, LLC.

Thomas L. Friedman, "The Dell Theory of Conflict Prevention" from *The World Is Flat: A Brief History of the Twenty-First Century*, further updated and expanded by Thomas L. Friedman. Copyright © 2005, 2006, 2007 by Thomas L. Friedman. Reprinted by permission of Farrar, Straus and Giroux, LLC.

Francis Fukuyama, "Human Dignity" from *Our Posthuman Future: Consequences of the Biotechnology Revolution*. Copyright © 2002 by Francis Fukuyama. Reprinted by permission of Farrar, Straus and Giroux, LLC.

Roxane Gay, "Bad Feminist" is reprinted from the *Virginia Quarterly Review*, Fall 2012, by permission of the publisher.

Daniel Gilbert, Chapter 11, "Reporting Live from Tomorrow" from *Stumbling on Happiness*. Copyright © 2006 by Daniel Gilbert. All rights reserved. Figures 23 and 24 by Mapping Specialists, Ltd. Copyright © 2006 by Alfred A. Knopf, an imprint of the Knopf Doubleday Publishing Group, a division of Penguin Random House LLC. All rights reserved. Used by permission of Alfred A. Knopf, an imprint of the Knopf Doubleday Publishing Group, a division of Penguin Random House LLC. Any third party use of this material, outside of this publication, is prohibited. Interested parties must apply directly to Penguin Random House LLC for permission.

Robin Marantz Henig, "What Is It about 20-Somethings?" originally published in *The New York Times Magazine*, Aug. 22, 2010. Used with permission of the author.

Daniel Kahneman, "The Surety of Fools" appeared in *The New York Times Magazine*, Oct. 23, 2011 and was adapted from the book *Thinking, Fast and Slow*. Copyright © 2011 by Daniel Kahneman. Reprinted by permission of Farrar, Straus and Giroux, LLC.

Chuck Klosterman, "Electric Funeral" from *I Wear the Black Hat* is reprinted with the permission of Scribner, a division of Simon & Schuster, Inc. Copyright © 2013 by Chuck Klosterman. All rights reserved.

Maria Konnikova, "The Limits of Friendship" from *The New Yorker*, Oct. 7, 2014. Copyright © 2014 by Conde Nast. Reprinted with permission.

Ariel Levy, "Female Chauvinist Pigs" from *Female Chauvinist Pigs: Women and the Rise of Raunch Culture* is reprinted with the permission of The Free Press, a division of Simon & Schuster, Inc. Copyright © 2005 by Ariel Levy. All rights reserved.

Yo-Yo Ma, "Behind the Cello" was published in *The Huffington Post*, online, Jan. 21, 2014. Reprinted by permission of Opus 3 Artists LLC.

Richard Manning, "The Oil We Eat: Following the Food Chain Back to Iraq" from *Harper's*, May 23, 2004. Copyright © 2004 Harper's Magazine. All Rights reserved. Reproduced from the February 2004 issue by special permission.

Sharon Moalem, Chapter 3, "Changing Our Genes: How Trauma, Bullying, and Royal Jelly Alter Our Genetic Destiny" from *Inheritance: How Our Genes Change Our Lives and Our Lives Change Our Genes,* copyright © 2014 by Sharon Moalem. Used by permission of Grand Central Publishing.

Maureen O'Connor, "Is Race Plastic? My Trip Into the 'Ethnic Plastic Surgery' Minefield" from *New York* magazine, July 27, 2014. Reprinted by permission of the publisher.

Steve Olson, "The End of Race: Hawaii and the Mixing of Peoples" from *Mapping Human History: Genes, Race, and Our Common Origins.* Copyright © 2002 by Steve Olson. "Hawaiian Migration Map" copyright © 2002 by Steve Olson. Reprinted by permission of Houghton Mifflin Harcourt Publishing Company. All rights reserved.

Ruth Padawer, "Sisterhood Is Complicated: When Women Become Men at Wellesley" from *The New York Times*, Oct. 19, 2014. Copyright © 2014 by The New York Times. All rights reserved. Used by permission and protected by the Copyright Laws of the United States. The printing, copying, redistribution, or retransmission of this Content without express written permission is prohibited.

Nick Paumgarten, "We Are a Camera" from *The New Yorker*, Sept. 22, 2014, is reprinted by permission of the author.

Michael Pollan, "The Animals: Practicing Complexity" from *The Omnivore's Dilemma: A Natural History of Four Meals.* Copyright © 2007 by Michael Pollan. Used by permission of Penguin Press, an imprint of Penguin Publishing Group, a division of Penguin Random House LLC.

Jennifer L. Pozner, "Ghetto Bitches, China Dolls, and Cha Cha Divas" from *Reality Bites Back: The Troubling Truth about Guilty Pleasure TV* is reproduced with permission of Seal Press, a member of the Perseus Books Group. Copyright © 2010 by Jennifer Pozner.

Richard Restak, "Attention Deficit: The Brain Syndrome of Our Era" from *The New Brain: How the Modern Age Is Rewiring Your Mind.* Copyright © 2003 by Richard M. Restak, MD. Permission granted by Rodale, Inc. Emmaus, PA 18098.

Hanna Rosin, "Why Kids Sext" from *The Atlantic*, Oct. 14. 2014. Copyright © 2014 The Atlantic Media Co. All rights reserved. Distributed by Tribune Content Agency, LLC.

Dan Savage, "Introduction" by Dan Savage, copyright © 2011 by Dan Savage and Terry Miller from *It Gets Better: Coming Out, Overcoming Bullying, and Creating a Life Worth Living,* ed. by Dan Savage and Terry Miller. Used by permission of Dutton, an imprint of Penguin Publishing Group, a division of Random House LLC.

Urvashi Vaid, "Action Makes It Better" by Urvashi Vaid from *It Gets Better: Coming Out, Overcoming Bullying, and Creating a Life Worth Living*, ed. by Dan Savage and Terry Miller. Reprinted by permission of Urvashi Vaid.

Julia Serano, "Why Nice Guys Finish Last" from *Yes Means Yes!: Visions of Female Sexual Power and A World Without Rape* edited by Jaclyn Friedman and Jessica Valenti. Copyright © 2008 by Jaclyn Friedman and Jessica Valenti. Reprinted by permission of the Seal Press, a member of the Perseus Books Group.

Peter Singer, "Visible Man: Ethics in a World without Secrets" from *Harper's Magazine*. Copyright © 2011 by Harper's Magazine. All Rights Reserved. Reproduced from the August issue by special permission.

Rhys Southan, "Is It OK to Make Art?" from *Aeon*, online, March 20, 2014. Reprinted by permission of the author.

Sarah Stillman, "Hiroshima and the Inheritance of Trauma" from *The New Yorker*, Aug. 12, 2014. Copyright © by Conde Nast. Used by permission.